FOUR AFRICAN LITERATURES
Xhosa · Sotho · Zulu · Amharic

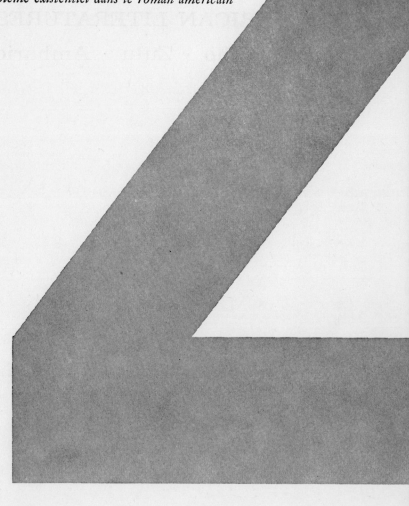

ALBERT S. GÉRARD

FOUR AFRICAN LITERATURES

**XHOSA
SOTHO
ZULU
AMHARIC**

UNIVERSITY OF CALIFORNIA PRESS
Berkeley, Los Angeles, London

University of California Press
Berkeley and Los Angeles, California

University of California Press, Ltd.
London, England

Copyright © 1971 by The Regents of the University of California
ISBN: 0-520-01788-9
Library of Congress Catalog Card Number: 74-126763

Designed by W. H. Snyder
Printed in the United States of America

TO MY WIFE, whose
unfailing patience with the
demands of scholarly life has made
the writing of this book
possible

Acknowledgments

The research that has gone into this book has been made possible by generous help from the Belgian Fonds National de la Recherche Scientifique, Brussels, the Institute for the Arts and Humanistic Studies of the Pennsylvania State University, and the Centre d'Etude des Pays en Developpement of the University of Liege.

It is impossible to provide a complete list of the authors and other persons to whom I am obliged for valuable information of many kinds. In a number of cases, I have acknowledged my indebtedness in the footnotes. I owe special gratitude to the patient kindness of Miss P.-D. Beuchat and Professor D. Ziervogel in South Africa, Father Marcel Ferragne in Lesotho, Mr. Kebbede Mika'el, Dr. Richard Pankhurst in Ethiopia, and Dr. Arthur K. Irvine of the London School of Oriental and African Studies. I wish also to express my heartfelt thanks to my daughter Christiane, who drew the maps.

Permission to use copyright material has been obligingly given by Professor Brom Weber for part of chapter 2; the editor of the *Journal of Ethiopian Studies* for part of chapter 4; the University of the Witwatersrand for Benedict W. Vilakazi's Ph.D. dissertation, "The Oral and Written Literature in Nguni"; the University of Natal for Raymond Kunene's Master's thesis, "An Analytical Survey of Zulu Poetry, Both Traditional and Modern"; Collins Publishers in London for *Blanket Boy's Moon* by A. S. Mopeli-Paulus and Peter Lanham; E. J. Brill in Leiden for quotes from G. C. Oosthuizen's *The Theology of a South African Messiah: An Analysis of the Hymnal of "The Church of the Nazarites"*; International African Institute for extracts from Bengt Sundkler's *Bantu Prophets in South Africa*; Howard B. Timmons for quotes from the Vilakazi poems.

Contents

MAPS

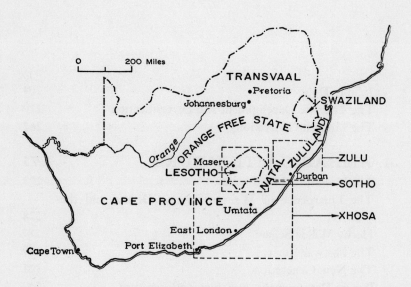

SOUTH AFRICA

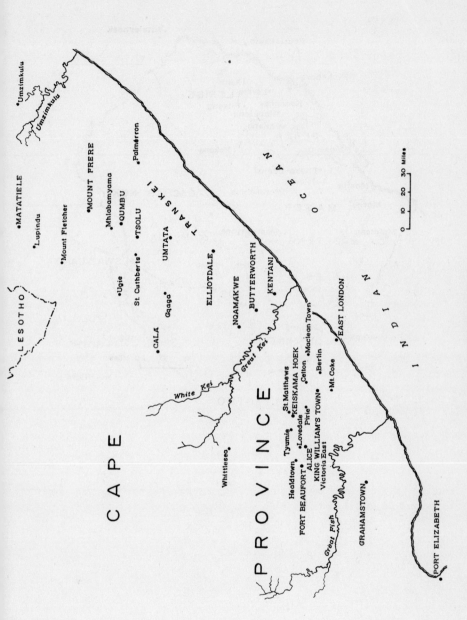

XHOSA LITERATURE

CAPE PROVINCE

LESOTHO

TRANSKEI

INDIAN OCEAN

•Umzimkulu
Umzimkulu

•MATATIELE
•Lupindu
•Mount Fletcher
•MOUNT FRERE
•Mhlobomyama
•QUMBU
•Palmérron
•Ugie
St. Cuthberts•
•TSOLU
UMTATA•
•Gqaga
•CALA
ELLIOTDALE•
•NQAMAKWE
BUTTERWORTH•
KENTANI•
Great Kei
White Kei
•Whittleseo
St Matthews•
•KEISKAMA HOEK
Tyumie•
•Lovedale
•Cotton
•Macican Town
•Berlin
•EAST LONDON
•Pirie
Heoldtown•
FORT BEAUFORT•
ALICE•
KING WILLIAM'S TOWN•
Victoria East•
•Mt. Coke
GRAHAMSTOWN•
Great Fish
FORT ELIZABETH•

0 10 20 30 Miles

LESOTHO

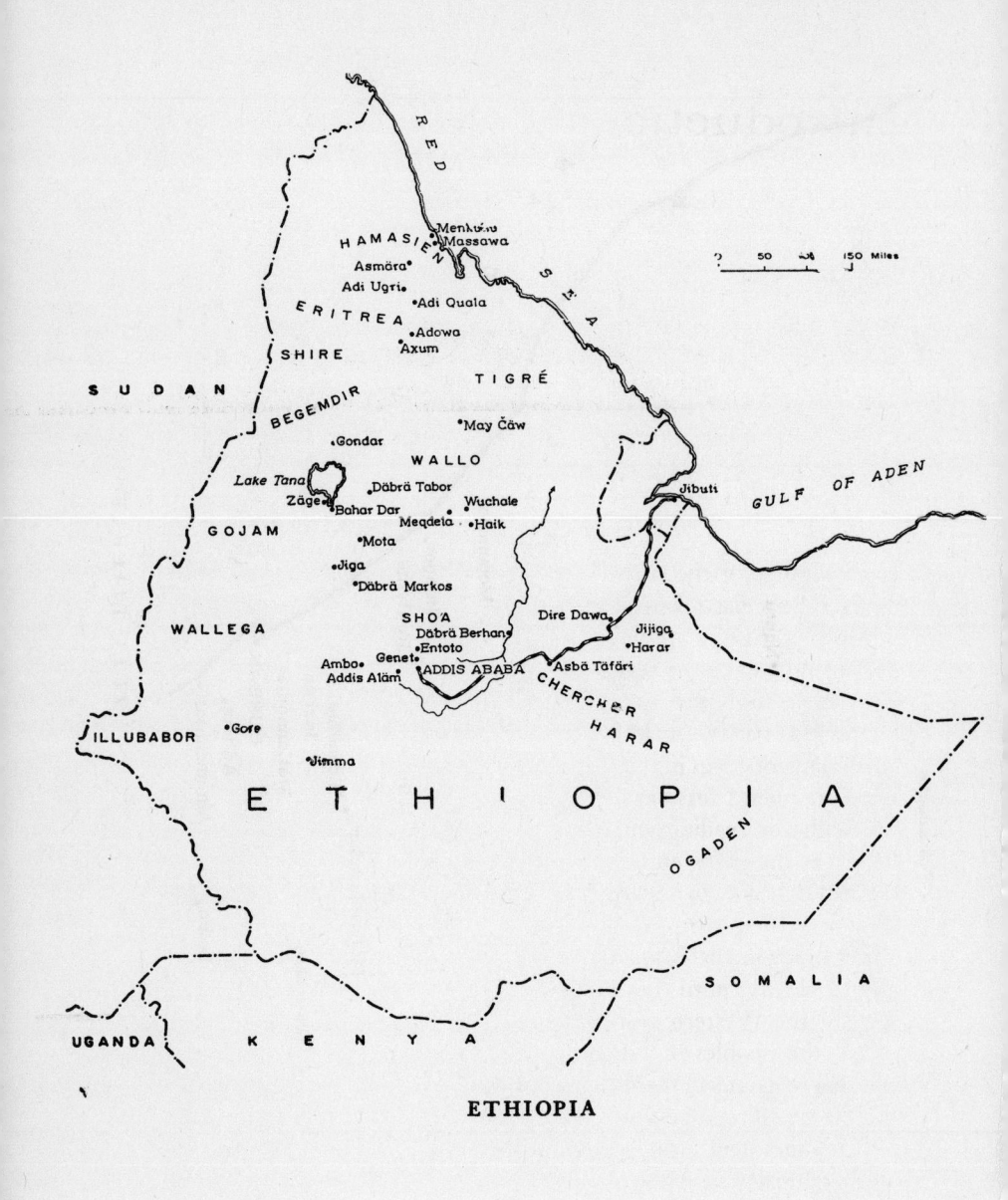

ETHIOPIA

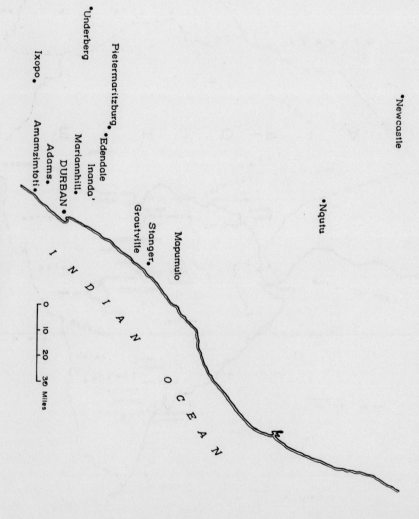

ZULU LITERATURE

•Newcastle

•Nqutu

•Underberg

Pietermaritzburg•

Ixopo
    •

•Edendale

Inanda'
Mariannhill•
DURBAN •
Adams•
Amamzimtoti•

Mapumulo

Stanger•
Groutville

INDIAN OCEAN

0
10
20
30 Miles

Introduction

In the course of the last century and a half, a most extraordinary development has taken place, almost unnoticed, in the history of world literature: a whole continent has been introduced to the art of writing and to the techniques of modern creative writing. This is an exceedingly rare occurrence, which certainly never happened on such a massive scale before. The most recent example in recorded history was in the centuries following the fall of the Roman Empire, when Christian missionaries brought both the Gospel and the skills for reading and copying it, across the Channel and the Rhine, to the Celtic and Germanic tribes, whom the Roman legions had never had a chance to tame and civilize. It took them centuries to worm their tortuous and dangerous way from the Christian strongholds in the Romania first to Ireland, and thence to Britain and Germany, until they reached even Ultima Thule on the confines of the Western world. Between the sixth and the tenth centuries, the peoples of Northwestern Europe were thus gradually enabled to extricate themselves from what is, for us, the dark limbo of oral art, illiterate culture, and literary prehistory, and to emerge into the incipient light, so comforting to scholars, of documented literary history. Very soon, as it seems to us at such a distance, they started enriching the literary patrimony of the world with masterpieces of their own devising—mainly epic poems and tales in Gaelic, Old English, Old High German, and Old Norse. Actually, as compared with what has been happening in Africa recently, the

1

process was an exceedingly protracted small-scale affair. We do not know how large the populations involved may have been. But obviously, in terms of square miles, the area where the technique of writing and the art of creative writing thus spread in the early Middle Ages was ludicrously dwarfish in comparison with the vast expanses of sub-Saharan Africa. On the whole, this area of Europe was not densely populated. Literacy was confined to the elect few who could gather and learn in sparsely scattered monasteries. It was not until four or five centuries had elapsed after Saint Patrick reached Ireland, that writing skill managed to spread to all corners of Northwestern Europe and to penetrate fairly thick layers of its population.

In Africa, on the contrary, the very same process, which started with the endeavors of philanthropists, missionaries, and traders in the early decades of the nineteenth century along the coast of western and southern Africa, was tremendously accelerated in the second part of the century, when an altogether different breed of colonizers explored and conquered the whole continent, and set up a fast-growing network of schools everywhere for purposes of their own. The reasons for this difference are obvious. In the Middle Ages, the devoted heralds of Christianity and civilization did not have steamboats or airplanes; they did not have printing presses; they were not supported by mighty armies sent out in the service of imperial prestige and economic profit. The results of this difference are there for all to see. It took Western Europe more than four hundred years to produce the body of literary writing that has been preserved: the Irish cycles and the Welsh bardic poetry, Caedmon's hymns and *Beowulf*, the *Hildebrandslied* and *Ruodlieb*, the Norse *Edda* and the Icelandic sagas. After 150 years —and in many cases considerably less—of exposure to the new-fangled technique of writing, black Africa today can boast several thousand printed imaginative works, composed by hundreds of writers, in about four dozen languages, most of them vernacular. A vast and rich new field has thus been opened for the student of literary history to graze at leisure.

Incipient trends in culture change usually start with a whimper rather than a bang; few people at the time are aware of their importance, and nobody can realize their true meaning until they have developed to more conspicuous proportions. In early medieval Europe, much information was preserved from the first concerning those writers who resorted to Latin; they belonged to the literary establishment. Vernacular composition, which was ultimately to prevail, was long considered an undignified activity, directed at the *vulgum pecus*, unworthy of serious or scholarly attention. Its initiators were accordingly consigned to oblivion. Something similar happened in Africa. Of course, there is no reason why we should expect missionaries and civil servants to have been interested in the scholarly study of literature. To the early missionaries, the composition of Christian hymns by native speakers of Xhosa or Yoruba or Malagasy was just part of the routine work of propagating the new faith, but the literary historian of today cannot help recalling Saint Colomba or Cynewulf. To the educational authorities in colonial Africa, the early written pieces of vernacular prose fiction were just part of the everyday business of providing appropriate reading matter for schoolboys. Until the mid-twentieth century, African creative writing was mainly considered as an instrument for ulterior purposes, religious or educational, or—by the scholarly—as a source of material for linguistic and anthropological studies. While these nonliterary viewpoints undoubtedly were, and still are, legitimate, the fact remains that the imaginative writing produced in Africa evidences the passage of numerous societies from oral to written art, and illustrates the birth and growth of a new African literature, the history of which specialized scholars will want to map out some day.

African literature is an immense field and (to vary the metaphor) a multilayered quarry. The bulk of it even now consists of oral folk art that, by its very nature, seems to be unsuitable for historical research. Yet, oral composition is still a flowering activity in many parts of Africa today. Indeed, in places like Hausaland and Lesotho, and, no doubt, others, there is some cause for believing that African societies are passing into a MacLuhanesque metaliterate era, where drama or poetry is no longer read but broadcast and televised! This type of contemporary literature is a suitable object for scientific study. True, much of the folklore of the past is now beyond the historian's reach. Nevertheless, in the early stages of contact with Europe, many bards were known of, and oral production was recorded by missionaries and explorers. Popular memory still possesses data, as yet unexploited. Recourse to oral sources as well as to memoirs by missionaries, travelers, and administrators could yield invaluable information about some of the illiterate poets who are responsible for the oral art of Africa.

Diachronically, the second layer of African literature is constituted by such writing as was produced before exposure to
Western influence. Ethiopia has been a literate country for nearly
two thousand years, and the Arabic script penetrated along the
fringes of black Africa at early dates through the action of Arab
traders, later bolstered by Muslim religious expansion. The Ge'ez
literature of Ethiopia has been studied very carefully for a long
time, presumably because Ethiopia is a Christian country. Until
recently no such attention was paid to the literature produced in
Arabic script in such places as Madagascar, the Swahili east coast,
and the Islamized areas on the southern outskirts of the Sahara. Yet,
Malagasy chronicles in Arabic script dating from the fourteenth
century were imported into France as early as the seventeenth century. For several years now scholars have devoted considerable
work to collecting, editing, and translating works in the Arabic
script written in Hausa in Nigeria, in Fulani in Guinea and the
Cameroons, and in Swahili along the coast of Kenya and Tanzania
and on the islands of the Zanzibar group. It can be expected that
the foundations for a historical account of those literatures will be
laid in a not too distant future.

The third stratification in African literature is made up of the
works that were written and printed under European influence.

This made a start in Europe itself at an unexpectedly early stage.
Few people are aware that the first "modern" African poet was a
Latin writer of the sixteenth century; indeed, he is known as Juan
Latino. He was brought to Spain as a slave boy in 1528, received
the best education available at the time, and became Professor of
Latin at the University of Granada in 1557. He is the author of
several Latin odes. Latino's accomplishment was exceptional, but,
in the eighteenth century, educational experiments by enlightened
philanthropists led to the emergence of a generation of black writers born in Africa, freed slaves all of them, who were active in Germany, the Netherlands, England, and the United States. Their
achievement did not pass unnoticed, and they were first studied as
a group in 1808 by the Abbé Henri Grégoire, bishop of Blois, in
his De la littérature des nègres.[1]

It was not until Europeans settled in Africa that literary activity
of a modern type could emerge on the black continent itself. Modern African literature, defined as creative writing by black Afri-

cans, seems to have begun—as far as the actual printing of books is concerned, and as far as can be ascertained in the present stage of our knowledge—in widely separated parts of Africa between 1890 and 1910. The first published volume of creative writing traced so far is a collection of poems in Portuguese ominously entitled *Delírios*, by an Angolan author, Joaquim Dias Cordeiro da Matta (1859–1899); it was printed in 1889.[2] Prior to this, a somewhat younger writer, Caetano da Costa Alegre, born in 1864 on the island of São Tomé and educated in Portugal, had produced a number of poems that, however, were not printed in book form until 1916, some twenty-six years after his untimely death. Meanwhile, an Ethiopian student, Afäwärq Gäbrä Iyäsus (1868–1948), had written the first novel in Amharic, which was printed in Rome in 1909. In the tiny protectorate of Basutoland (now Lesotho), a whole crop of writers had emerged between 1906 and 1912; the oldest of them, Azariele M. Sekese (1849–1930), had written an animal frame story that did not reach print until 1928. By 1910, the most gifted of them, Thomas Mofolo (1876–1948), had written his third novel, *Chaka*, modern Africa's earliest known major contribution to world literature. Some writing was done in German in the Cameroons, and in English in West Africa during the first decades of this century. And while vernacular literature was growing at an impressive pace in South Africa, the twenties and the thirties witnessed the birth of a literature in French in West Africa and in Madagascar; indeed, the island produced the first great lyrical poet using French in Africa, Jean-Joseph Rabearivelo (1901–1937). Portuguese literature also made progress in Angola and in Mozambique, and especially in the Cape Verde islands. All this, however, was on a strictly local scale, outside the ethnocentric pale of the "civilized" world's attention.

As a result of factors that were first disentangled by Lilyan Kesteloot,[3] World War II and the ensuing decade saw the elaboration and the dissemination of the negritude concept (or myth). Thanks to Senghor and other Senegalese and West Indian writers, the existence of African writing impressed itself upon the consciousness of the outside world, with the corresponding result that African writers became aware of their own intrinsic identity and worth. In most parts of the continent, this new self-awareness has led to a frantic outburst of literary productivity in the course of the last two decades, with British West Africa taking over the leadership from French West Africa, which is only now beginning to recover from its past obsession with negritude and anticolonialism.

A literary map of present-day black Africa would certainly hold some surprises in store for the lay reader. We all know that those areas of Western Europe which were integrated into the Roman Empire were so thoroughly deculturized that their intellectual elites never thought of using their own languages for literary purposes until the late eleventh century. Something similar occurred in what may perhaps be called Latin Africa, where the literary medium is French or Portuguese. Exceptions to this general statement are Madagascar, which did not come under French rule until 1896, Cameroun, which remained German territory until 1915, and the Islamic regions of West Africa. These seem to be the only parts of the former French empire where the vernaculars have been put to literary uses to any significant degree. On the contrary, in countries where British influence was paramount, English and the vernaculars are often thriving side by side, as in Ghana. English predominates in Eastern Nigeria, but there is also an important amount of creative writing in Yoruba done in Western Nigeria; Northern Nigerian literature, however, is wholly in Hausa. Although the only South African colored writers with an international reputation are those who use English, such as Peter Abrahams or Alex La Guma, by far the greater part of South African imaginative literature is in the vernaculars, which have almost unchallenged monopoly in the former protectorate of Lesotho and in the three countries that have arisen from the splitting of the Central African Federation. Swahili is still the most widely used literary language in East Africa, although an increasing number of writers now resort to English. And, finally, Ethiopia, which has managed to remain independent except for a five-year period of Italian occupation, has a vast literature in Amharic, although one or two writers now turn to English so as to enlarge their audience.

The first prerequisite for a truly scientific study of modern African literature is, of course, a reliable bibliographical foundation.[4] We need to know which books were written, by whom, when and where they were published. This need for a primary bibliography did not begin to be felt until 1959, when a German student of Africa, Janheinz Jahn, who has done so much to pro-

mote interest in African literature through his anthologies and his
bibliographical and historical studies, published *Approaches to
African Literature* (Ibadan, 1959), a slim thirty-nine page pamphlet to which was appended a reading list of some 230 items, prepared in collaboration with John Ramsaran, a West Indian scholar
working at Ibadan. This bibliography had the immense merits, but
also the inescapable shortcomings, of all pioneering undertakings.
It dealt solely with work that had appeared in French or in English.
Along with truly African writing, it included not only fiction by
the white writers of southern and eastern Africa, but also novels
by European authors handling African themes. In harmony with
the tenets of the negritude school, West Indian writers ranked as
Africans.

Interest, often somewhat amateurish, in the bibliography of
modern African literature, grew considerably in the early sixties,
when the decolonization process had made Africa fashionable in
the eyes of public opinion. But the standard work on the subject
appeared in 1965, when Jahn published *Die neoafrikanische Literatur. Gesamtbibliographie von den Anfängen bis zur Gegenwart.*
This is a highly ambitious venture, which purports in effect to list
the whole of Negro creative writing (for which Jahn coined the
word "neo-African") in African and in European languages, in
Africa, in Europe, and in the Western Hemisphere, from the sixteenth century to the present day. It is compiled very conscien-
tiously. It indicates the vernacular languages used; it provides
English, French, and German versions of all the titles; it lists the
anthologies where so many African writers first appeared in print;
it also lists the published translations of any particular work; it
often gives the dates of the various editions; it signals forgeries and
apocrypha; and it has a very useful index. As far as Africa is concerned, Jahn's *Gesamtbibliographie* is the most extensive and serv-
iceable reference work in existence. Although it lists 1,166 books
by 560 authors, it is still very incomplete. This is due partly to
Jahn's own definition of "neo-African," which excludes, for example, Amharic and Malagasy. But the gaps chiefly result from the
difficulty of tracing reliable information, not to mention getting
the books themselves. Since 1965, Jahn has been gathering a considerable amount of new data and preparing a new edition of his
Gesamtbibliographie.[5] Meanwhile, much complementary information can be found in a few other works of more restricted scope

such as Pierre Comba's *Inventaire des livres amhariques figurant dans la collection éthiopienne à la bibliothèque de l'University College d'Addis Abeba* (Addis Ababa, 1964), Marcel van Spaandonck's *Practical and Systematical Swahili Bibliography* (Leiden, 1965), Barbara Abrash's *Black African Literature in English Since 1952: Works and Criticism* (New York, 1967), and, for drama, in the bibliographical lists published from time to time in the *Afro-Asian Theater Bulletin*.

While a promising start has been made in the bibliographical listing of African creative writing, historical studies are still in their hatching stage. The earliest monograph dealing with the literature of any single African country is Jean-Marie Jadot's *Les Ecrivains africains du Congo belge et du Ruanda-Urundi* (Brussels, 1959). It is a very thorough piece of research, but as the Congolese themselves, for a variety of reasons, have not proved very productive in the field of creative writing, Jadot had perforce to deal chiefly with ephemeral work published in newspapers and magazines. In 1963, another Belgian scholar, Lilyan Kesteloot, attempted the more ambitious task of tracing the beginnings of the literature produced in French by black writers from Africa and the West Indies; her *Les Ecrivains noirs de langue française: Naissance d'une littérature* is a lasting contribution to the scientific historiography of African literature and of its interaction with Negro literature from the French West Indies. In 1966 Jahn published a volume with an all-embracing title, *Geschichte der neoafrikanischen Literatur*, which has since become available in an English translation. In less than 300 pages, it proposes to cover the same field as did the author's *Gesamtbibliographie*, including besides, the Negro folk songs of the Western Hemisphere, African oral art, and Hausa and Swahili literature written in the Arabic script. Apart from the latter, the treatment of African writing is actually limited to three vernacular literatures of southern Africa and to the negritude writing in French, with some rather desultory consideration of African writers using English. Jahn's book, although it undoubtedly provides some of the main guidelines and a wealth of valuable data for a future history of African literature, makes it clear that the time has not yet come for such all-inclusive ventures.

Before a historical account of creative writing in sub-Saharan Africa can be attempted with any hope of success, a considerable amount of research on the more modest scale exemplified by Jadot's book is obviously required. Indeed, 1966 also saw the appearance of two highly meritorious and useful monographs: *A Study of Cape Verdean Literature* by Norman Araujo, and *African Literature in Rhodesia*, a collection of essays dealing with modern Shona and Ndebele writing, under the editorship of E. W. Krog (Gwelo, 1966).[6] It must be admitted, however, that little historical research has been conducted so far, especially concerning the numerous vernacular literatures of Africa. One exception is the Amharic literature of Ethiopia, of which there exist several brief accounts, mainly by Italian scholars.

The reason for this dearth is almost self-evident. Anyone who has attempted to meddle with the history of the early centuries of Western literature—or, for that matter, of classical literature—knows what a thankless and irritating and frustrating and often fruitless labor that is. A great many works have been destroyed, documentary evidence is scant and unreliable, and we know nothing or next to nothing about even the most illustrious writers, their experience of life, their aesthetic and other purposes; very often, even their names are a mystery. Did Homer really exist? Who wrote such acknowledged masterpieces as *Beowulf* or the *Nibelungenlied*? Even the authorship of such comparatively recent works as the *Chanson de Roland* or the *Poema de Mio Cid* is likely to remain a mystery. In spite of technical progress and the printing press, much of this is true of African writing. Many works are issued in exceedingly small numbers, sometimes simply in mimeographed form. Because of the tropical climate and of carelessness in the matter of book preservation, it is quite conceivable and likely that a number of works may have disappeared forever. In the early stages, and even now, poems and short stories were printed in missionary newsletters issued by station presses in cyclostyled form, or in vernacular periodicals with limited circulation. Few people and few institutions have cared to preserve this ephemeral material. There are many cases in which it is simply impossible to find a complete collection of a given periodical printed in Africa. As recently as 1923, a magazine entitled *Revue Africaine des Arts et des Lettres* was printed in Dakar; no complete collection is still in existence; only a few stray issues have been preserved at the library of the Institut Fondamental d'Afrique Noire in Dakar. One of those issues contains one chapter of a novel written by Massyla Diop, which should perhaps be considered the first legitimate novel ever composed in French by an African. Nothing remains of its, except this one chapter.

Of the early authors, many have remained anonymous, many are dead, and only their names survive on tattered front pages. Nothing is known that might help the historian to understand why they wrote, and why they wrote the way they did. Gerald Moser recently revealed that the first volume of poetry printed in Angola was *Espontaneidades de Minha* (Luanda, 1849), by one José da Silva Maia Ferreira. We do not know the author's skin color, not to mention his birthdate, his education, his career, and all the elementary facts that the historian of any modern European literature takes for granted. Vernacular Christian hymns composed by native speakers were in existence among the Yoruba and the Malagasy as early as the 1830s; while many have been preserved in hymnbooks, no one ever bothered to record the names of those pious pioneers. Even today, many writers are ignorant of their birthdate, partly owing to the absence of parish registers, partly because until recently Africans boys who were too old to be admitted to schools were in the habit of falsifying any identity papers they might have in order to be able to learn the three Rs. Thomas Mofolo did not know when he was born (although we do); nor does Ahmadou Kourouma, a gifted young novelist from the Ivory Coast who now lives in Algiers and *assumes* he is in his early thirties.

The writing of this book has been undertaken with the strong conviction that to allow this ignorance to persist would be simply unforgivable. We have the scientific consciousness that makes us aware of the imperative need to record and preserve documentary historical evidence for the benefit of future scholars. We have evolved the most sophisticated methods of storing knowledge and of retrieving it in the history of mankind. It is a duty of present-day scholarship to see that the Malagasy student of the twenty-second century, writing his Ph.D. dissertation on the beginnings of his own literature will not be faced with the same penury of documentary evidence which our medievalists so helplessly deplore.

The primary, and very humble, purpose of this book in its embryonic phase was to trace, collect, record, and so to preserve and

make generally available, as much evidence as possible concerning
the beginnings and the development of written literature in selected parts of sub-Saharan Africa. At an early stage in the research, however, it became apparent that the available material was
considerably more abundant than had been anticipated. The word
"available" should of course be taken *cum grano salis*. There is as
yet no systematic bibliography of secondary sources for any particular literature of Africa, although the development of the African section in the MLA *Annual Bibliography* opens up very promising prospects with regard to current production. Much of the
required information about books and authors does exist in print
somewhere. The difficulty lies in tracing it. Linguistic and educational journals have published lists of creative works; a few African presses do issue catalogs. As early writers usually associated
with European missionaries, the latter's memoirs and reports are
an invaluable source of information. Many later writers were active in a wide variety of nationalistic (often disguised as cultural)
movements. Information about them can be gleaned from contemporaneous newspapers and in more recent historical studies of
African politics. Some of them have become diplomats and states-
men, and their life histories figure in biographical compilations
with varying degrees of thoroughness and reliability. It is further
possible to dig a rather astounding amount of book reviews from
the back files of educational, linguistic, and missionary journals.
While the reviewers may not have been genuine literary critics,
they generally provide useful information on such elementary but
basic matters as plot, theme, and style. And many living writers
show themselves willing to provide autobiographical information,
to discuss their works, and even to reminisce about literary activity
in their own countries during their formative years.

Consequently, it soon appeared possible, and therefore advisable,
to proceed a step farther; from the mere collection of factual data
and their arrangement in chronological order, to an admittedly
tentative and sketchy analysis of successive phases in the birth
and growth of some of the literatures of black Africa. As facts
were gathered, they could be seen to fall into definable patterns of
evolution which could be connected with the changing configuration of Africa's recent history. The introduction of writing and
of Christianity in Northwestern Europe from the fifth century
A.D. led to the emergence of written literatures, whose basic con-

stituents—Latin and the vernacular tongues, the Christian religion
and the traditional outlook—mixed variously from place to place,
so that Irish literature is different from Scandinavian, and Old
English from Old High German. In Africa as in Europe, the literary evolution of any given society has been part and parcel of the
wider process of culture change. Even in the present rudimentary
state of our factual knowledge, it is not utopian to frame hypotheses concerning the historical evolution of a number of the national literatures of Africa. It is quite clear, for example, that
African literature in French falls into three distinguishable periods:
prenegritude, negritude, and postnegritude. It is equally obvious
that English writing in West Africa took a sharp turn as the University of Ibadan began to exert an impact on creative writing.
Likewise, the adoption of the Roman alphabet by a significant
number of authors in Northern Nigeria and on the east coast during the thirties ushered in a new era in the literature of the Hausa
and Swahili people, which had traditionally used the Arabic script.

As more and more facts were seen to fall into definite patterns,
it appeared that modern African literatures arose from the interplay of two general factors: one is the indigenous cultural substratum; the other is the innovating impact of the West. And this
leads us to a third level of historical analysis.

Literary history as a science began in Western Europe at a time
when the acknowledged units of European history were the
nation-states. Accordingly, it developed along national lines, each
literature being examined independently of the other national
literatures. Goethe's concept of *Weltliteratur* was the first notable
hint that in literary historiography as in other fields of scholarship
and of action, the nation-states of Western Europe were just too
puny to be considered valid cultural units any longer. The growth
of comparative literature since the early years of the nineteenth
century has placed the emphasis on what the societies involved
have in common despite their undeniable diversity. This led to the
notion of a new, wider, basic unit whose frontiers are not yet quite
fixed. It certainly comprehends the whole of Europe and the
Americas, and its comparative homogeneity rests on centuries of
continuous close interrelationship. This is undoubtedly a more
fruitful, more enlightening, more enriching approach to literary
history than the narrow nationalism of earlier days. Clearly, the
new science of African literary history should be spared the Bal-

kanization that characterized the early stages of European literary history. It should be founded as soon and as firmly as possible on an international, comparative basis. In spite of the efforts of such pioneers as Jahn, little has been done as yet toward a study of African literature on a continental scale. Whereas English-speaking scholars are usually quite aware of the importance of Francophonic literature, the reverse is by no means true: ignorance of English and the dearth of French translations cause French-speaking authors and scholars to ignore the literary achievements of English-speaking Africa. Specialists in African literatures written in European languages such as French, English, or Portuguese tend to imagine that the modern literary contribution of vernacular languages is negligible, both in terms of quantity and of quality, although by far the greater amount of creative writing printed on the continent is in the vernacular tongues.

While there is, therefore, a real danger that African literary history may succumb to the narrow sectionalism and cultural nationalism that are still characteristic of much of European literary scholarship to this day, it is also necessary to beware of the equally perilous temptation of drawing hasty generalizations from an oriented selection of facts. Attempts have been made—most notably by Léopold Senghor, Kwame Nkrumah, and Janheinz Jahn —to elaborate the image of an all-African personality, or even of an all-Negro cultural configuration, which is generally subsumed under the concept of negritude. There may exist a nucleus of culture traits that all African societies have in common—in common, perhaps, with many other underdeveloped societies in the world. But it is a matter of ascertained scientific fact that various African societies have elaborated various civilizations that are all the more diversified, as they often grew without any intimate or prolonged contacts with one another. Some are democratic and others feudal or autocratic; some are pastoral and others urban; some are sedentary and others nomadic, and so forth. Each of these civilizations has its specific features that are reflected in its literary folk tradition and are likely to echo further in its written art.

Whereas, then, the first constituent of any African literature, namely, the indigenous substratum, offers a large spectrum of modulations, the other basic ingredient, the impact of Western civilization, is equally far from homogeneous and monolithic. Actually, it too should be considered not a rigid, fixed determinant, but a flexible series of variables. For one thing, it was not felt everywhere at the same time and in the same manner. It is hardly surprising that the societies of central Africa, which came latest under the influence of the white man, should have been the last to produce written literature on any significant scale; indeed, many of them have not even made a start. Further, European policies in Africa have covered a wide range of attitudes, from loose indirect rule to a strongly centralized policy of assimilation. It is presumably no coincidence that the African territories that were submitted to the Latin rule of the French and the Portuguese have resorted to the European language as their proper medium of literary expression and have hardly produced any writing in their own tongues. That the concept of negritude should have been concocted by thoroughly Frenchified intellectuals is a paradox only in appearance. Actually, negritude resulted from an aching awareness of, and a violent revulsion against, the very processes of deculturation and assimilation most successfully performed by the French. That this revulsion should have taken the form of a concept provides in itself evidence of the efficiency with which typically French modes of thought permeated the minds of the new black elite. And, again, awareness of this has turned such poets as David Diop or Tchicaya U Tam'si, such novelists as Mongo Beti or Ferdinand Oyono, into the shrillest exponents of literary anti-colonialism outside the Republic of South Africa and the Portuguese "Provinces." Looser policies—administrative, linguistic, and educational—in the greater part of British Africa did not lead to anything like the same degree of deculturation, or the same sense of alienation, or the same need for conscious reintegration. Even when they chose to use English, writers from British Africa such as Chinua Achebe or James Ngugi have kept in touch with their people and have maintained an organic relationship with their own society. Their general outlook on the great issues at stake since the mid-fifties has hardly been distorted by that feeling of estrangement that has afflicted their French-speaking colleagues.

The peculiarities of the British colonial nonsystem clearly offered greater opportunities for the indigenous substratum to assert itself in the new literature. A typical example of the ensuing variations is to be found in Nigeria. There it was that Lord Lugard sought to obviate the shortage of white administrative manpower by adapting a method of indirect government, which had proved

satisfactory in India. Throughout the wide expanse of Nigerian
territory, there was then an attempt to impose one single administrative regime over a great variety of societies—the most important
of which are the Hausa, the Yoruba, and the Ibo—while at the same
time the very looseness of that regime made it possible for each
ethnic group to maintain its own cultural personality. This is not
the place to expatiate on the political aspects and consequences of
such a situation. But the historian of Nigerian literature will have
to account for the astounding differences in the literary development of each group. Why have the Hausa stubbornly kept to the
Arabic script and the traditional genres, resorting only sporadically
to the Roman alphabet, to the Western-type novel, and not at all
to the English language? Why did the Ibo refrain from putting
their own tongue to modern literary use, while becoming the most
prolific producers of creative writing in English on the whole continent? And why is it that the Yoruba can boast two literatures,
one written in their vernacular and the other in English, both of
them equally interesting and impressive and, what is more, both of
them exhibiting similar stylistic and thematic features? The an-
swers to such questions cannot be given by any analysis of the
colonial system, which was homogeneous, but only by a careful
consideration of such indigenous culture traits as religion, social
organization, native regime, and the proportion of misoneism and
innovationism in each of the societies concerned.

The ideal historical and comparative study here advocated requires
a most astounding combination of skills—linguistic, anthropological, historical, and critical—which no normal person can be
expected to have accumulated. A really useful and scientific history of African literature on a continental scale can only be effected through closely coordinated teamwork. And it will have to
be done by African scholars. But until such are available in sufficient numbers and equipped with the necessary techniques, there
is no reason why a start, however unassuming, should not be made,
on however small a scale.

    Although African literary historiography ought to be com-
parative in approach and continental in scope, the first step is to
provide detailed studies of individual literatures. The phrase "national" literature, when used about Africa, is in need of redefini-
tion. In the present context, it will be assumed (a) that the "nation"

is the social unit to which an individual's allegiance goes, and (b) that the basic unifying factor is a common language that enables the members of the group to communicate freely with one another. In dealing with Africa, "state" and "nation" cannot be taken to coincide. The present states of the continent have maintained the artificial boundaries carved by the Europeans powers for their own purposes, which had little, if anything, to do with the spontaneous loyalties of the African people themselves. Only the smallest of the African states, such as Lesotho, can be described as national states. All the others are multinational entities, grouping into purely political and administrative units a number of societies that a needlessly derogatory tradition calls tribes. As at present, the members of each of those groups seldom have any genuine sense of ethical allegiance to the artificial state into which they are incorporated. Those among them upon whom the state has conferred certain powers feel it their moral duty to use this power for the exclusive benefit of their nation or tribe. This is the fundamental origin of the corruption that is so ominously prevalent in Africa today and has become a central theme in much of the latest African literature. Predominance of any particular tribal group in the state, however, is strongly resented by other member groups; because of this many African states have been, and still are, plagued by civil disorders. As with the tribal wars of yore, within any particular state, national or tribal groups tend to view one another as foreigners and enemies. However much this situation is to be deplored, it is a fact of African life in the present historical situation, and the study of literature must take it into account. In many cases, therefore, an African state has several national literatures in various vernacular languages, and although they may exhibit common features, each of them has its own definable identity based on causal factors. It is the historian's task to elucidate these as far as is feasible.

The basic determining element for the definition of a national group is language. There are multilingual nations in Europe, but Swiss people will tend to think of themselves primarily as Swiss citizens, regardless of whether their mother tongue is French, German, or Italian; most Belgians still think of themselves as Belgians, whether they speak Dutch or French. There are some signs of emerging national consciousness in Africa, although it is generally limited to minority elite groups. Some Nigerian writers, no doubt, would place their Nigerian citizenship above their Yoruba, or Ibo, or Hausa, identity, and this would be even truer of smaller ethnic groups that are hardly capable of playing any role in Nigerian power politics. In South African literature, there is some evidence of a sense of South African identity that outgrows the boundaries not only of linguistic and tribal definitions but also, sometimes, of race and color. In most instances, however, the sharing of a common mother tongue is still the prevailing ingredient in identity definition especially in literature. A complicating factor is that people who belong to the same ethnic group and share the same mother tongue may write in different languages. It is clearly perceptible, however, that works like D. O. Fagunwa's Yoruba novels, Amos Tutuola's highly idiosyncretic English stories, and Wole Soyinka's drama *A Dance of the Forests* have more in common with one another than they have with any work produced in English or in the vernacular by Ibo or Hausa writers. Conversely, a number of South African Bantu writers using English have been born and bred in completely detribalized urban communities, and there are many Cape Colored writers using Afrikaans, who have never been part of any tribal society. These, however, are at present exceptional phenomena, although they probably point the way to trends that may prevail in an unspecifiable future. Finally, it must be stressed that ethnic and linguistic definitions often cut across state boundaries, for homogeneous ethnic groups have often been divided, through the pragmatic phantasy of European power politics, between several modern states. The Ewe people spread on both sides of the Ghana-Togo border. The Fulani people have dispersed over a wide area that extends from the Adamawa in Cameroun to the Fouta Toro in Senegal, and includes sizable parts of Nigeria, Guinea, and other countries; nor is it always clear whether they still identify themselves as Fulani. Fulani writers in Northern Nigeria have been converted to the Hausa language. The Southern Sotho population overlaps the boundaries of Lesotho; for nearly two decades there have been writers who are ethnically Sotho, who use the Southern Sotho language, but who are nationals of the Republic of South Africa.

In the face of this extraordinary confusion and complexity, it has seemed advisable to focus each of the chapters of this book on the literature produced by one ethnic group. Even this definition, simple and straightforward as it may sound, should be taken as just a norm from which it will sometimes be necessary to depart. In

Portuguese Africa, and in the greater part of what used to be
French Africa, there are practically no vernacular writers, and
authors from widely separated areas are brought together by their
common participation in a European language and culture much
more efficiently than they are kept apart by traditional tribal al-
legiances. A considerable segment of Swahili literature has been
composed in Zanzibar and the neighboring islands by true-blood
Arabs, the descendants of fifteenth-century emigrants from Hadh-
ramaut, who have adopted, and indeed appreciably contributed
to Swahili culture. They are an integral part of Swahili society,
although they may be racially distinct from the bulk of the Swahili
population. Whereas all early Xhosa and Sotho writers composed
in their own languages, some of the first imaginative works by
Zulu authors are in English; it has seemed that they should be considered part of Zulu literature. To this must be added that not all
Ethiopian writers are Amhara. The Amhara are simply the dominant group in a polyethnic state, and in the absence of any reliable
census figures, they may well represent only a minority of the
country's population. Yet, theirs has become the official language
of Ethiopia. As biographical data are not always available, it is
sometimes impossible to decide whether an Ethiopian writer is
truly an Amhara or belongs to one of the other ethnic groups, such
as the Galla, whose traditional culture is extremely different. Until
more knowledge has been collected, it is wise to consider all literature written in Amharic as a unit, without losing sight of the fact
that, as among the Zulu, there are Amhara, or at any rate Ethiopian
authors, who use both the vernacular and English.

The four literatures discussed in this volume are Xhosa, Sotho,
Zulu, and Amharic. This selection is partly due to the mere fact
that, of all modern African literatures, these are the ones about
which it has proved possible to gather the largest amount of information in the course of the last ten years. At the present time,
they lend themselves better than others to historical treatment.
There is, however, a more relevant consideration, which justifies
this choice not simply on grounds of expediency but also at the
comparative level.

   The Xhosa, Sotho, and Zulu belong to the so-called Bantu people
of southern Africa. Until the coming of the white man, theirs were
illiterate societies and their religions were of the "animistic" type—

a convenient label to describe sets of beliefs of which little is known except that they are neither Christian nor Muslim. The Amhara of Ethiopia, on the contrary, are of Semitic origin. Their modern literature is the continuation of an ancient indigenous tradition of creative writing mainly inspired by Coptic Christianity.

In spite of important similarities in the subjacent native cultures, Xhosa, Sotho, and Zulu literatures first arose independently of one another, at different times, and developed along different lines. Comparative analysis of the three is bound to bring out the manner in which the diverse modalities of the Western impact affected the birth and growth of literature in Africa.

By the early years of this century, the Xhosa and the Zulu had been forcibly and completely subjected to European control, but the process did not occur simultaneously. The Xhosa had been in close touch with the white man for several decades when the first European traders ventured to Zululand. Whereas the conquest of Xhosaland—called Caffraria in the nineteenth century—proceeded with comparative ease, the Zulu put up fierce resistance until the crushing of the rebellion of 1906. So, although the Xhosa and the Zulu both belong to the same Nguni group and have extensive linguistic and cultural affinities, differences in the evolution of modern literature among them must be explained to a considerable extent by differences in the historical processes that led to their final absorption into the Union (now the Republic) of South Africa. On the contrary, Lesotho, as the British protectorate of Basutoland, already enjoyed a large measure of autonomy before it became independent in 1966. Its situation in this respect is closer to that of Ethiopia, which managed to elude European colonialism except for the brief spell of Italian occupation between 1936 and 1941. Whereas white supremacy was imposed upon the Xhosa and the Zulu, it is significant that the first bearers of Western influence, cultural and technical, should have been *invited* to Lesotho and to Ethiopia by such far-sighted innovating rulers as King Moshoeshoe and Emperor Menelik.

This volume consists of four monograph studies attempting to record and order all the data that have been traced so far. It is hardly necessary to state that these accounts are by no means intended as final. They have been allowed to reach print in the expectation that they may convince other, more competent scholars that historical study of modern African literature is both necessary and feasible, and so prompt them to find more evidence, fill gaps, correct errors of fact and interpretation, in order to complete, or completely to remold, the evolutionary patterns that suggested themselves as a result of my own limited research.

The concluding chapter will endeavor to frame some comparative generalizations—which should not be considered more than working hypotheses—along the lines suggested in the preceding paragraphs, in the hope that this research about the birth and early growth of modern literature in black Africa may contribute toward the solution of a problem that has proved most frustratingly puzzling to historians of classical and medieval literature—the problem of how creative writing originates in societies emerging into literacy.

Chapter **1** **Xhosa Literature**

The original inhabitants of southern Africa were neither black nor white: they were Bushmen, a yellow-brown race who came to the area one thousand years ago. But for several centuries before the first Portuguese sailors discovered the Cape peninsula on their way to India in 1497, the Bushmen had been gradually dispossessed by the more powerful Hottentots. These had come from the Great Lakes in East Africa, and were moving southwestward under Bantu pressure; they are supposed to have reached the Atlantic coast in the late thirteenth century. When the first Dutch colonists settled the Cape peninsula in 1652, they found a society where the Bushmen were subjected to the Hottentots.

As to the Bantu-speaking tribes, they had crossed the Limpopo River in the eleventh century at the latest. Recent historical research[1] suggests that by 1300 the various Bantu tribes had settled in the territories that they still occupy. There were two main groups. The Sotho-Tswana group was moving in the interior, parallel to the coast of the Indian Ocean; ultimately they divided into three distinct subgroups. The Tswana settled in the areas now known as Botswana, the Orange Free State, and western Transvaal; the Northern Sotho occupied central and northwestern Transvaal; the Southern Sotho came to constitute the kingdom of Lesotho. The Sotho-Tswana people, however, were preceded in their southward advance by the Nguni group, who were trekking along the coast; these divided into two main subgroups. Their vanguard was constituted by the Xhosa, who had settled north of the Kei River

21

in the sixteenth century and, by the mid-seventeenth century, had reached as far south as the Great Fish River. The Xhosa were followed by a number of other Nguni tribes that were later unified under the name of Zulu; these had established themselves in present-day Natal.

The Xhosa-speaking people are a large and diversified group divided into many tribes and clans. Indeed, some of them—such as the Hlubi, the Bhaca, or the Mfengu (known in European usage as "Fingo")—do not belong to the original Xhosa nation at all, but were driven from their own land by Zulu expansion in the first quarter of the nineteenth century. They settled in Xhosa territory and adopted much of the Xhosa language and culture.[2] These tribes maintained a tradition of mutual distrust and hostility well into the nineteenth century, chiefly because their pastoral economy made continuous expansion imperative, while European presence and power made it impossible for them to conquer hitherto unsettled land. Besides, frequent dynastic quarrels also made for inner divisiveness. Such disturbances offered welcome opportunities for white armed intervention and pretexts for European settlement. In 1865 the area between the Kei River and the Great Fish River, where many white colonists had already established themselves and which was known, therefore, as British Kaffraria, was formally incorporated into the Cape Colony. Further expansion north of the Kei resulted in the eventual annexation of the whole Xhosa territory by the government of the Cape of Good Hope in 1879. That was the area now known as the Transkei, which is inhabited by the majority of the 3,570,000 Xhosa people. Somewhat larger than Switzerland, it extends from the Kei River to Natal and from the Indian Ocean to the Lesotho border. In 1963 it became the first of a number of semiautonomous all-black states projected by the South African government, and commonly known as Bantustans.

If we are to understand how and why literature of a modern type, as contradistinguished from the oral tradition, originated where and when it did, it is necessary to dwell on some details of Xhosa history at the time of early contacts with white expansion.[3]

The earliest authenticated date is 1686, when a Dutch ship, the *Stavenisse*, was wrecked on the coast of the Indian Ocean. In their effort to reach the white settlement at the Cape, its survivors crossed the territories of many tribes, among them the Xhosa, whose paramount chief was named Togu. According to tribal accounts, this Togu was a direct descendant of Xhosa, who—allegedly in the first half of the sixteenth century—separated his own tribe from the Nguni nation. In the late seventeenth century, Togu was succeeded as paramount chief by his son Ngconde, then by his grandson Tshiwo, who died in 1702. In that same year, Tshiwo's heir was born; this was Phalo, who reigned until 1775. Phalo was succeeded by his son Gcaleka (1730-1792), who gave his name to Gcalekaland.[4] But in consequence of a dispute between Gcaleka and Phalo's eldest son Rarabe (1722-1787), the latter seceded and formed a separate clan, the Rarabe Xhosa. While Gcaleka was succeeded as paramount chief by Khawuta (1760–1820) and later by Hintsa (1790-1835), the Rarabe Xhosa had settled the part of the country that lies between the Keiskama and Buffalo rivers. When the lesser, semi-independent Xhosa clans established along the northern bank of the Great Fish River came into conflict with the whites in the so-called first Kaffir war (1779), Rarabe "sent word to the Boers dissociating himself from these disturbances." [5] As his rightful heir, Mlawu, died before him, the chieftainship of the Rarabe Xhosa came to Mlawu's son, Ngqika (1775-1828); but since the latter was a mere boy, his uncle Ndlambe (1755-1828) was appointed regent and ruled with undisputed authority for several years. By the time Ngqika came of age, Ndlambe sought to keep the overlordship of the Rarabe Xhosa for himself. In order to secure the assistance of the Europeans, he entered into an alliance with the Boers and fought for them against the other tribes during the third Kaffir war (1793). This attitude led to a division between his upholders and those of Ngqika. The tension was increased when Ngqika had an incestuous affair with the beautiful Thuthula, one of his uncle's younger wives. Meanwhile the British had taken over from the Dutch in the early years of the century, and Lord Charles Somerset met Ngqika. He recognized him not only as head of the Rarabe Xhosa, but also (presumably out of ignorance) as paramount chief of all the Xhosa, a title that, in accordance with customary law, was then held by Khawuta. As a result, the other chiefs sided with Ndlambe. Things came to a head in the so-called fifth Kaffir war (1818), when Ngqika was assailed by a Xhosa confederacy at the battle of Amalinde near the present city of Kingwilliamstown. But the English came to Ngqika's rescue and, as John Henderson Soga records "prevented his total destruction; whereupon Ndlambe, in great fury, turned

upon the Whites and attacked them at Queenstown, the result of
which action was that Ndlambe's power was completely destroyed." [6]

Another consequence of these events was that the early missionaries did not go to the hostile tribes along the border, but to
the Rarabe Xhosa who were on friendly terms with the Boers, and
later to the Ngqika Xhosa, who were on friendly terms with the
English. These were the first Bantu people to be exposed to Christian proselytizing and to receive a literate education. It was among
this particular section of the Xhosa nation that vernacular writing
originated. To a large extent, their geographical situation at the
turn of the century accounts for their prominent role in the development of modern Xhosa literature, and their historical experience
and internecine quarrels became an important source of inspiration
for later Nguni writers, both Xhosa and Zulu.

Ntsikana, The First Christian Bard

Even before the writing stage was reached, Xhosa literature[7]
offers an example of one of those transitional phenomena that must
not have been infrequent, but whose memory has usually disappeared. In precolonial Africa as in medieval Europe, poetic composition was usually anonymous because its function was primarily social. During the 1830s, however, British missionaries in Madagascar managed to record oral works by individual traditional
composers, whose names were thus preserved, together with some
valuable biographical information.[8] Whereas those Malagasy
poems were of pre-Christian inspiration, the earliest Xhosa author
whose name is recorded did not compose in the "pagan" tradition
but was inspired by the newly introduced ideals of Christianity.
This Christian oral poet was called Ntsikana, and as his life and
career were intimately bound up with events that have since become part of the historical and literary legacy of the Xhosa people, they are worth recounting in some detail.[9]

The first representative of the London Missionary Society, who
arrived at the Cape in 1798, was a Dutchman, Dr. Johannes Theo-
dosius van der Kemp (1747-1811). His purpose was not to help
the Moravian Brothers evangelize the Hottentots, but to go to the
"Caffres" [10] east of the Great Fish River, which was the agreed
boundary between the colony and the Xhosa. In September 1800,

van der Kemp passed into the territory of Chief Ngqika, whom he met at his "Great Place" in the Tyumie Valley. For several months he wandered between the Tyumie and the Buffalo rivers. This was the first direct contact of the Xhosa with Christianity. Rumors of impending tribal war constrained van der Kemp to leave Ngqika's country toward the end of 1800, and the government at Cape Town decided to allow no other missionaries to go there in spite of Ngqika's requests to that effect. This decision was not reversed untli 1815.

In April 1816 the Reverend Joseph Williams of the London Missionary Society crossed the river, and in July he took up residence with his wife and his infant son in Ngqika's territory. Williams died on 23 August 1818 and was not replaced until June 1820, when the Reverend John Brownlee settled at a place called Gwali, which Williams had built as an outstation, and which was later to be known as Old Lovedale. In a letter of 3 August 1822, Brownlee wrote as follows:

One of the strongest encouragements to Missions in this country is the blessing which seems to have accompanied the labours of the late Mr. Williams, not only among the people of the Institution, but also among those who were occasional visitors of which I shall give you an instance presently. There is a kraal of about one hundred population, who, from the time of his death to my entrance into Caffreland (a period of nearly two years) were accustomed to meet regularly for worship morning and evening, and to observe the Lord's day. The chief person of the kraal, who conducted the worship, died about two years ago. He composed a hymn in their language, which they still sing in their worship of God.[11]

This hymn, and its author's name, were first recorded in 1828 by Dr. John Philip of the Church of Scotland:

Among those to whom the labours of Mr. Williams had been useful, the Chief Sicana deserves particular notice in this place. This individual survived his teacher a few months only. Under his last illness, Sicana's mind was elevated above the world by the hope of eternal blessedness. . . . Sicana was a poet as well as a Christian, and though he could neither read nor write, he composed hymns, which he repeated to his people, till they could retain them upon their memories. The following may be considered as a specimen of his poetical abilities, and which his people are still accustomed to sing in a low monotonous native air.[12]

The hymn is here given in the more faithful translation of R. H.
W. Shepherd:[13]

> He, the great God, high in Heaven,
> Great "I am" of truth the Buckler,
> Great "I am" of truth the Stronghold,
> Great "I am" in whom truth shelters.
> What art Thou in Highest Heaven,
> Who created life around us,
> Who created Heaven above us,
> And the stars, the Pleiades.
> We were blind until He taught us.
> (Thou mad'st us blind, it was Thy purpose.)
> With a trumpet gave the message,
> As he hunted for our spirits.
> Toiled to make our foes our brothers.
> (Thou our leader who dost guide us.)
> Then he cast His cloak about us,
> Cloak of Him whose hands are wounded,
> Cloak of Him whose feet are bleeding,
> See the blood that streameth for us;
> Flows it, though we have not asked it?
> Is it paid without our praying?
> Heaven our Home with no beseeching?

Professor Archibald C. Jordan, himself a Xhosa novelist of note
and the best authority on the history of early Xhosa literature, has
pointed out the importance of this poem: not only is it "the first
literary composition ever to be assigned to individual formulation—
thereby constituting a bridge between the traditional and the post-
traditional period," but moreover, being a Christian poem composed in the traditional manner of the praise poetry devoted to
chiefs and ancestors, it shows that "the idioms, style and technique
of the traditional lyric are easily adaptable to new conceptions." [14]

Thanks to the written evidence of Ntsikana's earliest disciples,
which has been studied by Jordan, and to his biography written in
Xhosa by the Reverend John Knox Bokwe, it is now possible to
give a more detailed account of the poet's life.

According to Bokwe, Ntsikana was born around 1783. His
father, Gabo, belonged to the Ngqika tribe; his mother was Gabo's
second wife; her family were followers of Ndlambe. Out of jealousy, Gabo's first wife accused her of sorcery, and she had to run

away to her own clan for her life. Ntsikana was born there, but when he was twelve or thirteen, his father had him brought to the Ngqika clan, where he later heard the teaching of van der Kemp. After the missionary's departure, he was schooled and circumcised according to custom, and his father presented him with some cattle and two wives. Jordan tells us that he "lived and enjoyed the pagan life as fully as any man of his social accomplishments. He was a great composer, singer and dancer, as well as a polygamist, adulterer and diviner." His gifts as a "prophet" raised him to a position of some eminence at Ngqika's court. This drove him into bitter rivalry with his opposite number on Ndlambe's side, a prophet known as Nxele or Makhanda. Consequently, Ntsikana became deeply involved in the dynastic feuds of the Xhosa chieftains, and the fact that Ngqika was supported by the British goes a long way to account for his interest in the white man's religion.

Although dating is hazardous, both Ntsikana and Nxele had been exposed to Christian teaching, presumably under van der Kemp as well as Williams.[15] When Ntsikana's conversion actually occurred is unknown; in all likelihood, it was the outcome of a slow evolution. He himself traced it back to a visionary experience in which he said he was born anew. One morning, as he was looking at his favorite cow, he saw a strange radiating light that others around him did not perceive. During this illumination of the soul, he realized that his life task was to spread the word of God. On another occasion soon after, a mysterious wind thrice arose to prevent him from taking part in a tribal dance. He then went to the river to wash off the ritual paintings with which his body was covered; apparently, this was as near to baptism as he ever came. According to some of his later disciples, the vision occurred before he had ever met a white missionary, but this does not seem very likely. In any event, after Williams's death in 1818, Ntsikana set up his own "school" at Makanzara, where he proclaimed "this Thing" that, he said, had entered him. Apart from the hymn quoted above, he composed a number of songs for calling his adherents to prayer, or for choir singing. He taught them to give up heathen dances and traditional face-painting. He spent most of his time in prayer and preaching, advising his followers to suffer persecution for the new faith. Ngqika himself almost became his first convert. But Jordan quotes the words of Makhaphela Noyi Balfour, a son of Noyi, Ntsikana's leading disciple and successor, to

the effect that because Ngqika "adhered so much to this outmoded
Xhosa way of life, he was easily led away from his aim by his
councillors." This episode was later dramatized in a long narrative
poem by the Reverend James J. R. Jolobe, *Thuthula.*

Throughout the first quarter of the century, the dynastic feuds
of the Xhosa were closely interwoven with the wider trends of
colonial enterprise. At an early stage, Ndlambe and his followers
had been defeated by Ngqika's warriors and had been constrained
to infiltrate in growing numbers into an area west of the Great
Fish River, within the colony, where there occurred constant
clashes with the Boer farmers. In 1812, the authorities at Cape
Town chose to consider that the Xhosa had no right to be there,
and they made it their policy to drive them back across the river.
By then, it had become impossible for Ngqika and his people to
accommodate several thousand refugees on their own land, even
supposing they had been willing to try. The consequence was the
fifth Kaffir war. After being defeated by Ndlambe and his allies
Ngqika turned in wrath against his Christian advisers. Ntsikana
and his disciples had to flee for their lives. But as the officially
recognized paramount chief, Ngqika appealed for British support,
which was gladly supplied. Ndlambe was finally defeated in 1819.

What little is known of Nxele's teachings point to a stark contrast with Ntsikana's.[16] British help to Ndlambe's opponent
prompted Nxele to deviate from the orthodox type of Christianity
taught by the missionaries, and to evolve one of the earliest syncretic cults on record in southern Africa, with a tribal god alleged
to be stronger than the white man's God. He reverted to polygamy
on the grounds that the Xhosa god wanted his people to multiply
and populate the earth, and he advocated a return to traditional
worshiping practices. It is likely that Nxele too composed songs
and hymns. The result of Ndlambe's defeat of 1819 was to drive
his adherents underground, so that orthodox Christianity and, with
it, literacy and the use of printing, became a monopoly of their
adversaries, the Ngqika Xhosa.

Ntsikana himself must have died about the end of 1820 after
recommending to his disciples that they never return to the traditional way of life and that they follow the teachings of the missionaries. More important, perhaps, than his own literary achievement,
is the fact that as Jordan says, "through his influence, a few young
disciples were introduced to the arts of reading and writing, and

that, inspired by his exemplary life and teaching, these men became the harbingers of the dawn of literacy among the indigenous peoples of Southern Africa." More specifically, he should be considered the initiator of original Bantu hymn-writing, which was to gather momentum at the end of the century, as "students who were given a sound musical grounding in training institutions, and others who developed without a specialised background but as a result of their own intense eagerness, their talent and the help of their fellows . . . emerged as hymn-writers and composers of both serious and light, religious and secular choral music."[17] Immediate literary developments, however, were intimately bound up with the intervention of the Glasgow Missionary Society, and with the history of its schools and printing presses.

The Glasgow Missionary Society and Early Xhosa Writing

The first agents of the Church of Scotland reached the Cape in 1821. In December 1823 they established themselves in the Tyumie valley, where John Bennie and John Ross set up their first printing press. In 1824 they moved to a place called Gwali, which was renamed Lovedale in 1826, in honor of the secretary of the Glasgow Missionary Society, Dr. John Love, who had died in 1825.

The uses to which the press was put followed the pattern that was standard practice throughout Africa.[18] First, the Xhosa language was reduced to writing, and the missionaries composed a word list and an elementary grammar to help them both in their dealings with the population and in the preparation of Bible translations. The first major work to come out of the Lovedale Press appeared in 1826 under the title *A Systematic Vocabulary of the Kaffrarian Language in two parts; to which is prefixed an Introduction to Kaffrarian Grammar.*

The next task was the publication of scriptural material. Already in the twenties, John Bennie had translated parts of the Bible into Xhosa, but this work had remained in manuscript. Actually the first printed Xhosa version of scriptural material was *Luke's Gospel*, which was brought out by two Wesleyan missionaries, William A. Boyce and Barnabas Show, on the Methodist Press at Grahamstown.

Xhosa journalism was also inaugurated by the Wesleyans. In

July 1837 they published the first issue of a paper called *Umshumayeli Indaba (The Preacher's News)*, which appeared at irregular intervals until April 1841. It was succeeded by *Isibuto Samavo (A Collection of Stories)*, seven issues of which were printed at three-month intervals, from January 1843 to July 1844. In spite of these Methodist initiatives, it was the Scottish mission that really became the focus of native Xhosa writing.

The Gwali station and its press were destroyed in the sixth Kaffir war in 1834. Five years later, a second press was sent to the Tyumie valley as part of the equipment of the new Lovedale station, near the present-day town of Alice. In 1841 the mission school was attended by nine white and eleven black pupils. In that same year, the missionaries launched a Xhosa magazine, *Ikwezi (Morning Star)*, of which four issues were printed between August 1844 and December 1845. There, as Jordan points out, we find "the earliest records of anything ever written by a Xhosa speaker in Xhosa." Native contributions were mostly the work of the first converts, disciples of Ntsikana who must have learned to read and write in their old age. The most important of those early writers included Ntsikana's son William Kobe Ntsikana, Zaze Soga, and Makhaphela Noyi Balfour. They wrote mainly of the wars between Ngqika and Ndlambe, and of the rivalry between their respective advisers, the two "prophets" Ntsikana and Makhanda. This they did in the spirit of the old oral tradition. Jordan emphasizes that "none of these disciples set out to write history as such. They set out to write about their mentor, and the chiefs are mentioned only insofar as their rule affected Ntsikana."

Meanwhile, competition for land in Xhosa territory was involving not only rival native groups, but also a growing number of European farmers. When the seventh Kaffir war, known as the War of the Axe, broke out in 1846, it was no longer a dynastic feud of the old type. It started as a popular rebellion against the Cape Town authorities' determination to ensure the maintenance of what they considered law and order even beyond the Great Fish River. Lovedale was closed, the missionaries were dispersed, and the first principal, the Reverend William Govan, returned to Europe. He took with him the most promising of his young scholars, who was to become the first ordained Bantu minister, and who reached fame through his literary achievements.

This young man was Tiyo Soga.[19] He was born at Gwali in
1829. His grandfather, Jotelo, who is reported to have been killed
in the battle of Amalinde in 1818, was a trusted adviser of Ngqika.
So was his father, Soga. The latter had eight wives and twenty-
nine children, but, according to R. H. W. Shepherd, "he was not
merely an unprogressive pagan, for he was the first African to
use a plough in his district and the first to make a water-furrow."[20]
Soga was opposed to the ninth and last Kaffir war of 1877-1878,
and did not fight in it; yet, he refused to desert the Great Chief
Sandile and to seek some safe shelter. He was killed by Fingo
auxiliaries of the colonial army in 1878.[21]

Tiyo's mother was a Christian and sent her son to school at
Gwali under the Reverend William Chalmers, who found him a
bright boy and sent him on to Lovedale for further education.
When Govan took him to Scotland in 1846, Tiyo attended the
Glasgow Free Church National Seminary until 1848. He then
returned to Africa with the Reverend George Brown to do
catechetical work at the Umondale Mission in the vicinity of
Keiskamahoek.[22] The eighth Kaffir war began at the end of 1850,
and Tiyo Soga returned to Scotland to prepare for the ministry.
He took the arts course at the University of Glasgow, and received
his clerical training in the Theological Hall of the United Presbyterian Church. In 1856 he became the first African minister to be
ordained in Great Britain. The following year, he married a Scottish young lady, Janet Burnside, and the couple soon left for
Africa, where Tiyo Soga founded a mission station at Emgwali
in the Stutterheim district, among the Ngqika Xhosa.

His first dedication was to the healing of the wounds that the
Xhosa people had inflicted upon themselves in the course of an
astonishing, gruesome episode that took place in 1856-1857 and
that was to haunt the imagination of poets and playwrights for
several generations.[23] In March 1856, Mhlakaza, councillor of the
Paramount Chief Sarili, was told by his daughter Nongqause that
she had had a vision of strange people and cattle. Soon after, he
too claimed to have seen, in the words of Charles Brownlee's
report,

a number of black people among whom he recognized his brother
some years dead. He was told by these people that they had come from
across the water; that they were the people—the Russians[24]—who had

been fighting against the English with whom they would wage perpetual warfare; and they had now come to aid the Kafirs, but before
anything could be done for them they were to put away witchcraft,
and as they would have abundance of cattle at the coming resurrection,
those now in their possession were to be destroyed.[25]

This prophecy kindled bitter conflicts. Tiyo's father, one of
Sarili's Christian advisers, joined the white missionaries in trying
to prevent the wholesale sacrifice of the cattle, but to no avail.
The situation of the Xhosa was indeed desperate. As Monica
Wilson points out, they had "lost the greater part of their land
to the whites, a little to the coloured people, and some to the
Mfengu refugees, who became allies of the whites. They fought
bitterly to retain it but the inequality in arms (most Xhosa fought
with spears and all whites with firearms); the fact that the whites
were mounted, whereas the Xhosa mostly fought on foot; and
above all the power of an organized state as opposed to fragmen-
tary chiefdoms, outweighed superiority in numbers."[26] A feeling
of utter impotence prompted Chief Sarili and the majority of
the people to resort to supernatural means and to obey the ancestors' injunction, with the predictable consequences in terms
of destitution and starvation: "At least 150,000 to 200,000 cattle
were killed. By February 1857 the whole countryside was starv-
ing. . . . The population of certain chiefdoms between the Kei
and the Fish was estimated to have dropped from 104,721 in
January 1857, to 37,696 in December—a loss of over 67,000.
Brownlee estimated that of these, 20,000 had died, and 30,000
moved into the colony for employment." In analyzing the significance of those events, Monica Wilson concludes as follows:

The cattle-killing was clearly, in one aspect, a "resistance movement," in which people participated in the hope of getting rid of the
whites and recovering their land. It was also a "revivalist" movement
involving purification from witchcraft; and it was a fusion of old and
new religious ideas. The symbolism was rooted both in ancient notions
of the shades and revelation through diviners, and in Christian teaching
of the apocalypse.

Tiyo Soga returned to Africa in the midst of the famine and
for several years was mainly engaged in rehabilitation work

among his people. It was, however, during that period that he began writing hymns.

While the earliest printed books or booklets published by Protestant missionaries were mostly translations from the Bible, at a very early stage they also produced hymnbooks. Anglo-Saxon Protestantism and African cultures share a common taste for community singing. Throughout Africa, the first hymns in vernacular languages were composed, more or less knowledgeably, by the missionaries themselves, but the rapid development of the schools soon led them to encourage composition by their more gifted native students. Indeed, the very first written poems by native speakers in Yoruba and in Malagasy and, presumably, in a number of other languages, were hymns. The success of the genre is not to be explained solely on the grounds of missionary concentration on devotional writing. A Christian hymn, after all, is little else than a praise song to God, and early African writers were bound to find the genre congenial, as it enabled them to put traditional literary taste and poetic techniques in the service of their new beliefs. The case of Ntsikana is especially significant in this respect. Tiyo Soga started writing hymns on his return from Scotland in 1857, when he produced "Lizalis' indinga lakho" ("Fulfil Thy Promise"), and he went on doing so until his death. The best known of his compositions are "Khangelani nizibone izibele ezingaka" ("Open Your Eyes and Behold How Great the Blessings Are")and "Sinesipho esikhulu esisiphiweyo thina" ("We Have a Great Gift Which Was Given Us"). Many of his hymns were incorporated into the Xhosa hymnbooks produced by the Glasgow Missionary Society and other missionary presses. They are still favorites in Xhosa church services today.

From 1862, Tiyo Soga participated in the restoration of Xhosa journalism, which had gone through many vicissitudes since the Methodist missionaries had founded the first vernacular newspaper twenty-five years earlier. The war of 1846 had been responsible for the end of *Ikwezi*. No attempt was made to start a new Xhosa paper until 1850, when the Wesleyan missionaries started a magazine entitled *Isitunywa Senyanga (The Monthly Messenger)*, which was printed in Kingwilliamstown. It went through five issues only, as its publication was interrupted after the issue of 21 December 1850 by the eighth Kaffir war. The next journalistic

venture originated at Lovedale in 1862. It was a monthly magazine
entitled *Indaba (The News)*. Edited by William Govan, it printed
contributions both in Xhosa and in English, and it lasted until 1865.
From the first issue, Tiyo Soga was a regular contributor to *Indaba*
under the pseudonym of UNonjiba Waseluhlangeni ("The Dove
of the Nation"). Most of his articles were didactic and moralizing,
although they had a characteristic humorous twist. But he also
published recordings of oral art, fables, legends, proverbs, praise
songs, and genealogies, of which he was an eager collector. Contrary to what is often claimed by the ill informed and the preju-
diced, those early Christian writers were no renegades. They and
their elders had lived and were still living in societies torn by
tribal strife. They adopted the Gospel of love which was preached
to them because they found it better than the sectional ethos of
tribalism. They did so all the more eagerly because during the
first half of the century the missionaries were undoubtedly the
most fervent defenders of the black man's rights against white
encroachment. But within the framework of the new belief and
the new morality, they remained true to their own people. They
respected most of the tribal customs and traditions, and they did
a lot to prevent oral lore from falling into oblivion. In many cases,
the missionaries were willing enough to make room in their magazines for records of ethnographic and literary material. But their
primary purpose was the spreading of the Gospel. Quite naturally,
of the total mass of early writings, those that dealt with devotional
and educational topics got into print more readily than the recordings of folk traditions. Much of the material gathered by Tiyo
Soga has never been published, and though this is the first, it is by
no means the last, such occurrence in this pioneering period of
modern African literature.

It was, however, chiefly as a translator that Tiyo Soga was
renowned in his own day. He was a respected authority on the
Xhosa language, and in the late sixties he sat on the interdenominational committee appointed to revise the Xhosa translation of
the Bible. Already in the late fifties, he had embarked on a vernacular rendering of *Pilgrim's Progress*. Of the whole corpus of
European literature, Bunyan's masterpiece is the most widely translated work in Africa. Because of its edifying purpose and allegorical structure, the missionaries found it eminently suitable for
African readers, and it exerted considerable influence on the early

stages of creative writing in Bantu languages. Tiyo Soga finished translating the first part, as he noted in his diary, on 21 November 1886. The book came from the press in 1867 under the title *U-Hambo lomhambi*; it was dedicated to William Govan. It is considered a Bantu classic in its own right, and Jordan claims that it had "almost as great an influence on the Xhosa language as the Authorized Version of the Bible upon English." [27] The second part was to be translated by Tiyo's son, John Henderson Soga, in 1929.

In 1866 Tiyo Soga left Emgwali to establish a new mission north of the Kei, at Tutura, near Butterworth, where he died on 12 August 1871, from acute congestion of the lungs, while translating the *Acts of the Apostles*.

Tiyo Soga was in many respects an exceptional figure. He was the first black Southern African to be favored with a university education. He was one of the privileged few who had been able not only to travel to, but also to live in Europe. He was the first to enter the church ministry and, as such, to occupy a position of spiritual prestige and authority within the new order that was beginning to take shape. His missionary protectors and friends were opponents of the concept of white superiority and supremacy. His work reflects the comparative smoothness with which the acculturation process occurred for him. It falls into a pattern that will remain basic, although with significant modifications. His hymns, scriptural translations, and other devotional writings testify to the depth and genuineness of his Christian faith. His concern with the recording and preservation of folk material shows a sense of identification with the traditions and dignity of his own people. In his life and work, both attitudes are harmoniously reconciled. Although he considered that material civilization without the Christian faith would destroy the traditional culture utterly, he was equally convinced that Christianity without African access to educational and economic opportunities would merely keep the Xhosa in their inferior status. In the 1850s, this was the prevailing viewpoint among the missionaries, in contrast to the colonists, whom Tiyo rebuked because they "do not like the elevation of the natives, whom they would fain keep down as men and maid-servants." [28] As the settlers' policy of white supremacy increasingly submerged the genuine Christian outlook of the missionaries, and as white power tightened its hold over Xhosaland, younger writers soon found it impossible to achieve the inner poise and the singleness of mind characteristic of Tiyo Soga. Of these, the first and most important was William W. Gqoba, whose literary career illustrates the growing dichotomy with which the changing course of events was inevitably to plague the African's mind.

William Wellington Gqoba was born into the Ngqika clan near Gaga in 1840. After attending elementary mission school at Tyumie, he was sent to Lovedale in 1853. There he learned the trade of wagon-making, a job that he pursued for the next ten years. But he was gifted in other ways as well. He was highly esteemed for his knowledge of English, and for his teaching and preaching abilities. In the late 1860s, the Reverend Tiyo Soga invited him to teach at Emgwali. He later went to Kingwilliamstown, where he taught until 1873. Then he became pastor of the Native Church at Rabula, where he worked for four years. The year 1877 marked the outbreak of the ninth and last Kaffir war, which was to initiate the formal annexation of Xhosaland to the Colony. Gqoba left for Peelton, a small place west of East London, and worked for a while as an assistant preacher in the church there. He was also employed for a time as a translator at the Native Registry Office in Kimberley. He then returned to Lovedale as an assistant in the translation classes.

Meanwhile, at Lovedale, *Indaba* had been succeeded in 1876 by a bilingual monthly, *The Kaffir Express* and by an English journal, *The Christian Express*, which was to become, in 1922, the *South African Outlook*. *The Kaffir Express*, however, was soon replaced by *Isigidimi samaXhosa (The Xhosa Messenger)*, written entirely in the vernacular. In 1884 Gqoba became the editor of *Isigidimi*, to which he was also a frequent contributor. He died suddenly on 26 April 1888, and the journal disappeared with him.

Gqoba was a prolific writer, and his works fall into two categories—Christian inspiration and folk inspiration—thus following the pattern set by Tiyo Soga in his endeavor to reconcile the old tradition and the new faith. But the modulations to be observed are immensely significant.

Like Tiyo Soga, Gqoba remained deeply immersed in the customary life of his people. Like many other African writers, he felt the need to preserve in writing the wealth of oral wisdom that had found expression in a vast number of proverbial sayings. These he gathered and recorded and explained in modern Xhosa prose. Further, as the *Ikwesi* contributors had done in earlier days, he also wrote accounts of important events in Xhosa history, past and present. Indeed, his narration of the cattle-killing episode, which took place when he was an adolescent, is the earliest printed source in the vernacular.

Unlike earlier writers, however, Gqoba was not concerned solely with his own tribe. Although the Ngqika Xhosa had been only very indirectly affected by the tremendous upsurge of Zulu power in the first quarter of the nineteenth century, Gqoba wrote a historical account of the scattering of the tribes under Chaka's reign, *ImBali yaseMbo* (*History of the North-Eastern Peoples*), which illustrates a budding awareness of the interdependence of the black peoples faced with the European threat throughout the subcontinent.

As had been the case with Tiyo Soga, much of Gqoba's writing was not printed during his lifetime, but a number of his unpublished notes and essays appeared in 1906, in Walter B. Rubusana's Xhosa anthology, *Zemk' Inkomo Magwalandini* (*Away Go the Cattle, You Cowards!*)

As to Gqoba's Christian inspiration, it chiefly appears in two long didactic poems that have been conveniently analyzed by Jordan:[29] the *Discussion between the Christian and the Pagan* (850 lines), and the *Great Discussion on Education* (1,150 lines). In form, both are allegorical debates, the characters of which bear such Bunyanesque names as Present-World or Sharp-eyed, Miss Gossip or Miss Upright; but the participants often make their various points in typically African fashion, introducing gnomic folktales and historical precedents to buttress their arguments. These poems are the first imaginative treatment of two themes which were to remain central in African thought: Christianity and education. The fact that they are debates suggests that both topics were already becoming consciously and articulately controversial. Their apologetic tone indicates that the growing impact of European power was being felt, criticized, and resisted, not only in terms of material interests and physical fighting for survival but also in terms of its ethical relevance or otherwise. As Jordan shrewdly observed, although the purpose of Gqoba was to vindicate Christianity and, to some extent, the ways of the white man, the characters who stand in opposition to the new way of life build up an impressive case.

In the *Discussion between the Christian and the Pagan*, Present-World is the upholder of heathenism, for which he brings several pungent and often—at that early stage in African writing—singularly effective arguments. He claims that pagan life is fuller and richer, not only because it is less hampered in its enjoyment of the good things of this world but also because it is not vitiated by fears of everlasting punishment in the next. He further points to the hypocrisy of the Christian converts, many of whom advocate virtue while being addicted to liquor. Finally, he observes that conversion does not bring the material rewards that were expected from it, since the white authorities contemptuously subject all black men, whether pagan or Christian, to the same hard laws:

> Deserting your Chiefs, you came to the White Man;
> Destroying our rule, you side with the enemy;
> But now your faith is lean and shrivell'd
> Even like a chameleon whose mouth is smear'd
> With nicotine on a sultry summer's day.

To all this, World-To-Come can only reply that the evil of alcohol had been prophesied by Ntsikana, that heathens are exposed to the same diseases and sufferings as are Christians, and that they will undergo eternal damnation and torture in Hell.

The *Great Discussion on Education* is more complex, as a larger number of participants of both sexes are involved, defending a greater variety of views. Criticism centers on two aspects of the educational system of the day: it deliberately refrains from giving the black man the full knowledge that he is capable of absorbing; and it does not provide for adequate recognition or reward since the main purpose of the colonial order is to keep wages low, even for educated black Africans. This leads to a wider condemnation of the sway of the white man, which had been welcomed by many in the hope that it would bring a better life, whereas it has only resulted in land spoliation and heavy taxes. To those arguments, the reply is that the white man has in fact brought some good things, and that the full blessings of modern civilization can only be acquired the hard way. Those reasonings convince Ungrateful, who in conclusion advises the participants to "go seek learning" and to "love the White people."

African critics have no high esteem for Gqoba's talent. Although his literary abilities were held in some regard during his lifetime, Benedict W. Vilakazi later claimed that "he lacks originality. He simply wrote as he felt, saw and experienced. His writings are those of a man who knows what he wants to say, but fails to say it adequately for lack of style and apt words." [30] This failure may be due either to deficient training or to insufficient enthusiasm. The fact is that Gqoba's two long poems sound like halfhearted, last-minute attempts to restore his readers' confidence in Christianity and Western civilization.

When British Kaffraria was incorporated into the Cape Province, *Isigidimi* at first appeared as a forum where the young Xhosa intellectuals could discuss events and their implications with a certain amount of freedom. The official view, voiced by Gqoba, was that all this was an unhappy episode in the struggle between heathenism and Christianity, between savagery and civilization. But this view was questioned, more or less openly, in articles, poems, stories, and readers' letters. As war activities against the natives were spreading in the late seventies to include Zululand (1879) and Lesotho (1880-1884), Xhosa writers in *Isigidimi* turned more and more skeptical. They became acutely aware of the overall discrepancy between Christian doctrine and the white man's actual purposes and practices. The larger scale of military operations awakened a new sense of solidarity between the various Bantu-speaking peoples, and the less engaging aspects of European contribution to African life were stigmatized in unequivocal terms. Jordan summarizes one of the stories that was printed during the period of Gqoba's editorship in illustration of the havoc wrought by alcoholic beverages imported by European traders:

Death issues a proclamation that he will award a prize to the courtier who brings the greatest number of subjects to his Kingdom. A number of courtiers come forward and take turns in giving an account of their stewardship; among them, Asthma, Fever, Cyclone, Accident and Liquor, in that order. When Liquor enters, he is not steady on his legs, and his speech is thick. But he is sure of himself. He shows that he has served his king more loyally than the others have. Among other things, he has made young men age before their time and die. He has picked on the most beautiful girls, destroyed their virginity, deprived them of their youth and beauty, and finally brought them to the King of Death. After listening to Liquor's account, the King of Death does not wait to hear any more. Satisfied that Liquor is the most loyal of all his courtiers, he awards him the prize.

Although to most Xhosa readers such a story would appear as an indictment of the demoralization wrought by the European impact, neither the official authorities nor the missionaries could possibly have found anything reprehensible in it. But other writers were more outspoken.

Among the most talented was Jonas Ntsiko,[31] a blind catechist at the St. John's Mission, Umtata, who was well known as a hymn writer. Nineteen of his hymns appeared in the 1881 edition of the Church Xhosa Hymn Book, printed in Grahamstown; the collection comprised altogether 130 hymns. For his contributions to *Isigidimi*, Ntsiko styled himself "Uhadi Wase-luhlangeni" ("The harp of the nation"). He voiced the discontent of many of the paper's readers, both in verse and in argumentative prose. His minimal demand was that the editor allow the African point of view to be expressed as fully as the official positions of government and church. In an article published in April 1883, to illustrate what he meant, Ntsiko inserted a poem in which the Sotho are invited to beware of Queen Victoria, described as "that rabbit-snake with female breast," and to rise up in arms against the "white Hyena, All ravenous for the bones of Moshoeshoe." By 1 February 1884, he had reached a stage of utter disillusionment, even with the Christian faith, and vented his feelings in a pathetic poem, where he shows himself conscious of introducing a new strain into Xhosa writing:

> Some thoughts till now ne'er spoken
> Make shreds of my innermost being;
> And the cares and fortunes of my kin
> Still journey with me to the grave.
>
> I turn my back on the many shames
> That I see from day to day;
> It seems we march to our very grave
> Encircled by a smiling Gospel.
>
> For what is this Gospel?
> And what salvation?

> The shade of a fabulous ghost
> That we try to embrace in vain.

This was one of Ntsiko's last contributions. Later in that same year, an article that he had submitted to Gqoba, who had by now assumed the editorship of the journal, was rejected for being "too hostile to British rule." The young African intellectuals soon lost all confidence in the paper. Gqoba's endeavors were of no avail, and the magazine vanished in 1888.

The death of Gqoba and the end of *Isigidimi* mark the close of a period in the history of Xhosa literature, as the ninth Kaffir war and its sequels close a period in the history of the Xhosa nation. Until then, the Xhosa had been able to preserve a not inconsiderable measure of independence, and the missionaries had often taken sides openly and with some efficiency in favor of the Africans against the growing tide of imperialism and racism. With the annexation of the Transkei, a new situation to which the Xhosa had to adapt themselves was created, and a new challenge had to be met if they did not want to disappear. They were fully conscious of their physical weakness and powerlessness. The way to salvation as they saw it was defined by another *Isigidimi* poet, I. W. W. Citashe:

> Your cattle are gone, my countrymen!
> Go rescue them! Go rescue them!
> Leave the breechloader alone
> And turn to the pen.
> Take paper and ink,
> For that is your shield.
> Your rights are going!
> So pick up your pen.
> Load it, load it with ink.
> Sit on a chair.
> Repair not to Hoho,[32]
> But fire with your pen.

The Emergence of Political Consciousness

The advice in Citashe's poem was heeded by four writers, born in the late fifties, who rose to prominence at the end of the century, all of whom are characterized by their acute awareness of their nation's need for modern education, for pride on its own cultural achievement, and also—but with meager results—for political action on a multitribal basis. In these respects, three events were of capital importance in Xhosa life during this period: the publication of the first Xhosa-managed newspaper, the foundation of the South African Native National Congress in 1912, and the opening of Fort Hare College in 1916.

The main personality of this generation was John Tengo Jabavu, who was born of Christian parents at Healdtown in 1859. He attended the Methodist mission school there and qualified as a teacher in 1876. While teaching in Somerset East, he also worked as a printer's apprentice, which gave him the opportunity to learn a great deal about journalism and politics. Besides, he wrote a number of articles and letters in English, many of which were printed in the *Cape Argus*. In 1881 he went to Lovedale for higher education. Because of his previous experience, he was appointed editor of *Izigidimi samaXhosa*, a job that he held until 1884, when he was succeeded by Gqoba. In 1883 Jabavu passed the matriculation examination at the University of South Africa in Cape Town, the second African to achieve this distinction. His stay in Cape Town afforded him the possibility of studying the workings of colonial government at close quarters and strengthened his interest in politics. He also established connections with white liberals and with journalistic circles; these provided the financial backing he needed to strike out on his own. On 3 November 1884, he issued in Kingwilliamstown the first number of a bilingual weekly, *Imvo Zabantsundu (Native Opinion)*. The style and format of the journal changed several times: on 2 January 1895 it appeared as *Imvo Neliso Lomzi (Native Opinion and Guardian)*, and on 6 April 1898, as *Imvo Zontsundu (Nelizo Lomzi) (Native Opinion)*; but Jabavu soon reverted to the original title, which the paper has kept to this day. During the last few years of the century, he was assisted in his editorial work by another prominent Xhosa intellectual, John Knox Bokwe.

Bokwe was born on 18 March 1855 at Ntselamanzi, a village near Lovedale where the boy received his education. Aged ten, he was a pupil of William Kobe Ntsikana. From 1869 to 1872, while still studying, he was acting as private secretary to the principal, James Stewart. In 1873 he was put in charge of the Lovedale Telegraph and Post Office. Meanwhile, he had become active as a writer of hymns, for which he composed both the words and the music.

These were published in *Izigidimi*, and a number of them were collected in *Ama-Culo ase-Lovedale (Lovedale Hymns* [1885]), which seems to have been the first hymnal to have been published by a black South African.[33] Vilakazi points out, besides, that "the poetry in these songs is the first noteworthy single effort of really good original Nguni verse set to music." [34] In fact, Bokwe's real fame among the Xhosa was due to his music, and when he visited the United Kingdom, he sang his own hymns with marked success at numerous public gatherings.[35]

This is perhaps the place to emphasize that lyrical poetry designed to be sung, not read, has kept, in many of the written literatures of Africa, the function and importance that it is trying to recover in the West today. Many musicologists have signaled the highly musical qualities of African languages. Dealing with Xhosa, J. F. A. Swartz lays particular stress on its richness in vowels, which, he claims, surpasses Italian, its greater variety of consonants owing to the clicks introduced under Hottentot influence, its hum-like syllabic *m*, and its flair for onomatopoeic ideophones. But little historical information is available about the evolution of the modern African lyric. Speaking of composers whose work has actually reached print, Swartz makes a rough distinction between two generations: "The older generation were all missionaries and quite naturally they seem to have written nothing but sacred songs. From the point of view of the development of African music, this older generation of songwriters may have no significance or they may have significance only in the negative sense of exemplifying the stranglehold church music gained on the minds of the educated African. Culturally, however, the work of these older songwriters is very interesting." By "missionaries," Swartz, of course, means African hymn writers, and he makes a point that "old Ntsikana" "has become immortal among his people through the Bell Song he used to sing to call his congregation to his church services. . . . In the Eastern Province it is hard to find an educated Bantu who does not know the name of Ntsikana." Bokwe was also a representative of this older, Christian school, as was Enoch Sontonga, of whom more later. On the contrary, Swartz goes on, "the work of the more serious-minded section of the new generation of Bantu songwriters is characterised by an attempt—generally not very successful attempt—to break away from the sacred song. A hangover of the hallelujah-style of singing encouraged by the older generation of

Bantu songwriters can still be discerned in many of the secular songs of these present-day songwriters." Among those later poet-composers whose work became available in printed form, Swartz mentions T. T. Matshikiza, whose lyrics are "typical of the efforts of the serious-minded present-day Bantu songwriters who are trying hard (perhaps too hard) to shake off the hold Western church music has on them." And Vilakazi has called attention to the popularity of Ben Tyamzashe, who was educated at Kimberley and Lovedale, taught at Tiger Kloof institution and at Cala,[36] and who, Swartz adds, gained special renown after World War II for his V-Day celebration songs. More research into the history of the African lyric is certainly called for.

To return to John Knox Bokwe: he resigned his postmaster job in 1897, in order to help Jabavu with the editorship of *Imvo Zabantsundu*, to which he contributed articles in Xhosa and in English. But he soon left journalism to return to preaching. He was ordained a minister around the turn of the century and was put in charge of the Presbyterian congregation at Ugie. He had differences, however, with the church authorities about the use of money he had collected in Scotland, whereupon he set up his own church.[37] His closest association with Jabavu was connected with the foundation of Fort Hare College.

Momentous events came to pass in South Africa during the first decade of the century. In 1902 the Boer War came to an end. The Transvaal Republic and the Orange Free State became colonies. Negotiations were in progress for grouping them together with the Cape Colony and Natal into an autonomous Union with Commonwealth status. The status to be granted to the black population was only a minor preoccupation with most of the white politicians involved in the discussions. To the Bantu themselves, however, the franchise was a paramount problem. While there was no legal color bar in Cape Colony or in Natal, the constitutions of the Transvaal and Orange River colonies had maintained the rigid white manhood suffrage that had been established in the Boer republics. For the African elite—which, apart from a few educated Tswana and Zulu, was chiefly composed of Xhosa—and for such white liberals as were prepared to fight for their principles, the danger was that the color bar might be inscribed in the Union constitution (as it actually came to be in 1910), even though non-European franchise might be retained in the Cape Province and in Natal. A delegation was therefore sent to the British government in 1909. It was headed by a former premier of the Cape Colony, W. P. Schreiner, and it comprised John Tengo Jabavu and another Xhosa man of letters, Walter B. Rubusana.

Rubusana was born into the Cira clan on 21 February 1858, at Mnandi near Somerset East. After beginning his studies at Peelton in 1874, he attended Lovedale from 1876 to 1882. He obtained his teacher's certificate and worked in Peelton until 1884, when he was ordained a minister of the Congregational church.

In the course of the next twenty-five years, Rubusana proved himself a prolific writer in three areas. The greater part of his activity at first was devoted to the writing of pious articles and the translation of religious books and pamphlets: in 1905 he took part in the revision of the Xhosa Bible. But like Tiyo Soga and Gqoba, Rubusana was dedicated to his people's folklore. He collected a vast number of proverbs and praise poems that were printed, together with a glossary and some of Gqoba's unpublished material, in a 570-page anthology entitled *Zemk' inkomo mag-walandini (Away Go the Cattle, You Cowards)* in 1906; some of this had already appeared in the Xhosa newspaper *Izwi Labantu (The Voice of the People)*, which had been founded in 1897 by Nathaniel Cyril Mhala. Rubusana became closely associated with this journal, and turned to politics of a more progressive kind than that of John Tengo Jabavu. He wrote a *History of South Africa from the Native Standpoint*, for which it is said he was awarded an honorary Ph.D. by a Negro college, McKinley University, when he visited the United States.[38]

In the course of the first decade of the century, the Reverend Rubusana made himself known as a champion of native rights and soon became involved in political action. In 1909 he took part in the National Convention that met in Bloemfontein to discuss the forthcoming union of the various South African territories and its consequences for the natives: "this was the first occasion on which politically-minded Africans came together from all corners of South Africa to discuss common problems."[39]

In spite of a common general purpose, there was no love lost between Javabu and Rubusana, who were supported by rival factions among white politicians. Rubusana was more radical than Jabavu, and in the elections of 1910, he was put forward as an African candidate to the Provincial Council in Cape Province. He became the first black provincial councillor, much to the chagrin of Jabavu and his supporters, who claimed that Rubusana's success would provoke a white backlash and so in fact damage the native cause. In 1912 the South African Native National Congress was formally founded at Bloemfontein; Rubusana presided at the first meeting, and Jabavu attempted to build up a rival organization of his own. At the Cape Province elections of 1914, Jabavu managed to split the vote, so that Rubusana lost his seat on the Provincial Council.

Rubusana, however, remained a popular figure on the wider scene of the Congress. In August 1914 he took part in a delegation sent to London to fight against the Native Land Act of 1913, which aimed at establishing segregation in land ownership and occupation, and which had the approval of Jabavu. Although the protest was ignored, Rubusana wrote to the British foreign minister in 1915, offering to recruit black soldiers to help the white South African forces against the Germans in South-West Africa; the offer was politely declined on the ground that His Majesty's government was "anxious to avoid the employment of its Native citizens in a warfare against Whites." Rubusana died in August 1916.

Meanwhile, Jabavu had been busy with more constructive occupations besides undermining his rival's prestige or supporting land segregation. Early in the century, he had tried to enter his son Davidson into Dale College at Kingwilliamstown, but it was against the rules of the institution to admit native scholars. In his frustration—and in accordance with his political views—Jabavu then began to militate most actively for the creation of a Bantu college. He attended the various preparatory conventions that were held at Lovedale in 1905, 1908, and 1913, and he participated in fundraising campaigns in southern Africa and in Britain.

Throughout these strenuous efforts, he had the active help of Bokwe, who, at the same time, was working on a biography of Ntsikana, *Ibali likaNtsikana*, which was printed at Lovedale in 1914. When Fort Hare College was formally inaugurated in February 1916, Bokwe was responsible for the organization of the opening ceremonies where Prime Minister Louis Botha was the guest of honor. Jabavu's son Davidson later became the first black African lecturer on the staff of the college. John Tengo Jabavu died at Fort Hare on 10 September 1921, John Knox Bokwe, who had retired in his hometown of Ntselamanzi, died on 22 February 1922.

The fourth major representative of this generation was Tiyo Soga's second son, John Henderson Soga, who was born in 1859. He was first sent to Scotland at the age of three and he received his education there, attending the Glasgow High School from 1870 to 1873, and the Dollar Academy from 1873 to 1877. He followed the arts course at Edinburgh University from 1886 to 1890 and received his theological training at the United Presbyterian Divinity Hall from 1890 to 1893. Like his father, he married a Scotswoman, Isabella Brown. After his ordination, he returned to South Africa and founded the Mbonde Mission in the Mountfrere district, among the Bhaca.

Being a mulatto, John Henderson Soga kept aloof from the political controversies of the time. In his writing, he followed in the steps of his father. He too composed many hymns, a number of which made their way into the Xhosa Presbyterian hymnbook, *Amaculo ase-Rabe*. In 1910, he started work on a Xhosa translation of Aesop's fables, which has remained unpublished.

In 1916 he was transferred to the Miller Mission, Elliotdale, to succeed his brother, Dr. W. A. Soga, a medical missionary who had just died there. He went on with his translation work, devoting most of his endeavors, like Bokwe, to Xhosa renderings of religious works; three of these were printed between 1924 and 1927. But his chief contribution in this respect was his translation of the second part of *Pilgrim's Progress*, which was brought out by the Society for the Promotion of Christian Knowledge in 1927. Soga also wrote several books in English, such as *The South-Eastern Bantu (Abe-Nguni, Ama-Mbo, Ama-Lala)*, published by the Witwatersrand University Press at Johannesburg in 1930, and *Ama-Xhosa Life and Customs*, printed at Lovedale in 1931. In his preface to the former, he wrote that his purpose "was to place in the hands of the rising generation of the Bantu something of the history of their peoples, in the hope that it might help them to a clearer perception of who and what they are and to encourage in them a desire for reading and for studying their language."

In 1936 John Henderson Soga retired from the ministry. He spent the remaining years of his life in England with his family. In March 1941 he was killed together with his wife and son during a German air raid in Southampton.

As we survey this first century of modern Xhosa literature, we are struck by its extreme geographical concentration. Most of the writers originate in a small area formed by the present towns of Healdtown, Kingwilliamstown, Peelton, and Keiskamahoek. This was the territory under Ngqika's control when the first missionaries came to preach the Gospel. The center of learning was Lovedale, where most of the writers were educated. This was only a tiny section of Xhosaland. There were other Xhosa tribes; there were other mission stations in other parts of the Xhosa country; there were other printing presses and schools besides Lovedale. An interesting example is supplied by the Reverend C. E. Earle Bulwer:

It is said that as early as 1862 a small press was established at St. Matthew's Mission, Keiskama Hoek, by the Rev. W. Greenstock (1859–1870), and that about 10 years later it was removed by the Rev. A. J. Newton, the Missionary at Gwatyu and situated about halfway between St. Mark's and Whittlesea, and said to be an offshoot of St. Mark's Mission. Mr. Newton had a small printing-press already in operation at his mission, and found the St. Matthew's plant very useful. In 1878, however, the Gwatyu Mission was destroyed.[40]

Meanwhile the Reverend Newton had managed to publish several books, among which was the first Church Xhosa Hymnbook printed in 1869 and twice enlarged, in 1873 and again in 1877. He was also responsible for publishing the first Xhosa translation of Aesop's fables, which appeared in two parts, in 1875 and 1877. But this was an exception. For some reason that cannot as yet be defined, but that must be related to the personal outlook of the missionaries involved, mission presses other than Lovedale concentrated on purely educational and religious material.

It goes without saying that the gift of literary expression was not confined to the Ngqika Xhosa. While the felicitous combination of native literary talent, opportunity for learning, availability of printing presses, and missionary willingness and encouragement, turned Lovedale and the adjacent area into the cradle of modern Xhosa literature, elsewhere in Xhosaland, oral composition must have been going on much as usual. Indeed, during that period, by far the greater part of literary activity in the Xhosa language must have remained unwritten and is, therefore, mostly lost to us. But we can get a glimpse of it in the contemporary praise poems that were recorded by Gqoba and Rubusana, and analyzed by Jordan.

The writing produced in the Tyumie valley flew forth from two main sources of inspiration, which reflect the duality of African experience under the impact of Europe. The earliest writers found it easy, it seems, to reconcile their African identity with the new faith that was the central element of Western civilization as they received it at first. They used the new writing and printing techniques both to record their oral lore, their "history" and the customs of their people, and to produce the educational material, the religious treatises, and the Christian hymns that were designed to help their people on their way to civilized advancement and to spiritual salvation. The conflicts between white and black, which resulted in the first Kaffir wars must have appeared to those first educated Xhosa as just a new version of the kind of tribal fighting for land and cattle, with which they were familiar. Racial antagonism could hardly be perceptible, as the South African authorities often acted as allies of the Ngqika Xhosa against their tribal enemies.

It was not until the middle of the century that the Kaffir wars definitely took on the form of a colonial imperialistic assault against the black man as such. The cattle-killing episode of the fifties shows that the Xhosa people had sensed the change long before this awareness made its way into literary expression. But the ninth Kaffir war of 1877 and the annexation of Gcalekaland clarified the issue in most unambiguous fashion. In the literary field, the results were felt in the last two decades of the century: directly, through such writers as Jonas Ntsiko, whose contributions to *Isigidimi* illustrate two important new trends: first, his sense of the need for all-Bantu solidarity in facing the white man's threat; second, his increasing disillusionment with Christianity itself. Indirectly, Gqoba's apologetic and rather unconvincing pleas testify to widely felt resentment against the white man, his religion, and the colonial regime that he was bent on establishing.

It is true that the missionaries had been, from the beginning, very active in protecting native rights, and they allowed some outspoken contributions to be printed in the Lovedale magazine. But in the last quarter of the century, as the scramble for Africa was gathering momentum, in Xhosaland as in many other parts of the

continent the spiritual power of religion, charity, and humanitar-
ianism revealed its weakness and futility as compared with the
ruthless efficiency of firearms. To many Africans, Christianity was
no longer the best path to the all-important purposes of terrestrial
betterment and eternal salvation. It began to be considered as truly
the opium of the people, a spiritual weapon auxiliary to the white
man's imperialistic aims. While men like Bokwe and Soga went on
working along the lines set by an earlier generation in different
circumstances, Jabavu and others strove to create newspapers uncontrolled by the missionaries. In the early years of this century,
this trend overflowed the boundaries of newspaper discussion and
led to political action.

The manner in which the Xhosa were exposed to Western civilization certainly accounts for the small share of imaginative writing
in the early growth of vernacular literature. The literate Xhosa
were faced with two problems in succession. During the first half
of the century, the educated converts were deeply concerned with
the spiritual salvation of their people from the bonds of heathenism.
During the latter part of the century, it was the very physical and
cultural survival of the Xhosa and neighboring nations that became
of primary importance. Given the crucial significance of both issues, it is understandable that the literate class should have devoted its newly acquired skills to religious, didactic and, later,
political writing. Further, it must be remembered that the oral
tradition was not equipped with the requisite literary techniques
to cope with issues arising from the introduction of radical culture
changes into basically conservative societies. The techniques and
aims of praise poetry could be transferred to hymn writing, but
the more internalized forms of lyricism were hardly practiced at
all. Ntsiko's effusion on his own anguish when faced with the
hideous truth behind the white man's Christian mask is exceptional
and gives the measure of the writer's originality. Finally, not until
further research has been done will it be possible to determine
when and how far (if at all) the educated Xhosa was exposed
to the Western genres of personal lyricism, prose fiction, and
stage drama. The only model the early writers followed—perhaps
because it was the only model they knew—was *The Pilgrim's
Progress*, which inspired a number of allegorical moralizing tales.

The birth of imaginative writing as it is commonly understood
in Western culture, should probably be considered a response to

the challenge of the desperate historical predicament of the Xhosa as a result of the constitution of the Union of South Africa. It had become obvious, on one hand, that the kind of tribal warfare which had been resorted to in the Kaffir wars was of no avail against overwhelming European armed power. On the other hand, direct political action as practiced in the Bantu-owned papers and by the South African Native National Council had proved unable to overcome Boer racism and British indifference. Very soon, the council itself split and became impotent, as a result of personal quarrels among its members. The educated Xhosa now began to realize that any betterment in his people's predicament would be a lengthy process that could only succeed on a mass basis. It was necessary to start with the grass roots and to raise the common man himself, through more education, to intelligent and active aware-ness of his plight and needs. Hence, the concentration of the elite on the extension and improvement of educational facilities for the Bantu; hence, too, the emergence of modern genres on the Xhosa literary scene. For obviously the novel, the short story, and stage drama, were better suited to disseminate new ideas among the ever-growing semiliterate audience than were abstract political discussions. This was the work of a generation of writers who were born in the seventies.

The Birth Of The Novel

In non-literate societies, imaginative oral art is the undifferen-tiated medium of all intellectual activity. It contains the whole body of the group's knowledge—philosophical, historical, and scientific. Myths embody man's earliest accounts of the events that are supposed to have given rise to his own existence and to that of the surrounding universe. Narrative poems, carefully preserved through the centuries, contain the records of the high deeds that justify the tribe's sense of dignity and continuity. Praise poems extol the valor of the warriors, in whose prowess and conquests the honor and the power of the society originate. Folktales con-tain the patrimony of wisdom and skills which has been bequeathed by generations precariously fighting for the inner cohesion of the tribal group and for its subsistence in the hostile world of men and natural forces. The primary purpose of oral composition does not reside in aesthetic achievement. Art and beauty are subordinated to the expression, preservation, and communication of memories and values that are essential to the survival of the society and to its sense of collective identity. The clear-cut demarcation established by modern Western thinking between scientifically ascertained fact and imaginative interpretation is therefore irrelevant: any amount of hyperbolic or allegorical distortion is legitimate provided it serves the ultimate societal purposes. Writing and the cultural attitudes with which it is usually associated gradually introduce a previously unknown division of labor. This is a very protracted process in a society that is left to its own devices. In medieval Europe, although abstract philosophical writing separated from creative art at a fairly early stage owing to the subordination of intellectual activity to the needs of the Church, it took a few centuries before a clear-cut division was made between fiction and history as well as between fiction and the natural sciences.

Another significant feature of most oral art is that it focuses on society rather than on the individual. Close attention is paid to the individual only insofar as his activity affects his society, favorably or adversely. Hence, the stress laid on warlike action, and the comparative neglect of purely private emotions. Love and sex, being private concerns, are not deemed worthy of the care and labor of literary treatment, except to the extent that they may threaten societal cohesion, as can be seen in the Deirdre story of the Irish saga. The shift from group-oriented to person-oriented inspiration also takes a long time. In Europe, it was not until the twelfth century that personal passion became a worthy topic for written composition. And this interest in the individual as such, his personal emotions and experiences, gave birth to literary genres that were no part of oral art: the modern theater, aesthetically formalized as the stage representation of individuals in conflict, at length emerged from ritual drama and from festive pageantry, and the novel emerged from the epic.

The two basic evolutionary processes did not require as much time in modern Africa as they did in medieval Europe. Africa was not left to its own fumbling devices, but was submitted constantly and intensively to the pressures and the challenge of European culture. All the same, the process of acquiring the basic techniques of modern imaginative writing has normally extended over several generations. The first generations of Xhosa writers put the new skills to two main uses: the recording of traditional lore, and the composition of Christian hymns. It was not until the beginning of the twentieth century that the Western genre of imaginative prose fiction was introduced into Xhosa literature, most prominently by a man who—somewhat paradoxically—was also perhaps the last of the great tribal bards.

Samuel Edward Krune Mqhayi[41] was the great-grandson of Mqhayi, a one-time councillor of Chief Ngqika, who was killed by the English in 1835. Mqhayi's son, Krune, was born in 1800. He was converted to Christianity and attended Lovedale for some years. He died in 1895. His own son Ziwani became a preacher and died in 1920 in Grahamstown. Samuel was born on 1 December 1875 at Gqamahashe on the banks of the Tyumie. When he was six, he was sent to school at Evergreen. In 1885 the family moved to Kentani near Butterworth, where they settled close to the homestead of the boy's great-uncle, Chief Nzanzana. During the six years that he spent there, Mqhayi, while attending school intermittently, acquired a remarkable knowledge of his people, their history, and their language. "It was there," Jordan writes, "that he first listened to *izibongo* (praise-poems), and himself began to 'lisp in numbers,' praising favourite oxen, other boys or himself. It was there that he began to appreciate the beauty, dignity and subtleties of Xhosa, and to acquire the amazingly wide vocabulary that even Tiyo Soga would have envied." He used to listen to the stories of the wars that the old men of the village told in the evenings. He learned how to extemporize praise songs in honor of his cows, his dogs, and his friends. And he also watched with fascination the judicial proceedings at the court of Chief Nzanzana.

In 1890 Ziwani left Kentani for Grahamstown, and the boy's sisters took him to Lovedale, where he was enrolled in April 1891. Although he belonged to a family of long Christian standing, he entered the circumcision school, contrary to the prescriptions of the missionaries: "I knew," he writes in his autobiography, "that the missionaries were violently opposed to circumcision, but I did not hesitate for a minute: I had rather be expelled from school than give up the prospect of becoming a man. I realized that I would never be able to help my people if I did not become a man like them." He was circumcised on 6 March 1894, but after a while the Lovedale authorities pardoned him and allowed him to return to school. In the same year, he married the daughter of one of the disciples whom Ntsikana, from his deathbed, had sent to the missionaries.

After training as a teacher, he taught for a time in East London. But he was not really interested in teaching, and he soon left to become secretary of the congregation of the Reverend Rubusana, who fostered his growing concern with social and racial problems. He contributed, like Rubusana, to Mhala's newspaper, *Izwi Labantu*, and later became one of its editors. After a new stay at Kentani, he resumed his work on *Izwi Labantu* but the journal had to stop publication for lack of funds and because of differences of opinion among the editors. Mqhayi again went to East London as a teacher, and assisted Jabavu in the editing of *Imvo Zabantsundu* from the turn of the century until Jabavu's death in 1921. His first poems were printed there.

Mqhayi's poetic talent soon caused him to be known as "the poet of the race." As a result of his linguistic abilities, he had been appointed in 1905 a member of the Xhosa Bible Revision Board. At that time, Dr. William Govan Bennie (1868-1942) was chief inspector for Native Education in the Cape. He sought Mqhayi's help in standardizing Xhosa spelling and in codifying Xhosa grammar. From then on, the young man devoted himself mainly to writing. His first published book was *U-Samson*, an adaptation of the Bible story of Samson.

Mqhayi's first original work was *Ityala lama-wele (The Law-Suit of the Twins)*, which was printed in 1914,[42] quite some time, he claims in his autobiography, after he had actually composed it. As a result of this publication, Z. K. Matthews writes, Mqhayi "sprang into fame at once as one of the best Xhosa writers, to be classed with men like Soga and Rubusana." [43] The story takes place during the reign of Hintza, chief of the Gcaleka Xhosa, who was killed while attempting to escape from British imprisonment in 1835. The plot was suggested by the story of the birth of Thammar's twins in Genesis 38:27-29. It concerns a legal dispute between twins over who is the elder and therefore entitled to their father's inheritance. Mqhayi's memories of Nzanzana's court enabled him to provide, as Alice Werner pointed out, "a very illuminating picture of native judicial procedure." [44] But Mqhayi's purpose was by no means merely ethnographic or antiquarian. The theme of justice is an important one in all literatures, as justice and law are the very

foundation of the social order. A large portion of early narrative
writing in Europe focuses on the theme of revenge. The trial of
Ganelon in the *Chanson de Roland*, the *Njalssaga*, for example,
illustrate the conflict between the primitive practice of private vengeance on the one hand, and the social and religious requirements
of impartial and impersonal justice on the other hand. This was still
a major theme in serious drama of the Renaissance and of the seventeenth century throughout Western Europe. Other aspects of justice preoccupied African writers during the early years of the
twentieth century. The contribution of Azariele Sekese in Lesotho
will be discussed in the next chapter. But it is important to notice
that there is considerable difference in approach between Sekese
and Mqhayi. The former, living in a British Protectorate where
the native judicial system was not threatened by the European
authorities, felt free to criticize its abuses from inside. The situation was by no means the same in South Africa. By the end of the
nineteenth century, Xhosa chiefs in the Ciskei had seen their authority and their judicial privileges eroded by the setting up of
district councils whose members were appointed by the Cape authorities.[45] Whereas Sekese wanted to criticize the chiefs' courts
in the hope of improving them, it was Mqhayi's aim to vindicate
traditional native justice threatened by the colonial administration. He made this clear in the foreword to *Ityala lama-wele*: "Although I am no kind of expert on the legal affairs, I have, however, the conviction that the legal system of the Xhosas is not in
the slightest degree different from that of the enlightened nations.
When the white races came to this country, they found that the
people of this country are virtually experts—all of them—in legal
procedures." He even goes so far as to claim that "the white races
took for themselves a considerable share of the customs and laws
of the Xhosas." The chief virtue of Xhosa law, he says, is that it is
based upon jurisprudence. Consequently, he goes on, "in this short
tale I am endeavouring to show the efforts, the pains, and the time
that the Xhosas take when they research into the origin of law, for
they are trying to base it upon precedent." In the story itself those
efforts, described in minute detail, come to nothing since the case
appears to be one for which there is no precedent, even in the
memory of the oldest man of the tribe. In his foreword, Mqhayi
further claims that he is trying to show "that the king is not the
final arbiter of affairs by himself, as foreigners believe is the case

with us." Actually, in the tale it is the chief who makes the final decision, a highly subtle and ambiguous one, although he first has all the evidence gathered and listens to the advice of all the notables. At the end of the trial, the author describes the reactions of the people as follows:

And concerning the judgement, some were mumbling, finding fault, and seeing many errors. But the majority did not forget a case that had proceeded with decorum and justice, and that had been spoken well, in which all aspects had been examined, and the judgement given with great skill.

The second part of the volume contains a historical account of the Xhosa nation through the nineteenth century and up to the famous *Mendi* episode, when a ship loaded with South African soldiers was sunk by a German submarine in the early months of World War I. By this time, as Jordan rightly observes, "the subject is no longer the Xhosa alone, but the Bantu of South Africa," one more interesting example of the growth of intertribal solidarity in the early decades of this century.

In 1922 Mqhayi was invited to teach at Lovedale, but he could not come to an agreement with the missionaries as to how Xhosa history should be taught,[46] and he desisted, though, as he says in his autobiography, without rupture or bitterness. In 1925 he published *UBomi buka J. K. Bokwe (Life of J. K. Bokwe)*, a biography of the Reverend Bokwe. This was followed in 1927 by a collection of poems for children, which was printed at the Sheldon Press in London: *Imihobe nemibongo (Songs of Joy and Lullabies)*.

In 1929 Mqhayi produced his escond important work of prose fiction which is also the first Xhosa utopia, *U-Don Jadu*. This book, which provides the writer's picture of an ideal South African society, has been usefully summarized and discussed by Jordan in his article on Mqhayi. It describes how

through the influence and guidance of Don Jadu, a highly educated African, the *amaRanuga* (detribalized Africans) of the Eastern Province acquire land of about the area of the Transkeian Territories. All kinds of industry begin to spring up in the new province of Mnandi (Sweetness). As a result, in a few years the population is double that of the Transkei. The Union Government become interested and vote large sums of money to promote the scheme. Self-government is granted to the people of Mnandi and, the Union Government having disappeared from the scene, Great Britain assumes guardianship. Don Jadu is the first president.

There is neither racialism nor isolationism in Mnandi. Immigration is encouraged, and experts of all races and shades of colour come from the four corners of the earth to make a permanent home there. There is full social, economic and political equality. According to the constitution, women are free to go into parliament, but the sensible women of Mnandi decline this offer on the grounds that there is enough work for them to do at their homes! Mnandi is a Christian state, and Christ is the "President" of the Ancestral Spirits. Ministers of religion are officers of state, and their stipends come from the general revenue. Magistrates and ministers of religion work in close co-operation. In fact, Church and State are so closely knit together that there is no distinction between the police and deacons' courts. Education is compulsory. Xhosa is the first language, but English is such an important second language that no one who is not strictly bilingual may hold an office of state. Baby boys are baptized and circumcised in the Temple eight days after birth, and Holy Confirmation forms part of an initiation ceremony held in the Temple between the ages of fifteen and twenty. All these ceremonies are supervised by the magistrate and the minister of religion together. The marriage ceremony is conducted by the magistrate and subsequently blessed by law. The importation or sale of liquor is prohibited by law. Home-brewing is allowed, but anyone found drunk in public places is locked up in a lunatic asylum, dressed in the uniform of the asylum and is for seven days subjected to the same treatment as the legitimate inmates of that institution. People who are sentenced to penal servitude receive wages for their labour. There are no prisons.

It is interesting to compare Jordan's analysis with the harsh judgment passed upon *U-Don Jadu* by a European critic, John Riordan:

The hero passes from town to town, solving all problems overnight, and leading raw tribesmen from a primitive state to an advanced civilization in a matter of weeks. Thus does Mqhayi allow his imagination, fostered by a repulsive hunger for self-glorification, to run riot and escape into a world of pure fancy, where probability is grossly violated and logical development unknown. True, Mqhayi's imagination is colourful and productive, but it is not disciplined. His mastery of lan-

guage is undoubted, but he blatantly tries to impress by playing with
big words and archaisms. His glittering facade of words is unsupported
by any real substance.[47]

Obviously, Riordan had expected what Mqhayi never intended
to give: a realistic, social, and psychological novel of the Western
type. Jordan too recognizes that "Mqhayi is not a great creator of
individual character," and that "hardly any character stands out in
this story." This is a critique frequently leveled at the African
novel in general, whose failure in character depiction must be
ascribed to two main causes. First, concern with the individual
personality is not a feature of traditional oral literature any more
than it is of traditional tribal society. The individual apprehends
himself first and foremost as part of the group, rather than as a
separate personality endowed with its own rights and privileges.
Literature is a public activity dealing with matters of public interest, and purely private experiences and emotions are seldom
deemed worthy of literary treatment. Second, this particular trend
in the native culture was further reinforced by the historical situation. In his autobiography, Mqhayi explains that the idea for
U-Don Jadu can be traced back to his school years at Lovedale. He
used to make frequent visits to his father in Grahamstown, and
during those trips, he had to pass through the little town of Alice.
There it was, he tells us, that he became aware for the first time of
the antagonism between black and white. So far, he had lived a
sheltered life at the court of his great-uncle and in the quiet multiracial seclusion of Lovedale. But in Alice, he witnessed how Xhosa
cattle was requisitioned out of the common pastures to make room
for the white people's cattle, and he realized the growing hostility
between both racial groups. As cattle was the foundation of Xhosa
economy, and therefore of Xhosa society, this was a problem of
life and death for the Xhosa nation as a whole. *U-Don Jadu* grew
out of these experiences and this realization. It was not meant as a
realistic description of a situation that every one knew anyway. It
was designed as a blueprint for the future coexistence of both races
in South Africa. And it was conceived in a spirit of compromise
and syncretism. There are only three things that Mqhayi forcefully
rejects: the South African government, the prison system, and
imported hard liquor as opposed to the native home-brewed beer.
His ideal state is not a preliminary study in Bantustan. It is a multi-

racial society that places a high premium on education and progress, and it is a Christian society that has incorporated many of the beliefs and customs dear to African hearts. In the elaboration of this Bantu utopia, Mqhayi exhibits uncommonly powerful intellectual imagination. In 1935 he won first prize in the first May Esther Bedford Competition for the third part of *U-Don Jadu*.[48]

Mqhayi's next book was a biography of the Gold Coast scholar and advocate of Pan-Africanism, Dr. J. E. K. Aggrey, whose visit to South Africa in 1921 had initiated, if we are to believe Vilakazi, "a new spirit of co-operation and understanding between Africans and Europeans." [49] Actually, this new spirit is more likely to have been restricted to a few intellectuals of both races. But there is little doubt that Aggrey's presence and utterances brought immense encouragement and hope to the Bantu elite, who had been disheartened by the dismal failure of the Congress in the previous decade. Mqhayi's biographical account was a translation of Edwin S. Smith's *Aggrey of Africa*.

In 1936 Mqhayi took part in the Conference of Bantu Authors convened at Florida (Transvaal) by R. H. W. Shepherd, director of the Lovedale Press.[50] The next year, Mqhayi published a collection of eight cantos on Chief Hintza, *U-Mhlekazi U-Hintza (Hintza the Great* [Lovedale, 1937]). At the same time, he was writing his autobiography, which was first published in German, in Diederich Westermann's collection, *Afrikaner erzähler ihr Leben* (Essen, 1938), before it appeared in Xhosa under the title *U-Mqhayi wase Ntab'ozuko* [51] *(Mqhayi of the Mountain of Beauty* [Lovedale, 1939]). His last volume was one more collection of poems, entitled *I-nzuzo (Reward* [Johannesburg, 1942]).[52] In the late twenties, Mqhayi had settled on Tilana's Hill, near Berlin. He had renamed the place "Ntab'ozuko" (The Mountain of Beauty). This was on the territory of the Ndlambe clan, and at the same time that he established a model farm for the benefit of the Xhosa peasants, Mqhayi acted as poet laureate and secretary to the Ndlambe chieftain. He died there on 29 July 1945.

It was perhaps as a poet that Mqhayi was chiefly valued by the Xhosa audience, not least because he had completely mastered the form and the spirit of the traditional praise poem *(izibongo)* while adapting it to modern circumstances and topics. He was known as *imbongi yesizwe* ("Poet Laureate"), and Vilakazi calls him "the Father of Xhosa poetry," because "he is responsible for a transition

from the primitive bards who sang the *izibongo*." [53] The main
function of the tribal bard *(imbongi)* was to strengthen the cohesion of the group, usually by celebrating the glorious figures of
the past and extolling the authority of the reigning chief. Mqhayi's
volume on Hintza is an example of this, as are the obituary eulogies
of local figures in *I-nzuzo*. But since the central preoccupation of
the izibongo in its purest form is to promote the prosperity and
the greatness of the group, it does not deal solely with the chiefs,
but also with any public events that may be significant in that respect. Hence Mqhayi's poetic treatment of topics that, to the European reader, sound hardly promising: *I-nzuzo* contains a poem
written in appreciation of the bimonthly agricultural journal published at Umtata! Throughout the year, seasonal festivals offer
opportunities to remind the tribe of its past achievements and to
advise it for the future; therefore, the many New Year poems that
Mqhayi composed. As Jabavu wrote, "the topic of the expiration
of one year and the incoming of a new one is almost Mqhayi's annual exercise and monopoly, and he does it with gusto." But
Mqhayi's inspiration also reached beyond the traditional tribal
basis, and he wrote abundantly, in poetry and in prose, about
prominent Africans of past and present. Further, his Christian beliefs merged into the edifying and societal purposes of traditional
poetry in moralizing pieces dealing with such abstract subjects as
Truth, Hope, and Love. If we are to believe Vilakazi, Mqhayi's
attempts at innovation were not always successful. His poems dealing with nature, the Zulu critic says, are "dull," and those on
religious subjects are "mere oratorical exercises" when compared
with those of his successor Jolobe. Mqhayi "excelled in heroic
poetry of the traditional type, and showed great skill in weaving
his people's customs, legends, and myths into his poems." [54]

The imbongi's role was not simply to praise the chief. As his
major concern was with the welfare of the nation, he often felt
called upon to criticize any abuses by the powers that be. On this
score, too, the tradition was modified and enlarged by Mqhayi in
the light of a historical situation where actual authority was vested
in European hands. When the Prince of Wales (later Edward
VIII) visited South Africa in 1925, the poet was entrusted with the
privilege of delivering an izibongo of his composition. Jordan informs us that the poem began in the usual fashion, with "a succession of metaphors and similes, in which he likens the prince to all

the mighty fabulous animals of Bantu Folklore." Then comes a
section that is here quoted in Jordan's translation:

> Ah, Britain! Great Britain!
> Great Britain of the endless sunshine!
>
> She hath conquered the oceans and laid them low;
> She hath drained the little rivers and lapped them dry;
> She hath swept the little nations and wiped them away;
> And now she is making for the open skies.
>
> She sent us the preacher: she sent us the bottle,
> She sent us the Bible, and barrels of brandy;
> She sent us the breechloader, she sent us cannon;
> O, Roaring Britain! Which must we embrace?
>
> You sent us the truth, denied us the truth;
> You sent us the life, deprived us of life,
> You sent us the light, we sit in the dark,
> Shivering, benighted in the bright noonday sun.

Jordan quotes this passage to show "that the idiom, style and technique of the traditional praise-poem can be applied most effectively
to modern themes." [55] But in its own right, it is a little masterpiece
of irony and conscious artistry. It may be pure coincidence that
the translation appears as a sort of inverted Elizabethan sonnet,
with the couplet at the beginning instead of the end. But the structure of the poem is as carefully devised as that of a sonnet. It falls
into two main parts, each of which is announced by an apostrophe
("Ah, Britain!" "O, Roaring Britain!"), and each of the three qua-
trains is a clearly distinguishable step in a continuous process of
heightening tension. The first quatrain, describing Britain's universal power, is in the third person, objective and impersonal in
tone, although a note of subdued irony creeps in as Britain's victories over nature (oceans, rivers) appear as an icon of her conquest
of men (nations), and as the effects of her might are couched in
increasingly destructive terms (oceans laid low, rivers lapped dry,
nations wiped away). The last line is probably designed as ambivalent, referring both to the physical skies conquered by air power,
and to the way the British manipulate the heavenly Gospel for
purposes of their own. This, at any rate, is suggested by the mention of "the preacher" at the beginning of the second quatrain.

This third stanza has a more direct personal character ("She sent

us the preacher") and refers to the particular experience that
Mqhayi and his people have gained of British power. This experience is tersely described in its fundamental ambivalence: while
England sent the Africans the light of Christianity, she also introduced them to liquor and firearms, both of them agents of destruction. The modulation in the second apostrophe ("Roaring Britain" instead of "Great Britain") contains an ominous, although
hidden and implicit, answer to the question in the quatrain's last
line. The main attribute of England, the source of her political
greatness and power, is not the "sunshine" of Christian civilization,
but the roaring, destructive might of artillery. It is not likely that
Mqhayi, a devout member of the Presbyterian church, wanted to
invite his people to use violence as a response to violence. The
interrogative form of the line suggests the pathetic perplexity of
the African in general, and intimates how tempting it is for him to
conclude that only armed power, not the Christian faith, can redeem the African from the quandary where Britain herself placed
him.

The gradual heightening of emotion reaches its climax in the
last stanza, where Britain is now directly and aggressively apostro-
phized: the "you-us" relation replaces the "she-us" of the second
quatrain and the impersonal "she" of the first. At the same time,
the poet relinquishes metaphorical language and indicts Britain in
straightforward terms, for bringing the truth of religion in theory
and ignoring it in practice, and for bringing the light of progress
and civilization while depriving the black population of its livelihood. The last two lines of the poem revert with deadly irony, to
the light imagery of the beginning. Although Britain, the land
where the sun of Christianity and modern civilization shines end-
lessly, sent the light to Africa, the African remains in the cold and
the darkness of oppression, with only his native, physical "bright
noonday sun" to console him. The translation can only preserve
the bare bones of the poem's structure. There is little doubt that a
study of the musical and connotational values of the Xhosa original
would enhance our appreciation of this brief masterpiece, the
quality of which certainly suggests that more of Mqhayi's work
should be made available to an international audience.

To the same generation as Mqhayi belongs Mankayi Enoch Sontonga, who was born in Lovedale in the early 1870s. He is perhaps

the first Xhosa writer who was not a member of the Gcaleka tribe. His family was of Tembu origin and came from a more northern part of the country. After leaving school, Sontonga taught, at the end of the nineteenth century, in an African township near Johannesburg. He is chiefly known as a composer of songs; he wrote both the music and words. In 1899 he formed a church choir in the African Presbyterian church. His songs were very popular, but the best known of them is entitled *Nkosi sikelel' i-Afrika* ("God Bless Africa"), which he composed at the turn of the century.[56] Sontonga died in Johannesburg in 1904, but at the first meeting of the South African Native National Congress held in Bloemfontein on 8 January 1912, this song was sung by the participants at the opening ceremony, immediately following the prayer. The Congress adopted it in 1925 as its national anthem; it is now the official anthem of the Transkei. According to Swartz, *"Nkosi sikelel' i-Afrika* was the first song by a Bantu to be published in staff notation as a complete piece of music," and not in the simplified system known as tonic sol-fa introduced by the missionaries.[57]

Sontonga's Tembu origin is a symptom of the way the recruiting area for Xhosa writers began to widen after the annexation of Xhosaland to the Cape Province. Another writer to come from outside the Gcaleka Xhosa was Henry Masila Ndawo; he belonged to the Hlubi tribe,[58] which had left its original habitat in Natal as a result of the Chaka wars, and had settled among the Xhosa as part of a motley mixture of immigrant groups collectively known as Mfengu or, in European usage, Fingo. Although his birthdate has not yet been traced, Ndawo must have been roughly contemporary with Mqhayi. He too was trained as a teacher, and he taught for a while in Matatiele.

On a distinctly lower level than Mqhayi, his work exhibits the same duality characteristic of so much African writing. In the present state of our knowledge, he should be considered the founder of the Xhosa novel with *Uhambo luka Gqoboka, (Gqoboka's Journey)* which was printed in Lovedale in 1909. It tells the story of an African's indomitable struggle to give up heathenism and embrace the Christian faith. The book clearly exemplifies the influence of *Pilgrim's Progress*. It purports to describe allegorically the evolution of an African from heathenism to Christianity, but, as Vilakazi observed, Ndawo was unable to master the allegorical technique of Bunyan. The central character, fighting against wild

beasts, and men, and the elements, is not symbolical, but straight-
forwardly anecdotal.[59] Yet, this little work was not without its at-
tractiveness. Jordan informed me that it was "a set work at junior
secondary school at Lovedale in 1926." [60] It went through several
editions.

During the twenties, Ndawo relinquished his attempt at acclimatizing the novel in Xhosa and turned for inspiration to the traditional sources of Xhosa folklore and history. Here, too, however,
he was something of an innovator. *Inxenye yen-Tsomi zase-Zweni
(Selection of Folktales)*, which was published by the Catholic
mission press at Mariannhill in 1920, is one of the very few, and
certainly the first, book-length collection of popular tales in Xhosa.
Whereas this genre was one of the first and the most widely popular manifestations of creative writing among the Zulu, Ndawo
next gave way to the typical Xhosa taste for collections of praise
poetry. In *Izibongo zenkosi zamaHlubi nezamaBaca (Praise
Poems of the Hlubi and the Bhaca* [Mariannhill, 1925]) and *Iziduko
zama Hlubi (Clan Names of the Hlubi* [Lovedale, 1939]) Ndawo
brought together Hlubi and Bhaca praise poems in the same way as
his predecessors had done for the Gcaleka Xhosa.

Ndawo turned back to the novel in the early thirties encouraged,
perhaps, by the example of some of the younger writers. *U-Nolishwa* (Lovedale, 1931) shows less ambition and greater skill than
Gqoboka. It is the simple life story of a Hlubi girl who is first led
to evil because of her bad upbringing in a small urban community.
She kindles quarrels between teachers and parents; she raises the
African and Colored people against each other; she indulges in
thieving and is convicted. Meanwhile, her lover, Msi, has gone to
the mines in Johannesburg to earn the bride money. The news of
the girl's imprisonment brings him to the verge of mental collapse,
and he meets with an accident. On learning this, Nolishwa in despair first decides to commit suicide. On second thought, however,
she chooses to undertake the long and hazardous journey to Transvaal to seek Msi. This act of selfless love puts her on the path to
moral salvation. After Msi's recovery and the young people's marriage, Ndawo significantly brings them back to their home place in
the country, where—as in an early Sotho novel by Everett L.
Segoete which will be discussed later—the simplicity of tribal mores
is more conducive to the Christian way of life than are the sophisticated allurements of city experience.[61]

Unlike Mqhayi's, Ndawo's inspiration in his first two novels is definitely Christian rather than syncretic. Nevertheless, it was probably under the influence of *U-Don Jadu* that he attempted to fuse his religious beliefs and his racial pride in his third and last novel, *U-Nomathamsanqa no Sigebenga (Nomathamsanqa and Sigebenga* [Lovedale, 1937]), an allegorical story of mankind led astray, but redeemed by the eldest son of an African chief .

Henry Masila Ndawo was killed in a railway accident in 1949.

Two other writers were responsible for the emergence of Xhosa prose fiction during the second decade of this century. One was the first Xhosa woman writer, L. Kakaza. She wrote a thirty-one-page novella, *Intyatyambo yomzi (The Flower in the Home* [Gcuwa, 1913]) dealing with the fortitude of a girl who overcame temptations until the day of her death. This was followed by *U-Tandiwe wakwa Gcaleka (Tandiwe, a Girl of the Gcaleka)*, a longer tale that was published in 1914 by the Methodist Book Room in Cape Town. The other was Enoch S. Guma, who studied at the Anglican Training College of the St. Matthew's Mission. His only known work is *U-Nomalizo okanye izinto zalomhlaba ngamadingiqhiwu*, which was printed in Tsolo in 1918. An English translation entitled *Nomalizo, or, The Things of This Life are Sheer Vanity* was published in London by the Sheldon Press in 1928 and was reprinted in 1951.

The heroine, Nomalizo, is courted by two young suitors: Mxabaniso, who is a bad boy, and Bangela, who is a good boy. She herself is of preternatural virtue and piety. She submits with extraordinary resilience to the many calamities that befall her: her father's cattle die from some disease; her mother dies from worry; her father soon leaves this world, too. Nevertheless, she refuses the comparative safety and prosperity offered her by Mxabaniso, who has dropped out of college to become a thief. He even kidnaps her, but the timely intervention of a priest prevents her from being raped. She comes under the care of her aunt, who takes her to Kingwilliamstown. This is the place where Bangela's family had moved some time earlier, and Nomalizo's aunt has been receiving help from the young man and his sister. On renewing their acquaintance, Nomalizo falls in love with Bangela. But Mxabaniso in his jealousy plants stolen goods and money in the latter's house and manages to have him arrested. Bangela is condemned to life imprisonment. Fortunately, the policeman who arrested him re-

morsefully confesses he had been bribed by Mxabaniso, so that
Bangela is freed and can marry Nomalizo.

Although this Sunday-school novelette has little intrinsic value,
it is of some historical and sociological importance. In the preface
to the 1918 edition, the Reverend Godfrey Callaway claimed that
the book gives "just the very conditions of life which now prevail
when the old jostles with the new. To my delight, I found that the
old was not treated with contempt and that the new was not treated
without discrimination." Indeed, *U-Nomalizo* is the first Xhosa
piece of prose fiction to treat African city life with any degree of
realism. Mxabaniso and his lazy parents illustrate the moral disintegration that is one of the results of urbanization: they are addicted
to drinking and smoking, and he ends up a rapist and a thief. Later
South African fiction, especially in English, was to make us familiar
with the widespread hooliganism in African townships. One of the
aspects of this moral disintegration is the new attitude to love and
sex, which often violates both tribal and Christian ethics. Mxabaniso, Guma says, "was not urged by true love, but by evil desires. He was attracted by her face and figure, things which never
can of themselves keep alive the love of those who are to be separated only by death. . . . They are attractions that come to an
end. . . . We think this is one of the reasons why there is so much
separation nowadays between husbands and wives. We plunge into
marriage without thought, and understanding, and deep consideration" (pp. 24-25).[62]

In spite of Callaway's claim, however, the book makes little mention of the traditional way of life, which is not surprising as the
story takes place in an entirely urban environment. About the only
allusion to the old outlook is a condemnation of sorcery: "Charms
and other evil works of witchcraft are among the things which
take the chief place in the minds of our people. It is sad to find that
even Christian people are not able to stand against the tide of false
belief." Guma is strongly critical of those native Christians who
deviate from the teaching of Christ, who believe in witchcraft,
who drink and lie.[63] Their bad conduct is the greatest obstacle to
the conversion of pagans. But he also condemns the lack of adaptation to modern ways that have nothing to do with Christianity. He
considers, for example, that Nomalizo's father is responsible for his
own ruin because all his wealth was in cattle, as was the custom in
the old pastoral days: "The foolishness of well-to-do natives is an
amazing thing. . . . Had he been a rich man with money, these

things would never have happened to him. Yes, he knew about banks, but he placed no reliance on them and did not trust them" (p. 30). It is the first time in Xhosa writing that Bible and bank are brought together as joint emblems of what is best in modern civilization.

It is perhaps meaningful that the Reverend S. J. Wallis, who translated the book in 1928, found it advisable to warn the English reader against taking the episode of the corrupt policeman as a faithful picture of the workings of the law in South Africa: "The description of legal proceedings in Chapters XIV and XV should be read with an entirely uncritical mind; nor must it be taken as in any way an accurate account of the administration of justice, even in an out-of-the-way country like Kafirland" (p. vi)!

The Growth of the Novel and the Birth of Xhosa Drama

Whereas Sotho literature had known its golden age in the years between 1906 and 1912, the twenties witnessed a remarkable development and diversification of Xhosa writing. Not only was the decade illuminated by the work of Mqhayi and, on a lower level, Ndawo, but it also attended the emergence of a generation of younger writers, who were born at the turn of the century. They introduced new themes and new genres, and their activity reached its apex just before World War II.

The first of them was Guybon B. Sinxo,[64] who was born on 8 October, 1902, at Fort Beaufort (C.P.), where his father was an interpreter at the magistrate's office. After receiving his primary education there, he was trained at St. Matthew's College, where in 1920 he qualified as a teacher. He taught for some years in the Cape Province. His first novel, *U-Nomsa* was printed at Lovedale in 1922. It was followed in 1925 by a collection of school plays, *Imfene kaDebeza (Debeza's Baboon)*, which dealt with such varied topics as superstition, countryside life and mentality, the disturbances brought about by men's entanglement in women's affairs, and the like.[65] While Zulu school drama had emerged a few years earlier in the colleges of Natal (see pp. 193–195), Sinxo's little book marks the intrusion of Western-type formal playwriting in Xhosa literature.

In 1924 Sinxo had married Mqhayi's eldest daughter, Beula

Nohle, who was to die in 1929. To her he dedicated his second
novel, *Umfundisi wase-Mthuqwasi (The Priest of Mthuqwasi*
[Lovedale, 1927]), the hero of which is a teacher who has to give up
his job because he is too poorly paid. He opens a small business and
is fairly successful, until he has a dream of his late father, who had
been a Christian and had wanted him to become a minister of the
church. In compliance with his father's will, Thamsanqa takes up
the ministry. He is sent to a destitute station, at Mthuqwasi, where
he marries. Sinxo's purpose is obviously to extol this African minister's selfless devotion to what he considers his filial and spiritual
duties. Thamsanqa lives in utmost poverty. He also has to face the
hostility of one of his parishioners, who sues him. Thamsanqa is
only redeemed from jail through the intervention of his brother-
in-law Blankethe. When he dies exhausted by hard work, the same
Blankethe will take care of his family in the old spirit of clan
solidarity.

Such a plot testifies to the educated African's puzzlement and
bitterness as he observes how the new society treats him, even when
he devotes himself to the diffusion of the higher aspects of Western
civilization: education and the new faith. A similar perplexity was
later to be reflected in an English novel, *The Catechist*, by Joseph
Abruquah from Ghana. It is significant that genuine charity is
chiefly to be found in the heart of Thamsanqa's brother-in-law.
Indeed, the latter is the most attractive figure in the book, and the
center of an important subplot. Even as a child, he is in love with
Thamsanqa's sister Yalezwa, who is studying to qualify as a nurse.
A stammering illiterate, he is a clownishly amiable character. As
Vilakazi observes, both young people "represented groups of society that appeared as opposite camps—the literate and the illiterate." But Yalezwa is not insensitive to his devotion and his warm
human quality. She agrees to marry him on condition that he will
learn how to read and write. Sinxo's portrayal of Blankethe is a
labor of humor and love. Blankethe's attitude to Thamsanqa's family singles him out as an exemplary model of the new African, in
whom the allurements of modern civilization have not smothered
the traditional virtues of clan solidarity. His fate also contrasts with
that of Thamsanqa, who is driven to suffering and death by his
idealistic acceptance of Western values that white South African
society preaches but does not practice.

Sinxo was employed for some time by the Lovedale Press, but he soon left to seek work in Port Elizabeth, where he wrote *Umzali wolahleko (The Lost Parent* [Lovedale, 1933]). With this third novel, he turned to a problem that Ndawo had handled two years earlier in *U-Nolishwa* and that had also been discussed in Guma's *U-Nomalizo*; the problem of the moral education of children in the family and of its consequences. Mojaji has married a widower, Menzile, who already has a son, Ndimani. She bears him a son, Ndapho, and a daughter. While she treats her stepson with the utmost harshness, she spoils her own children. As a result of her quarrels with teachers and with the other boys' parents, Ndapho has to leave school and goes to Johannesburg, where he works in the mines and soon turns to evil ways. His sister likewise goes to town and becomes a moral wreck. Ndimani, on the contrary, learns how to earn his own pocket money by buying bags of mealies during the reaping season and selling them at a profit when they get scarce. In time, he manages to buy a small farm where he gains an honest maintenance raising cattle and fowl.

As most African writers were schoolteachers, they were genuinely concerned with educational problems. They viewed with anguish the steady disintegration of family life in the new urban context. Two themes grew out of their anxiety. One was the dismissal of parental authority that used to be unquestioned and provided the most potent factor of moral righteousness and social harmony in the tribal world. The second was the corroding effect of city life on youngsters whose moral fibers had been weakened, or rather had never been developed, because of their parents' permissiveness. Although the social analysis does not probe very deeply, the new Xhosa novelists proved very sensitive to the particular climate of each South African town. While places like Port Elizabeth and East London are bad enough, Johannesburg figures prominently as the acme of evil. In most novels, the demoralization wrought by city life can only be counteracted by Christian piety, or by the return to the bucolic honesty of village life.

After these two novels, Sinxo grew more and more absorbed in popular education. In 1934 he joined the staff of the Johannesburg *Bantu World*, where he edited the Xhosa pages until about 1938, when ill health forced him to resign. In 1935 he had helped W. G. Bennie with the preparation of the Stewart Xhosa Readers, a series of anthologies for schools which were printed in Lovedale. Not until 1959 did he return to creative writing, in the form of traditional praise poetry, with *Thoba sikutyele, amabali emibongo angama—76 (Bow Down, So That We Can Tell You. 76 Praise-Poems* [Lovedale, 1959]). He also adapted into Xhosa several popular English novels, such as Anthony Hope's *The Prisoner of Zenda* and H. Rider Haggard's *She*. But the most significant works of the late years before his death on 14 June 1962 are to be found in a collection of short stories, *Isakhono somfazi namanye amabalana (A Woman's Dexterity and Other Stories* [Johannesburg, 1956]). The title story, *Isakhono somfazi*, tells of a boy whose parents have made considerable sacrifices as domestic servants in Johannesburg in order to pay for his education. After graduating as a teacher, he becomes a popular writer. He leaves his country school for Johannesburg in the hope of gaining more experience in life, as indeed he does, for he allows himself to be ensnared by the wiles of one of the loose women who prosper in the big cities. Fortunately, he is ultimately rescued by his fiancée. Another story in the same volume deals with a country boy who comes to Johannesburg and falls into the hands of robbers; they are about to kill him when their leader recognizes him as the son of a man who had once helped him. The moral message is orthodox enough, but Sinxo resembles the South African Bantu authors who were writing in English during the fifties, by the outspokenness with which he describes the prostitution and hooliganism that plague the African townships of big cities. His frankness even earned him some words of mild reproof from Shepherd, who wrote that "Sinxo's work is of merit, but he has a tendency to depict town life with its undesirable features"! Actually, it is this realism that is Sinxo's chief merit and has earned him an important place in the historical development of Xhosa literature. Like most of the early writers everywhere on the African continent, he considered that it was the educated man's duty "to preach, not only from the church pulpits, but from the pulpits of the world, to a world congregation." [66] And Vilakazi, speaking of his first works, observed that "the constant harping on religion in Sinxo's novels forces him to drift unnecessarily into moralizing in every chapter." Even in that early phase, however, a realistic trend was apparent in his handling of the language. Where earlier writers, and especially Mqhayi, strove for conscious artistry, exploiting to the utmost the resources of traditional Xhosa literary style, Sinxo innovated by using in prose fiction the language actually spoken by the people. As C. M. Doke pointed out in discussing *Umzali wolahleko,* "in much of the conversational part, he fearlessly introduces the type of speech, affecting a knowledge of English, which is so often heard mingled in Bantu conversation of to-day." [67] In the light of his later works, it appears that this realism in style was only a prelude to an increasing realism in subject matter, as Sinxo came to concentrate on the demoralization and seaminess of African life in the native locations of such big South African cities as East London, Port Elizabeth, or Johannesburg.

The best Xhosa writer of this younger generation was James J. R. Jolobe, who was born at Indwe in 1902.[68] His father was a church minister. He studied at St. Matthew's, where he displayed precocious interest in writing. He is one of the few African writers who has left some reminiscences of himself,[69] and these are of interest for the study of the literary life of his generation:

When I was at St. Matthews as a young student many years back there was in that institution a student by the name of Enoch Guma. This student used to disappear from the College and what surprised us most was that when he returned he was not expelled. One day the whole institution was pleasantly surprised to learn that Enoch Guma had writen a book which was actually printed and published. We read the book *uNomalizo* with great interest.

Soon after, four or five of us formed a club which we called by a big name of the Witenagemot although I am sure there was nothing wise about any of its members. Its aim was that once a fortnight each should place before the others some small piece of writing he had done. I chose verse. It happened that a lady teacher in the Practising School there heard of our club and managed to get hold of some of our boyish writings. One day she called me to her classroom and made her pupils to recite some verse of mine. I wished that day the floor could open and swallow me. I was young and shy. As the children recited at the top of their voices, they seemed to be accusing me saying "Jolobe does murder verse." From that day I gave that teacher's classroom a wide berth. But I realised years later when I thought of the incident that it was her practical way of encouraging me.

Sinxo, too, was a member of the St. Matthew's Witenagemot.

Jolobe also attracted the attention of Canon J. K. Mather, with whom he carried on correspondence for a long time after leaving school, when he became a teacher in Mount Frere:

In one of his letters he suggested that I should write a book. I did not think then I was equal to the task. But it happened that I had to teach in a small village school at the back of beyond, as people say. Church people in that village could be counted on the fingers of one hand . . . and in many ways it was lonely. It was then that I remembered the suggestion of Canon J. K. Mather. I started drafting and writing my first book. . . . Presses in those days did not often take the risk they are taking these days of publishing manuscripts at their own expense and I had no money. Canon J. K. Mather kindly offered to pay for the publication of the book. I am afraid he had to wait for a long time to get his money back. Books then sold very slowly. It was before the days when books were prescribed for Xhosa classes. And even if they were I am sure mine could not have been prescribed. There was nothing wrong with the matter. But in language it did not conform to the Standard Xhosa of these parts. I had grown up in a Hlubi area and it was freely sprinkled with Hlubi idiom. Years after when I had learnt more standard Xhosa and the book had reached the stage of a second edition I had occasion to revise it and I was myself surprised at the frequency with which I met Hlubi expressions. But I am glad to say it survived the storm, as it is still on the market today, thirty years after its first publication.

This book was the short novel *U-Zagula* that was printed in Lovedale in 1923. In the words of a Xhosa critic, it describes "the terribly negative influence that the belief in magic had and still has on the social structure of Xhosa society." [70]

It was followed, five years later, by a story for boys, *Iindlela Ezahlukeneyo (Different Paths)*, which won a prize in a competition organized by the Society for the Promotion of Christian Knowledge.

By that time, Jolobe was a student at Fort Hare, where he had matriculated in 1926. The principal, Dr. Kerr, strongly encouraged him to go on with his writing. In 1931 the *South African Outlook* published an English essay of his which had gained first prize in a Fort Hare essay competition: *The Prospects for a Native of South Africa After Completing a Course of Work and Service Among His Own People*. While at Fort Hare, Jolobe went on writing poems:

I used to send some of these to the *Imvo zabaNtsundu* and the Editor of that paper was kind enough to publish them. It was his way too of encouraging me, and I am thankful for this.

There was at that time an Inspector of Schools who was also a Xhosa scholar, Dr. W. G. Bennie. He was a reader of the *Imvo*. He made cuttings of these poems and of contributions by other writers. When he was compiling his now famous series of Xhosa readers, the *Stewart Readers*, he used some of the poems. In this way he was encouraging unknown and struggling writers.

Later I collected my poems and sent them to Dr. Shepherd. He was sympathetic. But even then Xhosa stories were only beginning to sell steadily, while it was another story about poetry. He suggested that the manuscript should be sent to the University of the Witwatersrand Press as there Dr. Doke and Mr. Rheinalt Jones were publishing any good manuscript which could not be published profitably by ordinary Presses. This was yet another way of encouraging African writers. The manuscript was sent with Dr. Shepherd's recommendation and it was accepted and became no. 2 of the now famous series called "The Bantu Treasury."

This book, Jolobe's first major piece of creative writing, was *Omyezo (The Orchard)*, which appeared in 1936. In his review, Professor D. D. T. Jabavu emphasized the novelty of the experiment, observing that the author "specializes in topics rarely utilized by African poets, such as The Shepherd, The Death of an Infant, The Lament of the Ass, Admiration to the Butterfly, The River, One Day, Far Hills, Grandmother, The Spring, Our Cat, and so on." [71] The Xhosa critic also noted that Jolobe did not try to imitate European rhyme, but Professor Nyembezi was later to state that the poet "first experimented with rhyme in his poetry and when he thought that the result was not altogether satisfactory he did not hesitate to discard it." [72] Four of those poems were later published in Jolobe's own English translation as *Poems of an African* (Lovedale, 1946). Two of them, a sonnet entitled "To Light" and a long poem in memory of his mother, are of Christian inspiration. "To the Fallen" was written in honor of the black soldiers from southern Africa who died in World War I, supposedly in defense of democracy. It combines the yearning for political and social recognition with the traditional native notion that spoils are the legitimate material reward of the man who has proved his manhood in fighting; only, in this case the spoils are not to come from the vanquished Germans:

We look for spoil, for true reward from home,
From those defended with such cost of life:
The smooth fat cow—Impartiality,
The ox—Full-opportunity-for-growth.
From tree of life we long for leaf to chew
That we may live like races of the world.
When once a lad is asked to arm for war,
That hour he wins the standing of a man.
Consideration, honour, all are his
In days of peace when men assess the past.

(P. 3)

The last translated poem, *Thuthula*, which earned its author the first prize in the May Esther Bedford Competition for 1936, is a short epic romance dealing with the Ndlambe-Ngqika rivalry that had been the undoing of unity among the Gcaleka Xhosa. Thuthula was the youngest wife of Ndlambe; she was abducted by Ngqika, and the poet interprets this event both as the cause of the fifth Kaffir war, and as the outcome of a plot by Ngqika's heathen advisers to halt the progress of Christianity under the influence of Ntsikana. In his version of the story, Ngqika and Thuthula meet and fall in love with each other before the girl's marriage to Ndlambe. The sacredness of love is celebrated in Christian terms:

This thing called love is sacred, holy, pure.
It is the better self—man's complement,
It is a thing of worth, a royal gift,
More precious than all else we equally prize.
No bar nor gulf should ever rise between
Two hearts, two souls, two twins that yearn in love
For one another's company on earth.

(P. 13)

On the basis of this Christian and romantic exaltation of love, which was alien to the native cultures of South Africa, Jolobe utters his critique of traditional marriage conceptions:

Those days the chief vocation of the maids
It was to marry, find a lord and home.
Lobola cows were paid for virgin maids.
To gain this end the mothers too did strive
To guard and foster innocence of maids.

> Alas! again because of this same end
> Their happiness was often sacrificed
> To loveless marriage without a choice.
>
> (Pp. 15-16)

Thuthula's fate illustrates this sad predicament: she is made to marry the old chief Ndlambe, who already has more than a dozen wives. While she thus goes to live on the kraal of Ndlambe, who by then has moved across the Great Fish River, Ngqika almost forgets her. He comes under the influence of Ntsikana and leans toward Christianity. This rouses the fear and wrath of his other advisers:

> They were not ready yet for any change
> In ancient order, custom, life and faith.
>
> (P. 20)

Accordingly, they plot to have both Ngqika and Ntsikana properly chastised by Chief Ndlambe. They decide to engineer a war by having Thuthula abducted. Very cunningly, they play on both the old love and the chiefly pride of Ngqika, claiming that, as the most beautiful woman of the tribe, Thuthula should be his own wife:

> And thus they touched the king at his weak spot
> As one who loved supremacy and power;
> And thus again they did revive the fire
> Of love, which was well-nigh extinguished then.
>
> (P. 21)

It is therefore with Ngqika's consent that they call on Thuthula and ask her to join him. This precipitates an inner conflict in the mind of the young woman, between her infatuation and the sacredness of marriage vows, "between her pleasure and this holy thing" (p. 24). And Jolobe leaves us in no doubt of his judgment as she finally resolves to follow Ngqika's messengers:

> Alas! Thuthula, thou didst bring disgrace
> and shame on marriage vows. . . .
> Perhaps 'twas love that tempted thee, poor dame,
> The pain of being weaned from thy soul twin,
> On altar of *lobola* sacrificed.

> Forsooth, that was a death in life, but this
> Is death, and yea, a death seven times o'er.
>
> (P. 25)

The last section of the poem describes the battle that resulted from Thuthula's elopement.

This verse narrative, which is interspersed with traditional praise poems, is a good example of the best Bantu writers' tragic insight into the predicament of the African, torn between ancestral custom and the new faith. Jolobe, it will be perceived, rejects the traditional mores wholesale: the happiness of Thuthula and Ngqika is first prevented by the tribal conception of marriage, which encourages parental greed; and the uneasy peace of Xhosa society is destroyed because of the hostility of Ngqika's advisers to Christianity. Only complete adherence to the Christian gospel of love will restore orderliness in the body politic and fulfillment in private life. It is to this that Jolobe looks forward at the end of the poem:

> Those days the sun was rising in the east;
> To-day, rejoice, the sun has left the hills.
> It will ascend the Sky of Africa,
> Until the gloomy shadows of our land
> Of darkness and ignorance are gone,
> Such as did bring about the bitter wars,
> Like this great war for dame Thuthula sweet.
>
> (P. 31)

The publication of *Omyezo* in 1936 was a landmark in the history of written Xhosa poetry. The earliest authors had collected preexisting praise poems and composed Christian hymns. The greatness of Mqhayi lay, as Vilakazi put it, in his "combining and using the knowledge and craft of the dead *imbongi.*" Jolobe, too, is a Christian, who has, to quote the Zulu critic again, "a reverent approach to sacred things," and "sees the hand of God in every day happenings"; and he too draws inspiration from the tribal past. But his peculiar contribution, and that of his lesser contemporaries, consists in a spirit of "experimentation and innovation, backed by their knowledge of past history, and in the delicate culture of minds drilled in the study of European literature which generates true poetic poise." [73]

On 30 September 1937, Jolobe was invited, together with Mqhayi, as a Xhosa representative to the African Authors' Conference held in Johannesburg. In 1938 he was appointed assistant to Dr. Grant, to teach at the Lovedale Bible School.[74] And in 1940 the Bantu Treasury Series published *Amavo (Personal Impressions)*, the first collection of essays by a Nguni writer.[75]

No creative writing seems to have come from Jolobe's pen during the forties, but the early fifties were particularly fruitful and rewarding years. Apart from a Xhosa translation of Booker T. Washington's *Up from Slavery* (1951) and an adaptation of Aesop's fables (1953), he published a collection of poems about the little town of Alice near Lovedale, *Izicengcelezo zaseDikeni (Detailed Accounts of Alice* [Lovedale, 1952]). In 1952 he was awarded the Vilakazi Memorial Prize for Nguni writers. In 1953 he won the first prize in a competition organized by the Afrikaanse Pers-Boekhandel in Johannesburg. And in 1957, he received the Margaret Wrong prize and medal "for outstanding services to literature in South Africa." At that time, Jolobe was a member of the Lovedale Press Committee, of the editorial committee of the *South African Outlook*, and of the Xhosa Language and Literature Committee.[77] In 1958 the Afrikaanse Pers-Boekhandel printed his novel *Elundini lo Thukela (On the Horizon of the Thukela Valley)* and a one-act play in eight scenes, *Amathunzi obomi (The Ups and Downs of Life)*, which is sometimes claimed to be the first Xhosa stage drama. This is far from accurate, and at this point, it is necessary to interrupt our account of Jolobe's career and to consider the emergence of dramatic activity of a modern type in Xhosa.

Apart from Guybon Sinxo's school plays of 1925, formal drama among the Xhosa appeared in the early thirties with the founding in 1933 of the Bantu Dramatic Society by members of the Bantu Men's Social Centre in Johannesburg. This was a club for educated Africans who, as teachers, mine clerks, and other professionals, had become more or less detribalized town dwellers. The president of the club was R. F. A. Hoernlé, to whom we owe an account of the beginnings of Xhosa drama.[78]

The Bantu Dramatic Society's aim was "to encourage Bantu playwrights and to develop African dramatic art," in the awareness that "Bantu life is full of great and glorious incidents and figures that would form the basis of first-class drama." Nevertheless, the society first faced the public in Oliver Goldsmith's *She Stoops to Conquer*, which was performed twice in Johannesburg and once in Pretoria. This choice, Hoernlé says, was "due to the fact that this play had, some months previously, been performed by a visiting English company in His Majesty's Theatre in Johannesburg." At the time, this theater was "unique among South African theatres in that it lowers the colour-bar usually maintained in places of entertainment for Whites, by admitting Bantu spectators to the gallery when there is room. This gave the Bantu players an opportunity of studying a model of the acting and stage-management with which the play is put on by a White company. In addition, several members of the Johannesburg Amateur Dramatic Society interested themselves in the new venture and assisted the Bantu players with coaching and advice."

Later in 1933 the company added to its repertoire the first play ever written in Xhosa. This was *UNongqause*, which had been published in 1924 by a white South African woman, Mary W. Waters. It dramatized the cattle-killing episode of 1856, and it would be of interest to enquire into its relationship to a later English drama on the same subject. *The Girl Who Killed to Save* (Lovedale, 1936) by a Zulu author, Herbert I. E. Dhlomo. According to Hoernlé, Miss Waters's play was no masterpiece of stage-craft: "It is a very difficult subject to handle, and the authoress possessed none of the qualifications for handling it beyond her excellent command of the Xhosa language. Thus, in her hands, the story never rises above the level of jejune, uninspired chronicle . . . a series of scenes, or tableaus, without any dramatic quality, whether taken singly or as a whole." Further, "the authoress complicates her tale by trying to point a moral through contrasting the superstition-ridden heathens with the Bible-reading missionary" in a number of edifying speeches. As Hoernlé aptly comments, "you cannot make an actable drama out of harangues, unless you are a Bernard Shaw."

The Empire Exhibition held in Johannesburg in 1936 was one of the many occurrences that stimulated cultural effervescence among black South Africans in the mid-thirties. André van Gyseghem, who was pageant-master at the Exhibition subsequently gave an address on African drama to the British Drama League in London. Not only did he collect information about the Bantu Dramatic

Society who, at the time, had added that most unlikely play *Lady Windermere's Fan* to their exotic repertoire, but, as Vilakazi recalls:

He also offered his services to a society called "Bantu Peoples' Theatre," which proved willing to learn something new, and with this group he produced *The Hairy Ape*. The American slang was translated into "Kitchen-Kafir" and the results were intensely interesting. The show was given at the Bantu Men's Social Centre in Johannesburg and it was an eye-opener to many European producers and African actors. It attracted large crowds. . . . But van Gyseghem stressed the grave danger of imitation, and urged producers and writers to encourage Africans to preserve their culture and to exhibit it in their dramatic art. He was fortunate to meet "The Lucky Stars," who were then ripe for theatrical work, and he commented favourably on the abundance of their talent.[79]

The Lucky Stars was a Zulu company and will be dealt with in a later chapter. It is important to note, however, that Johannesburg in the mid-thirties became a cultural crossroads where Bantu intellectuals of various tribes and languages could meet and cross-fertilize one another's literary activities.

Contrary to expectations, the Bantu Dramatic Society does not seem to have led to any significant developments in Xhosa drama. It may have performed *Iziganeko-zom-Kristu (Tales About a Christian)*, a play based on the ever popular translation of *The Pilgrim's Progress*, which had been printed at Lovedale in 1928.[80] But it was not until more than twenty years after its start that playwriting in Xhosa was resumed and began really to develop, however clumsily at first. The way was opened by a member of the younger generation, M. Mbidlana, who published, in 1954, a mediocre play dealing with the custom of the bride-price. But before the movement gathered some momentum in the late fifties, a Xhosa translation of Shakespeare's *Julius Caesar* had been published in 1956 by Bennett B. Mdledle, who belonged to the same generation as Jolobe, as he was born in Victoria East on 20 February 1899.[81] He attended a junior certificate course at Lovedale, and was trained as a teacher at Healdtown. In 1920 he joined the Lovedale staff and pursued his teaching career until 1958. In 1926 he had matriculated by private study and obtained a B.A. degree, partly by private study, at Fort Hare in 1937. He was a frequent reviewer of Xhosa books in the *South African Outlook*. After retiring, he embarked on a new career as a politician. In 1963 he was elected to the Transkei Legislative Assembly, and he became the first minister of education in the Transkei. Through a reshuffle in 1966, he became minister of justice. The Afrikaanse Pers Beperk published his translation of *Macbeth* in 1959. In 1961 the Lovedale Press printed his Xhosa version of *Twelfth Night*.

Although Jolobe, then, was by no means the founder of Xhosa drama, nevertheless his turning to this comparatively neglected medium must have encouraged writers of the new generation who were entering the literary scene in the late fifties. The play he published in 1958 *Amathunzi obomi* has been conveniently summarized in a review by Mdledle:

It depicts the life of a widow with her two boys in an urban area. She continues the family worship in the evenings, even after her husband's death. Her influence for good is felt in church circles, but straitened means push her to the underworld. She indulges in illicit liquor traffic. She quickly piles up money. Within a short time, she has £500 in the bank. At length she is arrested and fined £10. A kind European woman finds her work at the factory. She retrieves her steps and is welcomed back in church. Her elder boy who has joined the tsotsi [hooligan] gang is arrested with others for housebreaking. He is sent to the Gompo Reformatory.[82]

Such as it is, the play is rather typical, in its choice and handling of the situation, of the main trend of this generation, whose formative years came after the constitution of the Union. As a result of the rapid growth of industry and industrial cities in the country, writers tended to concentrate more and more on the problems raised by the squalid way of life characteristic of urbanized black Africans in native townships. Ever since Guma's *UNomalizo*, the emphasis had increasingly come to rest on what Dr. Shepherd had called, in a memorable understatement, the "undesirable features" of city life. But the rebellious spirit of the previous generation seemed to have toned down considerably. The play does not entail any serious analysis, not to mention any serious criticism, of the social and economic factors inherent in colonial racism, although these issues were largely responsible for the situation described. Discrimination is taken for granted in a mood of impotence. No explicit connection is established between racial oppression and the inner disruption of urban African society. The only remedy offered is of a strictly ethical nature: Jolobe calls for forbearance on the part of the derelict black man, and charity on the part of the privileged white. The fate of the heroine intimates that virtue is always rewarded and vice always castigated, the latter statement being bolstered by the arrest and imprisonment of her hooligan son.

In 1959 Jolobe published a new collection of poems, *Ilitha (A Ray of Life)*, some humorous, most of a narrative kind, dealing with, among other things, the traumatic cattle-killing episode.[83] He also produced a translation of Rider Haggard's *King Solomon's Mines*.[84] Besides, he contributed a paper on the problems encountered by African writers at the African Authors' Conference that was held at Atteridgeville (Pretoria) on 7–9 July 1959. It was in the same year that he left the Lovedale Bible School to go back to his congregation at New Brighton, near Port Elizabeth,[85] where he still was living in 1966.

Jolobe's long career should not obscure the fact that the period of expansion and diversification in Xhosa creative writing mainly covered the twenties and the thirties, when a number of lesser authors also experimented with the novel.

The second Xhosa woman writer, Victoria Swaartbooi was born at Emgcwe in the district of Nqamakwe on 27 September 1907.[86] There she attended the Methodist school of which her father was principal. In January 1924 she entered Emgwali Training School. From 1926 to 1928, she studied at Healdtown, where she gained her junior certificate. In January 1929 she was appointed to the Emgwali Girls' Practising School. Her only novel, *U-Mandisa* (Lovedale, 1935) has obvious autobiographical overtones, being, as Vilakazi put it, "the life-history of a little girl born and brought up in the age of civilisation, where children play with dolls and later go to day school and pass on to boarding school, where they are trained as teachers." [87] According to the Zulu critic, there is "nothing striking" in the "language and style" of the book, and a Xhosa critic recently added that "the unnatural goodness of the heroine fills one with distaste, and it will inspire no child to follow her example." [88] Victoria Swaartbooi died at the Emgwali institution on 23 September 1937 after a short illness.

There were a few writers of whom even less is known. The Reverend John Solilo, of Cradock, published a collection of poems, *Izala (Miscellany)* during that period. *U-Nozipo* (Lovedale, 1923), by Stephen Mlotywa and *U-Ntsizi* (Palmerton, E. Pondoland, 1924) by Gilbert B. Makalima, were stories of native life, which Doke described as "not outstanding." Julius J. J. Walaza had *Inkwenkwe izala indoda (From Boyhood Stems Manhood)* printed in Johannesburg in 1929. B. A. Bangeni's *Kuphilwaphi? (Where Do People Live?* [Lovedale, 1934]) was characterized by Shepherd as "a vivid story full of incidents."

Although a few books in Xhosa were printed in various towns and mission stations, Lovedale remained the stronghold of Xhosa writing throughout the years from 1920 to 1940, and could even improve its position in the late twenties through a grant of about £2000 from the Carnegie Trust "to aid in equipping Lovedale with modern bookprinting machinery"; as a result, "in 1929 arrangements were made with Mr. W. G. Bennie, B.A., who was retiring from the position of Chief Inspector of Native Education in the Cape Province, to edit a new series of Xhosa School Readers, which were to be known as the *Stewart Xhosa Readers*." [89] As we know from Jolobe's later testimony, this was an efficient way of opening channels of publication for deserving Xhosa authors as well as providing suitable reading matter for Xhosa schoolchildren. Equally important was the publication by Bennie of his notable anthology *Imibengo (Titbits* [Lovedale, 1936]), in which thirty Xhosa and two European writers were represented, and work by six early authors such as Ntsikana, Tiyo Soga, and Gqoba, as well as extracts from *Indaba* and *Isigidimi*, was included. *Imibengo* supplemented Rubusana's earlier anthology in giving the Xhosa people knowledge of and pride in their literary legacy.

But the best work of that generation and, so far, probably the only Xhosa novel that can bear judgment by the most exacting criteria universally applied to modern prose fiction was not to appear until the eve of World War II. Its author, Archibald Campbell Jordan,[90] was of Hlubi stock like Ndawo; his ancestors came from the Tugela district. He was born on 30 October 1906, the son of a minister of the Church of England, at the Mbokothwana Mission in the Tsolo district of Pondoland (Transkei), where he attended primary school until 1921. After studying at the St. Cuthbert

School, he was awarded an Andrew Smith bursary, which enabled him to proceed to Lovedale, where he obtained his junior certificate. He was trained as a teacher at St. John's College, Umtata. He won another merit scholarship on the basis of which he went to Fort Hare College. He obtained his education diploma from the University of South Africa in 1932, and his B.A. in 1934. He then took a teaching post at the Bantu High School in Kroonstad, in the northern part of the Orange Free State, where he remained for ten years, becoming an executive member and later president of the African Teachers' Association. Daniel P. Kunene, who began junior high school at Kroonstad in February 1938 has provided the following picture of Jordan as a teacher of English language and literature:

Because of his intimate knowledge of his subject and his interest in sharing this knowledge with his students; because of his genuine concern for his students, and his efforts to understand their backgrounds with a view to assisting them more effectively, he displayed tolerance for attitudes universally associated with youth and always frowned upon by their elders (of whom Jordan would say that they did not temper their attitude with a frank admission that they, too, were once young). Because, while affable and loving, he yet retained enough authority to command respect and obedience—because of these and other qualities too numerous to recount, Jordan was admired by his students and held in high esteem by his colleagues.

It was also during his days in Kroonstad that Jordan started his literary career. As Kunene recalls:

In 1936 he published several of his poems in the newspaper *Imvo Zabantsundu,* and in 1958 several in *Ikhwezi lomso.* The poems were in Xhosa, some accompanied by English translations prepared by Jordan himself. The English verision of one of these poems has been included in many anthologies of African literature under the title, *You tell me to sit quiet.* In this work the author shows his deep involvement in the South African political scene where the deprived are indeed "told to sit quiet" or else face harsh punishment. The poem reflects the anger of a man who had, since 1936, been actively involved in the political struggle for the liberation of the Black people of South Africa. His involvement was through teachers' associations and more directly through political organizations dedicated to the eradication of the cruelty and immorality of the South African situation, a situation which was later to reject him.

But in the years following his poems of 1936, Jordan seems to have devoted himself to the writing of his first and only novel. As a student and as a teacher, he had been in the habit of spending frequent holidays at home, where Hlubi leaders told him about the customs and the history of their people. In 1933 he became acquainted with some Mpondomise chiefs, and a visit to the place where their ancestor Majola was buried[91] appears to have kindled his desire to write a book about social change among the Mpondomise. This was *Ingqumbo yeminyanya (The Wrath of the Ancestors* [Lovedale, 1940]), a novel that deals simultaneously with two of the major problems facing the acculturating societies of Africa: the theme of modern education versus traditional belief, and the theme of individual love and Christian marriage versus traditional custom and polygamy.

The plot is based on a dynastic quarrel similar to those that have frequently disturbed the course of Xhosa history. Dingindawo has usurped the chieftainship of the Mpondomise tribe from his nephew Zwelinzima. For fear he might kill his victim, a group of loyal tribesmen help the young man seek refuge outside the territory controlled by his uncle. This enables Zwelinzima to attend school at Lovedale, and thus to become a symbol of the modern educated African chief as opposed to the conservatism of his uncle. Further, Zwelinzima falls in love with Thembeka, who is a student at Lovedale too. As she responds to his feelings, he incurs the jealousy of another student, Mthunzini, whom she has jilted in his favor. When Zwelinzima, after completing his education, returns to the Mpondomise to claim his legitimate rights, a complex conflict develops. He has to face Dingindawo, who wants to keep power for himself and for his son Vukuz'umbeke, but he also has to face the vengefulness of Mthunzini, who, under cover of doing historical research, strikes an unholy alliance with the usurper. The distribution of forces within the novel intimates that education is by no means to be equated with everything that is good, or traditionalism with everything that is bad. Indeed, while Mthunzini puts his education in the service of self-seeking jealousy, Vukuz'umbeke, although an uneducated man, is presented as an idealist, who is aware of his father's guilt, helps the victim, and loses his own life in doing so.

Zwelinzima's victory and consequent accession to the throne, however, is only the beginning of the real problem and tragedy.

First, the new king finds himself at odds with his people with regard to his own marriage. They want him to marry a tribal girl, or at least to take one as his second wife. The young chief, however, has his way and marries Thembeka. Further, he irritates his subjects by his hasty and premature efforts to modernize the Mpondomise way of life. As Riordan observed, "He thinks he can change human nature and the face of the world in one day. He sees only the beauty of the ideal of civilization which he cherishes." [92] In this respect, his character might indeed be considered an ironical comment on the facile utopian idealism evinced by such elder writers as Ndawo in *U-Nomathamsanqa no Sigebenga* and especially Mqhayi in *U-Don Jadu*. The difference, however, which testifies to the considerably greater subtlety of Jordan's insights as against the oversimplified views of his predecessors, is that his hero comes to recognize his own errors. Not that he abjures the ideal to which he has committed himself, but he understands that the old order and the traditional customs are valuable in many ways, and that, insofar as they ought to be changed, any attempt at too sudden an eradication of familiar beliefs and standards can only lead to chaos.

According to Riordan, the tragedy of Zwelinzima is that he acknowledges this too late: "Rash youth has moved too fast, and he must pay the price." While this is true, Jordan's story is not merely the account of an individual failure. And Vilakazi asked the right questions when he wondered: "Does Jordan fear that the powers of darkness, embodied in the authority of the primitive and uneducated chiefs, will finally overcome the powers of the best in African and Western culture and civilization? Why does he kill the holders of Christian chieftainship?" [93] Indeed, it seems obvious that in Jordan's view the tragedy is not solely in the character of the young chief, but inheres in the very processes taking place in Africa: a new society, a new culture cannot be born without some admixture of destruction, suffering, and chaos. This at least seems to be implied by the nature of the final crisis in the novel, a crisis that focuses on Thembeka. From the beginning of her reign, the young queen antagonizes the tribe because she goes about in short dresses and bareheaded. One day, she finds a serpent coiled near her child and kills it. Now, as anthropologists know, among the Pondos, "different clans regard a particular species of snake as being a manifestation of their *ithongo* (ancestral spirits), and treat

it with respect, not killing it or driving it away when it comes to
the *umzi* (compound, kraal), for it is *umninimizi* (the owner of
the *umzi*)."[94] Whether the snake is poisonous or not makes no
difference. Clearly, this is one of the points on which modern and
traditional attitudes cannot be reconciled. It is perhaps the most
important of such points, since devotion to the ancestral spirits is
the cornerstone of many traditional societies, with the consequent
belief—skillfully described by Jordan at the beginning of the book
—that the ancestors inevitably take revenge on those who harm
snakes. To the Western mind, in killing the snake, the queen has
courageously done her duty to save her child's life; in the traditional African view, she has committed the most grievous offense
that can be conceived. This antinomy is the real core of the tragedy,
and it is the source of further dilemmas and calamities. For the
tribe is so outraged that Zwelinzima, in order to keep the throne, is
compelled to renounce the queen to take another, more acceptable
wife. Thembeka, in her turn, is frenzied by the wreck of her love
and marriage; she drowns herself and her son, upon which the chief
himself commits suicide. The whole process is of course a case of
self-fulfilling prophecy: it is the tribe's belief in the wrath of the
ancestors which is responsible for those catastrophic events, which
in turn confirm and strengthen that very belief. This, however, is
not how Jordan's tribesmen view it. As I. Oldjohn put it at the
time, "To an educated Christian such a tragic end is a perversion
of the accepted moral standards, that is, a triumph of evil over
good. But to a Pondomise, whose religious outlook is different, the
tragedy is the inevitable retribution of the *iminyanya*, whose wrath
has been kindled by a wanton non-observance of the tribal customs on the part of the chief and his wife." [95] It is not surprising
that the novel should have produced among the Xhosa elite a mixture of fascination and puzzlement which has been aptly described
by Daniel Kunene:

Ingqumbo yeminyanya had burst into the South African Bantu-
language literary scene, and had immediately been recognized as being
a great tragedy, the creation of a master mind. Students at boarding
schools and colleges broke residence regulations by continuing to read
the gripping story after lights-off, with candles sheltered under blankets
against the tell-tale windows. Illiterate men who had heard about it
got school-boys to read it to them and would not let them be until

they had read the last word. Comments came thick and fast, both in reviews and in private conversation—"Why does he make forces of reaction and conservatism triumph?" "Why does he give it such an unhappy ending?" "Why does he seem to ally himself with the forces of paganism?" "Does he believe in ancestor worship?" "Which side is he on?"

Such questions, like those raised by Vilakazi, or the paradox defined by Oldjohn, or the response of Shepherd in *Bantu Literature and Life*—"At the close of the book, the forces of evil, of paganism, and reaction, win"—are enough to show that *The Wrath of the Ancestors* is a deeply disturbing novel, where the interplay of character and circumstance cannot be described in simple terms. As Harold Scheub convincingly demonstrated, in his article in *Contrast*,

The atmosphere of the novel is . . . one of objectivity bordering on starkness. The author chooses no sides in the conflict between the old and the new; no special value is placed on either, for the fundamental assumption of the work is the inevitability of change, and little time is wasted weeping for the past and glorying in the future. . . . The preoccupation of the novelist is not with the conflict of races, not with apartheid and the South African political arena; he does not affirm Christianity over the ancient religion of the Xhosa people, or *vice versa;* and he gives no clear indication that either the world of the ancestors or the world of the academics will prevail. These conflicts are on the periphery of the author's central concern. . . . What at first seems to be a novel concerned with the conflict of the old and the new with only scant attention paid to character is in fact a novel of character, the conflict of change being the battlefield which exposes the strengths and weaknesses of the several characters. . . . Jordan thus begins with the fact of change in its widest sense, narrows this to the conflict between tradition and progress, and then he finds his themes not in the conflict but in the heroism and tragedy of those men caught up in it. Against insuperable odds, man is bound to lose, but man fights nonetheless, and it is in the fight that the beauty of his manhood is affirmed.

Coming some thirty years after Mofolo's *Chaka, The Wrath of the Ancestors* should probably rank as the second masterpiece contributed to the world corpus of prose fiction by the vernacular literatures of southern Africa. It is clearly desirable that Jordan's own English version should be printed and thus made available to wider audiences.

While writing his novel, Jordan was also studying for an M.A. degree from the University of South Africa, which he obtained in 1942. At the beginning of 1945, he was appointed lecturer in Bantu languages at Fort Hare in place of Professor Jabavu, who had retired the previous year. He remained there for one year only; in 1946 he took a similar appointment at the University of Cape Town, where he introduced the direct method in the teaching of Bantu languages to non-Bantu-speaking students. The outcome of these experiments was his *Xhosa Manual*. They were also auxiliary to his dissertation on "A Phonological and Grammatical Study of Literary Xhosa," for which he obtained a Ph.D. degree in 1954. In its turn, this linguistic study of Xhosa literature led him to do research into the early history of Xhosa writing, the results of which were published in a series of articles in *Africa South* (later, *Africa South in Exile*) from 1957 to 1959. It is reported that in 1958 he obtained permission from the chief of the Mpondomise tribe to bring some of his European students to visit the site of his novel. In 1961 he was awarded a Carnegie travel grant to visit universities in the United States and in the United Kingdom, and to investigate the latest developments in linguistic methods. He was also offered a visiting lectureship in African languages and literature. As Jordan had publicly opposed various government measures, including the notorious Bantu Education Acts and university apartheid, he was refused a passport by the South African authorities in spite of representations from the University of Cape Town. He then left the country illegally and went to the University of California, Los Angeles, where he remained for two years. In 1963 he went to the University of Wisconsin as a fellow at the Institute for Research in the Humanities, and in 1964 he was appointed as a professor of African Languages and Literature, a post that he held until his death on 20 October 1968.

Pressures of Apartheid

Most of the developments that took place in Xhosa literature, as in the other vernacular literatures of South Africa after World War II, are mainly to be accounted for by the hardening and

systematizing of apartheid policy with the victory of Dr. Malan's
Nationalist party at the general elections of 1948, and more specifically by the Bantu Education Act of 1953. The act transferred
Bantu education from the provinces to the Department of Native
Affairs, headed at the time by Dr. Hendrik Verwoerd. In the
course of parliamentary debate, Dr. Verwoerd clarified the leading
principles behind the new policy with commendable frankness.
Until now, he said, the native child "has been subject to a school
system which drew him away from his own community and mis-
led him by showing him the green pastures of European society in
which he is not allowed to graze;" but "there is no place for him in
the European community above the level of certain forms of
labour;" and since "Education must train and teach people in accordance with their opportunities in life," it follows inevitably
that the purpose of Bantu education can only be to prepare the
native child for his low status in South African society. Some provision must of course be made for teachers, doctors, lawyers, and
the like to serve the Bantu community, but—and since the majority
of writers had come from the teaching profession, this is of paramount importance for literature—"the Bantu teacher must be integrated as an active agent in the process of development of the
Bantu community. He must learn not to feel above his community
with a consequent desire to become integrated into the life of the
European community. He becomes frustrated and dissatisfied when
this does not take place, and he tries to make his community dissatisfied because of such misdirected ambitions which are alien to
his people." [96]
  Such principles entail a particular attitude to language, which
has double-edged consequences for literature. Already in 1948, the
Afrikaner Institute for Christian National Education had issued a
pamphlet that emphasized, among other things, the notion that the
mother tongue "should be the most important secular subject, and
the only medium of instruction except in teaching other modern
languages." [97] This led, of course, to a considerable enlargement
of the market for vernacular literature, and provided encouragement not only to the new generation that emerged after the war
but also for older, often mediocre writers, whose work had not
reached print earlier. In the general context of apartheid, this was
but a minor achievement as compared with the general lowering of
educational standards, and it is interesting to quote the description,

provided in 1964 by Brian Bunting, a white South African journalist who is an opponent of government policy, of the African response to this measure:

Perhaps the factor which has caused most distress to the Africans themselves has been the enforced introduction of education in the vernacular, with the allocation of equal time for both official languages. Previously, education had been started in the vernacular, but after the first
couple of standards had been pursued in English (most of the schools
were English mission schools). Today all teaching is done through the
medium of the vernacular up to and including standard 6, and the aim
is to continue the process all the way to matriculation. . . . When
matriculation is taken in the vernacular, the African matriculant auto-
matically loses eligibility for entrance into any non-African university.
His "Bantu matric" will qualify him for entrance into his appropriate
tribal university—and nowhere else. He will not even be able to leave
the country and, on the basis of his educational qualifications, proceed
with his university studies elsewhere. . . . Vernacular instruction itself
has led to a startling drop in educational standards. There are seven
vernacular languages, with the result that there is a lack of suitable
textbooks, and for the most part the children have to rely on the instruction of the teacher. Then, after education through the vernacular
in the primary school, there is at present a sudden switch to the two
official languages as media of instruction in the secondary schools.
Children have found the whole pattern extremely unsettling, and the
standard of English in particular has dropped disastrously.[98]

One consequence of this new regime has been a tremendous quantitative increase in vernacular publications; more and more books
reach print, not only in the established literary languages which
are Xhosa, Southern Sotho, and Zulu but also in the four other
recognized vernaculars of South Africa: Venda, Tsonga, Pedi or
Northern Sotho, and Tswana.

With regard to quality, it has become exceedingly difficult for
the foreigner to find reliable information. Since the early sixties,
there has been a rarefaction of articles on and reviews of vernacular
creative writing in such journals as the *South African Outlook* and
African Studies, which were important sources of information.
Any knowledge of recent developments in Xhosa literature is
therefore practically restricted to the Xhosa speaker. From what
little information it is possible to collect, the general impression is
one of steep decline. The reasons are obvious. Literature, espe-

cially of the written kind, thrives on learning. Innate gifts are of course a necessary prerequisite, but it is a fact that throughout Africa, creative writing has improved in quality in close connection with educational development. In all African colonies, native access to university training has meant a sizable progress in the depth of insight, intellectual power, and technical skill of modern imaginative literature. Intellectual cross-fertilization resulting from better knowledge of worldwide languages and literatures provides new models, new sources of inspiration, and enlarged perspectives, through which literature enriches itself anywhere. Now, the new system in Bantu education in South Africa is expressly calculated to prevent all these things. To the would-be writer, mastery of English was the gateway to world literature; decreasing proficiency in English is bound to narrow the scope of models of which he can avail himself. The tribalization of higher learning, as exemplified by the turning of Fort Hare into a Xhosa university, can only hasten the process of cultural segregation, especially as it is the official policy of the Native Affairs Department that "steps will be taken deliberately to keep institutions for higher education, to an increasing extent, away from urban areas, and to establish them as far as possible in the Native Reserves," allegedly in order that "education should stand with both feet in the Reserves and have its roots in the spirit and being of Bantu society." [99]

Even more relevant to our topic has been the increasingly severe and wide-ranging use of censorship, culminating in the Publications and Entertainments Act of 1963. Under the terms of the act, any book can be deemed undesirable, and its circulation prohibited, if it or any part of it

(a) is indecent or obscene or is offensive or harmful to public morals; (b) is blasphemous or is offensive to the religious convictions or feelings of any section of the inhabitants of the Republic; (c) brings any section of the inhabitants of the Republic into ridicule or contempt; (d) is harmful to the relations between any sections of the inhabitants of the Republic; (e) is prejudicial to the safety of the State, the general welfare, or the peace and good order; or (f) discloses indecent or obscene matter in relation to reports of judicial proceedings.[100]

Obviously, any serious discussion of Christian beliefs or of the actual mores of allegedly Christian people, any analysis of the ethical, social, economic, and political aspects of apartheid, any criticism or irony leveled at the European ruling minority, is bound to fall within one or several of these categories. Some sort of control had been effective long before the act. Already in 1953, the organizers of a literary competition in Johannesburg had stipulated that the manuscripts submitted were to be suitable for schools and therefore must refrain from dealing with political or religious conflicts.[101] But censorship has now become far more systematic and efficient.

While the English-speaking Bantu authors in South Africa can have their works printed abroad, as many do, the vernacular writer is hemmed in by two main limitations: the greater part of his audience is made up of schoolchildren or semiliterate adults; and he is not allowed to deal with the controversial topics that are the obsessive concerns of his race. Whereas the number of Xhosa authors who have reached print has increased appreciably, the level of insight exhibited in their works has lowered perceptibly.

The two aspects of this evolution were evoked at the third African Authors' Conference that was convened in Atteridgeville (Pretoria) on 7-9 July 1959. In this respect, it is useful to quote two excerpts from F. J. van Wyk's report: [102]

When in 1936 and 1937 the Rev. Dr. R. H. W. Shepherd of Lovedale and others convened conferences for African authors of the Union of South Africa, they were able to invite only *eight* on the first occasion and *nine* on the second. Circumstances have changed very considerably since then, and when the Continuation Committee and Literature Commission of South African Churches [of which F. J. van Wyk was at the time honorary secretary] convened the 1959 Conference of African authors . . . the organizers found that considerably more than one hundred African authors in the Union were "entitled" to invitations by virtue of their having had works published.

Eventually, eighty-nine African authors from the Union, the High Commission Territories (Bechuanaland, Basutoland and Swaziland) and from the Federation of Rhodesia and Nyasaland attended the Conference, together with an equal number of white educationalists, missionaries, publishers, etc.

Many problems were discussed, among them the still large percentage of illiteracy and the plurality of African languages. But there was also "the problem of finding publishers," which was a harmless way of describing the effects of taboos and censorship, as it arose, says van Wyk, from

the fear among many authors that if they were to write on the political aspirations and problems of their people, the suffering and frustrations which their people experience in a white-dominated country, the deep hurt caused by discrimination, then they would probably be unable to find a publisher willing to publish their works. About this fear, the Rev. C. B. Brink [who was the Conference Chairman] wrote in *Die Kerkbode*, official organ of the Dutch Reformed Church in South Africa: "This is a great pity, because it would seem that it is precisely in this field that the Bantu author could make a very definite and positive contribution to the development of the racial pattern in our country and at the same time give valuable instruction to his own people."

Restrictive measures, such as censorship, combined with the increase in the teaching of Xhosa, cannot but produce highly ambivalent results. In poetry, some of the older men, who had never gone into print before, were able to start publishing their work. One such was R. M. Tshaka, who was born at Isomo in the Transkei on 14 January 1904; he is active as a bookbinder, and his first collection of poems, *Iintsika zentlambo ye-Tyhume (The Pillars of the Tyumie Valley)* was published at Lovedale in 1953.[103] He was also, with Jolobe, one of the contributors to an anthology entitled *Indyebo yesihobe (A Treasury of Songs)* which was printed by the Afrikaanse Pers-Boekhandel in Johannesburg. Of peculiar interest are the poems gathered by G. Soya Mama and A. Z. T. Mbebe in *Amaqunube (Brambles* [Cape Town, *cq.* 1950]); as Mdledle pointed out, they are "modelled on the style of the English verse as distinct from the ordinary Xhosa *'zibongo*, which are symbolic and metaphorical," although many of them are in effect praise poems about such notable African writers as Sol T. Plaatje, John L. Dube, Samuel E. K. Mqhayi, James J. R. Jolobe, or Benedict W. Vilakazi.[104] The best Xhosa writers so far had experimented with European prosody, but they had soon realized that it was not suited to the resources and poetic requirements of the Xhosa language. To them, modernization had consisted of enriching traditional lore with new topics. As late as 1955, Dr. Shepherd could claim that "a gratifying feature of recent literature is the attention given to recording traditional praise-poems and the com-

posing of new ones. . . . It is still the custom for a chief to have at
his 'great place' an *Imbongi*, or praise-reciter, whose duty it is to
extend a welcome in impromptu songs or orations to some important visitor, as well as to extol through such songs the virtues of
his chief. . . . The coming of the British Royal Family to South
Africa in 1947 brought every tribal *Imbongi* to a pitch of excitement and ambition." [105] And Dr. Shepherd provides the translation of a praise by Alfred Z. Ngani, whose collection of poetry,
Intlaba-mkhosi (War Cry) was to appear in 1952. Whatever the
formal merits of the poem may be, it is undiluted panegyric and
has none of the controlled irony displayed by Mqhayi on a similar
occasion some twenty-two years earlier. The setting up of a semiautonomous Xhosa Bantustan in the Transkei may well rejuvenate
the traditional genres. Conversely, it is to be feared that the corresponding lowering of modern educational standards will encourage ritualistic imitation of Western forms by semiliterate poets—
an unmistakable symptom of literary regression.

Nor is there much reason for short-term hope in the field of
prose fiction. In the same article, Dr. Shepherd recalls how "twenty
years ago, when I told in one of my books of African literary
tastes, I remarked how little place the African found for the novel.
Even a comparatively advanced group, such as Lovedale students,
had little inclination for novel-reading. They took reading seriously and to them fiction seemed a waste of time. To-day in the
same group the novel is the type of literature most sought after.
Last year [1954], of 8,335 books borrowed from the Lovedale library by African students, 7,191 were books of fiction. This swing-
over may be partly due to the fact that in no African language has
the novel found so prominent a place as in Xhosa." No doubt, this
phenomenon also resulted from increasing intellectual sophistication. The example of incipient middle-class literature in thirteenth-
century Europe shows that distaste for the fictional is a characteristic of emergent social groups that have to make their way in
the world and to come to grips with its harsh realities: to them,
indeed, fiction is a waste of time. It is only at a higher level of intellectual maturity that the subtler rapport between fiction and
reality in creative literature can be grasped. With Mqhayi, Jolobe
and, above all, Jordan, the Xhosa elite was obviously well on its
way toward that deeper understanding of the relevance of fiction
to experience. Of lesser writers, Shepherd was right to point out

in 1955 that "not so long ago most Xhosa novels were too slight, too much given to moralizing, and frequently obsessed with the unhappy external circumstances of life in city locations." More recent works may be bulkier, but they exhibit little improvement in imaginative integration. With the three great elders in mind, Xhosa critics have little difficulty in pinning down the deficiencies in recent novels and plays; it may be useful to discuss a few samples.

D. Z. Dyafta's *Ikamvu lethu* (*Our Ancestry* [Lovedale, 1953]) [106] is set in the Tyumie Valley and deals with two themes, which, by now, have become traditional and politically harmless in African fiction: education and marriage. The members of the small backward Gwala clan resent having to resort to some educated member of another clan to read and write their own letters. They therefore decide to collect the required money for sending one of their boys to school. Education not only brings literacy but also new ideas and desires. After getting his teacher's certificate, the young man tells his father he wants to marry. This upsets the clan, because it is contrary to custom that a young man should take the initiative, and what is worse, select a bride of his own choice. But modernity triumphs over tradition, and the young hero ultimately has his way. This, obviously, is a rehash of one of the themes much more elaborately and successfully treated by Jordan. The book further belongs in the category of the ethnographical novel, as Dyafta "gives a detailed account of all the formalities that precede a Xhosa marriage. There are some interesting discussions of the different forms of marriage—their advantages and disadvantages, the importance of lobola as a stabilizing factor, and its place in marriage that is contracted under European law." [107]

E. S. M. Dlova's novel, *Umvuzo wesono* (*The Wages of Sin* [Lovedale, 1954]), has the additional distinction of being composed in a reactionary spirit of tribal communalism.[108] The hero is one Twatwa, of very humble origin, who manages to get some elementary education and rises to be the chief's most influential adviser. This earns him the jealousy of Gezenga, a backward heathen Hlubi who is the villain of the piece. Gezenga murders Twatwa's son, who is studying at Lovedale; the bereaved father has to be taken to a mental hospital; Gezenga is arrested and executed; Twatwa recovers after three years and ultimately succeeds the headman. It is of interest to quote the appraisal of a Xhosa critic, R. M. Sobukwe:

There is next to no interplay of character. The hero is thoroughly noble and even his short-temperedness is presented as "righteous indignation," while the villain is thoroughly bad, with a shady past and a gloomy future. . . . The theme of good versus evil, with good reserved for the christianized and evil for the heathen, besides being hackneyed, is not realistic. . . . However, the book abounds in true Xhosa humour and wit with the Christians hard put to it to explain the queer ways of their God.

The writer correctly exposes the tribal antagonisms between "Fingo" and Xhosa, and Hlubi and Xhosa. . . . But his treatment of this subject lacks balance. In the first place, he makes a sweeping condemnation of both the Hlubi and the so-called Fingoes, who, evidently, are in his bad books. The Xhosa, on the other hand, are not once censured.

Another fairly popular, but equally orthodox and crude writer is Witness K. Tamsanqa. In *Inzala ka Mlungisi (The Progeny of Mlungisi* [Cape Town, 1954]), he achieves his moralizing purpose through the facile device of depicting the contrasted fates of two brothers, one of whom receives a good education, leads a Christian life, and becomes accordingly prosperous, while the other becomes a first-class hooligan, roams around the country from Durban to Bulawayo, commits an astounding variety of murders, confesses them in a fit of insanity brought about by his gnawing conscience, and receives the just reward of his criminal career.[109]

Tamsanqa later published a play in six acts, *Buzani kubawo (Ask My Father* [Cape Town, 1958]), which purports to demonstrate the power of love and to indict traditional marriage custom. The hero, Guguletha, had promised marriage to Nomampondomise, whom he had met at college, but his father, Zwilakhe, compels him to marry an uneducated local girl, Thobeka. Nomampondomise reads of the marriage in a newspaper and drowns herself in despair. As to Guguletha, he leaves home and goes to work at Umtata. After twelve years have elapsed, his father sends him his wife and the children she has had by another man. Guguletha promptly murders them all and is sentenced to death. S. Z. Qangule interprets the plot as a clash of personalities between Zwilakhe, "who is a custodian of tradition and Guguletha who has the influence of modern ways of living," both characters being "determined not to make a compromise," and he considers *Buzani kubawo* "easily the best play in what has been written so far" [110] in Xhosa. The decline seems obvious, nevertheless, when we compare this crudely sensa-

tional story with the sensitive treatment awarded to a very similar
theme by Jolobe in *Thuthula*. Nor are more fastidious critics, such
as R.M. Sobukwe, blind to the low quality of such writing:

In the preface, the playwright . . . pleads that since drama is still a
comparatively unexplored field in Xhosa literature, his readers should
adopt a tolerant attitude towards his play. And indeed such a plea is
necessary, for in spite of the dramatic potentialities of the plot, which
gives scope for the creation of a great play based on the age-old conflict between the old and the new, between domineering parent and
rebellious child, the writer's ignorance of stage-technique makes of the
work a dramatic novel rather than a play. . . . The chief character,
Guguletha, is very poorly drawn. He is extremely unpredictable, not
because of his character as such, but because the writer makes him so.
The result is that his "madness," for instance, is unconvincing, because
we do not see the reason why he should go mad. There is no element of
greatness in him and, therefore, there is no element of tragedy in his
fall. . . . The influence of the Elizabethan dramatists, notably Shakespeare, with his battle scenes and wedding scenes, armies and horses, as
well as soliloquies and asides, is apparent. So also is the influence of the
cinema screen, where scenes change rapidly. What the writer has over-
looked, however, is that Shakespeare's technique and dramatic devices
were always designed to meet theatre and stage conditions and the
limitations imposed thereby. Further, the writer seems to be unaware
that the cinema screen is a different medium from the stage.[111]

Such as it is, the purpose of the play is again to illustrate the antinomy of tradition and modern ideas, and the tragedy derives from
the obstinacy with which both the hero and his father cling to their
respective views. Few Xhosa writers of the present day have shown
themselves able to evade this obsessional theme, and the range of
modulations is unfortunately very narrow.

Some of the writers do their best to eradicate what they consider
the most damaging among traditional beliefs and customs. In
his drama *U-Dusha* (Johannesburg, 1958), Aaron Mazambana
Mmango, who was born at Mhlabamnyama (Qumbu) in December 1925, offers yet another denunciation of witchcraft; the title
is the name of the hero and also means "disturber." Mmango later
composed *Law-ilahle (The Glowing Coal Has Fallen* [Lovedale,
1960]), an educational play about the rewards of cheating, and
uDike noCikizwa, (Dike and Cikizwa [Johannesburg, 1962]),
which has been described as a "love tragedy." Witchcraft is also

the target of Marcus A. P. Ngani's *Umkhontho kaTshiwo* (*Tshiwo's Spear* [1959]), a historical play about the destruction of witches by Tshiwo, who was paramount chief of the Xhosa in the early eighteenth century. As Qangule has commented, "The incessant brutal killing creates an atmosphere of horror." Indeed, Xhosa playwrights chiefly rely on bloodshed for creating dramatic interest. Another play, *Inene nasi isibhozo (I Solemnly Declare* [Cape Town, 1961]), by Amos Mtingane, is a family tragedy based on seniority prejudices in connection with marriage: Maukude, a widow, does not want her stepson Themba to marry before her son Vama, fearing that no provision will be made for the latter. She therefore poisons Themba on his wedding day. To evade retaliation, she finds she has to poison one of Themba's relatives as well, but the cups are exchanged, and it is her own son, Vama, who drinks the poisoned tea. Further killing and suicide heighten the ending of the play—its only resemblance to *Hamlet*.

Following in the wake of Jolobe's *Thuthula*, the bride-price or *lobola* is a favorite butt for critics of traditional society. It is the theme of Mafuya Mbidlana's play *Zangen'iinkomo* (*Enter the Cattle* [Lovedale, 1954]), and especially of a novel by D. M. Jongilanga, *Ukuqhawuka kwembeleko* (*The Snapping of the Skin* [Lovedale, 1960]),[112] whose heroine, Zoleka, is first deprived of the benefits of education because her father wants to marry her off as early as possible so that he may pocket the bride money. He also ignores her love for a young man called Zet, and arranges her marriage to a man she does not know. Zoleka soon conceives such a violent hatred for her husband that she kills him with an ax. After spending some time in a reformatory, she resumes her affair with Zet; unfortunately, the latter is a flirtatious young man, and this eventually leads him to an untimely death, whereupon Zoleka commits suicide by drowning in the sea.

Qangule has pointed out that Xhosa works "have in the main a rural setting. This comes as no surprise since the vast majority of the 2,300,000 Xhosa live in rural areas." Life in a rural community is the subject of a satirical novel by Rustum Siyongwana, *Ubulumko bezinja* (*The Wisdom of the Dogs* [Cape Town, 1962]), which is a rather poor imitation of George Orwell's *Animal Farm*. The chief characters are three dogs who overthrow their masters in the name of democratic equality, but they soon reveal themselves as just four-legged power seekers.

There are, however, a few works that follow the example set by

Sinxo in dealing with city life. The hero of Bertrand Bomela's *Umntu akanambulelo (Man Has No Gratitude* [Johannesburg]), for example, is brought up in a rural area and is educated at the cost of considerable sacrifices to his family, but after completing his education, he goes to the city where he is enthralled by the poisonous glittering pleasures of town life and then falls in utter degradation.

A similar pattern underlies the first part of *Izinto zodidi (Things of Value* [Johannesburg, 1959]), a novel by Professor Godfrey Mzamane, a man of the older generation, who was born at Fobane (Mount Fletcher) on 7 March 1909.[113] His father was a lay preacher of the Anglican Church. He attended primary school at Umzimkhulu, at a French Evangelical Missionary School, and at the Bethesda Moravian Mission School of Lupindo. After matriculating from Standard 6 in 1921, he stayed at home tending the cattle. In 1926 he resumed his schooling, first at St. John's College, and then at Adams' Teacher Training College in Natal. A scholarship enabled him to go to Fort Hare for some time, but financial difficulties compelled him to take up teaching in 1934. From 1936 to 1939, he taught at a training school in Mariazell (Matatiele). He did not complete his B.A. studies until 1940, after which he started learning museum techniques in Cape Town. In 1942 he was appointed assistant curator of the F. S. Malan Museum at Fort Hare. When Jordan resigned his post in Bantu Languages there in 1946, Mzamane was appointed to replace him. In 1947 he obtained his B.A. in Bantu Languages, and in 1948, he was awarded an M.A. degree. Although he is still battling with his doctoral dissertation, he is now head of the Department of Bantu Languages at Fort Hare. The central character of *Izinto zodidi* is one Deyi, who leaves his wife at home and goes to work in Johannesburg; she feels so lonely that after some time, she joins him in the city, where she finds him leading the life of a gangster. When an attempt is made at Deyi's life, they hurry back home. At this point, the interest shifts to their son, Manzodidi, who distinguishes himself as a science student. He proceeds to the University of Toronto, where he makes some stupendous scientific discovery. There is a contrast between the fate of Deyi, who drifts into delinquency once he is deprived of the props and help of tribal morality, and that of his son, who achieves successful adaptation to modern society through high education.

Another type of edifying success story emphasizes the dangers

of affluence and self-indulgence, and the corresponding usefulness
of hardships and endurance in shaping a person's character and en-
suring his social promotion. D. M. Lupuwana's *Khe kukhiwe
iidiliya (The Grape Harvest)* "is a story of the difficulties that are
experienced by children who are orphaned at an early age. Nomandiya, the heroine, is bereaved. Her brother Reuben sends her to
Healdtown Institution. After Reuben's death, Nomandiya goes to
Ngcolosi where she trains as an auxiliary nurse. Later on she quali-
fies as a nurse at Umthatha. She goes to Johannesburg, is courted
by Shadrack Jwara and they marry. They return home and run a
prosperous business." [114] Likewise, the message of *Kufundwa
ngamava (We Learn by Experience* [Cape Town, 1951]), by a
woman novelist, Minazana Dana, "is that great heights are achieved
through endurance and that the way to success is fraught with
many pitfalls."

At first sight, prospects for Xhosa literature in the near future
certainly look far from encouraging. Lower educational standards
and the pressure for conformity may seem to make further decay
inevitable. The creative impulse, nevertheless, has its own ways of
meeting any challenge. Xhosa writers may find new strength and
new self-confidence in the mere fact of being thrown back upon
their own mental resources. Moreover, within the limits set by the
apartheid system, they may still expect guidance and encouragement from enlightened whites, many of them scholars and church
ministers. In 1962 the Department of Bantu Languages of the University of South Africa in Pretoria, launched *Limi,* a journal that
appears twice a year, and devotes increasing critical attention to
vernacular literature. Although the surveys, reviews, and articles it
has published so far are not of a very high scholarly level, yet they
are the work of native sons. They are the foundation on which an
independent Xhosa school of criticism is bound to arise some day.
And the appearance at Fort Hare University College, at the beginning of 1969, of a new, all-Xhosa, literary journal called *Dimbaza,*
which is published by the Xhosa Language Committee should be
taken as an intimation that Xhosa writers are determined not to
relinquish the obstinate effort that has already lasted for a century
and a half.

Chapter **2** **Literature in Southern Sotho**

Enclaved within the territory of the Republic of South Africa, the tiny kingdom of Lesotho[1] traces its origins back to 1823, when a raider chieftain called Moshoeshoe (d. 1870) succeeded in wielding together a number of small tribal groups that were striving to escape extermination during the *Lifaqane* ("wars of calamity," 1818–1830), brought about by Zulu expansion under Chaka and his successors. Their language is known as Southern Sotho. Through skillful diplomacy, Moshoeshoe managed to withstand not only Zulu imperialism but also complete conquest by the Boers, who had made occasional appearances along the Caledon River as early as 1831 and were soon to trek northward in considerable numbers. Those early contacts impressed the king with the superiority of European armed power, and he soon realized that no resistance could be successful unless he and his people were initiated into the secret of the white man's power. Accordingly, in 1833, Moshoeshoe gladly welcomed three French missionaries from the Société des Missions Evangéliques de Paris to his headquarters at Thaba-Bosiu.

These were very young men,[2] alert, eager, highly cultured, and exceptionally open-minded. Being French or Swiss citizens, they had no nationalistic interests of their own at stake in those days when conflicts between Boer and British were the only political factor in southern Africa. Their task as they saw it was of course to convert the Sotho people to Christianity; this often made for trouble, especially in connection with such deep-rooted customs as

101

witchcraft, bride wealth and polygamy, initiation schools and circumcision, and burial practices. Nevertheless, they strongly identified themselves with the determination of the Sotho to maintain
their own independence. They acted as trusted advisers to Moshoeshoe in his dealings with Boers and British. It was for this, we may
surmise, that they were chiefly valued. Not without reason, for it
was probably upon their recommendation that the king, as early as
1842, sought to obtain from Great Britain the formal status of an
independent protected state.

This is not the place to recount the political history of Lesotho.
What needs emphasizing, however, is the crucial fact that, in the
main, Lesotho was allowed to go its course as a fairly homogeneous
nation with a considerable measure of self-government under a
liberal system of indirect rule. In this respect, its situation showed
greater similarity with that of Madagascar before 1895 or of Ethiopia before 1936, than of any of the colonial territories of southern
Africa. Indeed, so liberal was the type of administration that the
British government introduced into Lesotho when it assumed responsibility in 1884, that Sir Alan Pim, reporting in 1935, could
claim that "there was then and there is now no rule either direct or
indirect by the British government." [3]

To this exceptional degree of political autonomy must be added
the fact that interracial contacts were kept at a minimum. White
civil servants were few until the mid-thirties. And apart from the
missionaries, white settlement was practically nonexistent. The
status of non-Sotho people in the country was and still is defined
by Moshoeshoe's so-called "Law of Trade" of 1859:

Any trader who wishes to establish a shop, must first obtain permission
from me. Should he build a house, I grant him no right to sell it. Further, I do not grant him liberty to plough the fields, but only to plant a
small vegetable garden. The trader who fancies that the place he is
sojourning belongs to him, must dismiss the thought; if not, he is to
quit; for there is no place belonging to the whites, in my land, and I
have granted no white man a place, either by word, or by writing.[4]

The main contribution of the West to Sotho life, therefore, has
been in the cultural fields of religion and education, which partly
accounts for the present economic backwardness of the country.
The Société des Missions Evangéliques missionaries followed the
pattern set by their colleagues of the London Missionary Society

and of the Glasgow Missionary Society among the Xhosa: they reduced the language to writing, set up schools, started printing religious material. Already in 1846, it had been decided to supplement the elementary school network with "a secondary school or seminary where Native Catechists and Basuto teachers would be trained." [5] In 1868 a regular Teacher Training College, known as "Sekolo sa Tabeng" (The Mountain School) was established in Morija. In 1882 a Bible school was set up, where courses in theology were given; these provided the nucleus for a theological school that was formally opened with three students in Morija on 2 June 1887.

By 1864 literacy had spread to such an extent that the Reverend A. Mabille started publishing a monthly paper in the vernacular, *Leselinyana la Lesotho (The Little Light of Lesotho).*[6]

The first printing press in Lesotho had been brought from England to Beersheba as early as 1841. In 1837 the missionaries had already published a little catechism in Southern Sotho at Cape Town,[7] where they also had translations of Mark and John printed in 1839. It was at Beersheba, however, that the first complete Sotho version of the New Testament was printed in 1845.

In 1848 the Beersheba press was damaged by fire and closed down. Not until 1861 was a new press set up, this time at Morija. One year later, a Book Depot was opened also in Morija, and very soon *Leselinyana* began to appear. Its publication was interrupted only twice, from 1865 to 1869, when the Boer settlers of the Orange Free State invaded and temporarily occupied the more fertile areas west of the Drakensberg, and the French (and Wesleyan) missionaries there were evicted because of their support of the natives; and again during the Gun War of 1890, when the Sotho successfully resisted the Cape government's decision to disarm them and to allocate Sotho land to white settlers.[8] During the first of these interruptions the Reverend Mabille started translating Bunyan's *Pilgrim's Progress*, a task that he did not finish until 1872; entitled *Leeto la Mokreste* the book proved extremely popular and ran through its seventh edition in 1945. In 1878 the complete Bible was made available; its publication, C. M. Doke observed, "had a powerful influence in stabilising the language. With the early translations, as Victor Ellenberger put it, Sesotho became a literary language." [9]

In 1902, the Reverend Casalis took over the management of the printing works; he brought modern equipment from Switzerland, and the new press began to operate in 1905. By 1908 some forty-five years after its first publication, the circulation of *Leselinyana* had reached 1,500 copies.

The first contributors were inevitably the missionaries, who had, from the very beginning, displayed enlightened interest in the study of the Sotho language, and in the recording of Sotho customs and folklore. But after a few years, the growth of literacy and the development of the Teacher Training College made it possible to print articles by Sotho authors. So it was that in 1889 one Chere Monyoloza contributed a series of articles on the art of divination.[10] After five installments, this description of pagan customs was brought to an abrupt end by the editor. A mild protest came from Azariele Sekese, who was then beginning his literary career as a frequent contributor to *Leselinyana;* he argued "that Monyoloza's interest in divination was purely intellectual, and did not mean that he believed in it." The missionaries were not of one mind in this matter. When Edouard Jacottet took over the editorship, he specifically invited essays on traditional Sotho customs and institutions, apparently with little success. Such controversies, however, stimulated interest in Sotho writing. By 1899 there was in existence another newspaper called *Lentswe la Batho (The Voice of the People)* which attacked the editorial policy of *Leselinyana.* But the fact remains that the mission press and the Sesotho Book Depot in Morija were to become, in the early years of this century, what Lovedale had been for Xhosa literature: the main, and, for a long time the sole, center of creative writing in Southern Sotho.[11]

A Precursor: Azariele M. Sekese

The earliest of the Sotho authors, Azariele M. Sekese, was born at Tsereoane (Berea) in 1849. He was one of the first students to enroll in 1866 in the newly founded Training College. After graduating in 1869, he became a teacher and a catechist at Tlepaneng in 1872. In 1881 he was appointed secretary to Chief Jonathan, a grandson of Moshoeshoe, and one of the more enlightened among the Sotho chieftains. Several decades later Sekese was to illustrate some of the praise poems in honor of Jonathan with a note on his ancestry.[12] He did not stay long in the service of the chief but was soon sent, again as a teacher, to Hlotse (Leribe), where he engaged in research on the history of the Sotho people. Dissatisfied with poor wages, he gave up teaching and worked in a trade store from 1884 to 1891. Then it was that Chief Jonathan appointed him as his personal secretary for the second time. He served in this capacity for another three years, and afterward acted as intermediary between the chief and the British assistant commissioner, Sir Charles Bell, until old age forced him to retire. He died in 1930.

In the 1880s and early 1890s, Sekese contributed numerous articles about Sotho folklore to *Leselinyana*.[13] These were gathered in 1893 into *Mekhoa ea Basotho le maele le litsomo (Customs and Proverbs of the Basuto)*, which was the first collection of its kind ever to have been published in book form by an African. It went through at least four editions under slightly different titles, as Sekese kept enriching it with stories, fables, and praise poems.

But his only important contribution to original creative literature is a satirical animal story, which he composed, possibly in collaboration with Job Moteane,[14] during the 1880s, drawing upon his experience of native justice at the court of Chief Jonathan in the same way that Mqhayi, a few years later, was to use his own knowledge of judicial procedure in native courts. Although the work was highly popular and was often performed in play form in various schools, it does not seem to have reached print until 1928, when it appeared as *Bukana ea tsomo tsa pitso ea linonyana le tseko ea Sefofu le Seritsa (The Book of the Stories of the Meeting of the Birds, and the Lawsuit Between Sefofu and Seritsa)*. The book was very successful and went through its sixth edition in 1955.

The Sotho *pitso* is a tribal assembly, in which laws are discussed and justice is rendered. Sekese's story tells how the birds have called such a meeting to protest against the hawk's greed, cruelty, and injustice. Each bird in turn lodges his complaint and claims justice from the vulture, who is both chief and judge. Although the hawk is obviously guilty, he is nevertheless absolved by the court, whose members, being prominent and powerful persons, are by no means innocent of pilfering and other abuses. The tale ends after the partridge, acting as a priest, has called on the hawk to search his heart and repent of his guilt, quoting the Bible to show that the powerful who misuse their might cannot escape God's punishment.

While Mqhayi's *Ityala lama-wele* was to be a vindication of Xhosa judicial procedure, Sekese's *Pitso ea linonyana* is a satire of a judicial system that was basically tribal and feudal. The British administration had allowed the Sotho to preserve native law and justice within liberal limits:

Each chief, as an administrative authority, had his court. The courts were arranged in an hierarchical stratification in accordance with the political status of the chiefs. A right of appeal existed from junior to senior courts with the court of the Paramount Chief as the final Basuto Court of Appeal.[15]

In Sekese's story, the vulture is obviously a higher chief than the hawk, against whom the common people are appealing. The tale exposes the abuses and corruptions of a system that was already resented in the late nineteenth century, when the work was composed, and grew worse as decades passed. Indeed, the topical interest and the lasting popularity of *Pitso ea linonyana* can only be fully understood by reference to historical events in Lesotho.

The Sotho nation, it will be recalled, was concocted out of the remnants of a variety of tribal groups. In order to wield them into some sort of unity, Moshoeshoe shrewdly placed relatives of his in positions of authority. Lesser chiefs, however, followed this example thus bringing about a steadily increasing feudalization of the country. By 1938, when steps began to be contemplated as a result of the Pim Report, there were no less than 1,340 chiefs for a country whose population did not even reach a million.

It was Moshoeshoe's view that chiefs (including the paramount chief) held and administered the land in trust for and on behalf of the people. Actually, soon after his death, the chiefs blissfully waived the duties that kept their privileges within reasonable limits. They considered judicial procedure as a legitimate way of eking out, through the fines that they pocketed, the taxes that were their main source of revenue. The creation of the Basutoland National Council on British initiative in 1903 did little to remedy this legal form of exploitation, as 95 out of its 100 members were themselves chiefs or representatives of the chiefs' interests.

Whereas the British authorities' policy was to support the chiefs, who were the legal rulers according to the law of the land, the French missionaries' sympathy went to the common people. It has been noticed that they "made no specific attempts to convert chiefs. . . . Instead they sought to build up a Christian community among ordinary folk." [16] Accordingly, whenever there was a conflict of interests between the chiefs and the common people, they tended to side—more or less overtly—with the people. In the first decade of the century, the Basutoland Progress Association was founded by a few teachers, traders, and clerks, who had been reared in mission schools. It acted as a sort of lobby trying to influence both the council and British authority. There is little doubt that the comparatively frequent school performances of *Pitso ea linonyana* should be considered part of a somewhat loose, and for a long time ineffective, campaign to remedy the most glaring abuses that the Sotho people were suffering under chiefly rule.

Popular resentment intensified as the situation grew worse and, in 1928, the very year when Sekese's work appeared in book form, proposals for defining the powers of the chiefs and the organization of native courts were actually drafted. In fact, the printing of the book must almost certainly be associated with what Lord Hailey called "a growing local demand for the improvement of the procedure of the Native Courts." [17] The tale and its popularity grew out of a situation similar in many respects to the situation that accounts for the success of the Reynard the Fox stories throughout Western Europe in feudal times.

The similarity is further enhanced by the use of the same frame-story technique: in both works a trial court provides a suitable and plausible opportunity for bringing together a number of stories and anecdotes, some of which are only thinly linked to the central theme. But they differ on an interesting and important point. The twelfth and thirteenth centuries in Western Europe are often considered, rather rashly, as the very model of a Christian civilization. Yet, the best product of the popular literature of the time, the Reynard epic, is fundamentally secular and anticlerical in outlook. No suprahuman justice is even hinted at, and the clergy is cruelly flogged for participating in the corruption of the mighty. Sekese, on the contrary, draws a neat distinction between the justice of man and the justice of God. That he was thus merely paying lip service to the Christian ideals is not likely. The French missionaries had no overt share in the exercise of political or judicial power, and what covert role they did play was usually in the interest of the common people. The book, therefore, casts an interesting sidelight on some of the reasons behind the comparative ease with which Christianity spread through the country. It undoubtedly reflects a state of affairs that was bitterly resented. The Christian message of love and justice must have appeared to many as a rem-

edy against the abuses of customary law. At the same time, the fact
that Sekese's partridge solely addresses the conscience of the guilty,
and threatens them only with God's justice, without calling for
popular rebellion or even for institutional reform, can be considered an illustration both of Protestant inwardness and of native
reluctance to question traditional institutions as such.

Thomas Mofolo

Although we do not know exactly when Sekese's *Pitso ea linonyana* was composed, it must certainly be considered the earliest
piece of written prose fiction in the literature of Lesotho. For all
its elaboration and literary quality, it is still deeply embedded in
folklore tradition, being in fact a collection of animal fables clev-
erly woven into a single design to provide a severe critique of
native justice. More research is needed to assess what part of the
stories Sekese created, and what proportion of them should be considered a recording or rewording of oral tales. But the foundation
of the novel in Southern Sotho must be ascribed to a man of remarkable genius, who belonged to the same generation as Mqhayi
among the Xhosa: Thomas Mofolo.

Thomas Mopoku Mofolo was born in Khojane (Mafeteng). He
himself was not sure about his birth date,[18] but the parish register
of Hermone, to which Khojane belongs, shows that he was born on
22 December 1876, the third son of Christian parents. He was baptized by the Reverend Hermann Dieterlen on 30 September 1877.
In 1880 his parents moved to the fertile Qomoqomong valley
(Quthing). At the elementary school there, his teacher was Everett
Lechesa Segoete, who was later to appear in one of his novels; in
turn, Segoete was to follow his former pupil in writing one of the
earliest Sotho novels. Mofolo further studied at Matatiele under
the Reverend D. F. Ellenberger. He then left for Morija, where he
became a houseboy in the service of the Reverend Alfred Casalis,
who was the head of the Bible School, the printing press and the
Book Depot. Because of his intelligence and eagerness to learn,
Casalis sent him to the Bible School in 1894 and to the Teacher
Training College in 1896. He had to leave after two years for lack
of funds, and he was thinking of seeking work in South Africa
when the Reverend R. H. Dyke, who was headmaster of the Train-

ing School, allowed him to resume his studies on credit. Mofolo obtained a teacher's certificate in 1898.

In 1899 he started working for the Reverend Casalis at the press and at the Book Depot; but at the end of the year, the Anglo-Boer war put an end to the publishing activities of the mission. Mofolo left Morija for Leloaleng (Quthing), where he studied carpentry for two years at a technical school that had been founded in 1888. He then entered teaching, first at Leloaleng, then at the Bensonvale Institution in the north of Cape Province, and subsequently at the Maseru mission school, run by the Reverend Dyke. In 1904 Mofolo returned to Morija as secretary to the Reverend Casalis and proof-reader for the press.

Mofolo's activities at the printing works fostered his interest in literature. Sir Henry Newbolt[19] claims that "he had read all the religious and historical books then published, some English his-torical books on South Africa, and some novels by writers like Rider Haggard and Marie Corelli." [20] He was strongly encouraged to do some writing of his own by several of the missionaries: Al-fred Casalis, who had managed the press since 20 May 1894, and who left the country in December 1905; S. Duby, who succeeded him at the head of the Book Depot; and the Reverend Jacottet. So it was that in 1905-1906 he composed the first Sotho novel. His sponsors were fully aware of the novelty of the thing. One of them said that it was "an absolutely original work of imagination," [21] and F. H. Dutton, one-time director of education in Basutoland was later to describe it as a "surprise": "it was a new product—not a history, but a novel describing native life in ancient days." [22] The book was *Moeti oa bochabela (The Traveller to the East)*, which was first serialized in *Leselinyana* in 1906, and appeared in book form in 1907.

Actually, it is more than a mere ethnographical novel. It is a quest story set in Lesotho before the coming of the white man. The hero, Fekesi, is an idealistic young man who is prompted by two impulses. One is of a moral nature: he is horrified at the evil ways of the village people, who live in drunkenness, quarrels, and sexual promiscuity; the other is intellectual, and has to do with the mystery of the origins of the universe. To Fekesi's inquiries, the old men of the village reply by telling him the story of Kgodumo-dumo, a giant monster who devoured people; but one woman miraculously escaped him, and she gave birth to a child who rid the country of this dreadful monster.[23] The people, however, did not remain grateful to him; they soon began to hate him, and finally they killed him. The old men also tell Fekesi how God once lived among men, but their evil ways caused him to leave them, and he returned to Ntswana-Tsatsi, the place in the East where the sun rises, whence the Sotho people are said to originate, and which is now God's abode. Fekesi prays for God's help, and he has a vision of a beautiful figure with very long hair haloed with thick mist, who lives in Ntswana-Tsatsi. He decides to seek this place, and he bids farewell to his herds by reciting praise poems in honor of his cattle: this fine lyrical interlude marks the end of the first part and intimates the magnitude of the sacrifice that Fekesi is prepared to accept in order to reach truth and goodness.

In the course of his eastward journey, Fekesi encounters other nations that are living in corruption like his own people. He finally reaches the sea in a state of utter exhaustion. He faints, and when he recovers consciousness, he finds himself surrounded by three white men, who take care of him, instruct him in their religion, teach him how to read and write, and take him to their own country. This is precisely the country about which he had been dreaming, where people observe God's decrees and live in honesty and virtue. At last, Fekesi is ready for baptism. During the church ceremony, Christ appears to him over the altar. A voice announces that he is admitted to eternal bliss because he has loved Christ above this-worldly things. When the congregation look up again, they find that Fekesi lies dead.

Moeti oa bochabela is, of course, a Christian tract, obstensibly based on the antithesis of Africa—"clothed in great darkness," "a fearful darkness," Africa is the place "in which all the things of darkness were done,"—and the radiant light of the white man and of his religion, "the light that has come." This somewhat obvious symbolism involves a measure of suppression, perhaps of insincerity. By the beginning of this century, the Sotho people had been in touch with Europeans far less commendable than their devoted French missionaries, and Mofolo certainly knew that the white man's society was no faithful materialization of the City of God. Although the overall symbolism is simple and rather inadequate, Mofolo is by no means insensitive to the more subtle relations between Christianity and African culture. His highly unfavorable presentation of allegedly actual African mores may have prompted, as a reaction, the glorification of old-time Lesotho in Segoete's *Raphepheng*, which was to appear in 1913. But the fact remains that underneath the disparaging depiction of the minor characters of the novel, there is—illustrated by the elders' speeches, the mythical story of Kgodumodumo, and the motivations of Fekesi himself —the memory of and the aspiration to a life of orderliness and virtue that are presented as independent of any Christian teaching. So that the hero's discovery of Christianity is, as much as a conversion to a new faith, a return to beliefs and manners that had antedated both the introduction of Christianity and the degradation of morality exemplified in the early chapters of the book. Mofolo's ideal, then, may be said to be less one of rejection of traditional values in favor of Christian standards, than one of syncretism. Christianity is the new way toward the restoration of ancient purity. Mofolo has his white characters themselves point to the similarity between the legend of Kgodumodumo and the story of Jesus Christ. As Miss P.-D. Beuchat has written, "*Moeti oa bochabela* is interesting in that it shows the merging of Sotho beliefs and Christian thought." [24]

Sotho readers can enjoy the outstanding style of that first novel. But everyone can appreciate its careful two-part structure of search and discovery, hankering and fulfillment, evil and good. Moreover, the writer makes skillful use of the allegorical vision. Miss Beuchat goes on to claim that "the novel ends with a highly mystical scene, a dream or revelation which little resembles anything that Mofolo might have been taught by the rather austere Protestant faith in which he was brought up." Yet, he could have drawn his inspiration from the Bible and/or from Bunyan. Jack Halpern has wondered "just what the Basuto of the 1860s made of *Pilgrim's Progress*, the first work to be translated and published." [25] The reply seems to be that they found it congenial to their own mode of thought, as did countless African readers in about three dozens of languages. And there is little doubt that Mofolo's example encouraged his former teacher Segoete to make use of the same technique—albeit with less skill—in *Monono ke moholi, ke mouoane*, which was to be printed three years later.

It is in character depiction that the book—like so many African novels—is defective. In tribal societies, little attention is paid to individual inwardness. A person's awareness of self is primarily as a

member of the group, and not—as is the case in Western society—
as an autonomous individual whose chief legitimate preoccupations
are with his own personal identity, rights, and privileges. This
fundamental culture trait has many literary implications. Not only
are African writers notoriously clumsy in the expression of strictly
personal emotions such as love but also, more generally, their interests are ethical rather than psychological, and they are seldom
able to present convincing individual characters. Their societal outlook drives them to turn character into type, so that the reader's
response is one of moral edification rather than imaginative em-
pathy. This is why Miss Beuchat can rightly say of *Moeti oa
Bochabela* that "one's sympathy for Fekesi . . . dwindles when he
becomes less and less human because he always does the right thing,
chooses the right path, and comes through all difficulties. Because
of his utter sanctity, and his constant luck, he becomes totally removed from our daily lives and thus the contact established in the
first half of the novel is broken." [26] This weakness is of course due
to an indifference to individual psychology which is built into the
African tradition, and which is manifest in literary art, whether
oral or written. This particular cultural trait makes it very difficult
even for Europeans versed in the African languages to provide a
balanced appraisal taking into account both the conscious purposes
of the writer and his society's notion of the function of literature.
To illustrate the kind of patronizing ethnocentricity to which
white readers are liable, I cannot resist quoting a pronouncement
made on *Moeti oa bochabela* by Professor W. A. Norton of the
University of Cape Town in 1921. He called the book "a charming
odyssey . . . which, with a little more bloodshed, might have been
saga, or, in verse, an embryo epic"! [27]

   Mofolo next embarked on a second novel, which was to have
been entitled *The Fallen Angel* (Sotho title unknown). According to the *Livre d'Or*,[28] the purpose of the book was to disprove
some unspecified theory of Marie Corelli's; whether this was actually so or not is open to doubt. As we have seen in connection
with *Moeti oa bochabela*, and as we shall see again when dealing
with *Chaka*, at least some of the missionaries displayed complete
lack of understanding in their interpretation of Mofolo's intentions.
Anyhow, the author showed his manuscript to a missionary who
disapproved of it; the work never reached print, and its where-
abouts are unknown, if in fact it still exists.

Mofolo's second published novel was *Pitseng*, which was serialized in *Leselinyana* before it appeared in book form in 1910. The title refers to a village in the Leribe district. One of the chief characters in the book is the Reverend Katse, preacher and schoolteacher in Pitseng. He is a portrait of Mofolo's former teacher, Segoete, and the writer insists on his selfless dedication to the task of converting the pagans and educating the young. There is, however, little connection between Katse's career and the love plot on which the book is flimsily built, except that a considerable amount of Katse's preaching has to do with love and marriage.

The love story focuses on two young people, Alfred Phakoe and Aria Sebaka. Katse has noticed them among his pupils for their seriousness and zeal. It is his wish that they should become man and wife, and take up his task in Pitseng after he has grown old. Meanwhile, Alfred is sent to high school in the Cape Colony, and Mofolo seizes this opportunity to make all sorts of observations about the other peoples of South Africa, not only blacks but also Indians and Chinese, especially with regard to love and marriage customs. When Alfred comes back to Pitseng, Katse has had to give up his work owing to ill health. Alfred and Aria, now an assistant teacher at the parish school, fall in love, and the novel ends with their marriage.

The many disquisitions on courtship and marriage in the book illustrate the confusion that, in Lesotho as in many parts of Africa, resulted from the intrusions of Christian ethics. The new ideal of genuine feeling, sexual restraint, and monogamy is extensively described in Katse's sermons and is enacted in the story of Alfred and Aria. These two, however, can hardly be said ever to come to life, so that there is a wide gap between the edifying purpose of the book and the realistic description of actual mores as observed by Alfred. Whereas Mofolo's earlier volume was marked by the unquestioning identification of European mores with the Christian ideal, *Pitseng* strongly emphasizes the contrast between this ideal and actual behavior among Christians, both black and white. In Pitseng and in the Cape Colony, he notices that native Christians do "like most white people who put God last in everything," and indulge in aimless flirtations and desultory promiscuity. And he comes to the unpalatable conclusion that "the heathens are telling the truth when they say that the evil influences come from the Whites and come into Lesotho with the Christian converts, because this habit whereby a young man decides independently upon marriage, consulting only with his girl friend, started with the converts. This attitude has completely destroyed the youth of Lesotho." [29]

Noting that proper respect for the sacredness of courtship and marriage is more often found among heathens than among Christians, Mofolo extols the time-honored ways of the Sotho: "a young man grew up and matured and became a man without knowing what courtship was. And when the time came when he wished to marry . . . he would take the cattle at early dawn, and they would go to the pastures unmilked. That was the sign whereby he informed his people that he was begging for marriage: for it was a shameful thing if he spoke with his mouth to his parents that he wanted to marry." But traditional marriage customs have other aspects than this restraint and this symbolic indirection in conveying personal desires, and they struck Mofolo much in the same way in which, a few years earlier, they had struck a white woman, Minnie Martin, who gave the following account in 1903:

When a youth wishes to marry, he does not go to his father and ask for a wife. Such a course would be most disrespectful, and altogether wanting in etiquette. The young men before marriage are not supposed to make requests, or to converse much with their elders. . . . When a youth wishes to marry, he gets up very early one morning and takes out his father's cattle to the pasture without milking the cows, and lets the calves run with their mothers, and drink all the milk. No notice of this is taken on his return, and the same course is pursued by him for thirty days. . . . On the thirtieth day his father says, "Surely my son wants to get married. . . ." No questions are asked as to whom the youth wishes to marry. His wishes are very secondary considerations, and not to be weighed for a moment against those of his father. If the wife selected by his father does not happen to be the "lady of his heart," he is at liberty to choose a second wife for himself, as soon as he can pay the dowry or persuade his father to pay it for him.[30]

These last two elements in traditional marriage, the bride-price and polygamy, are precisely those to which Mofolo takes exception, dutifully following the teaching of the missionaries, like so many of the early writers. His objection to polygamy is of course consonant with the overall Christian and Western concept of marriage. But his criticism of the bride-price seems to be more specifically an echo of French Protestant policy in Lesotho; the Société des Missions Evangéliques de Paris missionaries were forcefully opposed to the customary bride gift of cattle, whereas the Roman Catholic missionaries at a later date "grew aware that a girl, whether Christian or not, was not considered to have been properly married without a bride-gift," and "resolved that provided it was made absolutely clear that marriage was not marriage unless made in church, there need be no objection to the customary exchange of cattle." [31]

The main source of African puzzlement in this matter is of course the fact that "objectionable" traits cannot be separated from "approved" features in either of the two main conceptions that Christianization brought face to face. This appears clearly—although, no doubt, unintentionally—in the development of the love plot in *Pitseng*. Although Alfred and Aria avoid the "reprehensible" aspects of African courtship practice, that is, the bride-price and polygamy, and although they refrain from the promiscuity so widely spread, according to Mofolo, among the Christian village youth, yet they do not conform to the aspect of custom that the writer explicitly extols, namely, the total submission to parental will. Alfred and Aria select each other from the depth of their personal feelings, without previously seeking their parents' approval. Nor could it have been otherwise: the Christian insistence upon inner feeling and personal responsibility, and therefore upon personal freedom, was bound to disrupt the traditional morality. It is noteworthy that a similar critique was to be raised by Jolobe in *Thuthula* and, much later, in a Rhodesian novel, *Nhorvondo dzokuwanana (The Way to Get Married* [1958]) by a Shona author, Paul Chidyausiku.

While it is quite true, as Daniel Kunene points out, that the two young people "are, for most of the time, portrayed as statues of virtue, sitting upon their high pedestals and looking with disapproval and even dismay at the goings-on of ordinary mortals," [32] *Pitseng* contains all the data of the dilemma that the new view of marriage raised in most African societies. And although Mofolo fails, as he was bound to do, to provide a convincing picture of the ideal syncretism he advocates, this novel has more realistic subtlety than the previous one, because it is based on something that was fast becoming fundamental in the African mind: a clear percep-

tion of the antinomy between Christian theory and Christian practice. "Christianity," Mofolo writes, "is very good, it is better than
anything on earth, if only all Christians would behave as this man
[Katze] does." [33]

While he was composing *Pitseng*, presumably in 1909, Mofolo
was journeying through Natal on a bicycle, gathering historical
background information for a new novel, to be based on the life
of the early nineteenth-century Zulu conqueror, Chaka.[34] "At
Mgungundlovu, the capital of the former Zulu nation (today
Pietermaritzburg)," says Kunene, "Mofolo was welcomed and
fêted and an ox was slaughtered in his honor, and a hut for him
was erected by order of the chief. Here, Mofolo visited the grave
of Chaka and observed the ceremonies of the Zulu people." [35] The
result was *Chaka*, a genuine masterpiece of insight and composition, and perhaps the first major African contribution to world
literature.[36]

The Chaka of history was born between 1783 and 1787; his
father was chieftain of one of the many small Nguni tribes that
peopled the territory now known as Natal. His people owed allegiance to Dingiswayo, chief of the Mthethwa, who began to
conquer and absorb his neighbors in the early years of the nineteenth century. Chaka succeeded him in 1817 and under his reign,
"the policy of conquest and amalgamation was carried to an extent
hitherto unprecedented in Bantu history. By 1820, it has been estimated, Shaka had more than 100,000 warriors, and had added about
500,000 people to his rule, having deprived some three hundred
tribes of their independence," [37] and having united them under the
name of Zulu. "Before his assassination in 1828, Shaka and his
armies carried fire and slaughter over large parts of what are now
Natal and Zululand and possibly Pondoland. . . . Undoubtedly
many tribes were scattered and broken, and as many scores of
thousands are said to have perished from starvation and disease as
were slain in actual fighting." [38] At its apex, Chaka's empire extended from the Limpopo River to the vicinity of the Cape Province. Among the vanquished tribes were the Fingo, who sought
shelter as far as Southern Xhosaland, and also the various groups
that Moshoeshoe fused into the Sotho nation. It is, therefore, not
surprising that Mofolo, as an African and as a Sotho, should have
been interested in the momentous career of that Zulu Napoleon.

What is less expected, however, in view of the strictures legitimately leveled at the deficiencies of most modern African fiction both with regard to character depiction and plot organization, is that Mofolo's research and meditation and genius should have produced a work that is remarkable for the clarity of its structure, the sharpness of its psychological insight, and the depth of its ethical approach. Although *Chaka* has been variously described as "an historical romance" [39] and "a Bantu epic," [40] it is really a tragedy, both in terms of construction and significance. Peter Sulzer perceptively observed that "while it has the rhythm of an epic, its inner structure and tragic content bring it near the sphere of the dramatic." [41] *Chaka* can be defined as a narrative tragedy in prose, built along the simple curve of growth and decline which defines the structure of classic tragedy at its best.

The illegitimate son of a petty chief, Senzangakona, and of a girl called Nandi, Mofolo's hero is from his very birth a reprobate in the eyes of the tribespeople, who want him "to be killed as being born of sin" (p. 13). The word "sin" is both equivocal and anachronistic. In historical fact, the people's hostility to Chaka as a child had two reasons: Nandi belonged to the same clan as the mother of Senzangakona, so that the latter had obviously flouted the rules of exogamy; further, although Zulu society accepted premarital sexual relationship, called *ukuhlobonga*, self-indulgence pushed to pregnancy was considered a crime. "In those days in Kafirland, an unmarried girl who bore a child was put to death" (p. 6). It was only because the father was a chief and because "with the Black Races a chief is above the law" (p. 6), that Nandi and her child were spared. Kunene has put forward the view that "when Mofolo speaks of sin in this book, we know that he is speaking of sin in the Christian sense, and not of social sin in the context of the social milieu which constitutes the setting for his story." [42] It may also be that the novelist deliberately equivocates on the word "sin," using it to denote an infraction of accepted standards, whether Christian or pre-Christian. This would be in line with the syncretic tendencies that characterize all of Mofolo's work.

When the chieftain's legitimate wives at last supply him with male offspring, he loses interest in Chaka and in his mother, who are left to their own devices and face the increasingly overt hostility of the tribe. With great psychological acumen, Mofolo, in the first four chapters of the novel, goes to the very roots of his hero's fate. As Ezekiel Mphahlele rightly observed, "His career begin as a compensatory response to people's despise of him which arose from the fact that he was a chief's illegitimate child. It was also a response to his brother's lust for his own blood and to his father's ill-treatment of his mother." [43] In tribal societies, estrangement from the group is the worst fate that can befall an individual. The numerous outlaw stories in the Icelandic sagas are cases in point. Chaka's suffering at being rejected by the tribe is the primary conditioning factor of his later development. His sense of alienation and frustration kindles an unquenchable thirst for revenge and domination, which he will be able to gratify as a result of the bravery and resilience he has acquired in resisting the most cruel persecutions.

Chaka's boyhood comes to an end when he decides to seek redress at the court of his father's overlord, Dingiswayo, head of the Mthethwa. Historically, this took place in the early years of the nineteenth century. On his way through the forest, "he reviewed all his life since his childhood, and he found that it was evil, terrifying, fearsome" (p. 42). The philosophy experience has taught him is that "on earth the wise man, the strong man, the man who is admired and respected is the man who knows how to wield his spear, who, when people try to hinder him, settles the matter with his club" (p. 42). This realization leads him to the ethics of unlimited self-assertion which accounts for all his subsequent behavior. "He resolved that from that time on he would do as he liked: whether a man was guilty or not he would kill him if he wished, for that was the law of man. . . . Until now his purposes had been good. Henceforth he had only one purpose—to do as he liked, even if it was wrong, and to take the most complete vengeance that he alone could imagine" (p. 42). From a reluctant victim, Chaka deliberately turns himself into an unscrupled revenger. It is at that moment he has his first meeting with one Isanusi, whose name means "witch doctor" in Zulu.

The status of this supernatural character in the novel was bound to cause considerable attention among the critics, not least because the beliefs of Africans are usually supposed to be just crude superstitions. The earliest review that has come to my attention was published in 1931 by Alice Werner, a noted expert on the Swahili language and literature and on Bantu folklore. Although it is very short, it shows a great deal of critical perception. Miss Werner finds that "the circumstances of Chaka's birth, his cruel treatment at the hands of his half-brothers . . . combined to set him on the downward path, so that we view him, not as an extra-human monster, but as a man with noble possibilities gone tragically wrong." She thinks that Chaka's dealings with Isanusi in the novel "are due to Mofolo himself, and show an extraordinary degree of sympathetic insight." But on the whole, she considers that it was the witch doctor's "baneful influence" that "determined" Chaka's career.[44]

The next brief study of *Chaka* was done by an African critic who was also an intellectual leader of the Xhosa people, D. D. T. Jabavu, the son of John Tengo Jabavu. He remarked that the book

gives us a new impression of the redoubtable Tshaka in that instead of the hero of history who is rendered repulsive by his unbridled, unjustifiable and insatiable thirst for murder, we here get a human being we can sympathize with for falling through no fault of his, under the baneful influence of a sorcerer during his tender years that followed a miserable childhood in which he was treated with heart-rending harshness. We sympathize with him in the same way as we sympathize with Shakespeare's Macbeth whose blind ambition is constantly goaded by his callous wife.[45]

Obviously, those early critics appraised the book against the backdrop of the traditional image of Chaka as a bloodthirsty monster of motiveless malignity. They were struck by the fact that Mofolo's interpretation seemed to turn him not only into a human being with definable and intelligible human motivation, but almost into a victim of his malignant fate. Hence, presumably, they show a proclivity to overemphasize the role of Isanusi and to load him with full responsibility for Chaka's evil deeds. As late as 1947, we find M. Leenhardt still claiming that "les magiciens exigent la maturation du projet criminel." [46] But in 1948, Luc Decaunes, in what was at the time the best discussion of *Chaka*, hardly mentioned this supernatural element, but analyzed the book in terms of fate and freedom:

The role of fatality is not predominant. The themes of predestination and of personal freedom are here curiously fused together. Man is free to choose his destiny, and the hero enters the realm of tragedy in full knowledge. . . . In Chaka, the will to power is no innate tendency. . . . His fate is controlled by the persecutions and injustice to which he is submitted by his own people. Humiliated, betrayed, hunted from his village, disowned by his father, he first thirsts for revenge only, he merely wishes to restore his natural rights. But in fact, his status as an outcast has fostered an inferiority complex in him. This complex, nurtured by the spirit of evil, is the mainspring of the action.[47]

In this mention of "l'esprit du mal," we still find the notion that Isanusi is a genuine supernatural being and the decisive causal agent in Chaka's career. In 1953, without discussing the witch doctor himself, Sulzer stated that the two envoys whom Isanusi places at the disposal of the Zulu warrior "are personifications of the bestial features which take ever greater hold of Chaka." [48] Nevertheless, as late as 1963, Miss Beuchat wrote that in the person of the witch doctor "we are presented with a supernatural explanation for Chaka's succumbing to evil," because "at the most crucial moments, when subsidiary crises occur, the power is there to challenge Chaka's decisions and remind him of his previous undertakings." [49] And in the same year the Soviet critic L. B. Saratovskaya claimed that "Mofolo's book is permeated with the concept of fate, of a mysterious higher force which controls Chaka's actions." [50] Other recent commentators, however, have preferred to work along lines that had been suggested by Sir Henry Newbolt when he wrote that Isanusi is "the visible symbol of [Chaka's] own hardening ambition." "The witch doctor," said Mphahlele, "is a symbol of Chaka's other self," [51] and Claude Wauthier viewed him as a "personification of paganism." [52] More recently, Kunene has shrewdly noticed that "if we compare the thoughts of Chaka at the time he hears the wailing in the village while he is hiding in the forest, with Isanusi's words during his first meeting with Chaka, we see identical sentiments, almost identical words." [53]

It is as irrelevant to ask whether Mofolo actually conceived of Isanusi as a real supernatural being within the Chaka-world, as it is to discuss whether Shakespeare believed in witches.[54] The point is that the Sotho sorcerer fulfills exactly the same function as do the witches in *Macbeth*: he helps crystallize the hero's impulses; he coaxes him into articulate awareness of his own desires and of their implications. When Isanusi, speaking of Chaka's ancestor, says, "If thou dost not spill blood he will take no pleasure in thee" (p. 54), he simply confirms the philosophy of status through strength to which the young man had come unaided during his earlier meditation. And when the sorcerer adds, "The medicine with which I inoculated thee is a medicine of blood. If thou dost not spill much blood it will turn its potency against thee and compass thy death. Thy work is to kill without mercy, fashioning thyself a road to thy glorious chieftainship," he merely makes Chaka fully conscious of the logic and of the dangers inherent in the course he has already decided to take.

At that point, we must observe, Isanusi assumes that the young man merely wants to be reinstalled into his birthright as the eldest son and successor of Senzangakona. Chaka's ambition so far has nothing that could be called illegitimate. It is Chaka himself who makes Isanusi understand that his aspirations are of wider scope: "I see," Isanusi concludes, "thou dost not desire the chieftainship alone; thou longest for fame also stretching to the ends of the earth, such fame that when thy deeds are spoken of they will sound like fables. This fame thou dost crave for as for the chieftainship itself" (p. 55). To which Chaka lucidly and candidly replies: "Yea, fame is sweet. I would not be content if I were a great chief but without fame. And the fame I seek is fame in war, where spears are wielded, and big men with thick necks and mighty warriors perish. I desire that I myself may win my chieftainship [that is, not merely inherit it] that my fame may grow the more" (p. 55). This statement contains the seed of Chaka's political greatness and moral decay, but it will not germinate until much later. Meanwhile, as Sulzer pointed out in his *Nachwort* to the German version of the book, it is clear that Chaka is a fully responsible being. At every crucial moment, "the decision for death is in his hand, the witch-doctor allows him freedom of choice. . . . Everything that turns him into a liar, a murderer and a bloody tyrant, flows forth from his early choice in favor of power for its own sake."

At Dingiswayo's court, Chaka's story branches off into three narrative trends: his bravery against the chief's enemy, Zwide, earns him the honor of being placed at the head of Dingiswayo's army; he falls in love with the king's sister, Noliwe, who loves him too; at the death of Senzangakona (which actually occurred in 1816), Chaka is made chief in his father's stead, much to the fury of his half brothers. In each case, his success is facilitated by the intervention of Isanusi's mysterious delegates—Malunga, who represents bravery and strength, and Ndlebe, who represents intelligence and cunning. Thus far, however, Chaka's overt purposes have been legitimate. Nor has any actual evil been involved in their materialization, devious and uncommon though the devices of Isanusi's envoys may be.

But Chaka is not satisfied with the vindication to which he was justly entitled: "I still hunger, I still seek," he tells the witch doctor at the grave of Senzangakona. "Let the cow continue to give milk, Lord, I pray thee use all thy power and all thy wisdom that I may reach the goal wither thou art bringing me, and which thou in thy boundless wisdom alone dost know. As for the spear of which thou dost speak, it shall be red with blood on both blade and shaft" (p. 96). From then on, the forces of evil and deception begin to creep into the story by carefully graded steps. At first, Chaka himself does not participate in their work. When Dingiswayo dies (this was in 1817), Chaka is not aware that Isanusi's henchmen have made arrangements for the king to be conveniently killed so that the young chief can succeed him at the head of the Mthethwa. In a sense, this is a climax in Chaka's career. Although he has acquiesced in evil, he himself bears no actual guilt for the murderous treachery that has brought him to the throne.

The point of no return is reached when Isanusi reappears after Dingiswayo's death as he had reappeared at the grave of Senzangakona. He explains to Chaka that further progress in power entails a new dedication to evil: "In some respects it is a difficult matter to win the chieftainship thou dost desire, such a chieftainship that if a man were to leave the place where thou now art, in his youth, on foot, and go to the bounds of thy territory, he would be an old man before he returned. It is a difficult matter, for it is thou who must provide the right medicine, and not I" (pp. 121-122). This medicine, it soon turns out, is the blood of Noliwe, which must be mixed with the food of the warriors. And although Chaka is willing to sacrifice his beloved instantly, the witch doctor insists that he wait for a period of nine months, "in which to confirm his decision so that he might not wish to turn back too late when the work had begun" (p. 124). The true nature of Chaka's longing is made clear when he changes the name of his tribe from Mthethwa to Zulu (which means "People of Heaven"), "because I am great, I am even as this cloud that has thundered, that is irresistible. I, too, look upon the tribes and they tremble"—and Mofolo, for once, intervenes in the story to comment: "we . . . must wonder at the arrogance and ambition of this Kafir who could compare his greatness to that of the Gods" (p. 125), adding, "Then it was that he sacrificed his conscience for his chieftainship" (p. 129).

It is important to understand the peculiar significance with which the murder of Noliwe is endowed in the total symbolism of the work, for the character of the girl and everything that is connected with her seem to be of Mofolo's own invention.

Describing Chaka's reform of the army, Mofolo mentions that he forbade his soldiers to marry at the usual early age:

He said that the married man . . . thought of his wife and children, so that he ran away and disgraced himself. But the unmarried man fought to kill instead of being killed, and to conquer, so that he might enjoy the praises of the maidens. All the same, Chaka did not forbid them absolutely. He promised that the troops that surpassed the others in war would be released first from this bondage of celibacy, even if they had not remained long in that state: more, they would be given wives by the chief himself. (Pp. 136–137)

And the writer adds the following, highly meaningful, generalizations:

The reader must remember that above all else on earth the Black Races love to marry. Often in speaking of the good things of life people do not mention marriage, because *marriage is life*. Therefore we can understand well how hard the warriors of Chaka worked to gain this reward. To set his regiments an example, Chaka remained a bachelor till the end of his life. (P. 137; italics mine)

Mofolo provides another reason for Chaka's rejection of marriage. Marriage, Isanusi had advised him, "is a hindrance to a chief, and brings dissension in his house" (p. 119). Indeed, it was sometimes the custom in Africa for a newly enthroned monarch to kill, or otherwise dispose of, all potential pretenders. Chaka's bachelorhood and his enforcement of celibacy on his warriors are part of a pattern that culminates in the murder of Noliwe and signals the victory of the values of war and death symbolized by Isanusi over the values of love and life.

Most preindustrial societies are plagued with high infant mortality; abundant human fertility is therefore essential to the perpetuation of the group. This societal requirement usually receives some supernatural sanction that appeals to the individual's sense of

wider self-interest. In thirteenth-century Europe, it will be remembered, Jean de Meung had forcefully condemned the traditional Pauline asceticism of earlier official theology in the name of
God's command that mankind should grow and multiply. This
type of vindication of sex and procreation, not only as a natural
activity but also as man's legitimate way of cooperating in the
creative work of God, was later taken up by Chaucer in *The
Parliament of Foules*. In many African cultures, a similar valuation
of sex and procreation is operated through the widespread notion
that a man's life after death can only be ensured and maintained
through the cult rendered him by his progeny. Religious belief
thus sanctions the collective biological requirements of the community in its struggle for self-preservation. Sterility, then, is a
curse and a source of contempt and unbearable ridicule,[55] both because it makes a man or a woman completely useless to the survival
of the group, and because it ensures his or her complete annihilation at death.

Self-imposed sterility,[56] as in the case of Chaka, is viewed as so
unnatural an attitude in the African culture context that it can only
stir puzzlement and awe. But Mofolo turns it into an image of evil,
the symbolism of which is clinched by the murder of Noliwe. As
Chaka's beloved, as a woman, the instrument of human perpetuation, Noliwe is truly the embodiment of the forces of love and life
in Chaka. His falling in love with her was the sign that, at that early
stage in his evolution, he was still capable of redemption; it stood
on a par with his devotion to Dingiswayo. On the level of Chaka's
psychology, her murder illustrates his complete surrender to the
evil impulses of self-assertion. In the wider symbolism of the work,
it brings to its highest intensity the antinomy of fame and love, of
power and life. It is the most repellent aspect of the overall destruction that is the only way to worldly glory and might.

In the introduction to his French translation of the work, Victor
Ellenberg writes that *Chaka* is "the story of a human passion, ambition, first uncontrolled, then uncontrollable, which fatally grows
and develops, as if fanned by some implacable Nemesis, and con-
sumes everything until it ruins the moral personality and leads to
the unescapable punishment." This Nemesis, however, is no outward power. It is the very same immanent logic of crime and
punishment which was at work in *Macbeth*. The murder of Noliwe
marks the moment of Chaka's rupture with human nature, as does

the murder of Banquo for Macbeth. From that point on, bloodshed becomes an addiction. The tyrant's downfall is linked to his rise by an inexorable chain of cause and effect. The growing extent of his power also increases the number of his enemies and compels him to impose ever sterner control upon his warriors. He is, therefore, threatened from two sides: by those who resent his ruthless authority, and by those who want a larger share of its benefits—until his two half brothers, from whom he had wrenched the chieftainship at the death of their father, pluck up enough courage to kill him. Historically, this took place on 22 September 1828.

It is obvious that Mofolo had fully assimilated the Christian view of man as a free agent, totally responsible for his acts. Among Chaka's deeds, he makes a perfectly clear distinction between those that are prompted by legitimate justice, and those that result from a fiendish lust for power. At every decisive point, the meaning and consequences of contemplated actions are fully described by Isanusi, and Chaka always makes up his mind in complete awareness of what he is doing. Few African works exhibit such a profoundly integrated sense of the meaning of freedom and guilt in Christian ethics.

Although missionary enterprise met with considerable opposition in Africa, there can be little doubt that the early educated elite, especially in southern Africa, embraced the gospel of love wholeheartedly. They soon realized that it did not exert any great influence on the actual behavior of the average white man. The Christian ideal of universal brotherhood, however, seemed to them palpably superior to the traditional ethics of tribal identity and communal hatred. But while the central idea of *Chaka* is coherently and impressively Christian, it would be an oversimplification to suggest that any other types of outlook were altogether foreign to Mofolo. Indeed, the last page of the novel is unobtrusively marked by the emergence of two other standards of valuation.

It is all too often forgotten that as a Sotho, Mofolo participated in the vivid legacy of bloody memories that his nation had inherited from the times of the Wars of Calamity. The Sotho people had suffered grievously as a result of Chaka's imperialism, and national feeling may well have played its part, side by side with Christian inspiration, in Mofolo's choice of this particular evil hero. Some patriotic satisfaction, one presumes, was involved in illustrating the workings of immanent justice, not only on Chaka, but also on the Zulu nation as a whole. Before dying, Chaka prophesies for the benefit of his half brothers: "It is your hope that by killing me ye will become chiefs when I am dead. But ye are deluded; it will not be so, for Umlungu (the White Man) will come and it is he who will rule, and ye will be his boundmen" (p. 198). Writing those words, Mofolo may have felt some complacency at this reversal of fortune for the enemies of his people, particularly in view of the fact that Zulu resistance to white occupation had finally been put down in 1906.

But Mofolo was not only a Christian and a Sotho. He was also an African, whose native continent was being increasingly and irresistibly incorporated into the white man's sphere. Awareness of their identity and of the need to overcome tribal definitions and differences was spreading fast among African intellectuals in those early years of the century. Indeed, Walter Rubusana, who had edited the first anthology of Xhosa prose and poetry in 1906; Sol. T. Plaatje, who was to translate several of Shakespeare's plays into Tswana, and to write the first novel in English by a Bantu author; John L. Dube, who was to become the first Zulu writer of note in the thirties—these and others were at that time busy building up the South African Native National Congress, which came formally into being in January 1912. Owing to its privileged status as a British protectorate, Lesotho's active part in this movement was negligible. The feeling was there, however, and we catch a fugitive echo of it in the subdued pathos of the last paragraph of *Chaka*:

Even today the Mazulu remember how that they were men once, in the time of Chaka, and how the tribes in fear and trembling came to them for protection. And when they think of their lost empire the tears pour down their cheeks and they say: "Kingdoms wax and wane. Springs that once were mighty dry away." (P. 198)

It is difficult to escape the impression that at this final stage the Christian and the Sotho in Mofolo have made room for the African, who renounces, for a brief while, his tribal rancors and his new definitions of good and evil to ponder on the past greatness of his race and on its present subjugation, finding some undivulged hope, perhaps, in the notion that the white man's empire, too, will wane some day.

It may have been this final impression that, in later times, was to enable Senegal's Léopold Sédar Senghor and Mali's Seydou Badian to extol Chaka, in poetry and on the stage, as the heroic, self-denying ruler, who does not hesitate to sacrifice the tenderest passion of the heart in order to ensure the greatness and to defend the freedom of his people. Mofolo's conception of Chaka is entirely different and, as far as can be ascertained, much closer to historical fact. The Sotho author is by no means blind to his hero's inherent greatness, but he judges him and indicts him in the name of an essentially ethical view of life. Besides the technical skill and the depth of outlook which it evinces, Mofolo's novel is unique in its successful combination of traditional African and modern Christian elements.

But it is considerably more than a novel. Apart from the wider, universal ethical significance of the curve in Chaka's career—from innocence to evil, and from crime to punishment—the story also has that mysterious quality in which all myths partake. In his *Nachwort*, which is easily the most perceptive analysis of *Chaka* to date, Sulzer points out that the Zulu monarch is, in some respects, an inverted image of Christ, while exhibiting, in other respects, fundamentally Faustian elements. Ever since its inception in sixteenth-century Spain, the modern European novel has been essentially realistic. Yet, literary realism ignores the realities of mystery that are basic to human experience. However extensively the certainties of science and logic have grown, the fundamental questions—the whence, the why, and the whither—of human existence and behavior still remain unanswered. It is with these that myth deals, and the level of myth can only be reached through nonrealistic, nonrational channels. The mystery in *Moby Dick*, the madness in *Don Quixote* and *Hamlet*, the magic in *Macbeth* and *Faust*, these are the elements that raise such works to the higher levels of myth. If they are so undefinably satisfying, it is because they beckon to the dim reluctant awareness within us that in all important matters uncertainty is still our lot. Whether Mofolo's *Chaka* can be claimed to rank with them is a matter for cultured Sotho readers and critics to decide. The mere fact that the question can be raised is in itself significant.

Although *Chaka* was completed early in 1910, it was not printed until 1925. This delay raises the question as to why the Morija missionaries refrained from printing immediately a book of such outstanding quality, which is now widely recognized as the earliest modern Bantu classic, and which was to prove immensely popular.

It will be remembered that Mofolo had first become a writer upon the encouragement and advice, of Alfred Casalis and Edouard Jacottet. In 1906 Casalis left for France to take care of his children's schooling. In 1910 Jacottet was entrusted with the responsibility of the printing press. In 1912 the Société des Missions Evangéliques de Paris published the *Livre d'or de la mission du Lessouto*. This contained a chapter entitled "Les Bassoutos d'aujourd'hui" (pp. 441-512), written by H. Dieterlen and F. Kohler, three pages of which (pp. 507-509) were devoted to a highly ambiguous, not to say almost offensive, discussion of Mofolo and his work. The novelist is introduced as "un homme qui n'a pas eu de déception et qui, peut-être pour son malheur, est arrivé à produire, pour ses débuts, une sorte de petit chef-d'oeuvre." This "kind of little masterpiece" was *Moeti oa bochabela*. After a brief mention of his following two books, the authors of the chapter allude to *Chaka*: "Un quatrième manuscrit, consacré par le même auteur à décrire les moeurs des Zoulous, est en ce moment même entre les mains d'un missionaire auquel Mofolo a demandé des critiques et des conseils." And they conclude: "Une telle prolificité est imprudente"! What, if anything, they may have thought of Balzac has not been recorded.

It is not unlikely that the man to whom Mofolo applied for criticism and advice was his protector Jacottet, who may have been responsible for the appraisal of the book as a description of Zulu customs. While this is a stupendous distortion of its meaning and import, we must keep in mind that the French missionaries, although some of them were highly cultured men, were not literary scholars, and criticism before the New Criticism was usually impressionistic anyway. The novel being thus misinterpreted, it is not surprising that the missionaries should have been reluctant to print it. In fact, one rather wonders how it happened that the book was printed at all.

According to Jahn, it was printed in a slightly garbled version, and this, he seems to suggest, led to the resignation of Casalis.[57] Actually, Casalis had returned to Lesotho in 1920; he had resumed his various occupations, among others the management of the printing press. He tendered his resignation early in 1925. His age and health did not permit him to pursue his heavy tasks any longer. His departure was announced in *Leselinyana* of November 13, and he left in December. The first edition of *Chaka* came from the press in February 1926. The records of the "Conférence des missionaires du Lessouto" clearly show that Casalis was solely and entirely responsible for the publication of the book, which makes any tampering with the manuscript most unlikely.[58]

On 21 April 1926, one member of the conference forcefully deplored the printing of *Chaka*:

M. R. Ellenberger demande qui est responsable de la publication de ce livre, qui, à ses yeux, ne peut faire que du mal à ses lecteurs, car il est une apologie des superstitions païennes. Il est étrange qu'une oeuvre religieuse comme notre Mission publie un tel livre; il ne faudrait pas que la valeur littéraire d'un ouvrage nous fît oublier les effets pernicieux qu'il peut avoir.

There is no mention in the record of any intervention in favor of *Chaka*. Casalis had left, Jacottet had died in 1920, and it may well be that the other members had not read it. The conference therefore invited the Publications Committee to report on the problem. It added a recommendation that sounds like a warning to the new director of the press not to repeat the "errors" of Casalis: "La Conférence recommande au Directeur du Dépôt de ne rien publier sans accord préalable avec la Commission des Publications." Presumably, Casalis had failed to request the agreement of that committee.

One year later, on 8 April 1927, the report of the Publications Committee came before the conference. The committee was unanimously (although with one slight variant) in favor of the book:

Trois des membres de la Commission des Publications sont favorables à ce que ce livre soit écoulé, et même réimprimé; le quatrième demande l'adjonction d'une page d'explications, écrite par l'auteur.

The conference accepted the advice of the committee; it decided not to discontinue the sale of the book, and to reopen the discussion when and if the problem of reprinting occurred. René Ellenberger, however, did not desist and expressed "la grande tristesse que lui cause cette décision, car il considère *Chaka* comme un livre mauvais, bien qu'admirable au point de vue littéraire." Clearly, he kept to the interpretation that had been defined some fifteen years earlier in the *Livre d'or*. There is some irony in the fact that it was his own brother, Victor Ellenberger, who provided the French translation of the book.

Whether there were new discussions before *Chaka* was reprinted in 1937, I do not know. The fact is that it went through nine editions from 1926 to 1962, and that in all some 40,000 copies were printed, making it undoubtedly the most popular best seller in the vernaculars of southern Africa. It was translated into English (London, 1931) and French (Paris, 1940). Abridged versions were also published in English (London, 1949), German (Zurich, 1953), French (Léopoldville, 1958), and Italian (Milan, 1959). The work was even serialized in a magazine for teachers published by the Education Department of the Southern Sudan in the late forties.[59]

The printing history of *Chaka* illustrates the dilemma with which both African authors and Christian missionaries were faced, and which weighed heavily on the emergence of written literature in Africa. Quite obviously, the missionary presses were established, as Kunene acknowledges, "primarily for the purpose of bolstering up the Christian faith," [60] and not with a view to fostering imaginative literature. Throughout black Africa, the growth of a steadily increasing body of creative writing should indeed be viewed, from a historical standpoint, as a mere by-product of missionary work. It would be rather foolish to expect the missionaries to have rushed through their own presses works that could be construed as trying to celebrate and perpetuate so-called "heathen" practices and beliefs, however high their literary quality might be. The arguments of René Ellenberger on this point were perfectly clear and *nuancé* and, given his premises, legitimate. His error, and that of any others hostile to publication between 1910 and 1925, was in mistaking the book for an apologetic discussion of pagan customs. Whereas the present-day reader versed in the techniques of modern literary criticism cannot miss the ethical significance of the work, it is true that *Chaka* contains none of the overt propagandizing that Christian proselytizers usually seem to think is the most efficient way to spread God's message. Account should also be taken of the possibility, or even the likelihood, that the African readership might misread the work exactly in the same way that some of the missionaries did.[61] Actually, the fact that the manuscript was preserved for fifteen years and ultimately published suggests that some amount of heart-searching must have been going on among the Morija missionaries, and it is a comforting thought that taste and understanding should have prevailed over blindness and short-term strategies.

It must be acknowledged, however, that the procrastination over *Chaka* caused far-reaching damage to both Mofolo and incipient Sotho literature.

In 1910 while *Chaka* was under consideration at the printing press, Mofolo left Lesotho for South Africa, and stopped writing altogether. Jahn suggests that he was "disappointed by the narrow-mindedness of the missionaries" and turned away from literature to "hurl himself into various sorts of business ventures." [62] In the short biographical note used by G. H. Franz, Mofolo himself had stated that he left the Morija station for Lealui "whither I was drawn by the high wages." Jahn's statement, however, is based on evidence from the writer's friend, Zakea D. Mangoaela, as reported by Sulzer,[63] to the effect that Mofolo had been influenced by the hostility and the misunderstanding of the missionaries. Although this is plausible enough, it is not the whole truth. When the Reverend Albert Brutsch discussed the problem with Mangoaela, the latter at length mentioned that Mofolo had left Morija as a result of a scandal. This prompted Brutsch to consult the Morija parish register, where he found the mention "bohl. 3/10 F. 1910," meaning that Mofolo was found guilty of adultery *(bohlola)* in March 1910 and left the country that same year; his wife left Morija for Teyateyaneng in June 1910.[64] This, of course, leaves the possibility open that Mofolo, in his literary "failure," sought relief and forget-fulness in illegitimate passion.

After a brief stay in South Africa, Mofolo went to Lealui in Barotseland (Zambia), but because of the bad climate, he had to go back to South Africa, where he worked on the Rand. In 1912 he settled in northern Lesotho as a labor recruiting agent for the Eckstein group of the Central Mining Rand mines. He also took over the management of a thirty-mile postal route between Teya-teyaneng and Ficksburg (Orange Free State) until the end of World War I. In 1916 he had purchased a government portable steam engine and milling plant. According to some reports, his purpose was to relieve Sotho women from the heavy task of pound-ing their corn.[65] His wife had died, and he remarried in 1918.

After the war, Mofolo turned to politics. He became a member of the Basutoland Progressive Association that had been founded in the early years of the century and was critical both of the tra-

ditional chiefs and of the British administration. In 1919 the association was the first to press for part of the Basutoland National
Council to be elected instead of nominated by the paramount chief;
this request was rejected.[66]

In 1922 Mofolo left the Eckstein group to become an independent labor agent, recruiting workers for the Rand mines and for
the Natal plantations. In 1925 he opened a new branch in Teyateyaneng and put his brother Ben Mofolo in charge; but Ben gave
up the business in 1927. In the same year, Thomas's second wife
died; he closed his recruiting agency and sold his mill. In 1928 he
bought a store in Bokong, in the Maluti mountains, although he
went on living in Teyateyaneng. He married for the third and last
time in 1933. He sold his store in 1937, and left the mountains
where the high altitude was harmful to his health. He had been
invited to the Conference of Bantu Authors held in Florida (Transvaal) on 15 October 1936, but he sent an excuse.[67] Nor did he pay
any attention to a suggestion made by Doke that he might write a
life of Moshoeshoe.

After a short stay in Port Elizabeth, he decided to settle nearer
to his own people and in 1937 he bought a farm from a white
farmer at Matatiele, not far from the Lesotho border. But the
transaction was invalidated under the Bantu Land Act of 1913,
according to which, Kunene writes, "a Native could only buy land
bordering another African's land. Mofolo's property was just
touching another African's land, and so he took his case to court.
But he lost not only his case, but his health and wealth besides." [68]
A broken and sick man, he first tried without success to run a tea-
room in Matatiele, and in 1940 he returned to Lesotho. Sir Patrick
Duncan, the then governor general, awarded him out of his personal funds a pension of £3 per month, which he received until Sir
Patrick's death in 1943. In 1941, he had suffered a stroke that left
him speechless for several months. Thomas Mofolo died at Teyateyaneng on 8 September 1948.

Mofolo's Contemporaries

The success of Mofolo's first novel, *Moeti oa bochabela*,
prompted interest in modern-type prose fiction among a number
of educated Sotho of his, and even of the older generation. He was
thus the initiator of a national Lesotho imaginative literature,

which was the first to develop on a significant scale in southern Africa. The second novel in Southern Sotho appeared in book form in 1910; it was written by Mofolo's former teacher Segoete.

Everitt Lechesa Segoete was born at Morifi (Mohale's Hoek) in 1858; he was called "Lechesa," which means "fire," because the Boers had recently made incursions in the area and had burned down a few villages. After some time, his father moved to Maphutseng, where there was a mission school run by the Reverend D. F. Ellenberger, which the boy attended on and off when he was not looking after his father's cattle. Segoete followed Ellenberger when the latter went to teach at Masitise. He obtained his teacher's certificate from the school at Morija, but instead of entering the teaching profession, he left for the Cape Colony, where he fell a victim to various misadventures that were to provide him with material for the novel he was to write several decades later. A missionary's wife advised him to return home, which he did. For a while, he worked at the printing press in Morija, then left again to work for a newspaper in Aliwal North (Cape Province), where he met his future wife. He then went back home to Lesotho and was appointed headmaster of the school at Qomoqomong (Quting). His activity there was greatly appreciated, and he was one of the three students who were selected to attend the theological seminary that had been opened on 2 June 1887. He graduated in April 1896, at the same time as Edward Motsamai, who was also to become a writer. After his ordination in 1899,[69] he was sent as a minister to Hermone (Mafeteng), then to Koeneng (Leribe), then back to Hermone, where he died on 7 February 1923.

Segoete's initial contribution to Southern Sotho writing was *Monono ke moholi, ke mouoane (Riches Are Like Mist, Vapor* [Morija, 1910]), his only novel, and the first illustration of a narrative pattern that was to recur with increasing frequency in African literature: the story of the tribal boy who goes to town.

The first section is told in the first person by the hero, Khitšane, who seems to be just a namesake for the author. A ruined man, Khitšane leaves Lesotho for the Witwatersrand, where he comes for the first time in contact with white society. He is unable to see his way through the alien maze of white laws and regulations, and soon finds himself compelled to join the underworld. After sundry crimes and a number of calamitous adventures, he meets one of his former cronies who has become a Christian preacher, and who

converts him. Khitšane then returns to Lesotho, a cripple with a
wooden leg, but happy in the true faith and in his native environment. The second section of the book deals with the death of
Khitšane on Good Friday, after a mythical vision that leads him
from anguish and terror to eternal bliss. His corpse is discovered
by his neighbor Tim to whom he had told the story of his life. Tim
is a rich pagan, but he is considerably impressed by the life, and
especially the death, of his friend. The third section of the novel
describes how Tim too turns to the true faith after a rather ghastly
experience; for three days he lies buried in a tunnel while hunting
rabbits, and during that time he has a vision of Doomsday.

Although one is bound to agree with Werner that Segoete's
novel is little more than "a moral tale of the Sunday-school
type," [70] considering that the novel as a genre was entirely foreign
to the literary tradition of Africa, its structure is certainly remarkable. It falls into two parts, the first one, with its two sections, centering on Khitšane, and the other on Tim. Each is the story of a
conversion; each begins in naturalistic description and ends in
allegorical vision. Both neatly complement each other. Khitšane is
a poor man, who is driven abroad by sheer necessity and is led to
faith and virtue through his misadventures in the exotic world of
the white man. Tim is a wealthy pagan who has never left his home
place, but he is brought to religion through fear of imminent death.
Indeed, Tim's odyssey is an illustration of Khitšane's vision insofar
as Tim gains access to truth along the dark way of suffering and
terror. His stay in the tunnel is an allegorical image for the death
of the body which is a necessary condition for the awakening of
the soul. Both visions center on the narrow path that man must
follow, beset by darkness and horror, if he is to gain the eternal
bliss that is the lot of the redeemed.

Each of the two stories thus appears as a kind of parable: this
indirect, allegorical way of expressing wisdom is characteristic of
Africa's gnomic tradition. Whereas in oral art its import is chiefly
of an ethical order, it was apparently under the influence of Christian teaching that allegory became used, in African writing, to
describe spiritual and even mystical experiences. In the translations
of the Bible and of *Pilgrim's Progress*, early Sotho writers found a
way of conveying the truths of the new religion peculiarly suited
to the literary traditions of their people.

But the most significant feature of Segoete's novel, from the

point of view of African literary history, is to be found in its first
section, which announces the shortly to become familiar motif of
Jim-goes-to-Jo'burg. As will be the case in such later works as
Mopeli-Paulus's *Blanket Boy's Moon* or Peter Abrahams's *Mine
Boy*, it describes the fate of a young man who is driven by sheer
economic necessity to leave his native place and seek a better fate
in the city. This theme accurately reflects the actual social conditions that had been prevailing since the discovery of gold and
diamonds in Kimberley and Johannesburg had created a huge demand for cheap unskilled manpower. Lesotho is a very poor country with a subsistence economy based on cattle-raising. As Leonard
Barnes observed in 1932: "In Basutoland, the chiefs and the European administrators and traders alike think the country lucky in
having Union industry hard by to take the overflow of unem-
ployed and provide them with cash to bring back." [71] This was
already true in the early years of the century.

It was Segoete's purpose to warn the Sotho against the dangers
of slum life in the industrial cities, and he knew what he was talk-
ing about. In his largely autobiographical account, however, there
is no attempt to assign responsibilities, no critique of the new industrial society that was emerging in South Africa. The outlook is
both tribal and Christian. Khitšane's escape from his native environment is to be taken as an act of hubris. He is punished through
a fatal mechanism for which no one is responsible. The Sotho man
is unable to comprehend the intricate laws and regulations of this
alien world governed by the white man. He is thus led to infringe
them unwittingly and to delve deeper and deeper into lawlessness
and crime. The proposed remedy is not to reform this racist urban
society. Segoete merely invites the Sotho man to stay where he
belongs, in his own country, in his own culture. There only can he
be happy, destitute and maimed as he may be. This tribal aspect of
Segoete's outlook easily combines with its Christian aspect, for
crime is not only an infringement of the white man's law, but also
of God's moral decrees. Life at home may be one of dire poverty,
but it is also one of simple virtue; it therefore contains a promise
of redemption. Tim's story is, of course, designed to bolster this
view by showing that Christian hope is not merely an escape from
the woes of life but is equally necessary for those who have been
privileged with worldly prosperity.

His deep religious convictions inspired most of Segoete's other books. In the same year as his novel, he published *Mefiboshethe kapa pheello ea molimo ho moetsalibe (Mefiboshete, or the Patience of God to the Sinner)*, a collection of religious meditations that had been printed serially in *Leselinyana*.[72] And his last two books are also devotional works: *Moea oa bolisa (The Spirit of Shepherding* [1913]), and *Mohlala oa Jesu Kreste (The Example of Jesus Christ)*, which was printed posthumously in 1924.

In 1913 the Morija press had issued his *Raphepheng (Father of the Scorpion)*, a strange hotchpotch of a book, which illustrates the duality that had been observable among Xhosa authors since the middle of the nineteenth century. It is a random collection of traditional lore placed in the mouth of the title character. In the first section, Raphepheng describes and glorifies the customs of the Sotho people of the past and deplores the neglect into which they have fallen among the younger generations. It is written in a vein of romantic idealization rather unexpected in an ordained minister. The Sotho of old are alleged to have been all handsome and healthy. They lived in prelapsarian nakedness and did not know the uses and evils of money. They were wont to help each other selflessly and to take innocent relish in games and music. This first part describes in great detail the agricultural customs of the Sotho and even deals extensively with Sotho cuisine. Segoete is also intent upon proving that the Sotho did not lack scientific knowledge, and he next turns to ornithology, recording observations about the birds of Lesotho and also the traditional songs dealing with each of them. After providing a list of some of the riddles that are a favorite pastime of non-literate societies everywhere, he has a chapter on locusts and grasshoppers, which may have been inspired by Sekese's tale about the meeting of the birds: the locusts come together to choose a new king; the leader they elect is "a vicious, morose individual and rules his people with great cruelty. Thus do people only obey and respect those who are stronger than they"[73]—another piece of evidence about the educated Sotho's doubts concerning chiefly power. The main purpose of this section, however, is to show Sotho interest in the observation and study of nature. The book ends with descriptions of Sotho religious beliefs, traditional medicine, customary initiation, marriage customs, educational habits, and tribal justice.

In view of the strictures raised against Mofolo's *Chaka* a mere three years earlier, it is certainly surprising that *Raphepheng*

should have been allowed to reach print, for it is much more obviously a description of pre-Christian customs than Mofolo's novel.
The fact that Segoete was a minister of the church may have
whitewashed him of any suspicion of advocating a return to heathenism. Writing in 1930, G. H. Franz did not miss the main point
of the book, which, he says, "implies, rather than expresses, a
severe rebuke against our civilisation. We have overthrown nearly
all that is Bantu, and have given the people nothing in return. Our
civilisation has been a disintegrating factor in the lives of the
Bantu, and to-day they are divided into two camps. Some cling
tenaciously to the old, and consequently lag behind in the onward
march. The great majority have outrun the old civilisation and are
running blindly into destruction. Raphepheng's voice comes like
the call of the *Mankoetlana* (mourning dove) out of Nature's hidden recesses, and calls in vain."

To Mofolo's generation belonged Edward Motsamai, who was
born at Masite (Maseru) in May 1870. After attending the Bible
School, from which he graduated with honors in 1886, he went to
the Teacher Training College and took his teacher's certificate in
1888. From 1889 to 1892, he taught both at the Bible School and at
the Mountain School. In 1893 he started preparing for the ministry,
but owing to ill-health and the loss of his voice, he had to give up
his studies from 1896 to 1899. He worked for a while at the Morija
Book Depot and later resumed his studies. He was ordained in
1900. Sickness forced him to give up the ministry, but in 1901 the
synod assigned him to a post at Letsunyane in the Maluti Mountains, where he recovered fully.[74] He died in July 1959.

Motsamai was the author of one of the earliest printed books by a
Sotho writer, *Majoe a mahlano a molatsoana (Five Pebbles from
the Brook* [1907]), a collection of five meditations previously published in *Leselinyana*,[75] and composed with a view to warning
Christian youth against the allurements of paganism. His single
contribution to imaginative writing is a collection of short stories,
Mehla ea malimo (The Days of the Cannibals [1912]). Motsamai is
a very minor writer, and the eighteen stories in the volume read
like sketchy summaries of the folktales that he had gathered from
the mouths of the old men of Lesotho. They deal with memories
from precolonial days, and it is significant that they are imbued
with a strong sense of fear and horror. Five of them describe fright-

ful encounters between human beings and the ferocious beasts of
the jungle. The others are all about the gruesome time when the
wholesale destruction of villages, harvests, and cattle wrought by
Chaka and his warriors had reduced many tribes between the Indian Ocean and the Drakensberg to cannibalism. Though there is
only slight literary quality to Motsamai's tales, they are important
as genuine evidence of the way in which the Sotho converts envisioned their own past.

Motsamai then returned to religious writing with *Kereke* (*The
Church* [1925]), a disquisition on the Christian church. His last
book was a biographical account of Moshoeshoe, *Morena Moshoeshoe mar'a Mokhachane* (*Chief Moshoeshoe, Son of Mokhachane*
[1942]).

The last writer of this group, Zakea D. Mangoaela, was not born in
Lesotho, but at Hohobeng near Palmietfontein (Cape Colony) in
1883. His parents were Christians, and his father was able to read,
although he could not write. The family moved to Lesotho soon
after Zakea's birth, since he was baptized in that same year by the
Reverend D. F. Ellenberger in Masitise, where he grew up. He
attended school there in 1889. He was a brilliant child and passed
the Standard IV examination in 1895. As he was too young, he had
to wait until July 1897 before he could enroll in the Mountain
School. In 1900 he was temporarily excluded from school for unruliness and for keeping bad company. He obtained his teacher's
certificate in 1902.

He wanted to go to Lovedale, but his father was too poor to pay
for further study. In 1903, Mangoaela was appointed as a teacher
and preacher in a backward area of the Maluti Mountains. There
it was that he composed a first series of three graded Sotho readers
that were long in use in Sotho schools. In 1907 he was appointed
to Segoete's school at Koeneng, where he began to write stories
and historical articles for *Leselinyana*. In Koeneng he married
Berenice Sekokotoana, whose father was the author of several religious tracts. In 1910 he agreed to assist the Reverend Duby in his
various tasks as director of the Book Depot, headmaster of the
Bible School, and editor of *Leselinyana*. It was at that time he
wrote his first book, *Tsoelo-pele ea Lesotho* (*The Progress of
Lesotho* [1911]), an account of the advance of the country under
European influence.

His only contribution to creative literature was a collection of short stories, *Har'a libatana le linyamat'sane (Among the Animals, Big and Small* [1912]). The book contains fifty-four hunting stories similar in inspiration to those of Motsamai, but Sotho readers consider Mangoaela far superior to Motsamai in style and technique.

In spite of his remarkable gifts, this was to remain Mangoaela's sole venture in imaginative composition. His next volume, which did not come out until 1921, was *Lithoko tsa marena a Basotho (Praises of the Sotho Chiefs)*, the first collection of Southern Sotho praises to be printed in book form. Mofolo Bulane considers that "it was a great step forward in reducing this genre to writing, thereby preserving it and assuring its transmission to later generations. It is on this publication that many a Mosotho poet and writer has had to depend." [76]

During those years, Mangoaela also worked with Jacottet on the *Grammar of the Sesuto Language* which was edited by C. M. Doke in Johannesburg in 1917. From the twenties onward, he devoted most of his time to edifying writing. In 1937 he was appointed a member of the Regional Literature Committee for Sotho, set up by the Christian Council of South Africa and chaired by the Reverend G. Mabille. [77] From 1954 to 1958, he was the editor of *Leselinyana*. He died on 25 October 1963.

While this literary activity was going on at the Protestant Morija station, another culture center was slowly emerging in Lesotho under the aegis of a French Catholic missionary society founded in the early part of the nineteenth century by Eugène de Mazenod (1782–1861): the Congregation of the Oblates of Mary Immaculate. [78] The first two Roman Catholic priests reached Lesotho in 1862 and settled at a place that was first called Motse wa M'a Jesu (the village of Jesus' mother) before it received its present name of Roma—not, it would seem, as a somewhat delirious hyperbole, but because the station was the center of the Ba-Roma, the Roman Catholics. To those who questioned the wisdom of introducing this new Christian sect, Moshoeshoe replied "that churches were like doctors: it was best to consult more than one." [79] Development was slow at first. The first Catholic Sotho catechism and prayer book, issued in 1865, was printed on the press of the *Natal Mercury* in Durban. Experiments were made with a manual printing press on the spot between 1872 and 1880. A few religious works and school textbooks were printed there, but the attempt was given up when the Trappist Fathers founded a Catholic press in Mariannhill (Natal) in 1883. There it was that Father Odilon Chevrier, who had been appointed secretary of the Catholic schools in Lesotho in 1927, launched a teachers' monthly, *Molisa (The Shepherd)* which provided pedagogical advice and also reading matter, chiefly in the form of saints' lives.

For a long time, written composition came solely from the white missionaries who did not seem to be very much interested in fostering imaginative literature or publication by native writers. From the generation with which we are now dealing, only one Catholic writer is still remembered: Justinus Sechefo, who was born in the 1870s and who died in 1938. When Paramount Chief Nathanael Griffiths traveled to London in 1919, Father Chevrier prompted Sechefo to write an account of the journey. It is interesting to note that during the same period two Ethiopian writers were likewise recording trips made abroad by the then Ras Tafari. Sechefo's 164-page volume, *Molia oa la Morena e Moholo la ho ea England 1919 (The Party of the Day the Paramount Chief Went to England in 1919)* was not published until about 1930. The printing was done at Mariannhill, just before a Catholic press was built in Lesotho itself, at Mazenod. Unfortunately, the remaining copies of the book were destroyed on 19 June 1946 when the Mazenod printing works and book depot caught fire. At the time of writing (1969), a new, cyclostyled edition is contemplated. Until his death, Sechefo worked as a proofreader at the Mazenod press and as a frequent contributor to *Moeletsi oa Basotho (The Sotho Adviser)* which had been started there on 10 January 1933. The Mazenod press later produced some of his works posthumously in cyclostyled form, at uncertain dates. They include devotional pamphlets such as *Mofumahali oa rosari (The Lady of the Rosary)*, which deals with the apparitions of Our Lady of Fatima, a collection of biblical extracts entitled *Matsipa a Bibele (Extracts from the Bible)*, and *Re adoreng re hlonepheng (Let Us Worship and Respect)*, a Sotho version of meditations on the Holy Sacrament by the eighteenth-century bishop of Naples, Saint Alfonso de Liguori.

Sechefo's interest in traditional Africa made itself felt in two volumes in English, *Customs and Superstitions in Basutoland* and *The Old Clothing of the Basotho*, and especially in a twenty-seven-page collection of praise poems, *Kulile*, which appeared in 1964.

But he also wrote poems of Christian inspiration, one of which has been translated into French.[80] Entitled "Hurry, the Chief is Coming!" it describes in imagery drawn from native everyday life how a housewife feverishly cleans and adorns her hut in preparation for the coming of the chief; she is so busy that she can find no time to help a hungry woman, a tired old man, and a wounded child who come to her in succession. The chief is of course Christ, and when at last he visits her hut, he rebukes her severely for rejecting him thrice as he had come for solace and food and compassion.

Justinus Sechefo was a forerunner at Mazenod as Sekese had been at Morija. The flowering of Catholic imaginative writing in Lesotho was not to come until World War II.

Decline and Rebirth

This period that has been described as "the golden age" of Sotho literature lasted from 1906 (Mofolo's *Moeti oa bochabela*) to 1912 (the short stories of Motsamai and Mangoaela). Not unexpectedly, Sotho writers drew most of their inspiration from the two main sources to which Xhosa authors had resorted until 1884. With all the intensity of a fundamentally religious people, they had embraced the ideals of Christianity. The overriding experience of the Sotho nation in the pre-Christian past had been the Zulu wars. It was obvious to them that Christian morality with its conception of the universal brotherhood of men was vastly superior to the sectional ethics characteristic of tribal cultures. Mofolo's *Chaka* and Motsamai's tales of cannibalism testify to this awareness. They were aware, nevertheless, of the threat that Western civilization, however scant its material impact may have been in Lesotho, represented to the positive aspects of their traditional culture. This can be seen from Segoete's *Raphepheng*, from many passages scattered throughout Mofolo's novels, from Sekese's devoted recordings of traditional customs, proverbs, and songs, and from Mangoaela's publication of oral praise poems.

They were not ignorant of the discrepancy between the ideal standards and the actual mores of the Christians, black or white: to point out this discrepancy is precisely a central point in Mofolo's *Pitseng*. Nor did they identify Christianity and Western civilization. In fact, it was part of Segoete's purpose in his novel to show that the traditional society of Lesotho was more favorable to gen-

uine Christian conduct, and therefore to the salvation of the soul,
than were the industrial cities built by the white man in the Union
of South Africa. But owing to the protected status of the country
and to the rigid enforcement of Moshoeshoe's laws prohibiting
ownership of land by Europeans, the educated Sotho understandably felt less menaced by the white man than did the educated
Xhosa of the same period. Early Sotho imaginative literature, therefore, exhibits no sense of racial conflict, no questioning of the
Christian faith of the type that had been found two decades earlier
in the works of Gqoba or Ntsiko. Nor is there any evidence that
writers were involved in the development of political consciousness that took place in the Union during the second decade of the
century. Sheltered as they were against foreign encroachment by
British protection, Sotho literati were more concerned with crit-
icizing the abuses of the prevailing traditional system, especially in
judicial matters, than with justifying tradition against foreign innovation and constraint.

The major contribution of those Sotho authors to the growth
of imaginative writing in southern Africa is to be found in their
novels. Extended prose fiction is a genre that can only flourish in a
literate society. It is alien to the oral tradition of Africa, and this
accounts for the late birth of the novel in most parts of the continent, as well as for the general clumsiness with which its techniques are handled. It is not yet possible to elucidate the reasons
why both Mofolo and, to a lesser extent, Segoete managed to produce novels that certainly deserve serious consideration, while
Mofolo's *Chaka* is the first masterpiece of African prose fiction.

The decline in Sotho literature that set in after 1912 is probably
to be ascribed mainly to the hostility of a number of the Société
des Missions Evangéliques de Paris missionaries to *Chaka*. Sotho
authors were discouraged from engaging in serious fictional discussion of their experience, and most of the native writing that came
from the Morija press between the wars was of a devotional nature.
Even though the Reverend René Ellenberger had to yield on the
publication of *Chaka*, he obviously had his way on a more general
plane. For a long time, the mission authorities rallied to his notion
that the business of a mission press was to print works devoted to
the propagation of the Gospel.

This trend, no doubt, was reinforced by the severe decline in
missionary finances owing to a bad drought in 1923-1924, followed

by the Great Depression. Missionary revenue came from three sources: they had the money they could raise by their own efforts, either on the spot or from their headquarters in Paris; since 1906, they had received some financial assistance from the British treasury; whatever else was needed had to be met from Lesotho's budget. There is a Sotho proverb to the effect that education is "a three-legged pot standing on the legs of the missions, the people and the government." [81] Dwindling resources in Lesotho during the twenties and the thirties were not compensated for by any increase in contributions from Britain. Indeed, throughout that period education was cut back steeply, educational growth came to a stop, and the effects of this are still felt today. As Halpern points out, whereas "until roughly the turn of the century, Basutoland bore comparison with South Africa, since then it has increasingly lagged behind. This lag has been most painfully noticeable in secondary education. As late as 1936, there was only one secondary school in Basutoland, and that stopped two years short of matriculation. It was only when Fort Hare in South Africa discontinued its matriculation classes that, in 1939, Basutoland got its first proper high school. It was and remains a government school."

It was also suggested to me by Sotho informants that another cause for this decline may have been the stronger emphasis placed on the English language and literature as a condition for British subsidies to mission schools. Improved familiarity with English may have led to a decline both in the prestige and in the knowledge of the vernacular.

Whatever the causes may have been, the fact remains that only one writer emerged in the thirties: David Cranmer Theko Bereng, who was born in 1900, and whose *Lithothokiso tsa Moshoeshoe le tse ling (Poems in Praise of King Moshoeshoe)* was published at Morija in 1931. This was the first collection of original poems to appear in Southern Sotho, and most of them are composed in the manner of traditional praise poetry. But they are not slavish imitations. As Bulane observed, Bereng's "kind of epic form derives directly from the praise poem, which sweeps through the halls of stormy history reeking with blood. This he intersperses with personal reflections, thoughts, emotional outbursts, and experiences at once personal and universal. . . . In interpreting the world around himself, in transporting his impressions, he has imposed his thought, obviously enriched by the Gospel, the pastor's sermon, and wide

reading." [82] The volume centers on Moshoeshoe, who is identified
with the Sotho nation, not in a piously metaphorical way, but, as
it were, sacrally. The genuineness and intensity of this feeling appear in the eloquence of this fragment of the "Poem on the Death
of Moshoeshoe":

> Moshoeshoe is buried by heroes alone:
> The first to throw dust into his grave is Sekonyela.
> Moshoeshoe is buried by distinguished ones.
> When people were burying Chief
> With "mokorotlo," the war song of men,
> The mountains groaned and moaned,
> The heavens were torn asunder,
> Winds howled with the violence of thunder,
> Beasts took refuge among people,
> Hedges of reeds suddenly collapsed,
> Walls all over Lesotho fell down,
> Tigers and colts kissed,
> Jackals grazed together with lambs,
> Hawks flew together with pigeons,
> Water flowed back to the sources.
> Strange things happened
> When the Ruler of Lesotho was buried.
> We saw frightening scenes
> Because wolves and people walked together,
> Snakes moved away from the bush,
> When people buried the Chief
> With the war song of men echoing afar.

But remembrances of the great days of Moshoeshoe prompt the
poet to ponder on the present fate of his land, sunk in poverty and
shamelessly exploited by the ever-increasing number of petty
feudal chieftains:

> Thoughts will torture me.
> I shall not rest from thinking.
> I shall think of the government's success,
> Of its wealth and comfort;
> I shall also think of the poverty of nations.
> I shall study the history of fallen kings
> And seek the causes of their downfall.
> I shall think of administrative ways
> Of various governments,

> And end up by saying,
> "People are superior to the ruler,
> But the law is superior to the people;
> And God is superior to the law."

In spite of the obvious similarity in wording, this is not the type of anticolonial poetry that was to become familiar later in other parts of Africa. Those lines are the outcome of the poet's meditation as he reflects on the decay of the traditional system of chiefly government that had been disintegrating into feudal dispersion of authority and increasing abuse of power. The extent of the demoralization brought about by the uninterrupted multiplication of petty chieftains has been described by Halpern:

Inevitably, as the competition between chiefs became keener, many of them abandoned the custom that a chief's wealth existed only to be shared with his people. They continued to demand the traditional services, such as unpaid labour, but they stopped giving anything in return. Some even went further and transformed their courts into petty racketeering concerns. Unreasonable orders were issued, and defaulters heavily fined. Sometimes a chief would even enter into cahoots with cattle thieves in return for a share of their loot. Understandably, dissatisfaction grew over the years, to reach a climax in the thirties.[83]

Like Sekese, whose bird story had been printed three years before, Bereng is bitterly aware of the contrast between reality and the idea of law, between the people's poverty and the wealth of those in authority, and he places his ultimate hope in the justice of God.

The high quality of Bereng's poetry won immediate recognition. In recommendations issued in 1933, a group of South African scholars suggested that he should be encouraged to write more. But in 1941, Doke could only remark that "apart from occasional *lithoko* appearing in journals, we know of no further poetry being published. Bereng, who is now on military service, has prepared a poetical M.S. which awaits a publisher." [84] As far as I know, this publisher has never materialized.

In spite of this dearth in actual creative writing, the thirties can be said to have paved the way for the future rebirth of Sotho literature.

First, there arose in Europe and South Africa a considerable interest, linguistic, pedagogical, and humanitarian, in the promotion of vernacular literature. This took the form of literary competitions such as those organized by the International African Institute of London. The fact that eight Sotho manuscripts received prizes in 1933 demonstrates that the writing urge was by no means defunct, even though printing opportunities might have vanished. In 1935 Dr. and Mrs. Mumford in London created a yearly May Esther Bedford prize of £50 for original work by Bantu artists in literature, music, and the arts. The conferences of Bantu writers convened by Dr. Shepherd in 1936 and 1937—to which Thomas Mofolo was invited but did not go—could not but lead to a revaluation of vernacular writing, while the standardization of Bantu spelling initiated in 1934 was to make the practical task of writing and reading easier throughout southern Africa.

Equally important in respect to Lesotho itself was the tremendous growth of the Catholic church and of its educational system. The Roma mission had been making slow headway until 1924, when Belgian and Canadian Oblates were sent to Lesotho to help the French Fathers. Catholic expansion began to gather momentum. A seminary was set up to train Sotho clergy. In 1930 the Vicariate was transferred to the Eastern Province of Canada. Larger resources from the Western Hemisphere made it possible to build a local press at Mazenod, and to start *Moeletsi oa basotho (The Sotho Adviser)*, first issued in January 1933. As had been the case in Madagascar since the last quarter of the nineteenth century, there was no peaceful coexistence between the Christian sects involved. Since the Société des Missions Evangéliques missionaries had practically enjoyed an unchallenged monopoly in Lesotho, Catholic aggressive vigor was inevitably directed against them. By 1945 the Roman Catholics could boast 334 schools as against 459 administered by the Protestants. As Halpern mildly puts it, those "rival efforts at expansion have at times looked like a 'soul-catching' race," and he quotes the "tactful" 1960 Report of the Education Department, to the effect that "much of the notable improvement in accommodation and equipment standards in very recent years has resulted from healthy competition, but the Department has been hard-pressed at times to maintain the balance between denominational enthusiasm and genuine educational needs." [85] Nor were the Mazenod missionaries slow to realize how efficient a means of propaganda imaginative fiction could become in their fight against the Calvinistic heresy. In this connection, one of their earliest published novels, *Lilahloane* (2d ed., 1944) by Albert Nqheku is highly significant, although it would be wrong to describe it as typical of the whole of Catholic literature in Southern Sotho.

Albert Nqheku was born at Shoepane on 1 July 1912. He has been a teacher and a catechist for over thirty years. He was still teaching in 1969 at Marakabies, in the mountainous part of the Maseru district. The book was perceptively reviewed by G. L. Letele,[86] who noted that "one cannot fail to see that the story is told primarily to make the reader aware of the spiritual salvation one gains by becoming a member of the Catholic Church." The heroine, Lilahloane, is a girl who has been instructed in the Catholic faith by her grandmother, Maria Louisa. Both "are an example of what true Catholics should be: by carefully carrying out the precepts of their religion they have the strength to face all the difficulties which confront them. Maria Louisa dies with a song of praise on her lips, and a peace of mind which shows that she is assured of a happy rest in Heaven." On the contrary, Lilahloane's father, Selepe, has turned away from the church; he is a heavy drinker, and he insists on having his daughter marry according to pagan custom. Worst of all, perhaps, he wishes her to marry a Protestant. To this demand, Lilahloane replies: "What Church has the power to save the souls of people, other than the one under the direction of the Pope?" Indeed, her in-laws "are shown up in a very bad light, and only begin to be good after they have turned from their Protestant religion to join the Roman Catholic Church." So zealous is Nqheku's polemic intent that he even goes out of his way to throw a few insults at "the Communists of Mapoteng who call themselves *Lekhotla la Bafo*." [87] The story, Letele adds, is "quite entertaining since it is told in a lively manner and colourful language." It illustrates the general atmosphere of the denominational struggle at the time, but Nqheku's belligerence is by no means representative of all, or even most, of the fast-growing literary output from the Catholic printing press at Mazenod, where the interdenominational Organization of Sesotho Authors was founded in 1956.

The third element that accounts for the extension and the new orientations of Sotho literature was the increasingly stronger relationship between the Sotho nation and the Union of South Africa. This took several forms.

In 1852 the British government had recognized the sovereignty of the Boer Republic in Transvaal. This was followed by the granting of similar status to the Orange Free State. The Afrikaners were therefore free to undertake the conquest of Moshoeshoe's territory. The treaty of Thaba Bosiu, which the paramount chief was forced to sign in 1866 after several military defeats, gave the Free Staters a rich victory as the Sotho had to give up more than half their arable land. Part of this was retrieved by them in 1868, when Lesotho was proclaimed British territory, and the border then laid down has been maintained in substance ever since. On the lands annexed to the Orange Free State, the Sotho were "driven out or kept on merely as labourers, and the French and Wesleyan missions were closed down for having supported them." There was, therefore, a nucleus of Sotho population in an area that was later to be incorporated into the Union. Further, when diamond mines opened in Kimberley after 1870, "thousands of Basuto flocked there for short spells to earn money." [88] Although both the missionaries and such literate Sotho as Segoete were trying to counteract this trend, the allurement of cash—in spite of the hardships to be endured in the industrial cities—was bound to prevail, especially with the drought of 1923-1924 and the Great Depression. The number of migrant laborers from Lesotho increased dramatically, and quite a few of them settled in the Union permanently. The Sotho population of the country became important enough for Southern Sotho to be included among the seven official vernacular languages of the Union. According to figures published in 1936 by Lord Hailey,[89] the mines in one recent year had drawn 42,582 of their native employees from Lesotho. Other Sotho men were employed on the farms. It has been estimated that the annual labor exodus from Lesotho affected some 60,000 out of an adult male population of 120,000.[90] There thus arose a generation of Sotho writers who were natives of the Union, and some of whom may even never have set foot in Lesotho. Further, the teaching of Sotho in some Union schools provided a new outlet for Sotho writers, as Union publishers began to print Sotho works primarily designed as school readers.

The connection with South Africa made its consequences felt in yet another aspect of the educational field. Already before World War I, Mangoaela had hoped to pursue his studies at Lovedale; only lack of money had prevented him from doing so. But between the wars, as the Lesotho educational system remained stagnant, a growing number of young Sotho scholars managed to study in the Union schools, together with South African students, and with students from the other High Commission Territories of Swaziland and Bechuanaland. This was of crucial importance in two respects. First, it has been noted that "most of those destined to assume prominence in the Territories attended such institutions as Lovedale, Adams College or Fort Hare, centres of nationalist ferment in South Africa. . . . Consequently, their attitude toward politics was more sophisticated than in many parts of Africa," [91] more so than if they had been trained in their own native countries. Second, the education they could obtain in South African schools was of far better quality, at least until the Bantu Education Acts, than anything that was offered in Lesotho, where, as already observed, education had remained stagnant, if it had not actually declined. This lasted until 1953, when South Africa decided to bar Lesotho children from its schools. By that time, however, a full secondary school had been in operation since 1939, and the Catholic Pius XII University College, founded in Roma in 1945, had grown in enrollment and in quality. In 1964 it was to become an official institution known as the National University of Basutoland, Bechuanaland, and Swaziland.[92] This marked improvement in the quality of education available to a number of Sotho children, whether natives of Lesotho or of the Union, was accompanied by a considerable change of outlook. It is no coincidence that Ntsu Mokhehle (b. 1918), the founder of the first modern nationalist party, the Basutoland African Congress, was graduated with a master of science degree in zoology at Fort Hare in the midforties. The young men reared in the schools of the Union became aware of wider problems than were discussed in the somewhat parochial institutions of their country, and it is no exaggeration to say that the main consequence of their experience in South Africa was to modify the Christian outlook of the older Sotho elite and to foster a secular approach to the various problems that faced their nation. This change was conspicuously reflected in the literary output during the forties and after.

The Last Twenty-Five Years:
Genres, Themes, and Personalities

The results of this development became perceptible during World War II. First, it led to an impressive increase in the output of literary works. Among the Xhosa, quantitative growth was accompanied by obvious qualitative decay. But the Sotho had already evinced, at least in the field of literature, remarkable gifts for adaptation and innovation, were it only by producing the first regular novels in a Bantu language. There arose a number of writers who, without necessarily reaching the level of Mofolo, deepened and diversified the general trends of creative literature in Southern Sotho.

The most conspicuous aspect of this process of diversification is perhaps the introduction of new genres handled with increasing skill. Prose narrative continued to be the favorite medium of the new generation of writers who emerged in the 1940s. But formal drama also made its appearance. It had never been practiced by Sotho authors, although a play was in existence which was based on, or was the basis of, Sekese's bird fable.[93] As in Xhosa, the first formal drama printed in Southern Sotho was the work of a European, Father Chevrier, who, in 1930, published at the Mariannhill Mission Press a short fourteen-page play "for Native Schools in Basutoland," *Tarcisius momartiri oa sacramente e Halalelang (Tarcisius, Martyr of the Holy Communion).* It was not until 1939 that the first genuine Sotho drama was composed by Twentyman M. Mofokeng, whose example was followed, after World War II, by more gifted writers such as Bennett M. Khaketla and Jac. G. Mocoancoeng.

Written poetry had been a latecomer in Lesotho. Sekese and Mangoaela had contented themselves with recording traditional lithoko, which were meant to be spoken, almost sung, so that rhythm was the basic prosodic device. "In these poems," Miss Beuchat wrote, "one often notes a succession of contrasting rhythms—slow-fast, slow-fast. The faster the action, the faster the rhythm. As the emotions become calmer, as the dignity of the moment is to be emphasized, the verse becomes slower." [94] This was the prosody used by Bereng in his original compositions of 1931. But whereas traditional poetry, in Lesotho as in other Bantu nations, was mainly devoted to the praises of chiefs, Bereng had shown that its forms could also be successfully employed for the treatment of other themes. In 1940 George Lerotholi returned to the strict themes of praise poetry in *Lithoko tsa morena e moholo Seeiso Griffith (Praise Poems of the Paramount Chief Seeiso Griffith)*, in honor of the new paramount chief, Seeiso Griffith, who was born in 1905, was inaugurated in 1939, but was to die on 26 December 1940. Lerotholi, who seems to act as Lesotho's poet laureate, later produced *Lithoko tsa motlotlehi Moshoeshoe II (Praise Poems of His Excellency Moshoeshoe II* [Mazenod, 1954]), on the occasion of the marriage of Seeiso Griffith's successor, the present paramount chief, who has taken the name of Moshoeshoe II. But in 1942, Adam J. Selane had turned for inspiration to the other aspect of Bereng's poetry in *Letlolo la Mosotho (A Sotho Man Whose Progeny Had Died)*, published in the Union by the Nasionale Pers, which contains poems about subjects entirely foreign to traditional praise poetry, such as summer, a hailstorm, love, and even the airplane. While admitting that Selane's skill is not of a high order, Letele found it nevertheless "gratifying to note that Bereng's experiments, introducing a variety of subjects into Sotho poetry, have opened up a new line of literary development in the language." [95]

There was further innovation by Ntsane, with his collection *'Musa Pelo (Heart Restorer* [Morija, 1946]). Kemuel Edward Ntsane,[96] who belongs to the Kwena tribe, was born in Kolojane (Leribe) on 4 April 1920. His father was a schoolteacher. In 1934, after his primary studies at Mmamathe near Teyateyaneng, he went to the Morija Teacher Training College. After graduating, he first taught in Roma, where Mocoancoeng was also teaching, and later transferred to the Maseru High School. It was at this time that he published *'Musa Pelo*. In 1947 he left for London, to attend courses on the teaching of English. Sometime after his return, he gave up teaching and entered the civil service. In the mid-sixties, he tried to follow a course in journalism in Kitwe (Zambia), but was obliged to interrupt it because of ill health. In the early fifties, he produced a novel, *Masoabi, ngoan'a Mosotho 'a kajeno (Masoabi, a Modern Sotho Child* [1952]) and a book for juvenile readers, *Bana ba Roma* (1954), both printed in Morija. His more recent works are two short novels, *Mahumane (Titbits* [1961]) and

Nna Saejane Kobeloa C.E.D. (I, Sergeant Kobeloa [1963]), which appeared in Johannesburg. He also authored a Southern Sotho version of *The Merchant of Venice.*

In his poetry, Ntsane followed the example set by Bereng and Selane in handling subject matter that has nothing to do with praise poetry. This was found significant by a Sotho reviewer who saw fit to note that the volume contains "poems on trains and journeys to work from Basutoland, poems on rivers like the Caledon, on villages like Matsieng, the home of the paramount chiefs of Basutoland, poems on the Basotho soldiers in the recent war. There are also poems on such subjects as evening, sleep, love." [97] Two poems at least provide a picture of the hardships of life and advise the reader to seek comfort in the thought of the second advent of Christ. It seems, too, that Ntsane was the first to use rhyme fairly extensively, although Bereng had occasionally resorted to this European device, which does not appear to be very suitable for Bantu languages. But more important is Ntsane's introduction of humorous and satirical elements into written Sotho poetry. In "Lumelisa Base" ("Greet the Boss") he describes in an ironic way the vain advantages to be gained by apparent (and deceptive) servility to the white "boss"; and in "Bo-khoona-Tsoana" (Black White-People"), "he holds to ridicule his fellow Africans who imitate the European way of living: their dress, their habits half-European, half-African, their language, their starvation which stands out as a sharp contrast to their 'smart' dressing, and above all the way in which they despise their own brethern." This kind of inspiration was a direct result of intensified contact between the Sotho and the white-dominated South African society.

A. J. Moloi, one of the more exacting among younger Sotho critics claims that Ntsane is "the best Southern Sotho poet," an assertion for which he gives the following reasons:

His poetry covers a wide range of subjects: his soul's longing, his highest thoughts and intense feeling about the civilization of his nation and the improvement of his people's lot, his love for nature's beauty, his admiration for and experience about the outside world in general, are revealed in a lively language. His imagery is rich, varied and meaningful because figures of speech have been employed to bring, as near as possible to the reader, the essential qualities of his subject matter. The reader always feels that Ntsane has some experience or some exciting idea, thought or feeling to share with him. To accomplish this, Ntsane employs European techniques of writing poetry, but these do not affect the spirit of his message because he couples them with a thorough knowledge of, and insight into the structure and idiom of Southern Sotho. Rhyming and division into stanzas are regarded as a means to an end and not an end in itself. It is for this reason that the music of the lines flows naturally and does not sound artificial to the ear. There is always a definite balance between content and form i.e. the contents seem to control the tone of the poem, its rhythmic pattern, the length of the verses and the general grouping of sense units.[98]

Moloi favorably contrasts Ntsane's organic and functional manipulation of Western techniques with the mechanical imitation characteristic of most Sotho poets writing under European influence. He finds that such authors as E. A. S. Lesoro and J. J. Moiloa exhibit an unfortunate tendency to concentrate on formal values, regardless of their adaptation to meaning: they force European metrical patterns and stanza forms on their verses, and they are apt to belabor their imagery in an overly ornamental way. Nevertheless, the field of poetic subject matter was further enlarged when J. K. Ratau published a long narrative poem, *Khirimpana* (Morija, 1955) whose title hero goes to the gold mines of Johannesburg and to the diamond mines of Kimberley to secure the bride wealth that will enable him to get married. Although few subjects could be more "modern"—to the point, it must be admitted, of triteness—Ratau has handled it in the rhythmic style of the traditional praise poem.[99]

Prose fiction has inevitably remained the most widely practiced genre, but even here the process of discovery and innovation was at work. Whereas in the early decades of the century the short story had been a mere adaptation of traditional tales focusing on historical experiences and hunting adventures, short stories of a modern type—illustrating moments of crisis in contemporary experience—began to appear. And the spread of literacy as contradistinguished from education, coupled with the spreading of the secular outlook, led to the need for reading designed for entertainment rather than edification. In 1954 Sotho literature was enriched with its first thriller, a genre that was not to emerge in such other places as the Swahili coast and Eastern Nigeria until the sixties. It was Mackenzie Ntsala's *Sekhukhumi se bonoa ke sebatalali (A Man Is Seen in His Hiding-Place by Someone Who Does Not Hide)*, which was printed in Johannesburg. It tells how two men,

Pitsa and Senare, commit a murder; unbeknownst to them, the crime has been witnessed by one Khabeli. When the murder is discovered, the local headman summons his diviner, but the latter has been bribed by the murderers and points out Khabeli as the culprit. Fortunately, Khabeli's cousin calls on the European police just before the execution. The police investigation brings the real murderers to light. The plot is elementary, and there is no attempt at character depiction, but, as a Sotho critic has noted, "the author has succeeded in eliminating all things that do not contribute to the development of the plot; consequently the story moves rapidly and the reader's interest is captured to the end." [100]

The underlying theme of any detective novel is of course justice and the restoration of law and order. It is significant that although the main purpose of Ntsala's book is anecdotal entertainment, its underlying attitude is based on a repudiation of traditional justice characterized by the evil influence of the sorcerer over the headman, and on admiration for the honesty and efficiency of the white police. This is highly different both from Mqhayi's vindication of customary law procedure and from Sekese's condemnation of feudal abuses in chiefly courts; nor do we find here any hint of the more disreputable police methods evinced many years before by Enoch Guma in *U-Nomalizo*. Ntsala's story follows the orthodox line defined by South African authorities.

At the same time as the new genres, new themes were introduced into Southern Sotho creative writing. As is usual in modern African literatures, thematic range extends into two main directions: the reappraisal of traditional identity, and the discussion of the acculturation problems raised by Western impact.

In the literate society now emerging in Lesotho, historical prose fiction has taken up one of the main functions of oral lore; namely, to preserve the memory of the tribal past and of the high deeds that give the nation its sense of pride and dignity. This important trend is illustrated in the work of several novelists. Gabriel Manyeli, a prominent Catholic and a secondary-school teacher was born in 1901. In 1958 he founded the conservative Basutoland National party with the present prime minister, Chief Leabua Jonathan; he later became assistant speaker in the Lesotho House of Representatives. In 1954 he published *Liapola tsa Gauda (The*

Golden Apples), a novel dealing with the tribal wars of the past. The same theme was handled in *Tsoana-Makhulo (The Black One of the Pastures* [Mazenod, cyclostyled, 1964]) by L. E. Mahloane, who also published essays about Shakespeare *(Lipale tsa Shakespeare* [Johannesburg, n.d.]) and a Sotho version of *Romeo and Juliet* (Mazenod, cyclostyled, 1964).

As was to be expected, the life and times of Moshoeshoe have provided considerable inspiration, as exemplified in *Phakoanatsooana (Small White Hawk* [Mazenod, cyclostyled, 1964]), by Mofolo's Catholic-bred son Thomas T. Mofolo, or in James Machobane's historical novel, *Senate Shoeshoe 'a Moshoeshoe (Senate, Moshoeshoe's Flower),* or again in *Morena oa Thaba (Chief of the Mountain* [Mazenod, 1961]) by Simon Majara, who was born in Thaba-Bosiu in 1924, and in *Moshweshwe moshwaila (Moshoeshoe the Razor),* a historical drama published in 1965 by Mopeli-Paulus, who will be considered later. Pius Joseph Hlelele, who is an ordained Catholic priest, has written a tragic drama about Chaka's brother, *Dingane* (Mazenod, cyclostyled, 1965). Dr. S. M. Guma's historical novels go farther back in time and contain a genuine imaginative analysis of the factors that have governed the evolution of the political systems of the Sotho and kindred tribes. *Morena Mohlomi, mor 'a Monyane (Chief Mohlomi, Son of Monyane* [1960]), shows how a once unified tribe could split over a matter of customary belief: "Dibabatso, chief Monaheng's first wife remains childless for a considerable period. At last, with the aid of a Pedi witchdoctor, she conceives and bears twins. According to Kwena custom one of the twins has to be killed," but as a part of the tribe disagrees with this custom, they "break away from Monaheng in protest and go to stay at a new place." [101] In *Tsehlana tseo tsa Basia (Those Light-Colored Basia Girls* [Pietermaritzburg, 1962]), Guma describes how the survival and unity of the Tlokwa tribe was preserved by two clever and courageous women in times of unrest and warfare aggravated by the premature death of the chiefs.

Already during the first decade of the century, Thomas Mofolo had managed to weave Sotho myths and allegedly pagan beliefs into the basically Christian pattern of his novels. We have no means as yet of deciding whether later Sotho writers were influenced in this direction by the concept of negritude which spread from Paris in the late forties and early fifties. Senghor, it will be remembered, had insisted on the positive spiritual value of what goes by the name of ancestor cult. This is the subject of one of the three stories brought together by C. R. Moikangoa in *Sebologi sa Ntsoana-tsatsi* (*The Sentinel of Ntsoana-Tsatsi* [Mazenod, 1943]). Moikangoa, who was born in 1880, was one of the first two African inspectors of Native Education in South Africa. He retired in 1948,[102] and he died about 1951. The story in question almost reads like a deliberate vindication and revaluation of the ancestor cult: 'Maphunye, the title heroine, has been marked by the ancestral spirits as their own, and she is called to their dwelling-place, Ntsoana-Tsatsi, which Mofolo had made the abode of God in *Moeti oa bochabela*, and which is considered the original home of the Sotho people. There 'Maphunye stays for six days. She meets her grandparents, relatives, and other dead friends, and the ancestral spirits confer healing powers upon her. On the seventh day, she returns to earth, where she settles down to her mission of curing the sick and instructing the people into the mysteries of the ancestors' world. It is likely that this tale was composed much earlier than the date of publication. Indeed, the story that gives the volume its title was rewarded with a second prize in the first May Esther Bedford competition in 1935.[103] 'Maphunye, therefore, may perhaps be considered one of the earliest literary reflections of educated Africans' persistent adherence to the so-called pagan cult of ancestors. By far the best example, however, of the re-creation of ancient myths in modern writing is S. M. Mofokeng's *Senkatana*, which will be discussed more fully later.

The increasing encroachments of modern civilization have prompted quite a few contemporary Sotho writers to cast nostalgic glances at the more idyllic or picturesque facets of tribal life. Their purpose is partly antiquarian—to preserve the memory of fast vanishing customs and institutions—and partly educational—to instill into the minds of younger readers, brought up according to the newfangled ways, proper respect for the past and for the identity of their nation. This is the case, for example, with *Mossongoa* (Mazenod) by J. I. F. Tjokosela. Born about 1911, Tjokosela is a prolific Catholic writer and a teacher at St. Joseph's Training College in Maseru. He brought up to date the *Histori ea Basotho* (1965) of Father F. Laydevant (1878-1954). *Mossongoa* describes the life of a pagan girl, with particular emphasis on courtship and marriage customs.

Although considerable stress is laid on the bucolic facets of tribal life, its less attractive aspects are by no means ignored. As is well-known, witchcraft is still widely practiced in black Africa, and large numbers of Africans, even among the better educated, still believe in it. The fact that witchcraft is universally condemned in imaginative writing should not lead to inferences about the actual mores and beliefs of African societies. On the contrary, the literary uses of magic and sorcery should be considered part of the writers' attempt to change the prevailing outlook. In *Chaka*, we remember, the witch doctor Isanusi was presented as the embodiment of the inner forces of evil in the Zulu conqueror. In contemporary Sotho literature, witchcraft is more crudely exposed as the central evil in the old way of life. This is exemplified in Twentyman M. Mofokeng's *Sek'ona sa joala (A Calabash of Beer* [Morija, 1939]) the first formal drama by a Sotho author, which Letele summed up as follows:

A marriage contract has been entered into by Seobi on behalf of his son, Phephei, and Lefaisa on behalf of his daughter Kenewoe. Phephei has been away and has not met the girl he is to marry. Just about the time of his return from Sekhooeng a quarrel arises between Seobi and Lefaisa due to the fact that Lefaisa, for no apparent reason, upsets the drinking-vessel (*sek'ona*) in Seobi's hand just as he is about to drink beer out of it. Seobi takes a serious view of this, especially when Lefaisa refuses to give any reason for his action. The engagement is thus broken. This is the state of affairs when Phephei reaches home. When his sister and mother try to expostulate with Seobi, Phephei is turned out of the house. He leaves home ostensibly to return to the mines, but actually in order to find time to disguise himself as a witch-doctor and return to his people so as to probe the mystery of the *Sek'ona sa joala.* For many days he lives under the same roof as his fiancée who, however, does not recognise him: she is, nevertheless, much attracted to him, and he lends her manuscripts of his. Meanwhile his investigations lead him to suspect Morongoe, a minor wife of Seobi. Disguised as a doctor, Phephei is able to terrorise her into confessing that she had poisoned the beer Seobi was about to drink when Lefaisa knocked it out of his hands. Her motive in this attempted murder, she says, was to spite his other wife whom he loved more than he loved her. The mystery thus solved, Phephei brings together the parties concerned to the reconciliation,

after which he invites them to dinner. At this dinner he appears undisguised, and this ending is virtually the re-engagement of Phephei to
Kenewoe.[104]

The implausibilities of the plot will be obvious, but the interest
of the play lies rather in the attitudes of the various characters.
The central antithesis is between the old and the young. As Letele
further notes, "the place in which the drama is enacted is a Sotho
village of the modern type, in touch with western ideas and modes
of living." Phephei is a writer, Kenewoe has been to a training college. "Both the chief characters are enlightened enough to find it
difficult to accept unquestioningly all the beliefs and customs of
their people." It is equally evident, however, that the real human
problem the story could have encompassed, has been evaded:
Phephei falls in love with the girl his father originally intended him
to marry—a fairly frequent and highly revealing situation in African writing—so that there is no conflict between the old, author-
itarian family view of marriage and the new individualistic conception of love. But while it stretches credibility beyond all proper
bounds, and although it is generally unsatisfactory from the dramatic point of view, Mofokeng's play nevertheless deserves to be
considered a landmark in the history of Southern Sotho literature.
Here, indeed, the approach is no longer religious but secular; the
tension is no longer between Christian faith and morality and
Bantu heathenism. It is between behavior inspired by irrational
customs and superstitions, and the rational conduct of the educated
young. This is the approach that was, at the time, exemplified with
infinitely greater subtlety in Jordan's Xhosa masterpiece.

The most gruesome aspect of Sotho sorcery was undoubtedly
the ritual murder. It was widely believed that a most potent medicine could be concocted out of the blood of a living human victim, who was subsequently murdered. It happened that on the
death of Paramount Chief Seeiso Griffith in 1940, his father's senior
wife, 'Mantšebo, was appointed regent. The evicted pretender,
Griffith's eldest son, Bereng, tried to wrest power from her, first by
legal means and, when these did not avail, by resorting to medicine
murders. He was tried for this and executed in 1949. Meanwhile,
his example had been followed by some lesser chiefs who felt their
authority threatened under the new measures taken by the British
authorities:

After the reforms in chieftainship and native courts became effective in 1945, the incidence of such *diretlo* ritual or "medicine" murders increased to almost epidemic proportions. Between 1895 and 1938, only twenty-three suspected "medicine murders" had been reported. Between 1938 and 1950 there were seventy, and of these thirty occurred in the two years 1947 and 1948. There can be no doubt that a large number of lesser chiefs, bitter about official non-recognition or fearful of being deposed, resorted to "medicine murder" to reinforce or restore their position and prestige through magic.[105]

Not only was an inquiry set up by the British but these events became highly topical and inspired such works as *Liretlo (Ritual Murder* [Bloemfontein, 1950]), by A. S. Mopeli-Paulus, who will be discussed at greater length later, or *Katiba* (Mazenod, 3d ed., 1964), a very popular drama by a Catholic writer, Sylvanus Matlosa, who was born at Mafeteng on 25 December 1915 and who now teaches at the Masitise Secondary School (Quthing).

Turning now to the literary reverberations of the Western impact upon African societies, we find that, here as elsewhere, the theme of love has assumed an importance that it did not have either in oral art or in early writing. As we noticed in connection with T. M. Mofokeng's play and with several Xhosa works, the issues are seldom clear-cut. Many of those works follow the same pattern. Whereas family authority seems to be challenged at the beginning of the story, it is usually vindicated at the end, when the young heroes, who have been married without even being consulted, finally fall in love with each other, thus condoning an outside decision that had been previously presented in an unfavorable light.

This pattern can be observed in *Mosali eo u'neileng eena (The Wife You Gave Me* [Morija, 1954]) a play by Lesotho's first woman writer, Ntseliseng 'Masechele Khaketla. The heroine, Tseleng, is an orphan girl who lives with her uncle. She is hated and ill treated by the latter's wife who, out of malice, has her married to a dumb herdboy called Sootho, an ex-serviceman suffering from amnesia as a result of war injuries. Before the war, he was a minister of religion. Soon after the marriage, he becomes severely ill but, on recovering, regains memory and speech. Man and wife then leave Lesotho and return to the young man's original home in the Transvaal, where he settles down as a minister, and they live happily ever after. However lurid, the situation is not without literary parallels. S. M. Mofokeng[106] in his review mentions James Hilton's *Random Harvest*, and one might add William Faulkner's *Soldier's Pay*, supposing Mrs. Khaketla had access to this. But the main defect of the play, as the Sotho critic observes, is that "the story is not acted, it is presented to the audience as hearsay. Throughout the book the reader—or audience—learns of the leading characters from the conversation between Thato (Tseleng's friend) and her mother. The real characters of the drama are never seen in action." That this technique is reminiscent of European neoclassical drama in its early stage in the mid-sixteenth century is, of course, not due to "influence," but to the similarity in situation. In contrast with folk drama, formal or literary drama in its incipient phase often derives from straightforward narrative and merely adapts the latter's technique to stage conditions: events are not enacted on the stage, but reported by various characters. The objections directed at Mrs. Khaketla's play are the same as those to which such an early Renaissance tragedy as *Gorboduc* is exposed.

One theme that has suffered comparative neglect at the hands of Sotho writers is the obsessive preoccupation of a large fraction of Xhosa and, as we shall see, Zulu literature: the theme of African life in the seedy suburbs of industrial cities. The reason for this is that Lesotho has had both the privilege and the disadvantage of remaining immune to industrialization and urbanization. As was observed in connection with Segoete's novel, town life is a foreign and transitory experience. Nowadays, it is of serious concern only to those Sotho writers who live in the Republic. For others, it is superseded, as a literary motif, by the very acute problem of migrant labor. The first author of any significance to have dealt with this is Albert Nqheku in *Arola 'naheng ea Maburu* (*Arola in the Country of the Afrikaners* [Mazenod, 1942]). The book tells the story of a lad who goes to earn his livelihood on Boer farms. It was highly successful and went through five printings. It is of some interest to quote the extremely cautious appraisal of this book provided in 1968 in a South African journal:

Nqheku portrays friction between the Boers and a young Mosotho who apparently knows very little about the Afrikaner in the Free State. In fact, Nqheku has chosen extremists from both the Sotho as well as the Afrikaner groups. Arola leaves Lesotho to seek employment in the Free

State. On his arrival there, he comes across some of the most cruel and unfriendly farmers. A terrible clash between himself and the farmers develops. He is badly assaulted and as a result of this, Arola becomes extremely hostile towards the Boers. In the hands of people with an unbalanced mind, this book may easily cause strained relationships between these two racial groups.[107]

In 1959 Nqheku completed his imaginative survey of exiled workers with *Tsielala (Silence, Please!)*, which describes the life of the Sotho miners on the Rand. As long as Lesotho could relax in its protected status as a High Commission Territory, a few exceptional writers like Nqheku could afford to be fairly outspoken in their critique of race relations inside South Africa. The ending of *Molahlehi (The Lost One* [1946]), by Sylvanus Matlosa, who was born on 25 December 1915, is significant in this respect. The title character is lured into leaving college before completing his course by the attraction of the city; he goes to Johannesburg with a few of his friends. They mix with young delinquents and start living dissolute lives. The purpose of the book is clearly to emphasize the importance of formal education and the dangers of city life for the benefit of young readers, but after a number of misadventures, Molahlehi is killed by a white man over a fowl that he is alleged to have stolen. Now that Lesotho has become an independent kingdom at the mercy of the overwhelming power—economic and otherwise—of the Republic, this mildly belligerent trend is likely to be discontinued in favor of purely edifying, less controversial issues.

This has always applied, of course, to Sotho authors living and publishing in South Africa. A typical example is a play by Mocoancoeng, which was printed together with a few poems on various subjects, *Tseleng ea bophelo le lithothokiso tse ncha (The Path of Life, and New Poems* [Johannesburg, 1947]).[108] The play takes place in a native township in the Orange Free State; the characters are a teacher and a nice girl, who at first are happily married. Soon, however, the husband abandons the path of virtue. The inevitable *deus ex machina* intervenes in the shape of an accident caused by his drunkenness. This traumatic experience makes him aware of his guilt, and he returns to his earlier unobjectionable way of life.

But even among Sotho writers who are citizens of Lesotho and whose work is printed in their own country, the outlook tends to be unswervingly ethical, with complete disregard for the social, economic, and racial factors involved. The first two novels of Simon Majara, who was born in Thaba-Bosiu in 1924, are cases in point. In 'Makotulo (Mazenod, 1955), the title heroine is a frivo-lous and dissatisfied young female, who deserts her husband in the hope of finding excitement and opulence as a prostitute in the Union. The hero of O sentse linako (He Wasted His Time [Mazenod, 1955]) is a boy endowed with strong proclivities to truancy; his well-to-do father wants him to get the best education money can buy. Already at primary school, the boy seeks the com-pany of other disreputable little fellows, in spite of the severe floggings with which his escapades are rewarded. His opportunity for escape comes when he is sent to high school. He runs away to the Union in the hope of finding employment that will supply him with the required money for enjoying life thoroughly. His low educational level, however, entitles him only to the humblest and lowest-paid types of work. In his misery, he realizes that his lust for the pleasures of town life has led him astray from education, which is the only way to genuine happiness. But when he wants to go back to high school, he finds that he has passed the legal age for enrolling. Here, obviously, the city-life theme is merely incidental, and the author's main purpose is to stress the need for education, as Xhosa writers had done in the last decade of the nineteenth cen-tury.

The various innovations in genres and themes are exemplified in the work of the three best-known writers to have emerged in Southern Sotho literature since the end of World War II: A. S. Mopeli-Paulus, B. M. Khaketla, and S. M. Mofokeng.

Atwell Sidwell Mopeli-Paulus was born in 1913 at Witzieshoek, a Sotho native reserve in the Orange Free State. He was educated at Edendale (Natal) and at the Witwatersrand University, where he studied medicine for some time. He holds a certificate as an art teacher in non-European schools. During World War II he served with the Cape Corps and saw active service in East Africa and Egypt. After the war, he settled in Johannesburg, where he was employed in a law office. His best-known work is a long poem on the sinking of the troopship Mendi in World War I, when 600 Africans were drowned en route to France. He is the author of several books in Southern Sotho, such as a collection of poems,

Ho tsamaea ke ho bona: lithothokiso (*To Travel Is to See: Poems* [Morija, 1945]), *Liretlo* (*Ritual Murder* [Bloemfontein, 1950]), and a short story, "Lilahloane oa batho" ("The Poor Lilahloane" [Bloemfontein, 1950]). More important, he is the only Sotho writer part of whose work was originally printed in English in the form of two regular full-size novels, *Blanket Boy's Moon* (London, 1953) and *Turn to the Dark* (London, 1956), which were told by him and penned in English by Peter Lanham and Miriam Basner respectively.

Blanket Boy's Moon tells the adventurous life story of a Sotho man of the present day, and tackles many of the problems that face the African in a period of acculturation. The hero, Monare, is the son of one of the soldiers who died when the *Mendi* was shipwrecked. He is a Christian, but he is also an ambitious man, fascinated by the glittering thought of the South African metropolis and by the stories "of money to be made, of sights to be seen, and of the many strange races of the White Man who lived in the city built around the mine dumps" (p. 29). He obtains the chief's permission to go to Johannesburg. His experiences there, however multifarious, are mostly unpleasant or evil. He feels the impact of racial prejudice; he is robbed of his money by *tsotsis;* unwittingly, he buys stolen goods and is arrested; he relinquishes his religious habits; he falls into drunkenness, and although he is married, he allows himself to fall in love with Mary, the daughter of a Bantu minister. When he has managed to save enough money, he returns to Lesotho. For several years, he lives happily, prosperous and respected, but he is as unable to withstand the claims of tribalism as he had been unable to resist the temptations of modern life. In spite of the opposition of the parish clergyman, he has his son Libe circumcised. And later, he overrules the objections of his own conscience, and he obeys the chief who has ordered him to participate in a ritual murder to be perpetrated on the person of one of his own friends. Filled with shame for his deed, and with fear of being captured by the police, Monare returns to Johannesburg. This is the moral nadir in his life story: he tries to seduce Mary, and might have succeeded had it not been for the intervention of his son, who also comes to the Rand and who is in love with the girl too. In his frustration, Monare finds forgetfulness in dagga smoking, and sexual relief in homosexuality. Still fearful of the police, he then seeks shelter in Durban, where he works as a longshoreman. He is there at the time of the riots of 1949, when numerous Indians were massacred by the Zulu under the benign eye of the South African police. During the disturbances, Monare saves the life of an Indian Muslim, Abdul Hamid, who, in his gratitude, helps him cross the border into Mozambique. One day, however, Monare hears of a mining disaster on the Rand, where his son is one of the victims. He travels back to Johannesburg, to learn that his son's life has been saved by a white overseer. But Monare himself is caught by the police for his participation in the ritual murder two years earlier. The chief, who is a courageous man for all his barbarism, claims sole responsibility for the bloody deed, but Monare is nevertheless condemned to death.

The story of Monare, very simply told, but carefully constructed, enables the author to touch on most of the problems of South African society, and it is a grim picture that arises from the novel, even though one reviewer saw fit to describe it as "charming" and "delightful." [109] The root of the matter is formulated in the thoughts of the minister to whom Monare has confessed his participation in the murder:

How terrible it is to be born a Mosotho. To have the white man's religion, and yet to have the customs of the land as they had been before the coming of the missionaries. It would have been better to live in Lesotho a hundred years ago, or to have been born a hundred years hence. To live in these in-between times is difficult. (P. 107)

Monare too grows more and more lucidly aware of this predicament: "The Basotho people were forced to live in two worlds—the tribal world—ruled by the witch doctors, the chiefs, and by custom; and the white man's world governed by the white man's law" (p. 110). And when he is imprisoned for murder, he exclaims: "Better might it have been for our forefathers to have fallen on the soldiers of the white man and killed them, or themselves been killed! Had events thus fallen out, to-day we should have been enslaved by white men, or enslaved by Chiefs—but not by both!" (p. 289).

The extreme example of the conflicts wrought by this dual allegiance is connected of course with the ritual murder. This was of topical interest at the time, and the psychosocial process involved is explained to Monare by the clergyman. In 1944, he says, the

chiefs had agreed to the creation of a National Treasury fed by
taxes and from which they received a regular salary; the taxes were
henceforth imposed by the District Courts and no longer by the
chiefs. The result was that the population conceived greater respect for the courts, which wielded actual power, than for the
chiefs, who had "exchanged their birthright for a mess of potage"
(p. 293). Consequently, the only means they found to restore their
authority was the time-honored custom of *liretlo*: "Never in
Lesotho's history have so many Ritual Murders been ordered, as in
the past five years—since the Chiefs have been made as oxen!" (p.
293). But it appears that in spite of the decline in the chiefs' actual
power, and in spite of the influence of Christian morality, "the
respect of a Mosotho for his Chief is greater even than that which
he has for his father" (p. 304). Monare's participation in the crime
is the outcome of an inner conflict and of a decision to which a
number of Sotho people must have been exposed in the forties and
the early fifties.

Considerable emphasis is laid, throughout the novel, on the sex
problem created by interplay of three factors: traditional mores,
Christian morality, and the demands of South African industrial
society. Monare's having his son circumcised in spite of missionary
hostility is a reflection of the actual hold that custom has over
people. Mqhayi's autobiography shows that even among educated
Christians the old notion persists that no boy can become truly a
man unless he has undergone the tribal ritual of circumcision. But
the author also has some interesting comments on female circumcision (an apology for which had been produced earlier by Jomo
Kenyatta in *Facing Mount Kenya*), its rationale, and its effects in
the new circumstances of city life: "The performance of this
rite," he says, "tends to encourage chastity among the women, for
a circumcised girl can know little of the joys and passions of
physical love. . . . Lying with a woman, then, becomes a selfish,
rather than a mutual pleasure. Here in the very homeland, in this
circumcision of women, lie the seeds of the physical love of man
for man, which is brought to flower by the living conditions imposed on African mine workers by the white man" (p. 93). Since
no provision is made by the mines to accommodate the migrant
worker's family, he is inevitably driven to extramarital release of
sexual impulses. Mopeli-Paulus shows us his hero living in de-

bauchery, attempting adultery, yielding to homosexuality. When his son Libe leaves for the Rand in his turn, "to earn money to buy clothes and blankets and ornaments for his future bride" (p. 95), he warns him against the dangers of prostitution and venereal disease, advising him to turn rather to "the friendship of the hand" (p. 95).

Apart from those problems of private conduct, the book also discusses issues of wider importance, such as the value of Christianity for the South African Bantu. As Monare reaches Johannesburg for the first time, he is struck by the contradiction between Christian doctrine and the white Christians' behavior: "I have listened to their [the missionaries] praising of the white man's God. They say that before him all men are as equal. Yet not only do they forbid me to enter their churches, but they will not allow me to sit next to them in the trains or buses or bioscopes" (p. 35). A further source of puzzlement is the bitter fighting among the Christian denominations: "Here amongst us Africans we have the witch doctors and their followers, then the Catholics and the Methodists, also the Salvation Army and the Apostolics, the Blue Cross people and Jehovah's witnesses—and each calls the others liars and fights with them!" (p. 310). Which is why he eagerly turns to Islam, observing: "It seems a great pity that their [the Muslim] missionaries did not come to Lesotho rather than the Christians. For I see that in their religion is the dignity of man upheld, no matter how lowly may be his task in life. Amongst them seems to exist a freedom and a unity which Lesotho badly needs." (p. 310).

Perhaps the most surprising feature of the book is its undisguised admiration for the Portuguese colonization system and its description of Mozambique as "that paradise for the African with both will and desire to rise" (p. 256):

He learned that in the country of the Portuguese there was much freedom for the brown, yellow and black peoples. He found that his Indian friends could enter any shop or hotel or train that was open to the white man; the people of mixed race, known in Mozambique as the "mulattos," were also allowed the same privilege. To his even greater amazement, he was told that Africans, too, could rise to enjoy this same equality, provided that they were judged to be—after examination by the Portuguese—ready for "assimilation." As far as the Mosotho could judge, the qualifications required for assimilation were that an

African must read, write and speak simple Portuguese, that he must possess steady work, that he must live in a respectable quarter, and that he must have adopted the more hygienic habits and customs of the white man in respect of living and dressing. (P. 237)

This may seem less unexpected if we remember that the book was composed in the early fifties, at a time when African endeavor was not yet primarily directed toward political power, but toward human recognition.

The peculiarities involved in the writing and the publication of *Blanket Boy's Moon* make it impossible to decide how far it can be considered truly representative of Sotho writing. We have no means of knowing what amplifications, clarifications, or other transformations Peter Lanham may or may not have brought to the story as originally told by Mopeli-Paulus. As the book was first published in London and New York, and not in South Africa, the authors could afford to be more outspoken in their critique of South African society than could vernacular writers. The work obviously has more in common with English fiction by African writers from the Union, and with Xhosa and Zulu works printed before the apartheid system solidified in the late forties, than with anything published in Southern Sotho. As an objective depiction of Sotho life in South Africa, *Blanket Boy's Moon* is a most impressive work, which has been translated into at least four European languages, and which should certainly be reprinted.

Turn to the Dark, written in collaboration with Miriam Basner (London, 1956), does not range as widely as does the previous novel. Instead of taking within its scope the multifarious typical experiences that can occur to a black South African, it takes place entirely in Lesotho and focuses on ritual murder. The hero is a literate young man, but he has taken part in a student rebellion against the college authorities.[110] Lesiba is expelled from school and settles in his village, much to the chagrin of his father, who is a minister of the church. The psychology of Lesiba is analyzed with great care. He is highly critical of what is euphemistically called Bantu "education":

It's all religion and agriculture. They expect us to listen to more prayers and hymns than white children. And they make us spend hours cultivating their land. What white children have to dig the garden as part of their education? No wonder so many of us fail our examinations with such poor teaching. No wonder it is easy for white people to say it is we who are inferior to them, and will be, for ever and ever. (P. 23)

What drives Lesiba to rebellion and return to his people is a desperate hankering for recognition of his human identity: "Our people may be barbarians, but they speak to one another with respect" (p. 23). This deliberate turning back to traditional life and values, which may owe something to the new ideologies of negritude and the "African personality," makes him a rather exceptional character in Sotho and even in the whole of Bantu South African literature. Most of the time, the educated young man is presented as eager to help his own people on their path to modernization, or —in fiction written in English—as eager to subvert South African apartheid society. Lesiba's peculiarity is probably due to the fact that this is one of the few novels in English by an author and with a hero who still have very strong tribal attachments. The result at first is a revaluation of tribal culture, somewhat along the lines of the upholders of negritude in French West Africa. Lesiba comes back full of hope to his native land and is eager to integrate into customary life. He decides to attend the circumcision school in spite of his father's overt displeasure. And he is perfectly happy when Chief Johannes selects him as his secretary and trusted adviser.

But Mopeli-Paulus's purpose is not to extol the alleged values of traditional society, it is to explore the tragic dilemma of the African today. While Lesiba rejoices in his insertion into the organic harmony of simple village life, he also becomes involved in its concomitant ugly aspects, and it is his very devotion to the chief that will cause his downfall. In the eyes of the headman, the new laws, the droughts, the government measures for land preservation, are as many trends in the pattern of decline of his power, privileges, and prestige. A well meaning but illiterate man, he finds no way out of his puzzlement but to consult the witch doctor, with the approval of Lesiba, who is full of rash pride in his renewed identification with the tribe. The witch doctor, in his turn, hails this golden opportunity for reviving his own waning prestige. He recommends that the chief's main attribute, the Medicine Horn, be "refreshed" with the blood of a human victim. For all his reluctance and disgust, Lesiba feels he owes it to himself as well as to the chief and the tribe to act his part in the ritual murder.

Lesiba's is a truly tragic fate, in the sense that he is punished for a crime, the responsibility for which lies in the inherent antinomies of these "in-between times." In his imaginative reassessment of the two cultures that contend for the young man's loyalty, Mopeli-Paulus shows his full awareness that modern Christian education in South Africa today cannot be separated from humiliating exposure to racial prejudice and from spiritual solitude and alienation. Lesiba's father is an example of this. In his deep Christian piety, he has espoused the white man's misconception of many harmless or even beneficent beliefs and customs to which his people want to remain true. Likewise, tribal life is not wholly defined by the idyllic harmony that had been nostalgically celebrated by Segoete some forty years earlier; it is not all dance and tom-toms and clan solidarity. It also includes asinine superstitions and boundless cruelty. Like Jordan's Xhosa novel, Mopeli-Paulus's works illustrate the sense of tragedy and the despair characteristic of a phase in African history which has now been outgrown in many parts of the continent. It is their exceptional distinction that they managed to fuse into unified imaginative wholes contradictory approaches that other writers had, somewhat facilely, kept apart. They do not clamor for instant modernization of the African psyche. Nor do they advocate a wholesale return to a bucolic past that never was. Like such West African writers as Chinua Achebe or Cyprian Ekwensi, Mopeli-Paulus has been able to bring into focus the central dilemma facing Africa and its tragic meaning for the African.

While Mopeli-Paulus lives in the Republic of South Africa, the most important writer at work today in Lesotho is Bennett Makalo Khaketla,[111] born in 1913 into a peasant family in the district of Qacha's Nek. After qualifying as a teacher locally, he studied privately and obtained a B.A. degree in political science and the Sotho language from the University of South Africa. He first worked as a typist, but in 1946, he was appointed to the Basutoland High School in Maseru. He had married in January 1946, and his wife, Ntseliseng 'Masechele Khaketla, was to become, as we have seen, the first woman writer in Lesotho.

It was during that period that Khaketla composed *Moshoeshoe le baruti (Moshoeshoe and the Missionaries* [Morija, 1947]), a drama that is little more than a sequence of historical events presented in the form of dialogues.[112] It deals with the arrival of the French missionaries in Lesotho. According to J. M. Lenake, "the theme is again a clash between the traditional and Christian ways of life among the Sotho. We also get a vivid picture of the warfare and violence which reigned in that period." [113]

After being dismissed because of a reduction in staff at the Maseru high school in 1949, Khatekla worked briefly for the British administration in Lesotho, then left for the Union, where he resumed his teaching activities. During those years, he wrote his first novel, *Meokho ea Thabo (Tears of Joy* [1951]), which was printed in Johannesburg, as were to be all his later works. The hero of the story is one Moeketsi, whose father dies when he is still young. He is sent to the Mariazell Institution, a Catholic training college that had been founded by the Mariannhill missionary society in 1909. While being trained as a teacher, he falls in love with a girl from Matatiele. But his uncle, who is acting as his guardian, will have none of such a marriage. According to custom, he intends Moeketsi to marry a girl of the family's choosing. The boy adamantly refuses to submit and leaves for Durban where he works to earn his livelihood. In time, he forgets the girl from Matatiele, and falls in love with a girl called Fumane from Lesotho. He returns home with her in the hope of mollifying his uncle. The latter, however, remains steadfast in his sense of family discipline. Things clear up when it appears that the girl Moeketsi's uncle had chosen for his nephew is none other than Fumane. The Sotho critic who reviewed the book for *African Studies*[114] was very hard on the novel where, he claimed, all the emphasis is on the plot, while there is no depth of idea and the character analysis is superficial. Miss Beuchat, too, finds that Fumane "is convincing as a character only for the first part of the novel. Her rapid acceptance of the new life she meets for the first time in Durban, her immediate and startling integration into it, does not fit what we know of her: a nice, submissive, fairly well-educated girl, but not a sophisticated person. Suddenly, she becomes as much of a 'town person' as any of those who have lived in a big city all their lives. Abruptly she becomes very determined to act as she wants to, not as her family wants. The change is too sudden to be acceptable, and Fumane becomes unreal." [115] Finally, "the ending after the final crisis is quick, but is rather of the farce type, for the crisis is solved through a happy coincidence and not through the doings of the characters." But Miss Beuchat also cogently points out that Khaketla brings in a new aspect of acculturation which had been neglected by Sotho authors, although Jordan and others had handled it in Xhosa: "having love as a side line to the main theme is a new feature and not yet exploited in any Southern Sotho novel." This she finds of especial significance, for whereas in early Sotho writing "the westernization manifests itself mainly through religion," in this novel it appears in "the younger generation wanting to be free to act as it likes." [116] Equally significant is the fact that Khaketla, unlike Jordan, but like most African writers treating the marriage theme, does not face the issue squarely. One feels that few vernacular authors are yet prepared to probe the ultimate depths of the inner conflicts wrought by acculturation. Somehow or other they manage to reconcile, in a usually rather implausible way, the antagonistic claims of traditional family authority and modern individualistic impulse.

In 1952 Khaketla returned home. This was the year when the Basutoland African Congress was founded as the first modern nationalist party, which was to inagurate the awakening of political consciousness in Lesotho. While he was turning to politics, Khaketla wrote two further works, both of which were printed in 1954. *Tholoana tsa sethepu (The Fruits of Polygamy)* is a better drama than *Moshoeshoe le baruti*, in that it has, according to Miss Beuchat, "a very interesting and powerful climax." The same critic points out, however, that "the conclusion following the climax is too long, and the reader . . . loses interest." [117] The other book is a collection of poems entitled *Lipshamate*. It is of peculiar interest because of its thirty-eight page Preface, where Khaketla discusses some of the technical problems with which modern Sotho (and indeed modern Bantu) poetry has to grapple. Strangely enough, he blames Bereng and Lerotholi on the grounds that their work lacks rhythm. The reason is, as S. M. Mofokeng was to explain in his review,[118] "that the author's ideas are based primarily on English poetry," so that the kind of rhythm he favors "is the exception rather than the rule in Southern Sotho, and it is not surprising that the author finds its absence a weakness common to most of the poets." The Sotho critic dryly observed that Khaketla does not carry out his own requirements in his poetry: "Except for the subject-matter, his poems have taken the form of the very praise-poems which he finds deficient in feeling and to a certain extent in rhythm. Nor is this surprising because the form of the praise-poem is an indigenous one that comes naturally and that has stood the test." And Mofokeng concludes with the hope that Khaketla, "in his future attempts can rid himself of some of the ideas expressed in his preface and just rely on his instinctive feeling for what is good Sotho poetry."

A. J. Moloi reached the same conclusion in 1969.[119] Khaketla's verse, he says, "will not seem artificial if European metrical patterns are not forced on them. He is on the right path because he is conscious of the essential aspects of poetry." Even though the poet "intended modernizing Southern Sotho poetry by attempting to employ metre as understood in European languages, he did not allow outward forms to govern his poetry." After pointing out that "like Ntsane's poetry, Khaketla's covers a wide field: his philosophy of life, personal experience, nature and natural phenomena, moral lessons, great personalities, elegies, satires, etc.," the critic emphasizes the strongly and often aggressively nationalistic approach that differentiates Khaketla's work from most Southern Sotho poetry. This is exemplified in a poem entitled "Lesotho," where the country is described in traditional imagery as "the strong and youthful girl who loved Moshesh / [and who] now is a temptation in the heart of the Boer":

> Hybrid cow with the heavy udder,
> nations may despise you and in scorn
> say you are no hybrid but a weakling beast,
> but we who own you ever will sing your praise:
> Our first love, you who fill our calabashes up with milk,
> often we milk you and you brim our pail.[120]

In his bitterness at racial discrimination and oppression, Khaketla joins the rank of some of the Xhosa and Zulu poets in the Union. For example, Moloi points to the similarity in motif between Vilakazi's Zulu poem "NgePhasika" ("On Easter"), and Khaketla's "Morena Marena" ("Chief Marena"). Both writers contrast the meekness, patience, and humility of Christ with the arrogance of the white man in southern Africa. We may add that "Ntwa ya Jeremane" (1914), a poem on World War I, is reminiscent of Jolobe's Xhosa poem "To the Fallen." Both writers denounce the white man's failure to fulfill the promises he had made to encourage African soldiers to fight for him. And a poem to commemorate the Italo-Ethiopian war, "Ntwa ya Abisinia" illustrates a sense of Pan-African solidarity not often to be found among vernacular writers.

Not unexpectedly, Khaketla was becoming deeply involved in political activities. In 1955 the Basutoland African Congress sponsored the publication of *Mohlabani* (*The Warrior*) under his editorship. The first issue of the paper marked the beginning of the agitational phase of the Sotho nationalist movement. It argued for equal pay irrespective of race in the civil service and advocated drastic constitutional reforms. It also stressed the importance of education and the state's responsibility for it. As a result of its attempt to politicize the Teachers' Association, the BAC came into conflict with the local Catholic church. In spite of his editorial activity, Khaketla had not yet joined the BAC, reputedly because he objected to its then multiracial outlook. In 1958, however, he was elected its deputy leader, and kept the position when the association changed its name to Basutoland Congress party. In that same year, he produced his third drama, *Bulane*, which was to be followed, in 1960, by his second novel, *Mosali a nkhola* ("*What a Calamity that Woman Has Brought Upon Me*").

The first elections held in Lesotho in January 1960 led to the victory of the BCP. Khaketla was elected to the legislative council; on 12 March, he was elected a member of the Executive Council, with responsibility for Health and Education. But dissensions soon arose in the BCP and on 29 December 1960, Khaketla resigned from the party. He was later to claim that he had done so because the party sought "to interfere with my religious freedom and dictate how I should worship." [121] According to other reports, however, he disagreed with the extreme agitational methods advocated by the party.[122] In April 1961, Khaketla, together with some other ex-Congress members, launched a new party, the Basutoland Freedom party, which revealed itself as a conservative force, both in terms of the pace towards independence and of the proposed powers to be exercised by the paramount chief as head of the state. In January 1963, when a merger was arranged between the BFP and Chief Matete's conservative Marema-Tlou party, Khaketla became the vice-president of the new movement. In

1964 the secretary general, Dr. Seth Makotoka, attended the Addis
Ababa Conference of heads of African states as an observer and
presented a memorandum on behalf of the party, appealing to the
participants not to forget Lesotho and its unfortunate situation.
This displeased the more conservative members of the party and
precipitated a split in 1964. Dr. Matotoka gained control of the
party and was elected president, but although Khaketla remained
a member of the new executive committee, he declined renomina-
tion as vice-president. In the elections of April 1965, he ran as an
independent candidate, and lost. He was subsequently appointed
chairman of the university's senate and a member of King Moshoeshoe II's Privy Council.

Although Khaketla is the most important author inside Lesotho,
the best writer of Southern Sotho to have emerged since Mofolo
is also the first to have received full university training. His position, therefore, is equivalent to that of Jordan in Xhosa. Like
Mopeli-Paulus, he was a native of South Africa. Sophonia Machebe
Mofokeng [123] was born on 1 April 1923 near Fouriesburg (Orange
Free State). He was educated at the local Dutch Reformed church
primary school, the Stofberggedenkskool, and at the Adams Mission High School, Natal, where he matriculated in 1939 with distinctions in Southern Sotho and botany. From 1940 to 1942, he
studied at Fort Hare, where he obtained a diploma in education
and a B.A. degree with distinction in Southern Sotho. He entered
the teaching profession at the Johannesburg Bantu High School
while registering as a part-time student in the University of the
Witwatersrand for a B.A. Honors degree in history. In 1944 he
was appointed a part-time language assistant in the Department of
Bantu Studies. He completed his historical studies at the end of
that year, thus becoming the first African B.A. Honors graduate
in history of that university. In 1945 he was appointed full-time
junior language assistant and started reading for a B.A. Honors in
Bantu languages. This was awarded him in March 1947. In August
1947, barely a few months after his promotion to the rank of language assistant in Sotho, he was admitted to hospital with tuberculosis in both lungs, and underwent drastic treatment for eighteen
months. In January 1949, he was able to resume his duties, and
began working on his dissertation, "A Study of Folktales in Sotho,"
for which he was awarded an M.A. degree in 1951.

The following year, his first book, *Senkatana,* was published by the Witwatersrand University Press in their Bantu Treasury Series. This book, much of which had been written in hospital, deals with a popular Sotho legend that Mofolo had already used in *Moeti oa bochabela,* the story, says Miss Beuchat, "of the many-headed monster which swallows all the people and cattle of the country, and which is slain by the prodigious and insatiable youngster Senkatana. Mofokeng has been able to translate the old tale into a new idiom which is alive and convincing, he has transformed something of the past into something suitable for the present. . . . One is faced with a play which will remain a great work even when Bantu written literature has fully developed." [124]

Mofokeng's second book, *Leetong (On the Way),* much of which was also written in hospital, is the first collection of genuine modern-type short stories in Southern Sotho; it was published in 1954 by the Afrikaanse Pers-Boekhandel. About the same time, another volume of essays, *Pelong ea ka (In My Heart)* was accepted for the Bantu Treasury Series. In 1954, his outstanding abilities and the quality of his literary achievement so far were rewarded with his promotion to the rank of senior language assistant. And in March 1955, Mofokeng was awarded a Ph.D. degree for his thesis on "The Development of Leading Figures in Animal Tales in Africa." He was the first recipient of this degree from the University of the Witwatersrand. Meanwhile, he had been collaborating with Professor Doke in the preparation of a *Textbook of Southern Sotho Grammar.* Mofokeng, however, had never fully recovered from his illness, and he died on 6 June 1957 after several weeks in hospital.

Mofokeng's death was a major loss for literature in Southern Sotho. He was undoubtedly the most widely cultured of the Sotho writers, and at the same time, the most articulate in the language and the traditional myths of his people. It is a matter of observable fact that the availability of a full-scale university training is the main factor of qualitative improvement in African literature. There are exceptions, of course, such as Thomas Mofolo or Amos Tutuola in Nigeria or J. J. Rabearivelo in Madagascar. But throughout the continent, the men who brought modern literature —whether in European or vernacular languages—up to a level where it can compete with the other literatures of the world, were

usually among the first university graduates: men such as Leopold
S. Senghor, Chinua Achebe, Archibald C. Jordan, or James Ngugi.
Sophonia M. Mofokeng clearly belonged in this category.

A significant development in the literature of Lesotho is the
appearance, in 1968, of the first work of creative fiction composed
in English by a Sotho writer. *Masilo's Adventures and Other Stories* is a collection of traditional tales designed as a school reader by
B. L. Leshoai.

Benjamin Letholoa Leshoai was born in Bloemfontein (Orange
Free State) on 1 July 1920. After getting his teacher's certificate
at Healdtown Missionary Institution in 1944, he studied at Fort
Hare, where in 1947 he obtained a B.A. degree in English and
Native Administration. He then taught English at a high school in
Pretoria and was appointed headmaster in 1957. He resigned in
1960 because of a clash with the Department of Bantu Education
on a matter of principle. He went to Johannesburg, and because of
his keen interest in drama, he became assistant manager of the
Union Artists, promoters of the famous jazz operetta *King Kong*.
In 1963 he migrated to Zambia and taught English in Ndola. After
a one-year stay in the United States, where he obtained an M.A.
degree in Speech and Theater from the University of Illinois, he
returned to Zambia in 1965, as lecturer in English at the Mufulira
Teachers' College. In 1968 he left for Tanzania, as lecturer at the
Department of Theatre Arts of the University College in Dar es
Salaam.[125]

As missionaries and travelers used to do when they adapted
African folktales for a Western audience, Leshoai has wrought
significant changes into his material. Not only does he introduce
natural descriptions that are necessary to make the foreign reader
familiar with the African setting, but he also often distorts the
original meanings in order to curb them to the more conventional
Western type of school morality. An example is his rendering of
the Senkatana story, a favorite among Sotho legends, which had
been dramatized by Sophonia M. Mofokeng, and, at an earlier
date, incorporated by Mofolo into *Moeti oa bochabela*.

As a piece of folklore, the story was first recorded by Jacottet
in his two-volume *Litšomo tsa Basotho* (*Myths and Legends of
the Sotho*), which was printed in Morija in 1909 and 1911. Two
other versions have been published recently and translated by S.

M. Guma,[126] who points out that the young hero who released his people from the stomach of the monster that had swallowed them was turned into a Christ figure at an early stage in the process of evangelization:

There is an interesting analogy that some informants draw between the story of Senkatana and that of Christ. A few old men in the Roma valley of Lesotho insist on it. According to them, the snake in the garden of Eden is the Kgodumodumo, which they also equate with sin; the sole woman survivor who bore Senkatana, is the Virgin Mary, and Senkatana himself, the slayer of the Kgodumodumo, i.e., sin, is Jesus Christ.[127]

This sort of comment aptly illustrates the ease with which the new religion and the traditional beliefs managed to coalesce in Sotho thinking; yet, it is not reflected either in the recorded oral texts or in Leshoai's rendering. Indeed, except for the descriptive elaboration of natural scenery and of battle scenes, Leshoai remains true to the basic pattern of the story, as least up to a point.

For the tale has two other features that account for the equating of Senkatana with Christ: sometime after his victory over the monster, the Sotho redeemer was killed by the very people he had rescued, apparently with his own consent, and when he died, his heart escaped from his body, suggesting that he did not really die. Leshoai has altogether left off this ending, which is loaded with religious meaning; he has replaced it by the conventional happy denouement characteristic of European pseudo-folktales arranged *ad usum delphini:*

Senkatana was a very wise ruler and his subjects loved and respected him. His bravery and fame spread to many lands beyond the boundaries of Lesotho. And thus ends the story.

There is something deeply symbolic of Africa's complex predicament in Leshoai's turning to the Senkatana tale for inspiration and in the way he has manipulated it. In the first place, his resorting to English is a portent of the widening that is taking place in the somewhat parochial Sotho outlook as a result of educational progress and political independence. He is the first Sotho writer to feel the need to address an international audience directly, and thus to be faced with the crucial dilemma of many African writers today. The example of French-speaking Africa and of Nigeria shows that many African authors are endowed with the rare gift of expressing themselves satisfactorily in a foreign tongue. In all likelihood, the trend initiated by Leshoai will spread as more Sotho writers acquire sufficient mastery of the English language to use it for their own literary purposes. While this will enable them to bring the cultural legacy and the particular problems of their nation to the knowledge of the outside world, it may cut them off from the grass-root experience of their own people, as was the case with many Francophonic writers until quite recently.[128] Further, one may doubt whether it is possible, except in the rarest of cases, for a creative writer to express his inspiration as fully in a foreign language as he would be able to do in his mother tongue.

Also characteristic is the fact that this first English composition deals with the popular lore of myth and legend. Guma recently pointed out that "the yearning for the retention of traditional values, some of which are being replaced by undesirable modern features, is a note that comes up again and again in Sotho literature." [129] Actually, this is typical of modern writing throughout Africa: Birago Diop in Sénégal, Benjamin Matip in Cameroun, Joseph Brahim Seid in Chad, Djibril Tamsir Niane in Guinea, Amos Tutuola in Nigeria, were among the early founders of modern literature in their respective countries. They all devoted their talent to making the cultural legacy of their people available to the outside world in worldwide languages. More comparative research is needed to determine what happens to the material in the course of this transfer from oral to written art, from one tongue to another, and from a local to an international audience. As already pointed out, Leshoai's rendering of the Senkatana story shows that the modern author—whether he be black or white—is compelled to add much additional matter. He must convey information about the natural setting, about local customs, about fighting styles, and the like, which the native listener of oral tales takes for granted. The fact that Leshoai has felt it desirable to maim the ending utterly is indicative of the almost insuperable difficulties that the modern writer encounters in addressing a foreign audience. The full import of the Senkatana legend is hardly intelligible outside the total context of Sotho culture. Mofokeng was able to convey its tragic and heroic message in his mother tongue. Using a Western language, Leshoai has not been able to withstand the temptation of making the story more accessible to the English reader by inserting it into the hackneyed optimistic tradition of European fairy tales.

The future evolution of Southern Sotho literature will be worth watching at least in three respects. First, Leshoai has just laid the cornerstone for a Sotho literature in English, thus starting a trend that had been initiated in the Union by Tswana writer Sol T. Plaatje and had been observable among the Zulu since the late 1920s. Lesotho is joining the ranks of African countries whose literature is bilingual. This process, which has long been at work in British West Africa, has spread on a large scale to East Africa in recent years and is even making some slight headway in Ethiopia. It will be of considerable interest to compare the contributions that authors from so widely different cultures will make to the vast corpus of English literature.

Second, the University of Lesotho, Botswana, and Swaziland in Roma is likely to become an important cultural center and a meeting place for intellectuals with entirely distinct backgrounds. As Halpern points out,

There is no common patriotism shared by the Swazi, the Batswana, and the Basuto, though the latter two peoples are related, and even Basuto students, isolated in their little mountain enclave, understandably prefer to study overseas. But overseas study is expensive, and once the Territories' bottleneck in secondary education is broken, it is doubtful whether even the Americans—or the Russians—will offer enough scholarships to accommodate all aspirants. There should thus be an important role for Roma to play in the future of all three Territories.[130]

This is true specifically in the field of literature. Whereas some amount of creative writing has been produced in Tswana since 1945, there does not seem to be any modern Swazi literature as yet. Contact with Lesotho may foster the emergence and the development of literary activity in the other two areas. On the other hand, the growth of the institution should modify and widen the mostly conservative and parochial outlook characteristic of the majority of Sotho writers today.

Finally, it will be enlightening to compare the literary evolution of the two segments of the Sotho people. While the very existence of the university at Roma will presumably make for literary improvement inside Lesotho, the qualitative growth initiated by

Mofokeng in South Africa may be stopped by the decline in higher education for the Bantu under the apartheid system. But the possibility should not be excluded that South African pressure may assign severe limits to the writers' freedom of expression inside Lesotho. Indeed, it is perhaps not excessive to think that literary developments in the small Drakensberg kingdom will provide an index of the measure of genuine independence that Lesotho can really manage to maintain.

Writing of the growth of vernacular literature in South Africa, G. P. Lestrade observed, in the early thirties, that Southern Sotho and Xhosa were "the two languages that have shown most development in this direction; in the other languages, though there has been some production, the amount is small compared to that in Xhosa and Southern Sotho." [1] The backwardness of the Zulu in this respect had already struck Alice Werner, who had remarked, slightly earlier, that "Natal has not, as yet, produced native writers to anything like the same extent as the Cape Province." [2] Nor is this surprising when account is taken of the history of Zululand in the nineteenth and early twentieth centuries.

The Zulu were just one of the numerous small Nguni groups that had spread over the area now known as Natal, until Chaka undertook to wrest power from the then dominant tribes, the Mthethwa and the Ndwandwe. Chaka's Napoleonic career has already been told, but at this point, it is necessary to emphasize that he "was not content that the conquered tribes should become tributary, but determined that they should become integrated with the Zulu tribe." [3] This purpose was achieved through a military organization that was based on age groups and cut across tribal affiliations. By 1824 Chaka had established a mighty state, which his immediate successors, Dingane (d. 1840) and Mpande (d. 1872) managed to maintain and consolidate. It is true that British traders had appeared at the place later called Durban al-

181

ready under Chaka, but they were few in number and were interested in business only, although by the middle of the century a
handful of American missionaries had secured a foothold in the
neighborhood of Durban. It is also true that from the days of the
Great Trek (1837) the Boers had represented a permanent threat
to Zululand as they had to Lesotho, but the British had formally
recognized the independence of Zululand in 1832 and again in
1842, when the Natal-Zululand boundary had been clearly defined.
It was not until the annexation of the Boer Republic of Transvaal
to the British crown in 1877, that Boer and British interests combined to conquer Zululand. A beginning was made under Cetshwayo (d. 1884) in 1879, but the country was not annexed until
1887, when the new king, Dinizulu (d. 1913) was banished to St.
Helena. When he was allowed to return from exile, it was no
longer as paramount chief, but as head of a local tribe. Yet, European domination was not firmly and finally established over Zulu
territory until 1906 when the white authorities crushed the rebellion led by chieftain Bambata in response to seizure of Zulu land
by Europeans and to the imposition of a poll tax at a time of extreme poverty.

Consequently, missionary activity, which is of crucial importance to the introduction of writing and the formation of a written
literature, began about half a century later among the Zulu than it
did among the Xhosa. And although the early missionaries in the
Natal colony were as outspoken champions of the natives as were
their opposite numbers in Xhosaland and in Lesotho, the acknowledged independence of Zululand until 1879, and the existence of
an officially recognized boundary between that country and the
British-occupied area of Natal, combined with the Zulu's strong
sense of national identity and dignity, proved powerful obstacles
to the usual modernizing impact of the missionaries. Only a few
Natal Zulu had access to the new civilization and its skills before
the rebellion of 1906.

The language was reduced to writing at an early stage of European contact.[4] The first publications in Zulu—extracts from the
Scriptures translated by Newton Adams, a pioneer of the American
Board of Missions in Natal—appeared in 1846 and 1847. They were
followed by a steady flow of similar works by missionaries of various denominations and nationalities.[5] In 1855 the Anglican Bishop
John Colenso's *Elementary Grammar of the Zulu Kafir Language*

appeared almost at the same time as Perrin's *Kafir-English Dic-
tionary of the Zulu Kafir Language as Spoken by the Tribes of the
Colony of Natal*, and these were only the first of a fast-increasing
number of linguistic works. A translation of *Pilgrim's Progress*
was printed in Natal in 1895; it was the work of J. K. Lorimer, who
had been helped by a native Zulu speaker named Benjamin Zidoke.[6]
But it was not until 1922 that the first original work by a Zulu
author reached print. As C. L. S. Nyembezi cogently observed,
"The grammars and dictionaries were not mainly intended for
the Africans but for the missionaries themselves. They were intended to help new missionaries in the field to master as quickly as
possible the language of the people among whom they were to
work. . . . The Zulu, quite naturally, could not be expected to
make any significant contribution during the early period, and the
twentieth century was well in before Bantu writers began to take
a hand in the development of their literature." [7]

Those historical circumstances account for the peculiarities in
the birth and growth of creative writing in Zulu. But the delay
does not signify that literary activity was altogether absent.
While their sense of national greatness prompted the Zulu to fight
against the encroachment both of Western colonialism and Western civilization most stubbornly and much longer than was the
case with the Xhosa and the Sotho, it was also a powerful incentive to traditional oral composition, especially in the form of
izibongo in honor of the tribe and its leaders. Indeed, most Zulu
kings of the nineteenth century have kept such prestige to this day,
that their praises are still very much alive in folk memory. The
names of the most respected bards, such as Chaka's praiser Magolwane, or his successor Mshongweni, have been preserved,[8] and it
has actually been possible to do genuine scientific research on the
historical development of the Zulu praise poem since the mid-
eighteenth century.[9] This creative oral tradition was still flourishing in the recent past. In 1938, B. W. Vilakazi signaled that the
court poet of King Nkayishana (who was also known as Solomon
or Maphumzana, and who died in 1933) was "still living and has
composed in the same vein as the bards of the 19th Century. The
only difference is that the symbols used involve some modern concepts of life and western conditions, but they rest on the background of the Zulu heroic age." [10] And in 1945, the same critic
mentioned, among the more prominent Zulu poets, one A. H.

kaMeseni, who, he claimed, "occupies the same literary position in poetry as Mqhayi among the Xhosa. Meseni has composed more poetry than many other Zulu poets put together, but hitherto he has not put his work into publication." [11]

Transition: Isaiah Shembe

While oral composition remained the sole medium of literary expression among the Zulu well into the twentieth century, there nevertheless occurred one of those transitional phenomena of which the hymns of Ntsikana had been an illustration among the Xhosa. Only it came almost exactly a century later. Isaiah Shembe was born in the late 1860s.[12] According to his biographers, he was the illiterate son of a farm laborer. Like Ntsikana, he did not attend school and had little contact with the white man during his youth. It is, however, significant of the evolution of the minds during the intervening hundred years that while Ntsikana died advising his disciples to attend the missionaries' school, Shembe openly gloried in the fact that he had not been polluted by the white man's formal education. In one of his most important sermons, he addressed the missionaries as follows, speaking of himself in the third person:

If you had taught him in your schools, you would have had a chance of boasting over him. But God, in order to reveal His wisdom, sent this Shembe, who is a child, that he may speak as a wise and educated man.[13]

At an early age, Shembe evinced the qualities of a seer and soon became renowned as a healer. At an unspecified date, he came in touch with the Baptist mission that had been active in Natal since 1892. Again like Ntsikana, he had supernatural experiences in which Jehovah called him and ordered him to relinquish the immoral, polygamous practices that he shared with his people. He was baptized in 1906 by the Reverend Leshaga, a minister of the African Native Baptist church.[14] Gerhardus C. Oosthuizen claims that Shembe was most probably attracted to this particular church "because of its indigenous character, its literalism in Biblical exposition and the importance attached to baptism." Immediately after his baptism, as he was himself ordained a minister and started traveling "by foot or oxwagon in Natal, very seldom by bus or train, keeping himself busy in driving out demons, giving people

holy water as a way of healing or purification, preaching inspired
by 'the Spirit,' and in rain making. He preached under the open
skies, in kraals and alongside water pools." [15]

Unlike Ntsikana, however, Shembe grew disillusioned with orthodox Christianity, which, he found, was lax in the observance of
Saturday, the Old Testament Sabbath, the true day of the Lord. In
1911, therefore, he seceded from the African Baptist church[16] and
soon founded his own church, "iBandla lamaNazaretha," the
Church of the Nazarites. The reference was not to Nazareth in
Galilee. In 1913 Shembe visited Nhlangakazi, which became his
holy mountain, and in 1914, or, according to Bengt Sundkler,[17] in
1916, he founded his holy city, the new Nazareth, Ekuphakameni,
about 18 miles from Durban, in the vicinity of the school set up a
few years earlier in Ohlange by another prominent Zulu leader
who will be discussed at a later stage, John L. Dube. After his death
on 2 May 1935, the leadership of the church was taken over by his
son, Johannes Galilee Shembe, who had been born in 1904 and had
been trained as a teacher at the University College of Fort Hare.
But Isaiah Shembe is alleged to have risen from the dead in May
1939.

Shembe's church is of the Ethiopic kind, being both messianic
and nationalistic. Its nationalism is not Bantu, but specifically Zulu:
the Zulu people could not be redeemed but by a Zulu Messiah.
Indeed, in the teaching of Shembe, there was hardly any mention
of Christ, although both the Father and the Holy Ghost were
acknowledged.[18] The Zulu Messiah is Shembe, and in later years,
the adherents of the sect even came increasingly to believe that the
prophet was God himself.

Although Shembe was the greatest religious leader in South
Africa, his was by no means the first of the numberless independent
churches that have seceded from the orthodox mission churches.
Nxele's peculiar Xhosa brand of Christianity, born from internecine tribal rivalries as well as from the will to resist European
encroachment, was an early pointer. In 1884 an independent
Tembu church separated from the Methodist mission church, and
in 1898 a number of Fingo in Xhosaland left the United Free
Church of Scotland to form their own Christian community, while
the Xhosa themselves remained loyal.[19] It has been claimed, especially by Sundkler, that two central motives are responsible for
this Balkanization of African Christendom: the widespread black

revulsion against color-bar policies, and the denominationalism inherent in the Protestant outlook. Although the former is undoubtedly an important contributing factor, in the case of Shembe's Nazarite church, it does not seem as if "anti-white feelings were predominantly responsible for the formation of the movement." [20] Denominationalism is undoubtedly more important, especially when it is viewed as a formalization of Protestant insistence on every man's personal and direct relation to the divinity and on his right to his own interpretation of God's message. Seen from this angle, the African churches are simply the logical outcome of the African's claim to the right to interpret the Bible as he understands it within the peculiarities of his own cultural context. Although the Nazareth Baptist church had as many interdictions as the missionaries' orthodox Christianity, its appeal was primarily to the Zulu's pride in their own cultural identity. Not only was this gratified by the appearance of a black redeemer, but Shembe restored a number of customs that had been dismissed or condemned by the European missionaries although the Zulu were deeply attached to them. Traditional dances were reintroduced into religious worship. Polygamy was again accepted as a harmless and, indeed, economically and biologically indispensable part of customary society. In church ceremonies, particular respect was paid to the chiefs, whose authority, although despised by the white man, was the very backbone of traditional society. It is now generally admitted that the dissident churches of Africa result from an attempt by the African people to establish their own relationship with the Christian God introduced by the white missionaries—an attempt made necessary by the lack of understanding and the contempt evinced by the latter toward culture traits to which the Africans remain legitimately attached.

Such deviations from Western Christian orthodoxy lead to original forms of worship which have their significance for the literary history of the peoples concerned. As should be clear by now, religious poetry has been one of the earliest literary products of cultural crossbreeding in Africa as it was in the European Middle Ages. In Zulu many orthodox hymnals are of course in existence: Lutheran, Anglican, Methodist, and—most popular of all—the American Mission Board hymnbook, *Amagama okuhlabelela*, an early version of which was already in print in 1897.[21] The latter

occupied a special position in orthodox hymn-writing because of
the taste and talent evinced by Charlotte B. Grout in her selection
of English hymns for Zulu translation. She made skillful use of
repetition, which is the basis of rhythm, and she may have been
responsible for the introduction of rhyme into Zulu poetry. Her
example was successfully followed by two native writer-
composers, who contributed several songs to the hymnal: the
Reverend P. J. Gumede, says Vilakazi, "used the same style as Miss
Grout. There is a melancholy tone in his music as well as in his
versification, and his song [no. 264] ranks among the best in the
book." The other Zulu writer involved was Ngazane Luthuli, who,
in 1938, was the editor of *Ilanga laseNatal*. According to the same
critic, "Luthuli, though himself a better musician, does not show
Gumede's brilliancy in hymns. His musical taste is very high, but
it does not shine in the hymns." Vilakazi added in 1938, that "after
these two there is a great break, up to now. The field of hymns
seems to be dead. The example which was set by American Board
missionaries was not rivalled by other bodies. Even at this present
time it seems impossible to publish hymns originally composed by
the Bantu." The Zulu critic ascribes this decline to the way poetry
was taught in the developing system of Bantu education in the late
twenties and early thirties:

Even when most of the Zulus had gone through some appreciable
standard of education, those who have studied the system of Native
Education up to about 1930 in Natal and Zululand, will agree with me
that students were not introduced to the spirit of poetry. The only
poetry, which they could recite like parrots, was English. . . . The
result was disastrous because we cultivated a dislike for poetry in general. . . . Such a system of education, I presume, is largely responsible
for the lack of continuation of the work begun by Gumede and Luthuli, who themselves may have even forgotten what they did for the
beginning of a new era of poetry. . . . There was implanted in the
Native mind that to be educated was to assimilate European standards
without gradual absorption or discrimination. Not until lately, when
the educational standard was raised, did the Zulus feel the responsibility
they had for their culture. They began to look back to the *izibongo*.
This looking back was also greatly influenced by Stuart's Zulu books.
In these books there are many poems recorded, and they have done a
lot of good in laying the foundation for inspiration to many of the
budding poets.[22]

Most of the Zulu hymns, therefore, are the work of literate, mission-trained Africans. They are of comparatively late origin and are more or less successful translations or adaptations of European or American hymns. Among the Zulu, orthodox Christianity does not seem to have fostered anything like the amount of hymn-writing that was done in Xhosa at a much earlier date. They mostly indulge in what Sundkler calls "the foreign prefabricated stuff with its cheap verse-making." According to the same writer, even among separatist churches, for want of their own African hymns, the practice is to sing "Bible verses to some well-known Zulu tune. The leader intones the first words and the members of the congregation follow suit, all at the same time moving their bodies to the dancing rhythm of the tune." [23] There is reason to expect, as a matter of a priori principle, that the hymns produced by the independent churches are bound to exhibit greater originality than the orthodox type, to represent a different combination of western and traditional techniques, and a more original blending of Christian and indigenous beliefs. It is in his hymnal poetry that Shembe makes his unique contribution to Zulu literary history.

The hymns of Isaiah Shembe—together with a number composed by his son—were not printed in book form until 1940, under the title *Izihlabelelo zaNazarethe (Hymns of the Nazarites)*, a collection that, Sundkler claims, is "easily the most important source-book that we have for the emergence of Bantu syncretism in the independent Churches." [24] But a few of them were composed at a very early date and may well be the earliest Zulu literary products of the Western impact. "The first hymn," says Oosthuizen, "was sung by children with whom [Shembe] came to Natal in 1910; the second hymn came in 1913 as he started to ascend Nhlangakazi. According to the preface no hymns were composed from 1914 to 1919. But from 1920 he wrote much and started to write also the Morning, Evening and Sabbath prayers." [25] In all, Shembe probably composed the first 219 hymns in the volume. A few others, however, raise problems of authorship with which few literary historians have been privileged to cope, since some of them (differing in the various editions) are alleged to have been composed by the prophet after he had risen from the dead! [26]

Accounts of Shembe's method of composition are far from clear. The first hymn, in which the old Zulu religion and Jehovah are brought together, was almost certainly composed orally and should

perhaps be considered the earliest original poem composed in Zulu
under the impact of the new civilization. Although Shembe had
no formal schooling, it would seem that he did learn how to write
at some point in his career. But he was, Sundkler says, "deeply conscious that his hymns were inspired." [27] Sundkler reports a statement by Shembe's son to the effect that the prophet "sometimes
had auditions of a girl's voice singing the hymn, and immediately
after the audition he would write it down." The result is that his
hymns "have a freshness and immediacy born out of deep religious
experience."

Nazarite poetry has been studied fairly extensively for its ideological significance, and it seems possible to trace a distinct evolution in the prophet's development. The earlier poems "show often
spiritual depth" and are chiefly inspired by the Scriptures. The
latter part of the hymnbook, which begins about 1926, "is often
interspersed with nationalistic and dance songs in which [Shembe]
refers to his supernatural birth, his call and to himself as their
Liberator. . . . The continuous emphasis in this section on his person, on him as the Liberator, on Ekuphakameni, on Nhlangakazi,
on the Sabbath, on the book of life, on judgment, on the nation affects the spiritual depth of many of these *Izihlabelelo*. This is also
the case with the dance songs. In spite of this, the *Izihlabelelo* in
general carry with them deep concern and sincerity." [28] Yet, there
is an undeniable organic link between the two parts and their various aspects, however heterogeneous they may seem to the Western
mind. For what Shembe found in Christianity was a way to re-
vitalize traditional Zulu religion with new, more universal, beliefs.
The Hebrew doctrine of an elect people could not but be a powerful incentive to black nationalism:

> To-day you are the laughing-stock
> of all the Nations.
> Africa, rise!
> and seek thy Saviour.
> To-day our sons and daughters
> are slaves.[29]

Further, dissatisfaction with the white paternalistic Christ-image
offered by the missionaries prompted Shembe—as it did many
others—to envision himself as the black Messiah, the redeemer of

the Zulu nation. Several hymns expressly describe his career as a
reenactment of Christ's messianic appointment:

> They came, the wise men,
> arriving from the East,
> saying: Where is He,
> who is the King of the Jews?
>
> *Chorus*: So it is also to-day
>   on the hill-tops of Ohlange.
>
> In no wise art thou least
> among the princes of Judah,
> for out of thee
> prophets shall come forth,
> who will save
> the city of Ohlange.
>
> *Chorus*: So it is also to-day
>   on the hill-tops of Ohlange.[30]

Indeed, Shembe's religion at times appears less a way of acclimatizing Christianity to the demands of the African mind, than an attempt to rejuvenate the traditional faith with the help of Christian
elements. That the Zulu were adherents of the true religion even
before Western Christianity was brought to them, is more than
suggested in hymn number 216:

> Rise up with us today
> on this morning
> even today
> oh! *Nkosi*
> That you be a journey
> to those who are journeying
> and even those who are staying,
> let it be so
> oh! *Nkosi*
> That you keep them
> in their staying
> on that day
> of today
> oh! *Nkosi*
> We are the progeny,
> of that root,

> we do not lack,
> we are with Sendzangakhona,
> oh! *Nkosi*
> We of long ago
> we have long been drinking
> at that fontain
> of Sendzangakhona,
> oh! *Nkosi*
> Shaka said we are not even beatable
> to you Mhlangana and Dingaan
> and yet to day it is even so
> to you Mhlangana and Dingaan,
> oh! Nkosi[31]

This doctrinal syncretism has its formal counterpart. Sundkler claims that introducing sacred dances into Christian worship was Shembe's innovation. "Some of the hymns," he points out, "expressly describe themselves as dance hymns:

> I shall dance, I have hope,
> I am a Nazarite girl.
> I do not fear anything
> because I am perfect.[32]

While dancing externalizes the worshiper's exultation at being one of the elect, it is also a tribute to God, as it was in Solomon's day:

> We dance before Thee,
> our King.
> By the strength
> of Thy kingdom.
> May our feet
> be made strong.
> Let us dance before Thee.
> Eternal.[33]

And Sundkler contends that some of the hymns "are in their whole structure nothing but Zulu dancing songs." [34] Shembe's contribution to the evolution of Zulu culture has been aptly summed up by Oosthuizen:

The Western liturgy transplanted *in toto* gave to Shembe, as well as to his followers, no satisfaction. The concreteness of expression in ritual did not find the necessary attention. Spontaneity and gaiety are characteristics of Zulu worship but the formalism of the denominations did not understand this. A new way of life had to be implanted by frustrating everything indigenous, and the extreme reaction is the consequence. Shembe came forward with his own expression of the new religion in dance, songs and hymns which contributed tremendously to the growth of his movement. Not the spoken but the sung word transfers the message, and Shembe understood this very well.[35]

A substantially similar explanation for the success of Shembe's brand of religion and religious composition was provided in 1938 by Vilakazi, but in the slightly contemptuous tone typical of the educated black African and orthodox Christian:

The Zionist movement, to which Shembe belonged, has greatly influenced the religious outlook of the Natives in town, and today has the largest numbers of Natives in Johannesburg locations alone. There seems to be a secret behind this. The followers of the Zionist movement have incorporated into their services most of the first-fruits ceremonial observances in the purification of priest or king, colourful dresses and community singing, mixed with dancing, consisting largely in rhythmical raising of the feet, thundering stamp upon the ground, and a series of grotesque shuffles, interspersed with vigorous leaps by the leaders of groups. This has an attraction for the average Native, and he eagerly supports such a movement, for he has an active part to play, besides the priest.[36]

Yet the main reason Vilakazi has little to say on Nazarite poetry is probably that only a few of the hymns had been published, in Dube's biography of the prophet, by the time he was doing his research. There is greater sympathy and cogency in the analysis supplied by a younger Zulu poet, one who, unlike Vilakazi, has a definite political commitment to the African cause. In his unpublished dissertation, Raymond Kunene defined as follows the originality and peculiar quality of the Shembe hymns viewed in the general context of Zulu poetry:

The Christian religion is, by its very nature, suitable for a people torn by life and harassed everywhere by cruel reality. It found a fertile soil in the hearts of all those whose minds had tired of the constant wars, who wanted peace and happiness. Moreover, it was offered by a stronger group that made life secure, at least physically. There were, however, mental conflicts which arose from the situation. For though the Chris-

tians found life safe and secure they could not escape the feeling that
they sheltered under foreign rule, and that amongst their people they
were despised and regarded as traitors. They were, in addition, still
dogged by their cultural background. The only solution for all this was
the solace offered by religion, the religion that talked of a better world
beyond this one of troubles. The wave of sentimentalism in poetry that
has up to now remained high, originates from such circumstances. . . .
It is this spirit that has nourished modern Zulu poetry. . . . Amongst
the Shembites, where Christianity is adapted to the traditional way of
life, religious poetry tends to have a universal moral outlook rather than
a sectional religious one.[37]

Kunene's appraisal of Shembe's hymns is illustrative of a general
trend among the best-educated Zulu poets: they tend to react
against slavish imitation of the European types of poetic inspiration and technique exemplified in school anthologies, and to seek
for a syncretic adaptation of traditional forms to modern experience.

Drama and the Secular Song

While Shembe's hymn of 1910 should be considered—until we
gain more knowledge—the first imaginative composition produced
in Zulu under Western influence, the earliest works to reach print
belonged, somewhat unexpectedly, to the dramatic genre. They
originated in 1920 at the Catholic mission, which had been directed
by the Trappist order at Mariannhill since 1882. As was to be the
case throughout black Africa, they were devised as an adjunct to
more traditional methods of education, taking advantage of what
a social worker in Natal, D. R. O. Thomas, was later to call "the
primal ability for drama . . . that the Native possesses, and . . . his
strong accompanying sense of rhythm and of group action." [38] In
1932 Thomas could look back on experiments at Kafubu in the then
Belgian Congo, and at the Kabete Jeanes School in Kenya. In that
very year, school drama in French was making a start in the Ivory
Coast before spreading to the William-Ponty school in Sénégal.[39]
But the earliest records of vernacular school drama by native authors that have been unearthed so far concern the performances
organized at Mariannhill by Fr. Bernard Huss, who was head of
the Teacher Training College there.[40]

On 2 and 3 October 1920, the inspector of education, Dr. C. T.

Loram, his wife, and ten teachers from Adams College, Ohlange, and a few other institutions, were entertained at Mariannhill, where the pupils performed nine short plays, mostly adapted by Huss from English plays. The purpose was primarily pedagogic; the plays were intended to provide dramatic illustrations of episodes in the Scripture or in South African history. Grade III boys staged a little drama that was an episode from the life of General Gordon. But other plays dealt more directly with African subject matter, sometimes as adaptations of folktales. Thanks to Dr. Loram, two of these were printed in the *Native Teachers' Journal* in 1921. The January issue contains one that, Huss says, "was staged by Francis Mkize, a boy of our Standard IV. It was tried, staged and criticized four times before it was played for our guests." The story had been written down in Zulu by Mkize, and a short dramatization was done by two second year normal students: this Zulu text, with its stage directions in English, cannot but call to mind the manuscripts of some twelfth-century vernacular European plays, with Latin didascaly. The April issue contains another play of different composition. It was first staged in English by Huss as a European story. On seeing it performed, the author recalls, "Dr. Loram suggested that it should be made to suit Native conditions. . . . Three Native Teachers, Mr. D. Wesley, Mr. T. Ngubane and Miss I. Nkosi, then changed it into what they thought would be Native conditions."

Zulu drama thus arose for the same reasons and following the same process as French African drama was to do a dozen years later in the Ivory Coast, when Charles Béart, the headmaster of the Ecole Primaire Supérieure of Bingerville became aware of the theatrical abilities of African schoolboys and decided to put them to educational uses. In both instances, the pattern was that of the commedia dell'arte, the written text acting as support for improvisation. Huss noted that "the Native players are often clever and witty enough to enrich the play from their own stock of humour." Indeed, if we are to rely on Vilakazi's article, the chief merit of those early plays lay in the liveliness of the dramatic performance:

The importance of these plays . . . lies not in the style in which they were written, for this is very poor indeed, but in the rapid dramatic effect with which the movement and change of scene drift on the stage. The producer had to rely, not only on the written version, but on his knowledge of animal lore, language and behavior.

Vilakazi further states that "because there was no interest in literary art and stage production, the dramatic art died in its infancy." It might perhaps be more accurate to say that it remained confined to schools. But the seeds were sown. From Huss's modest experiments in Mariannhill, school drama spread to Adams and, presumably, to some other institutions whose representatives had attended the Mariannhill performances of October 1920. And, as Vilakazi himself claims, "the importance of these plays lies in their later effect on the minds of the students as they left schools." This effect began to make itself felt in the late 1920s.

In 1929 one Esau Mtetwa organized a company of amateur actors known as Mtetwa's Lucky Stars.[41] On the death of the founder, the management was taken over by his brother Isaac. All the players had regular employment in Durban, and for several years took part in this new venture as a hobby, although the group was in regular demand for performances at hotels and socials in the Durban area. Dr. T. C. Lloyd has left an account of an occasion when two plays were performed near Durban. *Umthakathi (The Wizard)* starts as a satirical picture of a shrewish woman who refuses not only to prepare food for her husband but also to extend the usual hospitality to a stranger. The latter is in fact a sorcerer, and at night he reappears and casts an evil charm upon the daughter of the house, who soon becomes grievously ill. From that point on, the play turns to serious drama, based on the distinction between the evil magic of the sorcerer and the beneficent magic of a woman witch doctor *(isangoma)* who traces the trouble to its source. At the end, the villain is dragged off to stand trial before the chief. Magic plays an equally significant part in *Ukuqomisa (Love Scene)*: the hero first tries to coax the girl he loves into accepting his advances. After being rebuked, he resorts to the advice of a more experienced friend, who gives him a magic potion that will ensure him the girl's love. The charm works most satisfactorily, but the girl's elder sister enters and berates her for improper conduct in securing a lover before her turn comes. The girls' brother soon arrives and sides with the elder sister; so does another relative, and after some fighting the unfortunate lover is compelled to flee most unheroically from the scene.

It is obvious that, in contrast with Xhosa drama of the thirties, those Zulu performances kept close touch with Zulu grass-roots culture. There was no attempt to imitate formal European drama

or to dramatize Western ideas. The values are those of traditional
kraal life. Magic in its various forms efficiently controls human
behavior. Seniority is the basic principle of social hierarchies. As
Lloyd observed,

This new departure amongst the black races is valuable in presenting
to the public, scenes of native domestic life with a realism which would
be otherwise unobtainable. Such education of the white man is a necessary preliminary to the understanding of Bantu problems.

Lloyd also commented on the ex tempore element in the acting:

These plays are presented with a naivete which would be impossible
for the white man to imitate. The style of acting is much more free
than we have been accustomed to see on the more civilised stage. The
producer is an educated Zulu, but the players have only a rudimentary
knowledge of reading and writing. Consequently the parts are learned
by word of mouth and no strict adherence to the original wording is
insisted on. Sometimes one or two of the actors may be unable to attend
a performance. There are no understudies, so that the play goes on
with a slight rearrangement to suit the depleted numbers. This induces
a freshness and vigour of presentation which is a welcome relief from
the too conscious players of our own stage.

The Lucky Stars' renown spread in time throughout the Union
and, Vilakazi says, "their seasonal visits were occasions looked forward to by both Africans and Europeans in South African towns.
As for the European audience, lack of acquaintance with Zulu was
never a handicap, for every one could follow the whole play
through the facial expression and gesticulations so well portrayed
by all the actors."
   Their impact on Bantu drama was chiefly felt during the Empire
Exhibition held in Johannesburg in 1936. So far, African drama in
Johannesburg had been dominated, it would seem, by the "sophisticated" outlook of the Bantu Dramatic Society (see pp. 77–79),
which strove to imitate European theatrical productions. Vilakazi
claims that as a result of the appearance of the Zulu company, dramatic performances in the African townships of Johannesburg became more purely African and people began to understand the
values of real African themes." The "value of African themes,"
however, was not likely to be the same to all audiences. Even such
a well-informed and well-wishing spectator as Dr. Lloyd merely

concluded that the two plays just discussed "show to how great an extent the credulous native is at the mercy of the charlatan witch-doctor, or of any one else who possesses muti (magic). With true Zulu tradition, the author of these plays has adhered to the popular superstition of the infallibility of muti and witch-doctors. This superstition prevails through thick and thin, and the magic is consequently victorious in each case." But it is likely that the native audience, while rejoicing in such realistic presentation of a traditional outlook from which it felt sadly estranged in the city slums, also perceived finer shades of relevant ethical significance, and relished the skillful dramatization of a double-barreled purpose in each play. *Umthakathi* first vindicates the African value of hospitality as against the shrewishness of the heroine, and then proceeds to restate the distinction, familiar to African tradition, between the evil magic of the sorcerer and the beneficent magic of the isangoma. *Uqukomisa* first warns against the hero's brutal clumsiness in trying to capture the attention of the girl he loves, and then restates the seniority principle in all matters of family etiquette and behavior.

In this new type of theatrical activity, Vilakazi goes on, "educators and legislators" thought they had a possibility for using "African drama as an agency to stamp out the widespread demoralisation in towns among children due to immoral films shown to them by unscrupulous bioscope managers." This idea had been expressed in condescendingly paternalistic terms by Lloyd:

It is undoubtedly a noteworthy performance when the subject race is able, in spite of hereditary disadvantage, to develop its intellect to the full. Such is surely the case when the natives are able to break away from the influence of the cinema and to produce plays of their own.

It is equally noteworthy that the Zulu dramatist found a way out of this demoralization not in education and the Christian religion, but in a return to the traditional values of hospitality, to absolute respect for one's elders, and to the distinction between black and white magic. This sharply differentiates Zulu drama, designed for illiterate masses alienated from their native tribal universe, from the contemporaneous written literature of southern Africa, which was aimed at a literate readership already well on its way to religious and educational Westernization.

Their very success proved to be the curse of the Lucky Stars, for, as Vilakazi points out, "some interested white producers . . . offered them trips overseas under their auspices. After this, however, they ceased as an organised company."

The dramatic movement of the twenties and the thirties had led to another development that is of great significance for Zulu literature. After summarizing the plays that he saw performed in Durban in the winter of 1934-1935, Lloyd notes:

The entertainment concluded with an epilogue of singing. This time the songs were historical. They traced the record of the Zulu nation through their kings. They sang of those who had wielded supreme power whether good kings or bad kings. Once again the colourful voices of the natives were heard at their best now in an epic theme such as the Saxon bards might have sung when the wassail was passed around.

As there is no mention of any singing in the printed version of the early Mariannhill plays, it is presumably the Lucky Stars that Vilakazi had in mind when he wrote, in his article of 1942:

During the years that saw the birth of drama, we find that the productions were short and could not keep the audience interested through the evening entertainment. So someone had to supply music with Native plays; songs in a foreign language were unsuitable.

The link between traditional tribal song and modern lyric was provided by one of the numerous undertakings of John L. Dube, who will be discussed subsequently. In the early years of the century, Dube founded the Ohlange Institute, the first school built entirely through Bantu initiative. In his attempt to maintain and rejuvenate what was best in Zulu culture, he had sought to foster interest in music by setting up a traveling choir that also served the auxiliary but by no means negligible purpose of securing funds for the Institute through their annual visits to Johannesburg.[42] Significantly, it was at Ohlange that the earliest and most prominent composer of secular songs in Zulu got his education. Reuben Tolakele Caluza was born at Edendale and attended school there before going to Ohlange. He then proceeded to complete the teachers' course at Mariannhill, where Huss, who was as interested in music as he was in drama, strongly encouraged him. His first published song, "Ixegwana," ("Little Old Man"), was printed in the *Native Teach-*

ers' Journal for January 1921.[43] His work attracted the attention of the Native Affairs Department, and in 1930 he was sent to London with a Zulu choir of five men and five women to make recordings to meet the growing demand for native music in South Africa. He described his work in London to H. W. Peet:

Our party which I have been training since early this year consists of teachers, students, and clerks, while one member is a native Methodist minister. We are recording about one hundred and twenty different selections, many of which are my own compositions, based on traditional Zulu music. The selections are in three chief categories, namely, records, specially for the "raw" native, for the partially civilized, and for the educated native. There are ancient folk songs, songs dealing with native customs such as weddings, sacred songs, mostly to European tunes, songs of national aspiration, and humorous songs.[44]

In 1931, Caluza studied music at the Hampton Institute and wrote at least one article in English briefly explaining the principles and themes of Zulu song and urging the need to record African music.[45] He returned from the United States with B.S. and M.A. degrees in music.[46] In 1945 he was in charge of the Music Department at Adams' College. His "Rondo for Orchestra: Reminiscences of Africa," a string quartette, is considered one of the best African works in the field of orchestral music.[47]

In 1928, Caluza had published a collection of his songs which, according to Vilakazi, was not only the first, but by 1941 was still "the only book of secular music ever published in Zulu." [48] Dr. J. F. A. Swartz has claimed that none of Caluza's songs "seems to have become a hit," [49] but both Benedict Vilakazi and Absalom Vilakazi apparently think otherwise. Significantly, the latter considers them a valid reflection of one of the more unfortunate transformations inflicted upon Zulu mores by the pressure of rapid urbanization. Some passages of his sociological analysis ought to be quoted as they are exceptionally relevant to future developments in Zulu and indeed South African writing:

In South Africa, the lure of the gold mines and the cities was responsible for large numbers of people who left the rural areas and flocked to the mining areas on the Rand and to the cities all over the country for employment. When they went to these places, they were required by industry and commerce to enter legal contracts and to earn

money as individuals rather than as members of families or tribes. This
insidious individualism which was being insinuated into their lives, far
away from the tribal setting and from the close kinship and family
group, began the destruction of the strong sense of social solidarity; for
here in the mines and in the cities there were few things, if any, which
reminded the men of their kinship or family ties and traditions. A man
found himself exposed to new ways of life, new associates, new forms
of entertainment, a different kind and order of morality and an absolute
lack of customary restraints.

In the entertainment world he was shown the moving pictures, and
the impact of the American Wild West was soon felt. There developed, at that point, around the 1920s, particularly, a new class of
Africans called *abaqhafi*, who have been immortalized among the Zulu
in R. C. [*sic*] Caluza's songs.

Umqhafi . . . developed in the mining areas and in the cities. He was
characterized by his absolute lack of respect for old traditions; his way
of affecting Western manners; and a particular form of dress which
showed very clearly the influence of the American Wild West. He
wore an open shirt with a black or multi-coloured muffler tied into a
knot around the neck; and pants which were tied just under the knee
in imitation of breeches. He wore, of course, a cowboy hat and had a
guitar or a concertina or a mouth organ which he carried with him
everywhere and with which he supplied free music to all.

This class of people was neither educated nor Christian. It had arisen
under conditions in which Christian missions did not operate. When
these men had finished their work contracts in the mines and cities,
they returned to the African areas and spread the general patterns
which they had developed in the mines and cities; and one found,
especially in the 1920s, that many youths in the rural areas had copied
the dress and manners of the *abaqhafi*. . . . The places in rural areas
where such people increased were the European farms which were
notoriously against African education and Christianization—European
protestations notwithstanding! . . .

The *abaqhafi* were also found in mission stations, but their numbers
decreased rapidly as more and more Africans in the mission stations
went to school and Christian social life and cultural institutions developed a definite character. By the 1930s, there were very few of them
in the mission stations until, by the 1940s, up to the 1950s, the term
abaqhafi had died out. . . . This is not because the class died out. It has
merely evolved into something new. In the urban areas, what would
have been the *abaqhafi* in the past are now called the *tsotsis*.[50]

The flamboyance of this American-inspired "tough guy" style
did not necessarily entail, but it often included, delinquency. How

disquietingly widespread the phenomenon became in the twenties
was illustrated in Enoch Guma's and Guybon Sinxo's Xhosa fiction
as well as in Caluza's popular songs. As is well known, it is presented as one of the more important and damaging consequences of
racial discrimination in much of present-day South African fiction
in English. The *tsotsi* is a major character in the short stories of
Alex La Guma and in the novels of Richard Rive and Bloke
Modisane.

It is of peculiar significance that modern song in Zulu was started
by the separatist hymns of Shembe and by the secular lyrics of
Caluza. Modern Xhosa song had arisen in the nineteenth century,
when missionary teaching was still the main agent of Westernization. There was no such period in Zulu literature, which had its
inception after South Africa had become politically autonomous
as a dominion and economically industrialized. From the very
first, Zulu writers were immersed in a world where racial segregation, social oppression, and ethical demoralization were omnipresent features, and this was reflected during the twenties, not
only in Caluza's songs but also in works of prose fiction that will
be dealt with later. Meanwhile, we may well wonder whether the
Zulu drama of the thirties was not a deliberate attempt to remind
city audiences of the values and mores of the tribal society from
which they were fast becoming thoroughly alienated.

Shembe's hymns were not printed in book form until 1940, and
Caluza's songs until 1928. The first Zulu drama to appear as a
separate volume was not published until 1937. Actually, the earliest
book by a Zulu writer was *Abantu abamnyama lapha bavela
ngakhona (The Black People, Where They Come From)*, which
was issued by the City Printing Works in Pietermaritzburg in 1922.
It was written by Magema ka'Magwaza Fuze, who was a much
older man than Shembe, as he had been a pupil of Bishop Colenso
in 1859.[51] It was Colenso's daughter who encouraged Fuze to put
down his recollections in writing.[52] The work cannot be considered creative literature in the accepted sense of the phrase:
"Magema Fuze's desire," Nyembezi says, "was to tell the story of
his people and to trace their origin." Alice Werner describes the
book as "a curiously mixed production; along with valuable first-
hand accounts of Zulu customs and of incidents which had come
within the writer's own knowledge—e.g. the events of 1888, with

the trial and subsequent exile of the Zulu chiefs—we find speculations as to the ultimate origin of the South African peoples from the Lost Ten Tribes. In fairness, however, it must be said that the latter occupy comparatively little place."

This first work is highly characteristic in three important respects. Indeed, it may be said to have set the tone for much of modern Zulu literature.

First, in its careful, loving description of the traditions and customs of the Zulu people, it evinces the same sense of national identity and value that had been exemplified in the earliest writings in Xhosa and Southern Sotho. It is of especial value as it contains and preserves much traditional oral poetry, although Benedict Vilakazi pointed out that this "is badly recorded, as verse form is not observed." [53]

Second, it illustrates the peculiar sense of historical greatness, which characterizes the Zulu mind more than that of any other ethnic group in southern Africa. Fuze's "historical" and nationalistic approach anticipates a number of later works by Zulu writers, such as P. Lamula, who was born in Qhudeni and was educated at the Lutheran Teacher Training College in Maphumulo. He was ordained a minister of the Norwegian church in 1915, but in 1926 he was to found the Bantu National Church of Christ. In 1924 he had published *UZulu ka Malandela (Zulu, Son of Malandela)*, an account, based on oral traditions, of the chief who gave his name to the nation that he led down the Mhlatuze valley toward the coastal area of Umzimkulu some time in the sixteenth or seventeenth century. According to Vilakazi, Lamula, who later wrote *Isabelo sika Zulu (Zulu Inheritance)* "was well-informed in history, and, unlike Fuze, his matter is original and worked in a style of his own, which makes his books readable and interesting. Unlike Rev. M. J. Mpanza, who in 1930 wrote *UGuqabadele*, Lamula does not mar his books with irrelevant and tiresome moralisations at the end of every chapter. Lamula, though dealing with all the kings contained in Mpanza's book, leaves the reader to draw his own conclusions from the statement of facts. Both Lamula and Mpanza give us valuable information in the line of ethnology, anthropology and Zulu history." [54]

The third important aspect of Fuze's volume is its keen sense of all-Bantu unity. We do not know with any accuracy when Fuze actually wrote his book, but it seems that he was strongly impressed by the attempt on the part of the South African Native Congress during the second decade of the century to abolish tribal rivalries with a view to resisting the white man's supremacy. Whereas the congress leaders were thinking in terms of political expediency, Fuze tried to provide some historical foundation for the desirable notion that Bantu people are one. Vilakazi notes that "he unites the different peoples in his book and tells them of their oneness, quoting in very good Zulu his sources of information. He visualises a united black people of the future in the light of their past history. The Congress stood for this unity." [55]

Fuze's work ought to be viewed in this wider context: because of its late appearance, Zulu prose writing, from its very inception, reached the stage of political and social awareness that it had taken the Xhosa elite several generations to achieve. Fuze's attempt is, albeit on a lesser scale, the Zulu equivalent of the work done almost two decades earlier in Xhosa, especially by Walter Rubusana. The purpose of both men was to prepare the black South African for a dignified future by making him conscious of the greatness of his own past history and cultural legacy.

It is indeed a constant feature of South African Bantu writing that it is as reluctant to abandon the old as it is eager to grasp the new. Even while they were embracing the new religion and appropriating the new literary media, Xhosa and Sotho writers were careful to record and preserve the rich ancestral lore, the time-honored tales of their nations. Lestrade once pointed out that Bantu authors concerned with oral literature had a predilection "for putting down, not so much the stories, riddles, and proverbs, as the praises, and for making collections of historical rather than of purely literary material." [56] Later historical research in Bantu writing has shown that this assertion is not to be accepted unreservedly. Many early Sotho and Xhosa authors produced collections of proverbs and traditional stories. It is true that if Sekese made use of Sotho animal fables, it was with a strongly topical purpose in view. But Zulu literature is the only one that really began, as Fuze's example shows, with a markedly historical and nationalistic outlook. This is because it did not emerge until the time when the educated black Africans throughout southern Africa were beginning to think that the praises and chronicle poems, being the records of the high deeds and the great men of their past, were the worthier part of their literary inheritance.

This did not prevent Zulu authors from showing concern with the other, less sublime, aspects of their folklore, and in 1927 two native teachers, Allen H. S. Mbata and Garland C. S. Mdhladhla brought out a little collection of animal fables, *uChakijina Bogcololo* (*The Small Mongoose, Younger Brother to the Slender Mongoose*) which was printed in London by Simpson and Marshall. Both men were born in the Nquthu area and were trained as teachers at St. Chad's College. "Being supervisors of schools, and discouraged by the type of reading matter available to school children, they decided to begin writing for schools." [57] They subsequently published *Uhlabanengalwi* (*He Conquers Without Fighting*) and *Uthathezakho* (*Take Your Sticks*). In 1933 they were awarded a prize by the International African Institute for a story entitled *Umxoxi*. Much of their work is designed for school reading, but *uChakijina* is "more than class-room material," and the historical importance of their production has been defined by Vilakazi: "With those two writers the oral literature of the people begins to live in written form." [58] This trend was to reach its apex in the work of Violet Dube in the mid-thirties.

John L. Dube

When writing skill is introduced into an illiterate society, growth of imaginative literature in the new medium proceeds by separate leaps. There is a first gap between the appearance of writing and of the new world view that goes with it, and the earliest use of it for literary purposes. While these are usually connected with the recording and adaptation of traditional oral genres, there is a further gap before the alien literary genres brought together with the alien technique become actively appropriated by native writers. To some extent, the early development of the novel in Lesotho is an exception, but it took Xhosa literature almost a hundred years of uninterrupted contact with Western civilization before the first Xhosa novel saw the light of day. The Zulu novel did not take off until 1930, when John L. Dube published *Insila kaShaka* (Mariannhill), a book that was later translated into English as *Jeqe, the Bodyservant of King Shaka* (Lovedale, 1951). Because of Dube's wide-ranging activities in the fields of religion, education, journalism, and politics, more information is available about him than about almost any of the other Bantu writers.[59]

John Langalibalele ("bright sun") Dube was born at the Inanda station of the American Board Mission on 11 February 1870. He belonged roughly to the same generation as Thomas Mofolo, Samuel E. K. Mqhayi, and Sol T. Plaatje. His father, James Dube, a member of the Qadi tribe, was of the royal blood of the Ngcobo chiefs. He was also one of the first group of native ministers ordained by the American Board Mission. John Dube first attended the American Board Mission School in Amanzimtoti, which was later to be renamed Adams College. In 1888 he was sent to the United States, and during the academic years 1888-1889 and 1889-1890, he attended the preparatory department at Oberlin College in Ohio, although he was never a student of the college itself.[60] On his return to South Africa, he married on 24 January 1894, and after an interval of teaching and evangelistic work, he became pastor of the Inanda church. But he realized that his theological training was inadequate, and he traveled back to America, where he studied for three years at the Union Missionary Training Institute in Brooklyn; he was ordained in New York, presumably in 1900.

Some time in 1897, Dube had met James Booth, an English Baptist missionary, and John Chilembwe, who was to play a conspicuous role in Malawi. At the time, people interested in the progress of Christianity in Africa were becoming aware of and concerned with a problem that only grew more preoccupying with the years. Owing to the tightening of European colonial enterprise, Africans had started questioning not only the legitimacy of the white man's domination, but also the adequacy of the Christian religion as taught by white missionaries. Ominously, a separate Zulu Congregational church had been set up in 1896, and Ethiopianism was fast becoming a serious challenge to orthodox denominations. It was in response to this threat that James Booth evolved his concept of "Africa for the Africans" in the 1890s, and, according to his testimony,[61] Dube, too, was of the opinion that the only practicable solution lay in the establishment of orthodox but independent native missions. Such a program necessitated African missionaries with sound educational training and the required teaching skills. For this, the government authorities in Natal could hardly be depended upon, since they were providing natives with education up to Standard IV only. Self-help was the only answer, and Dube received much of his inspiration in this respect from the example of such great American Negroes as Booker T. Washington of Tuskegee and Dr. John Hope of Atlanta University. Although he stayed in the ministry until 1906, describing his affiliation as Congregational, the first thing he did after his return to Natal in 1901 was to found the first native educational institution in South Africa. The Zulu Christian Industrial School at Ohlange was quite a success. While Dube was its superintendent—a title which was later changed to that of principal—the institution was governed by a board of trustees in South Africa, with an advisory board in New York. In its early years, it was largely financed by Dube's lecture tours in America.

In the course of the first decade of the century, Dube publicized his views about Christianity and education among the South African Bantu in articles that he wrote in English for the *Missionary Review of the World*.

The first article,[62] printed in 1901, made several shrewd and important points. Dube noted that the attitude of missionary societies and of colonial churches at the time was largely conditioned by the outlook prevailing among the white population at large, and he showed his awareness of the socioeconomic fears that were the foundation of white racism: "It is true that an educated native seeks better paying occupation than merely herding cattle. One who has had his faculties sharpened by attending school and by manual training will seek to compete with the white man, and the white man does not like it" (p. 422). In Johannesburg, he points out, "white miners oppose any reforming of native people, on the ground that the native may some day oust them from skilled labor, and that Christianizing them is a stepping-stone to this" (p. 425). His conclusion was that colonial life was actually a hindrance rather than a help to the cause of genuine Christianity. It was responsible for "the limited progressive spirit on the part of the missions, and the lack of missionary interest on the part of the colonial churches"; only "natives who are Christianized and taught trades" can be expected efficiently to inculcate in the natives genuine Christian principles (as opposed to "strictly denominational doctrines") as well as giving them a proper education.

The experience of the Ohlange Institute confirmed Dube's views, and in another article published in 1907,[63] he defined with remarkable clarity both the purpose of his educational action, and the predicament of the Zulu at that moment in their history:

My object in respect to the school is to make it practical and capable of turning out first-class Christian agriculturists; for I am of the opinion that of all industries, farming is by far the most important for our people. They have the land, but unfortunately do not know how to make the best use of it. The Zulus have been born to agriculture, yet have made no progress in this direction because they have delegated to their women all of this important work. The women were acquainted only with the most primitive methods of tilling the ground, while the only contribution made by the men in the way of food supplies consisted in the meat which they procured in hunt. Now the white man's rifle and shotgun have killed the game and the savage Zulu finds himself forced to accept the white man's civilization or to give up his land and become the practical slave of the more advanced members of the human race. He can no longer live by fighting, and as the Colonials are not much interested in his welfare, his only hope lies in the path of industry along which we are endeavoring to guide him. (Pp. 371–372)

"To accept the white man's civilization" meant not only to assimilate the modern agricultural techniques and the various small crafts that were taught at Ohlange in order to make the Zulu self-sufficient and self-reliant but it also meant ridding them of cultural attitudes and value systems that stood as obstacles on their way to economic progress:

Some of our boys prepare the meals and wash dishes—in fact, do all the housework connected with the boarding-school. To have asked a Zulu young man to do this in former days would have been a great insult. He would have said: "Am I a woman that I should cook and wash dishes?" But the white man's industrial education is rapidly changing this feeling. (P. 371)

In Dube's view, culture change could only be directed toward Christian ideals:

Our success will depend upon the acceptance by the Zulus of the Christian religion. If they are to become a truly great people, our first duty is to impress the boys with Christian ideals. (P. 371)

What he meant by "Christian ideals" did not consist of doctrines, but was something extremely pragmatic. Respect for the dignity

of work was part of it. So was respect for the dignity of woman-
hood:

Woman has from time immemorial been looked upon as inferior to
man, and in order to destroy this mischievous idea we desire to have
girls as regular boarders and to give them work with the young Zulu
men and boys. The latter will then get an idea of the intellectual
strength of womankind and lose his erroneous ideas of his own mental
superiority. We can not hope to raise the Zulu men to any very high
standard unless we show them that they are not superior to the women.
. . . If our educated young men are married to ignorant wives, they
can not expect to have happy homes. (P. 372)

In 1907 the union of the colonial territories of South Africa was
not yet contemplated. The Bantu peoples did not yet feel the
danger of a single massive threat from a unified white government,
nor, therefore, did they feel the need for unity that was to emerge
at the end of the decade. Hence the cocky note of tribal jingoism
at the end of the article:

God works through individuals and through nations. We know how
He used the Jewish people to introduce Christianity into the world,
and we believe that He has a work for the Zulus. Prior to the advent of
the white man the Zulus were the dominant race south of the great
Zambesi. To-day they are intellectually superior to many of the tribes
of South Africa, but apart from being specially gifted they have been
providentially watched over as their geographical position forces upon
them an association with the white man and his civilization more intimate than that of any other native people in South Africa. The Zulu is
thus in the happy position of being the first of the native races to have
civilization forced upon him in anything like a wholesale manner. Tho
he must inevitably suffer during the period of transition, he will be as
surely rewarded, so soon as he is fitted to receive the benefits which
civilization invariably confers. As the Zulus were conquerors and leaders of the native tribes of South Africa in physical warfare, has not
God ordained that they shall conquer these same tribes by peaceful
methods and lead them to industrial, intellectual, and spiritual advancement? (Pp. 372–373)

Without relinquishing his pride in his own nation, Dube was
soon to give up this Zulu messianism, which sounds all the more in-
congruous as there is ample evidence that the Xhosa were far more
advanced on the path of modernization at the time. Indeed, when

Dube launched his second venture in self-help, he followed the
example set by John Tengo Jabavu among the Xhosa and founded
the first African newspaper in Natal, *Ilanga laseNatal (The Sun
of Natal)*. It was first printed in Durban by Indian printers, but
by 1907, Dube had purchased a secondhand newspaper press, and
a printing shop had been added to the Industrial School at Ohlange.
The primary purpose of the journal was, of course, to disseminate
education and to spread the gospel of self-help and self-reliance,
which appeals so much to Zulu pride, and which has become typical
of the Zulu outlook. But Dube also hoped to foster literary creation in the vernacular: "We believe," he wrote, "that this printing
establishment will be the means of bringing into existence a new
and enduring literature of the famous Zulu nation" (p. 371). That
this target was reached is attested by historians of Zulu literature,
who state that *Ilanga laseNatal* provided "useful training ground
for Zulu writers," [64] and that it was "responsible for the appearance of much talent in writing throughout nearly the whole of
South Africa." [65] The paper appeared in Zulu and in English, and
about 1920 its editorship was taken over by Ngazane Luthuli, one
of the contributors to the American Mission Board hymnal.

As already mentioned, Dube played a decisive part in the re-
nascence of Zulu music. But perhaps the most important facet of
his activity was his intrusion into politics, at the time of the Great
Zulu Rebellion, not only in *Ilanga laseNatal* but also in the *Missionary Review of the World*. Although he felt that white missionaries
could hardly present the Gospel in a way fully acceptable to the
black man, he was careful to stress the difference between their
attitudes and outlook and those of the European settlers and administration. After the rebellion of 1906, while he was bitterly criticiz-
ing the execution of Zulu insurgents in *Ilanga laseNatal*, he showed
his sympathy with the plight and ambiguous position of the white
missionary in another article in English,[66] where he wrote:

Ever since responsible government was granted to Natal, there has been
an absence of proper consideration for the natives. The desire on the
part of the ruling race to use the natives for their own comfort and
aggrandizement has led the natives to resort to armed resistance. The
missionaries are blamed on all sides as responsible for this rebellion because they teach the natives that they also are men with souls like white
men . . . . If the Europeans wish to know the true cause of native
unrest they may find it in their own policy of administration of native

affairs. They have debased their national ideals, for instead of national righteousness, they have manifested national selfishness. This makes the missionary's daily example of faithful, unselfish living among the natives a constant rebuke to the colonists. Thus he is placed between two fires—on the one hand, hated by his white neighbors as encouraging the natives to be more independent; and on the other hand, suspected by the natives as a tool of the oppressors. (P. 205)

Because of his protests at the way the Bambata rebellion was crushed, Dube was jailed for a short time, although he was released without trial. This, together with the negotiations for union, awakened him to the need for political action and for all-Bantu unity. In 1909, he joined other black intellectual leaders and representatives at the Native Convention, which met at Bloemfontein and which paved the way for the South African Native National Congress. Because of Dube's education and of his official position as adviser to the paramount chief, he was already a prominent figure among the Zulu. When the congress first formally convened in 1912, he was elected its first president-general because the Xhosa delegates, though they had an outstanding representative in the person of the Reverend Walter Rubusana, "decided that the Cape should take a back seat in order to unite people from other provinces who besides suffered under greater restrictions." [67] Rubusana became one of the vice-presidents, and Sol. T. Plaatje, the secretary-general. In the spring of 1913, Dube wrote to the governor general, Lord Gladstone, in the hope that he might veto the Native Land Bill, which gave "the million whites . . . access to more than 90% of the country while the four million Africans would be restricted to 7.3% . . . much of this . . . of poor fertility. . . . The Bill also made it a crime for any but servants to live on white farms and ordered the immediate eviction of Native squatters. Nearly a million Africans were squatters on white farms, living there with their families and small herds in return for services to the farmer." [68] In the summer of 1914, Dube led the delegation that vainly appealed to the then colonial secretary and to the British Parliament.

During World War I, however, financial troubles and difficulties of communication led to personal quarrels among the members of the executive council of the congress. Dube was fiercely criticized and humiliated, and in 1917 he "withdrew from Congress to concentrate on advising the Zulu royal house and running Ohlange

Institute." [69] It was then that he composed his first book, *Isitha somuntu nguye uqobo lwakhe* (*The Black Man Is His Own Greatest Enemy* [Mariannhill, 1922; repr. 1928]), in which he emphasized the need for oneness, cooperation and self-reliance. Fuze too was insisting at the time on the unity of the Bantu people. Since 1905, the more clear-sighted among the African elite had recognized the necessity to give up tribal rivalries. As Vilakazi later pointed out, they realized "that the failure of the Black people is not wholly to be laid at the White man's door, but that most of it could be accounted for in the Black men's insincerity to one another." [70] For all his sympathy with his people's plight, Dube had never idealized them. Already in his article of 1901, he had admitted that "the African is slow to learn," a shortcoming that he attributed to the influence of heredity and environment: "He has inherited this from his ancestors. Even the white people coming to Africa begin to lose the energy they possess in colder climates. . . . [The natives'] own beliefs keep their mental and moral powers in an aimless condition, without any higher desire than to herd sheep and cattle and to have as many wives as they can support" (p. 422). This trend in his thinking was reinforced by his disillusionment with the political activity of the congress and in the course of the years, while doing his best to improve his people's lot in small concrete ways, he came increasingly to stress the black people's responsibility in their own predicament, their lack of thrift, their laziness, their want of perseverance, and their tribal divisions, which prevented effective cooperation.[71] His book of 1922 was an eloquent plea for inner change, self-reliance, and the overcoming of divisiveness. His awareness of the African's share of responsibility in his own miserable condition later earned him a good reputation as a moderate among white South Africans and a nasty one as a traitor among the younger black intellectuals.

Dube's effort at objectivity indeed constrained him to steer a difficult path between the extremes of passive acceptance and shrill revolt. From 14 to 21 August 1926, he attended the International Missionary Conference in Le Zoute, Belgium. Passing through London, he was interviewed about the new segregationist measures that were contemplated by the South African authorities, and he warned, most outspokenly: "The Colour Bar Bill seems more than we can patiently bear. . . . If the Government persists with its present attitude, we can only think that it desires to exterminate

us." [72] In the next year, the new leader of the African National
Congress, James Gumede, also went to Belgium, to attend a con-
ference of the Communist-led League Against Imperialism in
Brussels. He was invited to visit the Soviet Union, and returned to
South Africa filled with enthusiasm for what he had seen there.
But at the ensuing congress meeting, Dube accused him of "irre-
sponsibility," thus reflecting the anti-Communist attitude of most
Africans at the time.[73]

It may well be as a response to his bitterness and disillusionment
that Dube, who was in many respects an exceedingly forward-
looking man, turned back to the past of his nation and wrote the
first novel in Zulu, *Insila kaTshaka*.[74] It is the straightforward narrative of a man whose youthful bravery earned him the doubtful
privilege of becoming Chaka's personal bodyguard and factotum.
The story takes place at a time when "Tshaka was beginning to
lose the respect of the chiefs and the common people. In spite of his
gallantry and prowess in war, the people were growing tired of
the endless campaigning" (p. 12). Jeqe's career as told by Dube
offers many examples of Chaka's senseless cruelty. The young man
is ordered to kill with his own hands one of his friends who had
entered the women's quarters in the king's kraal. On another occasion, he is ordered to steal twenty oxen from a Tembu village,
just to show the king that idleness has not made him soft. At a later
point, Chaka makes him kill a pregnant woman and rip her open to
see how the child is lying in the womb. Whereas increasing opposition to Chaka is motivated by the people's weariness with war,
Jeqe is profoundly repelled because he has "no love for the killing
of men and thieving of cattle" (p. 19), but he is bound to the king
both by fear and loyalty. When messengers from Dingane, Chaka's
brother, try to enlist his help in a plot to murder the king, he refuses, saying: "I am deeply grieved to see our people murdered in
their homes, or perishing on distant battle-fields to satisfy the ambition of one man only. But I am bound to my king because of the
promise I made to serve him truly, and if need be, to die at his
side" (p. 25). Somewhat inconsequentially, however, Jeqe refrains
from reporting the plot, and the first phase of his life ends with the
murder of Chaka, which took place in 1828.

As Jeqe does not want to fall victim to the time-honored custom
of burying the king's body servant with the king's corpse, he manages to run away before the funeral, and the second section of the

novel begins with his dangerous journey to Tongaland, during
which he is almost overcome by sickness and fever and has several
encounters—the kind that Africans are so fond of telling—with a
variety of wild animals. Among the Tonga, however, he falls in
love with a girl called Zaki, who accepts him although she had
been chosen by the local chief's son. This results in a fight in which
Jeqe is grievously wounded and would have lost his life had it not
been for the intervention of a woman named Sitela, who is described as "the queen of the Tonga doctors and diviners" (p. 55).
After his experience of bloodthirtsy cruelty at Chaka's court, Jeqe
now completes his education in the opposite direction—medicine.
He is instructed in the art of healing, and also acquires magical
powers of foresight and divination. After two years on Sitela's
island, Jeqe, now a learned doctor, returns to Zika's village to claim
her. While the girl has remained faithful to him, a new obstacle
arises for "her parents were disgusted with her because she refused
to marry the young prince and give them an assured position in
the royal kraal" (p. 65). She is nevertheless prepared to follow her
lover straightaway, but Jeqe replied: "The Princess, who taught
me all I know, made me swear that I would not steal you from
your parents. I want our marriage to be an honourable one, that all
men may say I am as good a husband to you as the Chief's son could
have been" (p. 65). He then decides to leave for mountainous
Swaziland,[75] where he hopes to earn the cattle he needs for the
bride-price. This ushers in the third phase in Jeqe's life, and his
career as a healer of men.

As the Swazi are suffering under a severe epidemic of dysentery,
for which Jeqe has efficient remedies, he soon obtains the necessary cattle, and returns for a brief stay in Tongaland, where he is
married properly but in secrecy because the chief's son is still sore.
Jeqe then goes back with his wife to Swaziland, where he is appointed physician to king Sobhusa, who gives him two more wives.
With the passing of the years, Dingane hears of the famous Swazi
doctor without being aware of his true identity. When his favorite
wife and her children fall sick, he asks Sobhusa to let his physician
come to Zululand. As Jeqe wants to see his parents, he goes to
Dingane's kraal, his face covered by a long beard and loose plaited
hair. He has no trouble demonstrating his superiority over Zulu
doctors and diviners, and he meets his parents, who describe the
situation in Zululand: "Life is not worth living. We long for

Tshaka to come back, even though he troubled us with ceaseless warfare; but Dingane has destroyed the country by cold-blooded murder" (p. 75). Jeqe's father also reports on Mpande's hitherto unsuccessful plotting with the Boers to overthrow Dingane. As a result, Jeqe makes secret arrangements for his parents to accompany him to Swaziland. Shortly after their arrival, however, Zulu informers reveal Jeqe's identity to Dingane, who becomes afraid lest Chaka's revengeful spirit should make its power felt through his former body servant. He therefore sends a delegation to Sobhusa with the demand that Jeqe be sent back to Zululand. It is to the Swazi monarch's refusal to comply that Dube ascribes the launching of a bitter war that the Swazi won, he claims, thanks to "the power of the medicines with which [Jeqe] had strengthened the army" (p. 83). It is a matter of historical fact that Dingane was killed in Swaziland in February 1840.

Although the main action of the story is fairly clear, its outlines are blurred at times by the many ethnographical digressions in which Dube indulges, describing aspects of tribal life among the Zulu and among the Swazi. These are part of his purpose to preserve the patrimony of native traditions, but they are not always quite relevant to the tale itself. Whether he is always reliable is open to question; in the narration of Jeqe's stay on Sitela's island, there occurs the following passage:

One day at the beginning of the second year, he awoke before dawn and went to bathe in the river. Now, at this hour, the Princess was wont to take a steam bath. On the way down, Jeqe noticed a fire burning near a bush and a large number of animals, both large and small, surrounding a naked woman dripping with perspiration. The woman was exercising her body by straining and relaxing her limbs. Snakes, lizards and other reptiles were twined about her arms and neck. . . . The animals were leaping and rushing forwards and backwards, in wild excitement. As the light grew stronger, Jeqe could see clearly and only then did he realise that it was Sitela, the Princess. . . . Jeqe now understood how she obtained her power, but his lips were sealed. He feared that if he were to mention what he had seen, it might reach Sitela's ears and he would surely die. (P. 63)

One may pardonably wonder how much of this is genuine reporting, and how much fantastic romanticizing of the Rider Haggard type, with which Dube was no doubt familiar. Indeed, one Zulu critic considers that the book's "literary value is seriously marred by the introduction of legendary incidents." [76]

It must also be admitted that psychological analysis is simply skeletal in spite of the almost Cornelian possibilities of the story. Jeqe's predicament, torn as he is between human decency and loyalty to the chief, never becomes truly pathetic. At times, his motivation is hardly coherent. During his brief stay at Dingane's kraal, as he listens to his father, and as he surveys the wooded hills of Zululand where he had spent his "happy childhood days," Dube tells us that "he felt he could never leave his home again." Yet, he had already heard his father's account of turmoil and atrocities, which prompts him to take his parents back to Swaziland with him.

For all its clumsiness, *Insila kaTshaka* is of considerable historical importance as the first novel in Zulu literature. Besides, many of its features illustrate the peculiar situation of the modern Zulu writer. As an African, Dube is immensely concerned with both the past of his people and their traditional culture. It has been observed that "among the Zulu there is a fanatical allegiance to royalty, and this makes it most difficult for the Zulu to accept foreign leadership." [77] This accounts for the many semihistorical novels dealing with nineteenth century kings written in Zulu since Dube's book first appeared. As a Christian and a highly civilized man, however, it was difficult for him to condone the general violence and cruelty that prevailed under the reigns of Chaka and Dingane. And as a politically conscious intellectual leader, he could not but deplore the tribal hatreds and conflicts of the past. His choice of Jeqe as the central figure of the book was a way out of a number of dilemmas. Through Jeqe's eyes, the founder of the Zulu empire is portrayed in a sketchy but balanced way: "Even though our King loves to see the red blood flow, I am overcome with admiration for his peerless courage on the battlefield" (p. 19). Partly, no doubt, as a reaction against the painful remembrances of Zulu imperialism, the novel is set in a multitribal perspective, involving not only the Zulu, but also the Tonga and the Swazi, and each of these is shown to contribute something to the growth of the hero.

At Chaka's court, he gains his experience of evil. His revulsion echoes to some extent the weariness of the Zulu people in general, and their tragic predicament as they were caught between their unconditional allegiance to the king and their legitimate desire for peace and quiet. Dingane is the true villain of the story, because his own brand of cruelty is ingrained; it is not an amplification of past courage and greatness.

In Tongaland, Jeqe acquires his understanding of love and charity. This is premeditated. At the beginning of the novel, when someone extols the beauty of Tonga womanhood, Chaka exclaims: "You do not know the country, nor have you seen our girls. . . . No country in the world can show more lovely girls" (p. 12). Jeqe's falling in love with, and marrying a Tonga girl is deliberately meant to counteract this jingoistic outlook, which is all too frequent in traditional African societies. Further, it is at the Tonga school of medicine that Jeqe learns the skills and the ethics of healing. This fulfills the genuine aspirations of his heart, thus demonstrating that the Zulu are not just bloodthirsty warriors. It is significant that Jeqe's maturing takes place entirely within the world of Nguni tradition and owes nothing to Christianity. This, of course, is historically correct. But the fact remains that no Xhosa or Sotho writer had ever suggested that spiritual salvation and the milk of human kindness would flow from any other source than the new religion.

Like so many African novels, *Insila kaTshaka* is a *Bildungsroman* that projects the graded inner growth of its central character. After his formative years in Zululand and Tongaland, it is in Swaziland that Jeqe reaches power and recognition. Vilakazi reports that "Dube, in his prime, was a hunter and a great shot. He admired life among the Swazi people, where he hunted every winter. He is a great friend of the rulers of Zululand and Swaziland." [78] There is little doubt that he found, in Swaziland, a sort of prototype of the ideal that the Zulu themselves had been unable to materialize: a proud and sturdy nation, which had remained true to its traditions, which had proved its valor by successfully resisting the assaults of Chaka and Dingane, while managing, at a later date, to frustrate European imperialism. Before it became independent on 6 September 1968, Swaziland had enjoyed since 1903 protectorate status as a High Commission Territory.

Vilakazi pointed out that the book reflects Dube "as a man who knows his people's miseries and indignities and sees them with a penetrating and revealing mind." [79] He also observed that "although the plot is not delicately handled, the style itself is wonderful," and that Dube "has a very picturesque way of depicting scenery and battlefields." [80] In 1961, Cyril L. S. Nyembezi, after praising the book as "a lively story told in Dube's gripping style," noted that it had remained the author's "most important and best-known among the Zulus." [81] Although this first Zulu novel was Dube's only venture in the field of creative fiction, it set the direction for much Zulu writing, which is mainly concerned with recording and reassessing the major events and figures of the nation's past.

At the same time as he was writing about the most famous of the Zulu kings, Dube also turned his attention to the most important of his nation's religious leaders in *U-Shembe* (Mariannhill, 1930), a biographical narrative of Isaiah Shembe. He may have been prompted by the example of Mqhayi, who had published his Xhosa biography of John Knox Bokwe five years earlier. In view of current European prejudices about the primitive and irrational character of such messianic movements, it may seem strange that a man of Dube's educational training, moderate temperament, and progressive outlook should have been interested in Shembe. But, precisely, this interest should invite us to a more careful assessment of Shembe's motives and ideas and, more generally, of the significance of his and similar movements in African religious life. Dube was by no means unreservedly encomiastic. He even claimed that the prophet "was very clever in extracting money from people." This was vehemently denied by Johannes Galilee Shembe in the Preface he wrote for the book, where he stated, with an eye, no doubt, on usual practices among orthodox denominations:

My Father has never said that a man who does not pay his Church dues will perish, when coming to heaven. Anybody who makes such a claim is lying—he is abusive against us.[82]

To Dube, the Nazarite movement was a significant instance of the cross-fertilization that was bound to take place between the new and the old beliefs and rituals. This is a crucial problem in the eyes of all African intellectuals, who keep trying to influence the course of acculturation by constantly weighing the values involved. And it remained a central preoccupation with Dube, even though, after *Insila kaTshaka* and *U-Shembe* he devoted himself mostly to didactic treatises.

About 1933 he published a pamphlet on good manners, *Ukuzi-phatha kahle* (*How to Behave Oneself Well*), in which he compares the old and the new standards of behavior and, among other things, strongly condemns kissing, even between mother and child, as this is not a Zulu custom.[83] *Inkinga yomendo (The Problems of Marriage)* is "a humorous play dealing with girls who go out of their way to get husbands," [84] and provides an opportunity to discuss the problems raised by the confrontation of the old and the new ethics in connection with marriage.

On 30 September 1937, Dube took part in the African Authors' Conference that was held in Johannesburg and issued important "Proposals for the Development of Bantu Literature." [85] In 1937, too, as part of the graduation ceremony at Fort Hare, Dube became the first African to be awarded an honorary Ph.D. from the University of South Africa.[86] Miss Lavinia Scott, a member of the Inanda Seminary of the American Board Mission, commented at the time that this event showed "a wonderful change in the attitude of the European leaders to the Bantu as a whole." [87] Another view is that it was a reward for a change in Dube's attitude to the colonial system since his early radicalism. In bills introduced in 1935, the government had laid down that no more natives could register as voters. This, in time, would ensure the disappearance of native franchise in the Cape Province. Natives would be represented in Parliament by four white senators, and a Natives' Representative Council would be set up, with purely advisory functions. Here is the comment of Edward Roux, who was at the time a card-carrying member of the Communist party: "An All-African National Convention was announced for December 15, 1935, at Bloemfontein. . . . Over 400 delegates gathered at Bloemfontein. There was only one outstanding traitor: the Rev. John Dube publicly declared himself in favour of the Bills. But who cared for Dube? He was known to be a Government man." [88]

Dube had been for a long time the leader of the Natal Native Congress, which had been described, in an official document of 1931, as "a movement which is not to be coupled with the activities of communist agitators, but which is doing considerable good among the Natives [with] a membership of some 200 . . . who are steady and law-abiding." [89] At the other extreme of the political spectrum in Natal was George Champion, whose efforts to get support for the African National Congress Dube thwarted to the best of his abilities. "The Zulus were great believers in one supreme leader at a time and their Paramount Chief's failure to respond to

the challenge of events . . . had left those two political leaders
to compete for provincial leadership like two bulls in one kraal.
Although Dube's behaviour caused especial dismay, for he had
been a man big in mind and stature, he received more sympathy
because of his age and the fact that he was an institution." [90]
In 1937 Dube was elected as the Natal natives' delegate at the
Natives' Representative Council; he was the senior leader of its
twenty-two members.

Thus Dube's evolution had been from radicalism to acceptance
of colonial rule on the one hand, and to withdrawal into tribal
sectionalism on the other. The fact that he was getting on in years
became conspicuous in an odd incident that took place in 1939.
Dube had agreed to sit on the platform together with his old rival
George Champion at an A.N.C. National Conference held in Durban. But "as the Regent Paramount Chief of Zululand arrived and
began to walk down the aisle, Dube—by that time a large elderly
academic figure of a man . . . jumped up and performed a Zulu
dance of excitement. Several Europeans were so frightened by
what they thought to be a Zulu war dance and the cheers and
ululations of the women that went with it, that they rushed anxi-
ously out of the hall." [91]

Although Dube was already seriously ill in 1941, he was reelected
in 1942. At the last meeting of the Representative Council that he
attended, he had to be carried in and out of the hall. He died on
11 February 1949. His successor to the council was Chief Albert
Luthuli.

The Thirties: Development and Diversification

The belated emergence of creative fiction among the Zulu is of
course accounted for by the fact that they did not feel the influence of modern education to any sizable extent until the beginning
of this century. Whereas modern Sotho literature had made an
impressive start in the first two decades of this century, and Xhosa
literature as early as the second quarter of the nineteenth century,
Dube, who belonged to the same generation as Mofolo and
Mqhayi, was a lone precursor, and he did not venture into imaginative writing until the 1930s. But as far as political awareness
is concerned, he was on a par with his Xhosa contemporaries
Rubusana or Jabavu; indeed, although he was a dozen years

younger than either of them, he was chosen as first president of
the South African National Native Congress. Their own peculiar
experience had not lulled the Zulu into expecting that satisfactory
arrangements—political, social, and economic—could be entered
into with the white authorities and population without hard fighting. Although, therefore, they were certainly backward in the
field of creative writing, in other ways they were more progressive and pugnacious than the other Bantu peoples of South Africa.

That Dube's earliest published writings—his articles in missionary reviews—should have been in English is quite meaningful. Because of historical circumstances, the Zulu recognized, from their
first serious acquaintance with Europeans, that the impact of the
West was not simply a cultural phenomenon characterized by the
introduction of a new faith and of new skills. They saw that it was
a matter of power politics in which not only their culture but also
their freedom and even their well-being were endangered.
Throughout South Africa, the intellectual elites of the early years
of this century understood that fighting was hopeless if the Bantu
peoples did not overcome their traditional tribal rivalries, and the
only way to establish channels of communication between the
various ethnic groups on the subcontinent was through the medium
of the English language. Dube was probably the first who realized
that the struggle had to be publicized in order to arouse world
opinion; and this too could only be done in English. Some Xhosa
intellectuals, it is true, had used English. John Henderson Soga
was a case in point, but his English writings are academic, not
creative, nor do they have any political overtones worth mention-
ing. The Sotho, who felt fairly secure under British protection,
remained isolated in their vernacular. Apart from Dube, only Sol
T. Plaatje, whose mother tongue was Tswana, was fully aware of
the importance of English, both because there was as yet no tradition of creative writing in Tswana, and because he was so fully
immersed in the all-African struggle for recognition. It is therefore
not surprising that even before Dube produced the first novel in
Zulu, a member of a later generation had already published the first
Zulu piece of prose fiction in the English language.

Rolfes Reginald Raymond Dhlomo was born in 1901. He was
educated at Dube's Ohlange Institute and at the American Mission
Board School in Amanzimtoti, where he obtained his teacher's

certificate. In the early twenties, he became a regular contributor to Dube's *Ilanga laseNatal* under various pen names such as "Randite," "Rollie Reggie," and "The Pessimist." His vein was humor, and he later became famous as a humorist because of his essays in the *Bantu World*, where he signed himself "R. Roamer, Esq." In 1928, while he was working as a mine clerk with the City and Suburban Mine in Johannesburg, he published *An African Tragedy*, subtitled *A Novel in English by a Zulu Writer*. As he stated in the Preface, his purpose was to stay the decline of native life in large cities, but the work also contains some cogent criticism of traditional customs. It tells the sad, pathetic, and edifying story of a young teacher named Robert Zulu, who wants to marry Jane Nhlauzeko. In order to pay the enormous bride-price that Jane's Christian father demands, Robert goes to work for two years in Johannesburg. There he is lured into evil ways, becoming "a hopeless drunkard" and patronizing local brothels. One day, after a card game that ends in fighting and manslaughter, he leaves town for fear of the police and goes back home. Meanwhile, Jane has had ominous forebodings, but her mother rebukes her. "This," the author comments, "is a common error of many Christians today. They rarely encourage their children to voice their own feelings, even in matters which concern the children themselves. Many marriages are still arranged and conducted by many modern Christians without consulting the contracting parties" (p. 25). The marriage does take place, however, but is not blessed with offspring. According to custom, this is blamed on Jane: people say that those modern girls practice birth control. Actually, Robert is almost impotent owing to some venereal disease he contracted in Johannesburg. When at last Jane has a child, it is born blind and soon dies, the mother in her despair exclaiming that there is no God. As to Robert, he is attacked by tsotsis. Before dying he makes a full confession, and the novelette ends with a rather perfunctory hope that God will pardon him.

To the Western reader, this sounds like a rather low-type sub-Victorian Sunday-school story. No one would claim that Dhlomo has proved himself a master of the light touch. Nevertheless, his slim novelette is as genuinely an African tragedy as Dreiser's fat volume is an American tragedy. It truly describes the African predicament in modern South African society. Robert Zulu's evil course flows forth from his prospective father-in-law's greed, which grossly distorted the significance of the bride-price concept. This frequently occurred in African societies newly introduced to a money economy. The story's purpose is to show that in the minds of many average Africans, Mammon and Jesus Christ have received simultaneous and equal allegiance. Dhlomo, of course, stigmatizes the dissolute life to which young workers are exposed, and almost condemned, in the revolting slums of the big industrial cities. But he also protests against the custom of parental authoritarianism in deciding matters of love and marriage, which are, to the western mind and in the view of many educated Africans, of sheer individual concern.

It is not known whether Dhlomo had read or was able to read the Sotho novels of Mofolo and of Segoete, which deal partly with a similar experience of city life. As a Nguni, he probably knew Guma's Xhosa novel *U-Nomalizo*, which had appeared ten years earlier, but in which habitual drunkenness is ascribed to illiterate pagans. While *An African Tragedy* is the first novel printed in English by an African writer (Plaatje's *Mhudi* had been composed much earlier but was not yet in print), it is also the first piece of genuine prose fiction by a Zulu writer. It is the first fairly extensive and realistic treatment of the moral evils of city life to be written in a spirit of social criticism. Guybon B. Sinxo's Xhosa novels in the same vein were still to come.

The rapid growth of the city novel from the late twenties onward must be viewed and can only be understood as the literary aftermath of a number of segregational legislative measures beginning with the Native Land Act of 1913 which lay down severe restrictions to Bantu land ownership. The census of 1921 reveals that Natal had an area of 25,000 square miles and a population of 132,000 Europeans and one million Zulu; to the latter was ascribed an area of less than 4,000 square miles. The area of Zululand was 10,000 square miles; the Zulu were restricted to 6,000 square miles, the rest being apportioned to some 400 Europeans.[92]

The taxation policy was also responsible for the cityward trend of the Africans, many of whom had to find paid work in towns merely to pay their taxes. As a result of these and other causes, Zulu men flocked in large numbers to the towns, especially to Johannesburg. But legislation was passed protecting white interests that were mutually antagonistic, thus creating an impossible situation for the Bantu. The Urban Areas Act of 1923 established segregation in the towns with a view to satisfying the white farmers' demand for cheap labor, and the Colour Bar Act of 1926 protected white industrial workers by barring native laborers from skilled employment in the mining industry. This was the legislation that, over a period of less than fifteen years, brought city-life experience to numberless Africans, while at the same time condemning them to dramatic conditions of increasing poverty and squalor. It was the purpose of many Bantu writers to bring out the moral degradation resulting from such conditions.

An African Tragedy was the only book that Dhlomo wrote in English. Dube's *Insila kaTshaka* may have awakened him to the potentialities of the mother tongue for written literature as well as to the suitability of native history as a topic for modern writing. That there did now exist an audience for Zulu writing appears from the fact that the firm of Shuter and Shooter in Pietermaritzburg began publishing books in Zulu in 1935.[93] Their first title was Dhlomo's *Izikhali zanamuhla (Modern Weapons)*, which was followed by a series of semibiographical narratives about the Zulu dynasty. The first of these, *UDingane kaSenzangakhona* (1936), was about Dingane, son of Senzangakhona and Chaka's half brother and murderer. As Dube had made clear in *Insila kaTshaka*, Dingane had acquired the kingship through a series of political murders. He had also desperately tried to prevent the Boers from settling in Zululand, but he was killed in 1840 in Swaziland, either while fighting against the Swazi, or as some say, by followers of Mpande, whom the Boers had had proclaimed king of the Zulu. In 1937 Dhlomo published *UShaka*, which is an attempt to reassess the manifold personality of Chaka. He is described "as tyrant and merciless despot, respected and loving king; a warrior, a founder of the most aristocratic nation, a prophet; and a man who wanted to solve difficulties." [94] *UMpande ka Senzangakhona* (1938) deals with Chaka's younger half brother, who, feeling his life was threatened by Dingane, fled to the Boers with a fairly large section of the Zulu people. The Boers took advantage of this to install him as "Reigning Prince of the Emigrant Zulu" until he succeeded Dingane on the latter's death. A peaceful and intelligent man, Mpande signed a treaty with the British in Durban, and

Natal could look forward to a long period of peace. He was the last of Senzangakhona's sons and the only one of the twelve who reached maturity to die peacefully in his own kraal in 1872.

Dhlomo's journalistic experience had given him the special skills required for this kind of popular history. His main source was not the native oral chronicles, but Bird's *Annals of Natal*. After *UMpande*, he gradually turned to more fictional material. *UNoma-langa kaNdengezi* (*Nomalanga, Daughter of Ndengezi*), is a love story involving two of Chaka's lieutenants and the daughter of a prominent warrior. With *Indlela yababi* (*The Evil Way* [1946]), Dhlomo reverted to the inspiration of *An African Tragedy*, once more providing a dramatic account of Zulu life in the slums of Johannesburg. The book focuses on an immoral love affair between Delsie Moya and the Reverend Gwebu. To keep their relationship hidden from their own people, they elope to the city, where they become involved in delinquent practices that cost Gwebu his life. Filled with remorse, Delsie returns home.

In 1951, Dhlomo was selected by the University of the Witwatersrand as the first recipient of the Vilakazi Memorial Award.[95] In 1952 he wrote the last of his historical novels, *UCetshwayo*, the story of Mpande's ambitious eldest son, who was born in 1827 and gained control of royal power in 1856 until he succeeded his father in 1872. Unlike Mpande, Cetshwayo "was deeply imbibed with the vanished glories of the Shakan era, and bitterly aware of the contrast between the glory the Zulus had then enjoyed and the sorry pass his father had brought them to" because of his subservience to the white men.[96] His attempt to restore Zulu independence in its fullness was bound to fail in the face of superior power, and after a crushing military defeat in 1879, he was stripped of most of his authority until he died in 1884, presumably poisoned by agents of one of the clans that were hostile to him.

Vilakazi has pointed out that "in handling the plot of his stories, Dhlomo shows a masterful and adept treatment not found in the writers of the earlier age. This is due to his occupation as a journalist of recognised ability and a humorist able to read and dissect human character with the fair and balanced judgment of a biographer." [97] Indeed, by 1961 he had been appointed editor of *Ilanga laseNatal*. Meanwhile, he had written a novel dealing with the disturbances between Africans and Indians in Durban in 1949.

This book has never been published because of its political implications.[98]

While Dube should undoubtedly be considered the founder of Zulu fiction, Dhlomo is the one who brought its two main trends —the historical and the social, the reassessment of the past and the analysis of the present—to their early fruition. Yet, his younger brother was a figure of greater intrinsic interest. Herbert I. E. Dhlomo was born in 1905 in the village of Siyama near Pietermaritzburg. His first work is also the first drama published in English by a black South African author. Entitled *The Girl who Killed to Save* (Lovedale, 1936), it is based on an episode that actually occurred in the history, not of the Zulu, but of the Xhosa: the cattle-killing tragedy of 1857. The events had been recounted in writing for the first time by Gqoba, probably in one of his *Isigidimi* articles. This may have been Dhlomo's source, although the Zulu dramatist may also have been inspired by Mary Waters's Xhosa play of 1924. There is certainly room for a thorough investigation of the Nongqause motif in the Bantu literature of South Africa. In Dhlomo's dramatic interpretation, the story of Nongqause becomes an exemplum of the workings of Divine Providence. In the first two scenes, it appears that Mhlazaka, a renowned witch doctor, and Sarile, who is described as "the Paramount chief of the Ama-Xosa," took advantage of Nongqause's loveliness and popularity to fake the prophecy: "I did hear strange sounds—not voices—near the river. Father and the Elephant assured me (after using the bones and medicines) the sounds were the voices of our dead ancestors. But are their interpretations correct? Why did not the spirits speak to me in the language I understand instead of in the wonderful but meaningless sounds?" (p. 9). An explanation for the chief's behavior is tentatively proposed by a white missionary, who says: "I'm afraid the plot behind the whole movement is to starve the people into fighting the Europeans. The leaders are playing on the people's feelings to cause trouble" (p. 20). But the quest for motivation is not Dhlomo's major concern. He is more interested in what may be called the mystical and eschatological significance of the episode. He does little to clarify the presumably tortuous psychology of the chief. His mouthpiece is a character named Hugh, who is brother-in-law to the government commissioner among the Ngqika Xhosa, Charles Brownlee. This is a historical character, and the volume has a preface by Frank Brownlee, who writes: "In Hugh, Mr. Dlomo [sic] has described a dreamer, and his philosophy, he has done this so ably that one would think that he had known Hugh as he actually was in life, just as he has been shown here." Hugh intones in the following terms:

The transforming, liberating process of evolution is often slow and cumbersome. Not infrequently Fate turns on the more rapid, more consuming scavenging process of accident, when he wants things speeded up a little. The cattle-killing drama of the AmaXhosa is an example of this rapid scavenging process of accident. It is one of those human mysteries that, defying the laws of determinism, come either to help or hinder a people. (P. 24)

To which an anonymous missionary replies:

The Xosa nation is a nation searching its soul. The missionary has tried to help the nation find and save that soul. So far the people are blind, arrogant and benighted. But if this cattle-killing craze goes on ... Nongqause may reduce at a sweep what legislative and missionary endeavour have so far failed to fight against—the power and influence of tradition, the authority of the chief, the isolation of the Xosa nation. ... Nongqause will give the AmaXosa that dependence (by robbing them of their food and national solidarity) which spells progress. For it is one of nature's charming paradoxes that independence is born of dependence. (Pp. 24–26)

These words provide the writer an opportunity to place a nice piece of hindsight in the mouth of Hugh:

Yes, I know that historians and writers will condemn Nongqause as a fool, a traitor, a devil-possessed witch. But is that everything that can be said about this? I hope to God not. . . . There must be something deeper. I believe that in the distant future someone will catch the proper spirit and get the real meaning of the incident and write about it. (P. 26)

This unspecified future person is of course Dhlomo himself, who is at pains to find room in God's benign schemes for this insane incident. In order to turn his heroine into a suitable instrument of Divine Providence, he emphasizes her innocence, which makes her a guileless tool in the hands of the true villains—the chief and the witch doctor. Scene 4 is devoted to a picture of the white missionaries and their black servants doing all they can to help the victims, and the optimistic tone is maintained through some rapturous comments of Hugh's on the beauty of nature. The last scene exemplifies the good that comes out of evil. It shows the edifying death of one Daba, a Xhosa convert, whose friend Nomsa exclaims: "Before that great Nongqause-Famine, death was a fearful black thing. But to-day we know more about our Lord and Saviour of whom the good missionaries preach. To-day death means birth. We need not fear for Daba who is a baptised believer" (p. 37). And Daba expires peacefully as Tiyo Soga enters to take up his new post, an image of redeemed Negrohood.

What Dhlomo set out to do is fairly clear: he attempted to make sense of an otherwise senseless, traumatic episode in the history of the Nguni people. Lacking the tools of psychiatry and group psychology, he could only do this in terms of the Christian belief that the dialectics of history are controlled by the infinite and unfailing benevolence of God. At the end of the play, the dying Daba has a comforting vision of the Xhosa dead, now redeemed, who acclaim Nongqause as "their Liberator from Superstition and from the rule of Ignorance" (p. 41).

With its all too obvious defects, this pioneering work earned Dhlomo quite a reputation. In the thirties, he was appointed to the staff of the *Bantu World*. In October 1936, he was the only Zulu representative at the African Authors' Conference held at Florida, Transvaal; his brother had been invited but asked to be excused, as did Jolobe, Mqhayi, and Mofolo.[99] In late 1936, he was appointed Librarian-Organizer by the Transvaal Committee of the Carnegie Library Service for Non-Europeans, the first African to hold such a job.[100] On 30 September 1937, he attended the second African Authors' Conference, which was held in Johannesburg. Other Zulu participants were Dube and Vilakazi.[101] Meanwhile, he was showing exceptionally keen theoretical interest in drama, and contributed several articles on African drama to various journals.

A few weeks before *The Girl Who Killed to Save* was released, the *South African Outlook* published an article in which Dhlomo aired his views on the nature and the future of African drama.[102] This is the first essay in literary theory by a black South African.

Traditional drama, Dhlomo contended, "was a combination of religious or magical ritual, rhythmic dances and the song." It fulfilled two main functions. On one hand it was historical: "Some of the dramatic festivals were commemorative of some important event —e.g. a successful hunt or raid. In such ritual representations, the people acted the actual thing or experience that had taken place." On the other hand, there were also "what one may call anticipatory dances or ceremonies based on the principle of sympathetic magic. In these ceremonies, the people 'acted' not what had happened, but what they wished to happen," whether they wanted "to precipitate rain, to kill and conquer in battle, or cause pain to their foes." Tribal drama was what we would now call a *Gesamtkunstwerk*. It "was accompanied by dancing and by song," but the spoken word was equally important, as "inspired individuals and tribal bards would often burst out into poetic praises of ancestors, kings, leaders, tribes, places." Further, traditional drama was essentially a communal activity: "The tribal audience participated in the ritual plays. . . . Between the tribal spectators and the tribal performers there was no strict line drawn. In most cases the tribal spectators were in fact actors awaiting their turn. Unlike some modern audiences the tribal spectators came, not passively to be entertained, but to take an active part themselves. The people came because it was a need, a duty, besides being amusement." As a result of this kind of training, "Africans were great actors." Colonial conditions, he adds, have only strengthened their abilities in that direction:

How often one hears people say the African is happy and care-free because he smiles—ignorant of the fact that behind those smiles and calm expression lie a rebellious soul, a restless mind, a bleeding heart, stupendous ambitions, the highest aspirations, grim determination, a clear grasp of facts and the situation, grim resolve, a will to live.[103]

This talent, Dhlomo further claims, was only one aspect of a general skill in handling language, which is proper to illiterate societies:

The African has greatly developed powers of speech. In European countries the introduction, long ago, of reading and writing, despite its incomparable blessings and advantages, made for some slight deterioration in European faculties of speech—the art of the spoken word. Writing and reading made it possible and easy to communicate without actual speech. Thus we find that the average White person with no training in elocution has slightly less developed vocal powers than the average Black man. The African has always depended on the living spoken word. With all its grave handicaps this weakness has helped to preserve the Black man's faculties of speech. In Africa it is customary to tell stories around the home fires in the evenings. The very dim light of such fires compels the story teller to depend almost entirely on his powers of speech to convey the meaning and excitement of the hair-breadth adventures of the day, or the varying situations of a folk-lore story.

Dhlomo's considerations about the evolution of African drama in modern days bear the mark of his confusion as an experimenter, and appear at times as a mere *pro domo* plea. This is obvious when he claims that "the development of African drama cannot purely be from African roots. It must be grafted in Western drama. . . . The African dramatist should not fear being mocked as an 'imitator' of European art." Or when he seems to think that the primary purpose of modern drama in Africa is to "interest people in African history and tradition," adding that "the tragedy of a Job, a Hamlet, a Joan, a Nongqause, is the tragedy of all countries, all times, all races."

Nevertheless, Dhlomo was quite aware of the new trend toward more outspoken realism and social criticism that had begun to emerge in the vernacular fiction of the early thirties, and he clearly wanted modern drama to share in this new development:

The African dramatist cannot delve into the past unless he has grasped the Present. African art cannot grow and thrive by going back and digging up the bones of the past without dressing them with modern knowledge and craftsmanship. If it is true that the Past should form the background of African art, equally true is it that African art must deal with the things that are vital and near to the African to-day—the school, the church, the slums, the automobile, commerce, etc.

The African dramatist has an important part to play. In the story of African Travail, Birth and Progress, lies an inexhaustible source of African literary and dramatic creations. We want African playwrights who will dramatize and expound a philosophy of our history. We want dramatic representations of African Oppression, Emancipation and Evolution.

Dhlomo resumed his theoretical discussion of modern African drama three years later in response to Vilakazi's essay on "The Conception and Development of Poetry in Zulu," which had just appeared in *Bantu Studies*. Thus began what should probably be considered the first literary controversy in the history of African writing in South Africa. Its origin is to be found in an observation made in 1935 by Lestrade in a discussion of Bantu oral poetry, to the effect

that the language is in general difficult and obscure, that a very large number of words and phrases occur the true meaning of which is no longer known, that many archaic forms present themselves; that the construction of sentences tends to be laconic and staccato, and that the poems are all extremely rich in allusions whose significance has been lost in course of time, or whose meaning has been preserved only indifferently.[104]

This, it would seem, prompted Vilakazi to analyze the nature and structure of the Zulu izibongo. While claiming that it truly deserves to be considered poetry because it has both powerful emotion and strong rhythm, Vilakazi admitted that it was indeed exceedingly obscure, for the reason that the Zulu poet

describes his experience in associative images which, when analysed, present great difficulty in explanation, for the poet makes use mainly of private and personal imagery.[105] This creates symbols and figures of speech which embody for him a certain complex emotional experience, which he seems to use in most of his lines as emotional shorthand. And because such a language has been used by a Zulu poet, to a common reader his work is generally incomprehensible until it is interpreted. (P. 107)

Vilakazi also deplored, somewhat patronizingly and, we may feel, mistakenly, the absence of conscious critical self-examination among illiterate poets:

The written poem, of which the educated poet feels the need, always gives him time to reveal his thoughts with accuracy, and to be able to pass criticism on his own works. The illiterate man has not this advantage, but composes from pure and primitive inspiration. He has no ability to pass self-criticism, which I believe came into being only when man discovered the art of writing. No wonder, therefore, that the illiterate mind appears not to be analytic and direct. (P. 110)

This, Vilakazi thought, was responsible for the rambling structure, the lack of formal organization and integration in the traditional izibongo. Yet he sought to account for the apparent discontinuity and incoherence of any particular Zulu poem in terms of an underlying stanzaic pattern:

There does not seem to be a systematic treatment of the main theme so as to form one complete and analysable vista. There is lack of perfect continuous description of a mood. The poet seems to ramble without control over his subject-matter. But looking at it objectively, the whole poem is "laconic and staccato," the gaps between different treated headings demand mental experience of the whole poem before the analysing of its contents. Something needs to be filled in before the whole of the poem is discernible. When I read a primitive poem and come on a gap, there I discover the end of my stanza. Some of these stanzas will be long and some will be very short, according to the mood of the poet as he treats a particular heading in his poem. Stanzas in primitive Zulu poetry are like lights shed on a sculptured work from different angles. (P. 112)

Turning then to the prospects of written poetry in Zulu, Vilakazi advocates its formal improvement and modernization through adoption and adaptation of the Western poetic technique of rhyme and metrical composition. As he was fully aware of the dangers of slavish imitation, he added the following proviso:

There is no doubt that the poetry of the West will influence all Bantu poetry because all the new ideas of our age have reached us through European standards. But there is something we must not lose sight of. If we imitate the form, the outward decoration which decks the charming poetry of our Western masters, that does not mean to say that we have incorporated into our poetry even their spirit. If we use Western stanza-forms and metrical system we employ them only as vehicles or receptacles for our poetic images, depicted as we see and conceive. Criticism of Bantu poetry to-day confuses "form" and "spirit" of poetry. The latter is very important. (P. 127)

The controversy flared up in the spring of 1939, when Dhlomo offered his own views about Zulu poetry in several articles. In

March, *Bantu Studies* printed an essay in which he dealt with the
esoteric quality of the izibongo, contending that "the tribal literary
forms whose nature and construction have baffled many investiga-
tors, are in reality mutilated and distorted remains of primitive,
tribal dramatic pieces" (p. 33). This is not the place to go into
the details of his demonstration, but the essay contains a number of
remarks which are of interest for understanding Dhlomo's own
inspiration.[106]

For example, the idyllic-elegiac mood of his later poem, *The
Valley of a Thousand Hills* must be largely accounted for by a
romantic, primitivistic notion expressed in the essay of March 1939:

Before the rise of Shaka, the people lived a quiet, full and homely life.
They tilled, hunted, played, danced, feasted, loved and married freely.
Naturally, the tribal bards sang of all this, many of their compositions,
no doubt, being amorous. The coming of Shaka brought about great
changes and wide repercussions. Life ceased to be hedonistic, peaceful
and safe. The policy of *laissez-faire* succumbed to one of tyranny.
People became military-minded. Shaka's domestic and foreign policy,
his great wars of conquest, and his studied ruthlessness transformed
tribal life and gave it new patterns of behaviour, new channels of
thought, new political ideologies. The demon of war, the menace of
invasion, the fear of annihilation, the restlessness of whole tribal migra-
tions and endless group treks, shook the very foundations of African
life, and gave birth to a whole catalogue of changes, developments and
upheavals. (Pp. 36–37)

This negative view of Chaka, which Dhlomo shared with Dube, is
typical of the early, Christian generations of Zulu authors. It was
not until much later, as we shall see, that more highly educated
and more independent-minded Zulu writers were going to reassess
Chaka's personality and historical role.

More directly relevant to Dhlomo's creative writing is his attempt at reconstructing some of those tribal plays, of which the
izibongo were alleged to be vestigial remnants. Although the cor-
rectness of the theory is highly dubious, it resulted in modern
experiments that have unfortunately remained unpublished. In a
footnote, Dhlomo informs his readers that in order "to try to do
for Bantu tribal dramatic art-forms what scholars have done for
Hebrew and other literatures, the present writer has deliberately
grafted this tribal dramatic piece in his play, *Shaka*. Of this point

(the preservation of archaic tribal art-forms by grafting them into modern works, etc.), more is said in the manuscript of which this essay is but an extract" (p. 41). It would seem that neither the play nor the manuscript has been printed, although Dhlomo's various published essays of that period are undoubtedly all fragments of the same work.

Out of his own experience and meditation—but perhaps also from his reading of European ethnologists—Dhlomo emphasized some features of African culture which in those very years Césaire and Senghor in Paris were elaborating into the concept of negritude. Drama as a social art, he says, is "native to African Genius for Bantu life is social, communal" (p. 44). And he lays particular stress on "what anthropologists call Sympathetic Magic," that is, the African's sense of the unity of being, and especially his feeling "that he was related to the other forms of creation, even to the stars," and that "his slightest word or act might disturb the stellar world or beget a universal cataclysm" (p. 45)—a thought that he characterizes as both "childish" and "profound."

In his next essay, "African Drama and Poetry," [107] which was issued in April, Dhlomo reverted once more to Vilakazi's article and took him to task for advocating the introduction of rhyme in Zulu poetry. "Rhyme," he pointed out, "can be an exacting taskmaster and a cold tyrant. Pre-occupation with technique and rhyme may make for art that is too self-conscious. This is true especially in African languages, where words end almost invariably with a vowel, and where stress and accent play an important part in meaning." Although his ostensible concern was with dramatic poetry, he set up as a model "the poetic form used by the ancient Hebrew writers," of which it seems he knew through some works of Arthur Quiller-Couch and Laurence Binyon. To prove that this form "is natural to African genius and to our Native speech," he quoted the analysis of a traditional Sotho praise poem that Professor Lestrade had published in *The Critic*. But the main point of Dhlomo's article was to downgrade rhyme and extol rhythm:

Rhythm is essentially African. The tribal African was under the rigid rule of pattern. There were rigid patterns of behaviour, rigid patterns even in architecture (the hut) and in village or kraal planning. This love of pattern certainly had grave disadvantages, but it gave birth to a marked sense and love of rhythm. This sense of rhythm is seen even in the movement of tribal people: how rhythmically graceful and charming is the motion of tribal belles! how rhythmically powerful and warrior-like the trot of tribal males! The element is also well marked in African music and in tribal plastic art. The dances, too, are strongly rhythmical. In fact, one may almost say that the greatest gift of Africa to the artistic world will be—and has been—Rhythm.

It is of course significant that those words were printed at the same time that Aimé Césaire and Léopold Senghor in faraway Paris were building up negritude, which emphasizes the centrality of rhythm to the essence of Negrohood. But Dhlomo's concern with a concept of African personality was only incidental. His purpose was topical, for there was among Nguni poets a strong tendency to relinquish traditional poetic techniques and imitate European forms that, although they had already become obsolete in Europe itself, were the only ones taught in the schoolrooms of Africa. A few years later, Jabavu, reviewing Mqhayi's *Insuzo* of 1943, compared it in the following terms with Vilakazi's *Inkondlo kaZulu* which had been published in 1935, and for which the author's article of 1938 provided the theoretical foundation: "Both authors employ forms definitely imitative of English rhymes such as long and short meters, the sonnet and the heroic couplet. Both excel in their infinite variety of rhymes." [108] Dhlomo was the first to offer a theoretical justification of traditional poetic techniques.

In another article printed in April 1939, Dhlomo widened the perspectives for his plea in favor of traditional inspiration and forms.[109] He showed himself disturbed by the African intellectual's readiness to accept the European's image of Africa, with regard both to past and present, an image that he found rooted in ignorance, misunderstanding, and prejudice:

The European historian was handicapped by preconceived ideas and existing prejudices. He could not enter into the mind and the aspirations and the feelings of the black people of whom he wrote. . . . In South Africa the activities of great African geniuses and heroes such as Dingane, Moshoeshoe, Shaka, Nongqause and many others are treated superficially and dismissed as barbaric. The social, psychological, every day life of the people is shamefully neglected or misconstrued. Therefore, constant research, frequent revision, open-mindedness and industry are required if we would keep our historical facts up-to-date.

Anthropologists know that in any mixed society, the weaker group tends to accept and internalize the image of itself which is offered by the stronger group, with nearly psychopathic self-disparagement as an inevitable result. Although Dhlomo does not say so explicitly, it seems that some such idea was at the back of his mind when he recommended that African drama should be based on serious research so as to offer a truer and more convincing portrayal of the African past and present. Deploring that "no African can gain access into public libraries and archives in the country," he stated that

it would be a step in the right direction if the literary, archaeological and other collections of the Department of Native Affairs Ethnological Bureau, the Zulu Society, the Institute of Race Relations and other organisations of this kind, could be used to form the basis of an African archives department where African writers and scholars could find help.

But although "a dramatist must be a research worker," Dhlomo is aware that the mere recording of facts must be transcended. After blaming the "historians and writers who think they know all about the African because they have studied the subject scientifically," he adds that it is the dramatist's task to fuse the academic and the humane, to search for motivation behind action: "the real human drama lies deep in human fears and hopes, desires and intuitions, thoughts and emotions." It is significant, however, that the two most urgent tasks he assigned to scientific research in this context were the "collection and reconstruction of the Bantu dramatic 'izibongo'" and the "collection, for dramatic purposes, of biographical material of Bantu kings, heroes and other outstanding figures." As we remember, this gathering and recording of folk material had made a start a hundred years earlier among the Xhosa, and about fifty years earlier among the Sotho.

To Dhlomo's article, Vilakazi replied in a letter to the editor of the *South African Outlook* for July 1939.[110] Writing from the dizzying heights of his academic degree, he spoke contemptuously of Dhlomo's ignorance. His assumptions about Hebrew poetry, he said, are "a sheer display of ignorance in a field where he could have retained his proper status by solitude and reserved silence"; he "does not understand the form he is attempting to write about." Vilakazi poked fun at Dhlomo's reputation among the Zulu: "fame is so cheap in Bantudom and it is won very easily at the expense of

others." In spite of this nasty personal tone, Vilakazi was right in
pointing out that the Bantu "dramatists" of whom Dhlomo made
so much had simply not yet arisen, and in stressing the need for
scholarly discipline in the discussion of the nature and the prospects of Bantu literature. He ended his letter with a welcome
definition of what should properly be termed "Bantu literature,"
and with an act of faith in its future:

By Bantu drama, I mean a drama written by a Bantu, for the Bantu, in
a Bantu language. I do not class English or Afrikaans dramas on Bantu
themes, whether these are written by Black people, I do not call them
contributions to Bantu Literature. . . . For that matter English and
Afrikaans books with Bantu setting, written by all our White friends
are not Bantu literature. I have an unshaken belief in the possibilities of
Bantu languages and their literature, provided the Bantu writers *themselves* can learn to love their languages and use them as vehicles for
thought, feeling and will.

Vilakazi's contemptuous arrogance did not discourage Dhlomo,
who, for all his concern with vernacular literature, remained convinced that it was to the African's own advantage to write in a
European language. In 1941 he had a long poem in English about
his native country printed in Durban. *The Valley of a Thousand
Hills* is a lengthy elegiac effusion in the Romantic-Victorian manner. It is based on the contrast between the harmony of nature and
the cruelty and ugliness of human society. This leads him to a
Rousseauistic idealization of tribal life as he imagines it to have
been in the past. The disruption of African society under the impact of industrial civilization is somewhat weirdly impersonated
in the breasts of Zulu girls which he claims used to be "haughty,
full, defiant bulbs," and are now "drooping low with shame and
use." With sub-Wordsworthian (although, no doubt, genuinely
felt) oratory, Dhlomo's vision embraces past, present, and future.
Life in Zululand, once "a land of homes and only homes," he now
perceives as

> . . . a groaning symphony
> Of grim discordant notes of race and creed,
> Of writhing snakes of ideologies
> And twanging tunes of clashing colour themes,
> Where Wealth and Power and blood reign worshipped gods
> And Merit, Truth and Beauty serve as slaves!

and he can only gaze "Into a future tragic with Greed's way." The
most moving part of the poem comes at the end, when the writer
expresses—as Rabéarivelo had done in Madagascar in the previous
decade [111]—his tormenting sense of being an exile in his own country:

> This beauty's not my own! My home is not
> My home! I am an outcast in my own land!
> They call me happy while I lie and rot ·
> Beneath a foreign yoke in my dear strand
> Midst these sweet hills, and dales, under these stars.
> To live and to be free, my fathers fought.
> Must I still fight and bear anew the scare?

This ominous question remains unanswered.

However mediocre as English poetry, *Valley of a Thousand
Hills* is to be hailed as the first sustained attempt by a black South
African at composing a serious long poem in the alien language
of the dominant race. The literary influences at work in it are all
too obvious. It is significant, however, that Vilakazi dismissed it
somewhat summarily because it was not romantic enough:

This poem reflects the struggle of a black man's soul which, though
exalted at the sight of the "bushy-bearded hills" that "rail at me with
happy drunken sounds," yet feels fettered in his continuous and unsuccessful struggles with life. His sight of beauty in solitude is corroded
and overlaid with a reactionary attitude of bitterness. The life in nature
appears repulsive to him, and, though it inspires to poetic creation and
reveals his interpretation of nature and the soul, it is not the outcome
of a spiritual and harmonious union with nature.[112]

Later critics, on the contrary, were to blame Dhlomo because his
bitterness at the black man's present predicament does not drive
him to positive revolt but leaves him confined to elegiac inefficiency. "Even in his protest," said Ezekiel Mphahlele, "Dhlomo
remains a thoroughgoing romanticist." [113]

Valley of a Thousand Hills was Dhlomo's second and last
printed venture in the field of creative writing, although Vilakazi
reports that he composed a number of unpublished plays; one of
these, *Ruby*, "was acted and produced by the author himself."
Three others, dealing with Chaka, Cetshwayo and Moshoeshoe,
"were meant to be published in one book, which the author in-

tended to call *The Black Bulls*"; [114] apparently, none of these works ever reached print.

A few years after his English poem, Dhlomo reverted to the study of Zulu oral art in a series of articles [115] that illustrate his continuing concern with the problems raised by the urgent need for somehow adapting traditional forms and themes to the requirements of modern times, while keeping alive the African's sense of his own identity and dignity. A large portion of the series is of mainly antiquarian interest, but Dhlomo provides one of the most lucid expositions of the societal significance of folk art, and especially praise poetry, to have come from the pen of an African:

It would appear that some of the folk poems sprang from or with the dance. The dance is rhythmical, and rhythm is the essence of poetry. The disintegration of tribal society, the hostility of some missionaries to what they regarded as obscene exotic dances, and of some administrative authorities to what they feared might be performances to perpetuate the martial spirit, have all conspired to sweep away the rites in which these dances played a major part, but the poetic compositions have outlived the ritual and the dance. But the point is that in tribal society poetry and the dance played a living part and were inseparable twins (or triplets, if we include the music). The praise poems were used as an urge to courage and endurance. No one wanted to fall short of his "praises"; and as cowards were deprived of their "praises" and these bestowed on the heroes (as in *Macbeth*, Macbeth won the Thane of Cawdor's title), people would rather die than lose them. You could dance to the amount and the quality of your praise-poems only—and no more. The more you achieved in battle or in the tribal councils, the more and better "praises" you received. They meant support to you by the others—their evidence and report (like being mentioned in despatches or getting a military decoration; and, in times of peace, having an honorary degree conferred upon you). They were a recommendation to your king for favour and advancement, and it was the highest honour to have the king sing your praises. They were used to delight and excite, to appeal to and appease, to honour and humour a person. They were a fairly faithful and inspired record of your career and character. In youth they told your measure of promise, your inclinations and your dormant but dominant qualities; in advanced age, the story of your achievements and adventures. The king's "praises" were the longest and most laudatory. The heroes were allowed a certain liberal measure. The poems did not die with you, but remained as an ornament to your life, a reminder and treasure, an inspiration and a glory to your family, friends and clan. They were used to make contact with, and intercession to you when you became an Idlozi (ancestral spirit). That is why the tribal man will tell you that the Izibongo are the wealth of our country, the soul of the state, the dignity and meaning of the Race—are God himself!

But it was also Dhlomo's purpose to indicate how modern Zulu writers might profitably use the traditional poems as almost ready-made materials for a more ambitious, larger-scale sort of work:

I look forward to the time when some Zulu poet of genius, or a group of Zulu scholars, will merge the poems of kings and heroes (by selection, alteration, rejection, re-arrangement) into a great national saga or epic that may stand comparison with other sagas. In fact there are many points of similarity, in incident, between for example, the Iliad and these narrative folk poems . . . the tales of the combats of heroes, the employment of the simile to break the monotony of the narrative and to introduce nature poetry, intercessory appeals to the gods, certain customs in the prosecution of war, etc.

It is hardly likely that Dhlomo was acquainted with the then budding school of negritude writers, or with Father Tempels's pioneering work on Bantu philosophy. It is all the more interesting to observe that he too insisted on the intuitive sense of organic oneness that characterizes the African's perception of the world, and sets it apart from Western habits of rational analysis:

Tribal people regarded all life as one. Today, yesterday, tomorrow, are all one. . . . They go further and claim that even stones and dust, etc. are one with the highest. That is why the praise-poems, which, as we have seen, are regarded as God Himself, are given to sticks and stones (for these are the manifestation if not the actual breath of God). The tribal man did not think of a heaven into which he would finally escape, his "mind continue without a brain, or be miraculously provided with another—or suddenly awake to a consciousness in hell or heaven," and live happily or miserably ever after. Man is God; God, Man. All things are one.

Significantly, Dhlomo uses this definition of African cosmological intuition as a starting-point for a reassessment of Chaka's historical role, which he defines in terms entirely different from those of Dube, and for a renewed advocacy of unity—social, political and, above all, cultural—among the Bantu people of South Africa:

Shaka examplified this trend of thought. He wanted all Africans to be one—speak one language and be one strong united nation. . . . Today when the theories of certain scholars, the work of literary fanatics, the tactics of some politicians, and the poverty, exploitation and disintegration of our people, all combine to threaten Bantu unity, it is most important that this oneness of the African people should be broadcast from hilltops. These cultural elements will help the African writer not to vacillate between two points—the false foreign and the useless and ephemeral indigenous—but give him something substantial on which to hold.

For all his concern with the maintenance of traditional values, aesthetic and other, Dhlomo realized that "to-day, to thousands of Africans, the school, the train, the police, the automobile, the cinema, the ballroom dance, tennis, golf, economic problems of housing, trade unionism and trading, even the international situation and the world fiscal policies, are as much part of their life as anything else." But he was able to overcome the apparent antinomy between the world of tradition and the world of novelty, the contradictions inherent in "a time when an old indigenous culture clashes with a new civilisation," through a conviction that seems to be deeply ingrained in the best vernacular authors of South Africa, the assurance that "it is not tradition to neglect the contemporary scene."

Dhlomo was for a while assistant editor of *Ilanga laseNatal*. He died at King Edward Hospital in Durban on 23 October 1956.[116]

In spite of the historical importance and the popular success of men like Dube and the Dhlomo brothers, the best Zulu writer so far is Benedict Wallet Vilakazi, who was born on 6 January 1906 of Christian parents at the Groutville Mission Station. His father had worked for a commercial firm and had earned enough money to buy a small holding and settle down to farming. The boy went to the mission primary school, then attended St. Francis College at Mariannhill, where he obtained a teacher's certificate in 1923.[117] At 17, he began to teach, first at Mariannhill and later at the Ixopo Seminary. Those were the early twenties, when Zulu drama and modern song were making humble but promising beginnings at Mariannhill. Yet, if we are to believe Nyembezi, the young man was only dimly aware of this:

As a student at Mariannhill, Vilakazi acted as secretary to Father Bernard Huss. It was probably this association more than any other single factor or influence upon him that made Vilakazi long more and more for distant educational horizons. Father Huss was very interested in the young Vilakazi but although he probably encouraged him and acted as his advisor, the young man gave little sign of his ambition either at the Mariannhill college or when he became a teacher. It was apparently when he went to the Catholic Seminary at Ixopo in Natal and came under the influence of enthusiastic priests that a definite change came over him.[118]

Vilakazi, who had by now become a Roman Catholic, realized that his true call lay in learning and writing. "He had lived," Nyembezi comments, "with African graduates who despised and disparaged anyone who did not have a university degree. The young man had felt their scorn deeply and his determination to climb up the educational ladder—and to climb high—was partly motivated by a desire to retaliate on those who had sought to belittle him." While teaching, he passed matriculation and B.A. examinations by private study, and obtained a B.A. degree from the University of South Africa in 1934.

In 1932, he had submitted a novel entitled *Noma Nini (For Ever)* for the third competition of the International African Institute; this was awarded a prize in 1933. The book was printed in Mariannhill in 1935. The story takes place in the late nineteenth century during the reign of Mpande, when the first missionaries reached Groutville. It deals with a girl whose lover goes to work in Durban for bride money; she promises to wait for him as long as will be necessary. But during his absence, which lasts several years, the missionaries settle in Groutville, the girl becomes a Christian, and she works at the mission station, where a nice young man falls in love with her. She rejects him at first, but as the years pass and she has no news of her fiancé, she comes to think that the latter has forgotten her, and she agrees to marry her new suitor. But just as the marriage is about to take place, the young man returns from Durban after all sorts of misadventures and delays. He has never stopped thinking about the girl, and he is fortunately in time to marry her. The bride manages to find another suitable girl to bring solace to her second lover. This sentimental and rather pointless story is a good example of acculturation literature, where the Western concept of romantic love and the Christian ideal of premarital constancy are oddly fused with the much more matter-of-fact African view of marriage. Further, as one recent Zulu critic says, "characterization is not convincing," and the narrative "is overburdened with unrelated and irrelevant details of historical accounts." [119] Nevertheless, *Noma Nini* had the merit of being the first piece of imaginative fiction to handle modern subject matter in Zulu.

More important is Vilakazi's first collection of poetry, *Inkondlo kaZulu (Zulu Songs)* which was printed in 1935 by the University of the Witwatersrand Press as number 1 in their Bantu Treasury series. The first volume of poetry to appear in Zulu, it contains poems that had been published in native newspapers over a number of years. Some research should be done to establish their chronology, as many of them apparently reflect phases in the poet's evolution. The title, J. Dexter Taylor explained in a long review article,[120] "is the name of a certain Zulu dance. Its significance lies in the fact that the emotions of a people who lack means of literary expression find outlet in the dance." Actually, even in their illiterate days, the Bantu did not lack means of literary expression, but the words, the music, and the dance were not kept apart. The title, therefore, means that Vilakazi envisioned himself as a poet in the tradition of the tribal bard, the imbongi, but with an important difference that Taylor pointed out when he said that "Vilakazi in the richness of his Zulu vocabulary, in the truly African flavour of his imagery and in the exuberant extravagance of some of his descriptions is a true descendant of the *imbongi*. But the background of his thought is not that of the *imbongi*."

To begin with, as Nyembezi observed, "unlike the traditional poet who recited the praise of chiefs and heroes, Vilakazi wrote on a variety of subjects." [121] This widening of the scope of vernacular poetry was a common feature throughout Africa. It does not mean that traditional topics were abandoned; there are several poems about Chaka in the volume. It means that praise poetry was used for illustrious people other than tribal chiefs and heroes, even though Taylor may have been somewhat rash in asserting that "Aggrey is a greater hero to [Vilakazi] than Shaka." It also means that apart from praise poetry, the modern Bantu author deals with other subjects as well: "the clay pot family heirloom," says Taylor, "the song of the lark, the train that dashes by in the night, leaving him vainly waiting—all the little incidents of daily life serve as starting points for the flow of his verse." One of the best-known poems in the collection is a descriptive piece about the Victoria Falls, which, it is reported, Vilakazi never saw; it was translated by Taylor as an appendix to his review of the book.

A third difference lies in the emotional tenor of the poetry. Traditional poetry was fairly impersonal; because of the limitations in subject-matter, the only emotions it was called upon to convey and stimulate were admiration and wonder. But Vilakazi introduces the lyrical modes he had found in English poetry. In the words of Miss Beuchat, he "has been able to convey his feelings of frustration, of longing for the past, his aspirations and deceptions, in a style of his own, which is not that of the traditional poems, and not that found in any European either." [122] Because of this unique African flavor, Taylor considers Vilakazi as "the *imbongi* come to consciousness of the abstract and of the inner self, through contact with the work of other poets and through the unconscious influence of education and of European culture."

As to form, Nyembezi has noted that Vilakazi "was mainly responsible for developing poetry whose form departed radically from the traditional Izibongo (or praise). Instead of adopting the style and pattern of the Izibongo, he experimented with European forms. He divided his poems into regular stanzas. He also experimented with rhyme." [123] For this, as we know, he was to be severely rebuked by Herbert I. E. Dhlomo. But already in his review article of 1935, Taylor offered a balanced appraisal of Vilakazi's endeavors in prosody: "He attempts rhyme, but with limited success, as Zulu syllables, invariably, ending in vowels, do not present the variety of sound and tone that makes successful rhyming possible. Even the forms of English rhythm that he uses do not supply a perfect medium, for Zulu accents and stresses refuse to be bent into conformity with the beat of the music. But Mr. Vilakazi is an experimenter in a new field and is to be congratulated on the large measure of his success, rather than criticized for small failures."

The section entitled "Future of Zulu Poetry," in Vilakazi's article of 1938 in *Bantu Studies*,[124] was presumably written as a rejoinder to Taylor's mild strictures. The poet noted that "there is a feeling among European critics that Zulu can achieve only a limited success with rhyming, since most of the words in Zulu end in vowels, and thus do not permit variety of sound that makes successful rhyming possible." Indeed, Vilakazi stressed his agreement with Steere's remark, in his Preface to *Swahili Tales*, that in Bantu languages "the rhyme is to the eye more than to the ear, as all the final syllables being unaccented, the prominent sounds often destroy the feeling of rhyme." To obviate these difficulties, Vilakazi explained that he had evolved his own system, based on the notion that "in rhyming the Bantu syllables one has to take into account the penultimate syllable," so that "the poet will run his rhyming through two syllables: the penultimate and the final," thus achieving both the desired eye and sound effects. Vilakazi's poetic credo at that early stage in his evolution was defined as follows:

Form tends to reduce everything to mechanical standards and mathematical formulae. But we have to use some form to embody or clothe the beautiful spirit of our poetry. We have no definite form so far, and our starting point will be at the standards given by the Western education we have imbibed at college. We are beginning the work which may be given perfect form in generations to come. After all, our language is old and is fast accumulating new words and concepts. I believe therefore it is absolutely necessary that, in composing some poems, we ought to rhyme and decorate our poetic images with definite stanza forms.

It is worthy of note, however, that already in 1938, Vilakazi was aware that better education and the influence of Stuart's Zulu books were combining to turn would-be Zulu poets back to the virtues of the traditional izibongo.

Vilakazi's experiments with rhyme and stanza form should not be viewed as ritualistic imitations of English prosody, but as a brave attempt to enrich Zulu poetic technique and to make Zulu poetry intelligible and acceptable by Western standards. Obviously, "Inqomfi" ("The Lark") was inspired by Shelley's "To a Skylark" and "We moya" ("Hail, Wind") by the "Ode to the West Wind," and echoes from "Mont Blanc" can easily be detected in "Impophoma yeVictoria" ("The Victoria Falls").[125] Romantic influence on Vilakazi—and later on Herbert Dhlomo— should not be solely accounted for by the prominence of romantic poetry in the school curriculum. The sensitive African suffers under a sense of alienation and nourishes a yearning for a better world, which make him share in the fundamental *Weltschmerz* and *Sehnsucht* of Western romanticism. Just as Western romantics —from Walter Scott to James Fenimore Cooper and Victor Hugo,

and from James Macpherson to the Grimm brothers—turned to
folklore and to history for images of happiness and grandeur, so
the Zulu poet, for all his innovations, remained profoundly faithful
to the inspiration of the tribal imbongi. The best pieces in *Inkondlo
kaZulu* are genuine praise poems, as allusive as, but less elliptic than
the traditional izibongo. Indeed, if we compare the Chaka image
in several of those poems with the portrait offered by Dube in
Insila kaTshaka, it is clear that the younger writer, far from attempting any balanced moral valuation, reverts to the unreservedly
encomiastic attitude of the old bards. He likens Chaka to Caesar
and Charlemagne as the great conqueror, the military and administrative genius, the welder of many nations into one mighty empire. He strangely revels even in the sufferings inflicted by Chaka
on the conquered tribes:

> Let us tell how peoples reeled
> And died, their blood congealed with terror.[126]

For him, Chaka is an outsize figure, whose stature makes moral
judgment irrelevant:

> How unpredictable were you!
> You whose ambition slaughtered infants,
> Babies born and unborn babies.
>
> (P. 65)

The reason for this unexpected leniency in a poet so imbued
with the Christian religion is that Chaka is presented as the instrument and the embodiment of past Zulu unity and greatness, and a
source of everlasting inspiration:

> Still today we speak of you
> And swear by you with utmost faith;
> And all the problems of the Council,
> Discussed by those whom you inspired—
> Those you bequeathed to Zululand—
> We who are not deaf, hear clearly.

Indeed, in "Khalani Mazulu" ("Weep, You Zulu"), a dirge written
on the death of King Solomon in 1933, the decline and enslave-
ment of the Zulu nation are ascribed to the divisiveness and inter-

necine strife in the post-Chaka era, as symbolized in the battle of
Ndondakusuka in 1856:

> Have you forgotten what happened:
> The slaughter of one by another,
> The ruin at Ndondakuzuka?
> You died and the future was barren.
> Now see all the young ones
> Of Whites who despoiled us
> Suckled by cows almost famished,
> Those that were meant for the children—
> The offspring of Senzangakhona
> Who sired the breed of Cetshwayo?
>
> Do you forget then
> Our share of the penance
> Is this: to remember and ever
> Be haunted by Ndondakusuka?
>
> (P. 38)

The poem celebrates Chief Solomon's tireless efforts to restore the
"Inkatha," the secret tribal emblem of Zulu solidarity, which now
takes the shape of a fund constituted by the various Zulu chieftains
in order to carry out such national projects as the building of a
school for the education of chiefs' sons:

> For years counting thirty and seven,
> Did Solomon scheme,
> And plans for uniting the nation
> He formed, and he showed it the ways
> Of peace, and in place of the spears,
> The use of the armour of knowledge.
> He planned and constructed a school
> Where those highly born should become
> The pillars of African progress.
>
> (P. 41)

This leads us to the second main theme of *Inkondlu kaZulu*. For
the world has changed, and if the Zulu are to restore anything like
their former glory, it cannot be through warlike deeds, but through
learning:

> How does it serve to brood upon the past
> As though this period of enlightenment
> Offers no more than darkness and confusion?
>
> (P. 71)

This was the lesson taught by Dr. Aggrey, whose lectures in 1921, as a member of the Phelps-Stokes Commission sent out from the United States to survey the problems and prospects of African education, had made a deep impression on Bantu audiences, even though he had been received with contempt by the Afrikaner section of the population:

> And from the Rand, Paul Kruger's people
> Derided and belittled you,
> Seeing, they thought, a little jackal,
> No different from the other jackals,
> Black, white-toothed, this country's own!
>
> (P. 84)

In this praise poem addressed to Aggrey, Vilakazi recalls how

> I turned from you because I feared you,
> Dreaded to have my ignorance revealed,
> My nakedness displayed,
> When I had thought that I was learned.

But, he adds,

> When you had gone away, I stayed,
> Saw, with new eyes, my native land,
> How men stood firmly on their feet
> And packed their bags and went to learn.

And he proudly records the educational achievements of his people throughout southern Africa, at Lovedale and at Morija, at Amanzimtoti and Ohlange. Characteristically, the last poem in the volume is a long ode in celebration of the fiftieth anniversary of the monastery founded by Catholic missionaries from Germany and Austria. In traditional Zulu phrasing, Vilakazi sings of those white educators as

                                              the sons
Who left their homes
To wander far and wide;
Knotted their bundles and escaped,
Never to return again.
The dwellings of their ancestors,
The kinsmen tied to them by blood,
The soil that nourishes the fruit,
The noon-day heat of summer days,
The moonlight's glow on winter nights—
All this they left behind them.
They crossed the waters of the sea,
They reached the place of assegais

                                                        (P. 97)

to help the Zulu gratify

                       . . . the longing
Of their souls,
The longing for the flaming torch
Already lighted in the South [i.e. among the Xhosa]
And carried high by Grout
And Lindley too and Adams.

These were the American missionaries who had come from the
United States in 1840. The Reverend A. Grout had founded the
Groutville mission, where Vilakazi was born; the Reverend Lind-
ley had founded the Inanda mission, home of John Dube; and Dr.
Newton Adams had established the college at Amanzimtoti. Vila-
kazi's gratitude for devoted service to the Zulu people extends to
Protestants and Catholics alike.

   The years immediately preceding World War II were filled with
feverish activity for Vilakazi, who had become by now the first
Zulu man of letters with a full university education. His work on
the Zulu language for a B.A. had earned him a bursary from the
University of South Africa and he started working for an M.A.
degree in African Studies. The only place that offered senior
courses in African Studies was the University of the Witwatersrand, which, at the time, was in need of an African language assistant for the Department of Bantu Studies. Vilakazi was appointed
to this post in 1936, thus becoming the first African to teach at

university level outside Fort Hare. Because of his literary activities, he was invited to attend the first two African Authors' Conferences of 15 October 1936 and 30 September 1937, where he, together with Herbert Dhlomo, represented emergent Zulu writing.
In 1938 he was awarded an M.A. degree with a study on "The
Conception and Development of Poetry in Zulu," the substance of
which was printed in *Bantu Studies*. Simultaneously, he wrote a
biographical novel about Shaka's protector, *UDingiswayo kaJobe*
(Dingiswayo, Son of Jobe [London, 1939], and carried on a controversy with Dhlomo about the nature of traditional izibongo, the
significance of Zulu drama, and the future of Zulu prosody.[127] But,
as Nyembezi recalls:

Vilakazi's appointment to the University of the Witwatersrand aroused
opposition among a section of the Africans in the Transvaal. Its effect
was to make him recoil into his shell so that he appeared to shun the
company of Africans of his class. He became a controversial figure
among the African people. The educated Africans respected him for
his academic achievements and for his contribution to Zulu literature.
But they regarded him as cold, aloof, haughty—a man who was not
easily approachable. They found him abrupt in his manner and sometimes deliberately rude. The illiterate Africans on the other hand,
found him a pleasant character and easily approachable. . . . Yet . . .
there were those who accused him of being insufficiently conscious of
their sufferings and disabilities. He did not take an active part in politics. It was his firm belief that he could not serve two masters and that
he could not participate in politics and still perform his academic work
satisfactorily.[128]

We have seen Vilakazi's somewhat abrupt, haughty manner during his controversy with Dhlomo. His sense of isolation found
utterance in the poetry of those years, which he collected in 1945
under the title *Amal'ezulu (Zulu Horizons)*. A poem like "Im-
fundo ephakeme" (Higher Education") traces his evolution from
his youthful hopes of smooth synthesis between tradition and
novelty to the more mature awareness of inherent conflict, which
grew in him as a result of his experience of life in Johannesburg:

> When my thinking was but folly,
> Then I dreamed of satisfaction
> If I read my books and studied,

> Pondered learning, mused on wisdom,
> Striving for some understanding:
> Now, to-day, my mind is weary.
>
> I have spent so many years
> Turning over leaves of books
> Whose authors' skins were white;
> And every night I sat alone
> Until the new day's sun arose:
> But now, to-day, my eyes are throbbing.
>
> And poets who were black I called on,
> Those who sang of kings' ambitions,
> Those who praised our brimming bowls,
> And their wisdom too, I thought on,
> Mixing it with white men's teachings:
> Now my mind's a battle-field.[129]
>
> (P. 115)

This intellectual confusion leads him to doubt the value of learning:

> He who does not know these things,
> And sleeps untroubled through the night,
> Never reading till the dawn,
> Not knowing Cicero or Caesar,
> Shaka, Ngqika or Moshoeshoe:
> He, to-day, is light of heart.

A further source of despondency is his estrangement from other Africans, the prosperous bourgeois class, who have fully embraced the white man's creed of material success:

> Those I grew with, those unlettered,
> When they meet me, they despise me,
> Seeing me walk on naked feet
> While they travel in their cars,
> Leaving me to breathe their dust:
> These to-day are chiefs and masters.

This tragic inner conflict finds resolution in acceptance of both the costs and the rewards that go with the author's dedication to learning and poetry:

> So I absorb and add and store
> Wisdom for the Zulus' children.
> The day may come to have discussions
> And learn from all my nightly writings,
> Never written from ambition:
> For you, ancestral spirits, urged me,
> Inspiring me through hours of darkness!
>
> But then I shall be here no longer.

The main direction in Vilakazi's development, therefore, lay in ever deeper reverence for the Zulu tradition. Many of the poems in this second volume deal once more with the great events and figures of the past, the beauty of the Natal landscape, the cult of the ancestors, African respect for the wisdom of old age, or the mission of the poet in Zulu society. The writer's technique also demonstrates that he was not happy with his experiments in the earlier collection. He now discards rhyme almost completely, thus rallying to the views expressed by Taylor and Dhlomo.

But a new orientation also emerges as Vilakazi shows himself more subtly aware of the complex pathos in the modern African's situation. He describes the bewilderment of the tribesman who is compelled to leave his kraal and come to the white man's city of brick and concrete:

> Tell, O tell me, white-man's son,
> The reason you have brought me here!
> I come, but O my knees are heavy
> And, as I think, my head is swimming;
> Darkness descends for me at noon
> And each day's sun becomes a moon.
>
> (P. 119)

In "Ukuhlwa" ("Nightfall"), he evokes the filth and insecurity of the native locations:

> Now, as the streets are lit,
> I fear the lurking thieves
> Who seek their prey like hunters.

> Here, there is no grass,
> But dust from off the mine-dumps
> Like smoke is drifting skyward.
>
> (P. 125)

In "Imifula yomhlaba" ("The Rivers of the World"), he relives
in a dream the occupation of African land by the white invaders:

> And then I saw Retief and all his men
> Scurrying, hurrying through the land,
> To scatter generations
> Of the nations of the white man.
> They wash in waters of the Orange,
> They cleanse themselves of filth;
> And we, the peoples who are black,
> Accepted that calamity,
> That evil weight that bowed our heads.
>
> (P. 147)

In "Izinsimbi zesonto" ("Church Bells"), he underscores the irony
of Christianity, which first seemed to threaten with extinction the
African's cherished beliefs and values:

> I heard the bells, the white man's bells!
> At first I heard them sullenly,
> Heard them toll with rising anger,
> Rage consumed me—then it left me.
>
> (P. 135)

but which has now become—unheeded by the white man, hypocritical, materialistic, and blind—the instrument of a new African
awakening:

> Ring out, O bells, O white man's bells!
> John Dube and his friends have risen
> And brought to life the black men's minds.
> Your call does not awaken them—
> Those looking on, the while they rang you!
> They waken us, yes us in darkness,
> Hidden in the white man's shadow.
> Ring out! the charge is yours, O bells!
>
> (P. 137)

And in "Ngoba . . . sewuthi" ("Because . . . You Say"), he denounces—in terms which are reminiscent of Dhlomo's article, if
only because they are a commonplace of African experience and
thinking—the comfortable blindness of the white man, who chooses
to remain unaware of the black man's sufferings and revolt:

> Because I smile continually,
> Because I even seem content
> And sing with all my voice
> Although you trust me underground
> Beneath the wealth so fabulous
> Of earth stained blue with diamonds—
> You say that I am like a post,
> A thing that feels no pain?
> . . . .
> Because I am, in truth, a dupe
> Who suffers through my ignorance,
> Not understanding all these laws,
> Though knowing I am used and plundered,
> And though the hut in which I live
> I've built beneath the mountain crags—
> My own true home is made of grass
> My own true garment is a sack:
> Because of this, you think me lifeless,
> Having not a tear to shed
> That issues from a living heart
> To fall within the spotless hands
> Of spirits holy and all-seeing.
>
> (Pp. 132–133)

Although Vilakazi did not engage actively in politics, it is clear
that his experience of township life in Johannesburg, because of
the contrast it offered with the sheltered seclusion of Natal mission
schools and with the comparative humaneness of life in Durban,
prompted him toward more explicit protest through his chosen
medium. This second orientation reached its climax in what is
commonly considered his best poem, "Ezinkomponi" ("In the
Gold Mines"), which deals with the black laborer's life on the
Rand. Vilakazi's mood and attitude are very close to those of
Dhlomo in *The Valley of a Thousand Hills*. The main difference
is that Dhlomo, writing in Durban, found his symbols of oppression in the "commercial dells" of the modern mercenary city,

whereas Vilakazi, writing in Johannesburg, found apt emblems of man's inhumanity to man in the industrial society and in the roaring machines that remain deaf

> To black men groaning as they labour—
> Tortured by their aching muscles,
> Gasping in the foetid air,
> Reeking from the dirt and sweat—
> Shaking themselves without effect.

Yet, the poet feels pity for the machines, that were brought from their faraway native land:

> You had no choice, you had to come;
> And now roar, revolve and toil,
> Till, thrown away, worn out, you rot
> On some neglected rubbish-plot.

But the miner's fate is even worse:

> We too, grow old and rusty in the mines;
> Our strength soon goes, our lungs soon rot,
> We cough, we cannot rest—We die!
> But you are spared that coughing—why?

Although Vilakazi's description of the cruel injustice of South African society is heartfelt and eloquent, it does not lead him to rebellion, but merely to what Mphahlele has aptly recognized as "romantic escapism." The poet can only dream ineffectually of "that far day" when

> we, at last, will cry: "Machines!
> You are ours, the black men's, now!
> . . . .
> "Dream that this land—my father's land—
> Shall be my fathers' sons' again."

For the present, his feeling is one of frustration and helplessness:

> But now I have no place to rest
> Though wealth is everywhere around me;
> Land that my fathers owned is bare

And spreads untilled before my eyes;
And even if I had some wealth,
This land my fathers' fathers owned
I may not purchase or possess.

. . . .

Every day this land of yours [i.e. the ancestral spirits']
Is seized and spoiled by those who rob us:
These foreign breeds enrich themselves,
But all my people and myself
Are black, and, being black, have nothing.

. . . .

Our hands are aching, always aching,
Our swollen feet are aching too;
I have no ointment that might heal them—
White men's medicines cost much money.

. . . .

Well have I served the rich white masters,
But oh, my soul is heavy in me!

The mood, however, remains elegiac, impervious to the revolutionary potentialities of the situation, and the only hope that the black miner entertains, as he once more addresses the machines at the end of the poem, is forgetfulness on earth and a better life hereafter:

Roar less loudly, let me slumber,
Close my eyes and sleep and sleep
And stop all thinking of tomorrow.
Let me sleep and wake afar,
At peace where all my forebears are
And where, no more, is earthly waking!
Let me sleep in arms long vanished,
Safe beneath the world's green pastures.

(Pp. 170–174)

It is noteworthy that the word "Zulu" does not occur in this poem. Vilakazi's move to Johannesburg had confronted him with greater misery, exploitation, and oppression than he could have witnessed in Natal. As the mining labor force on the Rand was multitribal, his turning to the social theme also meant a reorientation from Zulu particularism toward a new sense of all-African

solidarity. It is true that he remained faithful to his Zulu inspiration in his third and last novel, *Nje nempela* (*Truly, Indeed* [Mari-
annhill, 1949]). The book has been described as "one of the finest
expositions of the Bhambatha Rebellion of 1906," [130] and has also
been singled out by Zulu anthropologist Absalom Vilakazi as an
outstanding depiction of traditional life in a polygamous household, with the rivalries between co-wives, the suspicion, the ever-
present quarrels, and the tense relations marked by spiteful speeches
and public reprimands.[131] But while writing this novel, Vilakazi
was also working on a doctoral dissertation about "The Oral and
Written Literature of the Nguni," which made him the first African to obtain a Ph.D. degree of the University of the Witwatersrand on 16 March 1946. The Nguni are the branch of the Southern
Bantu which includes both the Zulu and the Xhosa; the two peoples speak kindred languages, and unsuccessful efforts had been
made in the previous two decades to bolster African unity by fus-
ing Zulu and Xhosa into one single language. This was also the
purpose of Vilakazi, who studied the traditional and the modern
literatures of both groups as if they were one nation. Although
the dissertation has never been published, it is the most important
single source of historical information for modern Xhosa and Zulu
literature.

Benedict Wallet Vilakazi died in October 1947.

Besides the publication of Dube's *Insila ka-Tshaka*, of Rolfes R. R.
Dhlomo's historical novels, and of Vilakazi's *Inkondlo kaZulu*, the
auspicious beginnings of Zulu creative writing in the thirties were
also marked by a few other writers. In 1935 the first Zulu woman
writer, Violet Dube, made herself known with *Woza nazo*. It was
printed in Cape Town, by the Oxford University Press, which had
started publishing creative works in the vernaculars. As Vilakazi
explains,

The title of the book derives from the practice indulged in by listeners
to folk-tales. As a narrator goes on with his story, he comes to a place
where he must rest; but he is always careful to leave off where his
hearers' minds are left in suspense. So they shout back to the narrator,
"Woza Nazo!" (Come along with them!) meaning that they are keen to
hear the rest.[132]

Judging from Vilakazi's analysis, *Woza nazo* is a motley collection of traditional tales, some of them based on the Chakijane motif
that had inspired Mbata and Mdhladhla some years earlier. But
the bulk of the volume deals with the adventure of a cunning hero,
Phoshozwayo, who manages to emerge triumphantly from many
strange ordeals. The first Phoshozwayo story tells how the hero is
wronged by his elder brother Qakala, who robs him of the two
horses that are his meager share in the rich estate of their father.
Qakala then attempts to murder his brother, but only succeeds in
killing their grandmother. Phoshozwayo retaliates by calling for
police help—an odd modern note. At last, he manages to get rid of
Qakala by having him tie a stone to his own neck and throw himself into a deep pool in order to discover a treasure that is alleged to
lie at the bottom.

Violet Dube seems to have graded her stories so as to bring out
with ever greater force the unbridled fantasy so often at work in
narrative folk art. The next Phoshozwayo story cannot but call to
mind some medieval Western romances dealing with the motif of
the impossible task. The hero is captured by a giant cannibal,
Nqaba, who lives in an impregnable fort in the midst of magic
country. The gate is guarded by two vicious dogs and a monstrous
snake. One of the impossible things Phoshozwayo is called upon
to do is to sow, to weed, and to reap a field on the same day and,
from the wheat, to bake bread and to bring it to the giant before
sunset. This he achieves with the help of an old hag called Shivane,
who has captured the giant's magic. Phoshozwayo is then ordered
to tame a wild horse that, Shivane warns him, is really the combined powers of all the inmates of the fort: Nqaba is the horse's
neck and forelegs; his wife is the tail and hindlegs; Shivane herself
is one of the horse's flanks. Phoshozwayo obtains a magic feather
from the giant's headdress and transforms himself into not one but
three church ministers who expatiate on the commandment "Thou
shalt not kill" in three different languages for the giant's edification. Nqaba's determination to destroy Phoshozwayo is shaken,
but his wife takes over and pursues the hero to a big river, which
swallows her. Phoshozwayo returns to his own people, who make
him their king.

Vilakazi claims high literary quality for Violet Dube's work,
which calls to mind the exuberance of Yoruba lore as recorded by

D. O. Fagunwa or transmuted by Amos Tutuola: she "is not concerned with inventing new forms of literature, but with perfecting
and building on the old"; "she puts her readers in possession of the
ardour and exultation, with which the oral narrator worked out
his arguments"; "her language abounds in pithy phrases and apt
epithets, coined mostly from words of onomatopoeic origin"; and,
what is highly remarkable in view of most African writers' prone-
ness to heavy-handed moralizing, she "has the story in view as her
first consideration and never punctuates her narration with philo-
sophising or moralising." [133]

In 1937, Zulu drama was at long last graced with publication in
book form when the Witwatersrand University Press issued a play
by Nimrod Ndebele, who had obtained a prize in a May Esther
Bedford competition. *UGubudele namazimuzimu (Gubudele
and the Cannibals)* tells how the title hero takes revenge upon the
cannibals who had eaten his father. Vilakazi considers it "a very
successful experiment based upon the short one-act plays found
written by College students in the 1920s," [134] but D. B. Ntuli finds
that it lacks "the tension that characterises a good dramatical work.
The grim and gory situations are recounted in humourous language
and the dramatic effect is diluted." [135] Nevertheless, Ndebele's
play initiates a new phase in the diffusion of a modern dramatic
tradition that goes back uninterruptedly to the early Mariannhill
plays, and reached popular success with the performances of the
Lucky Stars.

In the early months of World War II, a beginning was made
with original radio drama, a genre that developed rapidly on the
African continent, where the reading public and even more the
book-buying audience are comparatively small. One of the pioneers in this new form was K. E. Masinga, who was at the time
working for the South African Broadcasting Corporation in Durban. One of his plays, *Chief Above and Chief Below*, was translated into English in collaboration with an established white South
African writer Hugh Tracey, who explains how the book originated in his Foreword to the bilingual edition:

The play "Chief Above and Chief Below" came to life when I heard for
the first time the old Zulu legend told me by K. E. Masinga. It was a
very old story, he said: it had been told him by his mother and she had

heard it from her grandmother, and so on, back and back to the days of
the Great Chief. . . . The dialogue was decided upon between us and
written originally in Zulu to preserve the indigenous imagery. The
songs are entirely Masinga's, and based upon Zulu musical forms,
though only a few of them upon old melodies; the word tones and not
the melody being paramount in Bantu music one would not expect
otherwise.

The original legend apparently refers to an old fertility myth:
the daughter of "Chief of All-Above-Ground" refuses all suitors
until she is courted by "Chief of Down-Below-Ground," who has
his jester mesmerize her into marrying him. Chief Above is in-
censed at the disappearance of his daughter and forbids his people
to till the fields or feed the cattle until she returns. The search lasts
a whole year, and inactivity brings about a famine and much distress, until an old woman discovers by chance the subterranean
abode of Chief Below and effects the reuniting and harmonization
of what are obviously human action and the secret telluric forces
of the earth. As all resume work and celebrate, Chief Above's
daughter is hailed as Goddess of the Fields.

Chief Above and Chief Below is a musical play in the tradition
set by the Lucky Stars. Taking place entirely in the realm of myth
and legend, it shows no attempt at character depiction. The thread
of the story is conveyed through spoken comment. The theatrical
interest lies wholly in the songs and dances.[136]

The last writer of this promising generation that remains to be
considered is E. H. A. Made, who was born on 16 June 1904 at
Reichenau Mission near Underberg. After receiving his primary
education there, he entered the Mariannhill Training College,
where, from 1921 to 1923, he studied for a teacher's certificate.
He came back to Reichenau as a teacher and eventually became the
principal of the primary school in Sithebe outside Stranger.[137]
His first book and only novel, *Indlalifa yaseHarrisdale (The Heir
of Harrisdale)* was printed in Pietermaritzburg in 1940. The intro-
ductory chapters tell the story of a man called Muntukaziwa (Mr.
Unknown), who works as a cook on the farm of a white settler
named Harris. He is a thrifty and hard-working man, with great
ambitions for his only son. On Harris's suggestion, he uses what
little money he has been able to save to buy a farm for his son.

Later, Harris decides to dispense with his services. The cook
thinks he is fired, but in the long run he realizes that the white
man wanted to give him the opportunity to apply European ways
of farming on his own farm. Made describes Harris as "a benevolent king of a Whiteman to his devoted servants, unlike those
White people you know, my reader, who derive pleasure in kick-
ing about a Black man with their boots, who tie him at wagon heels
to flog him to death with a sjambok." To the black's awareness
that some white men are good, corresponds the white woman's
defense of the African when Mrs. Harris rebukes some of her
neighbors in the following terms:

You don't trust him because of his black colour. Why don't you reflect
on how many White farmers would ever prosper with so low a wage
as this one I pay him here at home? . . . I will not be blamed by a man's
colour to judge that every thing beneath it resembles it.

Muntukaziwa calls the farm that he has bought for his son, Harrisdale.

The hero of the story, however, is the boy, who receives a good
education at two of Natal's leading boarding schools. But as a
result of this education, he looks down upon farming as dirty
work, far below his dignity. Both Harris and Muntukaziwa are
puzzled and dismayed at this young man who seems to have no
desire beyond dressing up in expensive suits, which his father pays
for, and loafing around with other idle youngsters. He is a subject
of discussion among all the farmers, black and white, of the district. Finally, Muntukaziwa decides upon drastic action. Disregarding the tears and protests of his wife, he gives his son a long
lecture on industry, perseverance, and self-help, he hands him £30
in cash, and he tells him to go and not to come back home until he
has doubled that money. If we are to judge by Vilakazi's review
of the novel, this is a fairly frequent situation: "Muntukaziwa's
educated son is typical of many other sons and daughters of black
parents in South Africa. . . . They have never found a wholeness
in the entire synthesis of their tragic lives once they have been
educated. They therefore try to escape from reality through so-
cially more acclaimed and acceptable means within their reach, in
order . . . to exert the 'self' by self-expression in any way. Hence

excessive dressing, squandering of money in dance and social evenings, even practice of burglary and back-door traffic—and they land in jail." [138]

But Muntukaziwa's son has good stuff in him in spite of his parents' overindulgence. He determines that he will not use his father's money until he sees a good prospect of increasing it. He walks a hundred miles to Pietermaritzburg, where he goes through many sobering experiences. But he manages to gain the confidence of a European who advises him to try the poultry trade. This the young man does with such success that after a few months he has gained a capital of £150. He then becomes homesick, however, and returns home, fully prepared for hard work and frugal living on the farm.[139]

The purpose of the book was, of course, to emphasize the dangers of parental indulgence in bringing up children, to illustrate the dangers of academic education, and to promote that same gospel of self-reliance which John L. Dube had taught since the early years of the century. After *Indlalifa yaseHarrisdale*, Made seems to have given up fiction, turning his attention to the two volumes of *Amaqhawe Omlando* (*Heroes of History* [Pietermaritzburg, 1940 and 1942]), a collection of biographies of European and American great men and women from Drake to Livingstone and from Saint Teresa to Florence Nightingale, and to a volume of essays on miscellaneous subjects, *Ubuwula bexoxo* (*The Stupidity of the Frog* [1947]).

Made has also received some attention as a poet, although Zulu critics have dealt rather harshly with his endeavors in that direction. His collection *Umuthi wokufa* (*The Tree of Death* [Pietermaritsburg, 1951]) has the dubious distinction, according to Ntuli, of offering "very neat rhyming schemes in the fashion of Western poetry." [140] More outspokenly, Raymond Kunene denounced their "forced syllabic metre" and their "unnatural rhyme scheme." Their inspiration is twofold: some are elegiac praises, glorifying Africa and mourning for her glorious past, while in others, of a more personal character, the writer, says Kunene, "indulges in self-pity of the most sentimental type." [141] In "Ubhambatha kaMkhwata" ("Bhambatha, the Son of Mkhwatha"), a poem that was composed in commemoration of B. W. Vilakazi, the writer, Ntuli observes, "alternates the praise poem style with the modern poetic form. He is far more successful with the former. On the whole the poem does not have the dignity and solemnity we expect from a work of its nature."

The Modern Generation

The thirties were a period of fast growth for incipient Zulu literature. Since the war, however, the pace of its development has noticeably slowed down, at least in quality. It is significant that the saturation that Shepherd had mentioned with regard to the market for Xhosa literature in 1937 was observed a few years later in connection with the Zulu market. In a set of recommendations published in 1933,[142] it was suggested that Zulu authors should be encouraged to emulate Xhosa writers. In a report printed in 1942, C. M. Doke quoted D. McK. Malcolm to the effect that "the stimulation of Native [i.e. Zulu] authors has now come to the position when more material is being offered than the market can assimilate." Doke added, however, that "works that can be used as school books secure publication while others meet with extreme difficulty before they see the light of print." [143] The hardening of apartheid in educational policy in the last two decades seems to have had a similar effect on Zulu and Xhosa literature. While there has been in recent years a steady increase in the output of works of fiction designed for school use and hardly worthy of serious critical attention, only one name has emerged among the new generation that should have taken over after World War II.

Cyril Lincoln Sibusiso Nyembezi was born on 6 December 1919 at Babanango. He was educated in Natal and obtained an M.A. degree at the University of the Witwatersrand. After teaching in Natal, he was appointed language assistant in the Department of Bantu Languages of the University of the Witwatersrand. He then moved to Fort Hare as head of the same department there. He resigned at the end of 1959, when several English-speaking white members of the staff were dismissed because they were, in the words of the minister of Bantu Education, "destroying the government's policy of apartheid." [144] He is now working with the publishing firm of Shooter and Shuter in Pietermaritzburg.

Nyembezi's first work, *Mntanami! Mntanami!* (*"My Child! My Child!* [1950]) was dubbed "the best Zulu novel" by Miss

Beuchat. Like so much other South African prose fiction, it deals with

the life of a young boy leaving his home and getting into trouble in Johannesburg, but this novel reveals a high literary ability. The main characters behave according to their personality; all their actions are in keeping with their character and are the logical result of the inter- action of external circumstances and pressures with their personality. In this novel, conflicts between parent and child, and between two codes of morals, and internal conflicts are fully described. The resent- ment of the young boy when his parents misunderstand him, his loneli- ness in the big city where he has come to seek refuge, his struggle when he decides to choose between his accustomed patterns of behaviour and the new ones which he now faces, are all very realistically described.[145]

A Zulu critic, while admitting that this novel represents a seri- ous advance with regard to characterization and suspense, deplores that Nyembezi occasionally lapses into the kind of moralizing to which African writers are so regrettably liable. The novel is partly concerned, like Made's *Indlalifa yaseHarrisdale* and many other, more recent, Zulu tales, with the prodigal son theme and the evil effects of a too-permissive education, and there is a whole chapter of admonition to parents on how to bring up their children prop- erly.[146] It must be recalled, however, that the disruption of tradi- tional family discipline under the stress of apartheid and of Western-type individualism makes this an exceedingly important preoccupation in African experience.

Nyembezi wrote two more novels during the fifties. *Ubudoda abukhulelwa* (*Acts of Manhood Are Not Necessarily Performed by Grown Up Men* [1953]) is the edifying story of an orphan boy who manages to overcome the adversities of life. *Inkinsela yase-Mgungundlovu* (*The Squire From Pietermaritzburg* [1961]) is gen- erally considered his best novel. Dealing with a cunning rogue who cheats naive villagers disguised as a rich tycoon from the big city, it exploits a rich sense of humor that African writers all too often choose to repress.

Although he now seems to have given up creative fiction, Nyembezi has remained a very prolific and versatile writer. His works of the sixties include a Zulu translation of Alan Paton's

Cry, the Beloved Country, a collection of praises of Zulu and
Swazi kings entitled *Izibongo zamakhosi*, and several anthologies
and textbooks for the teaching of Zulu language and literature.
His *Review of Zulu Literature* is one of the most valuable sources
of information on the subject.

As is the case with Xhosa and Sotho, and for the same reasons,
information about the latest developments in Zulu creative writing
is anything but readily available. If any valid conclusions can be
derived from Ntuli's useful compact survey in *Limi*,[147] it would
appear that Zulu writers whose work reached print in recent years
have been slightly less interested than their predecessors in the
former greatness of their nation, and more preoccupied with the
social condition and moral degradation of present-day Zulu society.

After Rolfes R. R. Dhlomo and Benedict W. Vilakazi, the historical novel has been taken up by Kenneth Bengu. His novels,
which include *Ukhabetule* (*The One Who Draws While the
Others Are Silent*), *Ukhalalembube* (*The Snout of the Lion*
[1953]), *Umbuzo wezembe* (*The Question of the Awe*), *Ukade-
bona* (*The One Who Has Experienced a Lot* [1958]), and *UNyambose noZinitha* (*Nyambose and Zinitha* [1965]), usually have a
historical background. In Ntuli's opinion, "Bhengu seems to have
been motivated to write by his eagerness to glorify the valour of
the Zulus of old. Most of his heroes spear their way triumphantly
to kingship. . . . While the daring adventures of his heroes are
fascinating, the heroes' abilities are sometimes exaggerated and
superhuman." Several playwrights dramatize historical events. In
Ukufa kukaShaka (*The Death of Shaka* [1960]) Elliott Zondi
brings to the stage the plot that culminated in the assassination of
Chaka. In *Mageba lazihlonza* (*Mageba, It Has Tracked Itself
Down* [1962]), B. B. Ndelu has dramatized the battle for kingship
between Cetshwayo and Mbuyazi, a story that had also inspired
Vilakazi in one of his poems. Other dramatists use historical circumstances as a backdrop for their plots. Andries Blose's *Uqomisa
mina nje uqomisa iliba* (*You Are Courting Me, You Are Courting
the Grave* [1960]) tells of the tragic fate of two lovers who violated Cetshwayo's decree that girls of a certain age group be
forcibly married to soldiers belonging to some definite regiment.
Their fate is designed to awaken the audience's abhorrence for

traditional authoritarianism and for tribal violation of the rights of the individual and of the heart.

Most Zulu writers, however, draw their inspiration from the most glaring social problems of the present, that is, within the limitations imposed by apartheid legislation. In most cases, this takes the form of a straightforward life history. In J. M. Zama's *Nigabe ngani* (*On What Do You Rely?* [1965]), "Msweli and Hluphekile, the orphans whose childhood was full of hardships and miseries, grow to respectable citizens; on the other hand, Simangalise and Nomacala who were pampered and spoiled by their mother, develop into social misfits. Zama makes his readers conscious of the importance of home education in the later adjustment of an individual." In a way, this novel contains a compendious sampling of the various motifs used by Zulu authors. The problem of how to educate children in a fast changing culture had been handled by Made and by Nyembezi in his first novel.

The story of the virtuous boy who successfully struggles against adversity and reaches a measure of prosperity had been treated in Nyembezi's *Ubudoba abukhulelwa;* it is also central to much later fiction, such as *Uvelengazi* (*I Knew of Him When He Was Born*) by L. G. S. Mthiya, James Gumbi's *Ukuzalwa kukaMuntukaziwa* (*The Birth of Muntukaziwa* [1959]), Ntuli's *Ubheka* (*The Observant One* [1962]), M. R. Mseleku's *Uvumindaba* (*The One Who Masks the Matter*), or Mahlobo's *Umbubuli* (*The One Who Groans*). Many others, however, use the Jim-goes-to-Jo'burg motif as a way to warn their readers against the evils of city life, permissiveness, immorality, and crime. In J. M. Gumbi's *Baba ngixolele* (*Father, Forgive Me* [1966]), the young hero, Fikile, begins by showing disrespect to his parents, and ends in ignominious death. In *Wayesezofika ekhaya* (*He Was About to Reach Home* [1967]) the same writer "dwells on the hero's difficulty in getting permanent employment in Johannesburg. He is later persuaded by his friends to steal money from a bakery safe. He is arrested just before reaching home with the treasure." In *Ngavele ngasho* (*I Said So From the Beginning* [1965]), a drama by David Mkhize, "the hero goes to the city, joins a gang of thugs and finally lands in jail." In his novel *Ikusasa alaziwa* (*No One Knows What Will Happen Tomorrow* [1961]), O. H. Nxumalo tries to give this hackneyed structure "an interesting twist at the end by letting the formerly wayward hero repent and take up priesthood."

In M. Ngcobo's novel *Inkungu mazulu* (*The Fog, You Zulu People* [1957]), "the hero rises to fame, but through his irresponsibility regresses to a fully-fledged scoundrel."

Ntuli concludes his brief account of recent Zulu writing with the following observations:

In general the Zulu novelist uses his rich idiomatic language very successfully. We have mentioned the preponderance of the prodigal-son theme. There is a tendency to let the main character move from the rural to the urban area. Many novelists still step to the fore and become subjectively and openly didactic, thus hampering the natural flow of the story. This practice also deprives the intelligent reader of the pleasure of discovering for himself the writer's message as it can be deduced from the book. School life features regularly, probably because the author knows that the school is the main market for his work.

The Zulu critic does not have a very high opinion of the works he discusses, and his comments teem with rather damaging strictures: clumsiness in plot development, unconvincing characterization, unnecessary didacticism, weird improbabilities, and, with regard to drama, he claims that "the plays seem to have been written more for reading than stage dramatisation."

Clearly, most Zulu writing of the last few years deserves the sweeping judgment recently voiced by Masizi Kunene, who calls the greater part of the black South African output "situational literature," because, he says, "it deals with factual situations, without drawing any significant conclusions: never in our entire history has literature been so childish, so trite, so aimless; . . . the writers lend themselves to the requirements of the school audience and purge their works of any paragraph, word or phrase, that might be deemed subversive by missionary and government standards." [148] Yet, just because they deal with the actual facts of the African's predicament, such mediocre works can arouse valuable responses in the African reader. Lewis Nkosi recalls that he was awakened to literature by J. M. Zama's novel *Nigabe Ngani*, which he wrongly ascribes to J. Mthethwa. While the publishers describe the book as "a story which shows the importance of bringing up children the correct way"—a harmless enough purpose—what Nkosi found in it, in spite of its low aesthetic level, was food for vastly different thought. The writer, he reminisces, "brought out the clash between the traditional way of life and the new technical society created by the white man. The novel depicted what happened in a well-balanced African family when the white man brought industrialization. The result was perplexity, conflicts and the disruption of our ethical values; and with the departure of large numbers of Africans to the towns as industrial manpower, a frightening process of alienation took place among our people, who lost the highest of their African values, their tribal gods, and were not yet able fully to capture the roots and consequences of a Christian and technical society." [149]

After stating that "we still expect to see authors who have enough originality to explore new grounds," Ntuli claims that "judging from the more recent publications, we have good reason to be optimistic in this regard." It seems that in his opinion, one of the more promising among the young writers is Jordan Ngubane, who, he says, made a brilliant contribution with his *Uvalo lwezin-hlonzi* (*The Persistent Anxiety* [1957]). "In this satirical novel, the author ridicules the awkwardness of the lobola custom in modern Zulu society. He slashes fiercely at the practice of forcing a girl to marry a man of her father's taste. Bajwayele, the heroine, rebels against all this and disappears for good. There are many humorous situations; but these do not reduce the great impact the author's message leaves on the reader's mind." It can hardly be said, however, that criticism of the bride-price is a new theme in South African literature. Presumably, the novelty in Ngubane's story lies in its use of humor and satire.

In the field of drama, Ntuli singles out L. L. J. Mncwango, who, he says, "has contributed more than any single Zulu playwright in this field. His first drama was *Manhla iyokwendela egodini* (*The Day She Married the Grave* [1951]). Out of jealousy, Muzwa organises a plot to kill Siphango, his rival for the hand of Nontula. Siphango dies. After the unsuccessful application of love charms on Nontula, she also dies, leaving Muzwa insane with remorse. Apparently the author is trying to disprove the existence of witch-craft. . . . *Kusasa umngcwabo wakho nami* (*Tomorrow Is Your Fate and Mine* [1959]) is written in support of the campaign against T.B. The writer tries to advise the reader to abandon the traditional medical practices in favor of the modern scientific ones. In *Ngenzeni* (*What Have I Done?* [1959]), Menziwa the king tries in vain to make Zenzile, Hilwayo's rightful fiancée, his wife. The lovers flee and settle in Zululand as Shaka's subjects. Tension

mounts as one fears that Zenzile and Hilwayo might be caught
and perhaps meet an untimely death. The play is full of action."
Clearly, it is Mncwango's purpose to carry his audience forward
on the path of modernization, disregarding any romantic nostalgia
for the past.

It stands to reason that the modern writer in the Republic of
South Africa can hardly deal with the obsessional themes of African experience except in a cautiously descriptive way. Discussion
of causes and remedies is severely restricted by censorship. Though
the novelist may be fairly outspoken in his objective description
of the extant situation, when dealing with its origins and the responsibility for it, he is not permitted to lay the blame at any other
door but his own racial group's: hence, the emphasis on home education, the acquisition of learning, and the practice of Christian
virtue, to the exclusion of any overt concern with social reform.
As to the black South African writer who does not wish to comply
with the maiming requirements of apartheid policy, he has few
alternatives to choose from; while Alex La Guma has managed to
smuggle his fine short stories out of his prison, most of his fellow
writers are now living in exile—Peter Abrahams, Ezekiel Mphahlele, Bloke Modisane, Richard Rive, and others. These are city-
born, detribalized authors, who do their writing in English and
can therefore be published abroad. It is usually difficult to know
which ethnic group, if any, they belong to. One exception is Lewis
Nkosi, a Zulu born in Johannesburg. He too writes in English and
has become one of the most distinguished critics of African literature.

The special plight of the vernacular writer is illustrated by the
career of Raymond Masizi Kunene, one of the foremost younger
Zulu poets, who was born in Durban on 12 May 1930.[150] At the
precocious age of eleven, he was already submitting Zulu poems
to local newspapers and magazines. He obtained an M.A. degree
from the University of Natal with a thesis entitled "An Analytical
Survey of Zulu Poetry, Both Traditional and Modern." Although
still unpublished, this is an exceptionally valuable work because it
is not merely analytical but also outspokenly critical of the main
trends in modern Zulu poetry. Considering that modern Zulu
poetry has so far been submitted to three powerful influences—
traditional, Christian, and Romantic—he complains that the balance
has been heavily weighed to the advantage of the latter two. He

readily admits that "religious poetry did have some favourable
influence on the development of Zulu poetry. It introduced a
broader philosophy into Zulu poetry. . . . Humanity no more
meant the local group, but the whole of mankind." He also con-
cedes that English romantic poetry was influential not only because "it has for a long time been the only type of poetry read in
the High Schools," but also because "its melancholy and personal
nature appealed to the Zulu poet." [151] But the results, which he
states in unequivocal terms, have usually been escapism, sentimen-
tality, and lachrymose self-centeredness. Kunene also denounces
the ritualistic adoption of such Western poetic techniques as
rhyme, syllabic meter, or regular stanza forms, all of which, he
claims, are alien and even antagonistic to the very spirit of the
Bantu language. Given these premises, he can only be harshly critical of most Zulu poets. Of *Umyalezo (A Message)*, by E. T.
Mthembu, a schoolteacher who was born at St. Wendolin near
Mariannhill, he says that the writer "tends to be dogmatic, and
accepts religion without critically examining it. . . . The result
of this is that his poetry is didactic. . . . Many people find it dull
and uninteresting. . . . Everything is symbolic of some virtue or
vice. Even the sun that rises must chase away evil darkness." [152]
He is even more contemptuous of E. E. N. T. Mkhize's *Imbongi
kaZulu (The Poet of Zululand)*:

Mkhize's poetry is not of a very high standard. He catalogues platitudes without attempting to put his ideas into poetry. He has apparently not studied his art. Most of his poetry is didactic and commonplace. . . . He is absolutely devoid of originality, his poetry is further
weakened by the ever-present note of self-pity and sentimentalism. . . .
He has no philosophy and generally does not have a wide outlook of
life. He has a flimsy comprehension of the general which is not referred
to any particular situation. His ideas as a result hang in the air and
remain for the most part unconvincing.[153]

Yet, Kunene finds evidence of a welcome "change from servile
acceptance of new ideas to the revolt that sees some good in traditional life" in the poetry of some younger Zulu writers, such as
J. C. Dlamini, the author of *Inzululwane (A Dizzy Sensation*
[1958]); here, he says approvingly, "the critical attitude varies from
sincere questioning of religion to sacrilegious comment." [154]

In 1959 Kunene left for London as a bursary to complete his

Ph.D. dissertation at the University of London. In England, however, he became involved in political activities and gave up his academic pursuits to become the official representative of the African National Congress. Like Herbert I. E. Dhlomo and Benedict W. Vilakazi, he is a great admirer of traditional Zulu poetry, and an upholder of the communal values enshrined in it. While doing his political work and writing articles in English on African literature, he writes a great deal in Zulu, and is said to have been working at two major epic poems, one of which will deal with the history of the Zulu nation and propose a reappraisal of Chaka as a great political and military leader. Some of Kunene's poetry, in his own English translation, has recently been made available in *Zulu Poems* (London, 1970), which came out too late for detailed consideration in this book. The work of a poet who lives and writes in the freedom and estrangement of exile while striving to remain loyal to the literary tradition of his people, these poems may perhaps initiate a new phase in the history of Zulu literature. As English poetry, they rank with some of the best work produced by anglophone poets in Nigeria. But at a time when a disquieting amount of childish stuff is published for school use in South Africa, it is much to be deplored that the original Zulu version, never reaching print, should remain hidden from its natural, indigenous audience. This is perhaps a minor, but nevertheless pathetic aspect of the predicament of vernacular writing in South Africa today.

Chapter 4

Amharic Literature

In spite of their dissimilarities, the vernacular literatures of southern Africa all come from societies that have many things in common. Before the arrival of the Europeans, they were nonliterate societies. Their religions—which we commonly describe as animistic in order to veil our ignorance—were local cults, entirely unconnected with the worldwide beliefs and rites of, say, Christianity or Islam. At different periods in the nineteenth century, and with varying degrees of thoroughness and harshness, those societies came under European control.

In Ethiopia,* we are faced with an entirely distinct situation. True, Ethiopia, like South Africa, is a multinational state. It is governed by a strong Christian minority group, the Amhara; but although the Amhara, being Semites, differ from other groups in the country with regard to both racial identity and religious beliefs,

---

* There are no universally accepted principles for transliterating the Amharic script. Though I have used the system of Stephen Wright— the only critic to have written extensively in English about modern Amharic literature—no attempt has been made to unify the spellings found in the manifold sources that have been used.

As the Ethiopian calendar differs from the Gregorian calendar, and the Ethiopian year begins in September, it is customary, in Ethiopian bibliography, to signal the two Gregorian years corresponding to each Ethiopian year. Thus the Ethiopian year 1962 runs from September 1969 to September 1970 in the Gregorian calendar.

271

they form a larger proportion of the total population than does the white population of South Africa. Above all, they are undisputably indigenous. In their determined effort to unify the country under their sway, they have established their own language, Amharic, as the official language of the country, with such success that the amount of literary writing produced in the other Ethiopian tongues is negligible. Apart from a very few works in Tigriñña—and leaving aside, of course, the vast oral lore that each ethnic group in Ethiopia has produced and is still producing—the phrase "Amharic literature" can legitimately be used nowadays as a synonym for "Ethiopian literature." Indeed, there has been of late an increasing number of non-Amhara authors using Amharic for literary purposes.

Perhaps the most important difference between traditional South Africa and traditional Ethiopia lies in the field of religion. It is not necessary to recall the decisive part played by religious beliefs and rituals in the life of underdeveloped societies. Each group identifies with its god or gods as the source and mainstay of its identity and power. It often views the triumph of an alien people as evidence for the superiority of the latter's god. Its military defeats, if they are crushing enough, undermine its metaphysical roots and make it powerless to withstand not only the armed might of the enemy, but also what it easily takes to be the latter's spiritual superiority. The Amhara were Christianized as early as the fifth century, when Syrian monks, contemporaries of St. Patrick of Irish fame, came to evangelize the country as an aftermath of the Council of Chalcedon (A.D. 451). They produced vernacular translations of biblical texts, in the same way as Protestant missionaries were to do some fourteen hundred years later in other parts of the continent. As the Coptic Amhara belong to the so-called Oriental churches, they feel part of a large and powerful international creed. In the Middle Ages, they had fairly close links with Byzantium, including occasional military cooperation. Before the October Revolution, they sent out students to the Third Rome, Moscow, the capital of Orthodox Christianity since the capture of Constantinople by the Turks. However debased in its mores and petrified in its beliefs and rituals the Coptic church of Ethiopia may have been at the time when European imperialism first threatened to engulf the country in the 1890s, it certainly entertained no sense of spiritual inferiority before Western Christianity. It is not surprising, there-

fore, that Amhara culture proved as resilient and conservative in
the face of Western cultural aggressiveness as did the Islamized
societies of black Africa; the Hausa states of Northern Nigeria;
the Fulani areas south of the Sahara; and the Swahili culture, cov-
ering Zanzibar, the neighboring islands, and the eastern coasts of
Kenya and Tanganyika (now Tanzania).

This complete absence of a spiritual inferiority complex may
well have played a significant role in Ethiopia's successful resistance to colonialism. Before the Japanese victory in the Russian
war of 1904–1905, the troops of Emperor Menelik were the first
"underdeveloped" army to inflict a decisive defeat on a European
country, when the Italians were routed at Adowa in 1896. Except
for the brief period of Italian occupation between 1936 and 1941,
the vast and widely fluctuating territory known as Ethiopia has
been an independent empire since the early greatness of Axum in
the first centuries of our era. By 1936, Ethiopia was the only fully
independent country left in sub-Saharan Africa, with the exception
of Liberia. The self-confidence and pride that this entailed could
not but stimulate creative literature into developments that were
bound to differ in many important respects from those in the col-
onized parts of Africa.

The Literatures of Ethiopia

Even more crucial for our purpose is the fact that Ethiopia can
by no means be described as illiterate. It is true that even now the
percentage of nonliteracy is one of the highest in Africa. This
accounts for the prevalence of a highly diversified and elaborate
oral art in each of the languages spoken throughout the country.[1]

But epigraphic evidence demonstrates that an indigenous alphabet of Semitic origin was in use in Axum as early as the fourth
century A.D. Literary activity seems to have begun in the following
century, when the Bible, some of the Apocrypha, and several
theological treatises were translated from the Greek. The language
of the country was Ge'ez, which has remained to this day the language of the church, and which was almost the only language used
in writing until the mid-nineteenth century.[2] After the Axumite
period, there was a lull in Ethiopian literature. But in the late
thirteenth century, while Ge'ez was fast giving way to Amharic
as the spoken language, it enjoyed a literary renaissance that

reached its apex under King Zär'a Ya'cob (1434–1468). This was
due to the cooperation of the Coptic church and of a new dynasty
that had seized power in 1270. In order to vindicate the new monarchs' claim to legitimacy through continuous descent from Solomon and the Queen of Sheba, the pseudohistorical *Kebrä Nägäst*
(*Glory of the Kings*) was composed between 1314 and 1322. This
was an indication that Ethiopians were no longer concentrating on
translation, although after 1350, the Egyptian head of the Ethiopian
church, the Coptic Metropolitan Abba Salama, caused many devotional works to be translated into Ge'ez, no longer from the
Greek, but from the Arabic. But original composition swiftly
gained momentum in two main directions. Beginning with King
'Amdä Ṣeyen (1314–1344), the Ethiopian emperors, like the contemporary French kings and the Anglo-Saxon and Norwegian
monarchs of earlier centuries, got into the habit of having their
warlike deeds recorded and immortalized in the form of chronicles,
the last of which takes the history of Ethiopia down to 1840.[3]

In spite of official support for this secular type of writing, unchallenged supremacy went to devotional literature, which took
two forms. Whereas most theological treatises in Ge'ez are translations, indigenous hagiography began about 1400, reached its
golden age under Zär'a Ya'cob, and lived on until the eighteenth
century. The second form of original religious literature is to be
found in the hymnals, the earliest manuscripts of which date back
to the late fifteenth century. Ge'ez hymns are called *qené*, and an
Ethiopian scholar of the present day, Alämayyäwh Mogäs, claims
that the genre was invented in Gojam in the fourteenth century.
He also considers that qené is "distinctive of Ethiopia's spiritual
culture," because it "contains a unique kind of wisdom, dark and
deep. Instruction in this occult art of verse composition has traditionally been regarded as propaedeutic to the study of religious
texts. Partly this is because Ge'ez grammar, which must be known
in order to understand those texts, is normally taught only in the
schools of qené. The more philosophical reason given, however,
is that by affording exercise in fathoming secrets it 'opens the
mind' and thereby enhances the student's ability to approach the
divine mysteries." [4]

Since qené composition both in Ge'ez and in Amharic has been
practiced by a number of twentieth-century writers, it may be
useful very briefly to sum up the principles of the genre, the teach-

ing of which remained purely oral and highly esoteric until the
Swedish missionaries at Menkullu succeeded in inducing one of
the initiates to write an anonymous treatise on the subject at the
turn of the century. The essentials of Ethiopian rhetoric were first
expounded in Europe by C. Mondon-Vidailhet in 1907.[5] The best
description available today is to be found in Donald N. Levine's
Wax and Gold. Apart from its prosodic rules,[6] qené composition is
based on the wax-and-gold theory *(säm-enna wärq)*, which views
the poem as a core of deeper meaning (gold) set in an outer mold
of superficial sense (wax). Aristotle too claimed that metaphor is
the essence of poetry. Säm-enna wärq's peculiar feature—which it
shares, however, with the Old Norse *kenning* and many medieval
tropes—lies in the qené-writer's uncanny proclivity to obscurity
and intricacy. "The purpose, indeed," Mondon-Vidailhet commented, "is to create amphibologies by submitting the syntactical
system of the language to distortions which make the real meaning
of the sentence unrecognizable, under surface appearances which
seldom have greater clarity." Apart from such syntactic distortions,
the obscurity of the metaphorical language is further thickened by
recondite scriptural allusiveness, and by systematic recourse to
punning, to which the Amharic language lends itself with uncommon ease. The genre is highly praised for the reason that its composition and understanding require a sharp wit, considerable lexical
and grammatical knowledge and agility, and a thorough familiarity
with the Holy Writ.

While Ge'ez lingered on as the language of church and culture, it
began to be supplanted by Amharic as the language actually spoken
by the people as early as the tenth century. Yet, it does not seem
that Amharic was used in writing until the fourteenth century: an
interesting analogy with medieval Western Europe, where the
areas that had been part of the Romania did not produce any written vernacular literature until the eleventh century. The so-called
"Old-Amharic Imperial Songs" [7] must have been originally oral
praise poems of the kind that is so widely spread across most African societies. They are still in great official favor, and poems in
honor of the emperor and the imperial family have remained an
important branch of literary production in Amharic to this day.
   Strong impetus was given to Amharic writing by the arrival in
1557 of Jesuit missionaries in the wake of a small Portuguese army

sent out to reconnoiter the "Kingdom of Prester John" in 1541.
They became responsible for the earliest printed books in Ge'ez,
which were issued in Rome in the late sixteenth century. But they
also preached and wrote in Amharic, so that the Coptic clergy
were compelled to react in the same way. After Catholic priests
were expelled from the country in the mid-seventeenth century,
Amharic was given up as a literary language until the reign of
Theodore II (1855-1868).

In his own way, Theodore was a modern monarch, who aimed
at unifying his loose empire and centralizing its administration. He
was aware of the importance of the vernacular tongue as a means
toward that purpose. He broke with the old tradition of having his
exploits recorded in the erudite and confidential Ge'ez language.
The chronicle of the first part of his reign was written in Amharic
by his "Minister of the Pen," Däbtära Zänäb. A complete account
of Theodore's reign was composed somewhat later, under Menelik
II, by Aläqa Wäldä Maryam.

This political motive, however, was not the only one that
prompted the revival of Amharic as a written language. By the
time Theodore had himself crowned, a situation analogous to that
of the sixteenth century had been created: Western missionaries
were once more making their way into Ethiopia, settling on the
uncontrolled fringes of the flexible empire. "Men like Isenberg
and Krapf," says Stephen Wright, "devoted years of study in the
country to Amharic (as well as to Galliñña and other Ethiopian
languages). Isenberg in particular not only translated but actually
composed original religious works in Amharic,[8] and thus drew
attention to the fact that there was a public anxious to hear and, if
they could, to read books composed in their own vernacular."
Wright suggests that "it was probably the presence of foreign missionaries that encouraged Ethiopians to consider the possibility of
writing serious works in Amharic." It seems likely, however, that
devotional writing by Ethiopian priests also arose as a reaction to
the threat of Western Christianity. Whatever the reason, the fact
remains that in 1857 Theodore's chronicler, Däbtära Zänäb wrote
what Wright describes as "a little book of moral precepts with the
rather pretentious semi-Ge'ez title *Mäshafa Čäwwata segawi wä-
mänfäsawi*," which "consists of the sort of edifying, but not very
effective, moralising that preoccupies all too many Ethiopian
writers." [9]

The defeat of Theodore by the British expeditionary force of Sir Robert Napier, his suicide in 1868, the troublesome reign of King John IV (1872-1889), his fights against the Mahdi, his feud with Menelik, created favorable conditions for incipient European intervention along the coastal areas in the Red Sea during the early 1880s. Western missionaries reappeared, especially Swedish Protestants and Italian Catholics. A Swedish mission was set up at Menkullu, near Massawa in Eritrea, which had been occupied by the Italians in 1885. There it was that an Ethiopian convert, Gäbrä Giyorgis Terfe produced the first Amharic translation of the omnipresent *Pilgrim's Progress*. There was no printing press in Ethiopia at the time, and Martin Flad had the work printed at the St. Chrischona Mission Press in Switzerland in 1892, with financial help from the Ev. Fosterland Stiftelsens, the Religious Tract Society, and the London Society for Promoting Christianity Among the Jews. It was reprinted in 1946 by the United Society for Christian Literature in London.[10] According to Wright, "it is not a masterpiece of translation—a revision was made and published in Addis Ababa in 1958-59; but the book has probably had a profound influence, in respect to both form and content, on the formation of the new Amharic literature. After thirty years, its effects could be sensed in several works of Blaténgéta Heruy, and today many authors, including Ras Bitwädded Mäkonnen and a host of minor writers, obviously owe—though often indirectly and quite unconsciously—a considerable debt thereto." Apart from this, however, the part played by foreign missions in the birth and growth of modern Amharic creative writing is conspicuously unimportant as compared with their role in the literary history of other African countries. Even a sketchy summary of the introduction of printing in Ethiopia will substantiate this statement.[11]

The earliest Ethiopian printed book dates back to the sixteenth century: in 1513, a *Psalterium Chaldaicum sive potius Aethiopicum* in Ge'ez was printed in Cologne. But printing in the Amharic language began in the late nineteenth century under the aegis of the Swedish Evangelical mission in Eritrea. Its first Amharic books were printed in St. Chrischona, but after the conquest of the coastal town of Massawa by the Italians in 1885, a printing press was installed at Menkullu, somewhat farther south. It was transferred to Asmara in the mid-1890s, when the seat of the colonial government was shifted there. Many of their publications—including

Teresa de Pertis's version of *Pilgrim's Progress*, which appeared in 1934—were in Tigriñña, but whether in Tigriñña or in Amharic, those works have little to do with creative writing, being mostly of a didactic or devotional nature. So were the books published in Galla country by the Roman Catholic mission press set up in 1905 by the French Capucin missionaries in Dire Dawa, where they had been active since the mid-nineteenth century.

Meanwhile, however, printing had begun in Addis Ababa, with the encouragement of Menelik II. During the first decade of the century, a Greek named Kavadia used to produce twenty-four copies of a little periodical in Amharic, *Aimro (Intelligence)*, on a multiplying machine. The emperor helped him buy a small printing press, on which *Aimro* was published from 1914. This soon became known as the Imprimerie éthiopienne d'Addis Abeba, and was controlled by the capital's city administration. It produced at least one twelve-page booklet of poetry. But printing of creative work on any significant scale first began in 1921 when the regent Täfäri Mäkonnen instituted his own press, which was headed by Ethiopia's first major writer, Heruy Wäldä Sellasé. It thus appears that missionary presses, being peripheral to Amhara territory and mainly occupied with the publication of pious works and textbooks, often in languages other than Amharic, played little part in the emergence of the new national literature of Ethiopia, which was chiefly due to native initiative and to comparatively lavish financial support on the part of the regent.

The Emergence of Written Poetry, Drama, and the Novel[12]

As far as can be ascertained in the present stage of our knowledge, the first poet writing in Amharic was called Gäbrä Egzi'abehér. It would seem that he was born in Tigré in the early 1860s, but he spent the early part of his life at Säda Krestian (Hamasien) in Eritrea, where he attended primary school. He was one of the first of many Ethiopians who went to the Eritrean mission schools for their education, and then entered the service of the Ethiopian government. Indeed, before the Italian war, he had been collecting intelligence for the government of Menelik, and when war broke out, he was imprisoned by the Italian authorities at Nocra. After the battle of Adowa, he managed to make his escape to the emperor's court. It is said that he spent some more time in jail in Harar in 1902 for maintaining to Ras Mäkonnen that the earth revolves around the sun. He became "a kind of court satirist," and "started by trouncing the important men of state and by saying witty things at the great court banquets which Menelik held at the palace every Sunday, and later issued similar material in written form." It would seem that this "publication" took the shape of some fifty handwritten copies. Gäbrä Egzi'abehér's poems were therefore in the tradition of oral court poetry, but they were essentially didactic and political. They "emphasized the need for unity, strength and modernisation, and aroused considerable interest in court circles." [13]

Gäbrä Egzi'abehér is also alleged to have authored a seventy-page political pamphlet entitled *Advice for Seeking and Grasping the Best Way to Strengthen the State for the Benefit of People and Country*, which was printed anonymously outside Ethiopia in 1905-1906. On the occasion of the Libyan war between Italy and Turkey, he wrote a violently anti-Italian poem that prompted an anonymous reply ascribed to Afäwärq Gäbrä Iyäsus. Though his activities had earned him the title of Blatta, Gäbrä Egzi'abehér fell out of favor and died around 1914.

Gäbrä Egzi'abehér's poems did not reach print in his lifetime. It was as a by-product of the emperor's determination to modernize his country that a new creative Amharic literature in printed form was to emerge. Though he himself was not a very learned man, Menelik was shrewd, and he realized that two things were needed to maintain Ethiopia's independence. One, of course, was military strength. But in the long run, it was also necessary to reorganize the administration of the country, to get rid of an obsolete feudal system, to spread literacy and education, and to acquire the technical skills that made the European threat so formidable. The first step he took to that effect was to send some of his brighter young men to Europe. One of these was Afäwärq Gäbrä Iyäsus, who was to become Ethiopia's first novelist.[14]

Afäwärq was born on 10 July, 1868 on the Zägé peninsula of Lake Tana, which was a highly regarded center of traditional learning. His family, of half-Gondare, half-Gojame origin, were kin of Queen Taytu, wife of Menelik, who then ruled over only the independent kingdom of Shoa. While Emperor John IV was

fighting against the Italians and the Mahdists, Menelik was busy
conquering Harar. In 1887 he sent to King Umberto of Italy a mission headed by one of his nephews, Prince Gugsa, son of Ras
Dargé. This was an important step toward the Italo-Ethiopian
treaty of Wuchale, 1889, often referred to as the treaty of Ucciali.
Afäwärq accompanied the delegation and was entrusted to the
care of the Italian government in order to study at the Accademia
Albertina di Belle Arti in Turin. On his return to Shoa, he was
appointed to decorate with frescoes one of the churches recently
built by Queen Taytu in the old capital of the kingdom, Entoto.
It was then that he incurred the wrath of conservative Ethiopians
and of Queen Taytu herself because he had worked in the church
of Raguel without removing his shoes.

In late 1894, Afäwärq traveled back to Europe, together with
two other promising young men led by Menelik's Swiss adviser,
Walter Ilg. In Neuchâtel, Switzerland, he again met Gugsa, who
by now had become Menelik's opponent and was supported by the
Italian government because Ethiopia in 1893 had denounced the
treaty of Wuchale. He attached himself to Gugsa and left with
him for Eritrea, only to sail back to Switzerland after the battle of
Adowa in 1896. It was also in that same year that Afäwärq, who
had first been married to one of Ilg's relatives, became engaged to
Eugenia Rossi, whom King Umberto allowed him to marry in 1904.

After studying for some time at the Collegio Internazionale in
Turin, Afäwärq received an appointment as assistant to Professor
Francesco Gallina at the Istituto Orientale in Naples in 1902. Most
of his books were written and printed in Rome in the course of the
next ten years. They include three works on the Amharic language
written in Italian, a guidebook to Ethiopia in French and Amharic,
a biography of Menelik, a novel, and a collection of psalms in
Amharic.

In 1912, however, Afäwärq gave up Europe and the scholarly
life and left with his family for Eritrea, where he devoted himself to business. It was there that he entered into the controversy
with Gäbrä Egzi'abehér in connection with the Italo-Turkish war:
a pamphlet in verse published in Asmara in 1912 under the authorship of "a citizen of Asmara" is attributed to him. It was a spirited
defense of Italy's civilizing mission, in refutation of Egzi'abehér's
attack.[15]

While Afäwärq was in Eritrea, many things changed in Ethiopia.

Emperor Menelik died in 1913; he was succeeded by his grandson Lij Iyassu, whose undertaking to make Islam the official religion of the country prompted the Christian Amhara to rebel. In 1917 one of Menelik's daughters, Zäwditu, ascended the throne, with Ras Täfäri Mäkonnen as regent and heir designate.

In 1918 the empress and the regent called Afäwärq to Addis Ababa and sent him on a trade mission to the United States. In 1922 he was appointed director of customs at Dire Dawa with the title of Näggadras. At the end of that year, he accompanied Räs Täfäri to Jibuti, where the regent had been invited by the French authorities to visit the battleship *Jules Michelet*. His published account of the trip is the first example of a genre that was to become very popular in Ethiopia, as a means both of strengthening allegiance to the imperial family and of fostering a better knowledge of foreign countries.

In 1925 Afäwärq was appointed to preside over the special court instituted to try cases involving Ethiopians and foreigners. Provision for such a court had been made in the Franco-Ethiopian treaty of 1908, but it did not become operative until 1922, with Heruy Wäldä Sellasé as its first chairman. When the head of the Coptic church of Ethiopia, Abunä Matéwos died on 4 December 1926, Afäwärq sided actively with those who supported Ras Täfäri's request that Ethiopians might have a greater say in the affairs of their own church. Although the Holy Synod appointed yet another Egyptian metropolitan, the first four Ethiopian bishops were appointed in 1929.

In 1927, too, Afäwärq was sent to Rome by the emperor in order to initiate the negotiations that were to lead to the treaty of 1928. In 1931 he became his country's representative in Italy, whence he was recalled in October 1935 as a result of the Italian invasion. When the emperor left for his British exile, Afäwärq took part in negotiations held with the Italians in Jibuti in March and April 1936. During the period of Italian occupation, he was appointed Afä-Qésar, that is, supreme head of the native judiciary. Upon the liberation of Ethiopia in 1941, he was exiled and imprisoned in Jimma, where he died on 25 September 1947, after being struck with blindness.[16]

Afäwärq's was one of the earliest tragedies of intellectual acculturation in Africa. A highly gifted man, as Menelik had perceived, he had thoroughly imbibed the modes and values of Western civilization during his long stay in Italy. He was bitterly aware of the archaic elements in Ethiopian society and denounced them most outspokenly in his *Guide du voyageur en Abyssinie*. He realized that there were two major obstacles to the growth of Ethiopia into a modern country capable of holding its own in the twentieth-century world. One was the still prevailing feudal system, which made for continuous disorder through internecine war among the high feudal lords, and for ruthless exploitation of the common people by the military. The other was the misoneistic attitude of an illiterate population led by a clergy that was ignorant, corrupt, superstitious, and efficiently opposed to any kind of technological and scientific progress. For him, as for so many educated Africans of his generation, the model state was the European nation that he knew best, in his case Italy. And in his biography of Menelik, he succeeded, as one Italian critic put it, in setting a perfect balance between his Ethiopian patriotism and his love for Italy.

For although Afäwärq was fully Westernized, most of his books are devoted to promoting a better knowledge of the Amharic language abroad. We do not know why he gave up his assistant-ship at the Istituto Orientale, but the fact remains that after many years in Europe, he felt the need to go back to his native Africa. And when the empress called him back to Addis Ababa, he did not hesitate. But the best evidence of this deep attachment is perhaps to be found in *Lebb wälläd tarik* (*Fictitious Story* [1908]), the first novel in Amharic, and indeed one of the first to have been written in any of the vernacular languages of Africa.

By Western standards, *Lebb wälläd tarik* can hardly be considered an outstanding piece of prose fiction. It tells a rather complicated story based on the familiar folk theme of people getting lost and looking for each other. It takes place in an unspecified country where Christians and pagans are at war. A Christian general is made a prisoner, and his ransom is paid by a charitable merchant. The general's son, Wahed, tries to find the benefactor to show his gratitude but is himself captured and sold into slavery. The general leaves home, accompanied by Wahed's twin sister, Ṭobya, disguised as a boy, to recover his lost son. Unfortunately, both father and daughter fall into the hands of a pagan king, who behaves, however, in a most friendly way and summons all the slave merchants to rescue Wahed. Meanwhile, a lady of the court falls in love with Ṭobya, and the worried general reveals the whole

truth to the king. The latter becomes in his turn enamored with
Ṭobya and, after Wahed has finally been found, asks her in marriage, while the young man will marry the lady. Ṭobya refuses:
being a Christian, she cannot marry a pagan. Consequently, the
king adopts the only course open to him and becomes a convert
with all his people.

Quite justifiably, this rather naïve and, in some respects, almost
Victorian story, has been chiefly commended for its style. As
Luigi Fusella wrote, "Afäwärq's prose is by no means easy to
understand: the wealth of rare and far-fetched words, the long
complex sentences with a number of subordinate clauses, sometimes very far from the main clause, the vividness with which the
author personifies things and makes them talk, which leads to some
unexpected speeches, the habit of repeating the same thing with
different words—all this makes the writing of Afäwärq difficult to
understand even for Ethiopians, when they have not reached a
high level of education or are used to a less refined language." In
his article in *Something* Wright also comments that "Afäwärq
lapses into 'preciousness' now and then: like many experimenters
with language, he tends to 'overinvent.' Carried away by the thrill
of using words in new ways, he is sometimes led into unnecessary
originalities of spelling and usage." But in Amharic aesthetic
thought, it is just this wealth and complexity, this ability to sum-
mon up all the varied resources of the language, this virtuosity in
manipulating sound values, hyperboles, double entendres, and proverbs, which make the book worthy of admiration and account for
its popular success.

Literary realism is no part of the African legacy, and the Ethiopian reader has no objections either to the supernal virtues of
Afäwärq's characters or to the numberless coincidences that enable
his plot, such as it is, to progress. Indeed, nothing of this is really
implausible to the traditional Ethiopian mind, which has been
deeply affected by the high degree of fatalism inherent in Coptic
Christianity: since everything is in the hands of God, and since
God can perform any miracle, no amount of arbitrary coincidence introduced by the writer can strike the reader as lacking in
verisimilitude.

Although the actual religious life of Ethiopia had long been
marred by ecclesiastical corruption, popular superstition, and general ignorance, Christian ideals remained alive in the minds of the

learned. It had always been part of the function of Ethiopian literature, devotional and narrative, whether oral or written in Ge'ez, to remind listeners and readers of the true message of the Gospel. Christianity was not an imported product in Ethiopia as it was in the other parts of Africa. Whereas Afäwärq's *Guide* concentrated on the darker side of Ethiopian mores, his *Lebb wälläd tarik* must be considered an attempt to illustrate what was best in the native Christian tradition that had existed uninterruptedly since the fourth century. By writing this uninhibitedly edifying novel, where the virtues of family love, hospitality, and charity are extolled, where righteousness is always rewarded, where the true faith triumphs over heathenism by the meek force of virtuous example, Afäwärq transferred the moralizing intent of the traditional folktale to the modern creative writing of Ethiopia.

Two years after Afäwärq's departure for Switzerland, another group of five young men was sent to Europe, this time to Czarist Russia. This choice is perhaps to be accounted for by an age-old sense of kinship between Orthodox and Coptic Christianity: as early as the sixth century, an Ethiopian army helped by a Byzantine fleet invaded Yemen to protect Arab Christians there. Among the students sent to Russia was Täklä Hawaryat, whose single contribution to creative Amharic literature was to be of highly paradoxical significance.

Täklä Hawaryat was born in Kassat (Tägulät), Shoa province, in 1881.[17] After studying Ge'ez in Däbrä Berhan, he entered the service of Menelik II's trusted ally Ras Mäkonnen in Harar. He took part in the battle of Adowa, after which he was introduced to the emperor by his protector. In 1896 he and four others were entrusted to the care of Count Leontiev, who took them to the court of Czar Nicolas II. This Leontiev (1861-ca. 1911) was of genuine Russian nobility, although the title of Count had been bestowed upon him by Menelik, who later made him governor of Equatoria province with the title of Däjazmač. He came to Ethiopia in 1895 with Eliséiev's expedition, which was one more manifestation of Russia's interest in Ethiopia since the late 1880s. The death of Eliseiev enabled him to set himself up as an important intermediary, not only between Ethiopia and Russia, but also between the two camps in the Italo-Ethiopian war! When Täklä Hawaryat accompanied him to St. Petersburg, Leontiev had with him "two letters from Menelik, empowering him to negotiate peace terms with the Italians on his behalf, and a personal, and almost certainly forged, message to Nicolas II offering Russia a protectorate over Ethiopia." [18]

In Russia, Täklä Hawaryat associated chiefly with such representatives of enlightened opinion as Princess Volkonsky, the granddaughter of the well-known Decembrist leader, and Kochubei, himself one of the leaders of the Ukrainian nationalist movement. While thus imbibing the liberal ideas that were widely discussed in Russian aristocratic circles at the time, he attended the Mikhailovskaia Military School in Moscow and the Artillery School in St. Petersburg. After graduating, he was promoted to the rank of colonel in the Russian army.

He came back to Ethiopia in 1909, but after a few months he left again, this time in order to study modern methods of agriculture in France and in England. About 1912, he returned to his country, where he served in a great variety of capacities: he headed the Ethiopian mission during the negotiations with the English to define the Sudanese-Ethiopian border. He was for some time käntiba (chairman) of the Addis Ababa city council. He was also comptroller of the Addis Ababa-Jibuti railway line.

As a former protégé of Ras Mäkonnen, Täklä Hawaryat was a loyal follower of the latter's son, Ras Täfäri. He was one of the leaders who met, on 27 September 1916, to urge Abunä Matéwos to release the Ethiopian people from their allegiance to Lij Iyassu,[19] and he participated in the coup that ousted the latter from the throne in 1917. As a reward, he was appointed governer of the provinces of Jijiga and Ogaden with the title of Fitawrari. In 1923 he became governor of Chercher, where, according to Richard Greenfield he set up what might pass at the time for a model administration. He founded the new town of Asba Täfäri. He introduced "some rudimentary land measurement and reform." Under his administration, "taxes were raised in cash, local salaries were paid and the surplus, rather than a haphazard tribute, was remitted to Addis Ababa." He was keenly interested in public welfare, and subsequently wrote a book about tuberculosis and an agricultural primer.

In 1931 he was appointed minister of finance with the title of Bajerond. In this capacity, it was his privilege to deliver the parliamentary speech introducing the first Ethiopian constitution, which

he had helped prepare, taking as a model the 1889 constitution of
Japan. In 1933 he was sent to Paris as envoy extraordinary and
minister plenipotentiary to the European states. On that occasion,
he wrote a book of advice for Ethiopian travelers in Europe. He
also headed the Ethiopian delegation at the League of Nations.
When war broke out, he was recalled to his country and entrusted
with the task of defending the sector of the Awash valley. On 2
May 1936, Greenfield records, in the vicinity of Chercher, he
stopped the train carrying the emperor to Jibuti:

Takla Hawariat . . . was typical of many who saw the departure of an
Emperor abroad as a disaster of great and almost mystical dimensions.
Yet he was an educated and a travelled man. . . . With his rifle in his
hand, he greeted Hailé Sellassié and bluntly asked that his Emperor
journey with him into the hills and raise a Patriot force. Hailé Sellasié
was willing but the *rases* advised against it and the train moved on.
Some time later, Takla Hawariat himself was to go to Jibouti to help
the consul . . . organise relief for the many Ethiopian refuges. But when
pressed by newspapermen about his differences with Hailé Sellassié, all
Takla Hawariat would say was: "Our differences are personal—where
the country is concerned we are one."

This was diplomatic caution, for when Täklä Hawaryat left
Jibuti, he did not join the emperor, but settled in Madagascar; nor
did he return to Ethiopia until 1955, aged 74. Since then, he has
been living at Hirna (Chercher), experimenting with modern agricultural methods on his own farm.

   Täklä Hawaryat's sole and unique contribution to the creative
literature of his country was the first modern play in Amharic. It
is one of the most mysterious events in the nascent literature of
contemporary Ethiopia. Although accurate dating is not yet possible owing to discrepancies between the various sources,[20] it seems
to have been performed during the years following the author's
return from Western Europe, roughly between 1912 and 1916. It
has not been possible to trace its original title, which meant *Fables
and Animal Comedy*. The play was based on some of La Fontaine's
fables, which the writer dramatized in such a way as to provide a
scathing satire of the corruption, backwardness, and inefficiency
then prevailing in the Ethiopian administration. Although the first
performance was a success, the play, understandably enough,
caused considerable dissatisfaction in the powerful feudal-

bureaucratic circles that were the butt of its mockery. The result was a ban, not only on this particular play, but also on all theatrical performances. It was not until the coronation of Ras Täfäri as Emperor Haile Selassie I in 1930 that modern drama was revived in Ethiopia.

Heruy Wäldä Sellasé

Although Afäwärq and Täklä Hawaryat were creative writers only in an occasional and highly ephemeral manner, they nevertheless deserve recognition for initiating the modern genres of prose fiction and drama in Amharic writing. But the genuine founder of modern Amharic literature was a slightly younger man, Heruy Wäldä Sellasé, who was born on 7 May 1898 in Den, in the Shoan province of Märhabété.[21] The first forty years of his life are shrouded in secrecy, which he apparently did nothing to dispel. Ladislas Farago, who met him on his visit to Ethiopia in 1935 has the following story to tell:

Soon I discovered that a curious early history had created a legendary personality. He had been born the son of a slave, and was a slave himself in his childhood. Old Abyssinians remember the time when they saw him in the lowest ranks of Lidj Yassu's servants—at court the servants line up in order of precedence—carrying the ordinary rifle of his master.... Although he had to carry the king's rifle, he had other more responsible duties to perform and as this humble servant could never give offence to anyone, he was eventually given a post by the then Governor of Harrar, Ras Tafari, the present Emperor, and he was able to carry out his orders. He became the Governor's spy at the court of the unpopular king. He learned for his master about the royal intrigues and he made known the king's predilection for Arab and Mohammedan clothes, and when Lidj Yassu, thinking that he was among friends, wore Arab clothes instead of the Abyssinian shama, he was betrayed by Herouy.

When he was in court service, he was a faithful servant to Ras Tafari, who was told of the king's every movement and so enabled to make his plan accordingly, and when Lidj Yassu was driven out the servant was promoted to Foreign Minister.[22]

Elsewhere in his book, however, Farago reports that "Herouy studied the Amharic alphabet in the church school" adjoining a

monastery on the Entoto mountain.[23] He learned far more than
the alphabet, if we are to believe Adrien Zervos, who claims that
between 1895 and 1900 Heruy translated part of the Holy Scripture into Ge'ez, and edited the traditional code of civil and ecclesiastical law, the *Fetḥa Nägäst*. Hermann Norden further adds
that Heruy started his career as an assistant veterinary at the
French legation.[24] From other sources, it is possible to infer that he
married in 1902, that he entered the Civil Service as a secretary in
the Imperial Chancellery under Menelik, and that he visited Cairo,
London, Paris, and Athens in 1911. Obviously, the course of
Heruy's life before 1917 is in need of serious investigation.

The proclamation of Ras Täfäri as regent in 1917 meant for
Heruy the beginning of a meteoric career as a civil servant and
diplomat. He was appointed käntiba of the Addis Ababa city council and director of the Imprimerie éthiopienne.[25] Under his leadership, the press started publishing books, mostly of an educational
and devotional kind, in Ge'ez and in Amharic. In 1917 he also
launched a weekly literary journal, *Goha Ṣebaḥ (Dawn)*, which
had only a few issues consisting mainly of poems in praise of Ras
Täfäri.[26] Sometime between 1917 and 1922, the press issued an
undated twelve-page poem composed by Grazmač Webäté from
Harar, one of the official court poets, in honor of Empress Zäwditu
and Ras Täfäri. This is a traditional and highly popular genre in
Ethiopia as it is in many other parts of Africa. A large part of the
poetic output in the early days of printing, and even more in the
course of the past twenty-five years, consists of praise poetry
similar in function to the Nguni izibongo and to the Sotho lithoko.
One of the early publications of the Ras Täfäri Printing Press was
an ode in honor of the regent by Däbtära Yayu 'Aläm of Däbrä
Ragu'él, but the poetic vein of reform and modernization initiated
by Gäbrä Egzi'abehér was also continued. In 1921–22 an anonymous verse pamphlet entitled *So that the Sons of Ethiopia Should
Be Careful* reflected an outlook very similar to that of Afäwärq
in his *Guide*, advocating modern education in order to dissipate
past ignorance, and so to maintain the independence of the country. The following year, another anonymous poet, who had visited
American universities, published *So that the Sons of Ethiopia
Should Think*, a patriotic poem that drew an equally anonymous
reply entitled *Thoughts of the Heart* in the same year.[27]

But Heruy was the only writer of that generation who, besides his career as a civil servant, can also be considered a professional man of letters. His first work, published in 1911–12, testified to his scholarly interest in the literature of his country, since it was a catalog of the books in Ge'ez and in Amharic to be found in Ethiopia; a new, considerably augmented edition was to appear in 1927–28. Three further works of his were published in 1917–18, also by the Imprimerie éthiopienne. One was a short biographical account of Emperor John, based on an English book and on personal research in Gondar and Tigré. Another was a collection of funeral songs, providing an account of the circumstances in which each poem had been composed; some of these were later published in Italy by Enrico Cerulli.[28] The third was a collection of moral meditations, centered mainly on family education. The last of Heruy's works to come from the Imprimerie éthiopienne, was once more of moral and religious inspiration, purporting to illustrate the character and behavior of men through parables. First printed in 1922–23, it was exceedingly popular and was reprinted for the fourth time in 1956–57. After 1922, Heruy had his works published by the new press imported by Ras Täfäri.

In 1920 Heruy had obtained the title of Blatta, and in June 1922 he was appointed to preside over the newly created special consular court of justice, an office to which he was to be succeeded by Afäwärq in 1925. In 1922–23, he traveled a good deal, visiting Cairo, Jerusalem, Vienna, and Berlin, and taking part in the negotiations for the admittance of Ethiopia into the League of Nations. In 1923 he accompanied Ras Täfäri's wife, Princess Mänän on a pilgrimage to Jerusalem and wrote the official report of her journey to Palestine and Egypt. He accompanied the regent on an extensive voyage through Europe and the Middle East in 1924, of which he also wrote the official account. Coming shortly after Afäwärq's report of the regent's visit to Jibuti, "this attractive book," says Wright, "did more to shake the Ethiopian people into a realization of how the rest of the world was living and thinking and of the part therein which Ethiopia might be called upon to play than could have done any number of cold official communiqués."[29] During those years, Heruy also published several other volumes dealing with religion, practical ethics, and the history of Ethiopia and of her monarchs, as well as a collection of qené, some of them of his own composition.[30] In 1926–27 Heruy published *Goha Ṣebaḥ* (*Dawn*), an anthology of extracts from the Scripture,

from history and from various other works. He had used the same
title for his short-lived periodical of 1917, and he turned to the
same two Ge'ez words as a name for a new press that was set up
in 1927–28 at his own instigation, "for the purpose," says Wright,
"of printing more strictly 'literary' works than the existing Gov-
ernment-controlled presses could be expected to deal with." [31]
Goha Ṣebaḥ soon turned to other printing jobs as well, but its
main achievement, in the present context, remains the publication
of at least eight of Heruy's works.

Heruy's increasingly important official functions brought him
in contact with a number of foreigners, so that he is one of the
very few among early African writers of whom personal descriptions are available in print. James E. Baum, of the Field Museum
of Natural History in Chicago, who visited him in the mid-twen-
ties, met him as "confidential adviser to Ras Tafari, in the capacity
of Foreign Minister—a man who might be termed the Colonel
House of Abyssinia." Actually, Heruy had not yet received the
title of foreign minister, but was presumably acting as the regent's
trusted adviser on foreign affairs. Baum describes him as follows:

Small and rotund, dressed in the softest and cleanest of white shammas,
with his closely cropped beard, he was typical of the Abyssinian
grandee. And balata Herui is the last word in politeness. Quiet, unassuming for one in his high position, we found him one of the hardest
men to talk to we ever met.[32]

It seems that most of the conversation at luncheon was about modern warfare, on which Heruy displayed the utmost ignorance,
showing his disgust at the notion of trench warfare and at the fact
that Western generals do not lead their men to battle personally
in full regalia.

Norden, who met Heruy in the late twenties collected some
gossip:

Some people who have approached him claim he is gifted with hypnotic powers and consider him a new Rasputin. He certainly has a
remarkable physionomy, capable of expressing an uncommonly wide
range of feelings, from complete vacuity to irresistible force. . . . He
spoke some English as he had been in England on a political mission.
The handshake with which he greeted me was a concession to European mores.[33]

In 1929 Heruy was appointed director at the Ministry of Foreign
Affairs, and in 1931, after Haile Selassie's accession to the imperial
throne, he became foreign minister with the title of Blatténgéta.
In this new capacity, he was sent on a mission to Japan from 2
October 1931 to 28 January 1932. Later in 1932, after accompanying the empress on a new pilgrimage to Jerusalem, he visited
Greece once more. An American anthropologist Carleton S. Coon
met him in Dire Dawa as he was on his way to Palestine. He describes him as "a stocky man in native costume, with a violet cape
draped about his shoulders to indicate his high position. His face,
reddish-brown in color, was wide and well-modeled, and his fore-
head high and capacious. He looked and is reputed to be, a man
of great intellectual power." They talked about his trip to Japan,
and in 1934 Heruy launched a new journal entitled *Atbiya Kobäb*
create a certain sympathy for Japan among cultivated Ethiopians.
He, like others of his country, admired Japan for its ready adoption of modern civilization, while retaining the nobler aspects of
its ancient culture, and naturally envisioned a parallel development
in Ethiopia." [34] Coon wanted to take the minister's anthropological
measurements, but Heruy sent him the chief of the Dire Dawa
police instead!

The last few years of Ethiopian independence saw the appearance of several more works of a didactic and religious character,[35]
and in 1934 Heruy launched a new journal entitled *Atbiya Kobäb*
(*Morning Star*). Like so many of the early African writers, he
primarily thought of himself as a teacher, and he, too, attempted
the difficult double task of bolstering his readers' pride in their
national history and culture while urging upon them the need for
acquiring modern knowledge and modern skills. This he did
mainly through straightforward edifying works, but it was also
during this period that he wrote the two novels that have earned
him a significant place in the history of Amharic creative writing:
The Marriage of Berhane and Seyon Mogäsa in 1930–31 and *The
New World* in 1932–33.

The former narrates the very simple story of two young people
who wisely refrain from contracting an early marriage; accordingly, the girl retires to a convent for several years. When at last
they get married, they are blessed with numerous children, the
eldest of whom is named "the first-born of Sion," a rather facile
pun suggesting that he is to be the first representative of a new

generation and a new society. The purpose of the story is to indict the widespread custom of child-marriage.

But Heruy's most ambitious attempt in prose fiction is *The New World*,[36] the first Amharic treatment of one of the most prominent themes in the modern African novel: the young man who comes home to his traditional environment after receiving a modern education abroad.[37] The adolescent hero, Awwäqä, who is keenly desirous to know more about Europe and Western civilization, enters the service of a wealthy Frenchman who sympathizes with his aspirations and provides him with the necessary resources to study in France. After eight years in Paris, Awwäqä feels homesick and returns to Tägulät, which seems to be considered one of the most backward places in Ethiopia. The story then develops through two extended episodes focusing respectively on the death of Awwäqä's father and on the young man's marriage.

The father's illness and death provide Heruy with an opportunity for a biting satire on a number of superstitious beliefs and immoral customs. The family prefer to resort to the dubious competence of a sorcerer-priest and to his native medicines rather than call on a European doctor. They blame Awwäqä when he uses the telephone, that notorious tool of the devil, to recall those of his brothers and sisters who are away. The young man is indignantly taxed with hardheartedness when he refrains from the usual howling and shrieking to demonstrate his sorrow. He is severely rebuked by his father's confessor when he refuses to organize the customary funeral banquet, which is a costly and ostentatious occasion for drunkenness and rioting. Instead, Awwäqä gives the money to the church for charitable purposes, and this causes some of the more enlightened clergy to ponder, with a measure of approval, on his new-fangled manners.

The second part of the novel deals with marriage. In compliance with ancestral custom, Awwäqä's family selects a wife for him without consulting him. They are thunderstruck when he makes it clear that he intends to marry a girl of his own choosing, and that he considers marriage to be indissoluble. After finding a suitable bride in Addis Ababa, he further offends by arranging a church ceremony of the utmost simplicity, and by refusing to offer the huge feast that is an always welcome opportunity for excessive drinking and lewd singing. Instead of this, he scandalizes his family and neighbors by putting on his phonograph—yet another instrument of the devil—records of hymns to the glory of Christian marriage. His irate friends leave him, recounting on the way tales of their many marriages and extraconjugal affairs.

The story ends on a note of somewhat utopian optimism, when a synod of the Ethiopian church acknowledges that the evils of the time are mainly due to the ignorance of the lower, and the indifference of the higher, clergy, and promulgates an impressive number of reforms to put an end to the corruption of the church and to the greed and loose living of its priests.

Heruy's works had earned him quite a reputation in Ethiopia; unlike the earlier journalists and travelers, Farago, who visited him in the early months of 1935, was made aware of his literary activity. In reporting his interview with the minister, Farago first enlarged upon his alleged supernatural powers:

Heruy's name is well known amongst most of the African peoples, and in his own country, he is called the Rasputin of Africa. I was told about the hypnotic powers that he is supposed to possess; all kinds of unlikely stories of how his political opponents were overcome by his austere eyes, were spread abroad.[38]

As Heruy arrived at his office, Farago observed that "he was small and was wearing a tropical helmet on his grey head, and held a slim tapering stick in his hand. Otherwise, he was dressed, like the Emperor, in the national costume, with his black cape over his white shirt and jodhpur breeches." In the minister's office, Farago was introduced to Heruy's two sons, Sirak and Giyorgis, "who are now taking an important part in political life," and "were present as interpreters. George Heruy had studied at Cambridge and Sirak had just come down from Oxford. Both worked naturally in the Foreign Office without a salary and had been educated at their father's cost." Incidentally, Sirak Wäldä Sellasé Heruy was later to provide an Amharic version of Samuel Johnson's *Rasselas*, which was printed in Asmara in 1946–47. In the course of the conversation, Heruy proudly claimed that his sons were his "closest co-operators," and kept "in constant touch with the outside world, steering Abyssinia along the road of progress, and Europeanising Ethiopian life, as the Emperor wishes. I am rather too old for this perpetual work of reform," he said, "but I try to do my duty and never obstruct new plans. They further the Emperor's work un-

conditionally and pluck out and destroy the reactionaries." Farago
was slightly surprised as, after tea at Heruy's house, he noticed
that "there were no napkins and when the Foreign Minister had
finished his tea, he wiped his mouth on the table-cloth."

After the defeat of Ethiopia, Heruy Wäldä Sellasé—who, like
Täklä Hawaryat and unlike most *rases*, had been consistently opposed to the Emperor's departure and in favor of continued resistance—followed Haile Selassie in his British exile. He died in the
monarch's residence in Bath, on 19 September 1938, after several
months' illness.[39]

The accession of Haile Selassie to the imperial title in 1930 may
have encouraged Heruy to use prose fiction, which had lain dormant since Afäwärq's novel of 1909, as a vehicle for discussion of
topical themes and for the spreading of modern ideas. It is probably
no mere coincidence that the coronation provided an occasion for
resuming Täklä Hawaryat's aborted attempt at creating formal
stage drama in Amharic. Part of the festivities was the performance
of a play entitled *Vain Entertainment*, by Yoftahé Negusé.
Yoftahé [40] came from Gojam, had a church education, knew some
French, and had quite a reputation as a public speaker. He was
headmaster of St. George's School, which had been opened in September 1929 under the direction of a Swiss teacher called Bloch.

Vain Entertainment is an allegorical play describing the marriage
of Faith and Fortune decreed by King Solomon. The whole ceremony takes place on the stage. The characters' speeches are interspersed with many quotations from the Scriptures, for which
due references are provided in the text. The play ends with a
reading of the parable of the Wise and the Foolish Virgins in
Ge'ez with an Amharic translation. In conclusion, it is revealed
that the new emperor is the husband of the first of the wise virgins.

Yoftahé is known to have produced several other plays that do
not seem to have reached print. Two of them were performed at
the imperial palace in 1931–32 to celebrate the first visit of the
emperor's daughter Zännäbä-Wärq to Addis Ababa after her marriage to the son of Empress Zäwditu, Ras Gugsa Ar'aya of Eastern
Tigré. The most interesting, however, was staged at the court in
1932 on the occasion of the emperor's birthday. This was the year
when Ras Haylu of Gojam had rebelled in a last and vain attempt
to restore Lij Iyassu to the throne. In *The Punishment of Belly-*

Worshipper, Yoftahé dramatized those events in transparently allegorical form. The villain of the piece, who stands for Ras Haylu, is a dissolute young man who roams about the country disguised as a mendicant priest. In return for the charity extended to him by a good man, Bäggo-Säw, who is the impersonation of the emperor, he attempts to seduce the latter's wife and destroys his vineyards. He is caught, however, and taken to court, an episode that reflects the trial and condemnation of Ras Haylu. At the end of the play, the good man invites all his friends to a feast enlivened by Tigriñña dances—an allusion to the success met by the dances of soldiers from Tigré at the marriage of the emperor's daughter.

During the Italian war, Yoftahé composed a slim volume of patriotic poetry, which must have been one of the last publications of the Goha Ṣebaḥ press. He died in 1948–49.

Side by side with those court performances, interesting developments occurred in school drama, due chiefly to the encouragements provided by Sahlä Ṣädalu, who was in charge of the Department of Education. After his schooling under Egyptian teachers at the Lycée Menelik II, which had been founded in 1906, Sahlä Ṣädalu had worked in the Ministry of Foreign Affairs from 1915 to 1920. He then left for Paris to complete his studies, after which he became secretary general at the Ministry of Foreign Affairs. In 1930 he was transferred in the same capacity to the newly created Ministry of Education, of which he became the first titular minister (as well as vice-president of the Senate) in 1932, with the title of Blatténgéta. Sahlä was very much aware of the educational uses of playacting. He had a stage built in the Lycée Menelik II in 1934, and he encouraged both teachers to write plays and pupils to perform them.

An Egyptian scholar Dr. Zaher Riad has given interesting reminiscences of those early days of public theatricals in Addis Ababa:

The director of the school had to supervise printing the tickets and advertisements and distributing them in the different hotels of Addis Ababa as well as at the different offices of the Government and Companies. He was also the financial director of the theatre. Though the actors had to receive no salaries at all, he had to collect the prices of the tickets and deliver them to the minister to pay the instalments of the furniture of the theatre. . . .

In November 1934, the theatre began its work in a great festival.
Betwaded Wild Sadek, the Prime Minister, his colleagues and the
great dignitaries of the capital were the first visitors. . . . The spectators
were received by His Excellency the Minister of Education and were
led to the booking-office where they paid for their tickets. The visitors
took their seats in the Reservé while their wives were in the first class,
their sons in the second and the sons of their wives in the third. They
never sat together. The servants waited for them outside guarding their
mules. Acting began at four o'clock and ended at six before darkness
came.[41]

Farago, who visited the place in 1935, has supplied the explanation
for the lighting problem:

The Menelik School . . . possesses the only theatre in Abyssinia, a big
zinc shed: and the pupils performed a folk piece in English for my
benefit. We sat quite alone in the auditorium, and could only follow the
play with difficulty, because the stage of this unusual theatre is not lit.
Though the building is wired for electric light, there is no money for
fuel to work the dynamo.[42]

A number of the early school plays written in Amharic were not
the works of Ethiopians, but of foreign teachers. One example is
a comedy in eight acts entitled *The Adventure of Gäbrä Maryam
from Gondar*, which was printed in 1933–34. It is the story of
Gäbrä Maryam, who leaves Gondar in search of his daughter.
She had been kidnapped many years before, when she was barely
three years old, and is now in the hands of gangsters who benefit
from the protection of a corrupt judge. After many misadventures,
Gäbrä Maryam meets his daughter at last, but he does not recognize her, and he falls in love with her. At the end of the play, he
is falsely accused by the gangsters of having murdered the corrupt
judge, but his daughter's evidence exposes the lie. Whereupon
father and daughter recognize each other and travel back home.
This curious, but, it would seem, not untypical play, is the work
of one K. Nalbadiyan, presumably an Armenian, who has been
variously described as a music teacher at the Lycée Menelik II and
as the director of the musical school at Addis Ababa.[43]
    It would seem that the first school plays of undoubted Ethiopian
authorship were those attributed to Mäl'aku Bäggosäw,[44] who had
been appointed to the Lycée Menelik II without any teaching
assignment. But as he knew no foreign language and had never had

a chance to attend formal drama, it has been suggested by Riad that he was merely a namesake for Sahlä Ṣädalu himself, while Elena Sengal, speaking of his play *Being Deprived of What Others Have Causes Spite* says it was in fact written by a Greek. It must be added, however, that in his preface to the anthology, *In Praise of Independence*, which he published in 1941, Yilma Däräsa held up Mäl'aku Bäggosäw, among others, as an example of dramatic writing which younger authors ought to follow. The first of his plays, none of which seems to have been printed, was entitled *The Great Judge* and dealt with the biblical story of Solomon. It was staged at the opening of the school theater in November 1934, and was highly successful, being performed twice a week for four months. Mäl'aku's second play, *Zännäbäč*, was less popular; it described the experiences of a young girl through the various divorces and marriages of her lightheaded mother. After the Italian conquest of Ethiopia, Mäl'aku left the country and lived most of the time in Jerusalem, in an Ethiopian monastery. He died of tuberculosis in Cairo in 1940.

It is highly likely that other plays were composed and performed between the coronation of Haile Selassie and the beginning of the Italian conquest on 3 October 1935. Luigi Fusella mentions one Haddis Alämayyäwh, who was to publish a collection of fables some twenty years later, but very little of this dramatic production ever reached book form.

The growth of this budding literature of modern Ethiopia was prematurely interrupted by the Italian invasion. Here is how an Ethiopian writer of the present day describes the effect of this spell of colonialism:

The Italian fascist dictatorship systematically exterminated members of the Ethiopian intelligentsia who had acquired their modern education in Europe. It confiscated and made bonfires of books written in French or English and made the possession of them punishable by death. It then proceeded to implement the South African policy of Apartheid in education that coaxed Ethiopians to attend Italian schools but forced them to "graduate" from the third elementary grade. The result aimed at by this policy was the training of young Ethiopians in the mastery of the limited vocabulary of pidgin-Italian that employs only the infinitive of verbs among other niceties, so that the fascist masters will have an efficient cook, dishwasher, or general servant—

unable to read serious books in the proper Italian language. On top of
that fascist censorship allowed only sycophantic literature and pro-
Italian political propaganda to appear in Amharic, and ruthlessly
scotched the faintest stirrings of patriotic writing in the bud.[45]

Actually, the generation of younger men who might have ensured the succession of Afäwärq and Heruy, was severely deci-
mated in the so-called Graziani massacres of 1937. Further, the
Italian conquerors proved loyal to a Latin tradition of cultural
imperialism that dates back to the days of the Roman Empire, and
that has also affected French and Portuguese educational policy:
teaching in Amharic was forbidden. The racialistic purpose of
Fascist cultural policy was defined by Mussolini in 1938, when he
wrote, in an official publication entitled *Etiopia:* "It is necessary to
realise that the Empire is conquered by the sword but is held by
prestige. To maintain prestige we must have a strict and clear
racial consciousness, which will stabilize not only the difference
of race but also our absolute superiority." [46]

The application of this principle in educational matters was
promulgated in a number of official directives. On 5 June 1938,
General Guglielmo Nasi, governor of Harar, declared that "we
should reserve the strictly necessary education for the sons of
chiefs and more important notabilities only, because these can later
on succeed to the duties of their fathers, serve us as interpreters
and hold modest positions in offices." And on 16 October 1939,
the Duke of Aosta, governor general of Italian East Africa, defined
as follows the aim of all the schools for the "subject peoples":
"to train the pupils in the cultivation of the soil or to become qualified workers (not specialised) in order to create gradually native
skilled craftsmanship for all fields of labor where, for reasons of
climate, surroundings or race prestige, the use of Italian labour is
not admissible or convenient, and for the purpose of reducing the
cost of labour and production in general by making use of native
labour." [47] Significantly, scholarly discussion of the new Amharic
literature, which had been fairly frequent in such Italian learned
journals as *Oriente Moderno*, disappeared altogether, as if all mention of indigenous cultural modernization was to be erased. In
1935 all channels of progress were effectively suppressed for
Amharic literature.

The Postwar Revival

The Italian occupation did not last more than five years. Its impact could not have been very deep. Yet, such intimate and hostile contact with the West was bound to introduce interesting modulations in the way modernization was to be contemplated by future writers. Colonial experiences further provided imaginative talents with a new fund of themes and motifs. Of more immediate significance was the fact that colonial oppression inflamed Ethiopian patriotism, which has always been of a somewhat flamboyant kind, and stimulated loyalty to the emperor among the educated sections of the community. This response accounts for the tremendous explosion of literary activity that broke out almost as soon as Haile Selassie had returned to his capital on 10 April 1941.

The very first book to be printed in Addis Ababa after the liberation of the city was a 150-page anthology entitled *In Praise of Independence*, and subtitled *Hymns of the New Era by Young Ethiopian Writers*. It came out in 1941 from the Märḥa Ṭebäb press barely a few months after the liberation. This was the former Imprimerie du Gouvernement Ethiopien, which had taken over from the Imprimerie éthiopienne in 1922–23. It had never been used for printing literary works, with the possible exception of Heruy's *Dawn* in 1925–26.[48] But from now on it was to become a major instrument in the promotion of creative writing. This volume [49] contains some fifty poems, which are highly traditional in their spirit, motifs, and structure. They celebrate the emperor and the more prominent among the patriots who had fought for the independence of the country. They also voice the Ethiopian people's gratitude for the help received from the British. With the important exception of Käbbädä Mika'el, few of the contributors were to make their names in literature, although some of them— such as the historian Berhanu Denqé and the first two women writers of Ethiopia—did produce one or two works of creative writing afterward.

The anthology had been compiled by Yilma Däräsa,[50] a Galla of the royal house that had ruled over Wallega in the days of Menelik. Born in 1907, he had his early education in Addis Ababa. He then attended the Victoria College in Alexandria, and the London School of Economics, from which he was graduated in

1933. Later, he studied international law in Geneva, Switzerland. On the eve of the Italian war, he returned to Ethiopia to take up an appointment as legation secretary at the Foreign Office. He was, says Greenfield, one of a progressive "group known as the *Jeunesse d'Ethiopie*, most of whom had been educated to speak French," and who "congregated in a tin-roofed building in Addis Ababa and discussed the central government's attempts at reform and published a newspaper." Farago, who met him at the time, also observed that "he was a cultivated young man, who spoke English and French and was dressed in European clothes." He was a staunch patriot and supporter of the emperor. "We young Abyssinians," he told Farago, "are in duty bound to our country. We are the bridge that the Emperor has thrown across to European culture. . . . The Emperor . . . has a number of clever young Abyssinians educated in Europe at his own cost. This growing generation will complete the civilisation of our country." In this, he and his contemporaries were frustrated by the Italian invasion, and Yilma was one of the group of educated young men who rallied round Ras Imru Hailä Sellasé in 1936 to continue the resistance to the Fascist regime. He helped found the Black Lion guerrilla movement. He was captured in December 1936, together with Ras Imru, and exiled to Italy. Unlike the Ras, however, he was soon sent back to Ethiopia, where he was one of the few members of the young elite to escape the Graziani massacres. When the British crossed over from the Sudan in 1941, he joined a propaganda unit and accompanied the emperor as the latter entered the capital in May 1941.

In a way, of course, Yilma's anthology was a personal tribute to the emperor, whose photograph in full regalia adorned the first page. But it was more than that: he prefaced it with an important essay that delineated the main lines along which he thought Amharic literature should develop, as in fact it did. Although the book was a collection of praise poems, Yilma recommended that Ethiopian writers turn to more modern genres, such as the novel and the short story. He especially advocated drama as an educational mass medium, and as an example pointed to such earlier writers as Yoftahé Negusé, Haddis Alämäyyawh, and Mäl'aku Bäggosäw. He advised future authors dealing with the recent past to show themselves truthful and impartial, and he specifically recommended that the Italian period in Ethiopian history should not be judged merely from the viewpoint of the protagonists, or even of the country itself, but with a more universal outlook.

Although *In Praise of Independence* was to remain Yilma's sole contribution to Amharic literature, its importance should not be underestimated. First, as the editor's preface could not but reflect the conceptions of the emperor himself, encouragement coming from such high quarters gave unprecedented impetus to the new literature, which had made such slow beginnings with Afäwärq and Heruy. In the course of the last quarter of a century, more vernacular works of poetry, fiction, and drama have come out of Ethiopia than of any other African country with the possible exception of the Republic of South Africa. Another important point is that Yilma was the first Galla author in modern Amharic literature, which had been practiced until then only by Amhara authors. More writers of Galla and other origins were to crop up in the following decades, perhaps an indication that other segments of the polyethnic population of Ethiopia are finding their way to a genuine sense of national unity.

After 1941, Yilma's attention was absorbed by his political career. Partly because of his royal Galla background, and partly on account of his training in economics, he came to exert considerable influence on government activity. After becoming secretary general at the Ministry of Foreign Affairs in 1941, he was appointed vice-minister of finance in the following year. In this capacity, he headed several financial missions abroad, until he became minister of finance in 1961, the previous incumbent having been killed in the coup of December 1960. When Empress Mänän —who was of Galla origin—died in 1962, Greenfield points out, Yilma became perhaps the most influential Galla in Ethiopia; but by that time, the liberal of former days had come to be "regarded as a diehard conservative by the young élite." After holding his post for many years, he was reassigned to Commerce, Industry, and Tourism on 18 February 1969.

Two generations of authors emerged simultaneously during the forties. Although the renaissance was actually initiated by such men as Käbbädä Mka'el, who was younger than Yilma Däräsa, it seems logical to begin with an older group, who had reached manhood by the time the Italian war began, but did not reveal themselves as writers until the liberation. They belong roughly to the

same generation as the emperor himself, who was born on 23 July
1892. Each of them can be taken to represent a definite trend in
the fast diversifying literature of postbellum Ethiopia.

The most important of those elder writers was Mäkonnen
Endalkačäw,[51] who played a major part in the resurgence of both
the novel and the drama. He was born in 1892 and belonged to
the traditional class of feudal lords, being a scion of the powerful
Addisgé family from Tägulät. According to Ronald Segal, "he was
educated at Court and grew up a close friend of the present Emperor." Greenfield, however, claims that Mäkonnen was not on
very good terms with Ras Täfäri because "he had been a close
associate of Eyasu and had incurred disfavor following his elopement and marriage to Yashash Worq, daughter of Yilma, Haile
Selassie's half-brother; she was previously married first to Leul-Ras
Gugsa Aria of Tigré and then to Betwoded Makonnen Demissie."
Nevertheless, in 1924 he accompanied the regent to London,
where, incidentally, he was awarded an honorary O.B.E. Between
1924 and 1936, he occupied a series of important posts: comptroller
of the Addis Ababa-Jibuti railway, minister of commerce (1926–
1931), Ethiopian representative in England and at the League of
Nations (1931–1933), mayor of Addis Ababa (1933–1934), and
governor of Ilubabor Province (1935) with the title of Däjjazmač.
When the war broke out, he was put in command of the Ogaden
front, with special authority over one of the four armies defending
Harar. On 2 May 1936, Greenfield relates, as Mäkonnen and three
other generals were preparing for battle against Graziani, "a train
was reported to have reached Dire Dawa carrying the Emperor
and his entourage to Jibuti. Completely unnerved, they promptly
abandoned their forces and followed suit." But instead of accompanying Haile Selassie to Britain, Mäkonnen was, perhaps for that
reason, exiled to Palestine where he was to look after the many
Ethiopian refugees on behalf of the emperor.[52]

His main source of income while in Jerusalem was the sale of
his own religious paintings. In 1940 Haile Selassie called him to
Khartoum, where he was preparing the reconquest of the country.
On 29 January 1941, Mäkonnen was one of the party that crossed
over the border with the emperor into Ethiopia. In the spring, he
was one of the little group who were sent by air to Addis Ababa,
in the face of considerable British reluctance, to make the neces-

sary arrangements for Haile Selassie's return. Later that year, he
was made minister of the interior. He gained great influence at
court, and in September 1942 was appointed to the newly created
office of prime minister with the title of Bitwädded. He was an
important member of a conservative group of feudal lords and
high clergy who were trying to counteract the modernizing and
democratic forces at work in political circles. On 26 October 1957,
he became president of the senate with the rank of Ras Bitwädded,
an exalted title that is awarded only once in a monarch's reign;
the office of prime minister remained vacant until March 1961.
"When seen with his dogs in his country house," Greenfield recalls, "Makonnen seemed almost the prototype English aristocrat."

He had started his literary career in the late forties, and with
the years, his writing had become more and more important to
him. Because of his failing eyesight, he was afraid lest he might
not be able to write down all that he had to say. In December 1960
he therefore traveled to Asmara for medical advice and treatment;
he was thus absent from the capital during the coup engineered by
some progressive army officers. But he was among those who
greeted Haile Selassie at the Asmara airport when the emperor
returned from Brazil to reestablish his authority. Mäkonnen
Endalkačäw retired in 1961 and died on 27 February 1963.

Antebellum Amharic writers were change-oriented. In Gäbrä
Egzi'abehér's poems, in Afäwärq's *Guide*, in Heruy's novels, there
is an overt critique of Ethiopian society and mores. All emphasize
in varying degrees the need to abolish the exorbitant privileges of
the feudal overlords, to outgrow obsolete superstitions and degraded customs, to accept technological change. They were eager
propagandists for the modernizing line prescribed by the regent
and emperor, in the face of stubborn opposition from the clergy,
the feudal class, and the inert mass of the population. As a leading
member of a traditionally privileged group, Mäkonnen's work is
entirely different. It should probably be regarded as the perfect
expression of what was best in a doomed tradition, both religious
and political. The writer embodies an idealized self-image of the
feudal class, which is jealous of its rights, and therefore dubious
about the enlightened despotism of the regime. It justifies its traditional privileges in the name of its sense of responsibility toward
the people, and it reviews itself as the God-ordained secular arm of

the divine will, unquestioningly faithful to the sacred tenets of
Coptic Christianity. Three major trends, therefore, characterize
Mäkonnen's plays and prose fiction.

Probably the most important single feature of Amhara culture
is its built-in transcendentalism—its sense of the unbridgeable gap
between man and God, its stressing the overwhelming and unac-
countable power of God, and, consequently, the irremediable
weakness of man and the utter vanity of the world. "The concept
of fate—*eddel*—," says Levine "is invoked by Amhara to account
for the various accomplishments and peripeties of their lives. *Eddel*
is the working of divine will as it affects human purposes, and it
is believed to be more important than human effort to attain any
end." [53]

The very title of one of Mäkonnen's first published works, *The
Inconstant World* (1947–48) [54] intimates this obsession with the
unreliability of the world and, consequently, with man's duty to
earn God's rewards through humility and acceptance. The heroine
of this novel, Yayné Abäba is first presented as a young girl who is
hideously ill treated by an old woman. As she grows up, she finds
it impossible to bear such harshness, and she flees from home. On
her way, she meets a nice young man who is the son of a priest. As
he appears willing to help her, she agrees to marry him. On their
journeying, they are assaulted by bandits while crossing a desert,
and the young husband is brutally killed. Yayné Abäba manages
to escape. At the end she finds shelter in a convent, where she
meets her mother, who had taken refuge there after the death of
her husband and the kidnaping of her daughter. The central idea
of the story is that life is a source of unending pain and unhappiness, and that quietness is only to be attained in the detachment of
monastic life. Indeed, as the author says at the end of the novel in
his address to the reader, it is the function and the justification of
the world that "unhappiness purifies the just." The meaning of the
tale is synthesized in a dream allegory: Yayné Abäba dreams of a
man who reaches a town and succeeds in entering the palace of
Queen Aläm Wärätägna (Inconstant World); he falls in love with
her, and she has him raised to the rank of Ras, but the following
morning she refuses to see him. He is so bewitched by her charm
that he stays on, in the hope that her mood will change again, but
the king returns and kills his wife's unfortunate lover. The king's
name is "Mot," which means Death.

This work has been described as "a collection of moralities." [55] And, indeed, to Mäkonnen as to almost all Amharic writers until quite recently, imaginative literature has had a very definite single purpose. Speaking of Ethiopian culture in general terms, Levine has made the following observations:

The Amhara's essentially pessimistic estimate of man's potentialities does not . . . imply a dogmatic or emotional rejection of man. . . . The institution and norms of the Amhara are shaped not to overwhelm man with guilt for his shortcomings, not to pressure him into personal or social reform, not to deprive worldly existence of all enjoyment and significance, but rather to accommodate human reality and transcendental values to one another in such a way that neither is seriously compromised. The negative propensities of man are simply acknowledged and taken into account.[56]

But while the Amhara code of ethical behavior is notoriously lax, the function of literature is to remind man of the transcendental values, which he is allowed freely to infringe upon in his day-to-day conduct. This leads to heavy-fisted moralizing, to the tireless insistence on edifying statements that, to Western ears, sound painfully platitudinous, and to the unceasing emphasis on the fickleness of the world, on the insecurity of this-worldly life, and on the need for total acceptance. It is significant that when he turned to contemporary events and wrote *The Voice of Blood* (1947–48), a play about the Italian occupation, Mäkonnen did not choose to extol the resistance of the patriots, but dramatized the martyrdom of Abunä Pétros, the head of the Ethiopian church, who was shot by the Fascists. Martyrdom is the acme of acquiescence in God's will, as was well known to the Counter-Reformation writers of Europe, who wrote countless martyr dramas in the seventeenth century.

This emphasis on the higher virtues of selflessness, abnegation, humility, and acceptance is constant throughout Mäkonnen's works and is the central purpose of most of them. In his novel *Do Not Say I Am Not Dead*, printed in a collection entitled *Advise Me* (1952-53), he turned back to the Italian war, to describe the tribulations of Ato Tämačču, whose home is disrupted by the war. Although the story necessarily contains some indictment of white colonialism, its purpose is to stress the necessity for forbearance and virtue in the face of adversity. This philosophy, of course, applies chiefly to the poor, and one of the main functions of Mäkonnen's sermonizing is to convince them of their privileged spiritual status. Another part of his message is directed at the newly rising Ethiopian bourgeoisie, which he holds in no great respect. *The City of the Poor*, a short novel that appeared in the same volume focuses on the fate of a wealthy businessman named Habteh Yemar, who "was at all times so occupied with the latest development of the international market that he could hardly spare time to rest day or night, foreign currency in particular seemed to need all his attention to enquire its fluctuation by post, by telegram or by wireless." [57] About a third of the story describes a succession of warnings with which this tycoon is favored. He has a dream that his bank is on fire and that he commits suicide in his despair at losing his money. While visiting a graveyard, he meets a monk, Abba Säwbäkäntu, who reminds him that the church is the city of the poor and that "while the poor have no freehold on earth, there awaits freehold in the heavens for their immortal souls" (p. 120). The truth of this is impressed upon his mind when he meets a funeral procession. Habteh's faith in the transcendence of money is shaken by these experiences, but unfortunately "his multitudinous business interests" compel him to leave for London, Paris, and New York. At this point, Mäkonnen's didacticism turns to more mundane matters as he briefly describes his hero's strangely zigzagging journey and his visits to cathedrals, cabarets, and other places of touristic interest in a bewildering number of cities. On his way from Cairo to New York, Habteh narrowly escapes death in a plane crash; yet even this does not prevent him from being mostly preoccupied with the devaluation of sterling. But while sleeping at the Waldorf Astoria, he dreams of Hiroshima. Profoundly disturbed, he hires a cab and drives to a country churchyard; there he meets the soul of Abba Säwbäkäntu, who reminds him of his betrayal. Habteh falls ill and soon dies in hospital. As he has no heir, because in his exclusive love of money he had always refrained from marrying, his vast wealth ironically becomes the property of the government of the United States.

This unbearably sanctimonious story is illustrative of Mäkonnen's total subservience to the most unrealistic conventions of Ethiopian Christianity: crime is always punished, virtue eternally rewarded. Apart from the author's style, there is nothing to redeem his works from the abysses of triteness where much of Amharic literature is still immersed: no humor, no social analysis, no psychological insight or even interest. One of his last novels, Şähay Mäsfen (1956-57) deals with two young lovers in modern Addis Ababa; but it is yet another apologue exalting charity, devotion, and altruism as opposed to self-assertion based on instinct, wealth, or education.[58]

It is, of course, important to examine the relation between this almost Manichaean outlook and the trend of political thinking that is the second ingredient in Mäkonnen's literary inspiration. His concern with political matters, so conspicuously absent from the imaginative works of Afäwärq and Heruy, is already perceptible in *The Voice of Blood*. At the end of the play, a group of patriots from various tribes and various parts of the country discuss the bishop's execution with indignant emotion; his martyrdom shows them the way, and they all decide to join the underground resistance movement. At this point, they are interrupted by a Muslim woman, and they fear lest she might inform against them. But it turns out that the Abunä's death has kindled the same patriotic fervor in her heart:

When I saw this monk die with such patriotism, as though he knew it was a jihad, I honoured the Christian faith. (She falls on her knees.) What mighty strength! What glorious fate! What pride of motherland! To die in a jihad for his faith, for his motherland, for his Emperor's honour! Petros! Petros! Petros! If thou dost die, thy fame eternal shall not die! (She remains with her face covered by her two hands.)[59]

It is a well-known fact that the need to overcome denominational differences has been a central element in Haile Selassie's policy. While the main theme of the play is the power of sacrifice, expressed in the dictum that "the voice of blood cleaves the air as it ascends" (p. 79), all-Ethiopian patriotism is one of the values it advocates, and due homage is paid to the person of the emperor.

Nevertheless, Mäkonnen's deepest concern seems not to be so much with loyalty to the emperor as with the defense of Ethiopia's traditional feudal system. The whole of act 2 consists of a highly suggestive conversation between Abunä Pétros and his Ethiopian guards. These are common soldiers in the pay of the Italians, and it appears that they are perfectly satisfied with their conquerors:

Our mother Ethiopia has just married a husband, and she is flourishing and getting prettier all the time. . . . Long live the glorious Mussolini—

for he has thrown down off our shoulders the heavy load of our king
and chiefs and princes, who used to oppress us. (P. 93)

To this the Abunä replies with an apology for feudalism which is
a characteristic utterance of Mäkonnen's personal views:

Very well, my children: listen to me and I'll tell you. The first kings
and princes and chiefs who with their blood laid the foundations of
Ethiopia's liberty, valued men more than property. Property was
nothing to them—their property was in men. Therefore their estates,
including their private property, represented sustenance for your
fathers and fore-fathers. The property of these masters being the property of the people, any soldier or servant could call the master's house
his own house. Then when the master died, he would bequeath his land
and property, as to a son, to his followers and servants who had
rendered service to Ethiopia. The prosperity and wealth of these
masters was directed solely towards the security of their servants, and—
through maintaining their houses—towards their strength. Through a
unity of this sort between governor and people, the freedom of Ethiopia
was protected and lasted long. O my children, how many are the bene-
factions of which I could tell you, performed by governors in Ethiopia!
To sum it up, their houses were offices for the organization of poor
relief—they weren't private houses at all. (P. 94)

This piece of casuistry convinces some of the guards. It is also
an early and uncommonly explicit formulation of Mäkonnen's
faith in a utopian system of benign feudalism. That the writer was
not without misgivings about the imperial policy of centralized
power is suggested by the various portrayals of royalty in his
works. In 1949–50, Mäkonnen published a short piece of fiction,
David III, which was later turned into a play. This in turn was
translated into English by his son, Lij Endalkačäw Mäkonnen,
under the title, King David the Third.[60] The story takes place
under the Gondarine emperor who reigned from 1716 to 1721.
The choice is revealing, for David III was considered a heretic by
orthodox Ethiopian historians: in the theological disputes of his
day, he had sided with the so-called Unctionists, who maintained
that Christ's was a human nature made divine through the unction
of the Holy Ghost, against the orthodox Monophysite dogma,
which held that humanity and divinity are fused in the single
nature of Christ.[61]

Although the Preface claims that "the principal theme of the drama is the story of King David the Third, known as David the Singer," the central character is not the king but his son, Prince Jacob. There are a few allusions to some massacre of orthodox priests perpetrated by the emperor. In the main, however, his portrayal in the play enlarges on a suggestion offered in the Preface:

History does not know why and how King David the Third earned this strange nickname, but it would seem reasonable to imagine that it had been due to his excessive liking for music as a pleasant pastime which could lighten for him the heavy burden and responsibilities of government. But herein he was unlike the great majority of Ethiopia's sovereigns, who chose religion and morals as the main foundation of their service to the country, and thus made their reigns illustrious.

Indeed, scene 1 of act 2 chiefly consists of songs and dances, at the end of which the king intones the following verse:

> The man who finds no pleasure in a ditty
> Is out of place—in country, court, or city.
> Count him as good as dead—and spare your pity.

Upon which, according to the stage direction, "Prince Jacob, who has been looking sad and thoughtful during the proceedings, suddenly collapses and falls, head first, to the ground" (p. 35).

There is hardly any action, as the whole play consists of lengthy discussions between Prince Jacob and his philosopher friend Lij Mäsfen, whose advice the prince wants on how to govern wisely. But his main interest is to find peace for his soul, and he wants Mäsfen to tell him "the way by which I can escape and spend my days free from all the worries and cares of this world" (p. 21). This provides Mäsfen with a golden opportunity for narrating the nine-page-long story of one prince Gäbrä Krestos, who gave up his rights to the throne, lived for a while in a monastery, but, since he did not find there the "life of suffering and repentence" (p. 26) that he deemed necessary for the salvation of his soul, returned to the capital to live as a beggar until he died of "cold, starvation and illness" (p. 30). The unseemly dancing in act 2, scene 1 further strengthens Jacob's resolve; in a long conversation with the king (act 2, scene 4), he forcefully condemns the latter's unbecoming proclivity to worldly entertainment: "If my royal father inclines towards frivolous things, he encourages frivolity amongst the people. If you live a life of extravagance, you create a hankering after riches" (p. 39). The truth of this statement is evidenced in the two scenes of act 3: they contain the sixteen-page story of a talented woman, whose singing became so fashionable at court that she indulged in loose living. She fell perversely in love with a dirty wretch of a coachman, for, in Mäsfen's words, "once a human being has freed himself from his conscience, there will be no limit to what his ambition urges him to do. Once he has given free rein to his senses, and becomes the slave of wicked habits, he can find nothing on earth to satisfy him" (p. 50). All this brings ruin to the coachman's previously happy household. His only child dies in the gutter. Gnawed by remorse and fury, the poor man manages to drown his mistress, and goes to a monastery, where a monk tells him that the only way to atone is to put himself to death with suffering and repentance (p. 61). After a frightening dream about his mistress and his wife, he does indeed die, with the assurance that he has been absolved of his sins. This most dismaying chain of events, which is the result of King David's frivolousness, strengthens Jacob's melancholy: "Man is a candle that sorrow and illness burn out. I have neither wish nor hope to live in this world; I am only awaiting the day when the light of my life will put itself out" (p. 68)—which indeed it does with obliging promptness in the fourth and last act of the play.

However unengaging this drama may sound to a Western mind, it provides a good example of the theoretical hierarchy of values that most Amharic writing has illustrated until quite recently. There is an overall emphasis on otherworldliness, man's life on earth being painted in the most unattractive colors: man's fun is most blamable, salvation can only be obtained through sorrow and suffering. It is true that the better aspects of the king's outlook also receive expression. "You must realize, first of all," he tells his son, "that you can't have the best of both worlds. So long as you are in this world, you have to follow the way of all flesh. You cannot be in this world and live the life of another one" (p. 41). This is the compromise of practical Amhara ethics, described by Levine in a paragraph quoted earlier. But the sorrowful story of the coachman leads Jacob to discard it and to seek refuge in the other life. He does not even attempt to follow the early advice of Mäsfen, or the

example of King John the Righteous, which he himself quotes to
his father, that is, to shun flatterers, avoid business involvement
with his subjects, and distrust bad counselors (p. 18, 39). His
taedium vitae overcomes him, and it is certainly significant that
Mäkonnen should have chosen this reign of a bad emperor for his
setting, and the renouncement of an imperial throne for his topic.

Admittedly in the Preface to *King David the Third,* the author
extols the example of Haile Selassie, who "has substituted for the
pleasures of this world a life of prayer and devoted service." His
underlying attitude to imperial power, however, appears once
more in another historical novel, *The Bloody Era,*[62] which deals
with one of the last Gondarine monarchs, Täklä Haymanot II,
who reigned from 1769 to 1777. It is probably no mere coincidence
that Mäkonnen chose to present another king who had shown
hostility to the Ethiopian church, though not in the theological
field. In 1771 Täklä Haymanot had decreed—as Henry VIII had
done in Britain almost two centuries earlier—that all landed property formerly given by the king to the church should revert to the
king's own use.[63] This, however, was not the aspect selected by
Mäkonnen. The story begins with a reminder that Täklä Haymanot had ascended the throne after having his father Iyasu murdered. The main plot deals with the punishment of the rebellion
of one of the emperor's favorites, Wäräñña Fasil. After Wäräñña
has been in jail for a few years, his two brothers, who are after his
inheritance, engineer a clever plot to have him killed unwittingly
by the emperor himself. When Täklä Haymanot is informed of
what he has done, he is gnawed with remorse for infringing God's
command "Thou shalt not kill," and he goes to a monastery to end
his life in mortification. Although the king repents and withdraws
from the world, the book contains an oblique indictment of the
dangers and temptations of absolute power: the hero has murdered
his father in order to capture the throne, and corrupt nobles skillfully manipulate his power for their own selfish ends.

The same desire to warn against lust for and abuse of power can
be seen in Mäkonnen's last novel, *Taitu Bitul* (1957–58), whose
action takes place under Téwodros, who was born in 1818, was
crowned in 1855, and committed suicide after being defeated by
the British in 1868. Téwodros is a highly controversial figure in
Ethiopian historiography. While he initiated the effective reunifi-

cation of that vast country, he also did his best to curb the power
of the feudal nobility. The interest of Mäkonnen's novel for the
interpretation of Téwodros has been underscored by Greenfield:

In the 1950s and '60s the descendants of the great families of Ethiopia
still regarded Kassa or Tewodros as an upstart despite the fact that he
revived the great chronicles and claimed the Solomonic blood. There
have been attempts on the part of members of the aristocracy to defame
his memory. One such attempt . . . is [Mäkonnen's] historical novel
about a Gondarine woman named Taitu, related to Tewodros by marriage, whose husband was a *dejazmatch* and one of the Emperor's
soldiers. In general it discredits Tewodros and without historical foundation accuses him of sexual promiscuity. "Why does he want to speak
to me?" Taitu is made to cry out, when the Emperor calls while her
husband is away, "I am the wife of his honest servant!" However, this
work aroused considerable resentment, for Tewodros is highly thought
of by very many Ethiopians and particularly by younger folk of more
progressive outlook. His importance to younger Ethiopians is not unconnected with the fact that in his attempt to re-unify and modernise
Ethiopia he did not rely either on the Solomonic myth or the Ethiopian
Christian Church.[64]

This should not lead us to believe that Mäkonnen's imaginative
disquisitions about the ethical dangers of imperial power improp-
erly used might be the result of any democratic aspirations. On
the contrary, he should be considered the most vocal and articulate
exponent of the landed aristocracy, which is threatened both from
above, by the centralization of power in the hands of the emperor,
and from below, by the increasing pressure of modern democratic
ideas. Mäkonnen's ultimate message in this respect lies implicit in
the two installments of his autobiography, *The Good Family* and
The Course of Dreams, both issued in 1956-57, the latter as a photo-
graphed manuscript. As the leader of one of the most powerful
feudal families in the country, he used his reminiscences to draw
the picture of a social system in which the benevolent and enlightened aristocracy use their wealth and power for the benefit
of the common people.

While Mäkonnen thus illustrated, in his novels and plays, the ultra-
conservative outlook of the feudal class, a contemporary of his
represents the group of educated men of humble origin, such as

Afäwärq and Heruy had been, who have remained unconditionally and unquestioningly faithful to the emperor.

Wäldä Giyorgis Wäldä Yohannes was born at Bulga, in the Waged district of Shoa in 1896-97.[65] His father was a leather tanner or saddle maker. From 1907 to 1920-21, he attended various schools in the provinces of Gojam, Wadela, and Gondar. He studied the Ge'ez and Amharic languages and gained, he says "a deep knowledge of Qené, which gave me the intellect to understand things." Apart from Ethiopian history and something of world history, he also studied European languages. For a while he worked as an interpreter in Addis Ababa's Menelik II Hospital. He began his career as a proofreader in 1921-22. Several years later, he became assistant editor of *Berhanenna Sälam (Light and Peace)* which had been founded in 1924, a position that he held until the Italian invasion. Meanwhile, he had been promoted, says Greenfield, to "one of Haile Sellassie's lieutenants . . . when the Emperor sought to break the power of the great conservative barons. Before the Italian war he became a director in the Ministry of the Pen and he often acted as Haile Sellassie's secretary." On the eve of the war, Farago described him as "an important official who has to carry the responsibilities of whole ministries on his shoulders; . . . he was formerly in charge of the Foreign Office, and his youth is the only reason for his not being a full-blown minister. He works even harder than his master, starting at three in the morning and not stopping until midnight. He enjoys no holidays on Sundays or any other feast days, and often he is wakened out of his short sleep when the Emperor wants an order carried out during the night." [66]

In May 1936 he was one of the few who were candid enough to support Haile Selassie's opinion that the population would not go on fighting against the Italians, even though the Emperor should stay in Ethiopia. He followed the monarch into exile in Britain, and did much to thwart the plans of some of the resistance fighters, known as Patriots, who were in favor of setting up a republic in Ethiopia once the country was freed. He was also with Haile Selassie when the latter reentered his empire from the Sudan on 20 January 1941. He was then appointed editor of the newly founded daily *Addis Zämän (New Times)* and of the bilingual (Amharic-English) weekly *Sändäg Alamačin (Our Flag)*, both published by the Information Office of the Ministry of the Pen. Simultaneously, in 1941-42, he was appointed minister of the pen

with the title of Tsafahé Taezaz. "Ruthless and all-powerful," as
he has been described by Greenfield, he was largely responsible for
the modernization of the administration. "Under him, the central
government had been stabilized and a very firm control established
over the capital and the provinces."

Although he had no doubt contributed to the journals that he
had edited, it was during his period as minister of the pen that the
majority of his books were printed. *He Who Made History Does
Not Lie* (1946-47) is a historical work designed to glorify Ethiopia
and her monarchs; *The Way Of The World* (1947-48) contains
fables and tales to illustrate various aspects of human nature; *Prosperity Through Agriculture* (1948-49) is an agricultural treatise
interspersed with lyrical poetry; *After Work* (1950-51) is a collection of riddles; *Proper Conduct* (1950-51) is a moral and religious treatise; *The New Ethiopia* (1952-53) is an introduction
to present-day Ethiopia.

All these are mainly didactic. The bulk of Wäldä Giyorgis's
creative writing consists of four volumes of poetry printed for
the government information service: *The Glory of Kings* (1946-47), *Gift of Love and Peace* (1946-47), *Gift to Celebrate H. M.
Emperor Haile Selassie's 58th Birthday* (1949-50), and *The Gift
of Kingship* (1955-56) are collections of poems in praise of the
emperor, his warlike prowess, his civilizing achievement, and also
in praise of Ethiopia herself. In 1952-53, Walda Giyorgis also published a volume of poems on love and marriage, *Dialogue of Husband and Wife*.

The only novel he has written: *Ag'azi. I Had Gone Abroad*
(1955-56), is a historical and psychological story. The hero overcomes the entreaties of his family who want him to stay at home
instead of seeking impious knowledge in foreign schools. Whereas
the beginning illustrates the need to defeat traditional misoneism,
somewhat in the manner of Heruy's *New World*, the greater part
of the book is devoted to the student's experiences and impressions
abroad while his country is under Italian occupation.

Wäldä Giyorgis's tremendous power at court had intensified the
enmity of the great families and of rival claimants for the emperor's favor. It would seem that it had also provoked the diffidence
of the emperor himself. A series of intrigues led to the dismissal of
the minister of the pen in 1955. On being appointed to the
governor-generalship of Arusi, in semiexile, "he bowed low and

made no comment," says Greenfield, "for he knew he would have been arrested if he had." In 1961-62, however, he was recalled to Addis Ababa as director of the government newspapers and magazines, with the rank of vice-minister and the title of Blatta.

Another writer also gained some notoriety as court poet during that period. In 1946–47, Yaréd Gäbrä Mika'él, who was attached to the Ministry of Information, published a praise poem in honor of the emperor, a performance that he repeated yearly from 1952 to 1956. A slight variant was the composition of poems and biographical accounts on prominent members of the imperial family—for the fortieth birthday of the heir Prince Asfa Wäsän in 1955–56, after the accidental death of Duke Mäkonnen of Harar in 1956–57, and in honor of Empress Mänän in 1957–58. Like Wäldä Giyorgis, Yared also devoted some attention to the theme of love and marriage: *You and I* (1952-53) is a slightly fictionalized essay on the contrast between marriage customs in the countryside and modern city manners. In 1957-58 he published a philosophical poem entitled *The Prisoner of Love*.

In one of his informative essays on Amharic literature, Wright emphasized the peculiar situation of Wäldä Giyorgis and Yaréd as the only two authors of the present day "who may be called strictly 'professional' writers. . . . They occupy a position which perhaps derives ultimately from that of the minstrels at medieval courts—in Europe as well as in Africa—and faintly reflected in England today through the shadowy duties of the Poet Laureate. However, for these officials of the ministry of information it remains a full-time job, and one which demands not only expert technical skill in the composition of 'occasional' poems, but feeling for the 'mores' . . . of their country. The maintenance of this function is likely to have real value in keeping the new Amharic literature on coherent and realistic lines, especially if it is left in the hands of writers whose formal duties do not prevent them from exercising wit and imagination." [67]

Among this group of loyal supporters, and even devoted sycophants of the emperor, must be counted Mahtämä Sellasé Wäldä Mäsqäl, whose literary activity, however, was mainly directed toward the recording and preservation of folk literature and early Amharic poetry.

Mahtämä Sellasé[68] was born in Addis Ababa on 29 October 1905. His family came originally from Bulga in Shoa, and his father

was for a time minister of the pen. After going through primary
and secondary studies at the Menelik II school, he attended the
French lycée in Cairo. He then went to a college in southern
France and was graduated as an agronomist from the Institut National Supérieur d'Agronomie in Nogent-sur-Marne. On his return
to Ethiopia in 1930, he was appointed to establish a secondary
agricultural school at Ambo. In 1934 he became private secretary
to the crown prince. He was deported to Italy in 1937, and was
kept there until 1939. After the liberation, he was secretary general to the commissariat for the provinces of Wallo, Gondar, and
Tigré until 1946. In 1947 he was transferred to the Ministry of
Agriculture as director general and was promoted to vice-minister
in 1949.

He started his literary career with *Memories* (1949-50), which
provides a picture of Ethiopian institutions under Menelik and
Haile Selassie, and with *The Greatness of God* (1951-52), a religious meditation on God and Nature which he had composed
during his period of detention in Italy. He then turned his attention
to the traditional literature of Ethiopia, both oral and written. *The
Spirit Is Immortal* (1951-52) is a collection of more than three
thousand proverbs, which went through a second, augmented edition in 1953-54. It was also in 1951-52 that he published an agricultural treatise.

In 1954 Mahtämä Sellasé reached ministerial rank as head of the
Department of Agriculture, and in 1958 he became finance minister with the title of Balambaras. He contined his recording of
folk literature with a collection of sixty fables, *Selected Tales*. In
1960 he was appointed minister of state in charge of education and
the arts. During this period, he published a collection of hymns in
the traditional church style, *Amharic Poems* (1955-56), where
one can find, *inter alia*, couplets composed by the early nineteenth-
century king of Shoa, Sahlä Sellasé, and by the father of Menelik
II, Haylä Mäläkot.

During the coup of December 1960, Mahtämä Sellasé remained
loyal to the monarch and even participated in the sessions of the
counterrevolutionary group that decided to resist all attempts to
oust the emperor. From 1961 to 1966, he was minister of public
works and communications. He has also written a work on land
ownership in Ethiopia (1964-65), and in 1965 he was awarded the
Haile Selassie I prize in Amharic literature for the whole of his

work. In May 1966 he became a member of the crown council with the title of Blatténgéta.

The last representative of this first postbellum generation, who came to literature very late, was an important political figure, and a nobleman of even more exalted rank than Mäkonnen Endalkačäw, as he was second cousin to the emperor. Imru Haile Sellasé[69] was born in Harar on 23 December 1892. He attended the Menelik II school, and shared his cousin's progressive ideas. In September 1916, it was Qañazmač Imru whom Ras Täfäri sent to arrest Lij Iyassu in Harar (p. 139). Unfortunately, the telephone conversation was tapped and Imru was imprisoned by Iyassu. He was rescued by Täfäri's Shoan soldiers in late November.[70] In 1918 he was appointed vice-governor of Harar; he was transferred to the province of Wollo in 1929. After Haile Selassie's coronation, while the constitution was in its preparatory stages, he "opposed the inclusion of an article . . . stipulating that the imperial succession should henceforth be governed by what he considered to be the alien European custom of primogeniture" (p. 175). By 1933 he had been promoted to the rank of ras, and appointed to the governor-generalship of Harar (p. 173). Like Täklä Hawaryat—and unlike most of the feudal lords—he had an "early understanding of the necessity for an efficient civil service, loyal not just to the governor-general, but to the central government he represented," and in 1933 when he was transferred to Gojam after the deportation of Ras Haylu, "he left his entire provincial administration behind him in order to start again."

At the beginning of the Italian war, Imru was put in charge of an Ethiopian army of some 25,000 to 30,000 men, defending the western Eritrean border north of Gondar.[71] In December 1935, after the initial enemy advance, he was the first to stage a counteroffensive in the direction of Addi Quala in Eritrea (pp. 207–209); "he had met with considerable success . . . when . . . his men ran short of ammunition" (p. 213). Imru's army was decisively defeated in the battle of Shiré (29 February through 3 March 1936), and he had to report to the emperor that, as a result, "the greater part of the Gojjam troops have deserted and refuse to fight except in their own district" (p. 215).

Imru was back in the Gojam capital, Däbrä Markos, when a telephone call informed him, in May 1936, that the emperor had appointed him viceroy during his exile (p. 223). He then withdrew from Gojam to Gore in southwestern Ethiopia, intending to cross over to the Sudan with the remnants of his troops, but he was approached by a newly formed group of educated young patriots, who asked him to become their leader (p. 231). This he accepted, and they had many engagements with the Italians. They also had to face the hostility of the inhabitants and of the local officials of the provinces of Wallega and Jimma. In December 1936 (pp. 234-5), Ras Imru and his forces were surrounded by the Italians, who threatened to kill hostages and to use poison gas if he did not surrender. This was the end of organized resistance to Fascist occupation.

Imru was taken to Italy (p. 236) with several other leaders and their families. "There, the Italians screened them and those who were thought more likely to collaborate were returned first. . . . Ras Imru was not allowed to return" (p. 236). In fact, he was kept in Italy long after the liberation of his country. He was discovered in, a small village in Tuscany after a search conducted by the British and was flown back to Ethiopia in November 1943 (p. 277).

After his return, he was appointed governor-general of Begemdir. He was one of the few, among the surviving patriot leaders, who realized that the task of building the country anew "would not be resolved if narrow personal and provincial struggles were again to dominate the national scene" (p. 265). According to Greenfield, however, "Hailé Sellassié resented the considerable popularity of the former Regent. Ras Imru had been a progressive governor before the war and was remembered for his justice. . . . All admired his fight to the end against the Italians and he retained the respect and affection of the army officers. . . . Ras Imru . . . voiced his disagreement with some of Hailé Sellassié's policies on successive occasions. For example, although he himself speaks little of the language, he urged the Emperor to choose English rather than French as second official language to Amharic after the war. Partly to restrain his critic but also perhaps to neutralise a potential rival, Hailé Sellassié appointed (Ethiopians say 'exiled') the *ras* to embassies abroad" (p. 294). This was all the easier as Imru's progressive ideas had antagonized influential groups in Ethiopia besides earning him the esteem of the élite: "He had supported a controversial scheme to modernise the Amharic alphabet—a scheme incidentally opposed by the Ethiopian Christian Church which argued that it was sacrilegious because most Amharic letters were derived from Ge'ez, the language of the Church liturgy and literature. . . . He was feared by the more conservative of the court circles, who reminded the Emperor of the high regard in which the officers held him" (p. 353).

In 1946 Ras Imru Hailé Sellasié was appointed Ethiopian minister to the United States and received ambassadorial rank in 1949. He stayed in Washington until 1953, where, incidentally, he was "subjected to indignities on account of the colour of his skin" (p. 437n). When he came back, he received the title of Leul-Ras. But, says Greenfield, "he caused considerable alarm to the land-owning classes and even to some of his relatives by deciding to divest himself of his land in favour of his servants and their heirs. . . . His status in the imagination of the new élite—or as they described themselves enlightened Ethiopians—rose considerably, for he seemed to acknowledge the national need for land reform. Among the less sophisticated there grew up . . . 'the Imru myth'—a belief that his appointment as prime minister would liberalise the Ethiopian system of government overnight. Foreigners jokingly called him 'the red *ras*' " (p. 353). These hopes were damped by his opponents, who "argued that Imru was by then too out of contact with the country's administration to be trusted with ministerial office. Also Hailé Sellasié considered him to be too naïve, particularly with regard to Egypt and Islam, to be trusted with the Foreign Ministry" (p. 353).

In 1954 Imru was posted abroad for five more years, as ambassador to Delhi. His Addis Ababa residence "which had belonged to his father, was unused and Imru decided to allow graduates returning from overseas to use it as an informal club" (p. 353). It may have been there that the 1960 plot first began to take shape. He returned from India in 1959 and in 1960 was appointed ambassador to the Soviet Union.

He "was still making arrangements for his departure at the end of the year" when the conspiracy broke out. "Because of his popularity . . . no rebel group could afford to ignore him" (p. 385). Indeed, the young leaders of the conspiracy had hoped—not vainly as it turned out—to obtain his support. On 13 December 1960, as the coup had just been launched, Imru "was contacted and came to the head-quarters of the Imperial Guard" (p. 394). On 14 December, the twenty-five man Council of the Revolution announced that he had been appointed prime minister of the new government under the direction of Crown Prince Asfa Wäsän. He at once started negotiations to win over the counterrevolutionaries (p. 408). "He understood the masses and the political realities of Ethiopia in 1960, and on the 15th, he grew hourly more alarmed and said openly that much lay still unresolved. Although not completely informed, he sensed the impending crisis and sought desperately to avert bloodshed." He therefore wrote to the head of the Ethiopian church, Abunä Basilios, who replied "that he had already signed leaflets of excommunication against the rebels and, moreover, that the senior army officers with him did not wish for there to be any meeting" (p. 418). This decided the rebel leaders to resort to violence. Although he disapproved of the use of armed power, Imru stayed with them, whereas the crown prince hastened to join the Abunä and the counterrevolutionaries to meet the emperor at the airport. At the trial of the rebel leaders in February 1961, Imru was among the main witnesses for the defense (p. 443). He himself was not tried because the emperor believed, or pretended to believe, that his cousin had acted under duress.

While he was at his post in Washington, Imru Hailé Sellasé wrote his only novel *Fitawrari Bälay* (1955–56), an English translation of which appeared later (1961-62) in the *Ethiopia Observer*. While it may have some historical foundation, it is a very conventional and edifying story that betrays that obsession with family disruption through the hazards and general insecurity of life which has been a conspicuous theme in Amharic fiction since Afäwärq's novel of 1909. In consequence of political intrigues, Belay Kassa has been obliged to leave Gojam with his wife Tewabech and their two sons, Kassahun and Getaneh. While crossing a river, he nearly drowns and is separated from his wife and children, who, in their turn, are separated from each other when different people agree to take care of them. Tewabech is rescued by a kind Muslim who has been forcibly baptized under a decree of Emperor Yohannes; she eventually marries him in the belief that her husband is dead. Kassahun too is well treated by his benefactor. He becomes an officer in the army of Ras Makonnen fighting against the Italians. As we would expect, Getaneh is treated like a slave, but he manages to escape and to enlist in the same army. As to Belay, he has been rescued by a merchant and becomes Ras Makonnen's secretary. As a result of their various adventures, then, they are all gathered in the same place. When they are reunited, Belay magnanimously rejects the plea of his sons, who want their mother to leave her Muslim husband. This episode is characteristic of Imru's sense of tolerance and national unity as against the religious factionalism that had traditionally opposed Muslims and Christians in Ethiopia. The story as a whole has, of course, the trite moral significance that is to be expected from traditional Amharic writers. As the author says in the preface, it is "an expression of the belief that, sooner or later, bad men will be punished for their evil deeds. Good and kind-hearted men, on the other hand, shall always be protected by the grace of God." But he also claims for his tale a more esoteric significance on a political level: "implicitly, it is the story of the fall of Ethiopia under the rule of Fascism and of her eventual liberation." While the relevance of this late nineteenth-century story to the fate of Ethiopia in the 1930s may not be altogether clear, it is quite possible that the intrigues against Belay, his downfall, and subsequent triumph may refer to the experiences of the writer himself, who, in his Washington exile, may have wished to convey in this indirect manner his assurance that God's justice would see to his ultimate rehabilitation.

The New Generation

All the writers mentioned above were mature men when the Italian war broke out, and most of them were elderly persons when they entered the literary scene, usually in the 1940s. While Wäldä Giyorgis, who was fighting for the modernization of the country, kept to the tradition of the praise poem and did not turn to the novel until the mid-fifties, Mäkonnen Endalkačäw, whose political outlook was mainly conservative, was an important innovator in literature, inasmuch as he pursued Heruy's self-appointed task of acclimatizing the novel to Amharic writing, and also produced the first formal dramas on contemporary and historical subjects. In this, it seems he was preceded by a younger writer, who produced the first literary drama—albeit with a traditional allegorical subject —in Amharic in 1945-46, and who deserves to be considered Ethiopia's foremost playwright in the two decades following the liberation of the country.

Käbbädä Mika'él was born on 2 November 1915.[72] He was

twenty when the Italian war broke out, and consequently was unable to pursue his studies beyond secondary-school level, as were all young Ethiopians of the time. He worked by himself, however, reading voraciously and acquiring perfect command of French and Italian; he is also well versed in English. He started composing poetry when he was eighteen, and when Ethiopia was freed in 1941, he was one of the contributors to Yilma Därässa's anthology. In the same year, he published his first book, *The Light of Intelligence*, a collection of poems whose inspiration was drawn partly from his vast reading in Western literature, and partly from Ethiopian fables and folktales. He later published similar works, which are especially designed for school use. One of these was a volume in a series of school readers entitled *Story and Parable* (1942-43), of which Wright was to say that the first two "were botched-up translations of antiquated English storybooks, the third a much more highly polished collection of stories and poems by a young man named Käbbädä Mika'el, then only on the threshold of a distinguished literary career." [73]

In those early years of the postwar period, the emperor called Käbbädä's attention to an American novel that he had read with great pleasure. This was *Beyond Pardon*, by Bertha M. Clay, an American novelist of the late nineteenth century.[74] Haile Selassie asked Käbbädä if he could not translate it into Amharic. Instead of providing a straight translation, the young writer turned out an Amharic poem of some 1,500 lines with a detailed analytical preface, which appeared in 1943-44, became very popular, and was reprinted in 1951-52.

The crucial moment in his literary career occurred when he decided to turn to drama. He was familiar with the masterpieces of the European dramatic tradition. While he was a great admirer of Shakespeare—he was later to translate *Romeo and Juliet*—his own temperament was more adapted to the formal austerity and the intellectual and dramatic concentration of Greek and classical French tragedy. Käbbädä became the founder of serious modern drama in Amharic, doing away with the farcical and more crudely allegorical entertainments of the early thirties in favor of tragedies molded into classical form, which he constantly revises and improves upon. These plays were first performed in the theater of the Lycée Täfäri Mäkonnen.

It may seem surprising that Käbbädä's first play, *Prophecy Ful-*

filled (1945-46), which was later translated into English by Stephen Wright (Addis Ababa, 1953), should deal with a theme far remote from the usual preoccupations of modern civilization: the theme of prophecy. But Ethiopian Christianity is of the fundamentalist type, and it is significant that this widely cultured writer should have inaugurated his career as a playwright with a forceful reassertion of belief in prophecies and miracles. The play, in fact, is based on a situation not very different from that of Calderón's *La vida es sueño*, although whether Käbbädä knew the Spanish work is very doubtful. A pagan king learns that an astrologer's newborn son will later marry his daughter and evangelize the country. He tries to kill him twice: once as a baby, and again twenty years later. Each time, some miraculous intervention ensures the survival of the boy, who ultimately marries the king's daughter and sees that the prophecy is fulfilled by having the country converted to Christianity. Like Calderón's masterpiece, and all plays of this kind, Käbbädä's drama suffers from a basic psychological improbability: if the protagonist believes in prophecies, he must know that it is vain to attempt to thwart them; if he does not, there is no point in trying to prevent their accomplishment. In the second edition, which appeared in 1954-55, Käbbädä inserted a long soliloquy in which the king shows himself aware of this contradiction and attempts to resolve it in a manner that is not likely to convince the Western reader. Other alterations to the original version concern the technique of the play, which Käbbädä made more suitable for stage production by dividing the long sermon-like speeches and introducing livelier bits of dialogue. Equally significant, though in a different sphere, are further additions concerned with the duties, responsibilities, and burdens of kingship. Between the two versions, Käbbädä had been called to high office at the Ministry of Education and at the Ministry of Foreign Affairs, and he had represented Ethiopia as ambassador extraordinary to the Vatican at the opening of the Ecumenical Council. These new experiences in the field of public life were to turn his attention to problems less concerned with the supernatural.

Meanwhile, Käbbädä produced his second play, *The Storm of Punishment* (1948-49), which is an attack against materialism and atheism. The devil, disguised under the name of Qälil, avails himself of the despondency and bitterness of a poor man, Bälay, to turn him away from religious belief. He convinces him that man and his world are the ultimate reality, that God does not exist, and that moral values ought to be discarded—a combination of Marxist materialism and Nietzschean self-glorification. The bulk of the play is made up of philosophical conversations in the course of which Qälil persuades Bälay that ruthlessness and absence of ethical prejudices put in the service of science and a secular philosophy unhampered by religion, will result in man's total mastery over nature and in the creation of a breed of supermen. He thus plays simultaneously upon Bälay's lust for material rewards and upon his idealistic proclivities. He even promises him that science will soon be able to give him physical immortality. But at the end, after Bälay ruined one of his former friends and caused his death, Qälil reveals his identity and cruelly unveils the truth to Bälay, as the latter is about to be killed by some bandits. With its contrived action, implausible plot, and long-winded speeches, the play calls to mind Renaissance religious drama in Europe, in which the influence of Seneca's lyrical tragedy and of Christian ethics combined to produce static works, whose interest is literary rather than truly theatrical.

Indeed, the evolution of Käbbädä's dramatic inspiration followed paths similar to those of the sixteenth-century Western Renaissance, as he turned to history for his next play, *Hannibal* (1955-56). By that time, the writer had been appointed to various important public functions, and he had traveled abroad widely. What is more, in an attempt to define the cultural orientations that Ethiopia should embrace, he had made a thorough study of the history of civilization, and he had produced such works as *Ethiopia and Western Civilization* (1949), which appeared simultaneously in Amharic, French, and English; *Great Men* (1950-51), a series of biographical studies of Homer, Demosthenes, Cleopatra, Shakespeare, Peter the Great, Frederick the Great, and Napoleon; a monograph on *Alexander the Great* (1954-55); and the first volume of his *History of the World* (1954-55). He had also translated *Romeo and Juliet* (1953-54).

In Hannibal's career, Käbbädä selected the second Punic War, when the Carthaginian general, sending his army over the Alps into Italy, came nearest to achieving a final victory over Rome. In the play, he is prevented from doing so by the senators of Carthage, who deny him the financial resources he requests to conquer Rome itself. Their refusal is the result of intrigues instigated by Hanno, who fears that his power may be eclipsed by the prestige of the young general, and who instills into the minds of the senators the notion that Hannibal is after personal power. The crucial debate in the Carthaginian senate parallels a similar discussion in Rome, but while the Carthaginians resent the victories that Hannibal obtained without applying for permission, the Roman senators wisely refrain from blaming their own generals for their defeat, and they give Scipio the necessary means and authority for staging a diversionary invasion of Carthaginian territory. The senators of Carthage realize too late that their greed and envy have been the undoing of their city. The ethical implications of the play are fairly obvious. They are described by the author in the Preface, where he says that Carthaginian society was one "where love of wealth dominated all other passions, while factional strife was more violent than anywhere else." Indeed, the audience sees Hanno bribing another senator, and one of the main preoccupations of the senate is to know whether or not the war has brought huge personal profits to Hannibal, and what is to become of the spoils, if any. The central inspiration of the play, however, is not so much religious and philosophical as patriotic. The events described are of highly topical interest in a country like Ethiopia, which has had a long history of feudal strife and internecine war. Indeed, it has been suggested that one of the causes for Ethiopia's speedy collapse in the war against Italy was the reluctance of the feudal lords, who were also army commanders, to come to each other's rescue in case of need. Further, because of his inside knowledge of government, Käbbädä must have been aware of the kind of intrigues that had just led to the eviction of Wäldä Giyorgis. A dramatic call for selflessness and patriotic solidarity was no doubt to the point.

One other aspect of the play deserves comment. In his Preface, the author insists that his play is entirely based on historical sources, "without any attempt to make it more pleasing on the stage by means of imagined ornaments." It is all the more revealing, therefore, that he should have thought it advisable to put the following, somewhat anachronistic speech on the lips of an anonymous "passer-by" before Hannibal's defeat at Zama:

There is, moreover, a question of race and posterity. If the Romans are victorious, the whites will rule. They will possess all wealth and knowledge, and their power over the world will be eternal. They will guide the world. Europe will be the mistress of all nations. To her will go prosperity, science, power, On the contrary, if Hannibal triumphs, then prosperity will change camps, will leave Europe to come to Africa. Splendor, intelligence, grandeur, if transferred to the other continent, will lead to the decay of our race. Think of it; this war between Rome and Carthage, this merciless struggle, does not concern the two cities only. The victory of one or the other side will decide the fate of the peoples of the world. If Rome resists successfully, she will be able to break the development of Africa and to block her way to the future.[75]

This seems to be one of the earliest formulations of a sense of African solidarity in Amharic creative writing. The two centers of interest in Ethiopian literature have been Europe and Ethiopia itself. In the course of the last decade, concern with Africa has grown immensely among the younger generation of Ethiopian intellectuals, partly as a result of the role played by the emperor in the Organization of African Unity,[76] and partly because an important segment of the Ethiopian élite seems to feel that other new African states have made faster progress toward modernization and democracy than their own country. Until the mid-1950s, this trend of thought remained conspicuously absent from imaginative literature, which was dominated by an overriding concern to restore Ethiopia's greatness and the superiority that she allegedly owed to the fact that the Amhara were a Semitic, a Christian, and a literate nation. Indeed, the most cherished book of the Amhara, the Kebrä Nägäst, expressly states that "The will of God decreed sovereignty for the seed of Sem and slavery for the seed of Ham." [77] Given the fundamentalist character of Ethiopian Christianity, it is not surprising that racial prejudice should be strong among the Amhara and other Semitic groups. Käbbädä's pronouncement in Hannibal signals the emergence, in creative writing, of a sense that Ethiopian patriotism was not enough, and that the fate of the country should be thought of in the framework of continental solidarity.

Hannibal was performed at the newly built Haile Selassie I Theatre during the Silver Jubilee festivities, in costumes bought in Vienna. Apparently, this was the last of the author's plays to be performed. This falling out of fashion and of favor may partly be ascribed to intrigue, but another factor is to be reckoned with: the rapid evolution of Amharic drama during the late 1950s, which will be discussed later. All Käbbädä's plays are verse tragedies. They are intended more for edification than entertainment. The author has always been and still is greatly admired for his full mastery of the subtle resources of the language. His plays are the proper expression of a Christian and an élite culture, as was most serious drama in sixteenth- and seventeenth-century Europe. It is not to be expected that such works should greatly appeal, either by their style or by their ideas, to a popular, semiliterate audience. Nor is it surprising—although some may find it deplorable—that they should have been displaced, in popular, intellectual, and official favor, by the new type of drama, more realistic and more readily accessible, which was to be created by a later generation of playwrights.

In *Kaléb* (1965–66), Käbbädä brought to the stage an episode in the history of the Axumite kingdom. As the Ethiopian church had acknowledged the spiritual supremacy of the Alexandrine patriarch in the late fifth century, Axum had close links with Byzantium and was in fact a by no means negligible ally of the Eastern Roman Empire against Persia. For a long time Judaism had been very active in southern Arabia, where it was supported by the Persians. Toward 516, a Judaized monarch, Dhu-Nuwâs, took power in Yemen and threatened Arab Christendom. About 518, with the encouragement of the Byzantine emperor, Justin I (518–527), an Ethiopian expedition was sent to Yemen but was defeated by Dhu-Nuwâs, who started persecuting the Christians in their main center of Najran in 523. In 525, a new Ethiopian army, led by Emperor Kaléb, reached the city. Dhu-Nuwâs was defeated and killed.[78]

In a way, the new play is complementary to *Hannibal*, as it extols cooperation between Byzantium and Ethiopia in the service of Christianity. Like Carthage in the earlier play, Axum is carefully built up as a symbol for Africa. When the Byzantine envoys reach Kaléb's court, the monarch has just been listening to the report of an Ethiopian exploration of the African continent. He has reached the conclusion that "Africa, which is of our blood and of our race, must not fall under foreign domination," that it is his country's vocation "to take the lead on the African continent," and that the time has come to give up the traditional policy of eastward expansion over the Red Sea (Act 3, scene 1). But when the Byzantine ambassadors describe the sorry plight of the Arab Christians,

Kaléb immediately changes his mind, deciding, with full approval from Abba Pätäléwon, a church dignitary, that his most urgent task is to protect them against Jewish persecution.

The play ends as Kaléb, at the height of his power, withdraws to a monastery. Obviously, there is no room for great variety in the depiction of royalty in Amharic literature. Both Justin and Kaléb are perfect-ruler types: the will of God and the welfare of their countries fill all their thinking and determine their policies. The villain of the play is of course Dhu-Nuwâs, who lives in utter blindness. As was perhaps to be expected, he is also the victim of a self-fulfilling prophecy: he has seen in a dream that a Christian monarch would dethrone him. But, he says, "I made the mistake of seeking my rival amongst the Christians who lived around me, in my own country. And I hounded them, and wanted to exterminate them all. By so doing, I merely provoked Kaléb into declaring war upon me. Without that, he might not have attacked me. Such is man's ignorance; uncertain of everything I say, I can only conclude that destiny is not to be thwarted" (act 4, scene 2). Notwithstanding this belated acknowledgment, he sets out to fight and to meet his inevitable death.

In the Preface, Käbbädä points out with some justifiable pride that the Byzantine Empire was destroyed by the Ottomans in the fifteenth century, whereas Ethiopia managed to overcome her own enemies and to survive as an independent country. In the play, the main weakness of Byzantium is shown to be religious strife among her citizens. After discoursing on the fall of the Roman Empire and concluding that "every nation carries the seeds of its own ruin," Justin tells his prime minister: "We too have our own incurable sickness. You will see that our enemies' blows will be facilitated by inner strife due to religious disturbances. Priestly quarrels will cause the destruction of our country" (act 2, scene 1). This motif has little relevance to the main action of the play and has obviously been introduced by Käbbädä as a contribution to Haile Selassie's strenuous attempts to create unity in the country in spite of religious diversity.

After those two historical plays, Käbbädä turned to biblical history for inspiration, following, as he claims in the Preface to his next tragedy, the example set by Lewis Wallace and Racine! It is presumably the latter's *Athalie* rather than the former's *Ben Hur* which prompted him to write *Achab* (1967–68), a play about

Athalia's father. Achab, it will be remembered, had paid false witnesses to get rid of Naboth and, under the influence of his wife Jezabel, had introduced the cult of Baal into the kingdom of Juda. He had massacred a number of God's prophets and his ignominious death had been prophesied by Elijah. Like Shakespeare's Macbeth, Käbbädä's evil characters act in full awareness that God's justice will ultimately catch up with them. The difference, however, is of capital importance: where Macbeth clearly shows himself unable to resist the allurements of power, there is no such inner duality in Käbbädä's protagonist. One has a feeling that the author refrains from clarifying their motives out of a fear that evil may thus be made attractive. At the very moment when Achab, in spite of the warnings and prophecies of Elijah and Miceah, decides to wage war against Syria, he also utters edifying speeches showing that he does not entertain the slightest hope of evading God's wrath, even on this earth. He is carried all the time by forces outside his control so that he behaves, without any intelligible reason whatever, contrary to his own deep-felt beliefs. This is, of course, the inevitable reflection of Ethiopia's fatalism. If human destiny is fully in the hands of a constantly intruding God, it is obviously impossible to create credible tragic heroes endowed with a convincing responsibility for their own deeds. The motivation and the logic that must underlie Achab's criminal behavior never come to the surface. Although the play shows continued improvement in its construction and dramatic quality, the extreme idealism of Amhara culture obtrudes itself in moralizing speeches that are out of character.

Käbbädä's plays undoubtedly provide the most elaborate dramatic expression of a traditional Ethiopian outlook firmly based on Christian faith and national pride. But it must be viewed in the general configuration of the writer's thought as formulated in his many works on history and civilization. Whereas it had been Heruy's single-minded purpose to cure Ethiopian Christianity of its corruption and to help modernize Ethiopian society, Käbbädä's thinking evidences the traumatic impact of Italian colonization and of the swift penetration of the Western world view after World War II. Like Heruy, Käbbädä recognizes that if his country is to survive and prosper, she needs to assimilate Western scientific, technological, and economic progress. But by the mid-forties, this was a widespread opinion among the steadily growing Western-educated intelligentsia. It was clear that Ethiopia was irrevocably enmeshed, willynilly, in the mechanism of modernization. To the two generations of intellectuals who had known the period of Italian occupation, the danger was no longer stagnation, but an assimilation so thorough that it would lead Ethiopians to relinquish the ideals of the past.

In his discursive works, such as *Ethiopia and Western Civilization* (1947–48) and *Of Civilization* (n.d.), Käbbädä tried to maintain a balance between the obvious positive aspects of Western culture, and its negative features, which he defines as materialism, atheism, and a boundless lust for money and power. He often warns his readers against the tendency of the West to contaminate the whole world. In the latter work, he quotes the example of Japan, which he had analyzed in *The Modernization of Japan* (1953–54), observing that "when Japan finally reached the first rank of world powers, her attitude towards weaker nations was no different from that of European colonial powers; nor is there any reason to believe that China will evolve otherwise." [79] While displaying unconcealed admiration and love for the humanistic achievements of the West in literature, art, music and pure science, he is exceedingly diffident about Western thought, which he sees dominated by Marx and Nietzsche, and he urges his readers to turn for moral guidance to such Indian thinkers as Vivekananda and Ghandi—another meritorious African attempt at achieving syncretism. Of all this philosophical background, however, there are few echoes in the author's dramatic works, which are obviously designed to illustrate and preserve the Christian spirituality and the patriotic loyalty that, to Käbbädä as to most Ethiopian writers of his generation, are the most valuable features of the national culture.

Indeed, only one writer of the forties continued the modernizing trend that had been so characteristic of Afäwärq, Heruy, and Täklä Hawaryat. This was the latter's son, Germačäw Täklä Hawaryat,[80] who was born in 1915. After attending primary school in Ethiopia, he pursued his studies in France. He returned home on the eve of the Italian war and, following the Graziani massacre of February 1937, he was taken to Italy as a political prisoner. He stayed there until 1943. Two years after his return to his fatherland, he was appointed director general of the Press and Information Office. It was during this time that he contributed to the reawakening of

Amharic literature with a novel, *Ar'aya* (1948-49) and a play, *Tewodros* (1949-50).

Ar'aya, the hero's name, means "good example." As is usual in Ethiopian fiction, the story is a sort of exemplum that reverts to the technique and subject matter of Heruy in *The New World*. Like Heruy's protagonist, Ar'aya is a young Ethiopian who studies abroad. He attends the French Ecole Nationale d'Agriculture and comes back to Ethiopia to help in the modernization of his people. Though he, too, is disappointed, the reason does not lie—as it did for Heruy—in the general misoneism of the population and in the conservatism of the clergy: Ar'aya's endeavors are frustrated by reactionary intrigues in government circles.[81] The novel contains vestiges of the traditional moral outlook that was so powerful in Heruy's book: as the hero stops in Dire Dawa on his return journey, he is painfully struck by his fellow citizens' habits of drunkenness. But Germačäw introduces into Amharic prose fiction an element of descriptive realism which had been conspicuously absent from it before. The idealistic outlook of Ethiopian writers drives them to concentrate on moral ideas, preferably of a general order. Since the allegorical meaning is all-important, individual characterization is kept to a bare minimum and natural descriptions are felt to be pointless. Germačäw's depiction of the countryside along the railway track from Jibuti to Addis Ababa is the first of its kind.[82] But the author's education and his foreign experience enable him to go to the roots of the problem in a way that Heruy obviously could not have achieved. In *The New World*, it will be remembered, modernity is defined in two ways: it means the rejection of superstitious or degraded customs, and the acceptance of such minor and superficial aspects of Western technology as the telephone and the phonograph. But Germačäw knew, as his father before him had known, that the foundation of development is economic and administrative, and that the key to economic progress in Ethiopia is in agriculture. Ar'aya consequently becomes a gentleman farmer and shows the population how to till the earth in a rational and profitable way. This is the first Amharic work to have been translated into Russian and, subsequently, into Chinese.[83]

Germačäw's only play, which deals with Téwodros II, was printed in 1949–50, several years before Mäkonnen's *Taitu Betul*. It is one of the earliest manifestations of literary interest in the first emperor who fought for the unification of the country in the face of feudal privileges. Whereas *Ar'aya* took up the problem of modernization at grass-root level, the play discusses the same problem from the political viewpoint. Unlike Mäkonnen, Germačäw describes Téwodros not as a bloodthirsty upstart, but as a modern monarch, the precursor of Menelik II and Haile Selassie I. The hero's fate is genuinely tragic. His endeavor was in the right direction, aiming at setting up a modern centralized state, but it was frustrated for two main reasons: first, given the social-historical situation of the time, it was premature; second, in spite of the lengthy pleas that he devotes to justifying his plans, Téwodros makes the psychological mistake of strengthening feudal hostility because his impatience drives him to resort to violence rather than diplomacy and persuasion.[84]

In 1950 Germačäw was sent abroad as councillor and chargé d'affaires of the Ethiopian Legation in Stockholm. He later occupied a succession of important diplomatic posts. After a spell at the Ethiopian embassy in Rio de Janeiro (1954), he became a high official in the Ministry of Foreign Affairs (1956), then was appointed Ethiopian ambassador to Rome (1958) and, with the title of Blatta, to Bonn (1960). In 1961 he came back to Ethiopia as minister of information and was appointed governor general of Ilubabor Province with the title of Däjjazmac in 1965. He became minister of agriculture in 1966, and was moved to the Health Department on 18 February 1969. These diplomatic and ministerial activities brought a promising literary career to a premature end.

Bäemnät Gäbrä Amlak was born on 26 October 1920 in Adi Ugri, Eritrea.[85] He attended primary school at the Swedish mission there and at the Menelik II school in Addis Ababa. He studied privately for his secondary education, and, after attending the Hampton Institute in Virginia, he obtained a certificate in library science from the University of New South Wales in Sydney, in 1962.

By that time,[86] he had already published several didactic books: he had translated a pamphlet on altruism by Henry Drummond (1953-54) and an educational treatise by Jessie Hertslet (1955-56); he had also written a work on the origins of the Amharic language (1954-55). Although he claims that his main interest is in creative writing, he has only produced one novel so far: *Childhood Never Comes Back* (1956-57). This is a sort of narrative and edifying quartet that describes the various fates of four school friends. The first one is not interested in learning, as he wants to earn money and enjoy life as soon as possible; he leaves school prematurely and reaches an equally premature death at the hospital where alcoholism has taken him with a liver cirrhosis. The second goes through some elementary vocational training; because of his pragmatic, egotistic character, he drifts away from his family and finds himself living in isolation at a hotel. The third one, who is the central character, is aware of the value of the humanities; after completing high school, he studies abroad. On his return, he obtains a high-grade position and he even succeeds in marrying a charming woman whom he has chosen for himself in spite of the opposition of his conservative father-in-law. Typically, however, the last word remains with the fourth student, who has also sedulously applied himself to the pursuit of learning. After completing his studies, he has turned back to the true faith and has become a priest, and he denounces the obsession with material benefits to which Western education has led his friend: "With all your machines, *you* have become machines!" This novel, then, illustrates an interesting awareness of the paradox of modern education, which is both necessary for the development of Ethiopia, and dangerous to its soul. Like Germačäw's *Ar'aya*, Bäemnät's book has been commended for its realistic picture, not of nature, but of school life and of its hero's impressions as he travels abroad.

After his return from Australia, Bäemnät matriculated at the Haile Selassie I University in Addis Ababa, from which he was graduated with a B.A. degree in Ethiopian languages and literature in 1966. He is now a librarian and a graduate student in Addis Ababa.

Mäkonnen Zäwde was born in 1921-22 at Tenta, where his father was a parish priest in the Wärähimäno district of the Wallo province.[87] He got his elementary education in church schools in Tenta and in Boru, where he studied Amharic, Ge'ez, and the type of religious music called *zéma*. He went to Addis Ababa in 1932-33 and soon enrolled in the Boy Scouts' school founded in 1934, where instruction was given in French. At the time of the Italian invasion, he became an interpreter with the Belgian military mission that was then training Ethiopian troops. Young as he was, he accompanied the troops to the battlefield and was wounded at the

battle of May Čäw, which marked the ultimate defeat of the Ethiopian army on 31 March 1936. He returned to Tenta, but as his
father was an opponent of the Italians, he and his two sons were
imprisoned at Haiq, where Mäkonnen's father died in 1936-37. The
two brothers were later released at the request of the district
governor.

After the liberation, Mäkonnen became inspector general at the
Ministry of Education. It was during this period that he wrote the
two novels that he published in 1955-56: *The Wounded Man of
May Čäw*, tells the story of a sergeant, Bä-delu Tärräfä, who has
managed to survive the battle and becomes a leader of the underground movement during the Italian occupation; *Man's Career in
This World* deals with the problem of Ethiopia's access to the
modern world. The latter is fairly similar in technique and outlook
to Bäemnät's novel that was to come out the following year. The
story focuses on the experiences of two village boys, Gärrämäw
and Bezu-Ayyähu. Like the author himself, both leave their village
to attend a church school, and then go to the capital, where they
have their first contact with modern civilization. From then on,
their destinies begin to diverge. Gärrämäw goes on with traditional
studies and becomes a scholar in Ge'ez and Amharic. He remains
loyal to his origins and to his family, picking his way among the
various elements of modern civilization. Bezu-Ayyähu, on the contrary, yields to the allurements of the new way of life. He studies
administration abroad and becomes so thoroughly Westernized
that he even drinks his whisky straight. Back in Ethiopia, he rejects
his family, wastes his time dancing and drinking, gets into debts, is
dismissed from his employment, falls ill, and dies a miserable death,
forgotten by all except the good Gärrämäw, who has come to
assist him in his agony.

Such crude patterning is built into the Ethiopian writer's almost
maniacal preoccupation with moral teaching. It also controls the
structure of Mäkonnen's next novel, *The Sight of My Eyes* (1957-
58), which focuses on the problem of marriage. The antithesis is
between a husband who starts patronizing prostitutes, and his wife,
who remains a model of virtue and steadfast loyalty. It is noteworthy, however, that Mäkonnen seems to accept the Western
premise of free choice. The purpose of the book as he describes it
is to advise young people "to investigate the character of their
future husband or wife before getting married."

A similar combination of Western individualism and traditional morality is effected through the concepts of hard work and self-help in *Man and His Age* (1960-61). The main characters are once more a man and his wife, who come to grips with the hardships of life in town. Significantly, Mäkonnen departs from the modernizing attitude toward city life that had prevailed in early Amharic writing, and stresses its negative aspects as so many South African writers have done. His heroes do not find happiness until they leave for the country and engage in farming. "The main point of the book," the writer comments, "is to show that if a man endeavors to overcome the difficulties he meets in life he will succeed in the long run." And in recognition of the new trend toward social well-being through economic development, he adds that "the book also shows how a society could work and improve its standard of living."

But in his latest novel to date, *Endurance* (1963-64), Mäkonnen turned back to the otherworldly viewpoint so congenial to Ethiopian culture. The title character, Aschaläw, rejects the materialistic view that getting married and having children is man's best way to happiness. He therefore engages in study and altruistic work, building schools and hospitals in the hope of achieving good things that will live after him. Like Chaucer in *The House of Fame*—but, unfortunately, without Chaucer's humor—he comes to realize that wordly fame indiscriminately remembers and celebrates both good men and evil men. Thoroughly disenchanted with action in this world, he becomes a hermit in the desert.

It was also this generation that produced the first two Ethiopian women writers, Romanä Wärq Kasahun and Seneddu Gäbru, both of them contributors to Yilma Däräsä's anthology of 1941. In Ethiopia as elsewhere in Africa, there has been obdurate native resistance to any kind of modern education for girls. Indeed, the first modern girls' school was founded by Empress Mänän in 1931. Before that, only a few girls had enjoyed the privilege of being educated abroad. Among the first was the emperor's daughter, Princess Tsähay Haile Selassie, who studied in Switzerland before being trained as a nurse in London during her exile. She died in 1942, and in 1950-51 Romanä Wärq Kasahun published a play entitled *The Light of Science*, which was dedicated to her memory. Romanä Wärq, however, is better known as a journalist and a

broadcaster, and is the author of various pamphlets on the condition of women in Ethiopia.

Seneddu Gäbru was born in 1916 into an educated family in
Addis Aläm.[88] Her father, Gäbru Desta, had been sent by the missionaries to study in Jerusalem and Basel in the 1870s. He had been
mayor of Gondar in the last few years of the nineteenth century.
He then suffered a period of disgrace, which he spent in learned
studies, publishing an Amharic grammar in 1923. He was later to
become käntiba of Addis Ababa and, in 1931, vice-president of the
senate. In the late twenties, he sent his two daughters, Yubdas and
Seneddu, to St. Chrischona for their schooling; they later went to
France, studying in Montmirail and Morges. Seneddu subsequently
completed her education in Lausanne. In 1932 she returned to Ethiopia and started teaching. When war broke out, she became active
in the Red Cross. After the Italian conquest, she was arrested with
her father, who had been trying to organize guerrilla resistance in
Gore, and she was detained for a while in Italy.

After the liberation, she contributed to Yilma Däräsä's anthology. She was also asked by the minister of public health to organize
the Ethiopian Red Cross. Later, she was appointed headmistress of
the Empress Mänän Girls' High School. In 1949-50, she published
a volume entitled *The Book of My Heart*, which contains a verse
essay to the glory of the resistance fighters, a drama based on the
Graziani massacre, and another play in the moralizing trend.

In 1957, under the new constitution of 1955, she was elected to
the House of Representatives, of which she immediately became
vice-chairman. In 1960 she chaired a United Nations seminar on
the rights of man held in Addis Ababa, and in 1961 she was selected
as vice-president of the Red Cross at an international conference
held in Prague. She has traveled widely in Western and Eastern
Europe, and in India. She is the wife of Germačäw Täklä Hawaryat, and, like her husband, discontinued her creative writing after
1950 to devote herself to the service of her country.

The writers so far mentioned in this section are only a few among
those who contributed to the—by African standards—tremendous
literary outburst in Ethiopia during the fifties. As late as 1965,
Levine found it legitimate to deplore that "although Marcel Cohen
heralded the birth of a printed literature in Amharic as early as
1925, writing is still not very important on the Ethiopian scene,"

because "the output of original books and pamphlets in Amharic averaged less than fifteen a year over the last two decades." [89] As compared with other African countries, however, Ethiopia stands exceptionally high in the production of creative vernacular literature. The obstacles listed by Levine are real enough. The high cost of printing constrains most writers to find a patron in the crown; censorship inhibits overt expression of unorthodox views; the potential audience is small, owing to the high level of illiteracy and to the low intellectual standards of the modern elite. Yet, more creative work was printed in Amharic during those years than in any other single African language in the whole of sub-Saharan Africa. The quality of this writing will not be reliably assessed until Ethiopian critics conversant with the most sophisticated techniques of present-day literary criticism have been trained. At the present stage, it would seem that Ethiopian appraisal of written literature has been based on two main criteria: a writer is valued in proportion to the edifying character and the didactic significance of his message, and to his skill in handling the intricate possibilities of the language for ambiguous metaphorical expression. Such criteria obviously make for conformity, and Amharic writing, in this respect, is a faithful reflection not so much of Ethiopian society as it actually is but of a certain official idea or image of Ethiopian society and mores.

Ethiopia in the past was dominated by a coalition of the Coptic church and the feudal aristocracy, with the emperors fitfully trying to assert their authority. The task of unifying the empire and of centralizing its administration was achieved by Haile Selassie I, whose regime of enlightened authoritarianism is probably the best form of government that underdeveloped countries, with their largely illiterate population, their economic backwardness, and their lack of experience in handling the institutionalized forms of parliamentary democracy, can hope for, both at present and in the immediate future. In spite of his attempts to erect a facade of constitutional and parliamentary democracy, the emperor is the dominant factor in Ethiopian life. In Amharic literature, supremacy of his person is manifested in many forms. A large number of books are printed at official expense on the government press. Most of them open with a portrait of the emperor, sometimes in hideously crude color photography, and are prefaced with a poem or some dedicatory lines paying homage to his munificence, wisdom, and

universal greatness. There are poets such as Wäldä Giyorgis or
Yaréd, who consider it part of their duty, if not their main literary
occupation, to write gratulatory and encomiastic poems on the emperor's birthdays and other state occasions. The significance of this
was pointed out by Edward Ullendorff as late as 1965:

Exhortations and panegyrics are, perhaps, still the most voluminous
sector of modern Amharic poetry. Laudatory songs and poems in
honour of His Imperial Majesty's birthday somehow continue a trend
which began in the 14th century with the first Imperial songs in
Amharic. . . . Not all of the rhymes and verses produced for those
occasions can be called "literature," but they are genuine effusions of
respect and affection for a great King.[90]

While such poems should be considered the equivalents of the
numberless odes that were addressed to European kings and queens
in the days of absolute monarchy, Ethiopian drama and prose fiction have largely been concerned with extolling the greatness and
defining the duties and responsibilities of royalty. Perhaps the
closest parallel is with the religious and political outlook evinced
in Spanish drama of the Golden Age, where the monarch is constantly celebrated as God's vicar on earth, and is therefore described as the fountainhead of honor and justice. In fact, the greater
part of Amharic narrative and dramatic writing is swayed by a
concept much akin to what was called "poetic justice" in
seventeenth-century Europe. We have seen how, in Ras Imru's
Fitawrari Bälay, the virtues and loyalty of the main characters are
rewarded, after the many vicissitudes that put them to the test,
through the agency of Ras Mäkonnen.

The ruler's function of creating order, both on the moral and
the material planes, figures prominently in Mäzgäbu Abatä's novel
Tebäbä Sellasé (1955–56), which illustrates a typical Ethiopian
success story. Tebäbä is just a boy somewhere in Manz, but he has
premonitory dreams and is even visited by the Lord's angel, who
advises him to leave for the capital in spite of his father's opposition. In Addis Ababa, he fortunately meets the emperor, who is
struck by his bright intelligence, and entrusts him to the minister
of education. At school, Tebäbä swiftly goes through the whole
curriculum, always at the top of his class. He is sent to the University of Pennsylvania, where he masters naval engineering in
seven years, prudently refraining from playing football, and ad-

amantly resisting the multifarious allurements of American womanhood. On his return to Ethiopia, he first sets up a naval academy
and is soon appointed defense minister. In the midst of his official
duties, he finds time to look after his aged parents, and even to
marry a pretty graduate from Addis Ababa University College.
With its tiresomely explicit moralizing, this book admirably exemplifies the fundamental authoritarianism of Ethiopian society. What
primarily motivates the hero is not the individualistic impulse to
carve a position for himself in the world: it is obedience first to
supernatural visions, and second to the will of the emperor; the
rest is given to him. The rationale of such attitudes is always the
same: total submission to God and to the monarch necessarily
brings its rewards.

Exactly the same outlook is at work in a short novel in slightly
dramatized form, *Mother's Advice Is God's Advice* (1956–57), by
Näggädä Gäbrä Ab. The young hero, Zälläläw, is the son of a
Patriot killed at May Čäw. He enrolls in the army to acquire glory
by serving his country. His particular skill lies in the composition
of war songs, and his general is so impressed with his performance
in this field that he raises him to the command of a battalion. This,
however, arouses the jealousy of some junior officers who plot to
murder him. But Zällaläw's mother is warned by God in a dream,
and she gives her boy such good advice that his would-be murderers poison themselves. Ultimately, Zälläläw, like Mäzgäbu's
hero, rises to ministerial rank. The point is that God and the emperor join hands in rewarding the young man who has distinguished himself by his patriotic sense of duty and his filial devotion.

This cooperation of God and monarch in literary fiction reiter-
ates the concept of the divine nature of kingship as inscribed in the
constitution of 1955, which says that "By virtue of his Imperial
blood, as well as by the anointing which he has received, the Person of the Emperor is sacred, His dignity is inviolable and His
power indisputable" (art. 4). Indeed, the emperor's power and
dignity have remained undisputed, at least in literature. Even
Mäkonnen Endalkačäw, the most prominent representative of the
high feudal class among Amharic writers, while he showed peculiar
interest in imperial figures that had abused their power in various
ways, was always careful to contrast them with the great piety, the
love of learning, and the devotion to the nation's progress and welfare characteristic of Haile Selassie I. It would probably be a mis-

take to ascribe to his work any critical intention of a political order. It does not object to the imperial institution as such, but it emphasizes the danger of entrusting such limitless power to selfish or immoral individuals.

The second main source of power in Ethiopia today is the Coptic church. Although the present emperor did his best to weaken the overt political and administrative privileges of the clergy, he carefully avoided any open clash with the church. If anything, there seems to have been, after the liberation, a concerted attempt to strengthen the spiritual prestige of the national church. Of course, no questioning of church doctrine has ever been conceivable in Amharic literature. But at any rate, Heruy provided, in *The New World,* a realistic and outspoken indictment of clerical ignorance and corruption. This motif seems to have almost completely vanished from postbellum fiction and drama. It is true that a clerical character in Asäffa Gäbrä Maryam's novel *How She Left her Husband* (1953–54) asks this very revealing question: "If one stops drinking, what else is left in this world?"; [91] but this is not central to the story. It is the other aspect of Heruy's thought that has now come to the fore: the restatement and revitalization of Christian moral teaching in its pristine purity. The rationale for the evolution should probably be sought in a revulsion against the threat to faith and morals represented by the sweeping westernization of Ethiopia in the years following the liberation. This has been explained by Käbbädä Mika'él in *Ethiopia and Western Civilisations:*

Several countries realised their modernisation in times favourable to them, but Ethiopia came in contact with the modern world but recently, in an era of confusion, and her difficulties were hence increased. . . . The reason for this confusion is that men have become more materialistic and have deviated from the path leading to God; Christian nations are a great way off the spirit of Christianity, and the Gospel, which is its basis, is left neglected. . . . A child's character is formed according to the good or bad education he receives. In the same way a nation behaves according to the principles inculcated in it by those who roused it up from its torpor. Often this influence proceeds from the morality the people derives from books, theatre, poetry. . . . Rousseau's, Schopenhauer's, Spencer's, Darwin's, Voltaire's influence is harmful in the way that it deviates man's mind from religion. Such an error can be prevented, not by giving lessons from the Bible or the Gospel, but by convincing young people that outside Christianity, there is no supreme law for man's morality.[92]

This may well be a medieval way of viewing the evolution of man's mind, in complete disregard of the bewilderingly complex causations involved. We should do well to remember, however, that it produced the *Ancrene Riwle*, and Richard Rolle, and *Everyman*, and even *The Pilgrim's Progress*. Whether equal rank is to be granted to any Amharic literary work is a problem in comparative evaluation that is bound to remain unsolved pending the emergence of Ethiopian scholar-critics fully conversant with world literature. Meanwhile, it is perhaps possible to bring out the favorite themes handled by Amharic writers, as indicators of their deeper ethical and social preoccupations.

In a general way, Amharic novels and plays are very simply designed to condemn vice and extol virtue by showing that God always ensures the punishment of the sinners and the reward of the virtuous. Asäffa's novel deals with a woman who betrays her husband. At the end of the book, she crumbles under an avalanche of calamities—drunkenness, syphilis, and tuberculosis. Sometimes, in compliance with biblical teaching, the sins of the parents are visited upon their children. In a play by Haddis Wäldä Sadeq, *Woyzäro Aläm* (1956–57), the title character leaves her good husband under the promptings of Satan, who actually appears on the stage, and she goes to live with her rich lover, Baykädañ. She is punished in the person of her illegitimate son, Bä-käntu, who becomes a drunk and a womanizer, and who steals public money entrusted to his father, Baykädañ is jailed. Meanwhile, Bä-käntu resorts to burglary to get some money. He is killed by one of his victims. Baykädañ hangs himself in his prison, so that Aläm is left alone to repent and cry. Sometimes, too, punishment is effected through some miraculous intervention of the deity, as in Mogäs Keflé's *Unexpected Revenge* (1954–55), where a villager has to be duly chastised because he has killed his neighbor to get hold of the latter's wife.

Admittedly, sexual offenses are not the only form of immorality to be castigated in those works designed to discourage vice and promote virtue. In *Do Not Disown Me!* (1954–55) by Dässaleñ Harra Mika'él, the hero is not blinded by amorous lust, but by pride and greed; nor does he come to a bad end: he is saved because he listens to the advice of a good priest. Yet the fact remains that illegitimate sex is a central theme in the Amharic novel and drama. But contrary to South African literature, sin is not ascribed to any degradation of traditional mores for which Western influence might be held responsible. All students of Ethiopian society have noted that the Coptic church, which preaches an exceedingly austere theoretical morality, is also exceedingly pessimistic about man's ability to restrain his baser impulses. Consequently, it has proved remarkably tolerant and permissive with regard to the sins of the flesh, on which it has sought to impose a modicum of control through very lax divorce procedure. According to George Lipsky, writing in 1962,

Divorce is common: the estimated rate being between 60 and 90 percent. No exact statistics are available, particularly since only a small number of cases go through the courts. The divorce rate is reputedly highest for [Christian] Amharas and Tigrais, and divorces usually occur in the first marriage.[93]

But this is no novelty. Already in the antebellum period, Heruy and Mäl'aku had shown themselves deeply concerned with the widespread use of legal divorce. More recently, Täklä Maryam Fantaye, a prominent writer of educational treatise, authored *Truth, Foster-Mother* (1955–56), where he speaks up against divorce in the name of family stability. This is also recommended by Täfäri Däfärräsu in *The Ploughman and His Wife* (1956–57), a bucolic play celebrating the frugality and hard work characteristic of peasant life. It describes the courage and the resilience of a peasant and his wife, whose virtue is duly rewarded by an exceptional crop. At the end, they comply with the wishes of their families, and, out of gratitude to God, they change their civil marriage *(sämanya)* into a church marriage *(qurban)*.[94]

Such works represent a sustained effort on the part of novelists and playwrights to counteract, in the name of Christian morality, the degenerescence of the marriage institution. It is perhaps significant that until very recently few authors chose to handle the other aspect of traditional marriage customs that had been the butt of Heruy's criticism and had become such a favorite topic in South Africa. In Ethiopia, as in most parts of the continent, marriage was not viewed as the consecration of a personal love bond, but as a contract between two families. As Levine has pointed out:

The interests of the father are decisive in the selection of a marriage mate, and traditionally the boy has not even known what his bride looks like until the wedding itself. The boy who wants to choose a wife on his own commits an offence for which the father has the moral right to curse and disinherit him. Marriage is regarded as a bond between families, not individuals.[95]

Western insistence on individual freedom and personal choice was bound to challenge the assumptions underlying the old order of things. Heruy's hero was a precursor in this respect. But while young Awwäqä ultimately had his way, a more recent novel, by Azzanäw Alämé, ends in frustration and death. It deals with the unhappy love of a young prince, Gédéwon, and a shepherdess, Sännäyt, a theme highly characteristic of changing cultures, where the social hierarchies are being challenged by a new desire for self-assertion. Gédéwon's father had already arranged a political marriage, and since the young man refuses to bow to his decisions, he banishes him from his estate while the girl has to seek refuge in a monastery. There she languishes to an untimely death, while her lover is killed by bandits. The title of the novel, *This-Worldly Happiness? Vanity* (1956–57), provides the key to its real meaning. It is not designed as a vindication of personal love and an indictment of custom; it is one more illustration of the omnipresent *vanitas* motif. Whereas Heruy had openly aimed at reforming society and its mores, Azzanäw remains within the bounds of the fatalistic outlook that is so powerful in Ethiopia. He does not propose a remedy for the sufferings of his heroes. He merely advocates acceptance and self-denial. The regression is obvious.

There can be little doubt that the Italian occupation, brief though it was, bolstered Ethiopia's ingrained misoneism [96] and favored its emergence into the sphere of creative writing. Whereas the antebellum authors had seconded the emperor's policy of opening up the country to the intellectual and technological influence of the West, and whereas this influence became irresistibly stronger after the liberation, the Italian period and its aftermath prompted the writing elite to withdraw upon its national identity and to present a mostly unfavorable view of Western novelties. Germa-

čäw Täklä Hawaryat was one of the very few to use creative fiction as a vehicle for advocating administrative and technological
modernization. Usually, European mores were described as corrupt
and decadent in comparison with the Christian purity of Ethiopia's
traditional ideals. Revulsion against the Fascist regime prompted
a return to the fundamentalistic attitudes and beliefs that Heruy
had sought to discard. Admittedly, there were surprisingly few
works that overtly denounced colonialism in those years when
European imperialism was being successfully challenged throughout the continent. This was partly due to the Ethiopians' absence
of any sense of solidarity with black Africans. Nevertheless, the
antagonism between developed and underdeveloped nations is
the subject of *The Theater of Kidanä Qal* (1955–56) by Balambaras Aššäbber Gäbrä Heywät. One of the few attacks against
colonialism is a mild allegorical fable by Haddis Alämayyäwh,
which deals with a war between the kingdom of the cats and the
kingdom of the mice. Haddis's volume (1955–56) contains eleven
modern fables and is of a very high standard "both in form and
liberal content," according to Menghistu Lemma, who considers
that the writer "owes his great mastery of the Amharic language
and his refinement in it to the good classical background he has
of Qene Poetry," while "his knowledge of the English language,
his long career in the Foreign service have undoubtedly contributed to a more intimate contact with world literature and culture, that is reflected in the high quality of his literary creations." [97]
Haddis Alämayyäwh was minister of planning and development
when the emperor reshuffled his cabinet on 18 February 1969; his
ministry was abolished and he was appointed a senator.

In the main, however, whereas a large segment of African writing in French during the fifties focused on anticolonialism and
antiracism, these themes are hardly ever evoked in Amharic literature, except in novels and especially plays that deal with the purely
Ethiopian experience of Italian occupation. They handle it in terms
of national liberation rather than racial oppression, and extol the
exploits of underground heroes. The initiator had been Mäkonnen
Endalkačäw in *The Voice of Blood* (1947–48), which emphasized
the fusion of patriotism and religious loyalty in the martyrdom of
Abunä Pétros. In 1949–50, Seneddu Gäbru had published some
poetry in honor of the Ethiopian resistance movement, and a
drama about the sufferings of the nation under the government of

Marshal Graziani. Continuing interest in this subject matter was illustrated in the mid-fifties by two other plays: Yäşäwa Wärq Haylu's *Freedom, my Honor* (1954–55), and Atänäh Aläma's *History Dramatized: Zär'ay Däräs* (1955–56). The latter is the staged rendering of an episode, the memory of which is cherished by Ethiopian nationalists, and which Greenfield recounts as follows:

An Erythrean youth aged twenty-one named Zerai Deress was sent to Rome in 1937 [when] an imperial ceremony was held to commemorate the first anniversary of the occupation of Addis Ababa. [He was] to present some captured Ethiopian trophies, including a sword, to certain high officials at a function attended by both Mussolini and the King of Italy. Zerai did not know that he would have to present these in a public place where he could become an object of ridicule. In the middle of the parade his eyes lighted on the captured gold Lion of Judah which the Italians had removed from its stand near the Addis Ababa railway station. Identifying himself with Ethiopia's shame he knelt to pray. Two policemen tried to move him, but he turned furiously upon them, drew the ceremonial sword and killed five fascist officials before he in his turn was brought down by gunfire. He died in an Italian island prison. A statue and an Amharic booklet published after the war commemorate his patriotism. The first vessel of the new Imperial Ethiopian navy was called after him.[98]

The "booklet" was Atänäh's drama. It was followed by *Haylä Maryam Mammo* (1956–57), in which Te'ezazu Haylu celebrates the fame of another Patriot leader who gave his life against the Italians. Typically, to this thirteen-act tragedy is appended a philosophical essay that by no means glorifies man's determination to free himself and shape his own fate, but instead expatiates in conventional manner on the vanity of life and the unreliability of fate.

Even though it has adopted such Western genres as the novel and formal stage drama, Amharic literature has remained obstinately loyal to the wax-and-gold manner of qené composition. It cannot be called symbolic, because it lacks the concrete and individual truth that is essential to the symbol. As Pierre Comba aptly remarked, "apart from the moralizing impulse, which is present everywhere, psychological portrayal of the characters is often of the sketchiest and descriptive or picturesque passages are almost non-existent." [99] This all-pervading didacticism reaches its natural fulfillment in straightforward allegory, whose accomplished repre-

sentative in the late fifties seems to have been Gétačäw Awwäqä.
In his first novel, *Mahdärä Ṭebäb* (1955-56), the title-hero ascends
the Mountain of Knowledge under the guidance of his father. He
is furnished with such provisions as "audacity," "humility," and
"study." The top of the mountain is reached through the perilous
Ladder of Truth. But Mahdara's main concern is to make knowledge accessible to all. He therefore has the ladder replaced by
convenient and safe stone stairs. During the following year (1956–
57), Gétačäw published two more novels. *Aläm and Gännät
United by Spiritual Bonds* is ostensibly a love story. But the boy's
name, Aläm, means "this world," and the girl's name, Gännät,
means "Paradise." Aläm falls in love with Gännät, without ever
having met her, on the strength of what travelers have told him
about her. He seeks intermediaries who will bring him in touch
with her father. Two kind girls help him curb his impatience and
ultimately lead him to his goal: their names are Wängélu (Gospel)
and Ṭebäba (Wisdom). Although less ostensibly allegorical,
Gétačäw's third work is hardly less edifying. Characteristically
entitled *The Judge of Conscience: Of Two Young People and A
Criminal* (1956–57), this seven-act play in verse tells the story of
a girl whose parents are killed by the man who covets her. She
meets a young nobleman, by whom she has a son. The criminal
pursues them and burns their house. She thinks her child has died,
and she withdraws to a monastery while the child's father pursues
his own destiny and forgets her. But the son has not died: he has
been kidnaped. Later, he will bring his parents together again and
take vengeance on their persecutor. To a Western mind, God in
this play is little more than the *deus ex machina* who conveniently
organizes miracles and coincidences. But in Ethiopian eyes, the
supernatural occurrences, so frequent in Amharic fiction and
drama, are perfectly plausible manifestations of the infinite power,
justice, and benevolence of an omnipresent deity. Although this
is not an allegorical morality play as are the author's other works,
it is noticeable that the characters are not individualized. They are
not even supplied with personal names: they are called the Mother,
the Criminal, the Child's Father, and so forth. Straight allegory is
also to be found in a verse drama by Dawit Däggäfu, *The Man
Who Thirsts After Truth* (1956–57), which describes the struggle
of Truth and Lie—helped by such entities as Love and Honor,
Jealousy and Laziness—to obtain mastery over Man.

While moral teaching has been the self-appointed mission of most Amharic writers, patriotic inspiration has also led to the flowering of historical drama and fiction. Such works are usually designed both to remind—or to inform—the Ethiopian audience of the nation's great achievements in the past, and to infer from history topical lessons for the present and the future. During the antebellum period, this aim had been pursued in the straightforward historical and biographical writings of Afäwärq and Heruy. But the fifties were the years when Mäkonnen Endalkačäw produced his historical novels and plays, when Käbbädä Mika'él wrote *Hannibal* and *Kaléb*, and when Germačäw Täklä Hawaryat produced his drama on Téwodros II. Their example was followed by a number of others who also used imaginative fiction to disseminate historical knowledge, to instill patriotic pride, and to warn the people against the divisiveness and unruliness that had often proved the country's curse in the past. A professional historian, Berhanu Denqé, wrote *The Queen of Sheba* (1959–51), which brings on the stage the queen's visit to Solomon. As is well known, the main fruit of this state occasion was the birth of Menelik I, from whom any Ethiopian emperor must claim descent if he wants to be recognized as legitimate by his people. About Berhanu's play it has been observed that "the 'bedroom scene,' fraught with such historical consequences for the future dynasty of Ethiopia, is treated with ingenuity and tact." [100] Balambaras Aššäbber Gäbrä Heywät turned to the same subject matter for his second play, *The Historical Journey of the Queen of Sheba* (1958–59), which won a literary award at the University College in 1959–60.

Finally, mention must also be made of continuing concern with the traditional literature of Ethiopia, both the oral folk tradition and the written devotional tradition. Heruy had already evinced genuine interest in qené poetry, collecting Ge'ez poems and composing some of his own. Heruy's successor in this respect is Alämayyäwh Mogäs, who was born on 29 June 1922, in Gaveremma Mariam, near Baher Dar, into a learned family where both Ge'ez and Amharic were spoken.[101] His father was a teacher of qené and church music (*deggwa*). He began his formal schooling in 1929, under the traditional church school curriculum, and after completing the primary and secondary cycles, he studied qené under his father until the latter's death in 1938. In 1940 he pursued his studies in a church institution from which he was graduated as a teacher of qené in 1943. He then taught Ge'ez language and poetry for two years, studying Bible commentary at the same time. It was in 1945, he says, that he heard of the fame of Western civilization. He went to the theological college of the Holy Trinity in Addis Ababa, where he completed his education with studies of a more modern type. He was graduated in June 1949. In 1950 he was awarded a scholarship to study at a theological college in Istanbul, where he stayed until 1955. Since then, he has been teaching Ge'ez, Amharic, and the art of qené in various secondary schools and also at the Haile Selassie I University.

A very prolific and versatile writer, Alämayyäwh is also highly independent and outspoken, in spite of an upbringing that, compared with his contemporaries, was inordinately conservative. Indeed, nine of his books have been prevented from reaching print by censorship, and another one, *What Is a Motherland?* was banned after printing and caused him considerable trouble. His other published works include a collection of poems celebrating the natural beauty of Ethiopia; a play entitled *Why Is Marriage Hated?*, which deals with the deterioration of the marriage institution in Addis Ababa; and *Gäbrä Masqäl, the Slave*, one of the few literary works handling the problem of slavery. Alämayyäwh's main contribution to Ethiopian literature, however, is of a scholarly nature—collecting and editing of qené, both ancient and modern. His recently published report of one recording expedition shows both the importance and the peculiar difficulties of this type of research:

I set off to Washera with 4 Qene collectors, or copyists. The expedition was scheduled to last for 60 days, two months on the spot plus 8 days round trip from Jiga to Washera and Washera to Mota, almost 200 kms on foot. As there is not any modern transportation we hired mules for our luggage and instruments and walked most of the mountainous parts of Damot. We crossed many rivers by swimming because it was the rainy season and the rivers were in flood.

At first we were treated with great mistrust, but six days after our arrival I persuaded both the civil and the church leaders with long speech and careful conduct. After this Washera took the air as if it were during the time of Takle. To my surprise I was welcomed by 6 Qene masters, 2 apprentices, and 11 improvisors. To avoid conflicts which could have destroyed my expedition I hired all and one Qene collector for each. . . . I expected to get round eleven thousand stanzas but I got 24,473 pieces of Qene, the expedition was thus a huge success.[102]

The mention of "improvisors" suggests that in the Ethiopian countryside as in many remote parts of Africa, oral composition is flourishing as if the Gutenberg galaxy was still several light years off. Alämayyäwh's work also suggests that research in this recondite field is both possible and highly desirable.

Recent Developments in Ethiopian Literature

On 19 May 1965, *The Voice of Ethiopia* published an article entitled "Modern Amharic Literature," which contained a refreshingly sweeping indictment of a body of writing that had grown in self-enclosed complacency without being exposed to the slings and arrows of genuine literary criticism:

The vice that bedevils contemporary Amharic literature is not its preoccupation with topical subject matter and theme, but the flow of crude didacticism that overwhelms it. In such a state of affairs replete with all sorts of bogus profundity every peddler of moral platitudes assumes the role of the prophet and moral philosopher.

Actually, this statement by Menghistu Lemma was no longer quite true by the time it reached print. The late fifties had clearly initiated a new phase in the history of Amharic creative writing.

Most profound, perhaps, was the influence of modern-type education provided by new institutions such as the Haile Selassie I Secondary School, founded in 1943, or the General Wingate School, founded in 1946. According to Greenfield,

The impact of the new government schools was significant because they were orientated to what has come to be known as "western" philosophies and thought-patterns, and were not, like Menelik II's school had to be, largely staffed by the Egyptian Copts as a sop to the Ethiopian Christian Church. The conscious and unconscious democratic attitudes of the foreign teachers could not but be transmitted to the children, and the process at first received the full encouragement of the Emperor.[103]

The foundation of the University College (now Haile Selassie I University) at Addis Ababa in 1950, the promulgation of a new constitution in 1955, the institution of universal suffrage in 1957, the accession of many African nations to independent status, the installation of the UN Economic Commission for Africa in the Ethiopian capital in 1958—all this had favored acute intellectual fermentation and the growth of a keen critical sense in political and cultural matters. In a way, the new trends were a logical development of the policies pursued by Menelik II and Haile Selassie. Although the rate of illiteracy in the early sixties was still estimated at about 95 per cent of the population, the spread of education was gathering momentum, educational standards for the elite were rising swiftly, and the intelligentsia was opening to the modern civilization of the outside world in increasing numbers. In another sense, however, this evolution led to discontent with the emperor's policy. As more and more Ethiopians traveled and studied abroad and came into contact with representatives of the new African states, a growing number of progressive young men began to feel that the pace of economic development and political democratization was far slower than it should and need be.

Such educational and cultural developments are bound to reverberate in imaginative literature. There had been an unbroken trend of modernism that ran from Heruy to Germačäw, but as far as printed literature is concerned, it had been largely obliterated during the early fifties by a general distrust toward Western ideas and manners. There is some evidence, however, that it was maintained in some stage performances that apparently never reached print.

An article by American anthropologist Simon D. Messing contains a detailed discussion of a play which he saw performed in Addis Ababa under the patronage of the Municipality Theatrical Committee in the winter 1953–54.[104] The author, whose name is not mentioned, was, most significantly, an eighteen-year-old graduate of the Lycée Franco-éthiopien. The play was entitled *I and My Evil Deeds* and dealt with a peasant who is advised by a monk to leave for the city with his family. There his daughter goes to school despite the admonitions of the peasant's confessor from the country. The director of the school falls in love with her and, much to the father's displeasure, asks her to marry him. They marry without parental consent, and the peasant takes the young husband to court for abducting his daughter. He loses his suit and, still prompted by the confessor, he pays a sorcerer to poison the young couple, who are rescued in time, however, and duly recover.

Meanwhile, burglars steal the peasant's money, kill his wife, and burn his house. The man himself goes blind and turns a beggar. By accident, he reaches his daughter's house. She and her husband feed him and send him to the hospital, where he is cured of his blindness.

Messing's anthropological comments show in which sense such a play differs from the printed works of the period:

The play seems at first a rather obvious melodrama. But its value lies in the numerous instances of sharp self-analysis, both on the part of the author and of his audience with whom he never broke communication during the presentation.

In the beginning, the monk—who represents sincere religion as contrasted with the hypocritical, ignorant and greedy country cleric—is taught a sort of "social gospel" by the archangel. This . . . reflects the repeated requests of the Emperor to the coptic clergy to move in this direction.

The advice of the monk, that the peasant move to the city to seek a more respectable and less sinful life, runs counter to the Western views of the city as a place of greater wickedness than a rural community. But when one considers that feudal-type land-tenure continues in most of Ethiopia, and that modern legal safeguards for the individual are found, if at all, in the city, the new ethic is justified—certainly to an audience in Addis Ababa. Politeness and gentile [sic] behavior are correlated with urban, "urbane," and the concept of civilization is correlated with Western forms of etiquette in Addis Ababa. Of course the rural nobles have traditional patterns of politeness of their own, but the rustic peasant in his traditional role had little share in them. "Politeness" is part of the culture change he experiences in the city.

The modest and noble bearing of the young "director," who represents the young officialdom educated abroad at the Emperor's expense, and the patient wisdom of the city judges who preside over the changing legal concepts, are characterizations that cannot fail to please the sponsors. . . .

In conclusion, literature of this kind is increasingly being produced in many areas undergoing culture change, and offers valuable clues not only to parallel developments in Western history, but also to differentials in the urban culture.

It is probably not necessary to assume, as Messing does, that this play "was evidently influenced by the medieval European morality play," and that "the structural model of the play can be regarded as European." Actually, the Western morality play was the result of a culture-change situation similar in many ways to that of present-day Ethiopia, and equally characterized by a reassessment of traditional religious ideas and ethical norms of behavior under the influence of a growing literate urbanized middle class. Furthermore, the desire to convey the message in an efficiently pleasurable form led, in the best medieval moralities, to the same feature that Messing discerns in the Amharic play: "the humor arising out of keen, skeptical analysis of human behavior." Humor, we may note, is as conspicuously absent from printed Amharic literature as is psychological realism.

In the sphere of printed literature, as Lanfranco Ricci soon perceived with remarkable insight,[105] new portents of overt dissatisfaction with the sclerosis and irrelevance of the usually accepted motifs and style made their appearance in the year 1956–57. They were the work of two writers born in the early thirties. For them, the colonial period was already vanishing in a remote past; independence was an undisputed, unthreatened fact. Their eyes no longer turned solely to the past and to the need to preserve whatever may have been valuable in the cultural tradition. They were turned toward the future and the need to transform the Ethiopian outlook and society, if the country was to hold its own in a fast changing world, if it was to deserve its pride as the most ancient independent nation on the African continent.

Taddäsä Libän was born of a Galla family in Wallo Province. He was one of the first pupils of the Haile Selassie I Secondary School, which he attended from 1943 to 1949. In 1950 he joined the staff of the State Bank of Ethiopia of whose Addis Ketema Branch he has been manager since 1961. With *Mäskäräm* (1956–57) (the title is the name of the first month of the Ethiopian year), he became Ethiopia's first writer of modern short stories as distinguished from traditional fables and moral allegories. Taken as a whole, the five stories in the volume provide a balanced imaginative and critical assessment of the relationship between tradition and novelty in Ethiopian society. Whereas earlier writers had discussed things in the abstract and in the name of crudely high-flown principles, Taddäsä provides concrete realistic examples from contemporary experience.

The first story, "She Is a Hyena," satirizes both antiquated superstitions and the educated Ethiopian's continued subservience to them. Asäffa is a young student who has fallen in love with a village girl, Wäynitu, who is endowed with gorgeous hair. His mother warns him that she is a dangerous witch—she takes off her hair at night and changes herself into a hyena in quest of a prey. Asäffa refuses to believe such nonsense. But one night, when he has at last obtained the girl's favors, he is terror-stricken when he wakes up to find that his mistress walks around with no hair on her skull, and for a while, he really believes that she is a hyena. The explanation is that Wäynitu was badly burned when she was a child and has to wear a wig, but the point of the story is that Asäffa's spontaneous response was totally superstitious. On the contrary, the second story, "The Uprooted One," is a harsh indictment of the snobbery of the educated upstart. It tells of the sacrifices made by a widow so that her elder daughter, Roman, can have the benefit of a higher education abroad. When the girl returns after several years, she has become a pretentious prig, stuffed with contempt for the rusticity of her family.

The middle story, "That Guy," is a realistic vignette of city life. It tells how two young men attempt to seduce a pretty woman in a shop but are frightened off by her brother. The last two tales are symmetrical to the first two. "The Dog and His Ways" bitterly illustrates the erosion of the moral sense in an educated young man, who seduces pretty girls by promising to marry them. With "The Little Child," Taddäsä turns back to the satire of tradition: his butt now is family education, which is based on the very Victorian principle that children should be seen and not heard, so that when addressed by anyone in the presence of his family or of other elders, a child is expected to reply in a barely audible whisper. At the end of the tale, the little boy proudly explains to an adult friend that he never speaks up in the family circle because his parents do not like him to parade his vast knowledge.

In *Mäskäräm*, as in his second collection of short stories, *The Other Way* (1959–60), Taddäsä exhibits greater realism and psychological sophistication than could be found in any previous Amharic writer. Commentators of the time, however, were more impressed by the new style he introduced into Ethiopian writing, using short, crisp sentences instead of the long-winded, mellifluous rhetoric that was a traditional characteristic of good writing.

The same kind of style was resorted to by another writer of

Galla origin Beka Nämo in his novel *Let Us Look Inside* (1956–57), which offers an interesting example of literary syncretism. It deals with the well-worn theme of the separated twins already used by Afäwärq in *Lebb wälläd tarik*, but transfers it to a modern context and introduces a realistic picture of contemporary manners. Abäba has lost her parents as a result of Italian atrocities. She was adopted by a good man, Däraǧǧa, who enables her to get a modern education. She falls in love with a young man calle Feqré, who is an orphan too, and has a strange physical likeness to her. They become engaged, and, contrary to custom but in compliance with modern manners, Däraǧǧa allows them to travel to Asmara by themselves. In a restaurant, while Abäba is alone for a few minutes, she is solicited by an elderly gentleman who tries to kiss her. When Feqré comes back, there is a fight. The young man is wounded and taken to hospital; the girl is accused of shooting him and taken to prison. In order to pay the heavy fine that was levied against her, she tries to sell a medal that she has been wearing since she was born. Her aggressor recognizes the medal and realizes that he is the father both of Abäba and Feqré. This bare summary brings out the implausible coincidences that are a constant feature in Amharic fiction. The novel, however, boldly ignores the usual narrow conventions both in style and in subject matter. The short sentences and the jagged writing can be compared to Tadässä's manner. The kissing scene and the fight in the restaurant have no precedent in Ethiopian fiction and are in stark contrast to the habitual restraint of Amharic writing. There is also an obsession with murderous violence, which probably combines the Ethiopian tradition of insecurity with the influence of American movies.

The fact that those two innovators are Galla may be of some wider significance. Anthropologists have noted that Galla culture differs from Amhara in many important respects. The native system of Galla government is highly democratic, as it involves the periodic election of authorities by representative members of the various social classes. Moreover, as Levine pointed out, the Galla ethos "is relatively egalitarian: relations between the father and the rest of the family tend to be friendly and informal, and provision is made for the incorporation of strangers into local communities. . . . Of the small percentage of Ethiopians who incline to a republican form of government, the Galla appear to be over-represented." Such an outlook, on one hand, may account in part

for the attention that Galla writers are prone to pay to the real life
of everyday people, as distinguished from Amhara concentration
on dogmatic and allegorical definition of abstract ideals. On the
other hand, the Galla have their own language, which belongs to
the Kushitic group. By choosing Amharic as their literary medium,
both Beka and Taddäsä intimate that Ethiopia's official language is
being increasingly recognized as the genuine national *lingua
franca* and culture tongue. This would confirm Levine's observation that "even among those who are not Amharic speakers, those
who are aware of the situation elsewhere in Africa tend to take
pride in the fact that their national language is indigenous, not, as
is true in most other African countries, an alien tongue." [106]

The most prominent representative of the generation that emerged
in the late fifties and early sixties is Menghistu Lemma, who was
born in Addis Ababa in August 1925. He was first brought up in
Harar, where he received the traditional church education, studying qené and zéma, the religious music. He was also privileged to
receive a modern education, and after attending the Haile Selassie
I Secondary School in the capital, he traveled to England, where
he studied at the Regent Street Polytechnic from February 1948
to July 1949 and at the London School of Economics from 1949
to 1953. He was then employed in the Ethiopian Civil Aviation
Department. From 1957 to 1963, he was first secretary to the
Ethiopian embassy in India.

His first two works were a collection of philosophical and love
poems (1957–58), and a collection of traditional stories in verse
(1958–59). He then turned to the theater and did for Ethiopian
drama what Taddäsä Libän had done a few years before for the
short story: *Snatch and Run, or Marriage by Abduction* (1962) [107]
was performed at the Haile Selassie I Theatre in January 1963.

The theme of the play is the relevance of traditional customs to
modern life. The plot is based on a peculiar Ethiopian custom that
Lipsky has described as follows:

Variant types of marriage patterns are reported for Tigre and Shoa.
Marriage by capture is said still to exist under certain conditions. If, for
various reasons, such as poverty, a boy's family cannot properly arrange
a desired marriage, he may get a few friends together and kidnap a
bride. She may be compromised or simply taken for safekeeping to the
house of an elder. Through his parents or other elders, the boy may

send representatives to the girl's family to smooth over the difficulties
and get permission to marry. The kidnapping or seduction may take
place with the consent of the girl's family, if she has been betrothed to
another at a very young age and the family has changed its mind but
does not wish to break the contract. Marriage by capture may have
been much more common than it is at present.[108]

To understand how such an antiquated custom can provide a
plausible plot for a play dealing with a group of educated young
men, it is necessary to remember that Ethiopian society is still
uneasily trying to feel its way between the old mores, where marriage was usually taken care of by the family groups involved,
and modern individualism, where young people are supposed to
make their own choice. The result of this collocation of contraries
has been analyzed by Levine:

Since Ethiopian society still expects its maidens to be shy and retiring,
and to avoid social relations with boys outside their families, the boys
found few opportunities for getting to know members of the opposite
sex. Even in those few situations where sociability between the sexes is
publicly permitted, ingrained tendencies to segregate the sexes persist.
*The most liberal context for such sociability, the University College
campus, has witnessed relatively little interaction between male and
female students.* In spite of their occasional resolutions to act more
boldly, the college boys have in the past tended to shy away from the
co-eds except during such rare formal events as a college dance or off-
campus parties.[109]

The immediate concrete problem with which Menghistu's characters are faced is how to secure a suitable wife. They seek a
solution by trying to solve another larger problem: how to fuse
traditional and modern mores. Their first premise is that "the best
element in the modern European custom of marriage is its very
simplicity." In Europe or in the United States, one of them says,
"you jointly sign the document in the presence of two witnesses,
and after that without bothering about anything else, you simply
disappear and that is that." The trouble, apparently, is that, precisely because of traditional expectations of extreme modesty in
girls' behavior, none of them has found a suitable and willing part-
ner as yet. The real problem is sexual, rather than intellectual.
Returning to the ancient custom of marriage by capture is the only

"acceptable" means they find of procuring a wife, but they use a cultural and ideological alibi:

You may then ask what in our custom constitutes the simplest way of getting married, that which will avoid the paraphernalia, the huge expense, the show business, all this and that, etc.? My answer is marriage by abduction. . . Therefore, once we have isolated that particular element in our marriage custom that is really consonant with modern civilization, what we have got to do is simply to practice it with courage and determination.

Accordingly, they kidnap a pretty girl, whom they hardly know at all, and take her to the countryhouse of Wondayehu Marrine, where she will be married to Bezabih-Tori (whose name, incidentally, means "too many theories"). This act, however, raises the problem of love and consent. At the beginning of the play, Bezabih-Tori had argued that traditional marriage was arranged by the family and that boy and girl became man and wife without knowing each other: "Love in the days of our fathers and forefathers was the crowning glory of a long and successful married life; it was not a preface to it." But in act two, his friend Gelagle (whose name means "arbitrator") denies this interpretation of custom; he claims that abduction was usually arranged beforehand, and that abduction without previous agreement is "barbaric." "How can a marriage founded on compulsion, on brute force, be permanent?" In his view, love is the fundamental principle underlying both the traditional and the modern views of marriage: "You must remember that modern marriage is the fruit of civilization, based upon mutual understanding." To which the girl, Taffesech, adds, that "in this modern time in which we live, it is taken for granted for a young woman to get married to the man she likes and loves." Bezabih realizes he has violated the very spirit of marriage, whether traditional or modern, and telephones Taffesech's father to come for his daughter.

In this way, act three introduces the older generation. Wondayehu's father, who is a Fitawrari, arrives first. In the belief that it was his son who had kidnaped the girl, he congratulates him for "this great deed, this work of a real man." Incidentally, he recalls that he too had abducted his future wife. But it appears that he was in love with her, and the elopement had been arranged by common consent. When Taffesech's father arrives, he is deeply shocked at what he supposes to be his daughter's immodesty. But she informs him that she has meanwhile fallen in love with Bezabih and is prepared to marry him, so that everyone will know that she is a virgin—an allusion to the custom of publicly exhibiting proof of a bride's virginity after the consummation of marriage.

Discussing this play in his article on "Modern Amharic Literature," [110] Menghistu Lemma was careful to point out that "the actual process of abduction, which is the topical framework of the play, must not be taken too literally but as a symbol." Actually, he adds, the play "concerns itself with the problems of the transformation of a new generation of innovators equipped with a modern scientific outlook." But the point is that the representatives of this generation are wittily satirized for their failure to comprehend the very spirit of the tradition they strive to restore with impeccable but vain reasonings. As Menghistu further comments, "the innovators, if they are to achieve anything daring and decisive in the struggle for modernization, must acquire those qualities of character that made real men of Ethiopians of old." The rosy ending could be said to blur the issues at stake, but it too is symbolic: "the protagonist's failure to accomplish the 'manly deed' he set as his target was turned in the end into some semblance of success by the intervention of Fitawrari (a living representative of the old Ethiopians)." With a mild irony that is all too often absent from Amharic writing, the playwright provides a critique of the new elite, the young intellectuals, whose heads are filled with theoretical notions concerning cultural cross-fertilization, but who forget not only the real substance of traditional and modern outlook, but also the simple truths of common sense.

In 1963 Menghistu's *Marriage of Unequals*, which broaches on the marriage theme from a different angle, was produced at the Creative Arts Centre of the Haile Selassie I Theatre. Since then, the playwright has become a sort of unofficial mouthpiece for the new Amharic writers. In 1965 he took part in the Moscow conference of Afro-Asian writers, and in 1967 in the African-Scandinavian Writers' Conference held in Stockholm.

Between the present generation and the previous one, a fundamental rift has occurred. Earlier writers, who were trying to promote the modernization of their country, did so in the conventional spirit of ancient Ethiopian literature, which could be described as "normative." They took over the preacher's task of telling the people how to behave, what to eschew. They showed little interest in the complexities of real experience. For them, the issues were always clear-cut and lent themselves readily to allegorical impersonation, and they handled their topics in the refined oratorical style favored by Amhara tradition. The element of allegory is admittedly still strong in Menghistu's plays: the names of the characters point to their exemplary significance. Nevertheless, the dramatist shares with Taddäsä Libän a keen concern with actual individual experience in the present day. The result is that their writing is no longer normative, but mainly realistic and analytical. Their purpose is to bring out—sometimes with irony and wit—the perplexity and the confusion inherent in a changing culture, where man is no longer at ease but clumsily gropes his way through the puzzling antinomies of cherished, obsolete tradition and desirable, dangerous novelties. Their way of writing, like that of Beka Nämo, reflects this evolution in their rejection of time-honored stylistic habits and values, and in their revolutionary attempt to capture the living flavor of everyday speech.

This renewal of the very springs of literary inspiration has led other writers to consider in a new light some of the moral themes dealt with by many previous authors. Much of Ethiopian fiction had been devoted to fiercely sanctimonious denunciations of such immoral forms of behavior as drunkenness and sexual promiscuity. It evinced little inclination toward understanding or compassion; catastrophe was always the deserved reward of vice. In its rigidly moralizing outlook, it made no attempt at psychological or sociological analysis. A new note was struck in 1958-60 by Berhanu Zärihun who was born in 1933–34 in Gondar.[111] He had his elementary education at the Haile Selassie I School, and then attended a technical school from which he was graduated in 1955-56, specializing in radio mechanics. For some time, he taught as a shop assistant at the technical school, and then worked as a draftsman in the Geography Institute. After a few months, however, he turned to journalism, starting as a cub reporter for *Yä-Ityopya Dems* in 1957-58. Berhanu made swift progress and became editor of *Yä-Zaréyitu Ityopa* in 1960–61, before taking over the editorship of *Addis Zämän* in 1962-63.

Meanwhile, he had published his first book, *Two Letters of Tears*

(1959-60), an epistolary novel that deals with derelict woman-hood. It shows that prostitution is the only recourse left to an abandoned wife in traditional society, and it advises women to escape that fate by finding independent means of subsistence through education. This is probably the first time in Amharic fiction that immorality is not ascribed to the incurable weakness of human nature. The book is of particular interest because it contains an analysis of "vice" in sociological terms, and because it views the prostitute not as an image of evil, but as a victim of social circumstances. Berhanu Zärihun has since written a number of novels, but there is too little information on them for a discussion here. He has been commended by Menghistu Lemma for writing "clear, direct Amharic, on contemporary problems." [112]

Asräs Asfa Wäsän was born in 1936–37 near Däbrä Tabor (Begemdir).[113] He lost his parents at an early age. Thanks to the intervention of a Catholic priest, he was educated after the war as a ward in the household of Crown Prince Asfa Wäsän, whose name he adopted as his patronymic. After obtaining his teacher's certificate, he taught for two years, and then turned to journalism because of his interest in literature. As a result of some conflict with his editor, he gave this up and is now active as an accountant at the Haile Selassie I Military Training Center in Guennet.

His first published work was a collection of poetry entitled *Poet's Magic* (1957-58). It deals with heroism and love and, what is less common, also contains some nature poetry. The volume is curiously illustrated with photographs of armored vehicles and other war machines. Asräs then turned to narrative poetry and composed four verse novels, three of which focus on the tragedy of frustrated love. *Ideal Love* (1959-60) is the pathetic story of a girl who is acquired as a concubine by a wealthy old feudal lord; only after the man's death can she marry her lover. But in compliance with the somber Amhara view of earthly happiness, she soon dies in an accident, leaving the young man to lament over her grave. After this critique of an antiquated and unnatural custom, Asräs wrote *The Passion of Youth* (1962–63), in which the heroine is consumed by her vain love for a young intellectual who is utterly absorbed in his devotion to science and in his dedication to the promotion of his country.

In 1964–65, Asräs published *Rebel Against Injustice*, which seems to be an oblique imaginative comment on the coup of December 1960. This, we remember, had been engineered by a group of young radicals, several of them officers in the Imperial Guard, who wanted to dethrone the emperor and set up a more progressive regime under Asräs's patron, Crown Prince Asfä Wäsän. Four characters in the book represent the ideas and attitudes of the rebel group. They mock at a self-styled national hero whose inertia impedes the progress of the country, and they stigmatize the love of pleasure that has corrupted the whole regime. In their lust for revolution, they realize in time what the actual rebels of 1960 understood too late, namely that they would not be followed by the mass of the population, who still adhere to conservative and reactionary ideas. They therefore conclude that their primary purpose and the best way to ensure the ultimate triumph of their cause must be to educate the masses so that they shall understand the iniquity of the regime, and so pave the way for a genuine popular revolution.

In his latest novel to date, Asräs reverted to a safer theme. *The Flame of Love* (1965-66) is an imaginative rendering of Edward VIII's story. It is based on the autobiographical accounts of Wallis Warfield in *The Heart Has Its Reason* (New York, 1956), and of the Duke of Windsor in *A King's Story* (London, 1951). The purpose of the novel is to extol the supremacy of love over status and to indict the irrational and unnatural prejudices attached to the British conception of the duties of royalty.

After these remarkable changes in inspiration and style that began in the late fifties, the early sixties were marked by another, equally important phenomenon: the emergence of Ethiopian creative writing in English.

In 1964 there appeared in Addis Ababa a shoddy little book that is probably the first piece of creative writing directly composed in English by an Ethiopian. The author, Abbé Gubäñña, already enjoyed some popular favor for his Amharic works, one of which was a collection of poems warning the reader against unhygienic habits, alcoholism, venereal disease, and the like. While an English critic described those works as "more entertaining than significant," [114] Menghistu Lemma has claimed that Abbé is "a hardworking writer who has the distinction of having authored the first bestsellers in the history of modern Amharic literature." [115]

His first—and, so far, only—English book is a three-act verse

play entitled *The Savage Girl*. The heroine enjoys a life of prelapsarian happiness in the jungle, until she is taken to the city by
five hunters, who wear such clumsily transparent names as Mr.
Humane, Mr. Freeman, or—for the one who is in love with money
—Mr. Billman! Act two is improbably crowded with events. The
once savage girl, now called Mary, is received into the church. She
goes through the school curriculum with meteoric speed; she becomes acquainted with evil through the jealousy of Mrs. Humane;
she earns money, leads a "royal life" in a fine villa; and she becomes
engaged. The latter fact notwithstanding, she receives lecherous
proposals from a number of admirers, including a general, Mr. Billman, and the bishop. As she relaxes in bed after her heavy day, she
listens to the radio which speaks only of accidents and murders,
rebellions and civil wars, and thermonuclear bombs. The act ends
as a mullah and a rabbi ring at her door in the hope of converting
her, each to his own faith. When the curtain rises for the last act,
the fiancé has been murdered. Society chooses to pretend that he
has committed suicide because of the evil influence of Mary, who
is taken to jail. After thus living for six years in the city, the girl
reaches the conclusion that she "prefers the non-imposter beasts,
with all their vices, to men, with their false kind acts." She accordingly returns to her cave in the jungle, where her father's ghost
soon appears to comfort her:

> My dearest daughter the source of my grief and worry,
> To see you in such a state, I am truly sorry.
> Great was the tragedy of your life history.
> But you are a blessed one truly blessed one!
> All your conventions are unbroken,
> And all your beliefs are unshaken.
> Your fugivtive soul is about to rest.
>
> (Pp. 83–84)

And indeed, a "dragonic serpent" promptly arrives on the stage
and obligingly kills her.

Written in idiosyncratic—and at times, cryptic—English, *The
Savage Girl* nevertheless represents a very courageous and meritorious effort to convey the conventional Amharic view of life
through a worldwide medium. Its purpose, transparent though it
is, is described in the author's Preface:

This play is not written in connection with any particular society. It is only a modest attempt to give a bird's eye view of human society as seen by me.

I believe that unless any "civilized" society gives the highest priority to humanity's welfare there is no reason why we call it a civilized society. If the so-called civilized society is the source of trouble and disappointment to an individual, there is no reason too why a frustrated individual cannot curse the civilized society, and give his benediction to the good-old-care-free-days.

In his review of the book, William Prouty suggested that "perhaps the girl in this play is meant to represent Ethiopia and her new-found 'civilized' friends, foreign nations." The naïve contrast between idyllic primitive jungle life and the evils of modern civilization may seem to bear this out. But the play is interspersed with apothegms that go beyond this possible topical reference, and faithfully translate the dark, fatalistic, pessimistic world view so typical of Coptic Amhara culture.

In 1965 a second novel in English was printed in Addis Ababa. Entitled *Confession* and alluringly described on the front cover as "the most exciting, heart breaking story of an Ethiopian in the United States," "full of love," "full of hate," "adventurous," and "intellectual," it is the work of Ashenafi Kebede, who was born in Bulga (Shoa) on 7 May 1937.[116] His mother's father had been one of the very few Ethiopians who attended an Italian university in the days of Menelik. Ashenafi grew up in Addis Ababa, where he had his primary education at the Haile Selassie I School; he later was graduated from the Harar Teacher Training School. After teaching for two years, he left for the United States, where he studied languages and music education at the Eastman School of Music of the University of Rochester. After receiving a B.A. degree in 1962, he taught a summer course in music at Georgetown University in Washington, D.C., and then returned to his country. He was first assigned to teach music at the Täfäri Mäkonnen School. In 1964 he was promoted and became a music expert in the Ministry of Education and Fine Arts. He is now director of the National School of Music.

Apart from his main activity in composing musical treatises in Amharic, instrumental works and lyrics, Ashenafi made use of his experience abroad in *Confession*, the pathetic story of an Ethiopian

student's affair with a white American girl. Caroline belongs to a
nice, enlightened, upper middle-class, three-car family, who welcome the hero to their house as a friend of their daughter; but they
throw him out when her racist brother discloses that the "nigger"
is in fact her boyfriend. After the girl's failure to take her own
life, their love emerges, more unshakable than ever. During the
racial troubles of 1961-62, they both join a group of Freedom
Riders. Caroline, by now pregnant, is killed by the white mob in
Shreveport, Louisiana.

In the course of the last fifty years, large numbers of African
students have attended Western universities. Those who later
turned to creative writing usually built up Western university life
as an image of toleration, mutual understanding, and absence of
racial discrimination, contrasting favorably with race relations
and group attitudes in Africa. Their main interest was not their
experience on foreign soil, but the fruits it could bring forth at
home. Their usual subject had been the return of the student, a
theme that had been inaugurated, not only for Ethiopia, but for
the whole of sub-Saharan Africa, in Heruy's *The New World*.
Perhaps out of gratefulness for their host country, those who had
studied in America had tended to play down racial strife in the
United States, until Nigeria's John Pepper Clark published *America, Their America* in 1965. As a citizen of an African country that
had been fully self-governing ever since he could remember,
Ashenafi was more painfully struck by evidence of racism in the
States than any writer of his generation from any other part of
Africa could possibly be. If the theme of the African student
abroad does not die out, this approach is likely to acquire increasing
prominence. For most African intellectuals, America will soon be
the only place to which they have access and where large-scale
racial hatred can be experienced.

This aspect of Ashenafi's plot, therefore, provides further evidence of the new Ethiopian intelligentsia departing from the usual
pattern of parochial nationalism and acquiring a genuine sense of
Negro solidarity. This widening consciousness is further exemplified in the novel by other elements such as an otherwise irrelevant
discussion of disturbances in the Congo. These are naïvely ascribed
—by Caroline—to the fact that "when the Belgians left . . . they
destroyed everything in the Congo that they have built—everything that was possibly destructible—and they took every penny

they owned" (p. 75). That this allegation is contrary to established historical fact does not matter: it points to a widespread belief in Africa at the time, and, more especially, to a nascent sense of all-African solidarity among the new Ethiopian elite.

Another novelty of the book is that it introduces the theme of interracial love into the context of student life abroad. While this theme is frequent enough in American Negro fiction and in English works by such South African Colored or black writers as Peter Abrahams or Lewis Nkosi, it is exceedingly rare in sub-Saharan writing, where it usually crops up in connection with the theme of student life abroad, as it does in Ashenafi's novel. The closest example is *Mirages de Paris* (1937), by Senegal's Ousmane Socé. It is most unlikely that Ashenafi had read Socé's book. Yet, the two stories follow the same pattern: in both cases, the obstacle is the girl's family, described as decent, moderate, intelligent people, who think themselves immune to racism, yet, when faced with the problem, are unable to accept the idea of their daughter marrying a black man. Both stories end in a tragedy that has some symbolic intent inasmuch as the child of interracial love dies together with his mother. It is characteristic that this tragedy leads the Ethiopian writer to the rather lame conclusion that "accidents are the only instruments of Destiny that guide us to life and out of it again" (p. 121). To the Senegalese writer, on the contrary, the common suffering brings about a fruitful sense of shared sorrow and responsibility in both the white father and the black husband.

So far, the only Ethiopian writer of real distinction to have used English as his literary medium is Tsegaye Gabre-Medhin, who was born at Ambo on 17 August 1935. He received his LLB degree from the Blackstone School of Law,Chicago, in June 1960. He then studied stagecraft in Europe, working at the Theatre Royal, Windsor, and the Royal Court Theatre in London, and also visiting the French National Theatre in Paris and the Rome Opera. He started playwriting in Amharic. Two of his early plays—*Blood Harvest*, which handles the theme of the Fascist invasion, and *Listro or Shoe-Shine Boy*—were staged at the Addis Ababa Commercial School. Tsegaye also adapted and directed Molière's *Le Médecin malgré lui* and *Tartuffe*, and Shakespeare's *Othello*, *Macbeth*, and *Hamlet*. By 1966 he had been appointed acting director of theatricals at the Haile Selassie I Theatre. Meanwhile, he had been writing poetry in English, some of which was printed in the *Ethiopia Observer* in 1965.

His first English play, *Tewodros*, was performed on 5 May 1963 before the emperor, to inaugurate the Creative Arts Centre of the Haile Selassie I University. As he had done with his first Amharic drama, Tsegaye turned to a familiar topic in Ethiopian literature. His *Tewodros* can be described as the younger generation's rejoinder to the unfavorable view of the emperor put forward by Mäkonnen Endalkačäw a half-dozen years earlier in *Taytu Betul*. It is a chronicle play in two acts consisting of a succession of scenes that fade into each other. The author has thrown overboard the classical technique used by Mäkonnen and Käbbädä Mika'él and still preserved by Menghistu Lemma. Although there is some inevitable clumsiness in the handling of the language, and also in the use of a messenger to act as a chorus, the play is worthy of serious critical attention.

The first scene conveys young Kassa's intimation that he is called upon to become the Tewodros who, so the prophecies say, will establish unity, peace, and prosperity over the whole of Ethiopia. Tsegaye has gone through the main historical sources and interpretations, and both the construction of his play and his view of the emperor's character agree surprisingly with the conclusions of Tewodros's latest biographer, Sven Rubensson, whose *King of Kings: Tewodros of Ethiopia* was not printed until 1966. The first act covers the phase that Rubensson calls "the road to power," which starts with Kassa's marriage in 1846 to Täwabäč, daughter of Ras Ali and granddaughter of the Gondarine Empress Mänän; this is done in pantomime with dances and songs. In the eyes of Ali and Mänän, as the historian puts it, the aim of this marriage was "to secure Kassa's support in the unceasing conflicts and wars that went on between Ali and his vassals." [117] They were soon undeceived, and the end of the first act is devoted to the defeat of Ali's troops by Kassa in October 1846 and to the capture of Empress Mänän on 18 June 1847. The second act begins ten years later, when Kassa, now emperor of Ethiopia as Tewodros II, has started on "the road to failure." As the curtain rises, children at play make topical allusions to uprisings that had broken out among the Galla of Wallo in 1857. In the next scene, an interview with Menelik, then a twenty-year-old young man and the lawful heir to the throne of Shoa, partly serves as a reminder that Shoa too had re-

volted against Tewodros's rule in 1863. It is followed by an interview with the British consul, Captain Duncan Cameron, who is
taken prisoner together with the other "white faces" in the empire,
in reprisal for Queen Victoria's failure to reply to a letter of
Tewodros asking for her support against such infidels as the Turks
of Egypt. It was this action that prompted the British government
to send a military force into Ethiopia: in Rubensson's words, "at
the cost of £9,000,000 a British-Indian army of 32,000 men under
Sir Robert Napier was shipped to Ethiopia to carry out the task of
releasing the captives." [118] This was in the spring of 1868, and the
play ends as Tewodros shoots himself to avoid the dishonor of falling into the hands of the British, who have captured his fortress at
Meqdela.

Tsegaye's *Tewodros* faithfully reflects historical data not only in
its chronological structure but also, to a considerable extent, in its
interpretation of the emperor's character and fate. For the historian,
the two main problems have always been how to reconcile Tewodros's genuine concern with the welfare of the common people and
the bloody ruthlessness of his reign, and how to account for his
ultimate failure after the impressive successes of his early career. On
this second point, Sven Rubensson concludes as follows:

The fall of Meqdela by foreign guns and the death of Tewodros by his
own hand coincided. But it would be a mistake to believe that the
second was really caused by the first. As some foreigners had played a
role when Tewodros set his goals for a modern Ethiopian state, so they
played their part in his downfall by causing unnecessary misunder-
standings, frustrations, and rash actions, which Tewodros himself no
doubt regretted. But in neither case was it the major rôle. The British
came to Meqdela armed as if they had expected to meet the "invincible"
Tewodros at the head of a united Ethiopia. But long before they began
to contemplate the use of military force against him, Tewodros had
lost his Kingdom. It was internal political problems, not the British
army, that caused the fall of Tewodros.[119]

Such is also Tsegaye's view, at least if plot development is to be our
criterion. When Cameron is imprisoned, thus launching British
reprisals, Tewodros's power has already been successfully challenged by the Galla and Shoans, and is restricted to the vicinity of
his stronghold at Meqdela. But it is a sign of the present-day Ethiopian intelligentsia's growing concern with international issues, and

of its new awareness of a common African fate, that Tsegaye has
felt impelled to place in the mouth of some of his characters
prophecies and denunciations of colonialism that are clearly anachronistic. In a conversation with his wife soon after their marriage,
Kassa claims that he has heard voices that "warned of the coming
of powerful aggressors; foreign claws reaching out for the heart
of Ethiopia—for all of Africa" (p. 215).[120] Although Muslim imperialism is specifically referred to ("the evil intent of the Turkish
force"), other passages show that Tsegaye has Western imperialism
in mind as well. In a scene that takes place in 1846, one of Kassa's
faithful followers announces that "soon more white lice will come
from far away Europe to invade and thus to dominate us the way
they have our brothers in Africa" (p. 216)! And at the end of the
play, Tewodros warns his son against the British in the following,
hardly less anachronistic passage:

They . . . They will . . . may, take you; bring you up like a special
tool . . . take care of you like an expensive article . . . teach you . . .
how . . . "extremely powerful" their Empire is; how . . . how . . .
other nations should bow to them . . . how other people should toil
and bleed for them as they toiled and bled for the Romans. The
Egyptians and the Greeks did that to others even before the Romans;
some other nation may be doing it after the British. It may continue
like that; but it is *bad*, my son. (P. 225)

As to the fascinating problem of Kassa's personality, Tsegaye
has skillfully eschewed the onesidedness of those who consider him
an ambitious upstart and of those who treat him as an idealistic
figure thwarted by circumstances. This is effected in two ways,
which make Tewodros's character considerably more human and
convincing than any to be found in previous Amharic dramas.

First, Kassa is aware of the fearful dialectics of life, of "Nature's
ever unsatisfied lust . . . to kill all that she offers life to" (p. 214).
This is said in a conversation with his new wife, a perplexed and
lovable woman, who is—as Tewodros is later to reminisce,—"torn
between her duty towards her grandmother, the Empress Menen,
and her loyalty to her husband, yet to the end unable to answer
Kassa's bitter question" (p. 224). Tewabetch is disturbed with the
shedding of blood, while sensing all the time that it may be necessary for the fulfillment of her husband's dream: "The trouble with
God is that he seems to be on all sides at the same time. God is on

the side of Truth, but Kassa—how much Truth is there in a dream?" (p. 215). To this, Tewodros retorts that his visions are not mere dreams, and that there are two ways of losing blood: "one is by being sucked by life-long leeches, the other by spilling it at once and for all to make the cement on which a foundation is to be laid. Which of these do you consider a futile cause or a waste of lives?" (p. 215). This is the "bitter question" that Tewabetch cannot answer, because others, "who are at the mercy of lust and petty ambition," also use the vision "under the name of God, for which the peasant bleeds and suffers," while their "evil intention" is "to hook the ears, eyes and heart of one Ethiopia and tear her apart like wolves." "Many small powers behind the petty thrones declare that they are the chosen of God and declare themselves chiefs of the peasants of every Province and sub-Province of Mother Ethiopia" (p. 215).

In spite of her misgivings, Tewabetch remains obstinately loyal to Kassa, because her love for him is the only truth of which she is really assured. In this, the princess—who died in 1858—is in stark contrast to Tewodros's second wife Tru-Worq. Although the messenger describes the latter as "an impossible she-cat who scratched at his conscience with tearing claws" (p. 222), hers, too, however shrill, is the voice of pious womanhood:

You forced me into marrying you by imprisoning my father, when all I wanted was to serve God at the Monastery as Christ's bride. You made me bow and scrape at your Court, when all I wish is to be left alone in the worship of God and God alone, Emperor. . . . The only thing you learned from your British friends . . . was the evil act of war. This is what you are prepared to infect your child with, Kassa. The German Gospel missionaries, who came on God's pilgrimage to convert the non-believers, are instead converted by your Satan's Gospel to make fire-emitting modern ammunition, Emperor, dear! . . . What has become of the old vision and prophecy which you once promised an old peasant mother who died hoping it would come true? . . . Yesterday the Turks, today the chiefs from within, tomorrow the British, and then, and then, and then! No end while the evil wheel turns around in your head! . . . You dream of your mission far too much and live up to it far too little, wretched man! (P. 223)

The fundamental truth that Tsegaye wants to convey seems to be that Tewodros's failure should be ascribed to his resorting to violence only. The emperor may sincerely claim that "the petty, selfish lustful chiefs make me do it. They force me to shed the blood of the very people I would be more than willing to give my life for" (p. 221). His first action in the second act is to rob young Menelik of his father's treasure. By the time the play comes to an end, Tewodros has become a drunken, unbalanced, irritable and, at times, lachrymose wreck, whose last shred of dignity resides in his committing suicide. His inner tragedy is that he is aware of his shortcomings. When Menelik asks him if he is truly the man "who really knows the people, feels their hunger, their love and their hope," Tewodros can only reply in all honesty: "I try to be." And as Menelik persists in his doubts, the emperor finds himself reminded of his first wife's misgivings, so that the testimonies of all three characters—Tewabetch, Menelik, and Tru-Worq—converge to define the flaw in Kassa, his inability to imagine any other methods than those of self-defeating violence, in order that his beautiful visionary dream may materialize.

It is typical of the Ethiopian outlook that Tsegaye should have defined the origin of this flaw in terms of dynastic legitimacy. At the end of the first act, the Empress Mänän, now a captured old hag, predicts the failure of Kassa, whom she considers an usurpating upstart:

How about the ocean-deep history of Ethiopia's ruling blood? Through centuries the people's eyes were accustomed to looking up and following those who did not materialize from themselves, but those shepherds elect of God since David and Solomon! You need to have that blood running through your miserable veins before you talk big and all-knowing. Give it up, Kassa, before you are too late to repent. It isn't for you, fortune-hunting boy. . . . You don't have the blood for all that fantasy and myth, Kassa! (P. 219)

The course of events verifies this prophecy and, at least implicitly, vindicates Mänän's diagnosis. This suggests that although Tsegaye shares much of the Tewodros image elaborated by the new Ethiopian intelligentsia, although he admires the emperor's ideal and even seems to condone his hostility to the supremacy of the clergy —who are called "blaspheming, monstrous priests! those interwoven evil webs! those eye-piercing cheap candle lights" (p. 221)—yet he still clings to the traditional concept of legitimate descent. The scene with Menelik, for all its brevity, is very significant in this respect: like Tewabetch and Tru-Worq, Menelik has his doubts about Tewodros's methods in pursuing his ends. His gentleness and even his sympathy with the emperor—although he holds him responsible for his father's death [121]—should be taken as intimations of the distrust of violence which was to enable him to accomplish Tewodros's purposes through diplomatic rather than warlike means. According to official Ethiopian historiography, Menelik restored the imperial throne of the Solomonic line.

At the same time as *Tewodros*, the *Ethiopia Observer* printed another English play by Tsegaye, *Azmari*. "Azmari" is the name given to the numberless professional minstrels who used to sing poems, panegyric or satirical as the occasion required, to the sound of some string instrument. The Chadwicks summed up such information as was available about them in the 1930s:

They are everywhere, whether in the entourage of princes or wealthy men, in the houses of men of humbler rank, or wandering along the roads, and attending at all public gatherings, like the medieval minstrels to whom they are constantly compared by all travellers who have seen them. They live entirely by their wits, and have in consequence developed a quick and lively ability to hit off the foibles of their audience, to incorporate topical allusions, and to introduce puns and various other witty sallies into their poems.

The subjects of the songs of the *Azmaris* are generally contemporary events, or the characters or personal appearance of some prominent person in their audience. Their allusions are of the most outspoken, and, if they should chance to be offended, of the most outrageous character. More often they are complimentary, since this is the type of song most calculated to produce the desired reward. Witty and amusing allusions are liberally introduced and much appreciated by the audience, and the poetry in general represents a highly developed diction and art, if a somewhat limited range of form. . . . Wherever we find them, they appear to have no difficulty in obtaining an appreciative audience and an honourable reception. . . . Their persons are held sacrosanct, and it is said that in battle no one will touch them. . . . It is evident that the professional poet is a person of considerable importance and standing.[122]

Nevertheless, the Chadwicks refer to Plowden's observation in the mid-nineteenth century that female minstrels had the reputation of being dissolute courtesans.[123]

This may account in part for the fact that the heroine in

Tsegaye's play is a social and a moral outcast, who has been shamefully abandoned by her fiancé. But the main conflict in the drama
is between the girl's dedication to her art on the one hand and, on
the other hand, her mother's narrow preoccupation with down-to-
earth household matters, and the repellent materialism of the
brother, who earns money as a broker in the city. This is a new
theme in Ethiopian literature, and although the play is verbose and
even mawkish in places, it has the further interest of illustrating a
serious widening in the knowledge of world literature among
Ethiopian writers. Käbbädä had sought his models in Shakespeare
and especially in French classical tragedy; Menghistu has acknowledged the influence of Molière, Gogol, and Bernard Shaw; [124]
style, technique, and mood in *Azmari* point to serious acquaintance
with Chekhov and Western symbolist drama.

Tsegaye's best work in English so far is *Oda Oak Oracle*, which
evinces such skill in the handling of the language and in the creation of the mood, that it must have been written later than the
other two plays, although it was printed in London in 1965. This
terse, haunting drama takes place in a non-Christian society,
swayed by the ancestor cult and the cruel superstitious practices
that it entails. The oracle has decided that Shanka, "the strong son
of the Valley tribe," is to marry Ukutee, and that their first-born
son shall be sacrificed to propitiate the dead ancestors. Rather than
have his child killed, Shanka, in spite of his strong desire for
Ukutee, refrains from consummating the marriage, much to the
humiliation and distress of the bride, who exclaims:

> I'd rather live possessed
> In human passion
> For a short nine months,
> Than merely exist
> For an idle ninety summers.[125]

For this, Shanka is severely rebuked by his friend Goaa. Goaa had
once been taken away as a slave or a prisoner by foreigners. The
ship had been wrecked in a storm, and he had been able to return
to his own country. But he had been instructed in "the strangers'
wisdom," and he had come back praising the Gospel of Christ
and of love. The tribesmen therefore called him "the inhibited by
the strangers' way." To Shanka he argues:

The anger of our forefathers
Is only a nightmare
From the world of our dead,
While the bitterness
Of an ignored woman
Is the truer hell
Raging inside your hut.

(P. 3)

Goaa even promises to discuss the matter with the oracle in the hope of convincing him that Shanka and Ukutee should be freed from the curse that weighs upon them.

But although Goaa is the messenger of truth, he is a coward and a weakling, and he dare not face the oracle:

To face him
With my strange wisdom
Shall be my darkest sin.
Did I run from the strangers
Merely to be felled
By my own people
As one possessed by evil spirits?
Whatever spirit
I happen to be possessed of
I am not ready
To die for
Nor to die of, Shanka.

(P. 5)

And when Ukutee, from the depths of her frustration, challenges him to take her, he is unable to resist the temptation.

When the day of reckoning arrives, nine months later, Goaa, forgetting his principles, is abjectly afraid of the retribution that the oracle is bound to visit upon him. Even Ukutee's contempt— "Are you men / Never prepared / To pay for the happiness / You take out of life?" (p. 20)—fails to shame him, and he tries to shift the responsibility onto her, who tempted him. As the woman lies groaning in birth pangs, the Oda-man delivers his sentence: the child is "pronounced unworthy of life" and "unholy for the sacrifice." Goaa has angered the dead by his alien ideas and shamed the tribe by his illicit behavior. Shanka was the first to defy the ancestors. To appease the wrath of the spirits, says the Oda-man,

> The defiant . . .
> Shall be matched, in
> A combat to the death, against
> The coward who stole
> The bride of their choice. . . .
> After the battle
> The "undead" of the two defiant ones
> Shall be flogged out of the Valley
> By the woman under labour,
> Into the dark woods
> And into the lands of the strange ones.
>
> (P. 37)

Goaa is killed in the fight, but Ukutee dies while giving birth to a daughter. Shanka argues with the oracle and the elders in the hope of saving at least this "child of innocence," but the Oda-man can "interpret only wrath," and the tribe must have blood to appease the ancestors. As the curtain drops, Shanka, carrying the crying child, approaches the mob, ready to die "for a forbidden truth condemned."

Oda Oak Oracle is one of the finest plays to have been written in Africa. Profoundly religious though it is, it contains none of the tiresome preaching that mars much of Amharic literature. The spiritual issues involved are handled with remarkable subtlety and impersonality. The cruelty of the tribespeople is not without pathos, and Tsegaye had admirably succeeded in conveying the underlying, irrational logic of ignorance and fear. Goaa impersonates the destructive impact of Western beliefs and ways upon African society. Such knowledge as he has of the strangers' wisdom does not lead him to true wisdom, but merely rids him of the beliefs that had provided the foundations for the ethical norms of tribal society. It is Shanka's inner revulsion against the senseless cruelty of the old culture which points to the true spirit of the new outlook, although Shanka has had no direct contact with the strangers.

After the emergence of Galla writers using Amharic, after the introduction of realistic drama by Menghistu Lemma, the English works of Tsegaye Gabre-Medhin open up new vistas for Ethiopian

literature. The example set by Abbé Gubäñña was not very encouraging, and this may be one of the reasons why Menghistu
wrote a spirited defense of vernacular writing in 1965:

The language of a people is very much more than a mere means of
communication or expression. Embedded deeply in its collective unconscious, it has emotional and spiritual roots that may not be visible
at all to the foreign observer. People dream in their own language. It
should therefore be obvious that Ethiopian writers using the medium of
a foreign tongue (like English) however plausible might be their external, facile mastery of it, can never hope to fully profit by the finer
distinctions, nuances, music and rythm of that language on an equal
footing with those whose mother-tongue it is. Such writers voluntarily
forswear intricacy and depth of expression; and have no alternative but
to be "quaint" in the touristic sense of the word, spoiling somebody
else's language into the bargain.[126]

There is much uncontrovertible truth in this. Yet, many writers,
throughout the course of world literature, have been able to produce works of genuine quality in languages other than their own.
Until the seventeenth century, and even later, many Western
poets used Latin with great success. Milton also wrote in Italian;
Conrad and Nabokov are obvious cases in point. The phenomenon
is even more widespread in Africa today. Hardly any writers in
the former French colonies and in the Portuguese "provinces"
have resorted to their mother tongues. The French poetry of
Rabéarivelo in Madagascar and of Senghor in Senegal, the English
novels of Chinua Achebe, the plays of Wole Soyinka and John
Pepper Clark in Nigeria, the novels of James Ngugi in Kenya, are
all decisive proof that the vernacular is by no means the only valid
medium of literary expression in modern Africa. If the fate of
Latin in Europe is of any relevance, Western languages will, in
all likelihood, remain in use for a long time as the vehicle through
which Africa can convey its literary message to the world audience. It is all the more significant, therefore, that even Tsegaye
should agree with Menghistu in the basic notion "that the language
any 'native' dreams in is the one nearest perfect tool to record or
recount his experiences in." [127] For Tsegaye, using a Western language is a matter of sheer expediency. Africa should not abandon
"these useful tools of communications," which alone can create
"a dialogue of understanding between the 'mass' of the outside

world and the African Public." Since the vernaculars are as yet
too numerous, too little known outside Africa, and "all too limited
in scope to accommodate sufficient expressions for a modern
thought," he claims, "it is by recording ideas in the very language
one dreamt in, first, and then having the same translated into other
foreign languages second, that the recognition and growth of vernaculars into wider instruments of literature is guaranteed." This
view might perhaps not be shared by the Francophonic writers of
Africa. There is little doubt, however, that the vernacular tongues,
being the organic medium of self-expression, will ultimately prevail, as they did in Europe—albeit in a future that may be quite
remote.

Conclusion

A brief comparative discussion of literary developments in southern Africa and in Ethiopia may be of some use in view of the many hasty generalizations that have gained currency since the emergence of modern creative writing on the continent was brought to the attention of the outside world. The foregoing chapters will, it is hoped, have helped concretize the diversity of African literature. Two basic factors must be held responsible for this diversity. First, there was a great variety in the native cultural substratum. The Bantu societies of southern Africa were animistic and non-literate, whereas the Amhara of Ethiopia were Christians with a twofold literary tradition—one written and one oral. Further, in contrast with the Sotho and the Xhosa, the Zulu and the Amhara could draw on the glorious remembrances of an imperialistic past of their own.

Second, diversity originates in the timing and modes of Western impact. The Xhosa—or, rather, the Ngqika Xhosa—were the first to be exposed to close, continuous contact with the Europeans. In spite of frequent border clashes, the main agents of cultural penetration were the missionaries. Until the 1880s, therefore, culture change developed among the converts, on the whole in an atmosphere of eager acceptance, of mutual understanding, and of friendliness. This was also true of the Sotho, with the added observation that Lesotho remained sheltered by protectorate status after the Xhosa had been completely subjected to white supremacy. The less desirable aspects of Western influence were felt by the Sotho outside their own country, in the mines of the Rand and on the farms of Natal. One of the consequences was that anticolonialism did not appear as an important theme in Sotho literature until the

377

1940s. There was no such comparatively smooth transition for the Zulu, who remained largely unaffected by missionary enterprise until they were forcefully integrated into a unified South Africa officially committed to white racism, hence the belated appearance of literary writing among the Zulu; hence, too, its characteristic nationalistic coloring, evinced, for instance, in Shembe's hymns and in the success of the historical novel. As to Ethiopia, creative writing in the vernacular did not develop as a direct outcome of missionary work, but as a by-product of a preventive policy of modernization designed by forward-looking leaders in order to protect the country from foreign imperialism. The early emphasis, therefore, was on grafting Western techniques onto the native Coptic culture. Even more brutally than in Zululand, wholesale contact with Europe was concurrent with the worst forms of colonial racism and exploitation, but the liberation of the country in 1941 gave Ethiopian writers greater freedom to vent their revulsion against Western civilization than Zulu authors could possibly have enjoyed at any time.

Yet, for all the diversity illustrated in the choice of themes, in the adaptation of Western literary techniques, and in the writers' attitudes toward both the old culture and the new, modern literature, whether in Amharic, Zulu, Xhosa, or Southern Sotho, originated everywhere in response to the Western challenge. It shaped itself into diverse patterns, all inevitably controlled by the complex interplay of tradition and innovation.

Innovation produced phenomena that have their parallels in the past history of European literature. For example, urbanization and the need for mass entertainment fostered the emergence of formal stage drama, much as had happened in thirteenth-century Europe. The introduction of the printing press and the gradual spreading of literacy favored the birth and growth of the novel as they had done in Europe in the Renaissance. Knowledge of such Western works as were studied in schools or were available in school libraries, acted as a stimulus in the same way as Seneca's tragedies and Aristotle's *Poetics* had done in sixteenth-century Europe. The aesthetic quality of such works, admittedly, is often of the slightest. But for any objective appraisal, we must remember how bad neoclassical drama was before Shakespeare and Lope de Vega and Corneille. The reason was that the humanists were slavishly trying to imitate ancient forms, the function of which was still a closed mystery to them. Likewise, a large part of the new African literature is the product of a ritualistic endeavor to emulate Western achievement at the most superficial level of literary forms and commonplace morality.

Clearly, the most important literary effect of European influence was the introduction of the novel and—in a later phase—of stage drama, new genres completely alien to traditional art. But both the novel and stage drama are the outcome of a particular form of civilization, the premises of which are entirely at variance with those of indigenous African cultures. They are the favorite medium of an individualistic society; they focus on the exploration of individual character; they feed on the analysis of private emotions and motivations and experiences. On the contrary, like most technologically underdeveloped, small-scale societies, whose survival can only be ensured by the closest group cohesion, African cultures are based on values that are primarily societal. The main functions of literature are: to preserve the religious myths of the group, to perpetuate the memory of its past in semilegendary chronicles and so to bolster its sense of collective identity and dignity, to record the wisdom pragmatically accumulated by generations of ancestors in proverbs and gnomic tales, and to celebrate the prowess of the kings and warriors, whose mighty deeds have ensured the power and the glory of the group. This is why so many African novelists and playwrights have been unable—as has often been observed and deplored—to achieve convincing individual characterization. In many cases, they continue the folktale tradition of emphasis on anecdotal incidents or on allegorical morality. The absence of any native tradition in those genres also accounts for clumsiness in plot management and in the depiction of personal emotions: constant resorting to implausible coincidences and awkward handling of the love theme are illustrative of the difficulties that they will have to overcome.

Contact with Western civilization was also responsible for the chief original theme of African literature, the theme of acculturation, with its many subordinate motifs: industrialization and technical development, impact of city life and the new money economy on ethical behavior, transformation of marriage customs and sexual mores, contrast between modern education and ancient wisdom and superstitions, and exciting and perplexing experiences of the privileged few who have gained first-hand knowledge of Europe or America. Indeed, the chief interest of African literature for the non-African reader is, perhaps, that it provides a key to the African's own awareness of the problems raised by his emergence into the modern world. This awareness appears to be rather different from the abstract patterns constructed by Western economists and sociologists using the thought categories peculiar to their own culture. As exemplified in his literature, the African's awareness of his own predicament is characterized by utter ambiguity and confusion. On the one hand, he is exceedingly sensitive to the higher ideals of Christianity, as distinct from the tribal ethics and "pagan" superstitions in southern Africa and from the corrupt mores of the clergy in Ethiopia. As a member of the educated elite, he is attracted by modern education and science, and by the enjoyable benefits of Western-type economy and technology. On the other hand, he remains deeply attached to the values of his tradition: the fatalistic otherworldliness of Coptic Christianity, the ancestor cult, group solidarity, and the rustic decency of tribal society. Western and traditional values are obviously antinomic: fatalistic acceptance and overriding group consciousness can hardly foster the aggressive individualism that is the foundation of progress in the Western sense of the word. The African's puzzlement is further compounded by his realization that the enviably prosperous and powerful white man pays only lip-service to the loftier ideals of his own religion.

Seen through his own literary production, the modern African thus appears to be caught between two antagonistic and irreconcilable forces: the conservative power of tradition, and the innovational appeal of modernization. His is truly a tragic predicament, and a considerable amount of creative writing seeks to frame some solution to this obsessive, traumatic problem. Some sort of syncretism is bound to arise, but in the present phase of history, no solution that can be imagined is of any validity. The Church Fathers and those who built the Roman basilicas could not possibly have foreseen that the cross-fertilization of Latin and Germanic cultures would produce the *Summa theologica* and the Gothic cathedrals! As things are, Ethiopia and southern Africa nevertheless provide examples of three attitudes that are widely spread throughout the literature of the continent.

The first attitude is one of unquestioning acceptance of such Western innovations as have impressed themselves most powerfully on the African mind in a definite area at a definite time. This is a feature that early Xhosa writers and Amharic novelists have in common. The Gospel of love was as eagerly embraced by Ntsikana and his successors, as technological progress was hailed by Heruy and Germačäw. Their work obviously had a topical purpose. It was the writers' aim to help their society on its path to material improvement and/or spiritual salvation. This kind of inspiration, distorted, it is true, by white supremacy and apartheid policy, is predominant in South Africa today. Many writers produce politically harmless works designed to instill a zest for education and virtue into the minds of younger readers. Existing law and order cannot be questioned. A more strictly literary aspect of this uncritical adherence to Western standards is exemplified in the work of many South African poets, who still believe that the quality of their poetry will be enhanced by ritualistic adoption of European poetic forms, however unsuited they may be to Bantu languages.

Of greater promise than this undiscriminating attempt at assimilation are the imaginative descriptions of the culture-change process itself, when they evince due regard for the power and value of the factors involved. History is the record of ceaseless dialectical interaction of the forces of permanence and progression; neither of these can ever be erased. Literary works that ignore either of them are, for that reason, irrelevant, whatever their aesthetic quality may be. But the complexity of the issue is such that it can only be treated satisfactorily by writers gifted with more than a common share of insight and talent. To realize this, we need only compare the tragic, objective description of the African dilemma in Jordan's Xhosa novel with Mqhayi's blissfully utopian attempt at solving it in *U-Don Jadu*. On a lower level of artistic achievement, it is suggestive of the African writers' deepest preoccupation that so many of them should be intensely concerned with the havoc and the demoralization wrought by the Western impact. The behavior patterns selected to illustrate this quandary are the same everywhere: alcoholism, sexual permissiveness, slum life, lust for money and pleasure, and conceited rebellion of the educated young against traditional hierarchies of clan societies. This concentration on the negative aspects of modernization is akin to the shrill anticolonialism and the negritude cult in the French literature of West Africa, and it largely reflects an immature tendency to let others shoulder all responsibility for Africa's present troubles. It is a token of the swift maturation of the African mind that a number of younger writers in the newly independent countries should resolutely turn to self-criticism of a highly pertinent, and often pungent kind. The latest works of Chinua Achebe in Nigeria, the recent novels of Ahmadou Kourouma in the Ivory Coast and of Yambo Ouologuem in Mali are cases in point. And so is Menghistu Lemma's *Snatch and Run*, with its ironic portrayal of Ethiopian intellectuals.

Nevertheless, many of the works centering on acculturation obviously verge on a third attitude that in psychological jargon should probably be called "retreatism," as they illustrate a withdrawal from the urgent problems of the day into exclusive concern with the preservation of tradition and traditional values. There is nothing psychotic in this approach, which raises the fascinating problem of the influence of tradition on modern African creative writing.

With regard to the writers' attitude toward language, the continent has come to be sharply divided along colonial lines. Owing, presumably, to the strong deculturizing effect of French and Portuguese assimilation policy, writers in those areas have opted for the European language as their favorite medium of literary expression; hardly any writing is done in the vernaculars. In territories under British administration, indirect rule and the concern of Protestant missionaries to make the Bible available to native populations have encouraged the new writers' attachment to their mother tongues. This is even truer of territories that remained semiautonomous—such as Lesotho, where Christianization was effected by French Protestant missionaries—or independent—such as Ethiopia, where Western Christianity exerted little influence. In South Africa, educational apartheid policy and the subsequent demand for reading matter in schools have led to an enormous quantitative increase in vernacular writing. But whether concentration on vernacular writing is a consequence of colonialism or of nationalism, its drawbacks are obvious. The most glaring one is that it prevents writers from conveying the realities of African experience to the outside world. Until the task of translating such writings as are worthy of it is tackled on a large scale, authors have only one means of remedying this isolation, and that is to write in European languages—hence, the fast development of English imaginative writing in East Africa since 1965. It is possible, and indeed likely, that the growth and dissemination of higher education and increased opportunity for study in the United Kingdom and the United States will stimulate the same trend in Ethiopia and Lesotho in the next few decades.

The African author's attachment to the language he dreams in is matched by his deep love for the traditional literature of his society. It is significant that the earliest writers of Ethiopia and of South Africa devoted a considerable part of their activity to recording oral lore: praise poetry, folktales, and proverbs. The exceptionally precocious implantation of the novel in Lesotho is perhaps due to the fact that modern culture was brought to the country by French missionaries. In Senegal, too, modern literature began in the 1920s and 1930s with the novels of Ahmadou Mapate Diagne, Bakary Diallo, and Ousmane Socé.

A good deal of oral art is of a historical nature. Indeed, recent ethnohistorians have come to the conclusion that such chronicles are more reliable than had previously been suspected. Their function is similar to that of most primitive epic tales. It is to extol the warlike achievements of the tribe, to glorify the heroes who have contrbuted to its greatness, and so to uphold the cohesion and pride of the group itself. The African historical novel and drama are obviously a new outlet for this old urge. Quite understandably, they have prospered more in strong, aggressive societies with a history of conquest and power behind them, such as the Zulu and the Amhara, than in the comparatively meek and weak Sotho and Xhosa nations, which have no past imperialistic achievements of their own to celebrate. As their function is encomiastic rather than analytical, the parallel is with medieval epics rather than with our modern historical novel.

Innovation has been strongly tinged by tradition not only with regard to language, content, and function, but also in form and style. Ntsikana's hymns, the earliest compositions produced on African soil under Western influence, turned the techniques of tribal praise poetry to Christian use. Many writers have remained faithful to the ancient types—the Nguni izibongo, the Sotho lithoko, the Ethiopian qené—even for compositions of their own dealing with modern topics. It is true that in southern Africa there has been, and still exists, a tendency to appropriate such Western poetic forms as were made available through the school curriculum: rhyme, syllabic meter, and regular stanzas. But the best writers eventually outgrow this ritualistic phase, a trend that is likely to be strengthened as more and more authors become aware of twentieth-century Western poetry and of the wide-ranging formal freedom it allows its practitioners.

Stage drama, too, which was certainly unknown to most, if not all, African societies, is strongly influenced by the precolonial techniques of ritual drama and popular entertainment. The French William-Ponty plays of the thirties are interspersed with dance and pageantry and vernacular songs. This was also characteristic of Bantu drama in South Africa and of Amharic drama during the same early period. Admittedly, most of the plays that reached print laboriously try to observe the outdated conventions of such Western drama as was taught in schools. Here, too, better information about contemporary dramatic developments in the West is likely to bolster the influence of the native tradition. In Madagascar, during the early years of this century, the introduction of the French *opérette* encouraged Malagasy writers to turn back to their ancient *Mpilalau* tradition, whose blend of dramatic action, erotic interest, song and dance, had aroused stiff opposition from the British missionaries. Increased acquaintance with present-day trends in Western drama will no doubt help close the gap that is so painfully obvious between "serious" literate drama and popular theatrical entertainment in southern Africa and in Ethiopia.

At the present, inchoative stage in the scholarly study of modern African literature, utter caution in drawing conclusions is advisable. It is clear, for example, that contrary to what is usually assumed, the bulk of modern African writing is in the vernaculars, even though almost exclusive attention from non-African critics has gone to works in European languages. It is equally clear, therefore, that extensive research is required before any balanced knowledge, understanding, and appraisal of the new literature of the continent can be expected. To be sure, this should primarily be the task of African scholars. At present, however, there are very few highly educated Africans who have both the inclination and the specialized skill and training for genuine scientific research in this new field. For all its glaring shortcomings, this book will have achieved a modicum of success if it has demonstrated that non-African scholars trained in the techniques of literary history can

contribute—in an admittedly limited, but nevertheless useful way—
to laying the foundations of African literary science.

The first need, of course, is for detailed monograph studies of
individual literatures. Many facts have been recorded, but strenuous research is necessary to unearth and collect them, and to arrange them into meaningful growth patterns. Literary scholars
gifted with the indispensable linguistic equipment should turn in
greater numbers to the task of critically assessing the value of
vernacular writings, of translating the best of them so as to make
them available to the world audience, of studying the influence of
traditional art on the new literary forms.

Specialists of comparative literature will have to analyze cross-
relations at several levels: interaction must have taken place in
various ways and in varying degrees among the literatures of
southern Africa. There has been no direct contact between the
vernacular literatures of South Africa and of Ethiopia, but we need
to know more about the influence of vernacular writing on English
works by black South African authors, who, in turn, are likely to
have influenced writers capable of reading English in other parts
of the continent.

But the network of literary influences did not operate *intra
muros* only. Extraneous factors have contributed to the shaping of
the new art, and it will be one of the main tasks of African literary
scholarship to identify them and to delineate the extent of their
impact in each case. Whereas, for example, Catholic missionary
influence contributed little to the emergence of creative vernacular
writing, Protestant missionaries were often the promoters of the
new national literatures. Here again, however, distinctions must be
made. The fact that Christianity and the Bible and Western civilization were largely brought to the Xhosa by British missionaries,
to the Sotho by French missionaries, and to the Zulu by American
missionaries (many of them Negroes), may account in part for
the specific orientations taken by imaginative literature in each of
those areas. And literary influence of missionary enterprise was as
slight in Ethiopia as it was in the Islamized countries of black
Africa.

Another major channel of Westernization was education, which
was not necessarily under complete control of the missionaries;
Ethiopia and French West Africa are similar in this respect. Every-

where, however, it was through the schools that African writers gained their knowledge of Western literature. It will therefore be advisable to investigate school libraries and curricula and to determine which literary works were influential in the shaping of African creative writing. Only when this point is settled will it be possible to define the extent and manner of influence with any degree of accuracy.

The above are only some of the directions in which future research is bound to move if African literary scholarship is to be based on secure scientific foundations. The ultimate purpose, however, is not merely erudite and antiquarian. For one thing, vernacular writing is certainly a most important potential source for our knowledge and understanding of the African mind in the present phase of acculturation. Until recently, the Western image of Africa was based on the findings of non-African scientists or on imaginative works written by Africans in European languages with an eye on the interests, requirements, and outlook of the Western reader. Composed by Africans for Africans, vernacular literature is bound to provide a more faithful reflection of African experience. But although the study of vernacular literature can play a most useful role in clearing misconceptions and in completing the patchy image of Africa which still prevails in the white man's mind, Ezekiel Mphahlele was right to protest—at the 1962 Conference of Africanists—against a widespread tendency to exploit African imaginative literature as a gold mine for sociologists. Literary works of any value have a way of outliving the particular human situation out of which they grew. Admittedly, the introduction of the printing press, in Africa as in Europe, has favored the production and dissemination of trash. It will be the overriding task of scholars and critics more competent than I am to single out such works as are worthy of serious attention, and thus to help the black continent bring its own contribution to the swelling flow of world literature.

Notes

INTRODUCTION

1. On precursors, see chap. iii of Janheinz Jahn's *Geschichte der neoafrikanischen Literatur* (Düsseldorf, 1966).
2. Gerald Moser, "African Literature in Portuguese: The First Written, The Last Discovered," *African Forum*, II, 4 (1967), 78–96.
3. Lilyan Kesteloot, *Les écrivains noirs de langue française: Naissance d'une littérature* (Brussels, 1963).
4. For further information, see Albert S. Gérard, "Bibliographical Problems in Creative African Literature," *Journal of General Education*, XIX, 1 (1967), 25–35.
5. See also Bernth Lindfors's useful "Additions and Corrections to Janheinz Jahn's *Bibliography of Neo-African Literature*," *African Studies Bulletin*, XI, 2 (1968), 129–147. More recently, Hungarian scholar Pál Páricsy published a continuation to Jahn: *A New Bibliography of African Literature* (Budapest, 1969).
6. See review articles by Beat Inauen, "Dix ans de littérature Shona," *Bethléem*, no. 5 (May 1967), pp. 154–156; Gérard, "African Literature in Rhodesia," *Africa Report*, XIII, 5 (1968), 41–42.

CHAPTER 1

1. Monica Wilson, "The Early History of the Transkei and Ciskei," *African Studies*, XVIII (1959), 167–179.
2. N. J. Van Warmelo, *A Preliminary Survey of the Bantu Tribes of South Africa* (Pretoria, 1935), p. 60.
3. On the history of the Xhosa as they themselves see it, cf. John Henderson Soga, *The South-Eastern Bantu* (Johannesburg, 1930), chaps. ix through xvi.
4. Gcalekaland is now one of the four areas of present-day Transkei, the others being Fingoland, Tembuland and Pondoland.

388   NOTES TO PP. 23-24

5. Soga, *South-Eastern Bantu*, p. 130.

6. *Ibid.*, p. 153.

7. Most of the general information in English about Xhosa writing is to be found in the books and articles of R. H. W. Shepherd: *Lovedale, South Africa: The Story of a Century, 1841–1941* (Lovedale, 1942); *Lovedale and Literature for the Bantu* (Lovedale, 1945); *African Contrasts* in collaboration with B. G. Paver (Cape Town, 1947); *Bantu Literature and Life* (Lovedale, 1955); "Literature for Africa," *South African Outlook*, LXVIII (1948), 4–6, repr. in *Books for Africa*, XVIII (Jan. 1948), 7–8; "The Evolution of an African Press: Lovedale's Outstanding Contribution to Bantu Literacy," *African World* (Nov. 1953), pp. 7–8; "Recent Trends in South African Vernacular Literature," *African World* (March 1955), pp. 7–8. See also D. D. T. Jabavu, *Bantu Literature* (Lovedale, 1921). The only fairly systematic account of the early stages up to 1884 is to be found in a series of articles by Archibald C. Jordan, "Towards an African Literature," in *Africa South* (1957–1959). A useful compendium of factual information has been compiled from those and a few other sources, such as obituaries and newspaper articles by Daniel Kunene and Randal A. Kirsch, *The Beginning of South African Vernacular Literature* (Los Angeles, 1967). Much can also be gleaned from Benedict Wallet Vilakazi, "The Oral and Written Literature in Nguni" (Ph.D. diss., Johannesburg: University of the Witwatersrand, 1945). For details of the latest developments, see S. Z. Qangule, "A Brief Survey of Modern Literature in the South African Bantu Languages: Xhosa," *Limi*, no. 6 (June 1968), pp. 14–28.

8. See for example William Ellis, *History of Madagascar* (London, 1838), II:276; W. E. Cousins, "A Native Malagasy Lyric," *Antananarivo Annual*, V (1896), 457–459; E. Baker, "On the Poetry of Madagascar," first published in the first volume of the *Journal of the Bengal Asiatic Society* for 1832, and reprinted in *Antananarivo Annual*, III (1886), 167–177; G. Mondain, "Note sur les tout premiers débuts de la littérature malgache avant l'arrivée des Européens," *Bulletin de l'Académie Malgache*, n.s. XXVI (1944–45), 43–48; W. C. Pickersgill, "Biazavola: A Malagasy Bard," *Antananarivo Annual*, III (1886), 247–249; Lucien Andrianarahinjaka, "Ramananato; An Early 19th Century Malagasy Poet," *Présence Africaine*, no. 55 (1965), pp. 45–73.

9. A Xhosa biography of Ntsikana, *Ibali likaNtsikana*, was published at Lovedale in 1914 by the Reverend John Knox Bokwe. For a summary of this, see Ernst Marx, "Ein Beispiel volkstümlichen Christentums unter der Kaffern Südafrikas," *Neue Allgemeine Missionszweitschrift*, XIII, 3 (1936), 95–103.

10. *Kaffir* is an Arab word meaning "infidel." It was used in South

NOTES TO PP. 25–40

Africa for the Bantu, especially for the Xhosa, whose territories were officially known in the nineteenth century as "Kaffraria."

11. This letter, published in the report of the Glasgow Missionary Society for 1823, is quoted in Shepherd, *Bantu Literature and Life*, pp. 18–19.

12. John Philip, *Researches in South Africa* (London, 1828), pp. 186–188, quoted by Shepherd, *Bantu Literature and Life*, pp. 19–20.

13. Shepherd, *African Contrasts*, pp. 164–165.

14. Jordan, "Towards an African Literature: (V) The Early Writers," *Africa South*, II, 4 (1958), 113–118.

15. Cf. Marx, "Ein Beispiel volkstümlichen Christentums," pp. 95–103.

16. O. F. Raum, "Von Stammespropheten zu Sektenführern," in E. Benz, ed., *Messianische Kirchen, Sekten und Bewegungen im heutigen Afrika* (Leiden, 1965), pp. 47–70.

17. Yvonne Huskisson, "The Story of Bantu Music," *Bantu*, XV, 7 (1968), 16–20.

18. For more detailed information, see Clement M. Doke, "Scripture Translation into Bantu Languages," *African Studies*, XVII (1958), 82–99.

19. John A. Chalmers, *Tiyo Soga* (Edinburgh, 1877).

20. Shepherd, *Bantu Literature and Life*, p. 38.

21. See the biographical notice prefaced to Soga, *South-Eastern Bantu*, chap. xii.

22. Vilakazi, "Oral and Written Literature," p. 297.

23. I have used the most balanced and best-informed account of the cattle-killing episode, which is provided by Monica Wilson, "Cooperation and Conflict: The Eastern Cape Frontier," in *The Oxford History of South Africa*, ed. Monica Wilson and Leonard Thompson (Oxford, 1969), esp. pp. 256–260.

24. Rumors of the Crimean War had reached Xhosa country, and it was widely believed that the Russians were black people who would come to rescue the Africans from the grip of English colonialism.

25. Charles Brownlee, *Reminiscences of Kaffir Life and History 1896* (Lovedale, n.d.), pp. 128–129, quoted by Monica Wilson.

26. Wilson, "Co-operation and Conflict," p. 252.

27. Jordan, "Towards an African Literature: (IV) The Dawn of Literature," *Africa South*, II, 3 (1958), 112–115.

28. Chalmers, *Tiyo Soga*, p. 313.

29. Jordan, "Towards an African Literature: (VII) Poetry and the New Order," *Africa South*, III, 2 (1959), 74–79.

30. Vilakazi, "Oral and Written Literature," p. 291.

31. Jordan, "Towards an African Literature: (XI) The Harp of the Nation," *Africa South*, IV, 2 (1960), 110–113; "(XII) The Mounting

Anguish," *ibid.*, 3 (1960) 112–116. See also C. E. Earle Bulwer, "Xhosa Language and Literature: The Contribution of the Church of the Province of South Africa, Part II," *South African Outlook*, LXXXVII (1957), p. 77.

32. Hoho was a forest stronghold in the mountains, where the Ngqika chief Sandile was killed in June 1878.

33. J. F. A. Swartz, "A Hobbyist Looks at Zulu and Xhosa Songs," *African Music*, I, 3 (1956), 29–33.

34. Vilakazi, "Oral and Written Literature," p. 296.

35. The date of this journey is given as 1874 by Kirsch and as 1892 by Shepherd.

36. Vilakazi, "Oral and Written Litterature," p. 317.

37. See S. E. K. Mqhayi's autobiography in Diedrich Westermann, ed., *Afrikaner erzählen ihr Leben*, (Essen, 1938); this book was later translated into French as *Autobiographies d'Africains* (Paris, 1943), p. 260.

38. Edward Roux, *Time Longer Than Rope* (Madison, Wisc., 1966), p. 73.

39. *Ibid.*, pp. 109–110.

40. Bulwer, "Xhosa Language and Literature: Part I," pp. 44–45.

41. This account of Mqhayi is indebted to the author's autobiography in Westermann, *Autobiographies d'Africains*. The most informative source in English is Jordan, "Samuel Edward Krune Mqhayi," *South African Outlook*, LXXV (1945), 135–138. See also Vilakazi, "Oral and Written Literature," p. 280.

42. A rather poor translation by August Collingwood is to be found in *New African* V, 1 (1966), 5–8; 3:41–44; 4:74–76.

43. Quoted in Kunene and Kirsch, *Beginning of South African Vernacular Literature*, p. 28.

44. Alice Werner, "Some Native Writers in South Africa," *Journal of the African Society*, XXX (1931), 27–39.

45. On this point, see Lord Hailey, *An African Survey* (2d ed.; London, 1956), pp. 348–353.

46. Westermann, *Autobiographies d'Africains*, p. 262. In his recent memoir as the first principal of Fort Hare College, Dr. Alexander Kerr dryly recalls that "Problems of adjustment . . . sometimes did arise, as when a student studying South African history remarked that it seemed a curious coincidence that the 'kaffirs' started each and every one of the whole series of 'Kaffir' wars." *Fort Hare 1915–48: The Evolution of an African College* (London, 1968), p. 61.

47. John Riordan, "The Wrath of the Ancestors," *African Studies*, XX (1961), 53–60.

48. *South African Outlook*, LXVI (1936), p. 23.

49. Vilakazi, "Oral and Written Literature," p. 230.

50. The tremendous contribution of Dr. Shepherd to the growth of African literature was aptly summarized in an anonymous review of his book *Lovedale and Literature for the Bantu*, which appeared in *Books for Africa*, XV (1945), 57–58: "The author, as principal of Lovedale Institution, as literature secretary of the South African Christian Council and as director of publications of the Lovedale Press, has given leadership and guidance in surveying and planning for literature development in the Bantu languages of South Africa. He has encouraged missionary forces to collaborate in making adequate plans for literature development; he was instrumental in arranging two conferences of Bantu authors which gave an opportunity for consultation both on the need of literature and on the difficulties faced by authors in the publication of their work; he has urged missions to collaborate with the Inter-University Committee on Bantu literature which has produced surveys of existing literature in the Bantu languages of the South and suggestions as to publications required. A joint committee was set up representing the Inter-University Language Committee, the South African Christian Council and the African Authors' Conference, which made important proposals for an academy of African languages and literature. This encouragement of Bantu authorship and surveying of fields in which literature should be produced, has given great stimulus to the development of Bantu literature in South Africa. In the fields of distribution, Lovedale has also done pioneering work both through providing books for sale and urging adequate library provision."

51. Reviewed by I. Oldjohn in *South African Outlook*, LXIX (1939), p. 229.

52. Reviewed by Jabavu in *African Studies*, II (1943), 174–175.

53. Vilakazi, "Oral and Written Literature," p. 302.

54. *Ibid.*, p. 305.

55. Jordan, "Towards an African Literature: (II) Traditional Poetry," *Africa South*, II 1 (1957), 97–105.

56. Kunene and Kirsch give the date as 1897, but in *The African Who's Who* (3d. ed.; Johannesburg, 1932), p. 78, T. D. M. Skota assigns the work to 1903.

57. Swartz, "A Hobbyist Looks at Zulu and Xhosa Songs," p. 31.

58. Vilakazi, "Oral and Written Literature," p. 334.

59. *Ibid.*, p. 308.

60. What little biographical information I have concerning Ndawo was kindly conveyed to me by the late Prof. Jordan.

61. Vilakazi, "Oral and Written Literature," pp. 308–310.

62. Quotations are from the English translation.

63. This attitude is also strongly characteristic of present-day Shona

and Ndebele literature in Rhodesia. This literature has been developing since the mid-fifties, under conditions fairly similar to those that prevailed in South Africa in the twenties. On the vernacular literatures of Rhodesia, see E. W. Krog, ed., *African Literature in Rhodesia* (Gwelo, 1966); Beat Inauen, "Dix ans de littérature Shona," *Bethléem*, no. 5 (May 1967), pp. 154–157; Albert S. Gérard, "African Literature in Rhodesia," *Africa Report*, XIII, 5 (1968), 41–42.

64. Most of the biographical information about Sinxo I owe to the kindness of Mrs. Lena Guybon Sinxo and of Prof. Jordan. There is an important section on Sinxo in Vilakazi, "Oral and Written Literature," pp. 321–327.

65. Qangule, "A Brief Survey of Modern Literature," pp. 22–28.

66. Quoted in R. M. Sobukwe's review of *Isakhono, somfazi namanye amabalana*, *African Studies*, XVI (1957), 193–194.

67. Doke, "A Preliminary Investigation into the State of the Native Languages of South Africa with Suggestions as to Research and the Development of Literature," *Bantu Studies*, VII (1933), 1–98.

68. Vilakazi, "Oral and Written Literature," p. 344.

69. The following quotations come from Jolobe's speech on being awarded the Margaret Wrong Memorial Medal and Prize for 1958. It was printed in the *South African Outlook*, LXXXVIII (1958), 170–172, which also contains Prof. Nyembezi's "Appraisal," pp. 156–158, and a "Tribute by Dr. A. Kerr," p. 169. Some additional information can be found in Harold Scheub, "Interviews at New Brighton," *African Arts*, III, 4 (1970), 58–63.

70. Qangule, "A Brief Survey of Modern Literature," p. 17.

71. Jabavu, in *Bantu Studies*, XIX (1937), p. 53. The poems are here quoted from the author's English version, *Poems of an African* (Lovedale, 1946).

72. C. S. Nyembezi, "Honour for an African Author," *South African Outlook*, LXXXVIII (1958), p. 158.

73. Vilakazi, "Oral and Written Literature," pp. 346–348.

74. *South African Outlook*, LXX (1940), p. 72.

75. The book was reviewed in *South African Outlook*, LXXI (1941), p. 62.

76. *Ibid.*, LXXXIV (1954), p. 96.

77. *Ibid.*, LXXXVIII (1958), p. 110.

78. R. F. Alfred Hoernlé, "The Bantu Dramatic Society at Johannesburg," *Africa*, VII (1934), 223–227.

79. Vilakazi, "Oral and Written Literature," p. 355.

80. "The Lovedale Press: A Review of Recent Activities," *South African Outlook*, LXI (1931), 46–48.

81. I am indebted to Mr. Mdledle himself for most of the following biographical information.

82. B. B. Mdledle, *South African Outlook*, LXXXVIII (1958), p. 32.

83. Reviewed by Mdledle in *South African Outlook*, LXXXIX (1959), p. 45.

84. Reviewed by *ibid.*, p. 32.

85. *Ibid.*, p. 160.

86. J. MacGregor, "The Late Miss Victoria Swaartbooi," *South African Outlook*, LXVII (1937), 267.

87. Vilakazi, "Oral and Written Literature," pp. 331–332.

88. Qangule, "A Brief Survey of Modern Literature," p. 18.

89. "The Lovedale Press," pp. 46–48.

90. I am indebted for biographical information to Prof. Jordan himself and to Miss P-D. Beuchat of the University of the Witwatersrand, as well as to the notice in Ronald Segal, ed., *Political Africa* (New York, 1961), p. 116. Complementary details have been found in Vilakazi, Oral and Written Literature," pp. 334–335, and in Kunene's obituary notice in *African Arts / Arts d'Afrique*, II, 2 (1968), 25–26.

91. Vilakazi, "Oral and Written Literature," p. 335.

92. Riordan, "The Wrath of the Ancestors," pp. 53–60. But the most perceptive analysis of the book so far is Harold Scheub, "Approach to a Xhosa Novel," *Contrast*, VI, iii (1970), 77–91.

93. Vilakazi, "Oral and Written Literature," p. 340.

94. Monica Hunter, *Reaction to Conquest: Effects of Contact with Europeans on the Pondo of South Africa* (London, 1961²), p. 260.

95. Oldjohn's review of the book appeared in *South African Outlook*, LXX (1940), p. 77.

96. Quoted in Brian Bunting, *The Rise of the South African Reich* (Harmondsworth, 1964), pp. 206–207.

97. *Ibid.*, p. 195.

98. *Ibid.*, pp. 212–213.

99. Hendrik Verwoerd, quoted *ibid.*, p. 217.

100. *Ibid.*, p. 242.

101. Peter Sulzer, *Schwarze Intelligenz* (Zürich, 1955), p. 95.

102. F. J. van Wyk, "African Authors' Conference," *Books for Africa*, XXX (1960), 1–5.

103. Reviewed by J. J. R. Jolobe in *South African Outlook*, LXXXIII (1953), p. 160.

104. Reviewed in *South African Outlook*, LXXX (1950), p. 80. Mama later edited an anthology of Xhosa poetry, *Indyebo ka-Xhosa* (*Treasury of Xhosa* [Johannesburg, 1954]). For autobiographical information on

Mama, see Harold Scheub, "Interviews at New Brighton," *African Arts*, III, 4 (1970), 58–63.

105. Shepherd, "Recent Trends in South African Vernacular Literature," pp. 7–8.

106. Reviewed by Mdledle in *South African Outlook*, LXXXIV (1954), p. 160.

107. Qangule, "A Brief Survey of Modern Literature," p. 18.

108. Reviewed by Mdledle in *South African Outlook*, LXXXV (1955), p. 79, and by Sobukwe in *African Studies*, XVIII (1959), 101–102.

109. Review in *South African Outlook*, LXXXVII (1957).

110. Qangule, "A Brief Survey of Modern Literature," p. 22.

111. From a review by Sobukwe in *African Studies*, XVII (1958), 230–232.

112. Meaning the "carrying skin," used by women for carrying children on their back.

113. Biographical information kindly supplied by Professor Mzamane.

114. Qangule, "A Brief Survey of Modern Literature," p. 19.

CHAPTER 2

1. The main printed sources for our historical knowledge of literature in Southern Sotho are G. H. Franz, "The literature of Lesotho," *Bantu Studies*, IV (1930), 145–180; Franz, "Die vernaamste Basotho skryvers en iets oor hulle werk," *Die Basuin*, I, 4 (1930), 12–15; Franz, "Die Literatur des Lesotho (Basutoland)," *Die Brücke* (Johannesburg), Wissenschaftliche Beilage, I (1931), 1–4; II–IV (1932), 1–4; P. J. Coertze, "Die literatuur van die Basoeto," *Die Basuin*, III, 6 (1933), 10–12; G. L. Letele, "Some Recent Literary Publications in Languages of the Sotho Group," *African Studies*, III (1944), 161–171; M. D. Mohapeloa, *Letlole la lithoko tsa sesotho* (Johannesburg, 1950); M. Damane, *Marath'a lilepe* (Morija, 1960); Albert S. Gérard, "Literature of Lesotho," *Africa Report*, XI, 7 (1966), 68–70; S. M. Guma, "Southern Sotho Literature Today," *Africa Digest* (Mazenod), no. 15 [1968], pp. 25–29; J. M. Lenake, "A Brief Survey of Modern Literature in the South African Bantu Languages: Southern Sotho," *Limi*, no. 6 (June 1968), pp. 75–81; A. J. Moloi, "The Germination of Southern Sotho Poetry," *Limi*, no. 8 (June 1969), pp. 28–59. For oral lore, see especially Guma, *The Form, Content and Technique of Traditional Literature in Southern Sotho* (Pretoria, 1967).

2. Claude-Hélène Perrot, "Premières années de l'implantation du christianisme au Lesotho (1833–1847)," *Cahiers d'Etudes Africaines*, IV, 1 (1963), 97–125.

3. Sir Alan Pim, *Report on the Financial and Economic Situation of Basutoland* (H.M.S.O., Cmd 4907) (London, 1935), p. 49.

4. Quoted in Jack Halpern, *South Africa's Hostages: Basutoland, Bechuanaland, and Swaziland* (Baltimore, 1965), p. 220. This well-documented book has been used throughout as my main source for relevant background information.

5. Victor Ellenberger, *A Century of Mission Work in Basutoland: 1833–1933* (Morija, 1936), p. 66.

6. The *Livre d'or de la mission du Lessouto* (Paris, 1912) gives contradictory information about this: the foundation of *Leselinyana* is dated 1861 on p. 653 and 1867 on p. 504. Ellenberger (*A Century of Mission Work*, p. 126) gives the date as 1863. The collection at the Paris headquarters of the S.M.E.P. begins with the eleventh issue, which is dated February 1865; the first issue, therefore, is likely to have been printed in April 1864. But if the paper was not issued regularly at this early stage, Ellenberger's may well be the right date.

7. On early devotional printing in Southern Sotho, see the relevant section in Clement M. Doke, "Scripture Translation into Bantu Languages," *African Studies*, XVII (1958), 82–99.

8. Halpern, *South Africa's Hostages*, pp. 72–74, 79–80.

9. Doke, "Scripture Translation," p. 89, quoting the French text of Ellenberger's book, *Un siècle de mission au Lessouto* (p. 52).

10. Daniel P. Kunene and Randal A. Kirsch, *The Beginning of South African Vernacular Literature* [Los Angeles, 1967], pp. 43–46.

11. Northern Sotho, or Pedi, which is mainly spoken in the Transvaal, has kept its own individuality and is now one of the seven official vernacular languages of the Republic of South Africa. Creative writing in Pedi did not make a start until the 1940s. According to various census reports, quoted in *The Oxford History of South Africa* (Oxford, 1969), p. 131, Northern Sotho is spoken by some 970,000 people and Southern Sotho by about 1,140,000 people in the Republic. To the latter must be added the whole population of Lesotho, which numbered 638,857 in 1956 and was estimated at 754, 626 in 1965.

12. "Note on 'Mamosa, the Mother of Jonathan," in W. A. Norton, "Sesuto Praises of the Chiefs," *South African Journal of Science*, XVIII (1921–22), 441–453.

13. In "A War Song of the Basotho," *Journal of the New African Literature and the Arts*, no. 3 (Spring 1967), pp. 10–20, Daniel Kunene has given a thorough analysis of one traditional poem published by Sekese in *Leselinyana* of 11 Feb. 1891.

14. *Livre d'or*, p. 503. Job Moteane was one of the first three students who were graduated from the theological seminary in 1887; he was ordained on 6 Sept. 1891 (pp. 391–392), one of the first two Sotho ministers.

15. V. G. J. Sheddick, *The Southern Sotho* (London, 1953), pp. 54–55.

On the administration of law and justice among the Southern Sotho, see J.-E. Casalis, *Les Bassoutos* (Paris, 1859; 2d ed., 1930); J. C. Macgregor, "Some Notes on the Basuto Tribal System, Political and Social," *South African Journal of Science*, VI (1909), 276–281; E. A. T. Dutton, *The Basuto of Basutoland* (London, 1923), pp. 53–59; E. H. Ashton, *The Basuto* (London, 1952), pp. 246–248.

16. Austin Coates, *Basutoland* (London, 1966), p. 103.

17. Lord Hailey, *African Survey* (2d ed.; London, 1956), p. 272.

18. Not an uncommon occurrence in black Africa. According to his brief autobiographical note printed by Franz, Mofolo thought he was born in August 1877. The correct date was given me by the Rev. Albert Brutsch of Société des Missions Evangéliques de Paris. Biographical notices on Mofolo are numerous: anonymous obituary in *Bantu World*, 9 Oct. 1948, p. 1; Georges Dieterlen, "Thomas Mofolo," in *South African Outlook*, LXXVIII (1948), 168–169, reprinted in *African Affairs*, XLVIII, no. 190 (1949), 74–75; Edwin W. Smith, "Thomas Mofolo," in *Africa*, XIX (1949), 67–68; Peter Sulzer's "Nachwort" to his German translation, *Chaka der Zulu* (Zurich, 1953); John Jacobs, "Thomas Mofolo en de Negro-Afrikaanse literatuur," *Vlaamse Gids*, XLVII (1963), 199–206; Kunene and Kirsch, *The Beginning of South African Vernacular Literature*, pp. 43–46. The most convenient general survey of Mofolo's writings is Kunene, *The Works of Thomas Mofolo: Summaries and Critiques* (Los Angeles, University of California African Studies Center Occasional Paper no. 2), 1967.

19. In his introduction to Thomas Mofolo, *Chaka* (London, 1931), p. ix.

20. Marie Corelli's works have been favorites with African readers. In an article on "Marie Corelli in West Africa," *Ibadan*, no. 5 [Feb. 1959] pp. 19–21, Molly M. Mahood offers the following reasons for this writer's unexpected popularity in Africa: her works were among the first available to Africans with a reading knowledge of English, her strong stand against secular education and the "new woman," her exuberant prose, and her zest for the supernatural.

21. *Livre d'or*, p. 508. This novel was translated as *The Traveller of the East* (London, 1934); part of it was also translated into French: "Géorgiques et voyages du chrétien au Lessouto. Fekesi," *Le Monde non-chrétien*, n.s. no. 11 (1949), pp. 349–358. For Ghanaian readers, there is even an Ewe version (London, 1948). Some of the earliest reviews are by Alice Werner, "A Mosuto Novelist," *International Review of Missions*, XIV (1925), 428–436, and G. A. Gollock, "*The Traveller of the East*, by Thomas Mofolo," *Africa*, VII (1934), 510–511.

22. Quoted by Sir Henry Newbolt, intro. to Mofolo, *Chaka*, p. ix.

23. This is a traditional Sotho myth. It was apparently first recorded

by Thomas Arbousset, one of the first French missionaries to reach Lesotho in 1833, when he was 22, with Eugène Casalis, then aged 19. The same story was later to be dramatized by S. M. Mofokeng in *Senkatana* (Johannesburg, 1952), one of the best creative works in Southern Sotho.

24. P.-D. Beuchat, *Do the Bantu Have a Literature?* (Johannesburg, [1963]), p. 18.

25. Halpern, *South Africa's Hostages*, p. 205. In "The Provision of a Christian Literature for Africa," *International Review of Missions*, XV (1926), 506–514, C. E. Wilson claimed that there were thirty-three African versions of *Pilgrim's Progress* in existence by 1923.

26. P.-D. Cole-Beuchat, "Literary Composition," in *The Teaching of Southern Sotho*, ed. James Walton (Maseru, 1961) pp. 56–68.

27. Norton, "Sesuto Praises of the Chiefs," p. 441.

28. *Livre d'or*, pp. 508–509.

29. The quotations from *Pitseng* can be found in Daniel Kunene's pamphlet on Mofolo. Peter Sulzer has prepared a German translation of *Pitseng*, which has not yet been printed, although one chapter appeared, with a brief critical introduction, in the *Zürichsee-Zeitung* of 28 March 1970. Sulzer has dealt extensively with this novel in an unpublished paper, "Was ist an der afrikanischen Literatur afrikanisch?" (1967).

30. Minnie Martin, *Basutoland: Its Legends and Customs* (London, 1903), pp. 80–81.

31. Coates, *Basutoland*, p. 107.

32. Kunene, *The Works of Thomas Mofolo*, p. 15.

33. Sulzer, "Der weisse Mann in schwarzer Sicht," *Afrikanischer Heimatkalender 1963* (Westhoek), p. 66.

34. Many English-speaking scholars spell the name Shaka, although Tshaka is also found occasionally. I shall, however, use Mofolo's French spelling, Chaka, which was taught him by the French missionaries.

35. Kunene and Kirsch, *The Beginning of South African Vernacular Literature*, p. 44.

36. The section on *Chaka* appeared, in slightly different form, as "An African Tragedy of Hubris: Thomas Mofolo's *Chaka*," in Brom Weber, ed., *Sense and Sensibility in Twentieth-Century Writing: A Gathering in Memory of William Van O'Connor* (Carbondale, 1970); it is here reproduced by permission of the editor.

37. *The Cambridge History of the British Empire*, VIII South Africa (2d ed., Cambridge, 1963), p. 38.

38. *Ibid.*, p. 307.

39. The English version by F. H. Dutton is entitled *Chaka: A His-*

torical Romance (London, 1931; repr. ed., 1968). Page references are to this translation.

40. This is the subtitle of the French translation by Victor Ellenberger (Paris, 1940).

41. Sulzer, "Nachwort," *Chaka der Zulu*, p. 240.

42. Kunene, *The Works of Thomas Mofolo*, p. 26.

43. Ezekiel Mphahlele, *The African Image* (New York, 1962), p. 171.

44. Werner, "Some Native Writers in South Africa," *Journal of the African Society*, XXX (1931), 27-39.

45. Review in *South African Outlook*, LXII (1932), p. 19.

46. M. L[eenhardt], "Chaka. Fidélité et infidélité chez les païens," *Le Monde non-chrétien*, I (1947), 346-348.

47. Luc Decaunes, "Une épopée bantoue," *Présence Africaine*, no. 5 (1948), pp. 883-886.

48. Sulzer, "Nachwort" to *Chaka der Zulu*, pp. 240-241.

49. Beuchat, *Do the Bantu Have a Literature?*, p. 19.

50. L. B. Saratovskaya, "Periodizatsia literatury Bantu v Yuzhno-Afrikanstrom Souze (nachalniy period)," *Narodi Azii i Afriki*, I (1963), 117-127. This critic also regresses beyond even Werner and Jabavu, claiming that Mofolo was subjected to the influence of the official South African historians who were bent on reviling the Zulus' heroic struggle against colonialism, so that he represented Chaka as a "beastly power-drunk creature."

51. Mphahlele, *African Image*, p. 172.

52. Claude Wauthier, *The Literature and Thought of Modern Africa* (New York, 1966), p. 96.

53. Kunene, *The Works of Thomas Mofolo*, p. 26.

54. See also on *Chaka*, Smith's review in *Africa*, IV (1931), 506-508; Jacobs, "Les épopées de Soundjata et de Chaka: une étude comparée" *Aequatoria*, XXV (1962), 121-124; O. R. Dathorne, "Thomas Mofolo and the Sotho Hero," *New African*, V (1966), 152-153.

55. This is the theme of *Song of a Goat*, a play by Nigeria's John Pepper Clark. Such attitudes are, of course, not restricted to African societies. It would be interesting to compare this trend in Mofolo's novel and Clark's tragedy with Federico Garcia Lorca's *Yerma*.

56. According to recent historians, Chaka was actually impotent. See for example Donald R. Morris, *The Washing of the Spears: A History of the Rise of the Zulu Nation under Shaka and Its Fall in the Zulu War of 1879* (New York, 1965).

57. Janheinz Jahn, *Geschichte der neoafrikanischen Literatur* (Düsseldorf, 1966), p. 108.

58. I am gratefully indebted to the Reverend Albert Brutsch for the information in the next two paragraphs.

59. *Africa*, XIX (1949), p. 337.

60. Kunene and Kirsch, *The Beginning of South African Vernacular Literature*, p. 8.

61. We may recall at this point that in 1636 Richelieu obliged Corneille to delete a few lines from *Le Cid* because they seemed to glorify the illegal custom of the duel. Actually, they were spoken in character, and the apology they contained is negated by the total context of the play. Richelieu, however, was not concerned with aesthetics but with consolidating absolute monarchy, and he feared—no doubt rightly from his political viewpoint—the electrifying effect that such lines, taken out of context, might have on a seventeenth-century aristocratic audience.

62. Jahn, *Geschichte*, p. 107.

63. Sulzer, "Nachwort" to *Chaka, der Zulu*, p. 253.

64. This information was most obligingly conveyed to me by the Reverend Brutsch.

65. *Le Monde non-chrétien*, no. 11 (1949), p. 350.

66. Halpern, *South Africa's Hostages*, p. 119.

67. *South African Outlook*, LXVI (1936), 254–256.

68. Kunene and Kirsch, *The Beginning of South African Vernacular Literature*, p. 45. This piece of information is derived from Sulzer, *Chaka der Zulu*, p. 254.

69. *Livre d'or*, p. 419.

70. Werner, "Some Native Writers," p. 38.

71. Leonard Barnes, *The New Boer War* (London, 1932), quoted by Halpern, *South Africa's Hostages*, p. 112.

72. *Livre d'or*, p. 505.

73. Franz, "The Literature of Lesotho," pp. 156–157.

74. *Livre d'or*, p. 414.

75. *Ibid.*, p. 506.

76. Mofolo Bulane, "Poets of Lesotho," *New African*, VI (Oct. 1967), 19–23. Bulane has discussed several of the poems recorded by Mangoaela in "Then and Now: The Praise Poem in Southern Sotho," *New African*, VII, 1 (1968), 40–43.

77. *South African Outlook* LXVII (1937), 303–304.

78. For a large part of my information on Catholic creative writing in Lesotho, I am personally indebted to the patience and kindness of Father Marcel Ferragne, O.M.I. Three of his essays (two of them mimeographed) seem to be about the only published sources on printing activities at the Mazenod Press: "L'oeuvre de presse catholique au Basutoland," *La Voix du Basutoland*, no. 54 (Jan.–March 1953), pp. 19–26, "Le Centre catholique de Mazenod, au Basutoland" (1965), and "L'oeuvre de presse catholique au Lesotho" (1967). More recently, the Social Centre in Roma issued Ferragne's mimeo pamphlet, *Essai d'his-*

toire de littérature catholique en Sesotho [1970]. Some useful background information can be found in a special Basutoland issue of the Catholic missionary review *Grands Lacs* (July 1949).

79. Coates, *Basutoland*, p. 103.

80. Justinus Sechefo, "Vite! le Chef arrive! . . ." *Grands Lacs*, LXIV (1949), 10/11/12, 52–54.

81. On all this, see Halpern, *South Africa's Hostages*, pp. 207–208.

82. Bulane, "Poets of Lesotho," pp. 19–23. The quotations come from that article. One of the poems, however, had been translated into French by Georges Dieterlen, "Bitleng la Moshoeshoe (A la tombe de Moshesh)," *Africa*, XVII (1947), 206–207.

83. Halpern, *South Africa's Hostages*, p. 118.

84. Doke, "The Native Languages of South Africa," *African Studies*, I (1942), 139.

85. Halpern, *South Africa's Hostages*, pp. 207–208.

86. *African Studies*, III (1944), 168–169.

87. The *Lekhotla la bafo*, or "Commoners' League," is an association started in 1919 by Josiel Lefela (born ca. 1890) in order to preserve the national rights of Lesotho and to improve the lot of the ordinary peasants. His first contacts with South African Communists took place in 1928. At about the same time, a Communist party was founded in Lesotho—the only Communist party then operating South of the Sudan. In May 1962, Joziel Lefela sent a letter to the Soviet government and to Khrushchev personally, requesting support for Lesotho independence at the United Nations. *Nizam Newsletter*, IV, 5 (1962), p. 4.

88. Halpern, *South Africa's Hostages*, pp. 74–77.

89. Hailey, *African Survey*, pp. 700–701.

90. International Labour Conference, *The Recruiting of Labour in the Colonies* (London, 1935), p. 36.

91. Richard P. Stevens, *Lesotho, Botswana and Swaziland* (London, 1967), p. 56.

92. Halpern, *South Africa's Hostages*, pp. 209–210.

93. Guma refers to *Pitso ea linonyana* as "the first attempt at written drama in Southern Sotho." *The Form, Content and Technique of Traditional Literature in Southern Sotho*, p. 31.

94. Cole-Beuchat, "Literary Composition," pp. 56–68.

95. Review in *African Studies*, III (1944), p. 162.

96. Lenake, "Satire in K. E. Ntsane se gedigte," *Limi*, no. 8 (June 1969), pp. 60–82.

97. S. M. M[ofokeng], in *African Studies*, VI (1947), 99–100.

98. Moloi, "The Germination of Southern Sotho Poetry," pp. 28–59.

99. Letele's review, *African Studies*, XVI (1957), 81–82.

100. S. M. M[ofokeng], in *African Studies*, XIV (1955) 142–143.

101. Lenake, "A Brief Survey of Modern Literature in the South African Bantu Languages," p. 77.

102. *Africa*, XVIII (1948), 74.

103. *South African Outlook*, LXVI (1936), 23.

104. *African Studies*, III (1944), 163.

105. Halpern, *South Africa's Hostages*, p. 124. For more details, see G. I. Jones, *Basutoland Medicine Murder* (London, 1951).

106. Review in *African Studies*, XV (1956), 154–155.

107. Lenake, "Brief Survey," p. 77.

108. Reviewed by G. Mabille in *African Studies*, VI (1947), 211.

109. *Times Literary Supplement* (6 Feb. 1953), p. 85.

110. This may be an allusion to some contemporary event, or a reminder of the student rebellion at Lovedale in 1920, when the theological students set fire to some buildings as a protest against bad bread. See Edward Roux, *Time Longer than Rope* (Madison, Wisc., 1964), p. 156.

111. As a politician, B. M. Khaketla has a biographical notice in Ronald Segal's *Political Africa* (New York, 1961); much information about his political career is also to be gleaned from the books of Halpern and Stevens.

112. Beuchat, *Do the Bantu Have a Literature?*, p. 22.

113. Lenake, "Brief Survey," p. 78.

114. *African Studies*, XII (1953), 139.

115. Cole-Beuchat, "Literary Composition," p. 63.

116. *Ibid.*, p. 78.

117. *Ibid.*, p. 66.

118. *African Studies*, XIV (1955), p. 142.

119. Moloi, "Germination of Southern Sotho Poetry," pp. 48–53.

120. From Daniel Kunene's translation in Jack Cope and Uys Krige, eds., *The Penguin Book of South African Verse* (Harmondsworth, 1968), pp. 262–264.

121. *Contact*, 23 March 1961, quoted by Segal, *Political Africa*, pp. 139–140.

122. Stevens, *Lesotho, Botswana and Swaziland*, p. 63.

123. See D. T. C[ole]'s obituary of Mofokeng in *African Studies*, XVI (1957), 177–178. For complementary details, I am indebted to Miss Beuchat of the University of the Witwatersrand. A critical article in Afrikaans on "S. M. Mofokeng: *Leetong (1954)*" was published recently by P. S. Groenewald in *Limi*, no. 10 (June 1970), 58–61.

124. Beuchat, *Do the Bantu Have a Literature?*, pp. 22–23.

125. Information kindly supplied by Benjamin Leshoai himself.

126. Guma, *Form, Content and Technique*, pp. 194–197.

127. *Ibid.*, p. 9.

128. See Gérard, "Littérature francophone d'Afrique: le temps de la relève," *Revue Nouvelle*, XLIX, 2 (1969), 198-204.

129. Guma, "Southern Sotho Literature Today," pp. 25-29.

130. Halpern, *South Africa's Hostages*, p. 213.

CHAPTER 3

1. G. P. Lestrade, "European Influence Upon the Development of Bantu Language and Literature," in I. Schapera, ed., *Western Civilization and the Natives of South Africa* (London, 1934), p. 124.

2. Alice Werner, "Some Native Writers in South Africa," *Journal of the African Society*, XXX (1931), 36.

3. Trevor Cope, ed., *Izibongo: Zulu Praise Poems* (London, 1968), p. 3.

4. Some general information about Zulu written literature can be found in Benedict W. Vilakazi, "The Conception and Development of Poetry in Zulu," *Bantu Studies*, XXX (1938), 105-134: Vilakazi, "Some Aspects of Zulu Literature," *African Studies*, I (1942), 270-274; D. McK. Malcolm, "Zulu Literature," *Africa*, XIX (1949), 33-39; Cyril L. S. Nyembezi, *A Review of Zulu Literature* (Durban, 1961); D. B. Z. Ntuli, "A Brief Survey of Modern Literature in the South African Bantu Languages: Zulu," *Limi*, no. 6 (June 1968), pp. 28-36; Daniel P. Kunene and Ronald A. Kirsch, *The Beginning of South African Vernacular Literature* (Los Angeles, 1967), contains short biographical notices of only two Zulu authors, John L. Dube and Benedict W. Vilakazi. The most informative source, however, is Vilakazi, "The Oral and Written Literature in Nguni" (Ph.D. diss., Johannesburg, 1945), a microfilmed copy of which was made available to me through the University of the Witwatersrand Library. Also useful is Raymond [Mazisi] Kunene, "An Analytical Survey of Zulu Poetry Both Traditional and Modern" (Ph. D. diss., Durban, 1961), a microfilmed copy of which was kindly supplied by the University of Natal Library.

5. Clement M. Doke, "Scripture Translation into Bantu Languages," *African Studies*, XVII (1958), 82-99.

6. Nyembezi, "Honor for an African Author," in *South African Outlook*, LXXXVIII (1958), p. 156.

7. Nyembezi, *A Review of Zulu Literature*, p. 3.

8. Mazisi [Raymond] Kunene, "Portrait of Magolwane—the Great Zulu Poet," *Cultural Events in Africa*, no. 32 (July 1967), pp. 1-14.

9. On the precolonial history of Zulu poetry, see the works of Trevor Cope, Benedict W. Vilakazi and Raymond Kunene.

10. Vilakazi, "The Conception and Development of Poetry in Zulu," p. 108.

11. Vilakazi, "Oral and Written Literature," p. 308.

12. The main printed source concerning Isaiah Shembe is his biography in Zulu by John L. Dube, *uShembe* (Pietermaritzburg, 1936). His work and ideas have been extensively studied of late, especially Absalom Vilakazi, " 'Isonto Lamanazaretha': The Church of the Nazarites" (Ph.D. diss., Hartford Seminary Foundation, 1954); Bengt G. M. Sundkler, *Bantu Prophets in South Africa* (London, 1948), which is here quoted in the 1961 edition; Gerhardus Cornelis Oosthuizen, *The Theology of a South African Messiah: An Analysis of the Hymnal of "The Church of the Nazarites"* (Leiden, 1967). See also E. L. Roberts, "Shembe, the Man and His Work" (M.A. thesis, Pretoria: the University of South Africa, 1936), F. R. Lehmann, "Eine Form von Religionsmischung in Südafrika. Die amaNazaretha-Kirche in Natal," in *Von fremden Völkern und Kulturen. Beiträge zur Völkerkunde, Hans Plischke zum 65. Geburtstag* (Düsseldorf, 1955), pp. 183–193; Katesa Schlosser, *Eingeborenenkirchen in Süd- und Südwestafrika. Ihre Geschichte und Sozialstruktur* (Kiel, 1958) especially pp. 243–245.

13. Dube, *uShembe*, p. 34; Sundkler, *Bantu Prophets*, p. 125.

14. According to Sundkler (*Bantu Prophets*, p. 50) "this was probably an offshoot from the Negro Baptist groups which had begun their work in Natal in 1899, and who as 'Cushites,' practiced the new sacrament of foot-washing. In Shembe's system of purification rites this sacrament occupied a prominent position."

15. Oosthuizen, *Theology of a South African Messiah*, p. 3.

16. Schlosser, "Profane Ursachen des Anschlusses an Separatistenkirchen in Süd- and Südwestafrika," in Ernst Benz, ed., *Messianische Kirchen, Sekten und Bewegungen im heutigen Afrika* (Leiden, 1965), pp. 23–45.

17. Sundkler, *Bantu Prophets*, p. 111.

18. Ernst Damann, "Das Christusverständnis in nachchristlichen Kirchen und Sekten Afrikas," in Benz, *Messianische Kirchen*, pp. 1–21.

19. Oosthuizen, *Theology of a South African Messiah*, p. 146.

20. *Ibid.*, p. 3.

21. Raymond Kunene, "An Analytical Survey of Zulu Poetry," p. 197.

22. Vilakazi, "The Conception and Development of Poetry in Zulu," pp. 124–127.

23. Sundkler, *Bantu Prophets*, pp. 194–195.

24. *Ibid.*, p. 196.

25. Oosthuizen, *Theology of a South African Messiah*, p. 20.

26. For a detailed discussion of the problems of dating and authorship, see *ibid.*, pp. 7–8.

27. For a detailed analysis of the hymns, see Sundkler, *Bantu Prophets,* pp. 194-197.

28. Oosthuizen, *Theology of a South African Messiah,* p. 9.

29. Hymn no. 46, Sundkler, *Bantu Prophets,* pp. 196 and 334.

30. Hymn no. 34, *ibid.,* pp. 283-284.

31. Hymn no. 216, Oosthuizen, *Theology of a South African Messiah,* p. 189. In Shembe's hymns, *Nkosi* is a term used to refer to Jehovah, to the Zulu kings, and to the prophet himself. *Ibid.,* pp. 37-41.

32. Sundkler, *Bantu Prophets,* p. 195.

33. *Ibid.,* p. 197.

34. *Ibid.,* p. 195.

35. Oosthuizen, *Theology of a South African Messiah,* p. 155.

36. Vilakazi, "The Conception and Development of Poetry in Zulu," p. 124.

37. Raymond Kunene, "An Analytical Survey of Zulu Poetry," pp. 198-200.

38. D. R. O. Thomas, "Drama and Native Education," *South African Outlook,* LXII (1932), 238-240.

39. See on this, F. J. Amon d'Aby, *La Côte d'Ivoire dans la cité africaine* (Paris, 1951), pp. 135-147, 154-163, and several articles by the promoter of the movement, Charles Béart: "Towards a French-African Culture (William Ponty Training Centre, Dakar)," *Oversea Education,* XVII (1946), 357-368; XVIII (1946), 403-418; "A propos du théâtre africain," *Traits d'Union,* XV (1957), 103-104; "Les origines du théâtre dans le monde. Position actuelle du théâtre africain," *Comptes rendus mensuels des séances de l'Académie des sciences d'Outre-Mer,* XXII, 4 (1962), 143-163.

40. Vilakazi was the first to call learned attention to those early dramatic activities in his 1942 article in *African Studies;* his account was enlarged in "Oral and Written Literature," pp. 315-316. It is based mainly on a few papers written or edited by Bernard Huss in the *Native Teachers' Journal* for 1921: "Education Through the Drama," pp. 48-50; "A Zulu *Inganekwana* Dramatized," pp. 50-52; "A Short and Easy Drama in Zulu," pp. 95-97.

41. Vilakazi's account of this second phase in Zulu drama in "Oral and Written Literature," p. 316, is based on an article by T. C. Lloyd, "The Bantu Tread the Footlights," *South African Opinion* (8 March 1935), pp. 3-5.

42. Vilakazi, "Oral and Written Literature," p. 317.

43. Huss, *Native Teachers' Journal,* II (1921), 58.

44. H. W. Peet, "Zulu Choir in London," *Southern Workman* (Nov. 1930), pp. 521-522.

45. R. T. Caluza, "African Music," *Southern Workman* (April 1931), pp. 152–155.

46. Vilakazi, "The Conception and Development of Poetry in Zulu," p. 132.

47. Yvonne Huskisson, "The Story of Bantu Music," *Bantu*, XV (1968), p. 19.

48. Vilakazi, "Some Aspects of Zulu Literature," p. 273.

49. J. F. A. Swartz, "A Hobbyist Looks at Zulu and Xhosa Songs," *African Music*, I, 3 (1956), 29–33.

50. Absalom Vilakazi, *Zulu Transformations: A Study of the Dynamics of Social Change* (Pietermaritzburg, 1962), pp. 76–77.

51. Nyembezi, *A Review of Zulu Literature*, p. 6.

52. Werner, "Some Native Writers," p. 36.

53. B. W. Vilakazi, "Oral and Written Literature," p. 295.

54. Vilakazi, "Some Aspects of Zulu Literature," p. 273.

55. *Ibid.*, p. 271.

56. Lestrade, "European Influence upon the Development of Bantu Language and Literature," p. 123.

57. Vilakazi, "Oral and Written Literature," p. 312.

58. *Ibid.*, p. 313.

59. Apart from the brief sketch in Kunene and Kirsch, *Beginning of South African Vernacular Literature*, there is as yet no full-scale biography of Dube. The following account has largely been reconstructed from the many isolated data scattered in such more general works as Edward Roux's *Time Longer Than Rope* (Madison, Wisc., 1949) or Mary Benson's *The African Patriots: The Story of the African National Congress of South Africa* (London, 1963).

60. Information kindly provided by Oberlin College.

61. See *African Sabbath Recorder*, 6 January 1913, p. 4, quoted in George Shepperson and Thomas Price, *Independent African: John Chilembwe, and the Origin, Setting and Significance of the Nyasaland Native Rising of 1915* (Edinburgh, 1958), p. 92.

62. Dube, "A Native View of Christianity in South Africa," *Missionary Review of the World*, n.s. XIV (1901), 421–426.

63. Dube, "Practical Christianity Among the Zulus," *Missionary Review of the World*, n.s. XX (1907), 370–373.

64. Nyembezi, *A Review of Zulu Literature*, p. 6.

65. Vilakazi, "Oral and Written Literature," p. 297.

66. Dube, "Zulu and the Missionary Outlook in Natal," *Missionary Review of the World*, n.s. XX (1907), p. 205.

67. Benson, *African Patriots*, p. 29.

68. *Ibid.*, p. 33.

69. *Ibid.*, p. 40.
70. Vilakazi, "Oral and Written Literature," p. 298.
71. See *South African Outlook*, LXXVI (1946), 63–64.
72. Quoted in Benson, *African Patriots*, p. 61.
73. *Ibid.*, p. 62.
74. Page references are to the English translation.
75. The Swazi are a Nguni people, whose culture is very similar to that of the Zulu. They were constituted into a unified nation as a response to the challenge of Zulu imperialism by Sobhuza I, who played much the same role as Moshoeshoe did among the Sotho. They received their name from Sobhuza's successor, Mswazi, who died in 1868.
76. Ntuli, "A Brief Survey of Modern Literature," p. 28.
77. Vilakazi, "Oral and Written Literature," p. vi.
78. *Ibid.*, pp. 298–299.
79. *Ibid.*, p. 289.
80. Vilakazi, "Some Aspects of Zulu Literature," p. 272.
81. Nyembezi, *Review of Zulu Literature*, pp. 6–7.
82. Quoted in Sundkler, *Bantu Prophets*, p. 160.
83. See review by Malcolm in *Bantu Studies*, XXVI (1934), 213.
84. Ntuli, "A Brief Survey of Modern Literature," p. 33.
85. *South African Outlook*, LXVII (1937), 246–249.
86. Alexander Kerr, *Fort Hare 1915–48: The Evolution of an African College* (London, 1968), pp. 201–202.
87. Communicated by Oberlin College.
88. Roux, *Time Longer Than Rope*, p. 288.
89. Bulletin on the position in Natal issued by the Department of Justice, April 22, 1931, quoted in Roux, *Time Longer Than Rope*, p. 251; see also Benson, *African Patriots*, p. 59.
90. Benson, *African Patriots*, pp. 90–91.
91. *Ibid.*, p. 93.
92. Figures drawn from Sundkler, *Bantu Prophets*, p. 33, and from W. M. Macmillan, *Complex South Africa* (London 1930), pp. 283–284.
93. Vilakazi, *"Oral and Written Literature,"* p. 332.
94. *Ibid.*, p. 333.
95. *South African Outlook*, LXXXII (1952), p. 77.
96. Donald R. Morris, *The Washing of the Spears: A History of the Rise of the Zulu Nation Under Shaka, and Its Fall in the Zulu War of 1879* (New York, 1965), p. 194.
97. Vilakazi, "Oral and Written Literature," p. 333.
98. Peter Sulzer, *Schwarze Intelligenz* (Zurich, 1955), p. 95.
99. *South African Outlook*, LXVI (1936), 254–256.
100. *South African Outlook*, LXVII (1937), 77.

101. *South African Outlook*, LXVII (1937), 246–249.

102. Herbert I. E. Dhlomo, "Drama and the African," *South African Outlook*, LXVI (1936), 232–235.

103. This passage was to be reprinted, in a more elaborate context, in Dhlomo's next published article, soon to be discussed, which appeared in *Bantu Studies* for March 1939 (p. 44).

104. Quoted in Vilakazi, "The Conception and Development of Poetry in Zulu," p. 108. Lestrade's article originally appeared in *The Critic*.

105. Actually, it is probably truer to say that the poet makes use of an imagery that is not private and personal in any European sense, but is readily understandable only to the limited social group for which he composes.

106. Dhlomo, "The Nature and Variety of Tribal Drama," *Bantu Studies*, XVIII (1939), 33–48.

107. Dhlomo, "African Drama and Poetry," *South African Outlook*, LXIX (1939), 88–90.

108. *African Studies*, II (1943), 175.

109. Dhlomo, "African Drama and Research," *Native Teachers' Journal*, XVIII (1939), 129–132.

110. Vilakazi, "African Drama and Poetry," *South African Outlook*, LXIX (1939), 166–167.

111. See Albert Gérard, "Le poète et les palmiers: sur un sonnet de J. J. Rabéarivelo," *Marche Romane*, XVI, 1 (1966), 15–20.

112. Vilakazi, "Oral and Written Literature," p. 278.

113. Ezekiel Mphahlele, *African Image* (New York, 1962), p. 186.

114. Vilakazi, "Oral and Written Literature," pp. 277–278.

115. Dhlomo, "Zulu Folk Poetry," *Native Teachers' Journal*, XXVIII (1947–48), 5–7, 46–50, 84–87.

116. See Dhlomo's obituary in *South African Outlook*, LXXXVI (1956), 163.

117. "Vilakazi Memorial Fund," *South African Outlook*, LXXVIII (1948), 159.

118. From Nyembezi's Introduction to *Zulu Horizons: The Vilakazi Poems* (London, 1962), pp. 5–8.

119. Ntuli, "A Brief Survey of Modern Literature," p. 28.

120. J. Dexter Taylor, "*Inkondlo kaZulu*," *Bantu Studies*, IX (1935), 163–165.

121. Nyembezi, *Review of Zulu Literature*, p. 8.

122. P.-D. Beuchat, *Do the Bantu Have a Literature?* (Johannesburg [1963]), p. 12.

123. Nyembezi, *Review of Zulu Literature*, p. 7.

124. Vilakazi, "The Conception and Development of Poetry in Zulu."

125. For detailed analyses of some of Vilakazi's poems, see Raymond Kunene's "An Analytical Survey of Zulu Poetry Both Traditional and Modern," pp. 205–215.

126. Vilakazi, *Zulu Horizons*, p. 64. All quotations are from this English version.

127. See above, pp. 230–237.

128. Preface to Vilakazi, *Zulu Horizons*, pp. 7–8.

129. Quotations are from the English version in *Zulu Horizons*.

130. Ntuli, "A Brief Survey of Modern Literature," p. 29.

131. Absalom Vilakazi, *Zulu Transformations*, p. 37.

132. B. W. Vilakazi, "Oral and Written Literature," p. 328.

133. *Ibid.*, pp. 328–331.

134. *Ibid.*, p. 352.

135. Ntuli, "A Brief Survey of Modern Literature," p. 32.

136. See Vilakazi, "Oral and Written Literature," p. 353.

137. I am indebted for these biographical data to Professor Trevor Cope of the University of Natal. See also notice in J. M. S. Matsebula's anthology, *Iqoqo lezinkondlo (A Collection of Poems)* (Pietermaritzburg, n.d.).

138. *Bantu Studies*, XIV (1940), 201–203.

139. See also Malcolm's discussion of the book in "Zulu Literature," pp. 38–39.

140. Ntuli, "A Brief Survey of Modern Literature," p. 34.

141. Raymond Kunene, "An Analytical Survey of Zulu Poetry, Both Traditional and Modern," pp. 216–217.

142. *Bantu Studies*, VII (1933), 28–31.

143. Doke, "The Native Languages of South Africa," *African Studies* I (1942), 138.

144. Brian Bunting, *The Rise of the South African Reich* (Harmondsworth, 1964), p. 218.

145. Beuchat, *Do the Bantu Have A Literature?*, p. 19.

146. Ntuli, "A Brief Survey of Modern Literature," p. 30.

147. Most of the information and quotations in the next few paragraphs come from *ibid.*

148. "Littérature et résistance en Afrique du Sud," *Oeuvres Afro-Asiatiques*, I (1968), 2, 90–99. Although printed anonymously, this report was the work of Raymond [Masizi] Kunene.

149. Lewis Nkosi, "Die afrikanische Literatur in Südafrika," *Afrika Heute* (1 July 1964), pp. 168–170.

150. See notice in *Cultural Events in Africa*, no. 32 (July 1967), p. 2.

151. Raymond Kunene, "An Analytical Survey of Zulu Poetry," pp. 201–202.

152. *Ibid.*, p. 220.
153. *Ibid.*, p. 223.
154. *Ibid.*, p. 202.

CHAPTER 4

1. See for example the sections on "Abyssinian" and Galla folk literature in H. Munro Chadwick and N. Kershaw Chadwick, *The Growth of Literature* (Cambridge, 1940), III: 503–568.

2. For authoritative historical accounts of Ge'ez literature, see especially Enno Littman, "Die äthiopische Literatur," in *Handbuch der Orientalistik*, Band III, *Semitistik* (Leiden, 1954), pp. 375–385; Enrico Cerulli, *Storia della letteratura etiopica*, 3d ed. (Florence, 1968).

3. A convenient selection of excerpts is to be found in Richard K. P. Pankhurst, ed., *The Ethiopian Royal Chronicles* (Addis Ababa, 1967).

4. Donald N. Levine, *Wax and Gold: Tradition and Innovation in Ethiopian Culture* (Chicago, 1965), p. 8.

5. C. Mondon-Vidailhet, "Le Rhétorique éthiopienne," *Journal Asiatique*, X (1907), 305–329.

6. Ge'ez prosody was first described in Europe by Job Ludolf (1624–1704). A recent and extensive bibliography of the subject will be found in Anton Schall, *Zur äthiopischen Verskunst* (Wiesbaden, 1961).

7. These poems were first printed in Europe by Ignazio Guidi, in "Le canzoni Geez-amariña in onore di Re abissini," *Rendiconti della giche*, V (1889). They were first studied by Littmann in *Die altamharischen Kaiserlieder* (Strassburg, 1914).
Reale Accademia dei Lincei, Classe di scienze morali, storiche e filolo-
8. Charles William Isenberg also wrote works of more secular inspiration, such as his 391-page Amharic *History of God's Kingdom from the Creation of the World to Our Day*, which was printed in St. Chrischona, Switzerland, in 1893.

9. Stephen Wright, "Amharic Literature," *Something*, no. 1 [1963], pp. 11–23.

10. Pierre Comba, *Inventaire des livres amhariques figurant dans la collection éthiopienne à la Bibliothèque de l'University College d'Addis Abeba. Avril 1959* (Addis Ababa, 1961), p. 94.

11. On the early history of printing in Amharic, see Eugen Mittwoch, "Literarisches Morgenrot in Abessinien," *Deutsche Literaturzeitung*, vol. XLV, n.s. I, (1924), col. 1869–1874; Marcel Cohen, "La naissance d'une littérature imprimée en amharique," *Journal Asiatique*, CCVI (1925), 348–363; Stephen Gaselee, "The Beginnings of Printing in Abyssinia," *The Library*, XI (1931), 93–95; and the notices in Wright, *Ethiopian Incunabula* (Addis Ababa, 1967).

12. Apart from the articles of Mittwoch and Cohen, and Cerulli's book already mentioned, the main sources for our knowledge of modern Amharic literature are: Guidi, "Contributi alla storia letteraria di Abissinia," *Rendiconti della Reale Accademia dei Lincei,* ser. VI, XXXI (1922), 65–94, 185–218; Cerulli, "Nuove idee nell' Etiopia e nuova letteratura amarica," *Oriente Moderno,* VI (1926), 167–173; Guidi, *Breve storia della letteratura etiopica* (Rome, 1932); Guidi, "Le odierne letterature dell'Imperio Etiopico," *Atti del Reale Istituto Veneto di Scienze, Lettere ed'Arti,* XCII (1932–33), 935–942; Cohen, "La langue littéraire amharique," *Comptes rendus du Groupe linguistique d'Etudes chamito-sémitiques,* II (1937), 95; Elena Sengal, "Note sulla letteratura moderna amarica," *Annali dell'Istituto Universitario Orientale di Napoli,* n.s. II (1943), 291–302; "Amharic Literature," in *Guide Book of Ethiopia* (Addis Ababa, 1954), pp. 407–416; Wright, "Literature and Fine Arts," in *Haile Sellassie I Silver Jubilee,* ed. David Abner Talbot (The Hague, [1955]), pp. 321–335; Comba, "Une année de publications en langue amharique," *Annales d'Ethiopie,* I (1955), 151–152; II (1957), 253–264; III (1959), 301–312. Martino Mario Moreno, "Letteratura etiopica," in *Civiltà dell' Oriente* (Rome, 1957), II: 27–58; Comba, "Bref aperçu sur les débuts de la littérature de langue amharique et sur ses tendances actuelles," *Ethiopia Observer,* II (1958), 125–128; Wright, "Amharic Literature," pp. 11–23; Comba, "Le roman dans la littérature éthiopienne de langue amharique," *Journal of Semitic Studies,* IX (1964), 173–186; Lanfranco Ricci, "Romanzo e novella: due esperimenti della letteratura amarica attuale," *Journal of Semitic Studies,* IX (1964), 144–172; Menghistu Lemma, "Modern Amharic Literature: The Task Ahead," *Voice of Ethiopia* (19 May 1965), pp. 2–4; Teferra Shiawl, "Äthiopiens zeitgenössische Literatur," *Afrika heute* (15 Dec. 1965), pp. 322–325; Shiawl, "Ethiopia's Literature Today: a Brief Survey," *Afrika* (Cologne), VII, 1 (1966), 14; Menghistu Lemma, "Introduction to Modern Ethiopian Literature," mimeo. paper read at the African-Scandinavian Writers' Conference (Stockholm, Feb. 6–9, 1967); Albert S. Gérard, "Amharic Creative Literature: The Early Phase," *Journal of Ethiopian Studies,* VI, 2 (1968), 39–59; this article is reprinted here in slightly modified form by kind permission of the editor. See also Wright's notice, "Ethiopian Literature" in the *Encyclopaedia Britannica.*

13. Pankhurst, "The Foundations of Education, Printing, Newspapers, Book Production, Libraries and Literacy in Ethiopia," *Ethiopia Observer,* VII (1962), 241–290. This article is an important source of biographical information about early Ethiopian writers. With regard to Gäbrä Egzi'abehér, other sources are Cohen's "La Naissance d'une littérature"; Sengal's "Nota sulla letteratura"; Dr. Mérab's *Impressions*

d'Ethiopie (L'Abyssinie sous Menelik), vol. III (Paris, 1929), especially pp. 359–360; Murad Kamil's *Das Land des Negus* (Innsbrück, 1953), p. 19. More research, however, should be devoted to this pioneer, four of whose poems are conveniently reprinted, with an English translation, in J. I. Eadie, *An Amharic Reader* (Cambridge, 1924), pp. 193–202.

14. The best extant biographical notice (to which my attention was obligingly called by Afäwärq's son Giovanni Ghevre-Jesus) is to be found in *Chi è dell' Eritrea*, s.v. "Afework, Ghevrejesus." More information can be gleaned from Pankhurst, "Foundations of Education," and from several of his other recent articles, such as "The Effects of War in Ethiopian History," *Ethiopia Observer*, VII (1963), 142–164, and "Misoneism and Innovation in Ethiopian History," *Ethiopia Observer*, VII (1964), 287–320; in those very informative articles, Pankhurst provides a full account of the *Guide du voyageur en Abyssinie*. On Afäwärq's other works, see especially Cerulli, "Recenti pubblicazioni abissine in amarico," *Oriente Moderno*, VI (1926), 555–557, which reviews the account of Ras Täfäri's journey to Jibuti and Aden, and two articles by Luigi Fusella, "Il *Lebb wållad tārik*," *Rassegna di studi etiopici*, X (1951), 56–70 and "Il *Dāgmāwi Mėnilėk* di Afawârq Gabra Iyasus," *Rassegna di studi etiopici*, XVII (1961), 11–44.

15. This was asserted by Sengal in "Condizioni ed esigenze dell'-Etiopia dopo il '96 secondo uno scrittore Abissino," *Atti del terzo congresso di studi coloniali* (Florence, 1937), VI:215–218, and confirmed in her article of 1943.

16. L. R., "Cronaca etiopica per il 1950," *Oriente Moderno*, XXI (1951), 26–31. See also *Il Tempo* of 10 April 1950.

17. For this biographical note, I am heavily indebted to the author's son, Däjazmač Germačäw Täklä Hawaryat, himself a renowned writer, at present minister of agriculture. Some printed information is available in Pankhurst's "Foundations of Education"; in two articles by Cerulli, "Nuove pubblicazioni in lingua amarica," *Oriente Moderno*, XII (1932), 306–310 and "Rassegna periodica di pubblicazioni in lingue etiopiche fatte in Etiopia," *Oriente Moderno*, XIII (1933), 58–64; in Adrien Zervos, *L'Empire d'Ethiopie: Le miroir de l'Ethiopie moderne, 1906–1935* (Alexandria, 1936).

18. Czeslaw Jesman, *The Russians in Ethiopia: An Essay in Futility* (London, 1958), p. 114.

19. Richard Greenfield, *Ethiopia: A New Political History* (New York, 1965), p. 139. There is a lot of information about Täklä Hawaryat scattered in this book. The quotations in the following paragraphs come from pp. 172 and 226–227.

20. Zervos, *L'Empire d'Ethiopie*, who provides the only printed reference I have seen about this play, says it was produced at the Hotel

Majestic; the context implies that this was under Menelik (p. 232). But according to the author's son, it was performed before the heir designate at the Cinema Terrasse (this was the cinema attached to the Hôtel de France, whose owner was a Frenchman named Terrasse). Germačäw Täklä Hawaryat gives two dates for this performance (1913 and 1916) and implies that the comedy was actually printed, but I have found no trace of it in any of the bibliographies I have used.

21. I derive most of the biographical information about Heruy from a note by Girma-Selassie Asfaw. See also Zervos, *L'Empire d'Ethiopie*, p. 118.

22. Ladislas Farago, *Abyssinia on the Eve* (London, 1935), p. 122.

23. *Ibid.*, p. 183.

24. Hermann Norden, *Le dernier empire africain: En Abyssinie* (Paris, 1930), p. 32.

25. Cohen, "La naissance d'une littérature imprimée," p. 350.

26. Gaselee, "The Beginning of Printing," p. 94.

27. On this early printed poetry, see besides Cohen and Gaselee, Cerulli's articles of 1926 and Wright, *Ethiopian Incunabula*.

28. Cerulli, "Una raccolta amarica di canti funebri," *Rivista degli studi orientali*, X (1924), 265–280.

29. Wright, "Amharic Literature," pp. 11–23.

30. For a discussion of the oldest hymns in this collection, see Aläka Yekunna Amlaka Gäbrä Selasse, "Early Ge'ez Qene," *Journal of Ethiopian Studies*, IV, 1 (1966), 76–119.

31. Wright, *Ethiopian Incunabula*, p. 49.

32. James E. Baum, *Savage Abyssinia* (New York, 1927), pp. 22–23.

33. Norden, *Le dernier empire africain*, p. 33.

34. Carleton S. Coon, *Measuring Ethiopia and Flight to Arabia* (Boston, 1935), pp. 45–46.

35. On Heruy's nonfiction, see especially Cerulli, "Nuove pubblicazioni in linguaggi etiopici," *Oriente Moderno*, VII (1927), 354–357; "Nuovi libri pubblicati in Etiopia," *ibid.*, XII (1932), 170–175; Moreno's review of Heruy's report on his journey to Japan, *ibid.*, XIII (1933), 279–280.

36. On this book, see Moreno, "Notizia su uno scrittore modernista abissino," *Oriente Moderno*, XIII (1933), 496–499.

37. It would be of interest to compare Heruy's attitude to this problem with the handling of the same situation in Sembène Ousmane, *O pays, mon beau peuple!* (Paris, 1957), or Chinua Achebe, *No Longer at Ease* (London, 1960).

38. Farago, *Abyssinia on the Eve*, pp. 121–129.

39. In his contribution to *Civiltà dell' Oriente*, Moreno gives the date of Heruy's death as 27 September 1939.

40. I owe these few biographical indications to Dr. Pankhurst. For accounts of Yoftahé's plays, see Cerulli, "Nuovi libri pubblicati in Etiopia," pp. 170–175 and Moreno, "L'episodio di Lǐǧ Iyāsu e di Rās Hāylu nelle manifestazioni letterarie abissine," *Oriente Moderno,* XII (1932), 555–563.

41. Zaher Riad, "The Foundation of the Ethiopian Theatre," *Bulletin de l'Institut des Etudes coptes* (1958), pp. 72–76. The article is in Arabic, with an English summary.

42. Farago, *Abyssinia on the Eve,* p. 170.

43. These early Amharic plays by non-Ethiopian writers are mentioned in Zervos, *L'Empire d'Ethiope;* Sengal, "Note sulla letteratura"; Fusella, "Recenti pubblicazioni amariche in Abissinia," *Rassegna di studi etiopici,* V (1946), 93–102.

44. For information about Mäl'aku, I am indebted to Dr. Zaher Riad's article, "Foundation of the Ethiopian Theatre," and personal letters.

45. Menghistu Lemma, "Introduction to Modern Ethiopian Literature," p. 2.

46. Quoted by Pankhurst, "Foundations of Education," p. 285.

47. *Documents on Italian War Crimes,* I:30–31, quoted *ibid.*

48. Wright, *Ethiopian Incunabula,* pp. 43–45.

49. See Fusella, "Recenti pubblicazioni," pp. 98–100. On this postbellum praise poetry, see Kamil, "Amharische Kaiserlieder," *Abhandlungen für die Kunde des Morgenlandes,* XXXII, 4 (1957), 1–50; Ricci, "Canti imperiali amarici," *Rivista degli studi orientali,* XXXV (1960), 179–189.

50. Biographical information about Yilma Deressa is available in a notice in Ronald Segal, *Political Africa* (New York, 1961). See also Greenfield, *Ethiopia: A New Political History,* pp. 101, 231, 281, 315, and Farago, *Abyssinia on the Eve,* p. 37.

51. Most of the following biographical information is derived from the notice in Segal's *Political Africa,* the writer's obituary in the London *Times* of 1 March 1963, a letter from Professor Ullendorff printed in the *Times* of 5 March 1963, and many data scattered in Greenfield, *Ethiopia: A New Political History,* especially pp. 203, 226, 247, 262, 281, 385.

52. According to the *Times* obituary, however, Mäkonnen first continued the guerrilla warfare after the departure of the emperor.

53. Levine, "Ethiopia: Identity, Authority, and Realism," in L. Pye and S. Verba, eds., *Political Culture and Political Development* (Princeton, 1965), p. 261.

54. This novel has been discussed in Shiawl, "Äthiopiens zeitgenössische Literatur," and in Comba, "Le roman dans la littérature éthiopienne."

55. See the anonymous article on "Amharic Literature" in the *Guide Book of Ethiopia*.

56. Levine, "Ethiopia: Identity, Authority, and Realism," p. 259.

57. Quoted from K. M. Simon's English translation in *Three Plays by Bitwoded Makonnen Endalkachew* (Asmara, n.d.), p. 113.

58. On this novel, see Comba, "Une année de publications en langue amharique: 1949," pp. 304–305.

59. Quoted from Wright's English translation in *Three Plays*, p. 106.

60. Quoted from Endalkachew Makonnen's English translation in *Three Plays*.

61. Levine, *Wax and Gold*, p. 26.

62. See Comba, "Une année de publications en langue amharique: 1947," p. 152.

63. *Ibid.*, p. 152.

64. Greenfield, *Ethiopia: A New Political History*, p. 75.

65 Much of the biographical information has been kindly supplied by the author. Further details have been found in Kamil, *Das Land des Negus*, p. 77, and in Greenfield, *Ethiopia: A New Political History*, pp. 222, 247, 296, 285, 296, 298.

66. Farago, *Abyssinia on The Eve*, p. 70.

67. Wright, "Amharic Literature."

68. There is a biographical notice in *Ethiopie: Bulletin d'information*, no. 42 (12 October 1965); this author is also mentioned in Greenfield, *Ethiopia: A New Political History*, p. 396.

69. The most informative source for the biography of Imru is Greenfield, *Ethiopia: A New Political History*; quotations in the next few paragraphs come from that book, except where otherwise specified.

70. Leonard Mosley, *Haile Sellassie, the Conquering Lion* (Englewood Cliffs, N.J., 1965), p. 96.

71. Alberto Pariani, "La conquista militare dell'Impero," in Tomaso Sillani, ed, *L'Impero* (Rome, 1937), pp. 17–43.

72. I am considerably indebted to Mr. Käbbädä. Over several years, he answered my many inquiries with unfailing patience and courtesy, and he even kindly made available to me his own French translations of several of his works and of some unpublished autobiographical fragments.

73. Wright, "Amharic Literature."

74. This was the pseudonym of Charlotte M. Braeme, who was immensely successful during the last two decades of the nineteenth century among the less literate class of American readers. *Beyond Pardon* (1884) may be said to have initiated her period of maximum productivity, since she occupies more than six columns in the *American Catalogue* for 1884–1890. Her first work had been *Lord Lisle's Daugh-*

ter (1876), and at the height of her teeming inspiration, she was responsible for such unforgettable masterpieces as *Fatal Wedding, Gilded Sin* and *Wife in Name Only.* Between 1900 and 1905, her complete works were reissued by Street and Smith as the Bertha Clay Library, a mammoth series that lists 246 titles.

75. Quoted from the French translation, Kebbede, *Annibal, Tragédie (en cinq actes)* (Addis Ababa, 1964), p. 46.

76. The second Conference of Independent African States was held in Addis Ababa in June 1960; it was attended by thirteen states. The Organization of African Unity was founded at Addis Ababa in May 1963.

77. Chap. 74. The *Kebrä Nägäst (Chronicle of the Glory of Kings)* "is held in Ethiopia to be a translation of a document found before A.D. 325 among the treasures of St. Sophia of Constantinople, but was written in its present form in the fourteenth century. An especially venerable copy of it had been taken to Britain by the Napier expedition after its victory over Tewodros." It was, however, returned to the next emperor, Yohannes, who "had said that his subjects would not obey without it." See Greenfield, *Ethiopia: A New Political History,* pp. 41, 84, 369.

78. Ludwig Brandl. "Frühes Christentum in der Sahara und im Sudan," *Afrika heute,* no. 24 (15 Dec. 1966), Sonderbeilage.

79. Kebbede, *De la civilisation* (author's typed translation), pp. 71–72.

80. Biographical information has been kindly supplied by Germačäw Täklä Hawaryat himself.

81. Wright, "Literature and Fine Arts."

82. Comba, "Le roman dans la littérature éthiopienne."

83. Menghistu Lemma, "Introduction to Modern Ethiopian Literature," p. 4. See also *Ethiopia Information Bulletin,* no. 4 (Oct. 1963), p. 25.

84. Wright, "Literature and Fine Arts."

85. I owe this biographical information to Bäemnät Gäbrä Amlak himself.

86. The best source of information for Amharic literature of the fifties is the three articles published by Comba in *Annales d'Ethiopie.*

87. I owe this biographical information to Mäkonnen Zäwde himself.

88. See Pankhurst, "The Foundations of Education," pp. 251, 278.

89. Levine, *Wax and Gold,* p. 192.

90. Edward Ullendorff, *An Amharic Chrestomathy* (London, 1965), p. 13.

91. Levine, *Wax and Gold,* p. 170.

92. Kebbede Mikael, *Ethiopia and Western Civilization* (Addis Ababa, 1949), pp. 83–84.

93. George A. Lipsky, *Ethiopia: Its People, Its Society, Its Culture* (New Haven, 1962), p. 60.

94. On marriage customs in Ethiopia, see *ibid.*, p. 176.

95. Levine, *Wax and Gold*, p. 101.

96. See on this Pankhurst, "Misoneism and Innovation," pp. 287–320.

97. Menghistu Lemma, "Introduction to Modern Ethiopian Literature," p. 4.

98. Greenfield, *Ethiopia: A New Political History*, p. 242.

99. Comba, "Bref aperçu sur les débuts de la littérature," pp. 125–128.

100. Wright, "Literature and Fine Arts."

101. I am indebted to the writer himself for the biographical information. Unfortunately, no accurate bibliographical references have been obtained.

102. Alemayyehu Moges, "Collection and Analysis of Contemporary Ge'ez Poetry," *Survey of Language Use and Language Teaching in East Africa Bulletin*, II, 3 (1969), 8–9.

103. Greenfield, *Ethiopia: A New Political History*, p. 317.

104. Simon D. Messing, "A Modern Ethiopian Play—Self-study in Culture Change." *Anthropological Quarterly* XXXIII, 3 (1960), 149–157.

105. Ricci, "Romanzo e novella," pp. 144–172. See also Comba, "Une année de publications en langue amharique: 1949," pp. 302–304.

106. Levine, "Ethiopia: Identity, Authority, and Realism," pp. 269–270, 273.

107. This is the title of the English translation that appeared in *Ethiopia Observer* in 1964; quotations are from this version.

108. Lipsky, *Ethiopia, Its People, Its Society, Its Culture*, p. 79.

109. Levine, *Wax and Gold*, p. 126. Italics mine.

110. Menghistu Lemma, "Modern Amharic Literature."

111. Biographical information kindly supplied by Berhanu Zärihun.

112. Menghistu Lemma, "Introduction to Modern Ethiopian Literature," p. 4.

113. Biographical information kindly supplied by Asräs Asfa Wäsän.

114. W[illiam] P[routy], "Three Reviews," *Something*, no. 4 (Feb. 1965), pp. 53–59.

115. Menghistu Lemma, "Modern Amharic Literature," p. 4.

116. Biographical information kindly supplied by Ashenafi Kebede.

117. Sven Rubensson, *King of Kings: Tewodros of Ethiopia* (Addis Ababa, 1966), p. 37.

118. *Ibid.*, p. 88.

119. *Ibid.*, p. 89.

120. Page references are to Tsegaye Gabre-Medhin, "Tewodros," *Ethiopia Observer*, IX, 3 (1966), 211–226. Author's transliteration of proper names has been maintained.

121. Actually, Menelik's father, Haylä Mäläkot, king of Shoa, died of illness on 9 Nov. 1855, while Tewodros was still busy preparing his final attack on Shoa.

122. Chadwick, *The Growth of Literature*, p. 525.

123. *Ibid.*, p. 526. The reference is to W. C. Plowden, *Travels in Abyssinia and the Galla Country, With an Account of a Mission to Ras Ali in 1848* (London, 1868), p. 407.

124. Menghistu Lemma, "Introduction to Modern Ethiopian Literature," p. 5.

125. Tsegaye Gabre-Medhin, *Oda-Oak Oracle* (London, 1965), p. 11.

126. Menghistu Lemma, "Modern Amharic Literature," pp. 2-3.

127. Tsegaye Gabre-Medhin, "Literature and the African Public," *Ethiopia Observer*, XI, 1 (1967), 63-67.

Bibliography

I. SOURCES[1]

A. *Xhosa*

Aesop. *Aesop's Fables* (Xhosa version). Gwatyu, 1875, pt. I; 1877, pt. II.
——. *Iintsomi zika-Aesop* (James J. R. Jolobe's translation of Aesop's fables). Lovedale, 1953.
Bangeni, B. A. *Kuphilwa phi?* (*Where Do People Live?*). Lovedale, 1934.
Bennie, W. G., ed. *Imibengo* (*Titbits*). Lovedale, 1936.
Bokwe, John Knox. *Ama-Culo ase Lovedale* (*Lovedale Hymns*). Lovedale, 1885.
——. *Ibali likaNtsikana* (*Life of Ntsikana*). Lovedale, 1914.
Bomela, Bertrand. *Umntu akanambulelo* (*The Ingratitude of Men*). Johannesburg, 1960.
Bonsels, Waldemar. *uMaya: Amahla-ndinyuka enyosi* (James J. R. Jolobe's translation of *Maya, the Bee*). Johannesburg, 1957.
Bunyan, John. *Uhambo lomhambi* (translation of *Pilgrim's Progress* by Tiyo Soga and John Henderson Soga). Lovedale, 1867, pt. I; 1929, pt. II; 1930, complete edition.
——. *Iziganeko zom-Kristu* (dramatized version of *Pilgrim's Progress* by E. U. Ouless). Lovedale, 1928.
Dana, Minazana. See Jahn 857 (1st ed., 1951).
Dazana, S. *Ukufika kukaMadodana* (*The Arrival of Madodana*). Johannesburg, 1957.

---

[1] The source bibliography has been prepared as a complement to Jahn's *Die neoafrikanische Literatur. Gesamtbibliographie von den Anfängen bis zur Gegenwart,* to which reference is made whenever possible in order to avoid redundancy. Translations of foreign works into African languages have been included because of their interest for the study of influences. School textbooks produced by creative writers have not been included.

419

Defoe, Daniel. *URobinson Crusoe* (Guybon B. Sinxo's adaptation). Cape Town, 1961.

Dlova, E. S. M. *Umwuzo Wesono (The Wages of Sin)*. Lovedale, 1954.

Dyafta, D. Z. *Ikamvu lethu (Our Ancestry)*. Lovedale, 1953.

Futshane, Zora Z. T. See Jahn 877, 878.

Guma, Enoch S. See Jahn 881, 882.

Gwashu, E. F. See Jahn 885.

——. *Intombi yolahleko (The Prodigal Daughter)*. Johannesburg, n.d.

Haggard, H. Rider. *UZibaningashekazi* (Guybon B. Sinxo's translation of *She*). Johannesburg, 1958.

——. *Imigadi kaKumkani uSolomoni* (James J. R. Jolobe's translation of *King Solomon's Mines*). Johannesburg, 1958.

Hamilton, Mary A. *UBomi buka Abraham Lincoln* (Guybon B. Sinxo's translation of the *Life of Abraham Lincoln*). Johannesburg, 1959.

Hobson, G. C., and S. B. Hobson. *UAdonisi wasentlango* (Samuel E. K. Mqhayi's adaptation from the Afrikaans of *Kees van die Kalahari*). Lovedale, 1947.

Hope, Anthony. *Umbanjwa waseZenda* (Guybon B. Sinxo's translation of *The Prisoner of Zenda*). Johannesburg, 1958.

Huna, Michael, See Jahn 890.

——. *Ulindipasie (The Rinderpest)*. Cape Town, 1966.

Jabavu, D. D. T. *Izithuko (Abuses)*. Lovedale, 1954.

——. *IziDungulwana (Titbits)*. Cape Town, 1958.

Jolobe, James J. R. See Jahn 759 and 901–908.

——. *Amavo (Personal Impressions)*. Johannesburg, 1947.

——. "Honour for an African Author: Mr. Jolobe's Reply." *South African Outlook*, LXXXVIII (1958), 170–172.

Jongilanga, D. M. *Ukuqhawuka kwembeleko (The Snapping of the Skin)*. Lovedale, 1960.

Jordan, Archibald C. See Jahn 909–910.

Kakaza, L. *Intyatyambo yomzi (The Flower in the Home)*. Gcuwa, 1913.

——. *UZandiwe wakwa Gcaleka (Zandiwe, a Girl of the Gcaleka)*. Cape Town, 1914.

Lupuwana, D. M. *Khe kukhiwe iidiliya (The Grape Harvest)*. Johannesburg, 1959.

Mafuya, Bele B. *Bhoto Nonceba (Greetings To You, Nonceba)*. Cape Town, 1966.

Magona, Jongilizwe. *Ulundi lamaphupha (The Horizon of Dreams)*. Cape Town, 1965.

Makalima, Gilbert B. *U-Ntsizi*. Palmerton, 1924.

Mama, G. Soya. *Indyebo ka-Xhosa (Treasury of Xhosa)*. Johannesburg, 1954.

——, and A. Z. T. Mbebe. *Amaqumbe*. Cape Town, 1950.

Mbidlana, Mafuya. *Zangen'iinkomo* (*Enter the Cattle*). Lovedale, 1954.

Mlotywa, Stephen. *U-Nozipo*. Lovedale, 1923.

Mmango, Aaron Mazambana. See Jahn 979,980.

———. *uDika noCikizwa* (*Dika and Cikizwa*). Johannesburg, 1963.

Mqhaba, Alton A. M. See Jahn 1039.

Mqhayi, Samuel Edward Krune. See Jahn 1040–1044.

———. *The Case of the Twins* (translation of *Ityala lamawele*, by August Collingwood). *New African*, V (1966), 5–8, 41–44, 74–76.

———. *UBomi buka J. K. Bokwe* (*Life of J. K. Bokwe*). Lovedale, 1925.

———. *U-Mhlekazi U-Hintza* (*Hintza the Great*). Lovedale, 1937.

Mthembu, R. H. See Jahn 1045.

Mtingane, Amos. See Jahn 1046.

Mtuze, P. T. *UDingezweni*. Cape Town, 1966.

Mzamane, Godfrey. *Izinto zodidi* (*Things of Value*). Johannesburg, 1959.

Ndawo, Henry Masila. See Jahn 1063, 1064.

———. *Uhambo luka Gqoboka* (*Gqoboka's Journey*). Lovedale, 1909.

———. *Inxenye yen-Tsomi Zase Zweni* (*Selection of Folktales*). Mariannhill, n.d.

———. *Izibongo zamaHlubi nezamaBaca* (*Praise Poems of the Hlubi and the Bhaca*). Mariannhill, 1925.

———. *Iziduko zama Hlubi* (*Clan Names of the Hlubi*). Lovedale, 1939.

———. *UMshweshwe*. Lovedale, 1951.

Ngani, Alfred Z. See Jahn 1073.

———. *Ibali lamaGqunukhwebe* (*History of the Gqunukhwebe*). Lovedale, 1937.

———. *Ubom bukaKama* (*Life of Kama*). Lovedale, 1952.

Ngani, Marcus A. P. See Jahn 1074.

———. *Abantwana bethu* (*Our Children*). Lovedale, 1959.

Nkhulu, W. Sob. See Jahn 1081.

Ntloko, President Mthetho. See Jahn 1084.

———. *Iqhashu* (*Roasted Mealies*). Cape Town, 1954.

———. *UNgodongwana*. Cape Town, 1961.

———. *Kukh'u thixo kulento* (*God Is Present in this Situation*). Cape Town, 1965.

Nyembezi, Cyril Lincoln Sibusiso. *Ubudoda abukhulelwa* (*Age Is No Criterion for Manliness*, D. M. Lupuwana's translation of Zulu novel). Johannesburg, 1959.

Nyembezi, V. A. B. See Jahn 1090.

Nyoka, M. E. M. *UHadi*. Cape Town, 1961.

Petana, D. S. See Jahn 1099.

Rubusana, W. B. *Zemk'inkomo magwalandini!* (*Away Go the Cattle, You Coward!*), Lovedale, 1906.

Shakespeare, William. *U-Julius Caesar* (B. B. Mdledle's translation of *Julius Caesar*). Johannesburg, 1956.

——. *U-Macbeth* (B. B. Mdledle's translation of *Macbeth*). Johannesburg, 1959.

——. *Ubusuku beshumi elinambini* (B. B. Mdledle's translation of *Twelfth Night*). Lovedale, 1961.

Sinxo, Guybon B. See Jahn, 1133–1138.

——. *Isakhono Somfazi namanye Amabalana* (*The Skill of a Woman and Other Short Stories*). Johannesburg, 1958.

Sisilana, G. S. Ghandi. See Jahn 1139.

Siwisa, L. K. *Ndibuzen' Amathongo* (*Ask Me About Your Ancestors*). Johannesburg, 1956.

——. *Amabali angemigudu* (*Stories of Adventures*). Cape Town, 1962.

Siyongwana, Rustum. *Ubulumko bezinja* (*The Wisdom of the Dogs*). Cape Town, 1962.

Soga, John Henderson. *The South-Eastern Bantu* (*Abe-Nguni, Ama-Mbo, Ama-Lala*). Johannesburg, 1930.

——. *Ama-Xhosa Life and Customs*. Lovedale, 1931.

Sontonga, Enoch. *Nkosi sikelel' iAfrika* (*God Bless Africa*). Lovedale, n.d.

Swaartbooi, Victoria N. M. See Jahn 1158.

Tamsanqa, Witness K. See Jahn 1159.

——. *Inzala ka Mlungisi* (*The Progeny of Mlungisi*). Cape Town, 1954.

——. *Imitha yelanga* (*Rays of the Sun*). Cape Town, 1967.

——. *Ukuba ndandazile* (*Had I Known*). Cape Town, 1967.

Tshaka, R. M. See Jahn 1167.

Tsotsi, Liziwe L. See Jahn 1169.

Walaza, Ngu I. I. *Inkwenkwe izala indola* (*From Boyhood Stems Manhood*). Johannesburg, 1929.

Washington, Booker T. *Ukuphakama ukusuka ebukhobokeni* (James J. R. Jolobe's translation of *Up From Slavery*). Lovedale, 1951.

Waters, M. W. *UNongqause*. Cape Town, 1924.

Williams, C. Kingsley. *UAggrey umAfrika* (Samuel E. K. Mqhayi's translation of *Aggrey of Africa*). London, 1935.

Yako, St. J. Page. See Jahn 1181.

——. *Umtha Welanga* (*Sunbeam*). Johannesburg, 1957.

Yali-Manisi, D. L. P. *Izibongo zeenkosi zamaXhosa* (*Praise Poems of the Xhosa Chiefs*). Lovedale, 1952.

B. *Southern Sotho*

Bereng, David Cranmer Theko. See Jahn 829.

——. "Bitleng la Moshoeshoe (A la tombe de Moshesh)." *Africa*, XVII (1947), 206–207.

Bunyan, John. *Leeto la Mokreste* (G. Mabille's version of *Pilgrim's Progress*). Morija, 1872.

Chaane, J. D. See Jahn 832.

Chevrier, Odilon. *Tarcisius momartiri oa sacramente e Halalelang* (*Tarcisius, Martyr of the Holy Communion*). Mariannhill, 1930.

Gugushe, B. T. N. *Naleli ea Meso* (*The Evening Star*). Bloemfontein, 1951.

Guma, S. M. See Jahn, 883.

———. *Morena Mohlomi, mor'a Monyane* (*Chief Mohlomi, Son of Monyane*). Pietermaritzburg, 1960.

Haggard, H. Rider. *Merafo ya morena Salemone* (translation of *King Solomon's Mines*). Johannesburg, 1963.

Hlelele, Pius Joseph. *Dingane*. Mazenod, 1965.

Hoeane, Z. L. See Jahn 889.

———. *Dithothokiso tse Kgethilweng* (*Praise Poems of Kgethilweng*). Johannesburg, n.d.

Khaketla, Bennett Makalo. See Jahn 918–922.

———. *Lipshamate* (*Delicacies*). Johannesburg, 1954.

Khaketla, Ntseliseng 'Masechele. See Jahn 923–924.

Khalala, J. Taunyana. See Jahn 925.

Koote, J. D. See Jahn 827.

Lamb, Charles. *Dipale tse tswang ho Shakespeare* (Z. I. Hoeane's translation of *Tales from Shakespeare*). Johannesburg, 1965.

Lebakeng, D. P. See Jahn 930.

Lekeba, S. P. *Gauta e Ntjhapile* (*The Golden City Has Rejected Me*). Johannesburg, 1961.

Lerotholi, George. *Lithoko tsa morena e moholo Seeiso Griffith* (*Praise Poems of the Paramount Chief Seeiso Griffith*). Morija, 1940.

———. *Lithoko tsa motlotlehi Moshoeshoe II* (*Praise Poems of His Excellency Moshoeshoe II*). Mazenod, 1945.

Leshoai, Benjamin Letholoa. *Masilo's Adventures and Other Stories*. London, 1968.

Lesoro, Ephraim Alfred Shadrack. See Jahn 931.

———. *Reneketso tsa bana* (*Tales for Children*). Cape Town, 1959.

———. *Mmitsa* (*The Talisman*). Johannesburg, 1961.

———. *Makodilo a bana* (*Rhymes for Children*). Johannesburg, 1963.

———. *Mathe-malodi* (*Niceties*). Cape Town, 1964.

———. *Tau ya ha Zulu* (*The Lion of Zululand*). Johannesburg, 1964.

Maboee, Austin Teboho. *Menyepetsi ya maswabi* (*Tears of Shame*). Johannesburg, 1963.

Machobane, James J. See Jahn 941–942.

———. *Senate shoeshoe 'a Moshoeshoe* (*Senate, Moshoeshoe's Flower*). Johannesburg, 1954.

Mahloane, L. E. *Tsoana-makhulo (The Black One of the Pastures)*. Mazenod, n.d.

Maile, Mallane Libakeng. See Jahn 947–951.

——. *Ba ntena ba nteka (They Worry Me, They Tempt Me)*. Cape Town, 1965.

Majara, Simon N. *'Makotulo*. Mazenod, 1955.

——. *O sentse linako (He Wasted His Time)*. Mazenod, 1955.

——. *Morena oa Thaba (Chief of the Mountain)*. Mazenod, 1961.

——. *Moroetsana oa Moshate (Chief's Daughter)*. Mazenod, 1964.

Malefane, Bantu. See Jahn 954, 955.

Manaka, Valentinus Solo. See Jahn 958.

Mangoaela, Zakea D. See Jahn 959.

——. *Tsoelo-pele ea Lesotho (The Progress of Lesotho)*. Morija, 1911.

——. *Lithoko tsa morena ea Basotho (Praises of the Sotho Chiefs)*. Morija, 1921.

Manyeli, Gabriel. *Liapola tsa gauda (The Golden Apples)*. Mazenod, 1954.

Mapetla, Joase. *Liphoofolo, linonyana, litaola le lithoko tsa tsona (Praise Poems and Descriptions of Animals and Birds)*. Morija, 1924.

Matlororo, Charles L. L. *Kate oa Gamtoos (Kate of Gamtoos)*. Morija, n.d.

——. *Lithoko tsa sekolo (Poems for Schools)*. N.p., 1929.

Matlosa, Sylvanus. See Jahn 968.

——. *Katiba*. Mazenod, 1960.

Matselesele, R. L. See Jahn 969.

Mocoancoeng, Jac. G. See Jahn 984–985.

Mofokeng, Sophonia Machabe. See Jahn 989.

——. *Leetong (On the Way)*. Johannesburg, 1954.

——. *Pelong ea ka (In My Heart)*. Johannesburg, 1954.

Mofokeng, Twentyman M. See Jahn 990.

Mofolo, Ovid. *Lesiamo le Ema (Lesiamo and Ema)*. Mazenod, n.d.

Mofolo, Thomas. See Jahn 991–997.

——. "Géorgiques et voyages du chrétien au Lessouto. Fekesi." *Le Monde non-chétien*, n.s. no. 11 (1949), pp. 349–358. (French translation of part of *Moeti oa bochabela*.)

Mofolo, Thomas T. *Phakoana-tsooana (Small White Hawk)*. Mazenod, n.d.

Mohapeloa, J. Makibinyane. See Jahn 999.

Mohapi, M. Molelekoa. See Jahn 1000, 1001.

Mohome, Paulus Mokete. See Jahn 1002.

Moikangoa, C. R. *Sebonoli sa Ntsoana-tsatsi (The Sentinel of Ntsoana-Tsatsi)*. Mazenod, 1943.

Moiloa, James Jantjies. See Jahn 1003.

——. *Dipale le metlae (Stories and Jokes)*. Cape Town, 1963.

——. *Mohahlaula dithota* (*Traveller on the Plains*). Cape Town, 1965.

——. *Jaa o siele motswalle* (*Eat and Leave Something for a Friend*). Cape Town, 1966.

Mojaki, Philip J. *Makolwane a kajeno* (*Initiates of Today*). Cape Town, 1962.

Mokhomo, Makhokolotso A. See Jahn 1004.

Mokorosi, Emely Selemeng. See Jahn 1005.

Mopeli-Paulus, A. S. See Jahn 1008–1015.

——. *Liretlo* (*Ritual Murder*). Bloemfontein, 1950.

——. *Moshweshwe moshwaila* (*Moshoeshoe the Beard-shaver*). Johannesburg, n.d.

Mothibi, I. See Jahn 1018.

Motsamai, Edward. *Majoe a mahlano a molatsoana* (*Five Pebbles from the Brook*). Morija, 1907.

——. *Mehla ea malimo* (*The Days of the Cannibals*). Morija, 1912.

——. *Kereke* (*The Church*). Morija, 1925.

——. *Morena Moshoeshoe, mar'a Mokhachane* (*Chief Moshoeshoe, Son of Mokhachane*). Morija, 1942.

Motsatse, Ratsebe L. See Jahn 1020, 1021.

Nqheku, Albert. *Lilahloane*. 2d ed. Mazenod, 1944.

——. *Arola naheng ea Maburu* (*Arola Among the Boers*). Mazenod, 1942.

——. *Tsielala* (*Silence, Please!*). Mazenod, 1959.

Ntsaba, James Sefatsa. *Pelo e ja serati* (*The Heart Eats the Lover*). Mazenod, 1964.

Ntsala, Mackenzie. *Sekhukhumi se bonoa ke sebatalali* (*A Man Is Seen in His Hiding-Place by Someone Who Does Not Hide*). Johannesburg, 1954.

Ntsane, Kemuel Edward. See Jahn, 1085–1086.

——. *Bana ba Roma* (*Children of Roma*). Morija, 1954.

——. *Makumane* (*Titbits*). Johannesburg, 1961.

——. *Nna Sajane Kobeloa C.I.D.* (*I, Sergeant Kobeloa*). Johannesburg, 1963.

Ramathe, A. C. J. *Tšepo* (*Hope*). Johannesburg, 1957.

Ratau, J. Khathatso. See Jahn 1111.

Sebitloane, Sidwell Sabata. *Nteseng* (*Let Me Go*). Cape Town, 1965.

Sechefo, Justinus. "The Twelve Lunar Months Among the Basuto." *Anthropos*, IV (1909), 931–941; V (1910), 71–81.

——. *Molia oa la Morena e moholo la ho ea England 1919*. (*The Party of the Day the Paramount Chief Went to England in 1919*). Mariannhill, ca. 1930.

——. *Ba-shoela-tumelo ba Uganda* (*Martyrs of Uganda*). Mazenod, 1938.

———. *Mofumahali oa rosari* (*The Lady of the Rosary*). Mazenod, n.d.

———. *Matsipa a bibele* (*Extracts from the Bible*). Mazenod, n.d.

———. *Re adoreng re hlonepeng* (*Let Us Worship and Respect*). Mazenod, n.d.

———. *The Twelve Lunar Months Among the Basuto*. Mazenod, n.d.

———. *The Old Clothing of the Basotho*. Mazenod, n.d.

———. *Customs and Superstitions in Basutoland*. Mazenod, n.d.

———. *Kulile*. Mazenod, 1964.

———. "Vite! le Chef arrive! ..." *Grands Lacs*, LXIV (1949), 10/11/12, 52–54.

Segoete, Everitt Lechesa. See Jahn 1123.

———. *Mefiboshethe kapa pheello ea molimo ho moetsalibe* (*Mefiboshethe, or the Patience of God to the Sinner*). Morija, 1910.

———. *Moea oa bolisa* (*The Spirit of Shepherding*). Morija, 1913.

———. *Mohlala oa Jesu Kreste* (*The Example of Jesus Christ*). Morija, 1924.

———. *Raphepheng* (*Old Scorpion*). Morija, 1913.

Segwe, Francis More. See Jahn 1124.

Sekese, Azariele M. See Jahn 1126.

———. "Tsa Lesotho" ("About Lesotho"). *Leselinyana la lesotho*, April 1884.

———. "Tsa Lesotho." *Ibid.*, May 1884.

———. "Leeto" ("Journey"). *Ibid.*, February 1885.

———. "Ba hanang thuto" ("Those Who Refuse Education"). *Ibid.*, September 1887.

———. "Linku tse tsebang lentsoe la molisa oa tsona" ("The Sheep That Know His Voice"). *Ibid.*, November 1887.

———. "Litsela, le Mokaola, le Lingaka." *Ibid.*, January 1888.

———. "Paki oa 'nete" ("Witness of Truth"). *Ibid.*, June 1888.

———. "Maele" ("Proverbs"). *Ibid.*, January 1890.

———. "Maele II." *Ibid.*, February 1890. One article entitled "Maele" appeared every month until at least September 1891.

———. *Mekhoa ea Basotho le maele le litsomo* (*Sotho Customs, Proverbs and Tales*). Morija, 1893.

———. "Note on Mamosa, the Mother of Jonathan." In W. A. Norton, "Sesuto Praises of the Chiefs." *South African Journal of Science*, XVIII (1921–22), 441–453.

Selane, Adam J. *Letlotlo la Mosotho* (*Treasury of the Sotho*). Bloemfontein, 1942.

Sentšo, Dyke, See Jahn 1127.

Setloboko, Julius. *Monyaluoe* (*A Bride*). Mazenod, n.d.

Shakespeare, William. *Mohwebi wa Venisi* (Ntsane's version of *The Merchant of Venice*). Johannesburg, 1961.

Sutu-Mthimkhulu, Sam Duby Raymond. See Jahn 1156, 1157.

Taoana, B. K. See Jahn 1160.
Thakhisi, J. Kabeli. See Jahn 1163.
Thoahlane, A. B. T. See Jahn 1164.
Tjokosela, Joseph I. F. See Jahn 1165.
——. *Mosongoa.* Mazenod, n.d.
——. *Sarah.* Mazenod, n.d.
Tsephe, Joseph Sebata. See Jahn 1166.
Tsiu, Alf. K. *Lipapali le lithothokiso tsa Basotho (Plays and Praise Poems of the Sotho).* Morija, 1954.
Tsosane, W. L. N. See Jahn 1168.
Washington, Booker T. *Tokoloho* (Herbert H. Lekhethoa's translation of *Up From Slavery*). Morija, 1947.

C. *Zulu*

Bengu, Kenneth, See Jahn 827.
——. *Ukhabethule (The One Who Draws While the Others Are Silent).* Pietermaritzburg, n.d.
——. *Ukhalalembube (The Snout of the Lion).* Johannesburg, 1953.
——. *UNyambose noZinitha (Nyambose and Zinitha).* Pietermaritzburg, 1965.
Blose, Andries Jeremiah. See Jahn 830.
Bunyan, John. *Incwadi kaBunyane, okutiwa Ukuhamba kwesiHambi* (translation of *Pilgrim's Progress*). Pietermaritzburg, n.d.
Caluza, Reuben T. "Ixegwana" ("Little Old Man"). *Native Teachers' Journal,* II (1921), 58.
——. "African Music." *Southern Workman* (April 1931), pp. 152–155.
Dhlamini, Seth Z. S. See Jahn 858.
Dhlomo, Herbert I. E. See Jahn 859, 860.
——. "Drama and the African." *South African Outlook,* LXVI (1936), 232–235.
——. "The Nature and Variety of Tribal Drama." *Bantu Studies,* XVIII (1939), 33–48.
——. "African Drama and Poetry." *South African Outlook,* LXIX (1939), 88–90.
——. "African Drama and Research." *Native Teachers' Journal,* XVIII (1939), 129–132.
——. "Zulu Folk Poetry." *Native Teachers' Journal,* XXVIII (1947-48), 5–7, 46–50, 84–87.
Dhlomo, Rolfes Reginald Raymond. See Jahn 861–867.
——. *Izikhali zanamuhla (Modern Weapons).* Pietermaritzburg, 1935.
——. *UNomalanga kaNdengezi (Nomalenga, Daughter of Ndengezi),* Pietermaritzburg, 1934.

———. *Ukwazi kuyathuthukiza* (*Wisdom Elevates*). Pietermaritzburg, 1937.

Dlamini, John Charles. See Jahn 868.

Dube, John L. See Jahn 870–871.

———. "A Native View of Christianity in South Africa." *Missionary Review of the World*, n.s. XIV (1901), 421–426.

———. "Zulu and the Missionary Outlook in Natal." *Missionary Review of the World*, n.s. XX (1907), 205.

———. "Practical Christianity Among the Zulus." *Missionary Review of the World*, n.s. XX (1907), 370–373.

———. *Isitha somuntu nguye uqobo lwakhe* (*The Black Man Is His Own Greatest Enemy*). Mariannhill, 1922.

———. *U-Shembe*. Mariannhill, 1930.

———. *Ukuziphatha kahle* (*Good Manners*). Mariannhill, n.d.

———. *Jeqe, the Bodyservant of King Shaka* (J. Boxwell's English translation of *Insila kaTshaka*). Lovedale, 1951.

———. *Inkinga yomendo* (*The Problems of Marriage*). Pietermaritzburg, 1961.

Dube, Violet. *Woza nazo* (*Come Along With Them*). Cape Town, 1935.

Fuze, Magema ka'Magwaza. *Abantu abamnyama lapha bavela ngakhona* (*The Black People: Where They Come From*). Pietermaritzburg, 1922.

Gumbi, James N. See Jahn 884.

———. *Baba ngixolele* (*Father, Forgive Us*). Johannesburg, 1966.

———. *Wayesezofika ekhaya* (*He Was About to Reach Home*). Pretoria, 1966.

Haggard, H. Rider. *Imigodi yeNkosi uSolomoni* (J. F. Cele's translation of *King Solomon's Mines*). Johannesburg, 1958.

———. *Ulokokazi* (V. A. B. Nyembezi's translation of *She*). Johannesburg, 1959.

Hope, Anthony. *Isithunjwa saseZenda* (O. L. S. Shange's translation of *The Prisoner of Zenda*). Johannesburg, 1961.

Jobodwana, Edmund Dumani. *uNcuthu maZangwa* (*Very Nice, You of the Zangwa-clan*). Cape Town, n.d.

Khwela, Simeon T. Z. See Jahn 926.

Kunene, Mazisi. *Zulu Poems*. London, 1970.

Lamula, Petras. *Isabelo sika-zulu* (*Zulu Inheritance*). Pietermaritzburg, n.d. Repr. 1963.

———. *UZulu ka Malandela* (*Zulu, Son of Malandela*). N.p., n.d.

Made, E. H. A. *Indlalifa yaseHarrisdale* (*The Heir of Harrisdale*). Pietermaritzburg, 1940.

———. *Amaqhawe omlando* (Heroes of History). Pietermaritzburg, 1940 and 1942.

———. *Ubuwulo bexoxo (The Foolishness of the Frog)*. Pietermaritzburg, 1947.

———. *Umuthi wokufa nezinye izinkondlo (The Tree of Death and Other Poems)*. Pietermaritzburg, 1951.

Maduna, E. D. See Jahn 944.

Masuku, Thomas M'zwenduku. *Izikhali zembongi (The Weapons of the Poet)*. Pretoria, 1966.

Masinga, K. E., and Hugh Tracey. *Chief Above and Chief Below*. Pietermaritzburg, 1944.

Matsebula, J. S. M. See Jahn 763.

———. *Inkanankana (The Riddle)*. Pietermaritzburg, 1964.

Mbata, Allen H. S., and Garland C. S. Mdhladhla. *uCakijina Bogcololo (The Small Mongoose, Younger Brother to the Slender Mongoose)*. London, 1927.

———. *Uklabanengalwi (He Conquers Without Fighting)*. Durban, 1938.

———. *Uthathezakho (Take Your Sticks)*. Newcastle (S.A.), 1938.

Mbulawa, L. M. See Jahn 976.

Mdluli, S. V. H. *UBhekizwe namadodana akhe (Bhekizwe and His Sons)*. Pretoria, 1966.

Miller, Allister. *UMamisa iqhawe leSwazi* (translation by J. A. W. Nxumalo and S. W. Zulu of *Mamisa, the Swazi Hero*). Pietermaritzburg.

Mkhize, David. *Ngavele ngasho (I Said So From the Beginning)*. Pietermaritzburg, 1965.

Mkhize, E. E. N. T. *Imbongi yakwaZulu (The Poet of Zululand)*. Pietermaritzburg, n.d.

Mncwango, Leonhard L. J. See Jahn 981–982.

———. *Manhla iyokwendela egodini (The Day She Married the Grave)*. Pietermaritzburg, 1951.

Mpanza, M. J. *UGuqabadele*. Durban, 1930.

Mseleku, M. R. *Uvumindaba (The One Who Masks the Matter)*. Pietermaritzburg, n.d.

Mthembu, E. T. *Umlayezo (A Message)*. Pietermaritzburg, n.d.

Mthiya, G. S. *Uvelengazi (I Knew Him When He Was Born)*. Pietermaritzburg, n.d.

Ndebele, Nimrod N. T. See Jahn 1065.

Ndelu, Bethuel Blose. *Mageba lazihlonza (Mageba, It Has Tracked Itself Down)*. Pietermaritzburg, 1962.

Ngcobo, Moses John. *Inkungu mazulu (The Fog, You Zulu People)*. Johannesburg, 1957.

———. *Wo he Bantu (Well, That's That)*. Cape Town, 1964.

Ngubane, Jordan K. See Jahn 1076.

Ntuli, D. B. Z. *uBheka (The Observant One)*. Pietermaritzburg, 1962.

Nxumalo, Otty Ezrom Howard. See Jahn 926.

———. *Ikusasa alaziwa* (*No One Knows What Will Happen Tomorrow*). Johannesburg, 1961.

———. *Ikhwezi* (*Morning Star*). Cape Town, 1965.

Nyembezi, Cyril Lincoln Sibusiso. See Jahn 1088–1089.

———. *Ubudoda abukhukekwa* (*Acts of Manhood Are Not Necessarily Performed by Grown-up Men*). Pietermaritzburg, 1953.

———. *A Review of Zulu Literature*. Durban, 1961.

———. *Izibongo zamakhosi* (*Praises of Kings*). Pietermaritzburg, 1958.

Paton, Alan. *Lafa elihle kakhulu* (Cyril L. S. Nyembezi's translation of *Cry, the Beloved Country*). Pietermaritzburg, n.d.

Shabangu, Sydney Sipho. *Imvo yolahleko* (*The Lost Sheep*). Pietermaritzburg, 1966.

Shakespeare, William. *Umkhwebi waseVenisi* (O. L. Sibuso Shange's translation of *The Merchant of Venice*). Pietermaritzburg [1959?].

Sikanana, Jonathan Mandlenkosi. *Ikwezi likaZulu* (*Zulu Morning Star*). Johannesburg, 1966.

Stevenson, Robert L. *Isisulu sabaphangi* (translation of *Treasure Island*). Pietermaritzburg, 1953.

Tchmase, Ndodana J. E. S. See Jahn 1161.

———. *UGongoda*. Johannesburg, n.d.

Vilakazi, Benedict Wallet. See Jahn 1174–1180.

———. "The Conception and Development of Poetry in Zulu." *Bantu Studies*, XXX (1938), 105–134.

———. "African Drama and Poetry." *South African Outlook*, LXXIX (1939), 166–167.

———. "Some Aspects of Zulu Literature." *African Studies*, I (1942), 270–274.

———. "The Oral and Written Literature in Nguni." Ph.D. dissertation, Johannesburg, 1945.

Zama, Johannes Joel Mdelwa. *Nigabe ngani* (*On What Do You Rely?*). Pietermaritzburg, 1965.

———. *Ingwe idla ngamabala* (*A Man Is Known By His Deeds*). Pietermaritzburg, 1967.

Zondi, E. See Jahn 1182.

D. *Amharic*[2]

Abbé Gubeñña (እቢ ፡ ጉብኛ). ከመቅሠፍት ፡ ሠራዊት ፡ ይጠንቀቅ ፡ ሰውነት (*Let The Body Beware of The Army Scourges*). Addis Ababa, 1949.

———. ምልከአም ፡ ስይፈ ፡ ነበልባል . ၂ (*Melke'am, The Flaming Sword*). Addis Ababa, 1956.

———. የራኄል ፡ ዕንባ (*The Tears of Rachel*). Addis Ababa, 1956.

---

[2] Dates are given in the Ethiopian calendar. Dates in the Gregorian calendar are in italics.

——. የፍጡራን ፡ ኑር ፡ ፩ኛ ፡ የግጥም ፡ ትንሽ ፡ መጽሐፍ፡ (*The Life of Man: A First Little Book of Poems*). Addis Ababa, 1956.

——. ከልታማው ፡ እኅቴ. (*My Abused Sister*). Addis Ababa, 1957.

——. (Abbe Gubegna). *The Savage Girl*. Addis Ababa [*1964*].

Afäwärq Gäbrä Iyäsus (አፈወርቅ ፡ ገብረ ፡ ኢየሱስ). *Manuale di conversazione italiano-amarico con la pronuncia figurata*. Rome, *1905*.

——. *Grammatica della lingua amarica. Metodo pratico per l'insegnando*. Rome, *1905*.

——. ልብ ፡ ወለድ ፡ ታሪክ (*Fictitious Story*). Rome, *1908*. English version by Tadesse Tamrat: "*Tobbya.*" *Ethiopia Observer*, VIII (*1964*), 242–267.

——. *Guide du voyageur en Abyssinie*. Rome, *1908*.

——. ዳግማይ ፡ ምኒልክ ፡ ንጉሥ ፡ ነገሥት ፡ ዘኢትዮጵያ (*Menelik II, King of the Kings of Ethiopia*). Rome, *1909*.

——. ደዊት ፡ ዘተነትም ፡ በብሔረ ፡ ሮሜ (psalter published in Rome). Rome, 1902.

——. *Il verbo amarico*. Rome, *1911*.

——. የኢትዮጵያ ፡ መንግሥት ፡ አልጋ ፡ ወራሽና ፡ እንደራሴ ፡ ልኡል ፡ ተፈሪ መኮንን (Report of the Heir to the Throne and Regent of the Ethiopian Empire H.R.H. Täfäri Mäkonnen's journey to Jibuti and Aden.) Dire Dawa, 1915.

——. ነጋድራስ ፡ አፈወርቅ ፡ ከሥራው ፡ ወደ ፡ ገምሩክ ፡ የገባ ፡ ጊዜ ፡ ከመ ንግሥት ፡ ሠራተኛ ፡ ጋራ ፡ ሲተዋወቅ ፡ ከዚህ ፡ በታች ፡ የተጻፈውን ፡ ነገር ፡ ተናገረ ፤ የዚህን ፡ ጊዜ ፡ ብዙ ፡ ሰው ፡ ተሰብስቦ ፡ ነበረ ፤ ዋና ፡ ዋና ፡ ሰዎች ፡ ፊታውራሪ ፡ ይርዳው ፤ ቀኛዝማች ፡ ተፈሪ ፡ በለው ፡ አቶ ፡ ዮሴፍ ፤ ፈረንጆችም ፡ ነበሩ (On taking up duties at Customs and meeting state officials, Näggadras Afäwärq pronounced the following speech in the presence of many personalities, among them Fitawrari Yerdaw, Qäñazmač Täfäri Bäläw, Ato Yoséf, and many Europeans). Addis Ababa [1922].[3]

Alämayyäwh Mogäs (ዓለማየሁ ፡ ሞጋስ). ስዋስው ፡ ግዕዝ (*Ge'ez Grammar*). Addis Ababa, n.d.

——. ቀዳማዊ ፡ ምንባብ ፡ ግዕዝ (*A First Ge'ez Reader*). Addis Ababa, n.d.

——. የአቶ ፡ ዳኛቸው ፡ ወርቁን ፡ ምንነት ፡ ለመግለጥ (*To Explain Mr. Dañačäw Wärqu's Errors*). Addis Ababa, 1957.[4]

[3] Afäwärq is also claimed to have authored an anonymous verse pamphlet by "a citizen of Asmära" (Asmära, 1912) in defense of Italy's civilizing mission in the war against Turkey. No bibliographical information has been traced about several works—*Anthony and Cleopatra, When the Serpent Was Reigning* (a novel), and *Midas* (a novel)—mentioned in-Heruy's catalog, or about the articles Afäwärq published in Italian and other European journals according to *Chi è dell'Eritrea*.

[4] Dañäčäw Wärqu is the author of a verse drama published in 1950.

——. የድርስት ፡ አብነት. (*A Guide to Composition*). Addis Ababa, 1957.

——. እውነት (Truth). *Endihe Näw*, II, 1 (1958), 11.

Anonymous. ለኢትዮጵያ ፡ ልጆች ፡ ማመልከቻ (*So That the Sons of Ethiopia Should Pay Attention*). Addis Ababa, 1914.

——. ለኢትዮጵያ ፡ ልጆች ፡ ማሳሰቢያ (*So That Ethiopians Should Think*). Addis Ababa, 1915.

——. የልብ ፡ አሳብ (*Thoughts of the Heart*). Addis Ababa, 1915.

Antänäh Alämu (አንተነሁ ፡ ዓለሙ). ታሪክ ፡ በተያትር ፡ መልክ ፡ ዘርዓይ ፡ ዳረስ (*History dramatized: Zär'ay Däräs*). Addis Ababa, 1948.

——. የሰላም ፡ ጌታ (*The Master of Peace*). Addis Ababa, 1948.

Asäffa Gäbrä Maryam (አሰፋ ፡ ገብረ ፡ ማርያም). እንደወጣች ፡ ቀረች (*How She Left Her Husband*). Addis Ababa, 1946.

Ashenafi Kebede. *Confession*. Addis Ababa [*1965*].

Asräs Asfa Wäsän (አስረስ ፡ አስፋ ፡ ወሰን). የባለቅኔ ፡ አስማት (*The Poet's Magic*). Addis Ababa, 1950.

——. የፍቅር ፡ አውቶሟኪ ፤ የነቢዩና ፡ የአበባ ፡ እውነተኛ ፡ ታሪክ (*Ideal Love*). Addis Ababa, 1952.

Aššäber Gäbrä Heywät (አሽብር ፡ ገብረ ፡ ሕይወት). የኪዳነ ፡ ቃል ፡ ቲያትር (*The Theater of Kidanä Qal*). Addis Ababa, 1948.

——. የንግሥት ፡ አዜብ ፡ ታሪካዊ ፡ ጉዞ (*The Historic Journey of the Queen of Sheba*). Addis Ababa, 1951.

Azzanaw Aläme (አዛናው ፡ ዓለሜ). አዱኛ ፡ ብላሽ ፡ ልብ ፡ ወለድ ፡ ድራማ (*The Rubbish of This World*). Addis Ababa, 1949.

Bäemnät Gäbrä Amlak (በእምነት ፡ ገብረ ፡ አምላክ). የአንድ ፡ ቋንቋ ፡ እድ ገት ፡ ወይም ፡ አማርኛ ፡ እንደተከፋፋ (*The Formation of a Language: How Amharic Developed*). Addis Ababa, 1947.

——. ልጅነት ፡ ተመልስ ፡ አይመጣም (*Childhood Never Comes Back*). Addis Ababa, 1949.

——. " ሚካኤል ፡ ያየው " (*What Mika'él Saw*). *Endihe Näw*, I, 1 (1957), 26–28.

——. " ዘጓላ ፡ ደርሶ ፡ መልስ " (*Return Trip to Zegwala*). *Endihe Näw*, I, 1 (1957), 18–19.

——. " የቡና ፡ መዘዝ " (*The Dangers of Coffee*). *Endihe Näw*, II, 1 (1958), 9–10.

——. በዓለም ፡ ካለው ፡ ሁሉ ፡ ትልቁ ፡ ነገር (*The Greatest Thing in the World*) (translation of a work by Henry Drummond). Addis Ababa, 1946.

——. የልጆች ፡ ሁኔታ ፡ በቤትና ፡ በትምህርት ፡ ቤት ፤ የወላጆች ፤ የወጣቶችና ፡ የአስተማሪዎች ፡ መሪ (*Children at Home and at School. A Guide for Parents, Young People and Teachers*) (translation of a work by Jessie Hertslet). Addis Ababa, 1948.

Beka Nämo (ቤካ ፡ ነሞ).   ገሌጠን ፡ ብናየው (Let Us Look Inside).
Addis Ababa, 1949.

Berhanu Denqe (ብርሃኑ ፡ ደንቄ).   የሕፃናት ፡ ምሳሌ ፤ እንቆቅልህ ፡ ምን ፡
አውቅልህ ፡ በትምህርት ፡ ለማደግ ፡ ወጣቱ ፡ ዘ.ጋህ ፤ ሀ ብሎ ፡ ይጀምር ፡ ፊደል ፡
ነው ፡ ስምህ ፦ (Parable of Childhood). Addis Ababa, 1938.

——. ከወልወል ፡ እስከ ፡ ማይጨው (From Wäl Wäl to May Čäw). Addis Ababa, 1942.

——. የኢትዮጵያ ፡ አጭር ፡ ታሪክ   (A Short History of Ethiopia). Addis
Ababa, 1943.

——. ንግሥተ ፡ ሳዜብ ፤ ታሪካዊ ፡ ቲአትር ፤ በሰባት ፡ ክፍሎች (The Queen
of Sheba). Addis Ababa, 1943.

Bunyan, John.   የክርስቲያን ፡ መንገድ ፡ ከዚህ ፡ ዓለም ፡ ወደ ፡ ዘላለም ፡
ሕይወት ፡ የሚወስድ   (Gäbrä Giyorgis Terfé's Amharic version of
The Pilgrim's Progress). St. Chrischona, 1892.

——. የሃንስ ፡ ቡንያን ፡ ብሕልሚ ፡ ዝረአየ ፡ መገዲ ፡ ክርስቲያን
(Teresa de Pertis's Tigriñña version of The Pilgrim's Progress). Asmära, 1934.

Dässaleñ Harra Mika'él (ደሳለኝ ፡ ሐራ ፡ ሚካኤል).   እንዳትከዳኝ (Do
Not Disown Me). Addis Ababa, 1947.

Dawit Däggäfu (ዳዊት ፡ ደገፉ).   እውነት ፡ የጠማው ፡ ሰው ። ልብ ፡ ወለድ ፡
ድራማ   (The Man Who Thirsts After Truth). Addis
Ababa, 1949.

Gäbrä Egzi'abehér (ገብረ ፡ እግዚአብሔር).   አዋጅ ፡ የተፈለውን ፡ መንገድ ፡
ለመናፈቅና ፡ ለመያዝ ፡ ለሕዝብና ፡ ለአገሩ ፡ ይሀንነት ፡ እንዲበጅ
(Advice for Seeking and Grasping the Best Way to Strengthen
the State for the Benefit of People and Country)   (published
anonymously). 1897.

Germačäw Täklä Hawaryat (ግርማቸው ፡ ተክለ ፡ ሐዋርያት).   አራአያ ፡
ታሪካዊ ፡ ልብ ፡ ወለድ   (Ar'aya: A Historical Novel). Addis Ababa,
1941.

——. ቴዎድሮስ ፡ ታሪካዊ ፡ ድራማ   (Theodore: A Historical Drama).
Addis Ababa, 1942.

Gétačäw Awwäqä (ጌታቸው ፡ አወቀ).   ማኅደረ ፡ ጥበብ ፡ ማስተዋል ፡ ።መይ ፡
ልብ ፡ ወለድ ፡ መጽሐፍ (The Dwelling Place of Wisdom). Addis
Ababa, 1948.

——. ዓለም ፡ ገነት ፤ በሕሳብ ፡ ስንሰለት   (Aläm and Gännät United by
Spiritual Bonds). Addis Ababa, 1949.

——. የሕሊና ፡ ዳኛ ፡ ስለ ፡ ሁለት ፡ ወጣቶች ፤ ስለ ፡ አንድ ፡ ወንጀለኛ ፡ የልብ ፡
ወለድ ፡ ታሪክ (The Judge of Conscience: Of Two Young People and
a Criminal). Addis Ababa, 1949.

Haddis Alämayyäwh (ሐዲስ ፡ ዓለማየሁ).   ተረት ፡ ተረት ፡ የመሠረት
(Collection of Fables). Addis Ababa, 1948.

434   BIBLIOGRAPHY

——. የትምህርትና ፡ የትማሪ ፡ ቤት ፡ ትርጉም   (*The Meaning of Schools and Education*). Addis Ababa, 1948.

——. ፍቅር ፡ እስከ ፡ መቃብር ። (ልብ ፡ ወለድ ፡ ታሪክ ።) (*Love Until Death: A Novel*). Addis Ababa, 1958.

Haddis Wäldä Ṣadeq (ሐዲስ ፡ ወልደ ፡ ጻድቅ). ወይዘሮ ፡ ዓለም ። ታሪካዊ ፡ ቲአትር ፡ ልብ ፡ ወለድ (*Woyzero Aläm*). Addis Ababa, 1949.

Heruy Wäldä Sellasé (ኅሩይ ፡ ወልደ ፡ ሥላሴ).   በኢትዮጵያ ፡ የሚገኙ ፡ የመጻሕፍት ፡ ቀዋጥር   (Catalog of books written in Ge'ez and Amharic, to be found in Ethiopia). Addis Ababa, 1904.

——. የልቅሶ ፡ ዜማ ፡ ግጥም ። ምስጢሩ ፡ ከመጻሕፍት ፡ ጋራ ፡ የተስማማ (*Poems of Funeral Songs: Their Meaning in Harmony with the Scriptures*). Addis Ababa, 1910.

——. ኢትዮጵያና ፡ መተማ ። የአጼ ፡ የሐንስ ፡ ታሪክ ፡ ባጭሩ   (*Ethiopia and Matamma: A Short Biography of Emperor Yohannes*). Addis Ababa, 1910.

——. ለልጅ ፡ ምክር ፤ ለአባት ፡ መታስቢያ   (*Recollections of the Fathers, Advice for the Sons*). Addis Ababa, 1910.

——. ወዳጄ ፡ ልቤ ፤ የሰውን ፡ ጠባይና ፡ ኑር ፡ በምሳሌ ፡ የሚገልጽ (*My Friend, My Heart: The Character and Behavior of Man Unveiled in Parables*). Addis Ababa, 1915.

——. የልዕልት ፡ ወይዘሮ ፡ መነን ፡ መንገድ ። በኢየሩሳሌምና ፡ በምስር (*H. H. Princess Mänän's Journey to Jerusalem and Egypt*). Addis Ababa, 1915.

——. የሕይወት ፡ ታሪክ ። በኋላ ፡ ዘመን ፡ ለሚነሡ ፡ ልጆች ፡ ማስተወቂያ (*Biographies: Information for the Generations to Come*). Addis Ababa, 1915.

——. ስለ ፡ አውሮጳ ፡ መንገድ ፡ የምክር ፡ ቃል   (*Word of Advice on the Journey to Europe*). Addis Ababa, 1916.

——. ደስታና ፡ ክብር ፤ የኢትዮጵያ ፡ መንግሥት ፡ አልጋ ፡ ወራሽና ፡ እንደራሴ ፡ ልዑል ፡ ተፈሪ ፡ መኮንን ፡ ወደ ፡ አውሮፓ ፡ ሲሔዱና ፡ ሲመለሱ ፡ የመንገዳ ቸው ፡ አጎብኝ   (*Joy and Honor: Details of the Heir to the Throne and Regent of the Ethiopian Empire Ras Täfäri Mäkonnen's Return Journey to Europe*). Addis Ababa, 1916.

——. "Tutankh-Amen and Ras Tafari." *The Crisis*, XXIX (December *1924*), 64–68.[5]

——. መጽሐፈ ፡ ቅኔ ፡ ዘቀደምት ፡ ወደኃርት ፡ ሊቃውንቲሃ ፡ ወማዕምራኒሃ ፡ ለኢትዮጵያ   (*Book of Hymns by the Ancient and Modern Doctors and Masters of Ethiopia*). Addis Ababa, 1918.

——. ነጎ ፡ ጽባሕ ፡ ከቅዱሳት ፡ መጻሕፍትና ፡ ከታሪክ ፤ ከሌሎችም ፡ ከልዩ ፡ ልዩ ፡ መጻሕፍት ፡ ተለቅሞ ፡ የተጻፈ.   (*Dawn Has Come: Extracts*

[5] The writer's name is given as "Kantiba Nerouy."

From the Holy Writ, From History and From Various Other Books). Addis Ababa, 1919.

——. ዋዜማ ፨ በማግሥቱ፡ የኢትዮጵያን ፡ ንገሥታት ፡ የታሪክ ፡ በዓል ፡ ለማክበር   (*Vigil: To Celebrate Tomorrow the History of the Kings of Ethiopia*). Addis Ababa, 1921.

——. ሱላርና ፡ ወተት ፡ የልጆች ፡ ማሳደጊያ   (*Sugar and Milk to Bring Up Children*). Addis Ababa, 1922.

——. የልብ ፡ አሳብ ፡ የበርኔና ፡ የጽዮን ፡ ሞገሳ ፡ ጋብቻ   (*Thoughts of the Heart: The Marriage of Bernané and Ṣyou Mogasa*). Addis Ababa, 1923.

——. ጥሩ ፡ ምንጭ (ነቅዕ ፡ ንጹሕ) ፡ ዝውእቱ ፡ ዜና ፡ ሐዋርያት ፡ ንጹሐን   (*A Pure Spring: A History of the Pure Apostles).* Addis Ababa, 1923.

——. (ማኅደረ ፡ ብርሃን ፤) በገረ ፡ ጃፓን   (*The House of Light: The Japanese Country*). Addis Ababa, 1924.

——. መጽሐፈ ፡ እርስጣላብ   (*The Book of the Astrolabe*). Addis Ababa, 1924. (The author's name, ወዳጀነህ ፡ ወልደ ፡ ሥላሴ, is supposed to be a pseudonym for Heruy.)

——. አዲስ ፡ ዓለም ፡ የቅኖችና ፡ የደጋ ፡ አድራጊዎች ፡ መኖሪያ   (*The New World: Way of Life of the Just and of Those Who Behave Well*). Addis Ababa, 1925.

——. በዕድሜ ፡ መሰንበት ፡ ሁሉን ፡ ለማየት   (*To Stay Alive to See Everything*). Addis Ababa, 1926.

——. እኔና ፡ ወዳጆቼ   (*My Friends and I*). Addis Ababa, 1927.

Imru Haylä Sellasé (እምሩ ፡ ኃይለ ፡ ሥላሴ).   ፊታውራሪ ፡ በላይ ፤ ታሪክ ፡ በምሳሌ   (*Fitawrari Bälay*). Addis Ababa, 1948. (English version by Tadesse Tamrat: "Fitawrari Belay." *Ethiopia Observer*, V [*1961– 62*], 342–360.)

Johnson, Samuel. የራስሴላስ ፡ መስፍን ፡ ኢትዮጵያ ፡ ታሪክ   (Sirak Wäldä Sellasé Heruy's Amharic version of *Rasselas*). Asmära, 1939.

Käbbädä Mika'él (ከበደ ፡ ሚካኤል). ብርሃነ ፡ ሕሊና   (*The Light of Intelligence*). Addis Ababa, 1933.

——. መጀመሪያ ፡ እርምጃ ፤ ያአማርኛ ፡ መላመጃ ፡ መጽሐፍ   (*An Amharic Primer*). Addis Ababa, 1934.

——. ታሪክና ፡ ምሳሌ ፡ ፫ኛ ፡ መጽሐፍ   (*Story and Parable*, Part III). Addis Ababa, 1935.

——. ከይቅርታ ፡ በላይ   (*Beyond Pardon*). Addis Ababa, 1936.

——. የትንቢት ፡ ቀጠሮ ፨ (ቴአትር) ፡ ትራጀዲ   (*Prophecy Fulfilled*). Addis Ababa, 1938. English translation by Stephen Wright, 1953.

——. ኢትዮጵያና ፡ ምዕራባዊ ፡ ሥልጣኔ   (*Ethiopia and Western Civilization*). Addis Ababa, 1941 (with English and French translations).

——. የቅጣት ፡ ማዕበል   (*The Storm of Punishment*). Addis Ababa, 1951.

——. ፈለፀሁ ፡ ቱቀወዐ (*The Light of Intelligence*). Addis Ababa, 1942.

——. ታላላቅ ፡ ሰዎች (*Great Men*). Addis Ababa, 1943.

——. ጃፓን ፡ እንደምን ፡ ሠለጠነት ? (*How Did Japan Modernize Itself?*). Addis Ababa, 1946.

——. ትልቁ ፡ እስክንድር (*Alexander the Great*). Addis Ababa, 1947.

——. አኒባል (*Hannibal*). Addis Ababa, 1948. French translation by the author, *Annibal, tragédie en cinq actes*. Addis Ababa, *1964*.

——. የዓለም ፡ ታሪክ ፡ (፩ኛ ፡ መጽሐፍ) (*History of the World*, Part I). Addis Ababa, 1948.

——. ግርግዊነታቸው ፡ በሜሪካ ፡ አገር (*His Majesty's Journey to the United States*). Addis Ababa, 1951.

——. የቅኔ ፡ አዝመራ (*Poetry*). Addis Ababa, 1956.

——. ካሌብ ፤ ቴያትር (*Caleb. A Tragedy*). Addis Ababa, 1958.

——. አክዓብ (*Achab*). Addis Ababa, 1960.

——. ሥልጣኔ (*Civilisation.*) Addis Ababa, n.d.

——. የኢትዮጵያ ፡ የጥንፉ ፡ ሥዕሎች. *Old Ethiopian Paintings. Anciennes peintures éthiopiennes.* Addis Ababa, 1961 (with translation in English, French).

Mahtämä Sellasé Wäldä Mäsqäl (ማኅተመ ፡ ሥላሴ ፡ ወልደ ፡ መስቀል). ዝክረ ፡ ነገር (*Memories*). Addis Ababa, 1942.

——. ዕጹብ ፡ ድንቅ (*Great Marvel*). Addis Ababa, 1943.

——. ያባቶች ፡ ቅርስ (*Remains of the Fathers*). Addis Ababa, 1943.

——. ጥበበ ፡ ገራህት ፤ ፩ኛ ፡ መጽሐፍ (*The Art of Tilling the Earth: First Part*). Addis Ababa, 1944.

——. አማርኛ ፡ ቅኔ (*Amharic Poetry*). Addis Ababa, 1948.

——. እንቅልፍ ፡ ለዎኔ (*Seeking Sleep*). Addis Ababa, 1950.

——. ስለ ፡ ኢትዮጵያ ፡ የመሬት ፡ ሥራት ፡ አስተዳደርና ፡ ግብር ፤ ጠቅላላ ፡ አስተያየት (*Land Property in Ethiopia: A Survey*). Addis Ababa, *1957*.

——. ስም ፡ ከመቃብር ፡ በላይ ። የጸሐፊ ፡ ትእዛዝ ፡ ወልደ ፡ መስቀል ፡ ታሪኩ ፡ እጭር ፡ የሕይወት ፡ ታሪክ (*The Name Above the Grave: A Short Biography of Tesfahe Taezaz Wäldä Mäsqäl*). Addis Ababa, 1956.

——. የኛም ፡ አሉ ፡ እንወታቸው (*Let Us Know What We Have*). Addis Ababa, 1958.

Mäkonnen Endalkačäw (መኰንን ፡ እንዳልካቸው). ዓለም ፡ ወረተኛ (*Inconstant World*). Addis Ababa, 1940.

——. የደም ፡ ድምፅ (*The Voice of Blood*). Addis Ababa, 1941.

——. ሣልሳዊ ፡ ዳዊት ፤ ልብ ፡ ወለድ ፡ ታሪክ (*David III: A Historical Novel*). Addis Ababa, 1942.

——. አሳብና ፡ ሰው ፡ የልብ ፡ ወለድ ፡ ታሪክ (*Man and His Thought*). Addis Ababa, 1943.

——. አልሞትኩም ፡ ብየ ፡ አልዋሽም (*I Do Not Lie, Saying I Am Not Dead*). Addis Ababa, 1945.

——. ከቡታይ ፡ እስከ ፡ መኸር (*From Seed to Crop*). Addis Ababa, 1946.

——. የደም ፡ ዘመን ፤ ልብ ፡ ወለድ ፡ ታሪክ (*The Bloody Era*). Addis Ababa, 1947.

——. አርሙኝ (*Advise Me*). Addis Ababa, 1947.

——. መልካም ፡ ቤተሰቦች (*The Good Family*). Asmära, 1949.

——. የሕልም ፡ ሩጫ (*The Course of Dreams*). N.p., 1949.

——. ሰሐይ ፡ መስፍን ፤ ልብ ፡ ወለድ ፡ ታሪክ (*Ṣähay Mäsfen: A Novel*). Addis Ababa, 1949.

——. ጣይቱ ፡ ብጡል ፤ ልብ ፡ ወለድ ፡ ታሪክ (*Ṭaytu Beṭul: A Novel*). Addis Ababa, 1950.

——. *Three Plays: King David the Third, The Voice of Blood, The City of the Poor*. Asmära, n.d.

Mäkonnen Zäwde (መኮንን ፡ ዘውዴ). የማይጨው ፡ ቁስለኛ (*The Wounded Man of May Čäw*). Addis Ababa, 1948.

——. የዓለም ፡ ሰው ፡ እርምጃ (*Man's Career in This World*). Addis Ababa, 1948.

——. ያይኔ ፡ ብርሃን (*The Light of My Eyes*). Addis Ababa, 1949.

——. አስቻው (*Endurance*). Addis Ababa, 1956.

Mängestu Lämma (መንግሥቱ ፡ ለማ የግጥም ፡ ጉባዔ ፤ የፍቅር ፤ የጨዋታ ፤ የሐሳብ ፤ የተረት ፡ ግጥም (*Collection of Poems: Love, Entertainment, Philosophy, Verse Fables*). Addis Ababa, 1950.

——. የአማርኛ ፡ ግጥም ፨ ዓይነቱ ፡ ሥርቱ ፡ ሥርዓቱ ("The Technical Aspects of Amharic Versification"). *Journal of Ethiopian Studies*, I, 2 (*1963*), 133-151 (with summary in English).

——. ያላቻ ፡ ጋብቻ (*Marriage of Unequals*). Addis Ababa, 1957.

——. ጠልፎ ፡ በከሴ ፤ የቴያትር ፡ ጨዋታ (*Snatch and Run. A Play*). Addis Ababa, 1955. (English translation *Snatch and run, or Marriage by Abduction*. *Ethiopia Observer*, VII, 4 [*1964*], 321-360.)

Mäzgäbu Abatä (መዝገቡ ፡ አባተ). ጠቅል ፡ አብነቱ ፤ ፍዱም ፡ መድኃኒቴ (*Emperor, My Example and Complete Savior*). Addis Ababa, 1946.

——. የመንፈስ ፡ ማዕበል (*Tempest of the Spirit*). Addis Ababa, 1947.

——. ጠቅል ፡ ነህ ፡ መሪያችን ፡ ኑር ፡ መከበሪያችን (*Long Live the Emperor, Our Leader and Our Pride*. Addis Ababa, 1947.

——. ጥበብ ፡ ሥላሴ ፡ ልብ ፡ ወለድ ፡ ታሪክ (*Ṭebäbä Sellasé. A Novel*). Addis Ababa, 1948.

——. ምስኪኑ ፡ ድብ ፡ አርጋፈው (*Destroy Them, Poor Man*). Addis Ababa, 1956.

——. ፍቅር ፡ ምን ፡ ዕዳ ፡ ነው (*What Does Love Owe*). Addis Ababa, 1957.

Mogäs Keflé (ሞገስ ፡ ክፍሉ). አንደፍታ ፡ እንጫወት ፨ ፩ኛው ፡ ፎሊዩም (*Let Us Talk a While. First part*). Addis Ababa, 1943.

——. ሠላሰው ፡ ሌሊቴ (*My Thirty Days*). Addis Ababa, 1946.

——. ሳያውቀው ፡ ተበቀለው (*Unexpected Revenge*). Addis Ababa, 1947.

——. ዘመናዊ ፡ ኑር (*Modern Life*). Addis Ababa, 1949.

——. የሙሶሊኒ ፡ ምስጢር (*The Mussolini Mystery*). Addis Ababa, 1949.
Nabaldiyan, K. (ናባልዲያን).   የጎንደሬ ፡ ገብረ ፡ ማርያም ፡ አጥቶ ፡ ማግኘት
(*The Adventure of Gäbrä Maryam from Gondar*). Addis Ababa,
1926.
Näggädä Gäbrä Ab (ነገደ ፡ ገብረ ፡ አብ ፤). የናት ፡ መካሪ ፡ አያጥፋ ፡ ፈጣሪ ፡
አስደናቂ ፡ ትያትር ፡ ልብወለድ (*Mother's Advice Is God's Advice*). Addis Ababa, 1949.
Romanä Wärq Kasahun (ሮማነ ፡ ወርቅ ፡ ካሳሁን). ትዳር ፡ በዘ ፤ ትንሽ ፡
ምክር ፡ ለትዳር ፡ ወዳጆት   (*The Art of Family Life*). Addis Ababa,
1942.
——. ማኅቶተ ፡ ጥበብ ፤ ስለልዕልት ፡ ፀሐይ ፡ ኃይለ ፡ ሥላሴ ፡ መታሰቢያ. (*The
Candle of Wisdom: A Reminder About Princess Sähay Hoylä Sellasé*). Addis Ababa, 1943.
——. የሕይወት ፡ ጓደኛ   (*A Companion for Life*). Addis Ababa, 1948.
Seneddu Gäbru (ስንዱ ፡ ገብሩ). የልቤ ፡ መጽሐፍ   (*The Book of
My Heart*). Addis Ababa, 1942.
Shakespeare, William. ሮሚዎና ፡ ጁልየት ፡ ቴአትር   (Käbbädä Mik-
a'él's Amharic version of *Romeo and Juliet*). Addis Ababa, 1946.
——. የዮልዮስ ፡ ቄሳር ፡ አሳዛኝ ፡ አሞሙአት ፡ ቴአትር   (Bäqqälä
Tägäññä's Amharic version of *Julius Caesar*). Asmära, 1949.
Taddäsä Libän (ታደሰ ፡ ሊቢን).   መስከረም   (*Mäskäräm*). Addis
Ababa, 1949.
TäfäriDäfärräsu (ተፈሪ ፡ ደፈረሱ). ገበራውና ፡ ሚስቱ   (*The Ploughman and His Wife*). Addis Ababa, 1949.
Täklä Hawaryat (ተክለ ፡ ሐዋርያት). ስለ ፡ ትልቅ ፡ ሳልና ፡ ነቀርሳ ፤ የም
ክር ፡ ቃል (*A Treatise On Tuberculosis*). Addis Ababa, 1921.
——. ትንሽ ፡ መፈተኛ ፤ ስለ ፡ እርሻ ፡ ትምህርት   (*A Modest Attempt
at the Study of Agriculture*). Addis Ababa, 1922.
——. ጃንሆይ ፡ ቀዳማዊ ፡ ኃይለ ፡ ሥላሴ ፡ በፈቃዳቸው ፡ ሕግ ፡ መንግሥት፡
ስለማቆ ማቸው ፤ የገንዘብ ፡ ሚኒስቴር ፡ በጅሮንድ ፡ ተክለ ፡ ሐዋርያት ፡ በ፲፱
፳፬ ዓ. ም. ለመሳፍንቱና ፡ ለመኳንንቱ ፡ የተናገሩት ፡ ቃል
(Speech by Bajrond Täklä Hawaryat, Minister of Finance, made to
the princes and dignitaries in 1932 on the occasion of the grant of a
Constitution by His Majesty the Emperor Haile Sellassie I of his own
free will). Addis Ababa, 1932.
Täklä Maryam Fantayé (ተክለ ፡ ማርያም ፡ ፋንታዬ). እውነትም ፡ የአንጀራ ፡
እናት ፡ ልብ ፡ ወለዱ (*Truth, Foster-Mother*). Addis Ababa, 1948.
Te'ezazu Haylu (ተእዛዙ ፡ ኃይሉ). ኃይለ ፡ ማርያም ፡ ማሞ   (*Hay-
lä Maryam Mammo*). Addis Ababa, 1949.
Tsegaye Gabre-Medhin. "Poems." *Ethiopia Observer*, IX, 1 (*1965*),
50–59.
——. *Oda-Oak Oracle*. London, *1965*.
——. "Tewodros." *Ethiopia Observer*, IX, 3 (*1966*), 211–226.
——. "Azmari." *Ethiopia Observer*, IX, 3 (*1966*), 227–239.

——. "Literature and the African Public." *Ethiopia Observer*, XI, 1 (1967), 63–67.

Wäldä Giyorgis Wäldä Yohannes (ወልደ ፡ ጊዮርጊስ ፡ ወልደ ፡ ዮሐንስ) የወንድ ፡ ልጅ ፡ ኩራት (*The Pride of the Male Child*). Addis Ababa, 1927.

——. ጀግና ፡ ሰው ፡ ተጋዳይ (*The Brave Man Champion*). Addis Ababa, 1928.

——. ታሪክ ፡ ያለው ፡ አይሞትም (*He Who Made History Does Not Die*). Addis Ababa, 1939.

——. አምኀ ፡ ፍቅር ፡ ወሰላም (*Gift of Love and Peace*). Addis Ababa, 1939.

——. ክብረ ፡ ነገሥት (*The Glory of Kings*). Addis Ababa, 1939.

——. የዓለም ፡ ጠባይ (*The Way of the World*). Addis Ababa, 1940.

——. ብልጽግር ፡ በግብርና (*Prosperity Through Agriculture*). Addis Ababa, 1941.

——. ለግርማዊ ፡ ንጉሠ ፡ ነገሥት ፡ ለቀዳማዊ ፡ ኃይለ ፡ ሥላሴ ፡ የ፶፰ኛው ፡ ዓመት ፡ የልደት ፡ በዓል ፡ መታሰቢያ ፡ ገጸ ፡ በረከት (*Gift to Celebrate Emperor Haile Sellassie's 58th Birthday*). Addis Ababa, 1942.

——. ሥነ ፡ ምግባር (*Proper Conduct*). Addis Ababa, 1943.

——. ከሥራ ፡ በኋላ ፡ ሥራ ፡ ስትፈቱ ፤ እንቆቅልሽ ፡ ተጫወቱ (*After Work, Entertain Yourself with Riddles*). Addis Ababa, 1943.

——. የባልና ፡ የሚስት ፡ ጭውውት ፡ በእንካ ፡ ስላንቲያ (*Dialogue of Husband and Wife*). Addis Ababa, 1945.

——. አግአዚ ። ወደውጭ ፡ አገር ፤ ሔጄ ፡ ነበር ። ልብ ፡ ወለድና ፡ ታሪክ ፡ ወለድ (*Ag'azi. I Had Gone Abroad*). Addis Ababa, 1945.

——. አምኃ ፡ ንግሥ (*The Gift of Kingship*). Addis Ababa, 1948.

——. ታሪክ ፡ አይሙት ፡ እንዲያሜውት (*Entertainment Through History*). Addis Ababa, 1957.

——. አትሰረቅ (*Do Not Steal*). Addis Ababa, 1957.

Webäté, Grazmač (ውበቴ ፡ ግራዝማች). ለኢትዮጵያ ፡ ንግሥተ ፡ ነገሥታት ፡ ዘውዲቱ ፤ ለልዑልም ፡ አልጋ ፡ ወራሽ ፡ ራስተፈሪ ፡ ምከጋር (*Praise to Zäwditu, Queen of the Kings of Ethiopia and to Ras Täfäri, Heir to the Throne*). Addis Ababa, n.d. (between 1917 and 1922).

Yaréd Gäbrä Mika'él (ያሬድ ፡ ገብረ ፡ ሚካኤል). እንኳን ፡ የተወለድክ ፡ የነፃነት ፡ ጌታ ፤ ለኢትዮጵያ ፡ እንድትሆን ፡ መከታ. (*Not Only Born a Master of Freedom, You Should Be a Parapet for Ethiopia*). Addis Ababa, 1939.

——. ዕድሜና ፡ ሥራ ፡ ከጠቅል ፡ ጋራ (*Let Us Grow and Work with the Emperor*). Addis Ababa, 1944.

——. መዝገበ ፡ ታሪክ (*Historical Chronicles*). Addis Ababa, 1945.

——. እኔና ፡ አንቺ ፤ ጋብቻችን ፡ የተቀደሰ ፡ እንዲሆን (*You and I: Let Our Marriage Be Blessed*). Addis Ababa, 1945.

——. የታሪክ ፡ ጉልላት (*The Summit of History*). Addis Ababa, 1946.

——. ዕድሜ ፡ ከጤና (*Age and Health*). Addis Ababa, 1947.

——. የታሪክ ፡ ሰው ፤ ዜና ፡ ዕበየለቀደማዊ ፡ ኃይለ ፡ ሥላሴ ፡ ንጉሠ ፡ ነገሥት ፡ በጐል ፡ አውራኅ ፡ ወአዝማናት (Man of History: Chronicle of the Great Deeds of Emperor Haile Sellassie I, According to the Months and Eras). Addis Ababa, 1948.

——. የአፍሪካ ፡ ፀሐይ ፡ በኢትዮጵያ ፡ ሰማይ (The Sun of Africa in the Sky of Ethiopia). Addis Ababa, 1948.

——. የ፵ዓመት ፡ ጐልማሳ ፡ አጭር ፡ ታሪክ (Forty Years of Life: A Brief Summary) (A Biography of Crown Prince Asfä Wäsän). Addis Ababa, 1948.

——. ከለዑል ፡ መኰንን ፡ መስፍን ፡ ሐረር ፤ የሕይወት ፡ ታሪክ (Biography of H. R. H. Mäkonnen, Duke of Harar). Addis Ababa, 1949.

——. የፍቅር ፡ ምርኮኛ (The Prisoner of Love). Addis Ababa, 1950.

——. ግርማዊት ፡ እቴጌ ፡ መነን ፤ መዓምርቱ ፡ ለግርማዊ ፡ ቀዳማዊ ፡ ኃይለሥ ላሴ ፡ ንጉሠ ፡ ነገሥት ፡ ዘኢትዮጵያ (The Empress Etégé Mänän, Wife of Haile Sellassie I, Emperor of Ethiopia). Addis Ababa, 1950.

——. ስለ ፡ እንስሳት ፡ እገልግሎት ፡ ለሕፃናት ፡ በረከት (The Usefulness of Animals: A Present for Children). 7th ed. Addis Ababa, 1957.

——. ይምጡ ፡ በዝና ፤ አዲስ ፡ አበባ (The Call of Fame: Addis Ababa). Addis Ababa, 1958.

Yäšäwa Wärq Haylu (የሽው ፡ ወርቅ ፡ ኃይሉ). ነፃነት ፡ ክብሬ   (Freedom, My Honor). Addis Ababa, 1947.

Yoftahé Negusé (የፍታሄ ፡ ንጉሤ).   ጥቅም ፡ የሌለበት ፡ ጫዋታ (Vain Entertainment). Addis Ababa, 1923.

——. ጎበዝ ፡ አየን (We Saw a Brave Man). Addis Ababa, 1928.

——. አፋጀኸኝ (You Destroyed Me). Addis Ababa, 1958.

II. STUDIES

Aläka Yekunna Amlaka Gäbrä Selasse. "Early Ge'ez Qene." Journal of Ethiopian Studies, IV, 1 (1966), 76–119.

Alemayyehu Moges. "Collection and Analysis of Contemporary Ge'ez Poetry," Survey of Language Use and Language Teaching in East Africa Bulletin, II, 3 (1969), 8–9.

"Amharic Literature," in Guide Book of Ethiopia. Addis Ababa, 1954. Pp. 407–416.

Amon d'Aby, F. J. La Côte d'Ivoire dans la cité africaine. Paris, 1951.

Andrianarahinjaka, Lucien. "Ramananato: An early 19th Century Malagasy Poet." Présence Africaine, no. 55 (1965), pp. 45–73.

Ashton, E. H. The Basuto. London, 1952.

Baker, E. "On the Poetry of Madagascar." Antananarivo Annual, III (1886), 167–177.

Barnes, Leonard, The New Boer War. London, 1932.

Baum, James E. Savage Abyssinia. New York, 1927.

Béart, Charles, "Towards a French-African Culture (William Ponty

Training Centre, Dakar)." *Oversea Education*, XVII (1946), 357–368; XVIII (1946), 403–418.

———. "A propos du théâtre africain." *Traits d'Union*, XV (1957), 103–104.

———. "Les origines du théâtre dans le monde. Position actuelle du théâtre africain." *Comptes rendus mensuels des séances de l'Académie des sciences d'Outre-Mer*, XXII, 4 (1962), 143–163.

Benson, Mary. *The African Patriots: The Story of the African National Congress of South Africa*. London, 1963. Rev. ed. *South Africa: The Struggle for a Birthright*. Harmondsworth, 1966.

Benz, E., ed. *Messianische Kirchen, Sekten und Bewegungen im heutigen Afrika*. Leiden, 1965.

Beuchat, P.-D. *Do the Bantu Have a Literature?* Johannesburg [1963].

"Bibliography of Southern Sotho Christian Literature." *South African Outlook*, LXVII (1937), 229–230.

Brandl, Ludwig. "Frühes Christentum in der Sahara und im Sudan." *Afrika heute*, no. 24 (15 December 1966), Sonderbeilage.

Brownlee, Charles. *Reminiscences of Kaffir Life and History, 1896*. Lovedale, n.d.

Bulane, Mofolo, "Raymond Mazisi Kunene: The New Voice in African Poetry." *New African*, V, 6 (1966), 111–112.

———. "Poets of Lesotho." *New African*, VI, 2 (1967), 19–23.

———. "Then and Now: The Praise Poem in Southern Sotho." *New African*, VII, 1 (1968), 40–43.

Bulwer, C. E. Earle. "Xhosa Language and Literature: The Contribution of the Church of the Province of South Africa." *South African Outlook*, LXXXVII (1957), 44–45, 77–79, 90–91.

Bunting, Brian. *The Rise of the South African Reich*. Harmondsworth, 1964.

Casalis, J.-E. *Les Bassoutos*. Paris, 1930.

Cerulli, Enrico. "Una raccolta amarica di canti funebri." *Rivista degli studi orientali*, X (1924), 265–280.

———. "Nuove idee nell' Etiopia e nuova letteratura amarica." *Oriente Moderno*, VI (1926), 167–173.

———. "Recenti pubblicazioni abissine in amarico." *Oriente Moderno*, VI (1926), 555–557.

———. "Nuove pubblicazioni in languaggi etiopici." *Oriente Moderno*, VII (1927), 354–357.

———. "Inni della chiesa abissina." *Revista degli studi orientali*, XII (1929–30), 361–407.

———. "Nuovi libri pubblicati in Etiopia." *Oriente Moderno*, XII (1932), 170–175.

———. "Nuove pubblicazioni in lingua amarica." *Oriente Moderno*, XII (1932), 306–310.

——. "Rassegna periodica di pubblicazioni in lingue etiopiche fatte in Etiopia." *Oriente Moderno*, XIII (1933), 58–64.

——. *Storia della letteratura etiopica*. 3d ed. Florence, 1968.

Chadwick, H. Munro, and N. Kershaw Chadwick. *The Growth of Literature*. Cambridge, 1940.

Chalmers, John A. *Tiyo Soga*. Edinburgh, 1877.

Coates, Austin. *Basutoland*. London, 1966.

Coertze, P. J. "Die literatuur van die Basoeto." *Die Basuin*, III, 6 (1933), 10–12.

Cohen, Marcel. "La naissance d'une littérature imprimée en amharique." *Journal Asiatique*, CCVI (1925), 348–363.

——. "La langue littéraire amharique." *Comptes rendus du Groupe linguistique d'Etudes chamito-sémitiques*, II (1937), 95.

Cole-Beuchat, P.-D. "Literary Composition." In James Walton, ed. *The Teaching of Southern Sotho*. Maseru, 1961. Pp. 56–68.

Comba, Pierre. "Une année de publication en langue amharique." *Annales d'Ethiopie* I (1955), 151–152; II (1957), 253–264; III (1959), 301–312.

——. "Bref aperçu sur les débuts de la littérature de langue amharique et sur ses tendances actuelles." *Ethiopia Observer*, II (1958), 125–128.

——. *Inventaire des livres amhariques figurant dans la collection éthiopienne à la Bibliothèque de l'University College d'Addis Abeba. Avril 1959*. Addis Ababa, 1961.

——. "Le roman dans la littérature éthiopienne de langue amharique." *Journal of Semitic Studies*, IX (1964), 173–186.

Coon, Carleton S. *Measuring Ethiopia and Flight to Arabia*. Boston, 1935.

Cope, Jack. "South African Letters." *Landfall*, XVIII (1964), 258–263.

Cope, Jack, and Uys Krige, eds. *The Penguin Book of South African Verse*. Harmondsworth, 1968.

Cope, Trevor, ed. *Izibongo: Zulu Praise Poems*. London, 1968.

Cousins, W. E. "A Native Malagasy Lyric." *Antananarivo Annual*, V (1896), 457–459.

Damane, M. *Marath'a lilepe*. Morija, 1960.

Damann, Ernst. "Das Christusverständnis in nachchristlichen Kirchen und Sekten Afrikas." In Ernst Benz, ed. *Messianische Kirchen, Sekten und Bewegungen im heutigen Afrika*. Leiden, 1965. Pp. 1–21.

Dathorne, O. R. "Thomas Mofolo and the Sotho Hero." *New African*, V (1966), 152–153.

Decaunes, Luc. "Une épopée bantoue." *Présence Africaine*, no. 5 (1948), pp. 883–886.

Dieterlen, Georges. "Thomas Mofolo." *South African Outlook*, LXXVIII (1948), 168–169. Reprinted in *African Affairs*, XLVIII, no. 190 (1949), 74–75.

Doke, Clement M. "A Preliminary Investigation into the State of the Native Languages of South Africa with Suggestions as to Research and the Development of Literature." *Bantu Studies*, VII (1933), 1–98.

——. "Vernacular Text-Books in South African Native Schools." *Africa*, VII (1935), 183–209.

——. "The Future of Bantu Literature." *African Observer*, VI, 2 (1936), 18–22.

——. "European and Bantu Languages in South Africa." *Africa*, XII (1938), 308–319.

——. "The Native Languages of South Africa." *African Studies*, I (1942), 136–141.

——. "The Basis of Bantu Literature." *Africa*, XVIII (1948), 284–301.

——. "Scripture Translation into Bantu Languages." *African Studies*, XVII (1958), 82–99.

Dube, John L. *U-Shembe*. Pietermaritzburg, 1936.

Duncan, Cynthia. "Thomas Mofolo—Bantu Author's Contribution to African Literature." *African World* (March 1949), p. 13.

Dutton, E. A. T. *The Basuto of Basutoland*. London, 1923.

Eadie, J. E., *An Amharic Reader*. Cambridge, 1924.

Ellenberger, Victor. *A Century of Mission Work in Basutoland: 1833–1933*. Morija, 1936.

——. "Thomas Mofolo (1873–1948)" *Journal des Missions Evangéliques* (February 1949), pp. 77–79.

Ellis, William. *History of Madagascar*. London, 1838.

Farago, Ladislas. *Abyssinia on the Eve*. London, 1935.

Ferragne, Marcel. "L'oeuvre de presse catholique au Basutoland." *La Voix du Basutoland*, no. 54 (January–March 1953), pp. 19–26.

——. *Essai d'histoire de littérature catholique en Sesotho*. Roma (Lesotho) [1970].

Franz, G. H. "The Literature of Lesotho." *Bantu Studies*, IV (1930), 145–180.

——. "Die vernaamste Basotho skryvers en iets oor hulle werk." *Die Basuin*, I, 4 (1930), 12–15.

——. "Die Literatur des Lesotho (Basutoland)." *Die Brücke*, Wissenschaftliche Beilage, I (1931), 1–4; II–IV (1932), 1–4.

Fusella, Luigi. "Recenti pubblicazioni amariche in Abissinia." *Rassegna di studi etiopici*, V (1946), 93–102.

——. "Il *Lebb wallad tārik* di Afawârq Gabra Iyasus." *Rassegna di studi etiopici*, X (1951), 56–70.

——. "Il *Dāgmāwi Měnilěk di* Afawârq Gabra Iyasus." *Rassegna di studi etiopici*, XVII (1961), 11–44.

Gaselee, Stephen. "The Beginnings of Printing in Abyssinia." *The Library*, XI (1931), 93–95.

Gérard, Albert S. "Literature of Lesotho." *Africa Report,* XI, 7 (1966), 68–70.

——. "Le poète et les palmiers: sur un sonnet de J. J. Rabéarivelo." *Marche Romane,* XVI, 1 (1966), 15–20.

——. "Bibliographical Problems in Creative African Literature." *Journal of General Education,* XIX (1967), 25–35.

——. "La naissance du théâtre à Madagascar." *Bulletin d'Information CEDEV,* no. 8 (1967), pp. 28–35.

——. "African Literature in Rhodesia." *Africa Report,* XIII, 5 (1968), 41–42.

——. "Amharic Creative Literature: The Early Phase." *Journal of Ethiopian Studies,* VI, 2 (1968), 39–59.

——. "Littérature francophone d'Afrique: le temps de la relève." *Revue Nouvelle,* XLIX, 2 (1969), 198–204.

——. "An African Tragedy of Hubris: Thomas Mofolo's *Chaka.*" In Brom Weber, ed. *Sense and Sensibility in Twentieth-Century Writing: A Gathering in Memory of William Van O'Connor.* Carbondale, 1970, pp. 39–56.

Gollock, G. A. "*The Traveller of the East,* by Thomas Molofo." *Africa,* VII (1934), 510–511.

Greenfield, Richard. *Ethiopia: A New Political History.* New York, 1965.

——. "An Ethiopian Protest Poem: 'Submit to Cross-examination.'" *Literature East & West,* XII (1968), i, 22–29.

Groenewald, P. S. "S. M. Mofokeng: *Leetong* (1954)." *Limi,* no. 10 (June 1970), pp. 58–61.

Guidi, Ignazio. "Le canzoni Geez-amariña in onore di Re abissini." *Rendiconti della Reale Accademia dei Lincei. Classe di scienze morali, storiche e filologiche,* V i, (1889), 53–66.

——. "Contributi alla storia letteraria di Abissinia." *Rendiconti della Reale Accademia dei Lincei, ser.* VI, XXXI (1922), 65–94, 185–218.

——. "Le odierne letterature dell'Impero Etiopico." *Atti del Reale Istituto Veneto di Scienze, Lettere e d'Arti,* XCII (1932–33), 935–942.

——. *Breve storia della letteratura etiopica.* Rome, 1932.

Guma, S. M. *The Form, Content and Technique of Traditional Literature in Southern Sotho.* Pretoria, 1967.

——. "Southern Sotho Literature Today." *Africa Digest* (Mazenod), no. 15 [1968], pp. 25–29.

Hailey, Lord. *An African Survey.* 2d ed. London, 1956.

Halpern, Jack. *South Africa's Hostages: Basutoland, Bechuanaland, and Swaziland.* Baltimore, 1965.

Hoernlé, R. F. Alfred. "The Bantu Dramatic Society at Johannesburg." *Africa,* VII (1934), 223–227.

Hunter, Monica. *Reaction to Conquest: Effects of Contact with Europeans on the Pondo of South Africa.* London, 1961.

Huntingford, G. W. B., ed. *The Glorious Victories of 'Āmda Ṣeyon, King of Ethiopia.* Oxford, 1965.

Huskisson, Yvonne. "The Story of Bantu Music." *Bantu*, XV, 7 (1968), 16–20.

Huss, Bernard. "Education Through the Drama." *Native Teachers' Journal*, II (1921), 48–50.

——. "A Zulu *Inganekwana* Dramatized." *Native Teachers' Journal* II (1921), 50–52.

——. "A Short and Easy Drama in Zulu." *Native Teachers' Journal* II (1921), 95–97.

Inauen, Beat. "Dix ans de littérature Shona." *Bethléem*, no. 5 (May 1967), pp. 154–157.

International Labour Conference. *The Recruiting of Labour in the Colonies.* London, 1935.

Jabavu, D. D. T. *Bantu Literature.* Lovedale, 1921.

——. *The Influence of English on Bantu Literature.* Lovedale, 1944.

——. "The Origin of 'Nkosi Sikelel' in Africa." *Nada*, no. 26 (1949), pp. 56–57.

Jacobs, John. "Les épopées de Soundjata et de Chaka: une étude comparée," *Aequatoria*, XXV (1962), 121–124.

——. "Thomas Mofolo en de Negro-Afrikaanse literatuur." *Vlaamse Gids*, XLVII (1963), 199–206.

Jahn, Janheinz. *Die neoafrikanische Literatur. Gesamtbibliographie von den Anfängen bis zur Gegenwart.* Düsseldorf, 1965.

——. *Geschichte der neoafrikanischen Literatur.* Düsseldorf, 1966.

——. "The Tragedy of Southern Bantu Literature." *Black Orpheus*, no. 21 (April 1967), pp. 44–52.

——. *A History of Neo-African Literature: Writing in Two Continents.* London, 1968.

Jesman, Czeslaw. *The Russians in Ethiopia: An Essay in Futility.* London, 1958.

Jones, G. I. *Basutoland Medicine Murder.* London, 1951.

Jordan, Archibald C. "Samuel Edward Krune Mqhayi." *South African Outlook*, LXXV (1945), 135–138.

——. "Towards an African Literature." *Africa South*, I, 4 (1957), 90–98, II, 4 (1957), 99–105; II, 2 (1958), 101–109; II, 3 (1958), 112–115; II, 4 (1958), 113–118; III, 1 (1958), 114–117; III, 2 (1959), 74–79; III 3 (1959), 114–117; III, 4 (1959), 114–115; IV, 1 (1959), 117–121; IV, 2 (1960), 110–113; IV, 3 (1960), 112–116.

Kamil, Murad. *Das Land des Negus.* Innsbrück, 1953.

——. "Amharische Kaiserlieder." *Abhandlungen für die Kunde des Morgenlandes*, XXXII, 4 (1957), 1–50.

Kerr, Alexander. "Honour for an African Author: Tribute by Dr. A. Kerr." *South African Outlook*, LXXXVIII (1958), 169.

——. *Fort Hare 1915-48: The Evolution of an African College*. London, 1968.

Kobischanow, Y. M., "The Origin of Ethiopian Literature." In M. A. Korostovtsev, ed. *Essays on African Culture*. Moscow, 1966.

Krog, E. W., ed. *African Literature in Rhodesia*. Gwelo, 1966.

Kunene, Daniel P. "A War Song of the Basotho." *Journal of the New African Literature and the Arts*, no. 3 (Spring 1967), pp. 10–20.

——. *The Works of Thomas Mofolo: Summaries and Critiques*. Los Angeles, 1967.

——. "A. C. Jordan, 1907–1968." *African Arts / Arts d'Afrique*, II, 2 (1969), 25–26.

——. "Deculturation—The African Writer's Response." *Africa Today*, XV, 4 (1968), 19–24.

Kunene, Daniel P., and Randal A. Kirsch. *The Beginning of South African Vernacular Literature*. Los Angeles, 1967.

Kunene, Mazisi [Raymond]. "Portrait of Magolwane—the Great Zulu Poet." *Cultural Events in Africa*, no. 32 (July 1967), pp. 1–14.

——. "Background to African Literature." *Afro-Asian Writings*, I (1968), 35–40.

——. "Littérature et résistance en Afrique du Sud." *Oeuvres Afro-Asiatiques*, I, 2 (1968), 90–99.

Kunene, Raymond. "An Analytical Survey of Zulu Poetry, Both Traditional and Modern." Ph.D. dissertation. Durban [1961].

Laydevant, F. "La poésie chez les Basuto." *Africa*, III (1930), 523–535.

L[eenhardt], M. "Chaka, Fidélité et infidélité chez les païens," *Le Monde non-chrétien* I (1947), 346–348.

Lehmann, F. R. "Eine Form von Religionsmischung in Südafrika. Die amaNazaretha-Kirche in Natal." In *Von fremden Völkern und Kulturen. Beiträge zur Völkerkunde, Hans Plischke zum 65. Geburtstag*. Düsseldorf, 1955. Pp. 183–193.

Lenake, J. M. "A Brief Survey of Modern Literature in the South African Bantu Languages: Southern Sotho." *Limi*, no. 6 (June 1968), pp. 75–81.

——. "Satire in K. E. Ntsane se gedigte." *Limi*, no. 8 (June 1969), pp. 60–82.

Letele, G. L. "Some Recent Literary Publications in Languages of the Sotho Group." *African Studies*, III (1944), 161–171.

Levine, Donald N. *Wax and Gold: Tradition and Innovation in Ethiopian Culture*. Chicago, 1965.

——. "Ethiopia: Identity, Authority, and Realism." In L. Pye and S.

Verba, eds. *Political Culture and Political Development*. Princeton, 1965.

Lindfors, Bernth. "Additions and Corrections to Janheinz Jahn's Bibliography of Neo-African Literature." *African Studies Bulletin*, XI (1968), 129–147.

Lipsky, George A. *Ethiopia: Its People; Its Society, Its Culture*. New Haven, 1962.

Littmann, Enno. *Die altamharischen Kaiserlieder*. Strassburg, 1914.

———. "Die äthiopische Literatur." In *Handbuch der Orientalistik. III. Semitistik*. Leiden, 1954. Pp. 375–385.

Livre d'or de la mission du Lessouto. Paris, 1912.

Lloyd, T. C. "The Bantu Tread the Footlights." *South African Opinion* (8 March 1935), pp. 3–5.

"The Lovedale Press: A Review of Recent Activities." *South African Outlook*, LXI (1931), 46–48.

McDowell, Robert E. "The Brief Search for an African Hero: The Chaka-Mzilikazi Story in South African Novels." *Discourse*, XI (1968), 276–283.

MacGregor, J. "The Late Miss Victoria Swaartbooi." *South African Outlook*, LXVII (1937), 267.

MacGregor, J. C. "Some Notes on the Basuto Tribal System, Political and Social." *South African Journal of Science*, VI (1909), 276–281.

Macmillan, W. C. *Complex South Africa*. London, 1930.

Mahood, Molly M. "Marie Corelli in West Africa." *Ibadan*, no. 5 (February 1959), pp. 19–21.

Malcolm, D. Mck. "Bibliography of Zulu Books Presently Used by Missions." *South African Outlook*, LXXVI (1946), 146–148.

———. "Zulu Literature." *Africa*, XIX (1949), 33–39.

Martin, Minnie. *Basutoland: Its Legends and Customs*. London, 1903.

Marx, Ernst. "Ein Beispiel volkstümlichen Christentums unter den Kaffern Südafrikas." *Neue Allgemeine Missionszeitschrift*, XIII, 3 (1936), 95–103.

Mayhew, A. "Lovedale." *Oversea Education*, XV (1943), 4–8, 49–52.

Menghistu Lemma. "Modern Amharic Literature: The Task Ahead." *Voice of Ethiopia* (19 May 1965), pp. 2–4.

———. "Introduction to Modern Ethiopian Literature." Mimeographed. Stockholm, 1967.

Mérab, Dr. *Impressions d'Ethiopie (L'Abyssinie sous Ménélik)*. Paris, 1929.

Messing, Simon D. "A Modern Ethiopian Play—Self-study in Culture Change." *Anthropological Quarterly*, XXXIII, 3 (1960), 149–157.

Mittwoch, Eugen. "Literarisches Morgenrot in Abessinien." *Deutsche Literaturzeitung*, vol. XLV, n.s. I (1924), col. 1869–1874.

Mkentanne, Lincoln et al. "A. C. Jordan: A Tribute." *South African Outlook*, XCVIII (1968), 193–194.

Mohapeloa, M. D. *Letlole la lithoko tsa sesotho*. Johannesburg, 1950.

Moloi, A. J. "The Germination of Southern Sotho Poetry." *Limi*, no. 8 (June 1969), pp. 28–59.

Mondain, G. "Note sur les tout premiers débuts de la littérature malgache avant l'arrivée des Européens." *Bulletin de l'Académie Malgache*, n.s. XXVI (1944–45), 43–48.

Mondon-Vidailhet, C. "La Rhétorique éthiopienne." *Journal Asiatique*, X (1907), 305–329.

Moreno, Martino Mario. "Notizia su uno scrittore modernista abissino." *Oriente Moderno*, XIII (1933), 496–499.

———. "L'episodio di Lǐ̆g Iyāsu e di Ras Hāylu nelle manifestazioni letterarie abissine." *Oriente Moderno*, XII (1932), 555–563.

———. "Letteratura etiopica." In *Civiltà dell' Oriente*. Rome, 1957. II: 27–58.

Morris, Donald R. *The Washing of the Spears: A History of the Rise of the Zulu Nation Under Shaka and Its Fall in the Zulu War of 1879*. New York, 1965.

Mosley, Leonard. *Haile Sellassie, the Conquering Lion*. Englewood Cliffs, N.J., 1965.

Mphahlele, Ezekiel. *African Image*. New York, 1962.

Niemandt, J. J., comp. *Bibliografie van die Bantoetale in die Unie van Suid-Afrika. II. Suid-Sotho*. Pretoria, 1959.

———. *Bibliography of the Bantu Languages in the Republic of South Africa. V. Xhosa*. Pretoria, 1962.

Nkosi, Lewis, "South Africa: Literature of Protest." In Helen Kitchen, ed. *A Handbook of African Affairs*. New York, 1964. Pp. 275–284.

———. "Die afrikanische Literatur in Südafrika." *Afrika heute* (1 July 1964), pp. 168–170.

Norden, Hermann. *Le dernier empire africain: En Abyssinie*. Paris, 1930.

Norton, W. A. "Sesuto Praises of the Chiefs." *South African Journal of Science*, XVIII (1921–22), 441–453.

Ntuli, D. B. Z. "A Brief Survey of Modern Literature in the South African Bantu Languages: Zulu." *Limi*, no. 6 (June 1968), pp. 28–36.

Nyembezi, Cyril L. S. "Honour for an African Author: Prof. Nyembezi's Appraisal." *South African Outlook*, LXXXVIII (1958), 156–158.

Oosthuizen, Gerhardus C. *The Theology of a South African Messiah: An Analysis of the Hymnal of "The Church of the Nazarites."* Leiden, 1967.

Pankhurst, Richard. "The Foundations of Education, Printing, Newspapers, Book Production, Libraries and Literacy in Ethiopia." *Ethiopia Observer*, VI, 3 (1962), 241–290.

————. "The Effects of War in Ethiopian History." *Ethiopia Observer*, VII, 2 (1963), 142–164.

————. "Misoneism and Innovation in Ethiopian History." *Ethiopia Observer*, VII, 4 (1964), 287–320.

————, ed. *The Ethiopian Royal Chronicles*. Addis Ababa, 1967.

Páricsy Pál. *A New Bibliography of African Literature*. Budapest, 1969.

Paroz, R. A. "Bibliography of Southern Sotho Books Available or Temporarily Out of Print." *South African Outlook*, LXXVI (1946), 59–62.

Peet, H. W. "Zulu Choir in London." *Southern Workman* (November 1930), pp. 521–522.

Perrot, Claude-Hélène, "Premières années de l'implantation du christianisme au Lesotho (1833–1847)." *Cahiers d'Etudes Africaines*, IV, 1 (1963), 97–125.

Philip, John. *Researches in South Africa*. London, 1828.

Pickersgill, W. C. "Biazavola: A Malagasy Bard." *Antananarivo Annual*, III (1886), 247–249.

Pieterse, Cosmo, and Donald Munro, eds. *Protest and Conflict in African Literature*. London, 1969.

Pim, Sir Alan. *Report on the Financial and Economic Situation of Basutoland*. London, 1935.

Plowden, W. C. *Travels in Abyssinia and the Galla Country, With an Account of a Mission to Ras Ali in 1848*. London, 1868.

P[routy], W[illiam]. "Three Reviews." *Something*, no. 4 (February 1965), pp. 53–59.

Qangule, S. Z. "A Brief Survey of Modern Literature in the South African Bantu Languages: Xhosa." *Limi*, no. 6 (June 1968), pp. 14–28.

Riad, Zaher. "The Foundation of the Ethiopian Theatre." *Bulletin de l'Institut des Etudes coptes* (1958), pp. 72–76.

Ricci, Lanfranco. "Canti imperiali amarici." *Rivista degli studi orientali*, XXXV (1960), 179–189.

————. "Romanzo e novella: due esperimenti della letteratura amarica attuale." *Journal of Semitic Studies*, IX (1964), 144–172.

Riordan, John. "The Wrath of the Ancestors." *African Studies*, XX (1961), 53–60.

Roberts, E. L. "Shembe, the Man and His Work." Master's thesis. Pretoria, 1936.

Roux, Edward. *Time Longer Than Rope: A History of the Black Man's Struggle for Freedom in South Africa*. Madison, Wisc., 1966.

Rubensson, Sven. *King of Kings: Tewodros of Ethiopia*. Addis Ababa, 1966.

Saratovskaya, L. B. "Periodizatsia literatury Bantu v Yuzhno-Afrikans-trom Souze (nachalniy period)." *Narodi Azii i Afriki,* I (1963), 117–127.

Schall, Anton. *Zur äthiopischen Verskunst.* Wiesbaden, 1961.

Schapera, I., ed. *Western Civilization and the Natives of South Africa.* London, 1934.

Scheub, Harold, "Interviews at New Brighton." *African Arts,* III, 4 (1970), 68–63, 80.

———. "Approach to a Xhosa Novel." *Contrast,* VI, 3 (1970), 77–91.

Schlosser, Katesa. *Eingeborenenkirhchen in Süd- und Südwestafrika. Ihre Geschichte und Sozialstruktur.* Kiel, 1958.

———. "Profane Ursachen des Anschlusses an Separatistenkirchen in Süd- und Südwestafrika." In Ernst Benz, ed. *Messianische Kirchen, Sekten und Bewegungen im heutigen Afrika.* Leiden, 1965. Pp. 23–45.

Segal, Ronald, ed. *Political Africa.* New York, 1961.

Sengal, Elena. "Condizioni ed esigenze dell'Etiopia dopo il '96 secondo uno scrittore Abissino." *Atti del terzo congresso di studi coloniali.* Florence, 1937. VI:215–218.

———. "Note sulla letteratura moderna amarica." *Annali dell'Istituto Universitario Orientale di Napoli,* n.s. II (1943), 291–302.

Sheddick, V. G. J. *The Southern Sotho.* London, 1953.

Shepherd, R. H. W. *Literature for the South African Bantu: A Comparative Study of Negro Achievement.* Pretoria, 1936.

———. *Lovedale, South Africa: The Story of a Century: 1841–1941.* Lovedale, 1942.

———. *Lovedale and Literature for the Bantu.* Lovedale, 1945.

———. "Literature for Africa." *South African Outlook,* LXVIII (1948), 4–6. Reprinted in *Books for Africa,* XVIII (January 1948), 7–8.

———. "The Evolution of an African Press: Lovedale's Outstanding Contribution to Bantu Literacy." *African World* (November 1953), pp. 7–8.

———. *Bantu Literature and Life.* Lovedale, 1955.

———. "Recent Trends in South African Vernacular Literature." *African World* (March 1955), pp. 7–8.

Shepherd, R. H. W., and B. G. Paver. *African Contrasts.* Cape Town, 1947.

Shepperson, George, and Thomas Price. *Independent African: John Chilembwe and the Origin, Setting and Significance of the Nyasaland Native Rising of 1915.* Edinburgh, 1958.

Shiawl, Teferra, "Äthiopiens zeitgenössische Literatur." *Africa heute,* (15 December 1965), pp. 322–325.

———. "Ethiopia's Literature Today: A Brief Survey." *Afrika* (Cologne), VII, 1 (1966), 14.

Sillani, Tomaso, ed. *L'Impero.* Rome, 1937.

Skota, T. D. Mweli, ed. *The African Who's Who*. Johannesburg, 1930. 3d. rev. ed., 1932.

Smith, Edwin W. "Thomas Mofolo," *Africa*, XIX (1949), 67–68.

Stevens, Richard P. *Lesotho, Botswana and Swaziland*. London, 1967.

Sulzer, Peter. *Schwarze Intelligenz: Ein literarisch-politischer Streifzug durch Südafrika*. Zurich, 1955.

——. "Afrikanische Presse und Literatur." *Schweizer Monatshefte*, XL (1960–61), 435–437.

——. "Afrika-Literatur." *Schweizer Monatshefte*, XL (1960–61), 632–634.

——. "Afrikanische Prosa der Gegenwart." *Schweizer Monatshefte*, XLI (1961–62), 461–468. Repr. in *Die Muschel* (1962), pp. 50–56.

——. "Die Literatur der südafrikanischen Bantu und Mischlinge." *Afrika-Jahrbuch* (1962), pp. 282–291.

——. "Der weisse Mann in schwarzer Sicht." *Afrikanischer Heimatkalender 1963*. Westhoek, 1963. Pp. 61–69.

——. "Afrikanische Literatur." *Der Kontinent*, no. 13 (December 1963), pp. 118–124.

Sundkler, G. Bengt M. *Bantu Prophets in South Africa*. London, 1948.

Swartz, J. F. A. "A Hobbyist Looks at Zulu and Xhosa Songs." *African Music*, I, 3 (1956), 29–33.

Taylor, J. Dexter. *Christianity and the Natives of South Africa*. Lovedale [1928].

——. "Inkondlo kaZulu." *Bantu Studies*, IX (1935), 163–165.

Thomas, D. R. O. "Drama and Native Education." *South African Outlook*, LXII (1932), 238–240.

Ullendorff, Edward. *An Amharic Chrestomathy*. London, 1965.

Van Warmelo, N. J. *A Preliminary Survey of the Bantu Tribes of South Africa*. Pretoria, 1935.

Van Wyk, F. J. "African Authors' Conference." *Books for Africa*, XXX (1960), 1–5.

Vilakazi, Absalom. " 'Isonto Lamanazaretha': The Church of the Nazarites." Ph.D. dissertation. Hartford, Conn., 1954.

——. *Zulu Transformations. A Study of the Dynamics of Social Change*. Pietermaritzburg, 1962.

Vilakazi, Benedict W. "The Oral and Written Literature in Nguni." Ph.D. dissertion. Johannesburg: University of the Witwatersrand, 1945.

"Vilakazi Memorial Fund." *South African Outlook*, LXXVIII (1948), 159.

Wauthier, Claude. *The Literature and Thought of Modern Africa*. New York, 1966.

Werner, Alice, "A Mosuto Novelist." *International Review of Missions*, XIV (1925), 428–436.

——. "Some Native Writers in South Africa." *Journal of the African Society*, XXX (1931), 27–39.

Westermann, Diedrich, *Afrikaner erzählen ihr Leben*. Essen, 1938. French translation, *Autobiographies d'Africains*. Paris, 1943.

Wilson, C. E. "The Provision of a Christian Literature for Africa." *International Review of Missions*, XV (1926), 506–514.

Wilson, Monica. "The Early History of the Transkei and Ciskei." *African Studies*, XVIII (1959), 167–179.

Wilson, Monica, and Leonard Thompson, eds. *The Oxford History of South Africa*. Oxford, 1969.

Wright, Stephen. "Literature and Fine Arts." In David Abner Talbot, ed. *Haile Sellassie I Silver Jubilee*. The Hague [1955], pp. 321–335.

——. "Amharic Literature." *Something*, no. 1 [1963], pp. 11–23.

——. *Ethiopian Incunabula*. Addis Ababa, 1967.

Zervos, Adrien. *L'Empire d'Ethiopie: Le miroir de l'Ethiopie moderne, 1906–1935*. Alexandria, 1936.

Ziervogel, D. "Wat die Suid-Afrikaanse Bantoe op die gebied van die letterkunde presteer het." *Bantu*, no. 5 (August 1954), pp. 35–37.

——. "Bantu Literature, Writers and Poets." *Bantu*, XIII (1966), 384–86.

Index

453